ISBN 978-1-330-82532-7
PIBN 10110356

This book is a reproduction of an important historical work. Forgotten Books uses
state-of-the-art technology to digitally reconstruct the work, preserving the original format
whilst repairing imperfections present in the aged copy. In rare cases, an imperfection in
the original, such as a blemish or missing page, may be replicated in our edition. We do,
however, repair the vast majority of imperfections successfully; any imperfections that
remain are intentionally left to preserve the state of such historical works.

English
Français
Deutsche
Italiano
Español
Português

www.forgottenbooks.com

Mythology Photography **Fiction**
Fishing Christianity **Art** Cooking
Essays Buddhism Freemasonry
Medicine **Biology** Music **Ancient**
Egypt Evolution Carpentry Physics
Dance Geology **Mathematics** Fitness
Shakespeare **Folklore** Yoga Marketing
Confidence Immortality Biographies
Poetry **Psychology** Witchcraft
Electronics Chemistry History **Law**
Accounting **Philosophy** Anthropology
Alchemy Drama Quantum Mechanics
Atheism Sexual Health **Ancient History**
Entrepreneurship Languages Sport
Paleontology Needlework Islam
Metaphysics Investment Archaeology
Parenting Statistics Criminology
Motivational

HISTORY

OF

EDGEFIELD COUNTY

FROM THE EARLIEST SETTLEMENTS

TO

⊷ 1897 ⊶

BIOGRAPHICAL AND ANECDOTICAL; WITH SKETCHES OF THE
SEMINOLE WAR; NULLIFICATION; SECESSION; RECON-
STRUCTION; CHURCHES AND LITERATURE; WITH ROLLS
OF ALL THE COMPANIES FROM EDGEFIELD IN
THE WAR OF SECESSION; WAR WITH MEX-
ICO AND WITH THE SEMINOLE INDIANS.

BY

JOHN A. CHAPMAN, A. M.,

Author of SECOND PART OF ANNALS OF NEWBERRY; SCHOOL HISTORY
OF SOUTH CAROLINA, ETC.

NEWBERRY, S. C.
ELBERT H. AULL, PUBLISHER AND PRINTER.
1897.

INTRODUCTION.

The author of this book is a native of Edgefield District, born before it was shorn of its fair proportions, as it was in 1817, before a part was cut off to form the County of Aiken, and long before it was further divided to form Saluda County. He was born within three miles of Saluda River on the old Charleston and Ninety-Six Road, which, in Revolutionary times, was one of the main highways leading from the low country and the Congarees to Ninety-Six. The place is now in Saluda County.

From his boyhood the author was a great reader and student of history. Nothing pleased him better than to get hold of some good book telling of the deeds of other times, and stories of Marion and his men, and others of that heroic age. Unfortunately, books that told the history of that period were too few; but he had Weems' Life of Washington and of Marion, and a book of American Biographies published in 1830, all of which were well suited to cultivate a taste for history and make the reader long for more.

With such a training in early life it is not surprising that, as he grew older, he read everything that could throw light upon the early history of his State and the formation of the Union and the rights and duties of the States in the Union. In writing this book he has faithfully sought and drawn from every source of information available. All books, of which he could get hold, giving information of the first settlers and their struggles, he has used; and individuals and friends in all parts of the Counties of Edgefield and Saluda, and some outside, have freely and gladly helped him in his work. To these, one and all, he gives his grateful and heartfelt thanks. One dear friend, who loaned him many old books, and who assisted him greatly otherwise, has only recently, 1896, left this stage of life for a better, William G. Whilden.

Men of Edgefield and Saluda, and you children of Edgefield elsewhere, the author has done his best. This book now belongs to you and to your posterity; and the author cannot permit himself to believe that you will turn coldly from it because you may think that it has some errors and defects. Of one truth you may be sure, that it is absolutely impartial in its treatment of men and their deeds. Can you desire more?

HISTORY OF EDGEFIELD.

I.

FIRST SETTLEMENT.

Before the year 1785, Edgefield County was a part of Ninety-Six District, which then included a very extensive territory in the upper part of the State. By the Act of the Legislature of that year, March 12, 1785, Ninety-Six was divided into the Counties, afterwards called Districts, of Edgefield, Abbeville, Newberry, Laurens, Union, and Spartanburg. Augusta, as we shall see, was founded in the year 1736, and a very active and important trading post had been in existence already for some years at the place on the Savannah where Hamburg was afterwards built. Previous to its occupation by white people the greater part of the territory was in the possession of the numerous and war-like tribe of Indians, known as the Cherokees. The Southern part, lying on the Savannah River, was used by other tribes, Savannah, Creek, &c, as hunting grounds. Of these Indians, their habits, manners, customs, and traditions, it is not necessary at this time, to write, as our purpose is to give a history of Edgefield as it has been since its occupancy by Europeans and their descendants.

ROVING TRADERS.

For many years before there was any permanent settlement the whole upper country was traversed by roving traders, who bought skins and furs from the natives and made large profits by the trade. Beavers, buffaloes, bears, and other animals, whose skins were very valuable, as well as wolves, catamounts, and wild cats, were quite as plentiful as squirrels and rabbits are now. There were also many wild deer, and at one time the exportation of skins from the State, or colony, ran up as high as to two hundred and fifty thousand a year. As far back as the year 1690, some time before the English settlers on the Ashley knew that there was such a people in existence as the Cherokees, a man named Daugherty, a trader from Virginia, lived amongst them for purposes of traffic. From his

time many adventurers, in search of trade and fortune, frequented all the towns and war-paths of the nation. This
trade, for some years, was very profitable, for the Indians
knew little or nothing of the value of their goods, and for a
few showy trinkets, and gems of small value, the trader on the
Savannah, or the Catawba, could procure peltries which he
could sell in Charleston for many times their cost.

One of the first settlers of the upper country, Anthony Park,
who lived to a very advanced age in the adjoining County of
Newberry, travelled in 1758, several hundred miles among
the Indians to the west of the Alleghany Mountains. And
even then he found several white men who said they had lived
among the natives as traders twenty years; some forty or fifty,
and one as many as sixty years. One of these traders had upwards of seventy decendants then living in the nation. These
traders were mostly Scotch or Irish. These men, however,
were not settlers, in the proper sense of the word, although
they had lived for so many years in the nation. They were
only transient persons; pioneers of the true settlers, living in
the wilderness for the purpose of traffic,—a love of adventure,
and a desire to be rid of the restraints of civilized life. The
territory of Edgefield was traversed, time and again, by these
adventurers, as it lay in the direct line of route from Charleston and the Edistos to the rich, game-abounding country about
Ninety-Six and the country above.

From the best information obtainable, we find that the earliest permanent settlements within the limits of Edgefield
County were made about the year 1748. Ninety-Six was settled about that time. In May, 1750, a party of Monangahela
Indians, led by a Cherokee guide, passed down the Savannah
to attack the Euchees, who were friends of the English. These
Euchees lived about two miles below Silver Bluff. The Mo-
nongahelas were defeated and fled, the Euchees pursuing.
They passed through the pine woods about ten miles from
where Hamburg now is, moving in a direct line for the then
weak settlement of Ninety-Six. The pursuit was so close that
the fleeing Indians were compelled to throw away their guns,
blankets, and plunder. They avoided Ninety-Six and did not
stop running until they reached the Cherokee towns. We find
that one year later, May 7, 1751, Mrs. Mary Gould, called by

Captain John Fairchild Mrs. Cloud, living on Little Saluda River, was severely wounded by two Savannah Indians, who killed her husband and children and a young man who was sleeping on the floor. These murders were committed treacherously, the savages having entered the house in a peaceable manner and having been kindly entertained by Gould and his wife. Several distressed families in that neighborhood then deserted their homes and retreated down the country to the Congarees to avoid the Indians. In August of the same year Capt. Fairchild informed the Governor, James Glen, that he had ranged with his company as high up as Ninety-Six, and had built near that place a fort of puncheon logs for the protection of the people of that settlement. That fort was built on the north banks of John's Creek, where a flourishing civilized settlement was founded cotemporaneous with the first ever planted in any part of Ninety-Six District.

In May, 1751, Captain Francis, of Ninety-Six, urged upon Governor Glen to take into consideration the dangers to which the people there and on the Saluda were exposed from the incursions of the Northern Indians and the French. In July of the same year Captain Francis again wrote to the Governor, urging the necessity of building a fort, and of sending up a company of Rangers for the protection of the people. The fort was built in August by Captain Fairchild. At this time the Indians were committing considerable depradations. Indeed, from 1749, soon after the first permanent settlements were made in the District, to the close of Col. Grant's campaign in 1761, there was not a family in all this part of Carolina that was not exposed to serious danger from the inroads and attacks of the savages.

In the summer of 1753, Gov. Glen invited all the leading men of the nation to meet him in Charleston and hold a general conference for the settlement of difficulties. At this time some Savannah Indians were held as prisoners by the Governor for depradations committed on the whites, and Little Carpenter, a leading Chief of the Cherokees, said although he did not defend the Savannahs, yet, "if they are punished the path will be made bloody, and no white man will be able to come to our country." "You," he says to the Governor, "and those about you will be safe; but many a straggling white man will lose his life." The conference was long and closed apparently all right, as there were expressions of good will from both sides. But the good will was more apparent than real. A trader, named McDaniel, who had come down with the Chiefs, refused to return with them, because, he said, "it would be certain death for any trader to do so while the Savannahs were held as prisoners." We hear of these Indians again before they reach the end of their journey. They returned by the pathway, or trail, that led to the Congarees and to Saluda Old Town. On the Little Saluda lived Stephen Holston. His home was not far from the trail. By the time the Indians had reached the Little Saluda they had run short of provisions. The escort of ten soldiers, sent by the Governor, had left them at the Congarees, and there was no white man with them except perhaps the trader Butler, who had long been in their country. The Indians, forty in all, stopped at Holston's, surrounded the house and demanded a supply of provisions. Holston, himself, was absent, but Mrs. Holston readily supplied their wants, but in spite of her kindness they continued to show a restless dissatisfaction which it was impossible for her to appease. When night came on two of them insisted upon being permitted to sleep upon the floor of the house. This, after some hesitation, she permitted. About midnight, when she and her servants were fast asleep, those outside surrounded the house, and the two, who had been lying on the floor, opened the doors, and the whole party rushed in, whooping and yelling and firing off their guns. Mrs. Holston was terribly frightened, and finding that they were about to force open the door of her room, she seized her baby, jumped from the window to the ground and ran. She did not cease running until she came to the house of a neighbor several miles distant. The Indians did not pursue her, as they were not in a very blood-thirsty humor, but only sullen and discontented. They contented themselves with robbing the house of all the pewter plates and dishes, tea cups and a kettle. They took also thirty bushels of corn, and two valuable mares from the stables. When Holston returned home he found his property gone beyond hope of recovery. He laid his complaint before the Governor and petitioned for indemnity; but whether his petition was ever granted does not appear.

The reader will notice that amongst Mrs. Holston's losses mention is made of pewter plates and dishes. There are not a great many persons now living in Edgefield whose memory goes far enough back to remember when pewter plates and dishes were displaced by the introduction of delph ware. But it has not been so very long; nor has it been so very long since the old fashioned flax wheel and distaff were in common use. The present writer remembers sitting at table and eating off pewter plates, many and many times; and the heavy pewter dishes, or bowls, or basins, in which food was placed upon the table. All were thick and heavy. I remember also seeing a strolling manufacturer, with molds, who made thin light plates and dishes. These, however, were not nearly so good and durable as the old fashioned thick and heavy ones, though they were much nicer to look upon. When delph ware first came into use I found it exceedingly difficult to hold my fork to its place whenever I tried to cut a piece of meat on my plate. It would slip and run away. With a pewter plate there was no such trouble. The fork had firm holding ground as I could always make one, or both its tines, stick into the metal of the plate deep enough to hold. I have betrayed myself again—forks had only two prongs then. They were not split spoons, nor as well adapted to carrrying food to the mouth as those in use to-day.

BUILDING FORT KEOWEE.

A fort on the borders of the nation, or in the nation, had long been desired by the traders and settlers, and even by some of the best disposed Indians themselves. As early, even, as 1734, the importance of such a fort had been recognized in Charleston; but its erection had been put off, from time to time. And the colonists, instead of building the fort themselves, had petitioned the Parliament of Great Britian to build it. After years of delay the province was compelled to do the work at its own expense, and the Council directed that land be purchased from the Indians, and that the fort be erected as near as possible to the Indian town of Keowee. Accordingly Governor Glen, in the fall of 1753, visited the country of the Lower Cherokees, bought a quantity of land, and built the fort at Keowee. It was claimed that by this purchase the English acquired the territory now embraced in the Districts of

Abbeville, Edgefield, Laurens, Union, Spartanburg, Newberry, Chester, Fairfield, Richland, and York.   Whether this
claim is just or not, it is certainly true that from this time the
settlements began rapidly to extend.   But be this as it may,
the building of the fort, which was called Fort Prince George,
purchased only a brief peace for the nation and short-lived
confidence on the border.   Massacres soon began again, and
the savages were as restless and annoying as before.

CONFERENCE AT SALUDA OLD TOWN.

Governor Glen again invited the Chiefs to meet him in conference in Charlestown.   They refused to go to Charlestown,
basing their refusal, they said, on the fear of the fatal sickness
which they had before contracted there, and which they might
again contract.   They agreed, however, to meet at some place
between the nation and Charlestown.   The meeting took place
at Saluda Old Town in the summer of 1755.

Of what was actually done at this conference we know but
little; but an enthusiastic admirer of the Governor, a man
named Moses Thompson, writing to him in January, 1756,
says: "I cannot forget my impressions of your paternal care of
South Carolina since you came among us.   First, your journey
to Ninety-Six, to settle a peace with the Cherokees; and thence
to Savannah to make peace with the Creeks.   Second, your
long journey to the Cherokee Nation to build a fort.   Third,
your journey to Saluda, in the heat of summer, to settle a
second peace with the Cherokees in troublous times; which act
crowns all the rest; for I verily believe there never was such a
firm peace made with any Indians before, and all resulting in
the advancement of the indigo manufacture.   And likewise
your great care of our back-settlers; for when I was Major
under your Excellency; I cannot forget your care by your instructions to me on several occasions; besides your private
letters to me to inform your Excellency of any event, that
proper steps might be taken for our safety.   I think your successor will have nothing to do but to walk in your footsteps;
for you have paved the plainest road that can be taken, which,
I think, will keep your memory in the minds of the people
when you are dead and gone."

II.

SETTLERS OF VARIOUS NATIONALITIES.

Edgefield, like other parts of the middle sections of the State, was settled by people representing the various nationalities of Europe—English, Scotch, Irish, Welch, German, Dutch, and French—English predominating so greatly as to make the English language the language of the country; though several others are spoken in the United States in different sections and are the every day language of the people, especially German, Swedish, and French. Like other parts of the upper country, Edgefield received many settlers from the North, from Pennsylvania, Maryland, Virginia, and North Carolina; and also perhaps some few from colonies farther North. Some also came from Georgia, as in the early days of that Colony, there were laws prohibiting the sale and use of rum and other ardent spirits, and also the introduction of African slaves. Many Georgia settlers, not liking these laws, moved over into Carolina where the use of both was allowed. No matter from what region they came, nor of what nationality, they were a hardy, brave, energetic, industrious, adventurous set of men, such as pioneers must always be.

CULBREATHS, HAZELS, &C.

Among the earliest settlers on the Saluda side of Edgefield, was a Scotch family, or perhaps there were several families, who settled in the year 1756 about four miles south of where Chappell's Ferry now is, and near where afterwards was organized and built by them the Baptist Church of Chestnut Hill. This church, by the way, was named Chestnut Hill because it was built on a hill-side near where grew many chestnut trees, some very large. This growth was found nowhere else in the neighborhood. This settlement was called Scotland, and is still known and recognized by that name by some of the older citizens, though the descendants of the Culbreaths, the original settlers, are no longer there. Joseph Culbreath was born in Scotland, near Plymouth, in 1747, and was brought over to Edgefield by his father, Edward Culbreath, who settled there in 1756. Edward Culbreath, the father, lived only one year after coming to this country, dying in 1757. He left four sons surviving him, Joseph, John, Daniel, and Edward. These all lived to be over seventy years of age. Luke Culbreath, the grandson of Joseph (his father was John whom I remember well), was eighty-four years of age in May, 1891, and has lived sixty-two years at his present home near Pleasant Lane, ten miles north of Edgefield C. H. There were once many Culbreaths in "Scotland," but now there are none in that region of country and the name is almost extinct in Edgefield. James Y. Culbreath is a lawyer at Newberry. He is a direct descendant of Edward Culbreath, the founder of the colony at "Scotland." His father was William, a brother to Luke Culbreath, above mentioned.

There was a family named Hazel, Scotch also, who came with Edward Culbreath to seek new homes in a new world. The head of the family was Harry Hazel. Some of that family are still living in that part of the country not far from the original place of settlement.

Passing down Saluda, not far from "Scotland," and near Saluda Old Town, is an old settlement, now owned, that is part of it, by Johnson Hagood, and is cultivated as a grass farm, that is, the low grounds bordering on the river. The other part, which includes the original homestead, is owned by J. Y. Culbreath, and others, of Newberry. It was here at this old homestead where Capt. William Butler, of the Revolution, found his wife, Behethland Foote Moore. This place was settled a few years after the settlement at "Scotland," by Mr. Savage from Virginia, who had married the widow Moore the mother of several children, William, George, and Behethland.

ABNEYS, &C.

A little out from Saluda, and a mile or two below "Scotland," and on the old Ninety-Six Road, we find that land was granted to William Abney, February 14th, 1772, sixteen years after the Culbreaths came. William Abney settled and lived upon the land thus granted until his death. Some of his descendants, at least some of the Abneys, lived upon the place in the old house as long as it was a homestead—not a great many years since. William Abney was the ancestor of John R. Abney, a lawyer now living in New York City, and of Ben Abney, elected to the State Legislature from Richland County.

His home is in Columbia.   He also is a lawyer.   Near William
Abney settled Samuel Abney, a brother, I think, to whom land
was granted February 19th, 1772.   Michael Abney was in the
same neighborhood.   Land was granted to him October 3rd, 1771.
Lower down Saluda, just below Higgins' Ferry and lying on
the river, land was granted to Dannett Abney, June 14th, 1768.
From him descended O. L. Schumpert, Esq., sometime member of the Legislature, afterwards Solicitor of the Circuit in
which he resides.   His home is at Newberry.   Dannett Abney
met with a tragic fate during the Revolutionary war.   He was
butchered in his wife's arms by Cunningham and his men in
that celebrated raid of 1781, the sole object of which seemed
murderous revenge.   To Nathaniel Abney on the river, lying
just above and adjoining Dannett's, on both sides of the road
leading to the ferry, lands were granted October 5th, 1763,
and September 20th, 1766.

These Abneys all came from Virginia to this State.   The
family is Norman-English, Norman-French.   The name was
originally D'Aubigne, and was changed to the present form
four or five hundred years ago—about the middle of the fif-
teenth century.

Isabella Madison, the wife of Nathaniel Abney, was a great and
wise woman, ruling her household of children and servants with
a firm but gentle hand, wisely and well.   Twelve children were
the fruit of this union.   Their youngest son, Azariah Abney,
lived and died on the original homestead, and it is still in the
family, owned in 1891 by Joel Abney, a grandson of Azariah.
Dr. M. W. Abney, of Edgefield, was descended from this pair
through his mother, Martha Wills, who was a granddaughter
of Nathaniel Abney.   Isabella Abney Boykin, daughter of Dr.
M. W. Abney—died in 1889—was as queenly and wise as her
great ancestress.

Nathaniel Abney was captain of a militia company under
Major Andrew Williamson at Ninety-Six, November 15th,
1775, but what part he took after the war was fairly begun,
and after the Declaration of Independence, does not appear.
But he was on the side of Independence.

These Abneys all obtained grants of land before the Revolutionary war; but there were several others, not yet mentioned,
to whom lands were granted after the war.   John Abney, Febru-

ary 5th, 1798; Paul Abney, February 5th, 1798; Samuel Abney, January 7th, 1811.   As large as this family was at the
beginning of the century, and for some years afterwards, there
are but few persons who now bear the name in Edgefield
County.   I should have mentioned just above, that the Rev.
Mark Abney, so well known at Edgefield and in the county;
the good, the pious Christian and useful Baptist preacher, was
also a descendant, a grandson, of Nathaniel Abney and Isabella
Madison.

TOWLSES, CARSONS, &C.

The Towleses, very active and brave Whigs, were, I think,
settlers about the year 1760 above "Scotland," in the Half
Way Swamp country.   Between them and Ned Turner, in
fact between them and almost all Tories, burned the fire of
implacable hatred.   The Chappells were also in the same
neighborhood.   About Saluda Old Town were the Carsons,
brave and true Whigs.   Old Mr. James Carson used to tell an
anecdote of one of the family, his father, I think, very much
like one related by Kennedy of his hero in the story of Horse
Shoe Robinson.   He said that one day riding alone he
stopped his horse at a small creek, or stream of running water,
to let him drink.   While his horse was drinking, Mr. Carson,
not dreaming of danger so near, naturally let his head fall forward in a thoughtful, meditative manner.   When the horse
was through drinking and raised his head to go forward the
road was found to be full of Tories, ready and waiting and
completely blocking the way.   Mr. Carson's first impulse was
to turn and flee the way he had come, but, glancing back-
wards, he found the road barred in his rear also.   Without a
moment's hesitation he rode forward, extended his hand to
the leader of the band and said that he was very glad to meet
them; that he had given up the Whig cause as a failure and
had concluded to take the other side.   He affiliated with them
and so entirely disarmed their suspicions that they soon ceased
to watch him closely and in a little while he made his escape.

I do not know the exact time when many of these settlers,
Carsons, Towleses, Butlers (not Gen. Butler's family), Scurrys,
Andersons, and others, not far from Saluda, Scotland, and the
Island Ford, came into the country; but it was from 1756 to
1766, during which period the great wave of immigration

rolled down South from Pennsylvania, Virginia, and North Carolina into South Carolina; when sometimes the number amounted to as many as a thousand families a year, with all their movables and horses and cattle.

FERRIES—SALUDA.

In the year 1770, a ferry was established at Saluda Old Town, from the lands of Charles Carson on the south side of Saluda, to the opposite shore at the lands of William Turner. The ferry was vested in Charles Carson, his Executors, Administrators, and Assigns. By the same Act a road was ordered to be made and laid out from the south side of the ferry to the nearest and most contiguous part of the road lately laid out and established by the name of Kelly's Road.

Anderson's Ferry over Saluda was established December 19th, 1795. This, I believe, is the same as the Island Ford Ferry. At Abney's Ford and vested in Nathaniel Abney and Francis Higgins, December 19th, 1795. After some years this ferry was rechartered and vested in Francis Higgins alone, and I believe it is still known as Higgins' Ferry, though sometimes called Kinard's.

There was a ferry at Chappell's before the Revolutionary war—kept by the Chappells. On December 21st, 1792, a bridge was authorized to be built by Thom... Chappell, in whom the right of taking tolls was vested. I do not think the bridge was ever built, as a ferry at that place was rechartered, December 20th, 1800. And again in 1821, and vested in Charles Chapman. But in a few years it became Chappell's Ferry, which name it held for many years. Recently a bridge has been built, which is to be free. About the year 1845, Mr. John Chappell built a single span covered bridge at that place. The investment was not profitable and the bridge before many years washed away, and the ferry was reopened.

Previous to the year 1765, the Government of South Carolina had given the upper country very little attention, little more, indeed, than was found necessary to regulate trade with the Indians. The Governor and Council could do little more. In 1765 an Act was passed to establish a ferry from New Windsor to Augusta. New Windsor was where Hamburg now is. The place must have been named New Windsor by

John Stuart, Agent for Indian Affairs, as the ferry was vested in him.

By the same Act a ferry was established from the ferry of Moses Kirkland to the opposite shore on Saludy River—''Saludy'', so spelled in the old printed Act. This same Moses Kirkland became somewhat celebrated in after years as Agent of the British and Tories, acting in concert with John Stuart in rousing the Cherokees to attack the border settlements at the same time the attack on Fort Moultrie was made.

By the Act of 1768 a road was established from Orangeburg to Saluda and thence to Bush and Rayburn's Creeks—and also for making and establishing a public ferry over Saludy River, and vesting the same in Samuel Kelly and John Millhouse. The road thus ordered to be made from Orangeburg to Saluda is surely the same known as Kelly's Road, with which the road leading from Carson's Ferry at Saluda Old Town was to join at the most contiguous part.

Again in 1770 a ferry was established over Saluda River at the lands of Robert Cunningham—and another ferry over Savannah River, opposite to Augusta in Georgia.

The reader will notice that these roads and ferries were all made and established before the Revolutionary war. Others were opened soon after the war, notice of which will be made.

STEWART SETTLEMENT.

Just below Dannett Abney's, on Saluda River, was the Stewart settlement, notorious in local annals for devoted attachment to the Royal cause during the Revolution, and for their warm personal friendship for Ned Turner and Bill Cunningham. Their homestead was at or near the mouth of Tosty Creek, a small stream emptying into the Saluda, and called Tosty, or Tosta, by the natives. This settlement began as early as 1760, or about that time.

Mr. John Stuart, of New Windsor, on the Savannah River (whether connected with the Stewarts above named I do not know), was an officer of the Crown, wholly devoted to the Royal interest, and to him, for some years previous to the beginning of the war, had been committed the management of Indian affairs in upper Carolina. Under these circumstances he felt bound to exert his influence to attach the Indians to the Royal interest. Very early in the contest he retired to

West Florida, and from that province employed his brother Henry, a Mr. Cameron, and some others, to penetrate into the Cherokee country. A plan was settled by him in concert with the King's Governors, and other Royal servants, to land a British army in West Florida, to proceed with it to the Western frontiers, and from there, in concert with the Tories and Indians, to fall on the friends of the Revolution at the same time the attack should be made on the sea coast. Moses Kirkland was employed to proceed to Boston to concert with Gen. Gage, who then commanded there, the necessary means for accomplishing this design. The plan failed by the capture of Kirkland and the ship which was conveying him to Boston. The affair had made such progress, however, that the Cherokees began their massacres two days after the British fleet made the attack on Sullivan's Island. Of that war with the Cherokees, and of the part Edgefield people bore in it, something more will be said after awhile.

I introduced Mr. John Stuart here, under the impression that he might possibly be connected with the Stewarts of Tosty Creek, as they, too, were devoted friends to the Royal cause. In my boyhood I knew Alexander Stewart well. His home was at the old family homestead near the Saluda, where the family first settled. I have frequently heard it said that he kept and cherished fondly, as a precious memento of olden times, a British officer's old red coat, and epaulettes, which had been worn by an ancestor, or kinsman, in the Revolutionary war. I never saw these things, but I have no doubt of the truth of the facts stated.

III.

PERRYS, COLEMANS, TROTTERS, &C.

There were other early settlers in that part of Edgefield bordering on Big Saluda and Persimmon Creek, not yet mentioned. These were the Perrys, Colemans, Trotters, Berrys, Nunns, Summerses, Rileys, and McCartys, to say nothing as yet of the Brookses.

As the settlements in Abbeville began about the same time with those on the Saluda side of Edgefield, we will make a little excursion into that county. Both counties being parts of the original District of Ninety-Six their histories are necessarily very intimately connected. In the year 1756, the same year in which the Culbreaths came to "Scotland," Patrick Calhoun, with four families of his friends, settled on Long Cane in Abbeville. Before he came there were only two families, one named Gowdy, the other Edwards, in that extremity of the country. After 1763 the population increased rapidly.

INCONVENIENCES OF THE SETTLERS.

At this period of time the settlers in all parts of Ninety-Six District labored under very great inconveniences in regard to the administration of justice. Some of the new comers were not law-abiding, but quite the contrary. Some men were without families—mere adventurers, who had thrown off the restraints of civilized life, and felt as though they were amenable to no law except their own wills.

During the war with the Cherokees, which broke out in 1759, several settlements were broken up and property of various kinds was abandoned. After this war was over the evils generated thereby continued for some time. There were no courts for the trial of violators of law held outside of Charleston until the year 1770. The only legal authority in all Ninety-Six District was that of Justice of the Peace appointed by the Governor. In this unpleasant condition of affairs it is no wonder that well-disposed citizens were moved to take the administration of law and justice into their own hands. And this, although altogether justifiable at first, invariably leads to abuses. In this emergency arose the Society known as Regulators. These Regulators, in the year 1764, under the leadership of some of the best men in Ninety-Six District, such as Thomas Woodward, Joseph Kirkland, and Barnaby Pope, organized themselves and signed an instrument of writing in which they bound themselves to make common cause in pursuing and arresting all horse thieves and other criminals. Horse stealing was a very common offence; and the offenders when caught were tried by the Regulators and, if found guilty, were punished by whipping on the bare back, with many or few stripes, according to the number of their misdeeds. These provoked the horse thieves and their friends to take active measures to counteract the proceedings of the Regulators. Nearly all the inhabitants of the District took part on one side or the other. Those opposed to the measures of the Regulators made such representations to Lord Charles Montague, then Governor, that he took measures for their suppression. With this end in view he conferred a high commission on a man named Scovill, a man whom his neighbors, especially the Regulators, thought very unfit for the office. As though the District were in a state of rebellion, he erected the Royal standard and called upon the Regulators to submit. He arrested two of them and sent them to Charlestown, where they were imprisoned. The parties formed opposing camps prepared for war, but each one hesitated to begin the fray. They finally agreed to break up camp, go home, and that each party petition the Governor for redress of grievances. This was done, and the result was the passing of the Circuit Court law, which established Courts at Ninety-Six, Orangeburg, and Camden. A sullen peace was made, but the ill feeling between the parties did not die out. A few years afterwards, when the troubles with the mother country began, the Scovillites became Tories and the Regulators and their friends Whigs.

CHANGES IN THE NAMES OF PLACES.

It is curious to note the changes that have taken place in the names of some places since the country was first occupied by the whites. Hamburg was originally Savannah Town, taking its name from the native Savannahs. It was an im-

portant trading station, and about the year 1730 Fort Moore
was erected near it for its better protection. After that period
the place was usually referred to as Fort Moore. In the year
1747, a ferry over the Savannah River was established at the
garrison of Fort Moore in New Windsor—rechartered, as already mentioned, in 1765, from New Windsor to Augusta, Ga.
For some years Savannah Town, or Fort Moore, was a very
important trading station, the Indians, themselves, cutting a
trail from their upper towns down the east bank of the Savannah to that place. After Augusta was founded in 1736, the
trade was drawn off; Savannah Town was deserted, and Augusta soon became a large town, with many houses and people,
and a busy trading mart. This city is the first example on
the Continent of the rapid growth of a Western village into a
populous town.

Many years afterwards an enterprising Hollander, named
Shultz, of whom a sketch will be given further on, built
the city of Hamburg as a rival to Augusta. For a long
time it was an active busy place doing a large trade. It was
the terminus of the South Carolina Rail Road, which connected it with Charleston. At the time of its completion this
was the longest rail road in the world. Hamburg was a for-
midable rival to Augusta, but its glory has long since departed. Some time during the year 1862, or 1863, I rode
through it with a friend in a buggy, and it was then the most
lonely, desolate looking place I had ever seen. What it is
now I know not. I have never seen it since, except from the
windows of the rail road coach as I passed down the road.
Hamburg died, but Augusta still grows and has never faltered
nor halted on its way of progress from the year of its founding
until now

OPENING OF PUBLIC ROAD.

In the year 1770 a public road was opened and established
from Orangeburg Bridge to Indian Head; one from Indian
Head to the road which leads from the Ridge to Augusta; one
from the Ridge Road to Long Cane Creek; one from Long
Cane to Great Rocky Creek; one from Great Rocky Creek to
Mountain Creek, near Coffee Town; and one from Robert
Goudy's at Ninety-Six to the Ridge, and from thence to th

road that leads from Indian Head to Long Cane. The student of Edgefield history will see from the establishment of these roads, and also of the ferries across the Saluda and Savannah Rivers, that the progress of the settlements and the increase of population was quite rapid. Twenty years had made a wonderful change. But the same rapid evolution of life has been going on without cessation from that day to this. I remember when Chicago was a village in a marsh. I remember Fremont's expedition across the Rocky Mountains when his men were compelled to kill and eat their starving mules to keep themselves from starving. I remember when the West beyond the Mississippi was a region almost as little known as the interior of Africa is now. San Francisco was not: Texas was not, save as an unexplored Mexican province, the home of countless buffaloes and wild horses. We here have stood almost still, but the wave of population has rolled steadily westward, across mountains and rivers; building great cities as it moved, and making iron and steel roads for travel, until it has met the far Pacific in the West. Do the waves of Ocean stop the movement? Nay! Japan is quickened and awakes to a new life, feeling an electric shock from the land across the Sea.

CHRISTIAN PRIBER.

We have seen that although there were occasional wrongs done by both whites and Indians, yet it is probable that there would have been no general war between the English settlers and the natives of the upper country had it not been for the intrigues of the French. At an early day the French had occupied the northern portions of the Continent; they had passed westward through the Great Lakes; had found the upper part of the Mississippi; had explored that river to its mouth; had founded the city of New Orleans; had built a chain of forts from its mouth to its upper waters, and now aspired to the occupation of the larger part of the Continent by hemming in the English and confining them to the slope on the Atlantic lying east of the Alleghany Mountains. To be successful in this grand scheme, it was necessary that they should foment discord and keep up an endless war between the English and the native Indians. In these efforts they were only too successful, though the ultimate result was loss to themselves, and the surrender, after many years of bloody and useless war, of all their northern possessions to the English. Louisiana, an immense tract of country, comprising their southern and western possessions, was purchased from the Emperor Napoleon by Mr. Jefferson in 1803. One of the greatest, most artful, and most successful intriguers the French ever sent amongst the Cherokees was a man named Christian Priber, a German Jesuit in the service of France. He was sent amongst them as early as the year 1736, the year of the founding of Augusta. Although a man of great learning and intelligence; a Hebrew, Greek, and Latin scholar, yet he made himself, to all intents and purposes, an Indian. He married an Indian woman of great beauty and intelligence; painted himself as a son of the wilderness, and so completely identified himself with the natives that his most intimate friends could scarcely have distinguished him from the people with whom he lived. He entirely won their confidence and impressed their minds with feelings of hatred and contempt for the English, representing them as rapacious, greedy, and dishonest. Priber's object seems to have been the founding of a great Indian Empire, composed of the Cherokees, Creeks, Choctaws, and other tribes. Had he lived it is problematical whether he could have succeeded or not, but his career was cut short by his captivity and death. About the year 1741, business called him to Mobile, which was then a French town, near the head of navigation on the Tallapoosa, the English traders among the Creeks, suspecting the object of his journey, went in a body to the town of Tooka-hatchka, where he was lodging, and arrested him. They carried him to Frederica; delivered him to Gov. Oglethorpe, who put him in prision, where he soon afterwards died. But his influence did not die with him. He had filled the minds of the natives with distrust of the English, which never ceased to rankle in their hearts and always prevented a firm and settled peace. In the meantime, also, the use of rum had lowered and degraded their manhood, and the small-pox, carried up from Charlestown in a pack-horse train of goods, had further demoralized them by carrying off many in death, and disfiguring for life many of the survivors. All these evil influences combined produced a state of ill feeling in the nation, which was never entirely allayed, and finally culminated in the great war of 1760–61, at the conclusion of which the Cherokees parted with a large portion of their lands, and retired higher up the country, near and among the mountains. This war is usually known as Grant's war. Colonel Grant was a Scotchman, a colonel in the regular British service, and had general command of the forces engaged—the troops raised by the Province of South Carolina, as well as his own regiment,—though the South Carolina regiment was under the immediate command of Col. Middleton.

In this war first appear the names of Andrew Pickens and of others of Ninety-Six District; and Francis Marion, of the low country, who served with distinction and found it a good training school for service in that great war which was to follow not many years thereafter. Andrew Pickens was a native of Pennsylvania, and had moved to Ninety-Six District only a few years before the outbreak of this war.

IV.

OBSTRUCTING WATER COURSES.

In the early days of Edgefield fish of various kinds were so abundant, and furnished so much food for the people and of such excellent quality, that their preservation was considered a matter of prime importance. Owing to the increase of popu lation it became necessary to build mills for the grinding of corn into meal to supply the people with bread, and also saw- mills for the cutting of timber into plank for building pur- poses. This was before the days of steam, and dams across the streams became necessary in order to utilize the water power. These dams, of course, obstructed the free passage of fish, and especially shad, which in the early days of the colony, at certain seasons, were very numerous in all the larger streams nearly up to their sources. Here was a conflict of interests. The mills were necessary for the grinding of corn and also for the sawing of lumber, and the fish were a necessary article of food. The complaints of the people whose supply of fish was, in a great measure, cut off by the dams, became so earnest and troublesome, that the matter was made a subject of legislative investigation, and resulted in the passage of a Fish Sluice Law, March 26th, 1784. It was enacted that all owners of all dams, or other obstructions, on Broad, Saludy, Pacolet, Tyger, and Enoree Rivers, and Steven's Creek, should, within six months after the passage of this Act, build slopes, or make openings in their dams or obstructions, so that the fish at all times might freely pass up or down said rivers; in default whereof the per- son offending, shall on conviction, forfeit the sum of forty shillings for every day such obstruction should continue. But the necessity of having good mills was so great that it con- quered the supposed necessity of having a good supply of fish and the law at length became obsolete and died a natural death —I think it never was repealed. But the right to catch shad in Saluda, and the profit resulting therefrom, were not aban- doued without severe struggles to retain them; the last and most determined of which occurred in 1824. In that year a company of twenty men living near Saluda, in the·districts of

Abbeville and Laurens—none from Edgefield, it appears—
assembled at Swansey's Ferry, with a boat ready to float down
the river, with all necessary tools and implements for cut'ing
away the dam at Lorick's Mills—now owned by James Herbert—which obstructed the free passage of fish. The law
could not operate itself, and as the people in the neighborhood
of the dam did not seem disposed to enforce it, and as they
lived too far remote from the obstruction and from the Court
House of the District in which the obstruction lay, they preferred to carry out the provisions of the law in short form, the
due and ancient form being entirely too inconvenient. This
dam had been built, partly or entirely, at the expense of the
State under the auspices of Col. Blanding, as part of his great
scheme of making the Saluda a navigable stream. The canal,
which was dug in furtherance of the scheme, has never entirely filled up yet, and is still to be seen. It was dug on the
Newberry side of the river. The dam was very strongly built,
with heavy pens of rock below it to buttress and secure it.
Showing some respect for the Statute a small, narrow gap had
been left open, but not deep enough for the purpose required
by the law. When the party arrived at the scene of action
and saw the strength of the dam and considered the magnitude
of the work they would have to do if they accomplished their
purpose, their ardor was considerably dashed. However, they
concluded that it would not do to return home without having
done something, and so they bravely set to work and toiled
arduously for three days. In that time they opened a passage
six feet wide and considerably deeper than the original one.
Concluding this to be sufficient for the end designed, they de-
sisted and returned home. Numerous spectators had gathered
on both sides to witness the proceedings, but no one offered any
opposition. A short time afterwar.'s the breach was effectually
closed, and the dam made stronger than ever before. No
effort was ever again made to remove the obstruction.

EDUCATION.

Education has never been neglected in Edgefield by the people nor by the State. Doubtless there has been individual
neglect, and there still is, notwithstanding the universal free
school system. At all times since the first settlements were

made there have been many good schools in the county, and
it has always been possible for those persons who desired a
good education to get it.   On this subject I can write know-
ingly, for I am a native of Edgefield County.   All the education I ever received at school was received in the County, at
schools taught by teachers natives of the County, with the exception of three, and only two of the three were from other
States,—one from Maine, who married and lived in the County
the balance of his life—living at this time, 1891, I believe; the
other was from North Carolina; and, I fear, the least competent of all to teach what he professed.   One was a native of
York County, a brother of Gen. D. H. Hill.   One of my
teachers was Charles K. Johnson, a son of Rev. William B.
Johnson, of Edgefield, founder of the Johnson Female Institute
at Anderson.   Charles K. Johnson was a graduate of Yale
College; a ripe scholar—a man for whom I felt a reverence as
great as it is possible for a boy to feel towards any young man.
To me, whatever he may have been to others, he never spoke
a harsh word, but was always as mild and gentle as possible.
I shall always bear him in grateful remembrance and think of
him as the type of the perfect gentleman.   What he was in the
world I know not, I never knew; so I can only think of him,
and it does me good to think of him as all that was noble.
From him I learned the mysteries of English and of Latin
grammar, and learned to read a little Latin.   In the war
against the Seminole Indians, he was a volunteer and served a
three months term in Florida.   He afterwards went to New
Orleans, in which city he died.   In those days when I was a
pupil of Mr. Johnson's, short breasted, long-tailed, swallow-
tailed blue coats were in fashion, with bright, brass buttons on
the breast and skirt.   I can never forget how much I admired
the appearance of Mr. Johnson and his friend George Addison,
who was also a pupil, as they walked off together after school
was over for the day.   The tip ends of the long skirts of their
coats touched the calves of their legs, and they were both tall
young men.   It was at this school that I first saw Preston S.
Brooks, James C. Brooks, Thomas Butler, Butler Thompson,
Bart Blocker, Thomas Bird, John R. Weaver, George Blocker,
W. L. Jennings, George Bell, Mahlon Padgett, two or three
Tomkinses, W. W. Adams, and many others, some of whom

have long since gone to the land of the leal, and some still linger here.

As it was in the section where I was born and reared so I have reason to believe it was in all parts of Edgefield. The opportunity to acquire a common school education, if no more, was always there, even from the first. Some parents willfully neglected the opportunities and advantages before them and permitted their children to grow up in ignorance. I knew one family where the children grew up with very little knowledge of books and whose manners were rather uncouth and unrefined; but who, so far as money was concerned, were prosperous and well to do. Indeed, it was the love of money, the desire to accumulate, that caused the parents in this case to neglect the education of their children. Money was preferred to letters. Are there not some such cases yet? Not only were there schools in all parts of the county where reading, writing, and arithmetic were taught, and where these were, perhaps, the highest branches, with a course of Lindley Murray; but there were academies of a higher order in different parts of the State and county, in which a better education could be obtained. The same Legislature which divided Ninety-Six District into several smaller counties, chartered a college to be erected at Ninety-Six, and also other colleges at several other places in the State. On March 17th, 1785, five days after the passage of the Act for the division of Ninety Six-District, an Act was passed for erecting and establishing a College at Winnsborough, in the District of Camden; a college in or near the city of Charlestown; and a college at Ninety-Six, in the District of Ninety-Six, in the State of South Carolina. Similar Acts had been passed before the Revolution, and some were passed even during that stormy period. Nor was the State ever backward in appropriating money for Common School purposes. The appropriations were always liberal; amply sufficient, as was supposed, to meet all the exigencies of the case; that is, the education in the common English branches, of all who were not able to educate themselves. The public school system, as we have it now, is a creature of modern introduction, and the State pays, per annum, for each child so educated about two dollars. Under the old system each child, edacated by the funds appropriated for that purpose, cost never less than four dollars per year, and sometimes as much as ten in Edgefield. I do not wish to condemn our present school system, but it does not, and cannot, in the very nature of things, give an education worthy of the name. However, if one is thirsty and cannot have a full draught of water it is better to have a spoonful than none. For our present purpose it is enough to say that the cause of education has never been neglected in Edgefield. A county which has produced and reared such men as Maximillian LaBorde, A. P. Butler, P. M. Butler, the Bacons, Brookses, Charles K. Johnson, and many others, and which has been the home of the Hammonds, Chancellor Wardlaw, Carroll, Griffin, Spann, Moragne, McDuffie, General Gary, and others, whose names I cannot now call to mind, has no cause to be ashamed of itself. Of the living, as the Tillmans, Senator Butler, the pen of the historian should not write much; but as public men and servants have we any reason to be ashamed of them?

The Edgefield Village Academy was incorporated December 18th, 1824, though the village itself was not an incorporated town until 1830. The Academy was established and in successful operation some years before it was incorporated. James J. Caldwell, of Newberry, afterwards Chancellor, taught there in 1819. The village was made the county seat in 1791 and the first court was held there early in 1792. Certain escheated property was to vest in the village and the Society Academies to the amount of ten thousand dollars. In December, 1815, thirty-seven thousand dollars were appropriated by the State for general educational purposes, of which Edgefield received its due proportion. It was also enacted at the same time, that not less than that amount should be the annual appropriation. An inspection of the Acts of the Legislature will show that the State was never indifferent to the education of its children.

Professor La Borde received his early education at the Edgefield Village Academy, and thus writes of it: "Among my early teachers was Robert L. Armstrong, who taught for four years in the Edgefield Village Academy. He was from York District in our State, and a graduate of our College. He was remarkable for his industry and strict discipline. The Academy prospered under his direction—students poured in from the contiguous districts, and not a few from Georgia.''

At this time, 1891, there are graded schools in operation in the town of Edgefield, in which several hundred children, both black and white, receive instruction in the ordinary English branches at the public expense. Besides the public schools, which have proven insufficient for complete educational purposes, there are open, for eight or nine months in the year, not less than twenty good schools in which the pupils pay for their tuition.

V.

THE BUTLER FAMILY.

Passing out from Saluda to the neighborhood of Big Creek, near where Butler Church, Methodist, now stands, we find the old homestead of the Butler family. Capt. James Butler, the founder of the family in Edgefield, came from Prince William County, Virginia, a few years before the breaking out of the Revolutionary war, bringing with him his family.

FROM A. P. BUTLER'S FAMILY BIBLE.

The following entries are taken from an old Bible which James Butler had at his death:

William Butler, son of James Butler and Mary his wife (before marriage a Miss Simpson), was born December 17th, 1759.

James Butler, son of James Butler and Mary his wife, was born March 2nd, 1761.

Thomas Butler, son of James Butler and Mary his wife, was born November 4th, 1763.

Nancy Butler, daughter of James Butler and Mary his wife, was born September 27th, 1765.

Elizabeth Butler, daughter of James Butler and Mary his wife, was born 17th December, 1766.

Sampson Butler, the son of the above, was born February 18th, 1769.

NOTE.—What is found on this page was written by my grandfather before or during his imprisonment in Charleston.

The names of the two sons, Stanmore and Mason Butler, are from some cause omitted.

In another place in the Bible is this: Gen William Butler was born in Loudon County, Virginia, in 1759.

William Butler married Behethland Foote Moore June 3d, 1784.

Behethland Foote Moore was born near the Maryland line in Virginia, December 28th, 1764.

Mr. William P. Butler, in some notes that he gave me of the Butler Family, says: "We have no knowledge of Capt. James Butler prior to his emigrating from Virginia between 1680 and

and 1720." This is quite a mistake, as his son William was born in Virginia in 1759. He says also that: "Miss Sarah Butler, sister of Capt. James Butler, killed on Cloud's Creek, by Cunningham's band of tories, married first Capt. Smallwood Smith, by whom she had two children, recollected Jacob B. Smith and Sarah Butler Smith, wife of Ryden G. Mays."

Elsewhere it is stated that Sarah Butler married Jacob Smith of Mount Willing.

The following is a copy from a manuscript written by Hon. A. P. Butler:

FAMILY MEMOIR.

General William Butler, the subject of this memoir, was born in Prince William County, Virginia, in 1759. His father, Captain James Butler, removed with his family to South Carolina and settled in the District of Ninety-Six a few years before the Revolution. They were destined to take their full share in the stormy times that were approaching. Captain Butler, before he had time to attend his private affairs, was called upon to engage in the public concerns of the country. He served in the Snow Camp Expedition under General Richardson and was under General Williamson in his expedition against the Cherokee Indians. In 1779, upon the call of General Lincoln, who had assumed command of the Southern forces, he repaired to his camp near Augusta, Ga., but was taken sick and was unable to follow the army in the subsequent campaign.

From this period few events of Revolutionary interest occurred in the upper part of the State until after the fall of Charleston. The capitulation of the forces in the city and the dispersion or retreat of the small detached corps, which had kept the field during the siege, was regarded by the Royal commander as a restoration of British authority, and both civil and military organizations were engaged to maintain it. The inhabitants of the State were called upon to swear allegiance to the British authority and to take British protection. The village of Ninety-Six was designated as a place for the surrounding country to appear for the purpose. The proclamation was thought to be delusive and many persons appeared on the day without fully understanding its import.

Among these was Capt. James Butler, who, when informed of what was demanded of him, positively refused to conform to the terms of the proclamation. The British officers in command immediately put him in irons and threw him in Ninety-Six jail, from whence he was transferred to Charleston where he was confined in the provost for eighteen months. Upon his release, towards the last of the year 1781, from this severe and lengthened imprisonment he returned once more to his home, where he was fated to remain but three weeks before he was called on to seal with his life his devotion to the cause in which he had already suffered so much. The incidents of the bloody tragedy in which he died can be paralelled only in the annals of civil strife.

From the beginning of the contest with the mother country a difference of sentiment had existed in the State on this subject. South Carolina had been a pet province of the Crown. The grievances complained of by the commercial colonies were unfelt by her, and a strong conservative feeling pervaded a large class of her people. This feeling was strongest in the up country where the inhabitants took arms from the beginning upon either side of the quarrel, and the contest conducted by irregular troops assumed a savage guerilla character, in which, says General Greene, the inhabitants pursued each other like wild beasts.

A marauding party of Loyalists had made an incursion in the neighborhood of Mount Willing, near which Capt. Butler lived, carrying off considerable booty, and a band of Whigs being formed for their pursuit, he was called upon to take command of the expedition. At first he positively refused to go at all, saying that his hardships and privations already endured, and his recent return to his home ought to exempt him from such an undertaking. But his son, James Butler, one of the party, refusing to continue of the expedition unless his father assumed its direction, Captain Butler yielded to the appeal and consented to go as an adviser, the actual command being in Captain Turner. The Loyalists were overtaken, dispersed at Farra's Spring, in Lexington District, and the horses and cattle they had taken recaptured. Upon the return of the Whig party they stopped at Cloud's Creek and encamped, refusing to move onwards or to adopt the ordinary precaution against surprise, notwithstanding the urgent remonstrances of Captain Butler. It was not known then who were the Loyalists they had been pursuing, but the next morning demonstrated the wisdom of his advice. They proved to have been connected with a larger band, and about sunrise, the band amounting to some three hundred men, under the lead of William Cunningham, approached and attacked the camp. Taken by surprise and utterly disorganized, the little party of Whigs, about thirty in number, rallied and took shelter in an unfinished log house without doors or windows. They were fired upon by Cunningham's party, and a demand for surrender peremptorily made. Its terms were enquired by the Whigs and the response of the Tories was that they were unconditional, but that they would receive a communication from them.

Smallwood Smith was selected for the office; Cunningham's first inquiry was who are of your party? On hearing that young James Butler, the son who had been engaged in the affair in which Radcliff was killed was among them, he determined to give no terms that would exempt this young man from his sword. Cunningham was well acquainted with the father, Capt. Butler, having served with him in the expedition against the Indians, to which allusion has already been made. It is said he had rather a partiality for him and would have entertained terms of capitulation with the party had it not been for the presence of the son.

Capt. James Butler sent Cunningham a special message that if he would spare his son he would .make an unconditional surrender of himself. The young man, however, learning Cunningham's animosity to himself and entertaining the impression that his father or he would be sacrificed in the event of any surrender, determined to run all the hazards of a contest of arms, and exclaiming that he would settle the terms of capitulation, commenced the contest by firing his rifle and killing a Tory by the name of Stewart. It is said that negotiation had been commenced to save the officers and sacrifice the privates. But be this as it may, this demonstration of courage concluded the parley, and young Butler, but 19 years old, received a mortal wound while kneeling to pick his flint for a second discharge. The gallant but expiring boy called his father, who had gone upon the expedition unarmed in his character as adviser, to his side, handed him his rifle; and told him there were yet a few balls in his pouch. The father took the gun and discharged it until the ammunition was exhausted. But the death of the young man produced a panic in the little party contending against such hopeless odds, and an unconditional surrender was the result.

They were placed upon a ladder placed as a bench and heard the terrific order given to put them to the unsparing sword of retaliation and revenge, but two of the number escaped; the rest were slaughtered where they stood. Capt. James Butler caught up a pitchfork and defended himself until his right hand was severed by a sabre stroke.

The tragedy did not terminate here. A detachment of Tories, under the command of Prescott, a subordinate leader, was left to meet any burying party that might be sent to inter the mangled victims, and especially to meet the subject of our memoir, then a Captain of Rangers, who, it was expected, would hasten to the spot. But William Butler was too far from the sad scene to be present even at the funeral ceremonial. Women performed the melancholy rites. Mrs. Sarah Smith, a sister of James Butler, the elder, (his widow at the time being in a state of confinement) was summoned to the scene. Her brother's body was recognised by his hand being severed, but the rest could not be identified by their relatives. James Butler, the younger, was supposed to be identified. A large pit was dug, into which the unburied bodies were indiscriminately placed; but a separate grave was prepared by the direction of Mrs. Smith, in which the remains of the Butlers, father and son, were deposited and over which an humble monument with filial piety has since been erected.

WILLIAM BUTLER.

When Lincoln issued his proclamation from his camp near Augusta, William Butler repaired to his standard as a lieutenant of militia. The American leader's purpose was the invasion and reclamation of Georgia. Leaving a corps of observation at Purysburg, under Moultrie, he had scarcely crossed the Savannah River higher up when his sagacious adversary, Prevost, finding the way to Charleston open, made a brilliant dash for the capture of that city, and had nearly succeeded.

When he crossed the Savannah the city was without defences, and Lincoln believing the movement but a feint, delayed to pursue him; but Moultrie, throwing himself in his path, met him at Tulifiny and Coosawhatchie, and by a defensive retreat delayed his advance until field works sufficient to withstand an assault could be thrown up for the defence of the city.

The approach of Lincoln's force, as well as Governor Rutledge with militia from Orangeburg, forbade regular approaches, and Prevost commenced his retreat by way of the islands to Savannah. The militia from the up country were then discharged, but William Butler, who had been of the detachment engaged in the action of Stono, remained and attached himself to Pulaski's Legion, in which he remained during the campaign of 1779. He was with the gallant Pole until his death at the siege of Savannah, and always spoke of him as a bold, dashing dragoon officer. (He complimented his memory by naming one of his grandson's after him.)

During the captivity of his father in Charleston all the responsibilities of family obligations devolved upon William Butler. It was at that time, too, the time immediately succeeding the fall of Charleston, that that brilliant race of partisan leaders, whose achievements threw so much of romance over the war at the South, sprang into existence. And when General Greene took command of the Southern army in 1780, the depression which had followed the fall of Charleston disappeared entirely from public sentiment and South Carolina was once more the most warlike State of the Confederacy.

General Greene's movement upon Ninety-Six is a matter of history. At that time William Butler was serving under General Pickens on the Carolina side of the Savannah River near Augusta. He was at the siege of Augusta, and after the fall of that place, having been detailed by General Pickens to attend Colonel Lee to Ninety-Six, then also besieged, he was present at the interview between Greene and Lee, upon Lee's arrival, in the which the latter suggested the attack upon the stockade. General Butler always expressed himself with emphasis in speaking of this interview, repeating the words of Lee, that "the spring must be taken." Greene replied: "How can it be done without a general assault?" Lee responded: "Allow me to take the stockade on the opposite side

and my.guns will then drive them from the water." The
stockade was then taken and the garrison deprived of the use
of the spring, an operation which it has been conceded by
military critics if accomplished at an earlier period of the siege
would have resulted in the fall of the place before it could have
been relieved. As it was, Cruger, commanding the garrison,
managed to prolong his defence by sinking wells in the star
redoubt. Terms of capitulation had been proposed which
Greene refused, believing he could still take the place by
pushing the sap against the star redoubt under Kosciusko's
directions. The approach of Lord Rawdon with the relieving
force blasted his hopes.

A corps was detached to meet Rawdon while an assault
upon an incomplete breach was hazarded. Some skirmishing
between Rawdon's advance guard and this corps took place
near Saluda Old Town, in which some were killed and several
wounded. A young lieutenant from Virginia by the name of
Wade was shot, and as he fell from his saddle, with a genuine
trooper's care for his steed, forgetting himself, exclaimed
to his comrades: "Don't let my horse fall into the hands
of the enemy." He was carried to the house of Samuel
Savage and finally recovered. The Americans fell back
and the combatants had not long swept by when a young
dragoon officer with a white plume and the cockade of
the Whigs in his hat, and accompanied by an orderly,
rode up to Mr. Savage's and learned from his step-daughter,
who had just returned from the vicinity of Ninety-Six,
that the siege was raised and Greene in full retreat had
crossed Saluda at the Island ford, with Lee's legion bringing up
the rear. The young officer was William Butler, and this was
his first meeting with the lady whom he subsequently married.
He had been detached from the army of Ninety-Six upon some
separate service under General Henderson, from whom he
derived his first commission as captain in 1781. He at once
determined to join the retreating army, and being told that
two stragglers from Rawdon's force were down in Savage's
low grounds, taking the plantation horses, he took them prisoners, mounted one of them behind himself and the other
behind his orderly, swam Saluda near what is now called Boaz-
man's Ferry, and joined Lee about ten miles from the Island

ford on the Newberry side. He had learned from the prisoners that Rawdon had rushed forward a strong light corps, embracing both cavalry and infantry, in hot pursuit of the Americans. When William Butler came up with Lee he informed him of the pursuit, and the information came none too soon. Lee had halted his command and was lying on his saddle-blanket, making a pillow of his saddle. His prompt direction to Armstrong, one of his captains, was: "Form your troops in the rear and fight while we run." The legion was barely again on the march when the enemy appeared; but Armstrong made the required demonstrations with such gallantry and confidence that the enemy, apprehending an engagement with a stronger force, paused for reinforcements and Lee was enabled to put himself in close communication with the main body, which was then halted at Bushes Creek.

After this time William Butler was a partisan, sometimes serving as second in command under Ryan, and sometimes in the same position under Watson—both partisan leaders of local distinction. At a subsequent period he raised and commanded a company of mounted Rangers, under a commission from General Pickens, confirmed by the Governor of the State. While serving under Watson he was engaged in an expedition against a band of Tories, who had organized themselves on Edisto. The expedition rendezvoused at the Ridge, Edgefield District. Michael Watson, the leader, was a determined and resentful man, and consulted too much the counsels which these feelings suggested. When they met the Tories at Dean's Swamp the latter were stronger than had been expected, and though partly taken in ambush and the Tories occupying a strong position he disdained a retreat. The Whigs had fallen back at the first fire with symptoms of panic and a faltering response to the order to charge. But few obeyed with the stern alacrity they were wont to welcome it. Many obeyed not at all. Again driven back, the stern old warrior shouted his rally and ordered his men to stand to their duty. But about fifteen came up to the call. They had originally gone into the fight against superior numbers, and the Tories strongly posted in the swamp, which position they still maintained. Watson was mortally wounded by a ball through the hip while loading his rifle behind a tree. William Butler then assumed the command, giving his lieutenancy to John Corley, and, the danger of the party requiring a resort to desperate measures, placed him in rear with an order to cut down the first man that gave way. It happened that Joseph Corley, among others, was about to give way, which would have left the small remnant of the Whigs to certain destruction. John Corley, true to his instructions, with drawn sword menaced his brother with instant death unless he returned to his post. Joseph did return and behaved well afterwards.

Vardell had been killed, and before his breath left him he begged his comrades not to let his body fall into the hands of the Tories. The wounded Watson, lying between the contending parties, had made a similar appeal, specially to William Butler: "Billy, do not let them take me."

The Whigs made one more charge and carrying off their comrades retreated, but found time to bury poor Vardell under a clay root and cover him with their swords. At some little distance from the scene of conflict they took refuge in a wooden outhouse, being pursued, but circumspectly, by the Tories. Watson, severely wounded, and the sudden apprehension of death, still maintained a military resolution. A woman happened to be in the house in which they entered whose infant, some three weeks old, was in a dwelling some distance off. Watson insisted she should be detained; that their weakened condition required concealment and she might betray them. They found, means, however, to get information of their perilous situation to Orangeburg, and Captain, subsequently General Rumph, hastened to their relief. Under his escort Watson was carried upon a litter in a dying condition to Orangeburg where he expired and was buried. William Butler superintended the military honors of his funeral.

While serving with Ryan the subject of our memoir was engaged in another expedition against the Tories in Orangeburg District. They were in force near the Court House. A number of Tories, finding their condition desperate, deserted to the Whigs, and Ryan, distrusting them, placed them in front with instructions to his men to shoot them if they proved false. In the fight which ensued his chief was again disabled and William Butler assumed the command. The Tories were defeated.

In 1782 Cunningham made a second incursion into the Ninety-Six District. Perfectly familiar with the country in his youth, possessed of great sagacity, fertility in military expedients and endowed with all the physical qualities so essential to the partizan, he was no mean adversary to contend with. A favorite manœuvre with him was to divide his command upon the march into small detachments, to be concentrated by different routes near the point at which the blow was aimed. In this manner he had concentrated his force at Caradine's ford on Saluda. William Butler then was commanding a company of Rangers under the authority of General Pickens and, with a portion of his company marched to meet him. With a view to ascertain the enemy's position he resorted to a ruse. Approaching the residence of Joseph Cunningham, near the junction of Little Saluda with Big Saluda, he sent forward his brother, Thomas Butler, with Abner Corley to the house at night. Thomas Butler was an excellent mimic and, imitating the voice of one of William Cunningham's men, called Nibletts, asked from without where our friend Cunningham was. The wife of Joseph Cunningham replied that he had crossed at Caradine's ford. With that information William Butler himself rode up to the house and mounting Joseph Cunningham on a horse compelled him to guide the party across the ford.

They crossed the ford at 12 o'clock at night and next morning halted in a peach orchard near Bauknight's Ferry. The horses were unbridled but with the saddles on feeding upon peas out of a canoe when a grey mare, which Cunningham was known to have taken out of the neighborhood, was observed passing back, having escaped from his camp. This incident disclosed in some measure the state of affairs, and the Rangers received the orders to march. The Rangers numbered some thirty and Cunningham's men about twenty. The bloody scene of Cloud's Creek animated any encounter between Butler and Cunningham with more of the feelings of the duello than the battle-field. Approaching the Tory position unobserved, John Corley was detailed with eight men to gain their rear and upon a concerted signal to commence the attack, while the main body advanced under cover of a hedge. The Tories were drying their blankets by their camp fires; Cunningham, himself, was at a little distance off from his band. As it afterwards appeared, Butler's person being at one time exposed in advancing before the signal was given, he was observed by the Tories, but taken for their leader, for there was a striking personal resemblance between the two men.

Corley's furious assault, himself foremost in the charge, was the first intimation to the Tories that their exasperated foes were at hand. Cunningham was promptly at his post, but, taken by surprise and attacked by superior numbers, thought only of safety. Having no time to saddle his horse, but with partizan quickness seizing his holsters sprang to his seat, while Butler, singling him out, dashed in pursuit. Both men were remarkably fine riders and tradition has preserved the names of the horses they rode. Cunningham was mounted on a mare which had become celebrated in the service as "Silver Heels," while Butler rode a horse called "Ranter." As Butler carried only a sabre and Cunningham only pistols that had been rendered useless by the rain of the night before, for he snapped them repeatedly over his shoulders at his adversary as he fled, life or death hung upon the speed of the horses. As long as the chase was in the woods "Ranter" maintained his own, but when he struck an open trail in which the superior strides of Cunningham's thoroughbred could tell, turning in his seat and patting with triumph and confidence the noble animal that bore him, he tauntingly exclaimed, "I am safe," and dashing rapidly away from his adversary, he escaped by himself swimming the Saluda near Lorick's ferry. When William Butler returned from the pursuit of Cunningham he found a portion of his command assembled at the Tory camp under circumstances which gave him great concern. Turner, one of his prisoners, had been deliberately shot through the head after he had surrendered. When Butler sternly rebuked the act Seysin, who had done the deed, justified himself by reciting an outrage the unfortunate Tory had inflicted upon his mother. The verdict of the corps was in Seysin's favor and no court martial was held upon him. There was certainly strong palliating circumstances in the case. The Tory had stripped Mrs. Seysin to the waist and tying her had severely whipped her to force her to disclose where a party of Whigs, among whom was her son, were.

A pursuit of Cunningham's men was ordered for the purpose of capturing or dispersing them, and some were overtaken while crossing the river. Butler, finding his men disposed to fire upon them, ordered De Loach, who was raising his rifle, to desist. Sherwood Corley was then in the river, had snapped his pistol at the retreating party, not heeding the order, he deliberately primed it afresh while in the water and killed a Tory named Davis while he was ascending the Edgefield bank. The result of this action was the dispersion of Cunningham's famous band. He, himself, retired to Cuba where he died, being prevented from returning to his native State after the war by a proscriptive proclamation of the authoritives. He was awarded something like an ovation by the British. Goudy, a gallant partizan of the Revolution, visited Cuba after the war on account of his health. Cunningham, in the true spirit of hospitality, called upon him with an invitation to dinner. Whether Goudy accepted the invitation or not we cannot say; but Cunningham told him that on one occasion he had ridden up with an escort at his back to a house near Ninety-Six, in which Goudy and others were playing cards, with a view to ascertaining if William Butler was among them. "Why did you not fire upon us?" asked Goudy. "I had no temptation to kill you," said Cunningham, "but if Billy Butler had been there you would have had the floor flooded with blood."

From this time until after the close of the war, William Butler continued at the head of the Rangers, under command of General Pickens, and was considered his favorite captain. He had, however, very little duty other than patrol to perform. His company of Rangers was not discharged until 1784, more than a year after the peace.

With the resumption of the pursuits of civil life, the soldier's thoughts reverted to the young girl of Saluda with whom his meeting during Green's retreat from Ninety-Six has already been mentioned, Nor had she forgotten the young officer of the cocade and plume, for when the household rejected him, (the stepfather forbade him to visit her), she told him to come, she would see him. They were married the 3d of June, 1784.

Miss Behethland Foot Moore, whom William Butler had thus selected as the partner of his life, was a woman of strong, and in many respects remarkable traits of character. She always exercised great influence with her husband and he relied much upon her judgment and advice. He seemed to have inspired her with a deep feeling, almost amounting to a fascination; of itself a high tribute to his memory.

In 1794 William Butler was elected by the Legislature of South Carolina Sheriff of Ninety-Six District. He discharged few of the ministerial duties, however, leaving them to his brothers, Thomas and Stanmore, who were his deputies; but he always conducted the military escort of the Judge coming into the District and presided as High Sheriff during the sitting of the Court.

The sheriff of that day was an officer of distinction and was generally detailed upon offices of honor. William Butler, as Sheriff of Ninety-Six, received General Washington when upon the Southern tour, from the authorities of Georgia, and conducted him by the Pine House to the Ridge, which was near the termination of his territorial jurisdiction At the Ridge, General Hampton, then sheriff of what was called Camden District, received and conducted him by Granby, through Camden and thence to Charlotte, North Carolina, where the authorities of that State received the illustrious patriot. (There is certainly an error here. Washington passed through the District in 1791).

In 1796 General Pickens resigned the office of Major-General of the upper division of South Carolina militia and through his recommendation William Butler was elected by the State Legislature to fill the vacancy. In 1800 General Butler became a candidate for Congress against Robert Goodloe Harper, the incumbent from the Ninety-Six District. Mr. Harper had been elected as a Republican, but from conscientious motives joined the Federalists and supported what was peculiarly unpopular at the South—Jay's Treaty. This raised opposition to him at home and General Butler was selected as the opposition candidate, his old commander, John Ryan, moving the nomination. He succeeded in the election and took his seat in 1801.

When the resolution, charging General Wilkinson with complicity with Burr, in his attributed treason, was moved and adopted in the House of Representatives, the occasion gave rise to great sensation. A discussion took place upon the floor as to the chairman of the Committee of Investigation. A ballot was called for by Wilkinson's friends, the motion was overlaid and the duty of making the appointment devolved upon the Speaker. He appointed General Butler. Wilkinson made some offensive remarks. Something of this kind, that he was not only to be tried by a militia general, but that he was condemned before he was tried. This being reported to General Butler he resigned his position on the committee. Roger Bacon being appointed to succeed him and unfriendly communications were made between him and Wilkinson. They were, however, fully reconciled.

In 1813 General Butler resigned his seat in Congress, distinctly in preference to Mr. Calhoun, saying to him, "You can meet Mr. Randolph in debate, I cannot" His admiration for Randolph was very high, and notwithstanding they differed in opinion as to the war of 1812, they still continued to entertain friendly relations. Butler once spent some time with him at his house by invitation in returning from Congress.

In 1814 General Butler was called by Gen. Alston, in a very complimentary Order, on record in Washington, to command the troops of South Carolina at Charleston.

President Madison had, in 1812, offered him the commission of brigadier general in the United States service, but he declined it, saying he was a major general at home.

General Jackson was appointed to command the forces at New Orleans, while General Butler was to command in Charleston. They had been comrades in early life and Jackson sent him word that they were both called militia generals, but he knew whichever was attacked would do his duty. General Pickens desired to prescribe the mode of defence of Charleston. His plan was to allow the enemy to land and fight them in the streets from behind barricades. Butler's response to him, when he assumed the command, was that he expected to consult the dictates of his own judgment, and they should meet them in the water. An incursion was made upon one of the islands for the purpose of supplying provisions to the fleet off the coast, and a slight affair occurred in which Captain Dent of the navy was principally engaged. The incursion was repelled. This was the only engagement with the enemy of any portion of General Butler's command. It had fallen to the lot of his friend Jackson to vindicate the ability of militia generals. The war terminated with the battle of New Orleans and General Butler became a private citizen.

From this period to the close of his life he confined himself principally to the business of his farm. During the time he was in Congress his seat was twice contested, first by Dr. Scriven, a man of high character, and afterwards by Edmund Bacon, a man of mark. The last contest gave rise to the unfortunate issue known as the "old and new parties of Edgefield." It was bitter and led to many painful controversies. Mr. Bacon not only became reconciled with, but was afterwards a warm friend of General Butler's and frequently entertained him with a hospitality that would scarcely be recognized at the present day.

General Butler was a member of the convention held in Charleston in 1787 to consider the adoption of the Federal Constitution, and with General Sumter and others, whose names are to be found on the journal, voted against it. He was subsequently a member of the convention which framed our present State Constitution. (Constitution previous to 1868).

General Butler's brothers were Thomas, who was regarded a man of military talent; Sampson, who was Sheriff of Edgefield, and for many years represented that district in the State Legislature; Stanmore, who was a captain in the United States army during the time a war was expected with France, and was Clerk of the Court of Edgefield when he died; and James, who was killed in the Revolution, as already described. He had two sisters, Nancy and Elizabeth. The first married Elisha Brooks, who was a lieutenant in the Revolution; the latter married Zachariah Brooks, who was also a lieutenant in the Revolution and subsequently a colonel of State cavalry.

He had eight children. James was Sheriff of Edgefield and a colonel of State cavalry at his death. George Butler was a lawyer, and during the war of 1812 served as major in the regular army. William was a physician and was a surgeon in the army at New Orleans. He also served one term as Representative in Congress. Frank Butler was a lawyer. Pierce M. Butler was an officer in the regular army; was President of the Bank of the State; was Governor of South Carolina, and fell at the battle of Cherubusco at the head of the Palmetto Regiment.

Emmala, the only daughter, was married to General Waddy Thompson, who was a lawyer, a member of Congress and Minister to Mexico. Leontine died young.

Andrew Pickens Butler, the sole survivor, has been a lawyer, a Judge, and is now the senior United States Senator from South Carolina. (Judge A. P. Butler died May 25, 1857. A biographical notice of him is given elsewhere in this book).

General Butler was a handsome man, about six feet high, a good shot with a rifle, and excellent in woodcraft and horsemanship. His fondness for horses amounted to a passion, and he would have none but the finest blood upon his place. He considered it a defect in his sons not to ride well, and was in the habit of making them break his colts until, upon one occasion when a "Dare Devil" filly was to be mounted and two of the boys, Pickens and Pierce, were drawing lots to see who should do it. Mrs. Butler could stand it no longer. She interposed, telling her husband that they were her children as well as his, and if the horses were to be broken, put the servants at it. He yielded, carelessly remarking, "it would not hurt them to get thrown, the ground was plowed."

At one time he was engaged upon the Turf and ran his horses generally with success; but upon one occasion a demand was made upon him for a stake which he was unable to put up. Under the demand, however, he put up his family servant, Will. He won the race and it was his last. Returning home he told his wife what he had done and gave her a positive pledge, which he kept, never to run another race or to play another card. General Butler was a man of strong impressions and of great self-reliance. Though his connection with most of the events narrated was a subordinate one, he always had his own and decided opinions. He had not literary attainments, but in the school of experience he was a scholar that stood high. One strong peculiarity marked his character—an aversion to long letters and long speeches. He always spoke of John Rutledge as the best speaker he had ever heard; commending him chiefly for his brevity. He, himself, seldom wrote over a page, and that laconic and dispatchful. His sheriff's books, now in the possession of Hon. A. P. Butler, is a model of official neatness.

In his domestic relations he was absolute; making his sons

entirely subservient to his commands. His wife was devoted to him.

William Butler died in September, 1821, and was buried at the family burial-ground at Big Creek, in Edgefield District. He died with remarkable calmness. While he has left little that is remembered, save through tradition, he was a man of mark in his day.

Peace be to his ashes.

VI.

MUSTER ROLL—BROOKS' COMPANY.

General Butler's sister, Elizabeth, became the wife of Zachary Smith Brooks, Lieutenant during the Revolution and afterwards Colonel of State Cavalry. As it may possibly be of interest to some persons now living, I give here the muster roll of a company of cavalry commanded by Col. Brooks while he was still only a captain. I greatly regret that there is no date to the paper, but it is very old. Some of the names I cannot decipher and some are erased:

List of Capt. Zachary Smith Brooks' Company.

Zachariah Smith Brooks, Captain; Robert Christie, First Lieutenant; George Pope, Second Lieutenant; Joel Abney, Cornet; John Abney, Secretary; John Abney, First Sergeant; Hardy Matthews, Second Sergeant; Wade Carson, Bugler.

Cullen Lark, Azariah Abney, William Kennedy, Vincent White, Micajah Matthews, Jesse Hart, Joshua Burgess, Samuel Abney, Andrew Brown, Peterson Boram, John Blalock, Monte Towles, Nathan Spragins, Willis Boram, Henry Ethridge, Elijah Pope, Joseph Buffington, John Barnes, William Norris, John Cunningham, Stephen Norris, John Deshass, Nathan Norris, John H. Powell, Thomas Reynolds, Jones Willis, Thomas Mellon, Simeon Smith, William Nunn, Richard Eskridge, William Stuart, William Jay, C. Yeheets, Pointer.

I deeply regret that there is no date to this paper; but judging from the names I find and from the quality of the paper itself, it must be full eighty, or ninety, or perhaps a hundred years old. The George Pope, whose name I find as second lieutenant, was a brother of Sampson Pope, grandfather of Judge Y. J. Pope and Sampson Pope, of Newberry. Robert Christie, first lieutenant, was, I think, father of Simeon Christie, some time Sheriff of Edgefield District. Joel Abney, cornet, lived on Saluda River, near Higgins' Ferry, and was the father of Pope and Joel, and the Rev. Mark Abney, who was so well known at Edgefield some years ago. He was the father also of two daughters, Charlotte, who never married, and Elmina, who first married a Dr. Belden. When I first remember seeing her

she was a widow.   She afterwards married a Methodist minister named Rush. She became a widow again and died in 1889
or 1890, at an advanced age.   She was helpless and bedridden
for several years before her death.   Azariah Abney was a
brother of Joel and lived near him.   They married sisters
Joel, Elizabeth Pope, and Azariah, Mary—who were sisters of
George and Sampson Pope.   Wade Carson was of that same
family of Carsons, some of whom are living now not far south
of Saluda River; and one, Rev. James Carson, is a Baptist
preacher.   There were three John Abneys; one was the father
of Dr. M. W. Abney, whose home was at Edgefield, and who
died there about the year 1886.   Some of the descendants of
the others are still living in that section.   Of the descendants
of Hardy Matthews I know nothing, and cannot write with
certainty, though the name Matthews is still known in Edgefield, and a citizen of Newberry, E. P. Matthews, went from
Edgefield and having found great attractions in that county,
married and remained there.   And, in the year 1891, Mr.
Budd C. Matthews, grandson of a worthy citizen, followed
the example of E. P. and married in Newberry and deserted
the land of his birth.

   The names of Boram, Spragins, Buffington, Hart, Champion, Deshass, Nunn, Eskridge, and perhaps some others on
this roll, have disappeared from that part of Edgefield.   Of the
descendants of Captain Smith Brooks, the most celebrated and
best known is the Hon. Preston S. Brooks, who served his
country and State, commanding a company of volunteers during
the war with Mexico.   He was afterwards elected to the Congress of the United States—was expelled from the House for
caning Mr. Sumner, and was immediately re-elected.   Some
of the Willises and others, still live in the same section, not
far from their ancestral homes.

STORY OF GEORGE AND SAMPSON POPE.

   I have heard a story of the brothers George and Sampson
Pope, that may interest the readers of this book.   They were
both neighbors of Gen. Butler, and Sampson was warmly and
devotedly attached to him.   At some time, it appears, that
George was so unfortunate as to become very angry with
Butler.   In his anger and resentment he spoke very harshly

of him, which gave great offense to Sampson. He felt so em-
bittered by the abusive language George had heaped upon his
friend Gen. Butler, that it seemed to him they could no longer
live in the same neighborhood together. So he presented
George with a fine horse and a purse of five hundred dollars
and requested him to leave the District and go West, which
he did. Many years afterwards an acquaintance from Edgefield
travelling in Alabama, in search of new lands upon which to
settle, accidentally came across him, remained all night, perhaps longer with him; found him prosperous, if not rich;
very comfortably situated, and an influential local Methodist
preacher.

Of the sons of Sampson Pope, George was elected Clerk of
the Court of Edgefield, and died while in office. He was very
popular, and more than merely popular, he was beloved by the
people. Thomas H. made his home in Newberry—was a distinguished lawyer—was elected to the Legislature from that
county. One of his sons was, in 1891, Attorney General of the
State. Afterwards Associate Justice, and one was Clerk of the
Senate; they both having been previously members of the
Legislature. One son, Thomas H., became a Baptist preacher.
He was an earnest and good man. He died young, and his
body rests in Rosemont Cemetery in the town of Newberry. I
was writing "Within the Vail" and in the act of penning the
following lines when I was startled by the appearance of a
funeral procession passing with the body of Rev. Thomas H.
Pope to the grave. I dropped my pencil and paper and joined
the procession:

"The insect of to-day,
Whose little life is ended in a week,
Is as immortal as the god-like man;
It lives, grows old, and dies within a week;—
Three score and ten, the limit of man's life,
Is to eternity of equal date."

There are some other names on that roll of whom I never
knew anything. The very names are now strange in that section of the country.

ZACHARY SMITH BROOKS.

Capt. Zachary Smith Brooks I remember seeing often in my youth and early manhood. Zoar Methodist church, Persimmon Creek, as it was then called, was one to which I frequently went in my youth. Col. Brooks was a regular attendant. For many years, if my memory is not at fault here, his was the only carriage in all that part of the country, and the only one seen at that meeting house. It then seemed to me to be a very grand sort of life to be able to ride to church in a two horse carriage with a servant driving. And then when the carriage stopped to have him to let the steps down and help the master out! I remember the horses were bay, with nicked tails, as was the fashion in those days. I believe the first time I ever shook hands with Col. Brooks was at a Baptist camp meeting at or near Mt. Enon. Carriages and buggies became quite common in that community after awhile and the good old fashion of riding horseback to church gradually gave way, though it is not entirely abandoned yet. Horseback riding has its advantages—it gave young folks such splendid opportunities of cutting one another out, which, I dare say, the girls enjoyed, but some of the boys, especially those who were cut out, did not.

In the same general region of country, not far from Persimmon Creek, settled Crawford Perry and the Merchants, whose names are still well known in that community. The Barneses also came in at an early day. There was also a Captain John Hamilton and his brother Edward. These, however, did not come to Edgefield until after the Revolutionary War. Of this I am not right sure. Captain Hamilton was an officer in the British army, serving under his brother Col. Hamilton, who commanded a regiment in the left wing of the army at the Battle of Camden and aided greatly in the defeat of the Americans. These Hamiltons were Scotch, but they had been living in South Carolina—Lee, in his memoirs, says Norfolk, Virginia—engaged in mercantile pursuits before the war, but, unfortunately, took the wrong side in the contest, as many good men did. At their death they left very little property. I know of no descendants.

JOURNEY OF WASHINGTON.

When Washington, in May, 1791, passed through South. Carolina from Augusta to Columbia, the newly chosen capital of the State, his journey lay through the lower part of Edge-field. Of this journey Washington says: "Left Augusta about 6 o'clock Saturday, May 21st, and taking leave of the governor and the principal gentlemen of the place at the bridge over the Savannah River, where they assembled for the purpose, I proceeded in company with Colonels Hampton and Taylor and Mr. Lithgour, a committee from Columbia, (who had come on to meet and conduct me to that place), and a Mr. Jameson, from the village of Granby, on my route. Dined at a house about twenty miles from Augusta, and lodged at one Odem's about twenty miles further." The next day, Sunday, he rode about twenty miles to breakfast. Observe, that the Father of his country did not hesitate to travel on Sunday; but he foundered his horse and was compelled, in consequence, to remain in Columbia through Tuesday, the 24th, a day longer than he had intended. Of this route Washington says: "The whole road from Augusta to Columbia is a pine barren of the worst sort, being hilly as well as poor. This circumstance, added to the distant length of the stages, want of water and the heat of the day, foundered one of my horses very badly." His route lay by the Pine House and the Ridge. At every place along the road where he could be seen he was met by many citizens who were anxious to see and do honor to the great man. At one of these places he was seen by Mr. Crawford Perry, who lived at the time not far from the place now know as Perry's Cross Roads.

I think there is some land along that route the owners of which would not be pleased to have it now spoken of as a "pine barren of the worst sort."

ABNEY MEETING HOUSE.

Before I take a final leave of the Saluda near Higgin's Ferry, I may as well mention that a church, or house of worship, free to the use of all denominations of Christians, was once built on the road about a mile from the ferry, near Joel Abney's, and was known as the Abney Meeting House. All vestige and trace of it vanished from the earth long ago. In this meeting

House the eccentric Lorenzo Dow, on his journey northwards,
once preached. He also preached at Newberry Court House
the next day or evening, on the same journey. I have in my
possessson the original subscription list with the names and
amounts to be paid by each one. The money was to be paid
to the Trustees on the first day of January, 1803. There are
twenty-three names on the list of which seven are Abneys.
Francis Higgins subscribed ten dollars; William Irby five dollars; David Parkins five; and William Kennedy three dollars.
The whole amount subscribed was $156.00. Elias Boatner
subscribed two dollars. These names, Irby, Parkins, Kennedy and Boatner, though not strange to the country, vanished
from that section long ago. At what meeting house the
people of that section worshiped before the building of this
house I do not know. Evidently they must have had some
place, for too many years had elapsed since the first settlements were planted there for the people to be without divine
worship and religious instruction. Without churches and
school houses no people can be considered truly civilized, and
these always go wherever English speaking people go.

Before proceeding any further with this history I must beg my
readers,—if my accounts of the early history and traditions
of some sections are fuller and more complete than they are of
others,—to believe that of those particular sections I have been
able to obtain a greater amount of information, and not that I
have any special liking or partiality for those sections. I wish
to give a fair and impartial history of the whole county; but
wha: I do not know, or cannot learn, I cannot write.

VII.

ROADS AND FERRIES AFTER THE REVOLUTION.

By an Act of the Legislature, passed 22nd of March, 1786, a Ferry was established at Parkins' Ford on the Saluda River at the mouth of Bush River; one over the Savannah River by the name of Lemar's Ferry, in Edgefield County; one at a place called Snow Hill, in the County of Edgefield, on the Savannah River, to the land opppsite thereto, in the State of Georgia; and a road was ordered to be laid out and made the nearest and best way from Friday's Ferry on the Congaree, where Columbia now is, to the Ridge between the north and south forks of the Edisto—thence by the nearest and best way to the established ferry on the Savannah River opposite to Augusta; and also another road from the said ferry to Bevin's Bridge, on Horse Creek; from thence by the best and most direct way into the road leading from Fort Moore, (now Hamburg) to the White Ponds. This was partly the route of Washington. In 1788 a public road was established from Anderson's Ferry, on Great Saluda , to Mr. Enoch Grigsby's, and from thence to Captain Butler's, and from thence to intersect the road leading from Juniper to Orangeburg; also a ferry on Saluda, at the mouth of Rocky Creek, where the district line crosses;—and a road on the south side of the river was established from a place known as Weaver's Old Field to the said Waters' Ferry; and a ferry having been established in 1786 and vested in Philemon Waters, but no road leading thereto, laid out, a road was established and ordered to be laid out from, or near the Widow West's on the Ninety-Six Road, to the said Philemon Waters' Ferry, and Jacob Pope, Nathan Milton and William Boram were commissioners for laying out said road. In the same year, 1788, a road was ordered to be opened, by and under the direction of the Courts of the Counties of Abbeville and Edgefield, twenty-five feet wide, and leading the nearest and best way from Whitehall in the County of Abbeville to proceed near Samuel Anderson's in Cuffeetown, from thence to Charles Williams' on Turkey Creek, from thence to John Furman's on the Beaver Dam, from thence

to Charles Martin's on Horne's Creek, from thence to Seth
Howard's on Chaver's Creek, and from thence, in the most
convenient way, to the warehouse opposite the town of Augusta,—and that Seth Howard, Robert Anderson, John Thur-
man, James Hargrove and Fields Pardue be the commissioners
for opening the said road.

I am thus particular in noticing the opening of roads and the
establishing of ferries, because these show so clearly the needs
and wants of the people and their progress in improvements.
For the same reason we will take note of the building of railroads and telegraph lines, and of all other public institutions
which illustrate and meet the demands of the age.

MOUNT WILLING, S. C.

The History of Edgefield, says a friend—J. C. Edwards—
who has given me great assistance in the preparation of this
work, is grouped around four important centres, Mount Willing, Old Cambridge, or Ninety-Six, Edgefield Court House
and Hamburg.

Henry Mavson, who lived near Good Hope Baptist Church
for many years and died during the year 1891, at about eighty
years of age, was born at Ninety-Six. His father's house, in
which he was born, is the only building of that old time now
left standing there. After the decay of Cambridge Mr. Mayson removed to Hamburg, where he engaged in the mercantile
business in company with the late Colonel Thomas G. Bacon.

CATLETT CONNOR.

Catlett Connor, a very celebrated character in that day, and
who was elected to the State Senate over Eldred Simkins,
afterwards member of Congress and one of the most eminent
men in the State, lived near Ninety-Six in the house, the residence in 189., of Hon. Calvin W. Kinard. This Mr. Connor was
a blacksmith, a man of intelligence and of great force of character. Being considerably ambitious and jealous of the influence
of the Butler and Simkins families in the county, and thinking
that they were getting rather more offices than they were fairly
entitled to, wrote and published a pamphlet against them. He
was ably seconded by Mr. Matthew Jones of Ridge Spring,
father of General James Jones, Captain Lewis Jones of Edge-

field, and Major Edward Jones of Trenton; and the father-in-law of General Paul Quattlebaum of Lexington; Major Tillman Watson of Ridge Spring, and the Honorable William Gregg, the founder of Graniteville. Party feeling ran very high, so high, indeed, that Mr. Matthew Jones and Colonel Smith Brooks had a fight about the election at Mount Willing in which, it is said, that Colonel Brooks got the worst of it. Connor's gin house, said to be the first one built in Edgefield County, was still standing in the winter of 1890-91, and may be standing yet.

TOWNSHIPS OF MOBLEY, NORRIS, &C.

That part of Edgefield now constituting the townships of Mobley, Norris, Rhinehart and Huiett, used to hold their battalion muster at Mount Willing. At the beginning of the Revolutionary War this section was, perhaps, more thickly settled than any other part of the county. The original settlers came mostly, not from the lower counties of the State, but from Virginia and the Middle States. Many of them were noted for their independence and public spirit. Just before the breaking out of the war of Independence, there was not, perhaps, a happier, more prosperous, contented and independent people on the face of the earth, than the people of middle Carolina were—than the people of Edgefield were. The Indians were gone; much of the soil was fertile; game abounded in the forests and fish in all the branches, creeks and rivers. Taxes were light; so light, indeed, that the burden of taxation was not felt at all. He who was not able to live well and to grow rich was, indeed, one of nature's weaklings. It was, or might have been, equal to the poet's dream of life in Arcadia. The young men wooed and won the fair daughters of the pioneers who lived on the fertile shores of Cloud's Creek and Little Saluda, and built home nests of their own as cheerful and happy as the very birds that enlivened the forests around with their many and varied songs. But clouds came over the happy scene.

After the State threw off its allegiance to Great Britain, which was several months before the Declaration of Independence, by the General Congress at Philadelphia, it was necessary to have elections to fill all county offices, and also to elect members to the General Assembly. That election was held during the summer of 1776. Colonel Robert Cunningham was a candidate for election to the House of Representatives for the District of Ninety-Six. Cunningham was an avowed Loyalist, and sent·his relative, William Cunningham, afterwards the celebrated Bloody Bill, over to Mount Willing to look after the interests of that place. While the voting was in progress an unfortunate row occurred between the Whigs and the Loyalists, in which Cunningham and many others, on both sides, were beaten nearly to death. I think Cunningham was elected. Two years afterwards, in 1778, he was elected to the State Senate over Colonel James Williams, who was afterwards killed at the battle of King's Mountain.

1775.

But I must not omit to mention some events that occurred during the year before the Declaration of Independence. In this year, 1775, William Henry Drayton and Rev. William Tennant were sent by the Governor and Council of Safety into the upper parts of the State to conciliate the inhabitants and bring them to unite with the people of the low country in resistance to the arbitrary measures of Great Britain. In their progress through the up-country we find that Mr. Drayton had appointed a meeting to take place at the Ridge on Friday, the first day of September, 1775; but learning that Moses Kirkland had, without lawful authority, assembled men in arms in the district, and it being evident that, to his treachery against the Colony, he intended to add crimes of a deeper dye and, by force of arms, to violate the public peace, he declared that it was inexpedient for the meeting to be held, lest it should furnish occasion for bloodshed. He also declared that all persons following Kirkland and assembling in arms without authority, should be deemed public enemies, to be suppressed by the sword. This is the same Kirkland whose home was on Saluda, and who was captured while on his way to Boston to concert measures with General Gage for a general uprising of the Cherokees at the same time the attack should be made on Charleston by General Clinton. The British fleet was repulsed; the Indians made war as agreed, but the war ended in their total defeat and ruin.

From a letter from William Tennant to the Council of Safety in Charleston, September 1st, 1775, we learn that he was then on the south side of Saluda, and that Mr. Drayton had just gone on to Augusta. This letter was dated at Long Cane, in Ninety-Six District. Three volunteer companies were formed to repel the Indians and to keep the Tories in check. One under Major Terry; another under Colonel Pickens; and another under Captain James McCall. There was great terror felt by the well disposed inhabitants of the District.

On the 16th of September, 1775, a treaty of neutrality was formed between William Henry Drayton and Colonel Fletchall, and on the 21st Mr. Drayton wrote to Colonel Robert Cunningham, asking him if he considered himself included as a party to that treaty. Colonel Cunningham replied that he did not consider himself included as a party.

The following is taken from Gibbes' Documentary History of the American Revolution:

A report of the militia and volunteers on duty in the fortified camp at Ninety-Six on Sunday, the 19th of November, 1775, under the command of Major Andrew Williamson, by order of the Honorable the Provincial Congress:

NUMBER OF COMPANIES, COMMANDING OFFICERS, OFFICERS, SERGEANTS, AND PRIVATES

George Reed—1 officer, 2 sergeants, 22 privates.
Andrew Pickens—2 officers, 3 sergeants, 35 privates.
Aaron Smith—3 officers, 2 sergeants, 12 privates.
Benjamin Tutt—3 officers, 2 sergeants, 29 privates.
Andrew Hamilton—3 officers, 2 sergeants, 18 privates.
Thomas Langdon—2 officers, 1 sergeant, 9 privates.
Adam C. Jones—2 officers, 2 sergeants, 22 privates.
Matthew Berand—3 officers, no sergeant, 10 privates.
Charles Williams—1 officer, 2 sergeants, 8 privates.
Francis Logan—2 officers, 1 sergeant, 15 privates.
Alexander Noble—2 officers, no sergeant, 2 privates.
John Anderson—2 officers, 1 sergeant, 8 privates.
James Williams—2 officers, 2 sergeants, 24 privates.
Robert McCreery—3 officers, 2 sergeaats, 25 privates.
John Rodgers—3 officers, 2 sergeants, 15 privates.
Jacob Colson—2 officers, 1 sergeant, 15 privates.

Hugh Middleton—1 officer, no sergeant, 2 privates.

Francis Singuefield—2 officers, no sergeant, 15 privates.

James McCall—3 officers, 3 sergeants, 48 privates.

David Hunter—2 officers, 2 sergeants, 15 privates.

John Erwin—3 officers, 2 sergeants, 21 privates.

Robert Anderson—2 officers, 1 sergeant, 15 privates.

Nathaniel Abney—3 officers, 2 sergeants, 18 privates.

William Wilson—2 officers, 1 sergeant, 13 privates.

Jos. Hamilton's Artillery—1 officer, no sergeant, 16 privates.

Total: 25 companies, 55 officers, 36 sergeants, 432 privates.

N. B.—It is supposed that Major Mayson and his thirty-seven Rangers ought to be added to this return. William Abney, brother of Nathaniel Abney, was one of his officers.

These men were besieged in a fortified camp at Ninety-Six by Joseph Robinson, Patrick Cunningham, and Richard Pearis, and a strong force of Loyalists under their command. There was some fighting between the parties, and some loss was sustained by both sides. The men under Major Williamson were compelled to dig for water within their fort, as they were entirely cut off from a supply otherwise.

On the 22nd of November, 1775, a cessation of hostilities was agreed upon, a copy of which is here given with a letter from Major Mayson to Colonel Thomson enclosing a copy, and also giving an account of the affair; also a letter from Major Williamson to Mr. Drayton, giving an account of the siege, action, and treaty at Ninety-Six.

The following is taken from Gibbes' Documentary History:

Agreement for a cessation of arms between Major Joseph Robinson, commander of a body of his majesty's militia, now under arms for himself and the troops under his command, of the one part; and Major Andrew Williamson and Major James Mayson, commanders of the fort at Ninety-Six for themselves and the troops therein under the direction of the Provincial Congress:

1st. That hostilities shall immediately cease on both sides.

2nd. That Major Williamson and Major Mayson shall march their men out of the fort and deliver up their swivels.

3rd. That the fort shall be destroyed flat without damaging the houses therein, under the inspection of Captain Patrick Cunningham and John Bowie, Esq., and the well filled up.

4th. That the differences between the people of this District and others, disagreeing about the present public measures, shall be submitted to his Excellency, our Governor, and the Council of Safety, and for that purpose that each party shall send dispatches to their superiors—that the dispatches shall be sent unsealed and the messenger of each party shall pass unmolested.

5th. That Major Robinson shall withdraw his men over Saluda, and there keep them embodied, or disperse them as he pleaseth until his Excellency's orders be known.

6th. That no person of either party shall, in the mean time, be molested by the other party, either in going home or otherwise.

7th. Should any reinforcements arrive to Major Williamson or Major Mayson, they also shall be bound by this cessation.

8th. That twenty days shall be allowed for the return of the messengers.

9th. That all prisoners taken by either party since the second day of this instant shall be immediately set at liberty.

In witness whereof, the parties to these articles have set their hands and seals at Ninety-Six this twenty-second day of November, one thousand seven hundred and seventy-five, and in the sixteenth year of his Majesty's reign.

JOSEPH ROBINSON.
A. WM. SON.
JAMES MAYSON.

Present:

> PATRICK CUNNINGHAM.
> RICHARD PEARIS.
> ANDREW PICKENS.
> JOHN BOWIE.

MAJOR MAYSON TO COLONEL THOMPSON.

NINETY-SIX, November 24th, 1775.

I now enclose you a copy of the cessation of arms agreed upon by Major Williamson and myself the day before yesterday, by which you will be able to judge of the terms we are to abide by on both sides. The persons chosen to represent the matter before the Provincial Congress are Major Williamson, John Bowie, and myself, on the behalf of the associators for this Province; and Major Robinson, Captains Cunningham and Bowman, on behalf of the King. We who are appointed are to meet here on Monday next, the 27th inst., in order to proceed to town to settle this disagreeable business. I shall now give you a small narrative of our battle. On Saturday last, about 3 o'clock in the afternoon, we received intelligence that all the people assembled in arms over Saluda River, had marched over, and encamped about four and a half miles from our camps, in number about two thousand. We had, at most, not more than five hundred men. At first consultation with Major Williamson, we agreed to march and meet the opposite party and give them battle; but, upon consideration, we thought it most prudent to march all our men to Colonel Savages' old field, near Ninety-Six, as our numbers were small, compared with the other party, and to fortify the same with the rails thereabouts. We arrived there about day break, and in about two hours a square of one hundred and eighty-five yards was fortified in such a manner as to keep off the enemy; but before three days had expired our men began to be outrageous for want of bread and water, and we had not above sixteen pounds of gun-powder left. On Tuesday last, in the afternoon, the enemy held out a flag of truce and sent into our fort a messenger with a letter from Major Robinson to myself, which was the first beginning of this treaty. We have only one man dead since this battle, and eleven wounded; some will be mortal by the doctor's opinion. The enemy say they had but one man dead, who is a Captain Luper, and about the same number wounded as ours; by the best information they have buried at least twenty-seven men, and have as many wounded. I am certain I saw three fall at the first fire from our side. The swivels are to be delivered up this evening to us, although inserted in the articles of cessation as given by us up, as agreed to by the head men of the other party.

JAS. MAYSON.

———

Major Williamson to Mr. Drayton, giving an account of the siege, action, and treaty at Ninety-six:

WHITE HALL, Nov. 25th, 1775.

To the Honorable William Henry Drayton, Esq.:

SIR:—Your letter by order of Congress, dated the 9th inst.,

on the 14th, by the Express, and am happy to find my past conduct met the approbation of your Honor and the Congress. It shall always be my study to discharge my duty and the trust reposed in me by that respectable body. Before I received your letter I had reinforced Fort Charlotte with fifty-two militia and supplied them with provisions, and have since given orders for their continuing there one month longer; I have also furnished Captain Caldwell with iron for the carriages to mount the guns.

I should have had the honor of transmitting you an account of my situation before now, but could obtain no certain intelligence from the opposite party, until the seventeenth instant in the night, (notwithstanding I had used all possible endeavors and some expense to obtain some knowledge of their strength and designs,) when I learned their numbers amounted to at least fifteen hundred men, and understood that it was chiefly owing to an affidavit made by Captain Richard Pearis, that so many men were embodied—a copy whereof I now enclose you, as also a copy of the oaths they imposed on those who happened to fall into their hands, all of whom they disarmed, except such as were willing to join their party.

On the eighteenth, in the evening, I received certain information that they were crossing Saluda River on their march towards us, and then was joined by Major Mayson, with twenty-seven Rangers. I immediately ordered the men under arms, and took the resolution of marching to meet them, and demanding their intentions, and if they were determined to come to action, to be ready before them, and on acquainting the officers and men thereof, found them all cheerful and willing to proceed, but afterwards reflecting on the fatal consequences should we have been defeated, proposed in a council of war, consisting of Major Mayson and all the captains, to march from the camp near Ninety-Six into the cleared ground of Colonel Savage's plantation, where we could use our artillery with advantage, and there fortify our camp till we should receive more certain information of their strength (being in immediate expectation of being joined by Colonel Thompson and the Rangers at least, and also some men from the lower part of this regiment and Augusta,) which was unanimously approved of, and early next morning we marched to Ninety-Six

with all our provision and baggage, and in about three hours
erected a kind of fortification of old fence rails joined to a barn
and some out-houses, which, before we had quite completed,
they had surrounded us with a large body of men with drums
and colors. I then sent out an officer to demand their intention, who, on his return, reported that Major Robinson and
Mr. Patrick Cunningham refused to have any conference but
with the commanding officers. I then sent out Major Mayson
and Mr. Bowie, whom they and Mr. Evan McLaurin met be·
tween their men and the fort in sight of both, and after about fifteen minutes conference they returned and reported that they
insisted on our immediately delivering up our arms to them and
dispersing; which were the only terms they were determined
to grant us, and that at parting they told them to keep our
people within the fort, which was the only place where they
could be safe; and immediately they took two of our people
just by the fort, before my face, whom I gave orders to retake,
and a warm engagement ensued, which continued with very
little intermission from three o'clock in the afternoon of Sunday until Tuesday sunset, when they hung out a white flag
from the jail and called to us that they wanted to speak to
the commanding officers. I replied if they wanted to send an
officer or any message they should be safe. On which they
sent a messenger carrying a lighted candle and a letter from
Major Robinson, directed to Colonel Mayson, demanding of us
as before, to deliver up our arms and disperse, giving us one
hour's time to return an answer; to which Major Mayson and
myself jointly answered that we were determined never to resign our arms, and in about two hours Mr. Bowie, who carried
our answer, returned with a letter making the same demand,
and with him Patrick Cunningham, whom I met about fifty
yards from the gate, where we conversed for some [time, and
then he came with us into the fort, where, after some time, we
agreed to have a conference on the morrow, at eight o'clock.
Accordingly, on Wednesday morning Major Mayson, Captain
Pickens, Mr. Bowie and myself met with Major Robinson,
Messrs. Patrick Cunningham, Evan McLaurin and Richard
Pearis, and agreed to the cessation of hostilities now inclosed
you, which was lucky for us, as we had not above thirty
pounds of powder, except what little the men had in their

horns; but no scarcity appeared, as no person knew our stock but one gentleman and myself. We had thirty-eight barrels of flour with four live beeves in the fort, and got very good water the third day, after digging upwards of forty feet, so that if we had had a sufficiency of powder we could have stood a siege for a considerable time. It will appear to your Honor by the art'cles that we gave up the swivels; but that was not intended either by them or us, for after the articles were agreed on and were ready for signing, their people, to the number of between three and four hundred, surrounded the house where we were and swore if the swivels were not given up they would abide by no articles, on which the gentlemen of the opposite party declared upon their honor that if we would suffer it to be so inserted in the agreement they would return them, which they have done, and I have this day sent them to Fort Charlotte.

I am sorry to acquaint your Honor that some small difference arose between Major Mayson and me about the command of the militia, but flatter myself the service has not suffered thereby. To prevent any bad consequences I agreed that if he would come to camp I would receive orders from him for the militia and volunteers, and give them myself until a gentleman should arrive who would command us both, but when I received your letter with orders from the Congress, I thought myself no longer bound by that agreement, especially when he told me he was ordered to attend the Congress; I beg to be understood that I don't wish for command, but would willingly be of any service to my country that I possibly could.

I am obliged in justice to the officers and men on this expedition to declare that their behavior greatly exceeded the most sanguine expectation. They did not, during a siege of near three days without water, either murmur or complain, and cheerfully stood at their posts during three nights without any fire, nor was there any symptoms of fear to be seen among them. Our loss was very small, owing chiefly to blinds of fence rails and straw with some beeves' hides, erected in the night behind the men who would otherwise have been exposed to the fire of the enemy. We had only thirteen men wounded, one of whom is since dead, most of the rest very slightly. The loss of the opposite party is said to be considerable.

I have the honor to be, sir, your Honor's most obedient, and very humble servant,   A. Wm. Son.

This is the affair describing which, a resident in Savannah, Ga., to a gentleman in London thus writes:

"A Colonel Williamson, with twelve hundred men, first arriving, took possession of a stockade fort, where he was instantly besieged by Cunningham with his party. Williamson having remained confined for two days in the fort, destitute of provisions and water, was forced to sally with his men on the third day. But they were attacked by Cunningham in the attempt and totally dispersed. The Committee men made so good use of their heels that only twenty-five men were killed in the flight, for fight there was none."

Vlll.

In the Spring of 1776 George Mason collected a small company of men and marched with them to assist in the defense of Charlestown. He had the misfortune to lose a leg at the battle of Fort Moultrie, June 28th, 1776. Mr. Mason lived to be an old man and met his death by being drowned in Red Bank Creek while under the influence of rum or whiskey.

From the unsuccessful attempt on Fort Moultrie in 1776, to the Fall of Charlestown in 1780, matters were generally quiet in this part of Edgefield and the country was prosperous. However, in 1779, Benjamin Bell raised a company, composed of both Whigs and Loyalists, and joined Gen. Williamson in his expedition against the Cherokees. The Indians, in a spirit of derision, were accustomed to speak of General Williamson as a cow driver. Williamson retorted by calling them cattle. Captain Bell was killed in this expedition and I have been informed that some of his descendants think to this day that he was killed in the up-country while looking after his cows. Hon. John M. Bell, of Aiken, and the Daniels and Edwardses, are worthy descendants of this brave and worthy pioneer. A short time before his death he had been digging for silver on the south fork of Little Saluda, and his comrades, after their return from the expedition against the Cherokees, called it Mine Creek, which name it still bears.

After the Fall of Charlestown and the surrender of Lincoln's army, General Williamson, feeling that it was useless to struggle longer, submitted to the British authority, and took what is known as British protection. Very many good men did the same; among the number were Major Mayson and Colonel Pickens and Le Roy Hammond. Their condition was simply that of paroled prisoners, the same as that of the soldiers and garrisons in Charlestown. When called upon to take up arms by the British authorities, against their countrymen, many good Whigs refused and immediately took the field in the cause of independence, regarding the call to arms by the British as a violation of their parole, which it was. General Williamson, still regarding the Whig cause as entirely hopeless,

did not join them. For this his memory has always rested
under a shadow, and some have called him a traitor—the
Benedict Arnold of the South. This judgment is evidently
entirely too harsh. He never betrayed any trust. He never
sought any position for the purpose of betraying it. So far as
I have been able to discover he never did anything worse than
weakly yielding to what he thought was irresistible pressure.
He never took up arms against the State. He disbanded his
command and retired to his home. Ramsay, in his History of
South Carolina, says nothing of any treason—nor does Mills,
in his Statistics. Mills puts him in his list of eminent men of
the upper country, and says nothing of his treason. It is true,
however, that his act of submission gave great offense and was
a serious disappointment to many of his subordinate officers,
some of whom left the State. For the time they were helpless and the State was overrun. With all due deference to
great names and to the opinions of other historians of the State,
I submit that the proposition made by Governor Rutledge and
his Council of Safety to General Prevost to surrender the city
and State and hold them neutral during the war, was about as
shameful and disgraceful as any proposal well could be; and
equally as bad morally as General Williamson's course. It is
said that this was a mere *ruse*. General Moultrie and the soldiers did not so regard it.

In this particular part of Edgefield that now includes the
townships of Mobley, Norris, Rhinehart and Huiett, the Whigs
were in the majority, but the Tories had the assistance of the
British, which gave them confidence and the ascendency for
some time. Four companies of Whigs were raised and organized in these townships: One on Mine Creek, commanded by
Captain Solomon Pope, who lived on what is now known as
the Jennings Place, about one mile south of Red Bank church;
one on Cloud's Creek, commanded by Captain Mike Watson.
The present Rhinehart township was very thinly settled at
that time, but the men took a very active part in the war.
Captain James Butler, one of the heroes of Edgefield, lived
in that township on the place now owned (1891) by Dr.
John W. Kennerly. The Tory company was commanded
by Captain Neely Carghill and they lived mostly in the region
between the Little and the Big Saludas. This was the country

of Moses Kirkland and the Stewarts, though the Stewarts lived a little higher up. Captain Butler, with his company, was attached to the regiment of Colonel Le Roy Hammond of the Savannah side. The Tories under Carghill were subject to the orders of Colonel Robert Cunningham. ·Captain Pope's and Captain Watson's companies of Whigs also formed part of Le Roy Hammond's regiment.

SIEGE OF NINETY-SIX.

In the spring of 1781, when General Greene invested the fort at Ninety-Six, there was a general gathering of Whigs to his assistance, and of the Tories to re-enforce Colonel Cruger, the commander of the fort. Cruger himself was a Tory from New York, and all his garrison of five hundred men were Tories, two hundred from New York and three hundred from South Carolina, mostly from Ninety-Six District. The Tories under Carghill went up early in the spring to the assistance of ·Cruger. The Whig companies were ordered up in May.

General Greene, after besieging the fort for several days, hearing of the approach of Lord Rawdon with re-enforcements, was compelled either to raise the siege and retire or to endeavor to carry the place by assault. Could he have waited a few days longer, the place would have been his, but Lord Rawdon was too near; he could not wait. The assault was determined upon, but failed, and General Greene was compelled to retreat. He was pursued by Lord Rawdon across the Saluda and until he had crossed the Enoree. At that point Lord Rawdon ceased the pursuit, returned, and recrossed the Saluda, and sent word to Cruger to abandon Ninety-Six and go eastward, south of the Edisto, while he himself passed down south of the Saluda. General Greene, after crossing the Enoree, camped for a few days near Broad River. While he was here occurred that romantic episode of the war, the sending of Emily Geiger with dispatches to General Sumter, who was then on the Wateree. It would please me to tell at story here, but I am writing the history of Edgefield, and have already related it in the Annals of Newberry, and also in the hi ory of the State. Edgefield has its romances, the stories of which will be told in due season.

After Cruger left Ninety-Six, while passing down the country, he permitted Carghill's men to visit their homes, and they on their way passed the house of Captain Solomon Pope, where they found three of Pope's men, Aaron Wever, Joe Allen, and Fred Sissan, whom they made prisoners. Having no place of confinement after the loss of Ninety-Six, they took them into a swamp near by on Mine Creek and put them to death. Captain Pope immediately called his company together, hastened to Mount Willing and called on Captain Butler for assistance. With their united forces they met the troops under Carghill in the fork of Cloud's Creek and Little Saluda, where a bloody fight ensued, in which Carghill's men were completely exterminated. It is said that about half of them were killed after they had surrendered, so great was the exasperation of the Whigs at their conduct in murdering Pope's men a short time before. Only one man was left alive, Henry Etheredge, and he was saved by the interposition of Clark Spraggins, they being closely connected by marriage. Henry Etheredge lived to be over four-score years of age and died on Little Saluda in November, 1840. Captain Mike Watson followed the retreating Cruger as far as Orangeburg, where, or near which place, he was killed by the Tories in a severe skirmish. After his death Bud Eskridge, a brave but rather rash man, was placed in command.

TORY MARAUDERS.

Early in the fall of 1781 Pope and Lieutenant William Butler joined General Greene, who was then in the lower part of the State, leaving the militia in this part of Edgefield under the command of Captain Bud Eskridge. Soon afterwards a marauding party of Tories came up from Lexington into the neighborhood near Mount Willing, and carried off a considerable amount of booty. The Whigs immediately assembled for pursuit. They wanted Captain James Butler, father of Lieutenant William Butler, who was with General Greene's army at the time, to take command. But he begged to be excused, on the ground that the hardships he had so recently undergone had rendered him unfit to take command of such an expedition. He had only recently been released from prison in Charleston, where he had been closely confined ever since the British occupation of Ninety-Six, for having refused to take the oath of allegiance and accept British protection. The men were willing to excuse him, but his son James, who was quite a youth, refused to go with the party unless his father commanded. Captain Butler consented to go, but refused to take cammand, and would only go as an adviser. They pursued the Royalists, overtook them at Farrar's Spring, in Lexington, defeated and dispersed them, and recaptured the horses and cattle which they had carried away. On their return home elated with their success, contrary to the advice of Captain Butler, who urged them to push on without delay, they stopped at a tavern on Cloud's Creek kept by a Mr. Turner, to remain all night, thinking themselves safe from pursuit. Over confident and under the influence of liquor, they neglected to take the necessary precaution to post sentinels to guard against surprise.

The party of Tories, whom they had just defeated, formed part of Cunningham's band of raiders, then on their way through the up country on their last revengeful foray. This our party did not know, but they were soon aroused to a knowledge of the fact. The first intimation they had of the approach of Cunningham was given by Turner's daughter, who told young James Butler of his approach from the direction of Charlestown with several hundred men. There were in fact about three hundred. The house in which the Whigs had taken refuge was quickly surrounded by Cunningham, who demanded an unconditional surrender. He said, however, that he was willing to receive a communication from them. Smallwood Smith was selected by the Whigs to conduct the parley. When he presented himself Cunningham's first demand was: "Who are of your party?" When informed that young James Butler was one, he determined to give no quarter. The conflict then began by James Butler killing a man named Stewart. Butler himself was soon killed, and the whole party shortly afterwards surrendered. It is said that, after the surrender in a formal meeting of the Tory officers, Cunningham advised and ordered the massacre of the whole party. It was then that Captain James Butler caught up a pitchfork, which happened to be lying near, and defended himself until his right hand was cut off and he was shot dead. One man, Bartley Bledsoe, was spared as a compensation shown to Henry Etheredge a few months before.　Mrs. Sarah Smith, sister of Captain James Butler, with other women, wives, mothers, and sisters of the slain, went the next day with their negro servants, dug graves, and buried the dead as decently as possible.　Lot, a negro that belongéd to Smallwood Smith, told Mr. Edwards long afterwards, that he helped to burv three men, and that he saw a Tory strutting around, wearing a coat of his master's that had been badly cut with swords.

This butchery occurred during that celebrated raid of Cunningham's as far up as Hays' Station, in Laurens County, which he seemed to have made for the sole purpose of glutting a ferocious desire for revenge and getting one last copious drink of blood.　Such must have been the purpose, for it was impossible for the expedition to dɔ any good towards re-establishing the British authority.

CUNNINGHAM S RAID.

After this affair Cunningham, on his way up Saluda, devastated the property of the Whigs as far as he was able.　He burned the property of Dannett Abney, who was sick at the time and unable to make his escape, and slew him in his wife's arms.　He crossed Saluda with his men at Saluda Old Town or Anderson's, and passed through the upper part of what is now Newberry County, on his way to the Caldwell Settlement and Hays' Station.　In the upper part of Newberry he encountered a party of twenty men under Captain William Turner, who had fortified themselves as well as they were able in a strong log house.　These men he slew after they had surrendered, and after he had pledged his word to spare their lives. At Hays' Station, where there was a general massacre of all taken, Cunningham himself used his sword so unsparingly that his right arm became so weak and weary that he was scarcely able to raise his sword.　This was nearly the last of his butcheries and the end of this raid.

The present writer remembers seeing in his boyhood the charred remains of Dannett Abney's corn burned by Cunningham.　He made a clean sweep of everything combustible on the place.　On Cunningham's way back to Charlestown his party encountered, not far from Saluda Old Town, Oliver Towles, famous, as the Tories alleged, for stealing their cattle.

They hung him with a thong cut from the rawhide of a Tory's cow, so that he might meet his doom from that which he was so fond of lifting. A kind of grim humor not very humorous to all the parties concerned. Parties under Pickens, Le Roy Hammond, Butler, and others, started in pursuit. Seven fresh parties also started. Cunningham's party was broken up—his men were scattered and dispersed, many of them killed. Cunningham escaped, his fine horse carrying him safely through all dangers to Charlestown. Twenty-three days after reaching the city, Ringtail died, ridden to death, and his master wept like a child, Bloody Bill as he was, over the dead body of his poor friend. He buried him with military honors.

IX.

CONDITION OF THE COUNTRY.

As might naturally be expected, this part of Edgefield was in a very deplorable condition at this time and soon after the close of the war. A great deal of property had been wantonly destroyed—houses' had been burned—negroes stolen and carried away, and nearly half the men had either been killed or died of disease while in camp. I doubt whether any part of the State, or of the United States, suffered more from the strife between Whig and Tory than did this particulr section of Edgefield, the history of which we are just now trying to sketch. Cunningham was a man of strong will and of fine intellectual power, and, aided by such men as Ned Turner and the Stewarts, and Carghill and others, who lived on and near the Saludas, and, contending against such men as the Towleses, Butlers, Corleys, Edwardses, Brookses, Smiths and others of equal will and courage, the strife too often degenerated into one of mere personal animosity and bitterness. Men, in these intense, concentrated strifes, too often cease to contend for the original cause of quarrel, and fight and devour each other animated by a spirit of pure personal hatred.

Soon after the Whigs got the upper hand in this section they arrested Rev. Mr. Norris, of Cloud's Creek, for preaching the doctrine of non-resistance, and lodged him in jail at Ninety-Six. The imprisonment he, of course, bore with great patience, as it was a good opportunity to exemplify in practice what he taught so earnestly in preaching. After the war was over the State behaved with great magnanimity and forbearance towards all Tories and mal-contents. In many instances, and to large amounts, property, that had been confiscated and was already in possession of the State, was restored to the owners on condition of the payment of a fine of 10 per cent. Cruger, on the discharge of his men, many of whom were natives and citizens of Ninety-Six District, advised them to remain in the State and return to their old homes. Many of them did so, and some came to this part of Edgefield where they lived as good citizens, leaving large and respectable families when they died. Many also came over from the Catawba and Broad River sections of the State. Prominent among these were William and Abram Ferguson, brothers of Colonel Ferguson, who was defeated and slain at King's Mountain. These men lie buried at Denny's, just across the road in front of the store. They once owned the Mickler and Denny plantations.

In the year 1791, Washington, on his return North from his Southern tour, passed through this part of Edgefield. He visited Ridge Spring and shook hands with all who came forward to greet him—indeed, with the most of the ancestors of those who are living there now.

GREAT DEMORALIZATION.

In the early part of the century there was great demoralization in this part of Edgefield, as well as in other parts of the District and the country. The great besetting sin was the too free use of whiskey or rum; and to this may be added their usual accompaniments, card-playing, profanity and the disregard of the Sabbath. Many persons now living can remember when there was a grog-shop at every cross road, and sometimes between, when the cross roads were too far apart. Sometime, in the early part of the century, M. L. Weems wrote and published a history of Edgefield, in which he gives some account of the very deplorable state of morals then existing. He calls Edgefield a Pandemonium, which, being literally interpreted, means, I suppose, a home of all the devils. I hope it is some better now, and that some, at least, of the devils have been cast out. This book of Mr. Weems' I have never seen, but, judging from his Life of Washington, which I have read, and which I have now in my library, I am inclined to think that Mr. Weems was somewhat lavish in the use of glowing adjectives and strong language.

The state of morals was no doubt bad enough in all conscience, it always is for that matter. About the year 1809, a great reformation and revival of religion took place. It is said that in that year no less than sixteen hundred persons in Edgefield joined the church under the preaching of the celebrated Lorenzo Dow. In 1811 was the great earthquake, the greatest ever known in this State, with the exception of the one in 1886. Perhaps that also helped to deepen and render more firm the

religious convictions of the people; for, certainly, it is a little
startling and well calculated to impress us with the instability
of all earthly things to feel the solid earth beneath our feet
rise and fall and roar and quiver like the unstable waves of the
sea.

SETTLERS FROM MARYLAND.

In or about the year 1805, a considerable number of persons
came from Maryland and settled not far from the Saluda.
James Bonham and Jared Edwards were among the number.
Edwards first came to South Carolina as a soldier in the Maryland line under General Gates and was in the battle of Camden
when Gates was defeated, August 16, 1780. Not long after he
came to Edgefield he married Rebecca Bell, youngest daughter
of Captain Benjamin Bell, who was killed in the campaign
against the Cherokees in 1779. From this union sprang the
present large family of Edwardses.

James Bonham married Sophia Smith of Mount Willing, a
lady of rare intelligence and culture and noted for her extra-
ordinarily fine manners. Governor Milledge L. Bonham was
their youngest son.

During the war of 1812 the State was never invaded and,
consequently, there were no conflicts of armed forces on land,
though troops were raised and sent to the coast for defence.
The troops were commanded by Major General William But
ler. His son, George Butler, was commissioned colonel in the
regular United States Army. I have heard it related that he
was at home engaged in laying a brick walk from the door of
the dwelling house to the kitchen door for his mother's benefit,
when a courier rode up and handed him his commission in the
army. He sprang to his feet and, reading his commission, he
swore he would work no more that day. Samuel Mays was
brigadier general.   •

Before this time there had not been much migration from
Edgefield to the West; but the defeat of the Indians by General Jackson and the driving of them further towards the
setting sun, opened up vast fertile regions for the occupancy
of the white man, of which opportunity many in Edgefield
were not slow to avail themselves.

About the year 1820 the Legislature made an appropriation

of ten thousand dollars to Mrs. Randolph, the daughter of Thomas Jefferson. This appropriation caused great dissatisfaction in Edgefield and gave offense to many voters and tax payers. They construed it as an unlawful use of public money, as aiding in keeping afloat a decaying aristocracy, and not as a reward, a gift, a public testimonial, for the great services rendered to the whole country by her illustrious father, and entirely inadequate to those services. The opposition to the measure was led by Catlett Connor, a man of energy and intelligence, who denounced the appropriation in the strongest terms, and those members of the Legislature who had voted for it. A. P. Butler was one of them, and his popularity received a severe wound, but he bided his time and entirely recovered and reinstated himself in the affections of the people. He retained his popularity to the close of his life.

Colonel Ryden Grigsby, a brave soldier, died in 1825. He had represented the District in the Legislature. His daughter became the wife of Captain Jonathan Wever, a man of great wealth, who lived three or four miles north of where the town of Johnston now is. The only son of the marriage was the somewhat celebrated John R. Wever. He became brigadier-general of militia and a member of the Legislature. He was a man of free and easy manners and lavish in the use of his money. He was wealthy and lived as though he was seized, and possessed of the River Pactolus, the waters of which flowed full of gold, and the sands at the bottom were not common sands but diamonds and gold dust and silver. His property slipped through his hands; the stream of Pactolus ran dry; and from being a man of great wealth, he descended to very humble circumstances in life and died poor.

Rev. John Manly married a daughter of Zebulon Rudolph, of Red Bank, about the year 1825, and remained in Edgefield a good many years. The mention of Rudolph recalls to my memory an old Edgefield tradition that the celebrated Marshal Ney of France, the bravest of the brave, was a Rudolph, born on Red Bank, in Edgefield District, and that his name was Michael Rudolph; that, in his youth he went to France; enlisted in the army; soon became noted for his bravery; was made corporal, sergeant, lieutenant. At that period, in the history of France when promotion once began it was rapid, and before many years he rose to the highest rank in the army, that of Marshal of France. It is really wonderful how such traditions begin, and how they hold their own, once started. There is, however, this much of truth in the story to build upon. Ney's name was Michael. Alison in his History of Europe, and Ney's biographers, name the place of his birth, his education, his father, his enlistment, his rise from the ranks, &c. It is impossible for him to have been Michael Rudolph of Red Bank in Edgefield. But perhaps not, after all, for the Rudolphs of Edgefield were of noble German or Alsace origin.

There is a tradition also, that Jefferson Davis was a native of Edgefield. This is a mistake. He was born in Kentucky —his mother a native of South Carolina. But Edgefield can claim, as a well known and well established fact, that Lieutenant General James Longstreet, the right hand of Lee during the great war of Secession, was born in that district. The place of his birth is known as the "old Dent place," and is near the line of Aiken and Edgefield, a few hundred yards north of the north prong of a small stream known as Fox Creek, some seven or eight miles from Augusta, and about four miles east of the Savannah River. It is a rough, rugged spot, and has no house there now.

In the good old days there lived on Mine Creek an industrions man named Travis. His wife bore him no children and she was frequently begging her neighbors to make her a present of one; but the neighbors did not feel like parting from one of their own in this way. At last, however, her importunate prayer was gratified in a way she had not anticipated. Going out one morning to the cow pen as usual to milk her cows, she found hanging on the bars a little bundle carefully done up, which on examination she found containing a fine baby boy. She adopted him at once and named him Bar Travis from the place where he was found. He grew up a fine, healthy boy; became an active, energetic man, an honor to those who had adopted and reared him. In due time he married and finally settled a place one mile north of Bethlehem church—a place lately the home of Hon. W. J. Ready. It was here that Colonel William B. Travis, the commander and hero of the Alamo, was born in 1809. The grave of Bar Travis is still to be seen. William B. Travis emigrated to Alabama and from that State went to take part in the Revolution in Texas and was there murdered in the Alamo, March 6, 1836, by order of General Santa Anna, with all the other defenders of the place. Among them was the celebrated David Crockett, of Tennessee, and Colonel Bonham and Colonel Bowie. "Remember the Alamo!" was the war-cry of General Houston at the Battle of San Jacinto, where his great victory was gained and Santa Anna taken prisoner. A biographical sketch of Colonel Travis will be given further on and I hope to be able to say a little more about the others also.

During nullification times Press Bland was quite a prominent and influential character in Edgefield, though he never held any office nor aspired to any. He was a strong nullifier, and being a man of considerable wealth and strong will his influence was very decided and submissionists found no favor in his eyes. He left several daughters who were much esteemed. I have heard it related of Mr. Bland that he would sometimes on horseback, booted and spurred, visit Aiken, which in his day was a small railroad village. When ready to leave, inspired by the potent influence of John Barley Corn, he would mount his horse and ride through the town singing at the top of his voice:

Barnwell District, Aiken town;
O Lord in mercy do look down!
The land is poor, the people too;
If they don't steal what will they do?

During the war with the Seminole Indians in Florida, on the call for men from this State, David Denny raised a large company, of which he was elected captain, and took part in the campaign of 1836. Captain Denny was a brave and true man, and those who knew him well bear him in honorable and kindly remembrance. There were also the Huietts living in the same section of country. Colonel John Huiett was major during the service of the South Carolina Volunteers in the war in Florida. He was afterwards elected to the Legislature. He died in Augusta, Ga. His brother, George D. Huiett, I have heard mentioned as one of the best men that ever lived in Edgefield. He was industrious, honest and pious. If I am not mistaken he served a term of six months as an officer in the Second Regiment of State troops commanded by Colonel William Fort,

attached to the Brigade of General Walker, stationed at Pocotaligo in 1863–64. He died a few years ago—(I write this
September, 1891,) on the place where he was born in Huiett
township.

Very few volunteers went from the lower battalion of the
Tenth Regiment, South Carolina militia, to the war with Mexico. They were mostly from the neighborhood of Ninety-Six
and the Court House. A Roll will be given of all these, with
the casualties, as well as of all who entered the Confederate
service from the County.

Colonel Reuben Bouknight, a man of much promise and of
rather more than ordinary ability, was elected to the Legisla
ture from this section. He died at the early age of thirty-six.
Captain B. I. Bauknight, of Emory Chapel, is a son of his, and
a daughter was married to E. J. Goggans, of Newberry, who,
after marriage, deserted Newberry and made his home at
Mount Willing and the neighborhood, where he was living at
the close of the year 1891—living 1894.

We will now pass on into the neighborhood of the Ridge and
Cloud's Creek. Cloud's Creek, which bears the name of a man
who once lived there, is a lovely stream. Its source is a half
dozen small creeks which rise in the Ridge. They unite, forming Cloud's Creek; flow on through Rhinehart and finally
mingle with the turbid waters of Little Saluda. Cloud's Creek
has long been noted, and is yet noted for its quarries of fine
granite and millstones. This part of the Ridge is now Norris
Township. Before the year 1850, very few men in this section were aspirants for office or sought popular favor. About
that time James Cameron, a man of wealth and intelligence,
became a candidate for the Legislature. He was not elected,
and soon afterwards he sold his land, upon which he had built
a fine house and made a beautiful home, and went west. The
place is now owned by Dr. H. M. Folk. A few years afterwards Wade Holstien was elected, but his own affairs required
his exclusive attention, he retired from public life. Moses N.
Holstien is a son of his. Major Tillman Watson was a grandson of Captain Mike Watson of the Revolution, of whom a
biographical sketch will be found in this volume. He married
Elizabeth Jones, a daughter of Mr. Matthew Jones, who lived
near by. Major Watson was not a man of much education or

reading; but he was an honest and true man; of good natural ability, and had the respect and confidence of his neighbors and of all who knew him. He was once elected to the State Senate over Colonel James Carroll, one of the ablest lawyers of the Edgefield Bar and afterwards Chancellor. A good many stories illustrating the ignorance of Mr. Watson and showing his unfitness for public life, were told about this time. Here is one not at all to his discredit as an honest man, however much it might show that he was not well posted in public affairs. When State Senator he was asked what he thought of the Kansas-Nebraska Bill, which was then under discussion in the Congress of the United States. He at once replied: "Why, sir, if it is a just bill it should be paid." Mr. Watson was possessed of abundant wealth and being childless, he left it all to the children of his brothers and sisters.

X.

DR. J. C. READY.

I do not know any more appropriate time and place than the present to introduce a brief notice of Dr. John C. Ready, a physician of talent and of extensive practice, who lived for many years in Edgefield County and who died at his home on the Ridge in 1870 or 1871. Dr. Ready was born in Chester District in 1802. If I mistake not, I have been told that after taking his degree in medicine he practiced for awhile in Newberry District, but I may be mistaken in this. The first time I ever saw Dr. Ready was in Edgefield County, not far from the Saluda River at the muster ground of the Yellow Jacket Volunteer Company, during the nullification excitement—the year I do not remember. The doctor was then unmarried; a new comer into the county, and, being a good talker, of good education and of fine intelligence and ambitious of distinction, he was called upon to make a speech. There was a barbecue on hand, and, without doubt, a good supply of the ardent to stimulate the patriotism of the people, which was already glowing with considerable heat, burning in opposition to the high protective tariff measures of Congress. But in spite of our opposition; in spite of nullification, a high protective tariff has been imposed upon certain classes of goods from that day to this, and I suppose will be to the end, for it is the natural disposition of those who have the power to rob and oppress the weak. In fact, it may be laid down as a law, fixed and unalterable, that the weak have no rights that the strong are bound to respect. We see this principle, or law, established and exemplified through all animate and inanimate nature. Wherever there is life the strong and vigorous organization overshadows, oppresses, and destroys the weak. The strong man, the strong party, the strong nation, is only acting in accordance with fixed, unalterable law when robbing and destroying the weak. But a protective tariff that makes one industry pay for the support of another, more than the legitimate earnings of that other, is robbery all the same. Although it is robbery, yet what will we have? It is manifest

that laws were not made, and cannot be, for the strict administration and securing of positive and absolute justice. How
can the ends of justice be attained by law when no man is just?
After all, it is not justice that is desired, but order, which is
far more important.

"Order is heaven's first law, be this confest,
Some are, and must be, greater than the rest."

Yes, it is order that is the great desideratum, not justice.
After all, again, the tyrant of to-day; the oppressor is no happier nor better off than the oppressed. The autocrat of all the
Russias is a poor unfortunate wretch, whose nights and days
are dreams of terror. The wretchedest exile in Siberia is not
more unhappy than he. And, again, how can we have justice
in this world, when no man wants it, but wants, instead, to
get the upper hand of somebody else. After all, again, the
oppressor is no happier nor better off than the oppressed. Say
that he gets all he wants; let him pile up his millions; he cannot take them out of this world. They are of the earth and
must remain on the earth. But *he* dies and goes to hell, and
when he gets there he curses himself for being such a damned
fool while here. Even then, though, he would not change
himself, but his condition, for he can have no idea of any happiness, of any joy in life, except that which comes from self-
love and the gratification of all selfish desires and purposes.
If he ever hears or thinks of heaven, of a place, or State,
where men are happy and not wretched like himself, he only
thinks of those who are there as having been wiser and sharper
than he, and as having made a better bargain with somebody.
That his surroundings are himself, and that heaven and hell
grow out of the persons who are in them, is a thought that it
is impossible for him to entertain. But a tariff for protection,
that fosters one industry at the expense of another, is robbery
for all that, and everyone who receives any benefit from it is a
robber to that extent. Yes, it is order that the world wants,
not justice, not right; and let the robbery be done in due and
ancient form and no complaint should ever be made—that is,
ought not to be made. Though complaints will be made.
There are always some restless, dissatisfied persons who cannot
see, who *will* not see, rather, that order, the good order and
welfare of society, requires that things should always remain

as they are and never be disturbed. Robbery is robbery nevertheless, and protective tariff comes under that category.

It was on this theme that the doctor was holding forth the
first time I ever saw him. What he said I cannot remember, but
it was in opposition to the tariff. He was a good speaker, and
a very good practicing physician, but he was entirely unfit to
be a surgeon, on account of a weakness and unsteadiness of
nerve. I saw him once try to remove a small object from one
of the nostrils of a child. His hand shook and trembled so
much that it was impossible for him to insert the forceps into
the nostril, and he had to give it up and send the child away.
The object was soon afterwards removed by some one by the
simple process of pushing it back into the mouth.

During the great religious revival that swept over the country from 1830 to 1836, Dr. Ready became converted under the
preaching of Barnes, Hodges, and Worthington; joined the
church, and was himself quite a zealous Baptist preacher for
awhile. He married Miss Eliza Rook, of Laurens County, an
estimable and excellent lady. After marriage he settled at
Mount Enon and built him a good house where he lived for a
number of years, prospering and accumulating property. He
then sold his property and removed to the Ridge. His son
William J. Ready and some others of his children were born
at Mount Enon. I remember William as a boy, but do not
think I ever saw him after his father moved to the Ridge.

He, too, is gone, after an honorable career; having been an
officer in service during the War of Secession, and afterwards
elected to the House of Representatives and State Senator.
His estimable widow, in a few months after his death, also departed this life.

THAT YELLOW JACKET COMPANY.

I think this company should have more notice than the mention of its name, as it was certainly one of the most unique
institutions of the kind that ever was devised. It was a rifle
company and met on the old Ninety-Six Road, at the Sum-
mers' Place, not far from Perry's Cross Roads, and near a plantation belonging to Colonel Smith Brooks. It was at this place
that I first saw Colonel Brooks and heard him say something
to the people about having been an old Revolutionary soldier.

This was during the period of the nullification excitement.

The uniform of the Yellow Jacket Company was certainly one of the funniest ever devised by the ingenuity of man; but it had one exceeding great virtue—there was no excess of drapery about it. It was handy. The company was called the Yellow Jacket Company because the uniform was of a yellowish hue, nankeen or copperas, and cotton at that. The coat was a roundabout jacket, with the funniest little frizzled up duck's tail that I ever saw to a jacket, somewhat like that which race jockey boys have to their coats. The people I saw there, even all the boys that were with me that day when I heard Dr. Ready speak are all gone. My elder brother, Giles, was there. He was killed at the Battle of Buena Vista, in Mexico, when General Taylor gained his great victory that made him President of the United States. My uncle Daniel Abney was there—gone long ago. James Black, gone more than forty years ago. Mike Long—gone. I do not remember that I saw George Spearman that day. He is living yet. His mother was a Nunn—first married Abney—the grandfather of A. P. Coleman, who lives near the old cross-road—when a widow married Spearman, the father of George and Nancy, who are both now living. Nancy Spearman married Lewis Sample, the father of Frank and Sam. His widow lived and died near the place on which she was born, which was within a few hundred yards of the Yellow Jacket muster ground. At this same barbecue, of which I have been telling, I remember seeing Alexander Stewart, a scion of that Tory family of the Revolution, the same who preserved as sacred relics the red coat and other things worn by some of his people during that time. Aleck Stewart was himself of rather unsavory reputation, but I received treatment from him that day that warmed my heart towards him and kindled a grateful feeling that never has died out and never can. I was a very bashful and diffident boy, and have always been a very bashful and diffident man, though my friends might not know it, and might not believe it should I tell them, but it is true, nevertheless. Alexander Stewart seeing my diffidence and backwardness, took me up to the table, waited upon me and gave me whatever I wanted, and as much as I wanted to eat. I have never forgotten it. I am afraid of boys. It seems to me, sometimes, that a great many boys try to be smart, and make themselves too smart. They are not all so. Some are too diffident and back-ward, and in such cases if you can give a little kindly en-couragement, be it ever so little, you do a world of good and make to yourselves lasting friends. Girls always receive at-tention, it is their due; but boys often fail to receive the small sweet courtesies, when they would be of great and lasting benefit to them.

A FIGHT AT EDGEFIELD.

As I am now writing of events that occurred in the midst of Nullification times, the Yellow Jacket Company, being a red-hot nullification rifle company, I may as well relate an inci-dent that occurred at Edgefield Court House, in which a young Irishman or Scotchman, named Archibald Armstrong, who, I think, was a member of the company, was an interested party. One public day at Edgefield, whether Court-week or Sale-day, not now remembered, Armstrong was there, a jolly, rollicking young giant, ready for a fight or a frolic. In that day and time at Edgefield Court House one did not have to go far to find either a fight or a frolic. I am glad to say it is now a seat of culture and refinement. The crowd that day was de-cidedly a nullification crowd, and decidedly in earnest, as Edge-field crowds, in town or county, always are. There may have been some anti-nullifiers or submissionists there, but if there were any they found it necessary to lay low and keep dark. This crowd, seeing that Armstrong was a stranger, and some of them taking it into their heads that he was a submissionist, picked a quarrel with him and soon got into a fight. They put one of their best men forward, but after a few rounds he was used up and rendered unfit for further service. They tried him with another, and another, but he still remained master of the field and the situation. He then told them to come on one at a time and he would tan out the whole crowd if they wished; but they had enough, and no other one was found willing to tackle him. Armstrong had a friend present whom they all knew and respected; but until he spoke they did not know he was Armstrong's friend, as he had remained very quiet and was looking on to see fair play. He told them that Armstrong was as good and true a nullifier as any of them; that he knew him well and could vouch for him. This friend was James Boulware, of Big Creek, whom I knew well in my boyhood and early manhood. He moved to Alabama, and long afterwards I met him once at Edgefield Court House when he had passed the meridian of life; but he stood straight as an arrow and his step was firm. His beard was white, as white as snow, whiter than my own is now, and hung down upon his breast. His eyes were bright, his face was ruddy and full of health, and I thought him the finest looking man I had ever seen. Mr. William P. Butler of Edgefield, when I saw him last, a long while ago, was a very handsome man, but Mr. Boulware was larger, and there was a strength and vigor in his appearance, that impressed me so much that I still bear him in mind as the finest looking man I have ever yet seen. His brother, Humphrey Boulware, was Sheriff of Edgefield for some years. His grandmother was a Rutherford, of the patriotic family of Colonel Rutherford of the Revolution. She sleeps her last sleep at Red Bank Baptist Church, of which she was a member.

XI.

A REMARKABLE PHENOMENON.

Just before the great and decisive act of Secession, in the Fall of 1860, as I have been told it was, but my memory would place it a year or two earlier, in 1859, I think. I did not witness the phenomenon, but was told of it the next morning. I was absent from home in Laurens County, and the display occurred after the usual hour of retiring to sleep. It was a wonderful display of the Aurora Borealis. "I awoke," says my informant, "with a great thirst, being a little boy at the time, when my mother, of blessed memory, took me to the piazza to get some water. The whole element appeared to be a solid sheet of blood, and the reflection from the sky caused a pale yellow light to shine upon the earth. Many others saw it, and some say they heard music also. The old men called them 'war lights,' and said such things occurred to their fathers just before the Revolution." I did not see this magnificent disylay of the heavenly light, but remember hearing it spoken of as ominous of coming trouble. Comets were once so regarded and eclipses of the sun, and all unusual and remarkable displays of natural phenomena. Indeed, a great display of the Aurora Borealis is enough to strike any beholder with feelings of awe, and the unlearned with terror. It is a phenomenon which the most learned and scientific men of the age have never been able to explain satisfactorily. It is too hard for science. It seems to be one of those unexplainable phenomena. Similar phenomena occurred about ten years later, beginning in August and continuing almost nightly, until far into the spring following. Some of the auroras were exceedingly beautiful, rising in the northeast in great pillars of reddish light, passing westward across the pole and sinking in the northwest. As for the music, I know not whether any was heard then, but that music is sometimes heard in the atmosphere above us without any visible producing cause, I know; but whether it be an echo from music at a distance, or whether it be strains descending from supernal sources, I do not know. One day at the burial of a child in Rosemont Cemetery, New-

berry, officiating minister Rev. W. D. Kirkland, of the Methodist Church, I heard distinctly a strain of music, coming, it
seemed to me, from far above, yet floating around and near.
It might have been—I know not which—a response to the
hymn just sung at the grave, or a welcome from angelic choirs
to the soul of the child. Be its source what it may, I heard it.
Some years afterwards a friend told me that riding by the
same cemetery one evening near sunset, when everything was
quiet and still around, he heard similar strains floating in the
air far above him. Is it superstition to believe that there is
another and a better world very near to this, and that sometimes, whether by eye or by ear, or by some other sense, we
may have perception of its nearness?

SECESSION AT MOUNT WILLING.

When the State seceded, December 20th, 1860, the cannon
of rejoicing that were fired at Hamburg were heard as far as
Mount Willing, and even beyond. The cannon fired at Charleston, during the bombardment of that city by the Federals,
were heard very nearly as far as Ninety-Six; but they were of
much larger calibre than those at Hamburg. A few days after
the passage of the Ordinance of Secession, the lower battalion
of the Tenth Regiment was assembled at Mount Willing and a
company of volunteers was formed to go into service. David
Denny, the same man who commanded a company during the
Seminole war, was elected captain. This day will always be
remembered in the history of that battalion. A beautiful flag,
attached to a rope stretched from the top of the storehouse to
the limb of a large oak, was waving in the air. The ladies,
carried away by the enthusiasm of the time, waved their handkerchiefs and cheered their friends and relatives as they volunteered; while the band kept up a continual strain of music;
and the militia officers paraded and swore at a fearful rate, as
fully as terribly as ever our army did in Flanders. Aunt Fannie
Smith, a free colored woman, who sold ginger-cakes and beer
at musters, did a great business that day. Thomas L. Smith
was the Colonel of the Tenth Regiment of militia. When a
hundred men had enlisted and enrolled themselves, Miss
Lizzie Dozier, who, after the close of the war, married Captain Charlton, presented them their flag. J. C. McElroy re-

ceived it and assured the ladies that he would carry it from the Potomac to the Rio Grande, if necessary. He did his best during the war. He carried it beyond the Potomac, and his heroic dust now lies beneath the soil, or mingled with it, of one of the famous battle fields of Maryland. Several other companies were formed and went to the front. The names, as far as it is possible to procure them, of all, both officers and men, who went from the county, with the casualties, will be given before I close.

It is impossible in this book, nor does it come within its scope, to give a history of the War of Secession; but some incidents and anecdotes will doubtless be given before the work is done. Many brave deeds were performed, many lives were lost, and many cripples were made during that great contest; but the only question finally settled and decided was the relative strength and power of endurance of the parties. The great political question as to the relations existing between the States was left precisely *in statu quo ante bellum*. Slavery? That was a mere accident or incident of the quarrel, and not the question—not a question at issue between the parties. The real question at issue was: Whether a State, once independent, having formed a union with other independent States, could sever that union at will. We affirmed; they denied. The other side fought for the union, solely and simply, under any conditions. We fought for the freedom and independence of the States as States, without regard to any particular forms of government, whether Democratic, Republican, or Aristocratic. We were Greeks; they were Romans, who fought for empire. And as Rome conquered Greece in ancient days, so, in modern times, the Empire has conquered and the Greek States have perished. Let us see to it that Greek culture, Greek art, Greek thought, and Greek poetry, and Greek inspiration, have not perished, though the States have. In time we may reconquer the empire, as Greece through her letters at last conquered Rome.

Mr. Lincoln cared no more for the freedom of the negro than Mr. Davis did. His Emancipation Proclamation, which has been so much lauded by his admirers, was issued only as a war measure, in the hope that it would weaken the defences of the South by exciting insurrections, insubordination, and encouraging runaways from the Southern fields. It expressly excepted from its operation all States and parts of States not in rebellion against the government of the United States, and slaves in all such States and parts of States were to remain in slavery because their masters were loyal.

Men went to the front full of enthusiasm, leaving wives and children at home. In a little while it was impossible to go to church, or to any gathering of people, without seeing wounded soldiers at home on furlough, with arm in a sling or limping on crutches. Every mail brought news of a neighbor or a friend being wounded or killed in battle. The most distinguished officers that were killed from the section of country embraced in the lower battalion of the Tenth Regiment, were Lieutenants J. R. Bouknight, W. J. Denny, J. M. Daniel, Levi Crouch, W. A. Rutland, and Hiram Holstein; Captain Norris and Major John Crowder. These were all brave and patriotic men. No doubt there were many brave deeds done by private soldiers, as well as by the officers, that ought to be recorded; and the pen of this scribe would move gladly and swiftly in recording them, but no record was made of them at the time, and they have passed into the sum of all, lost, but not lost, as a drop of water in the sea.

Old soldiers still often speak of the unrivalled fun and courage of Loss Padget, a youth of twenty, who was killed in Virginia just before the surrender of Lee's army. The men now living who were most prominent in the war from the lower battalion, are Captain P. B. Waters, now a lawyer at Edgefield; James Mitchell, A. P. West, A. P. Bouknight, James Boatwright, Henry Vanzandt, S. L. Ready, and Colonel E. J. Goggans.

This war gave freedom to the negroes, but it settled no question of right or wrong. It did not even settle the right or wrong of slavery. It only settled the question whether it should be or not be—that is the question. If African slavery was wrong, it was wrong whether triumphant or not. That it was wrong, and a very great wrong, I never doubted from the time I was old enough to read and to think for myself. But I was a slave holder until the close of the war, and would be one even now, I suppose, if the institution had continued till to-day undisturbed. We did not fight for slavery, in itself considered—that was a mere side issue—as Lincoln and others never fought against it *per se*, but only as a means of hurting us. We fought for the States as States; for the right to pursue our own course, our own policy, to manage our own affairs, undisturbed and uninterfered with. We were Greeks, animated by the old horoic spirit of Greece, that led us to fix our affection upon our own State, and make it first and foremost, the glory of the world. The northern sentiment was Roman, with Lincoln as the head and chief exponent. That sentiment regarded the States as nothing, save as integral parts of the empire which centered at Washington, as the Roman Empire did at Rome. This question the war did not settle, and could not. It settled no question except the relative strength of the parties to the contest. Rebellion! He who uses that word as applicable to the people of the South is himself a tyrant or an ignoramus. We are a conquered people. Is it possible for a conquered people to love that power which conquered them? Is it possible for us to love a union which is forced upon us? We may acquiesce; we may faithfully do our duty as subject citizens; but that love, which ought to animate the heart and soul of every true citizen, must be wanting. The true union is free and not forced. I feel now as I have always felt, that the strongest bond of union possible to be devised, is for each and every State to have the acceded right and to be at perfect liberty to leave the union, with or without cause, whenever it might choose to do so. If the United States in 1860, or 1861, had said to South Carolina: "Well, you have left us; all right. You think you can get along without us; we know that we can do very well without you. Go in peace; let us live in peace." If this had been the ruling sentiment of the United States, South Carolina would have become the laughing stock of the world, and would soon have been knocking at the door for readmission into the Union. Suppose that now any State had the conceded right to leave the Union at once, if it saw proper, the State, of course, bearing its proper and proportionate share of the existing public debt. What could the State hope to gain by it? Nothing short of madness could induce any State to do it. But when the Union is one of force, when the chain that binds the States is one of iron or of steel, fast riveted, and not the golden fetter of good will and love and good fellowship, it galls and hurts, no matter how lightly and loosely and easily it may hang upon the limbs. It is a fetter imposed by force, and from that very fact becomes hateful, because the wearer knows that whenever the will of the master requires, it may be drawn so tight as to crush and destroy all freedom of motion. But I cannot doubt that a Divine Providence is in all human affairs, and that, in the War of Secession, God permitted the South to be beaten because slavery existed there, and *that* He wanted to destroy.

Soon after the war desperate white men, some of whom, it is said, had belonged to the Federal army, got in the Saluda country, and, there and elsewhere, committed robberies and other desperate deeds, that would do honor to the brigands of Spain, or Italy, or the James Brothers, or to the celebrated John A. Murrell. Major Hodge and a man named Thomas were leaders of these desperadoes. Thomas I saw once at a party, a social gathering in Edgefield County, in 1865, and again in my own bookstore in Newberry in the year 1866. He had bargained with a tobacconist from North Carolina, for the purchase of a wagon load of tobacco, with the wagon and :eam, to be delivered at a certain specified time and place; and they came into the store together to draw up the contract or agree- ment in writing. Soon after the tobacconist heard some rumors in regard to the reputation of Thomas and he did not appear and deliver the tobacco, &c., at the time and place agreed—probably from fear of being robbed and murdered. It was rumored afterwards that Thomas was hanged for some crime, and that Hodge was captured and hanged by the Fed- eral garrison at Augusta. This period of lawlessness lasted, perhaps longer than it would have done if the government of the State had not passed entirely out of the hands of the native white men, citizens, as one of the results of the war. David Graham, a full-blooded negro, who lived near Red Bank, was elected to the Legislature several times during the period from 1868. And nearly all the representatives and county officers were negroes.

MINISTERS OF THE GOSPEL.

Let us now notice some of the ministers of the gospel and teachers of the youth of this part of Edgefield. Rev. Henry

Herlong was a native of Orangeburg, though his home for
many years was in Edgefield near the Little Saluda River. He
was a good farmer as well as a good preacher and good man.
He was a Methodist preacher, but, I believe, never an itiner-
ant. He was the founder of Emory Chapel. I learned something from him once about the mixture of soils and earths,
which is worth remembering. Just below the public road and
on the east or right bank of Little Saluda, he had a small piece
of bottom land so crawfishy that it was worthless and unpro-
ductive. In course of time red clay from a hillside in the road
washed down upon it in considerable quantities, and the quality of the soil became entirely changed and produced heavy
crops of corn. He then made further experiments and found
the red clay upon such places to be most excellent manure.
Mr. Herlong was the father of Rev. Vastine Herlong, whom I
used to see frequently and to know well. Spann's was named
in honor of Rev. Henry Spann. Revs. Michael Rauch, Paul
Derrick, Emanuel Caughman, and A. M. Lindler have all, at
different times, preached the Word to the Lutheran churches
in this part of Edgefield. Their names will probably again
appear in a sketch of the Lutheran Church.

Revs. Mark Abney, George Bell, A. P. Norris, and Abner
Asbil were all acceptable ministers amongst the Baptists here.
Mark Abney and George Bell, this writer, many years ago,
knew well. Mr. Bell was a young man grown at Mount Enon
School in 1835, when the writer was a little boy. Being near-
sighted or having some defect in his eyes, he wore glasses,
which we little fellows thought very singular. He became a
very excellent business man, as well as acceptable preacher
and good citizen.

At the time of the ministrations of the Revs. Herlong and
Spann in this part of Edgefield, the people called Methodists
were not very numerous; but they were, and are, so active and
aggressive, and withal, so sympathetic, that they have increased greatly in numbers.

EDUCATION.

I have already written something on the subject of education, but it is never out of order to give additional information,
as the schoolmaster certainly occupies one of the most useful

and responsible positions in the world. There have been some very excellent teachers in the Lower Battalion. David Pugh, a graduate of Cambridge University, in England, taught for many years a large school near Mount Willing. Dr. John Barrett, another highly cultivated Englishman, spent a great part of his life as a teacher. Many of the prominent men of Edgefield for several generations , were students of theirs. It was the custom in those days for schoolmasters to work, like other people, the year round and all day, Saturday excepted. Now it is not thought necessary. Possibly ours is the better plan. It was quite common also in those days for educated men and women from the North to seek and find situations here as teachers. It is not so common now. The change in our domestic institutions has produced of necessity a very great change in our home life as well. At this time we have Training Schools for teachers, and many men, women and girls take pride in fitting themselves for doing the most perfect work possible, and our schools are taught mostly by trained teachers, "native and to the manner born." This is as it should be.

WATSON, BATES AND OTHERS.

Colonel Sam Watson was one of the most prominent characters of this section from 1850 to 1860. He lived where his son P. B. Watson now resides. He accumulated a very handsome property and died in 1873, about 57 years of age, leaving a large and respectable family. Captain Tom Bates was another prominent man at this time. His home was near the beautiful town of Batesburg, in fact, the place was named in honor of his family. Captain Bates married a daughter of Wade Holstien. He was quite wealthy. Alonzo Bates is his only son. William Padgett was also a worthy and prominent citizen of this section. He never sought nor held any public position. Indeed it may be said of the Padgetts that they are remarkable for their love of private life. William Padgett's wife was Margaret Denny, sister of Colonel David Denny, of whom mention has already been made. He was quite wealthy before the war but at its close he was not rich. For honesty, industry, and general integrity of character he had few superiors. Rev. Mahlon D. Padgett, of Mount Willing, and Mr. David Padgett, of the Ridge, are his sons. One of the loveliest characters I ever

knew was Mr. Mahlon Padgett, whose home is near Trenton—
hale and erect at the age of four score years—a man with a
small body but a large head and large heart. I knew him first
at school in the year 1835. We were students together in the
same class in English Grammar, of which Rev. George Bell
was also a member. Mahlon is still living and I hope that I
may meet him again. The last time I ever saw him was at
Edgefield Court House, many years ago, during or just
before the war, I do not now remember.

Mount Willing can boast of the largest and smallest man in
the county. Wesley Corley, the large man, is sixty-five years
old and weighs 350 pounds. Lewis Suddath is about sixty,
and weighs about 45 or 50 pounds. I have seen Mr. Suddath
several times—the last time was, I think, in the year 1885 or
1886, at O'Neall's church in Edgefield, near his home. Mr.
Corley I have never seen.

DIVISION OF THE DISTRICT.

Many years ago the question of the division of the District
was frequently discussed, being thought by many to be too
large. The idea then was to cut off the Tenth Regiment.
Hon. George D. Tillman, then a young, ambitious man—he
has since lost his youth but not his ambition—took a leading
part in the movement. The District has since been divided, but
not in the way then desired. Beech Island, including Hamburg, has been cut off and joined to a part of Barnwell, making the new County of Aiken. The old desire for division on
this side seems to have evaporated. It may be, too, that the
election of such good citizens from this side to the Legislature,
as D. B. Peurifoy, Rev. C. P. Boozer, J. B. Suddath, W. J.
Ready, has done much to cure the dissatisfaction.

Since this was written the District has been divided, and now
we have Saluda County.

XII.

MOUNT WILLING—ORIGIN OF THE NAME

Jacob Smith first settled Mount Willing. He had the old English custom of giving names to every farm and separate place he owned. He lived first at the place now (1891) occupied by Mr. Frank Boyd, which he called Flat Grove. His house was near the creek, near the old Smith and Bonham grave-yard. This place was very sickly at that time, which caused Mr. Smith to remove to a place which he called Wine Hall, where Mr. William Myrick now lives. Just before the Revolutionary War Mr. Smith built a tavern in the woods on the east side of Richland Creek. Soon afterwards a large number of men met at the tavern to see about opening some roads through the country. When they were through with the business of the meeting and all had agreed upon the location of the roads to be cut—the same, by the way, that cross there now—the Chairman or President of the meeting called out: "Let's Mount!" to which was replied: "Willing!" Mr. Smith, who was present, caught the words, and gave the place the name of Mount Willing, which name it has borne ever since. Jacob Smith married Sarah Butler, an aunt of General William Butler. Cunningham, while on his great raid, stopped there in order to refresh his men and also to put Smith to death, but a Tory begged Cunningham to allow Mr. Smith a few moments to pray, which request was granted. The Tory then ran to the house of Russell Wilson, who lived only a short distance from the store, north, and got Mrs. Carghile to help intercede for his life. Mrs. Carghile was Wilson's sister, and the widow of Captain Neely Carghile, who had been lately killed by the Whigs. She told Cunningham of Smith's great kindness to the widows and orphans of the murdered Tories, which saved his life. Jacob Smith was a man of great wealth, and many are the stories told of his liberality to the distressed families of both Whigs and Tories during the Revolution. He died in 1805 at about seventy years of age, and was buried at Flat Grove. Mr. Smith left a son, Luke, and a daughter, Sophia. Luke married Elizabeth

Loman, by whom he had two children, Jacob B. Smith and the exemplary wife of Dr. Rhyden G. Mays. Sophia married Captain James Bonham, a young widower from Maryland. Captain Bonham lived near Red Bank and died in 1815, at the age of thirty-nine. His oldest daughter, Sallie, married John Lipscomb; Julia married Dr. Bowie. His oldest son, Malachi, emigrated to Texas; James also went there, and was one of the victims of the massacre at the Alamo. Milledge was the youngest, and was regarded as a very pious youth; in fact, he used to preach sometimes. He read law; was a successful practitioner; was made Solicitor of his circuit, his home being at Edgefield; was a member of Congress when the State seceded; became Brigadier-General in the Confederate service; took an active part and rendered efficient service at the first battle of Manassas or Bull Run; was elected Governor succeeding Pickens, and held that office for two years during the war. After the war he held different public positions, and died in the service of the State. Mrs. Bonham, his mother, lived with him at the court house during the last years of her life. She was a lady of extraordinary merit. When she died the Goveruor had her buried by the side of his father at Flat Grove.

General William Butler had another aunt, Susan Butler, who married Enoch Grigsby. Mr. Grigsby lived near Mount Willing on the plantation occupied in 1891 by Dr. Unger. He left one son, Colonel Rhyden Grigsby, and four daughters. One of these daughters married Captain Jonathan Wever; one General Samuel Mays, of Big Saluda; one Lod Hill, who lived near Richardsonville in the Revolution; Thomas Butler, a brother of General Butler, married another. Lod Hill left two sons, Theophilus and Henry; and a daughter, who married Captain Bryant Dean, the father of Colonel A. B. Dean and Captain Theophilus Dean. Henry Hill was the father of Dr. Lovett Hill, of Ward, and the grandfather of John B. Hill, School Commissioner in 1891. Did he not also have a son named James? Theophilus Hill was the father of Lod Hill and Rhyden Hill, who are now dead; and also of Henry Hill, of Johnston; Dr. Walter Hill, of the court house; James R. Hill, of Richardsonville; Ben Hill, Dyson's; and a son Thomas, who was killed in the War of Secession. Captain Offie Dean, just mentioned, was living in 1891 at Mount Enon, in the house built by Dr. J. C. Ready. Many years ago Captain Dean was tax collector for the District, and may also have held other positions.

Colonel Rhyden Grigsby and Colonel Simpson Wilson married sisters, the Misses Mann'ng. Their brother, Luke, a very celebrated characte· in his day, is said to have killed three men in South Carolina, for which he was tried and found guilty of murder, but was reprieved each time. He finally went to Alabama, and there having killed a man, he was tried, found guilty of murder, and suffered the extreme penalty of the law. Colonel Grigsby died of consumption and his sons removed to Alabama. A Mr. Herbert, and John and Thomas Waters married hi daughters.

MAD BILL ABNEY.

Colonel Wilson and his son-in-law, Mark McKann, removed to Florida. Colonel Wilson was very wealthy, and had John Cronder and Mad Bill Abney employed to help superintend his business. Crouder went with him to Florida, but Abney remained at Mount Willing, then owned by Wilson, with a large number of negroes. The yellow fever raged in Florida from 1830 to 1832, with fatal effect. McKann and all his family died of it. Colonel Wilson sent Crouder back to arrange one of his plantations, so that he could move his family back to Edgefield. Crouder, immediately after his return, married Ellen Edwards, and just one month after his marriage died of yellow fever. The next fall his widow gave birth to a son, who was called John A. Crouder. More will be said of him after awhile. Crouder, Wilson, and McKann died in the year 1832. Colonel Wilson died in Florida, and his family all returned to Edgefield.

In the fall of 1832 Abney married the widow Stevens, a daughter of Colonel Wilson. A young gentleman from Newberry married another at the same time. Mrs. Stevens, who was famous for her beauty, had gone to Florida, where her husband died, leaving her a widow with three little girls. A dashing young colonel, who wore a gaudy uniform, made her an offer of marriage; but she told him if a lady like herself, with three little daughters, ever married again, she oug'it to try and get a man like Mr. Abney, who knew how to make

corn and potatoes.   Mr. Abney heard of the remark and afterwards courted and married her.   It is said that when the time
of the marriage came on and Mr. Abney went to the house to
be married, his modesty overcame him in the yard and he
could proceed no further.   He found it impossible to go into
the house.   His mother-in-law discovering his predicament,
and sympathizing with him in his embarrassment, walked out
to him and said very kindly: "Come in, Billy, the girls are
waiting." This relieved him of his embarrassment. Mr. Abney
afterwards sold the Mount Willing place to Jacob B. Smith, a
grandson of the original settler, and removed to Alabama,
where he prospered and all went well with him.   The epithet
of "Mad Bill" was applied to him on account of the grumness
of his countenance, and not on account of any harshness, nor
violence, nor irritability of temper.   This William Abney was
a son of Azariah Abney and grandson of Captain Nathaniel
Abney and Isabella Madison, who came from Virginia about
the year 1761.   I never saw Mad Bill, nor his brother Hardy.
I was at their father's house at the funeral of their sister, Miss
Elizabeth Abney, but I do not remember seeing them there.
The funeral sermon was preached by Dr. John Bolger, a great
Baptist preacher at that time, living on Turkey or Mountain
Creek, or somewhere in that region of country.   Dr. Bolger
was a connection of the family, he having married a widow
Wills, a sister of Azariah Abney, and who was also my own
great-grandmother.   Dr. Bolger was English by birth, and
came to this country in his youth or boyhood.   He raised a
family here in Edgefield, but after his death they all moved
away and, I think, Dr. Bolger has no descendants now living
in Edgefield.   Newberry's much respected citizen, Warren G.
Peterson, is a nephew of Mad Bill Abney.   So is Joel Abney,
of Saluda.

     Jacob B. Smith married Matilda Youngblood, of Edgefield
village.   He was elected Colonel of the Tenth Regiment of
South Carolina Militia, and also to the Legislature.   He died
in 1853, when only a little over fifty years of age.   After his
death the Mount passed into the possession of strangers, after
having been owned by some of the family for nearly a hundred
years.

     Feeling a deep interest in the welfare of my old comrades of

Company D, Nineteenth South Carolina Volunteers, I have learned, from inquiry, that Billy Reese, a litter-bearer, who helped to carry me off the field when I was wounded, and Lieutenant J. W. Denny, who became Captain of the company before the close, have died since the war. Sam. Edwards, Bas Peterson, James Crouch, and John G. egory, who was also a litter-bearer, were living in 1891. There were others whose names I cannot now recall. Sam. Edwards was wounded twice at Atlanta and taken prisoner. One of his legs was amputated. My brother, Sergeant Thomas Chapman, who himself was mortally wounded at Atlanta, sent word to Sam. Edward's father that Sam. was mortally wounded; but he survived and remained in prison at Camp Chase, Ohio, until released in he summer of 1865. J. D. Smith Livingston lives at Newberry.

JOHN A. CROUDER.

John A. Crouder helped to raise and organize Company D of the Nineteenth Regiment. He first belonged to a company commanded by Robert Meriwether, which went against Fort Sumter and then to Virginia. When the time of his enlistment expired he returned home and assisted Ira Cromley to raise Company D. Cromley was elected Captain; Crouder, 1st Lieutenant; E. B. Forrest, 2nd; and Isaac Edwards, 3rd. After a few months, Cromley, Forrest, and Edwards, who were too old for service, resigned and retired, and Crouder was promoted to be Captain. When the regiment was reorganized at Corinth, Miss., Crouder was elected Major, which position he held until his death, March 12th, 1863, from the effects of a wound received at the battle of Murfreesboro, Tennessee. His sword is now in the possession of his kinsman, John Crouder Edwards, who also bears his name—"and these," says Mr. Edwards, "are about all the evidence that any such man ever existed." I understand that John Crouder Edwards is a bachelor—not personally acquainted with him. He ought to marry and transmit the sword of his dead kinsman, who was a brave and honorable man, to his son, and son's son of coming generations, as a precious relic of the heroic, though dark days of the War of Secession.

Thomas G. Clemson, son-in-law of John C. Calhoun, once

lived in Coleman Township, near Red Bank. Mr. Calhoun
often visited Mrs. Clemson, and while on these visits it was
that I had the good fortune to see Mr. Calhoun several times;
and also Mr. Clemson. It was during the time that Mr. Calhoun's Dahlonega gold mines were at their best. Mr. Clemson was telling how rich the mines were, and by way of illus-
tration he took off an old fur cap which he was wearing, and
said that on one occasion he brought up from the mine in
which they were digging five hundred dollars worth of gold in
that cap. After Mr. Calhoun's death in 1850, Mr. Clemson
sold his farm in Edgefield to Colonel Alfred Deering, and
moved to Pendleton. By will, Mr. Clemson gave to the State
a portion of that property in Pendleton for the purpose of
establishing an Agricultural College, which has been named
Clemson College in honor of the founder.

William Gregg, the builder of Graniteville, was a native of
West Virginia, and came to Edgefield when he was about
twenty years old. He married Marina Jones, of Ridge Spring.
His brother-in-law, General James Jones, and Colonel John
Bauskett had built a cotton factory at Vaucluse and tried to
run and operate it with slave labor. Their success was not
great, the laborers not having the requisite skill and expert-
ness. Mr. Gregg concluded to use white laborers at Graniteville, and succeeded in his enterprise.

In 1858, Mr. Gregg and Colonel James Carroll, afterwards
one of the chancellors of the State, opposed each other for the
State Senate. The contest was very warm and spirited, and
resulted in the election of Mr. Carroll. About this time there
was some blockade running—importing negroes from Africa—
an importation which had a few friends, and very few in Edgefield, but which gave great offence to many persons. This
writer saw one young fellow belonging to a man who was living near Richardsonville, but who was preparing to move into
Georgia, who was said to have been brought from Africa. He
had not learned to speak English. It is said, but with how
much truth I do not know, that Mr. William Spires, of Hamburg, who was then Sheriff, had charge of the District of
Edgefield for the introduction of Africans.

DR. WILLIAM MOBLEY.

In 1854, Dr. William Mobley was elected to the Legislature. His grandfather, Jeremiah Mobley, came to Edgefield just after the Revolutionary War from North Carolina, and settled near Fruit Hill. His father, John Mobley, married Lucretia Simkins. They left three sons, William, Eldred, and John. William was born in 1809. He first married Harriet Goode, of Centre Springs. She died soon. He then married Susannah Neal, daughter of Hugh Neal, a wealthy gentleman of Irish descent. Dr. Mobley was a deacon of Red Bank Church for a long time. He was a man of very fine appearance, pleasing manner, and remarkable for his kindness to all classes of persons; traits of character which made him very popular both as neighbor and physician. He was first elected to the Legislature in 1854, to fill a vacancy caused by the death of Mr. John C. Allen, of Fruit Hill. He was re-elected several times, and was a member at the time of his death in October, 1866.

XIII.

WESTSIDE.

Let us give our attention for awhile to that part of Edgefield known as the Westside, lying on the Savannah.

The history of Edgefield on the side bordering on the Savannah, especially in the upper portion, is perhaps not so full of stirring incidents as some other sections of the county, but no part can properly be said to be without the material of which history is made. Man is the same in all ages and everywhere, and wherever man is, he is making history—history which, indeed, may never be wiitten, but which, if written, might be found full of absorbing and eternal interest. The record of the events now transpiring in any one day in South Carolina, would furnish a history, the darker pages of which would make the angels weep. We are always doing those acts, the record of which constitutes history. Some years are much more pregnant and fruitful in material than others; and some sections more than others; but no year, no day, and no section is entirely barren of material.

Since the earliest times the Savannah side of Edgefield has been tributary to Augusta, Ga., and its rival towns, Harrisburg and Springfield, on the Georgia side, with Campbellton opposite and a little above on the Carolina side. These villages, in the earlier times, were rivals, and owing to the growing wealth of the surrounding country, where, besides the traffic in pelts, hides, and other Indian products, tobacco soon became a staple product. In those primitive days the making of tobacco hogsheads in Augusta formed a considerable industry. These were very different from the tobacco hogsheads of recent times, and were necessarily made very much stronger then than now, as these receptacles of the tobacco crop were also the vehicles by means of which it was conveyed to market. This was effected by attaching a pair of extemporized shafts to each head of the hogshead, converting it into a huge roller, to which an animal was attached by these shafts, and the crop thus rolled to market.

As these rival villages were all at the head of navigation on the Savannah, and all situated at the falls formed by the granite formation, which traverses a greater portion of the two States, each seemed to possess equal chances of reaping the benefit of such natural advantages, and possibly becoming the chief infant city of these growing provinces.

Campbellton must have enjoyed the advantage of being the chief market town of Westside, Edgefield, as several roads and Indian trails centred at that point. Even at this time, 1892, the remains of an old trail leading up the Carolina bank of the Savannah are plainly visible. This trail came up the river to Stevens' Creek, which it crossed at a shoal near its confluence—later at a point a short distance above, known as the *free ferry*—both long since abandoned. After crossing Stevens' Creek it ascended to the ridge, which, by a succession of abrupt and broken hills, forms an uneven back-bone of lands about five miles in width, which divides these two streams for a considerable distance north, when it gradually subsides into a more even, but still hilly portion, marked by a pine belt twenty miles above. This trail describes almost a straight line to a point on the river known as Fort Hill, about two miles below the crossing known as Scott's Ferry, and where is still to be seen the remains of an old but diminutive earth-work, which served as a means of protection against the savages for trappers and traders, who either inhabited or visited this remote region. This ancient and almost obliterated structure stands upon a projecting point of ridge at the foot of the hills, and overlooking the river and the intervening lowlands bordering on it. While the soil is for the most part thin and rocky, the bottoms are quite fertile, and produce, even now, fine crops with fair cultivation.

As Campbellton declined in glory and wealth, and the necessity for a market on this side the river grew, Hamburg, the offspring of the enterprise and industry of an energetic and eccentric German named Shultz, came up out of the marshes and swamps scarcely two miles below. By the indomitable pluck and push of this remarkable man, aided by the advantages of locality, Hamburg, at one time, was no mean rival of Augusta, who had at this time swallowed up Springfield and utterly eclipsed Harrisburg in the cotton and grocery trade of all upper Carolina.

With the opening of the famous Augusta canal, which effectually killed the river trade, navigation by pole boats on the upper Savannah being both difficult and dangerous over the shoals below the locks at the head of the canal, and by the building not many years after of the Greenville and Columbia Railroad, Hamburg was doomed. Soon after the beginning of this decline, the South Carolina Railroad, which till then terminated at Hamburg, purchased a site for depots in Augusta, and extended its track across the river, thus sealing the fate of Hamburg, and giving great gain and new life to her rival. Yet, notwithstanding these fatal blows to the prosperity of Henry Shultz's hopes and lifework, Hamburg continued, even after the close of the Confederate War, to do a small cotton business. Reconstruction, with its hells and horrors, crushed out the last lingering hopes in the hearts of the property holders, and reached its climax in the now historic riot of '76, which culminated in the death of one of Edgefield's brightest and best boys, the young, the gallant, and fearless Thos. McKie Meriwether, who fell at the foot of the pier of the Columbia and Augusta bridge on that dark day.

Campbellton, Edgefield, and even the State of South Carolina, is adorned by another name made bright by the gallant deeds of its bearer, who had his home there, or at a place called New Richmond hardby, and who occupies a prominent place in the history of our State—Le Roy Hammond, or, as he was better known, Captain Le Roy Hammond, whose descendants still own the lands of New Richmond, and have figured in the civil as well as the military annals of Edgefield. Elsewhere in this book will be found a biographical sketch of Le Roy Hammond, with some account of his Revolutionary services.

Between Campbellton and the mouth of Stevens' Creek about five miles above Campbellton, were extensive and profitable shad fisheries, which gave employment and afforded revenue to the land holders on either side of the river. So abundant was the catch in the shad season that eight large roe shad would scarcely fetch a dollar, and in consequence a great portion of the season's catch was pickled and sent away to other markets. Round fish, such as suckers and red-horses, were a drug, and furnished food for hogs. Such was the providence of the early settlers of this rich and teeming portion of Edgefield.

Ascending the river over a broken and hilly country poorly adapted to agriculture, yet occupied by men who in the face of these adverse circumstances have been successful and prosperous farmers; and crossing Stevens' Creek, a more level and more productive country comes into view. As population increased and the products of the soil became more abundant, other and more convenient avenues of trade became necessary. About the year 1840, Delaughter, an enterprising citizen of the fork, conceived the idea of building a covered bridge across the creek two miles above its mouth, and obtained a charter for a new road, which afforded improved facilities for reaching market, but never realized his hopes of gaining wealth from tolls collected. This property soon passed into the hands of Colonel John Bauskett, a distinguished lawyer of the Edgefield bar, and who also owned a very considerable landed estate in the fork between the creek and river, and was long after known as Bauskett's bridge. This bridge went to decay and was never rebuilt, and necessarily caused the abandonment of the road. Long before the building of this bridge a road had been established by way of a ford at a shoal two miles higher up the creek, at which two brothers, George and Allen Anderson, had erected a grist mill, which, for a long series of years, furnished grist for a large portion of the neighboring country. These worthy men were most exemplary citizens, and have handed down a name for honesty, sobriety, and truth unexcelled by any and equalled by few names which now or have ever adorned the annals of this portion of Edgefield.

After passing out of the hands of the Andersons, this mill property fell into the hands of Captain Robt. Meriwether, a member of another quite prominent family, which figures in the history of Georgia. as well as in that of this State. He it was that gave material aid in establishing a school at Curryton, a village five miles from the mill, and named in honor of Joel Curry, who donated the lands, and otherwise aided in establishing two academies, male and female, the former under the management of a distinguished teacher, James Leslie.

This Captain Meriwether, when quite young, went as a soldier to the Seminole War, and after his return established

himself as a successful planter in Martinstown, whence he removed to the Ware place in the fork, only going to Curryton
to educate his children and build up a school. In company
with Dr. Hugh A. Shaw, who was another founder and trustee
of the Curryton Schools, and a popular and successful practitioner of medicine in that community, he remodeled and rebuilt the Anderson mill at considerable cost, but which still
stands as a work of the energy, enterprise, and industry of
these two men.

While writing of Captain Meriwether, it may be mentioned
that he was the first who raised a company and went to Charleston after Secession and aided with Gregg's regiment, of
which his company formed a part, in the reduction of Fort
Sumter. He afterwards went to Virginia with that famous
regiment, and returned home after the expiration of the term
of enlistment (six months) to form another company. Later
on he re-entered the service and surrendered as Major of the
Reserves.

Mortified at defeat, he resolved never to pay tribute to the
victors; he sold out his possessions and with his family sailed
to Brazil, where he, at last accounts, was still living, and engaged with his sons in coffee growing.

There is a wagon road running through Edgefield to Hamburg and Augusta called the Martintown road. Some short
distance above the old Collier place on this road many years
ago there stood almost in the edge of the road the remains of
an old rock wall, evidently the foundation and forming the
cellar of a barn or store house, probably the latter, which I
suppose was the centre of Martintown, and possibly the home
of the Martins of the Revolution (there were eight brothers),
the eldest of whom, William Martin, was Captain of Artillery,
and was killed at the siege of Augusta. Quite a number,
perhaps forty years ago, a family—at least two brothers,
Robert and Charles—an elder brother, George, having previously died, left the neighborhood of Horn's Creek Church and
went to Florida. Five or six miles lower down Horn's Creek,
near the Josia Sanborn place, there is an old plantation called
the Martin place, but I can trace them no further back. The
trading post located near Hamburg was probably just above
and at over about Campbelltown, which is about opposite

Harrisburg on the Georgia side, and once the rival of Augusta. Even within the past decade many Indian relics have been picked up about the site of old Campbellown, owned now, I believe, by the Hammonds, descendants of Colonel Le Roy Hammond of Revolutionary fame, who lived there also. The trail heretofore alluded to is doubtless the one mentioned as extending up the river on the Carolina side to another trading post, called Fort Hill, at which point, I have been told, the Savannah could be forded at low water, and where there was a ferry or other crossing for the inhabitants of Georgia who desired to avail themselves of this trade centre.

The author and compiler of this history inquired of Dr. McKie about Robert M. McKie, of Tennessee; to this inquiry he replied: "In tracing this family which came from the South of Scotland and settled in Virginia, probably no great way from Charlottesville, and afterwards to Horse Creek, below Hamburg, in this State, it has always been the rule to ask how it is spelled. If 'McKie' be the way, further inquiry may be made, otherwise not. Some of this family removed to Alabama, some to Mississippi, and possibly afterwards to Texas, but none to Tennessee that we know of. The Revolutionary ancestor left Horse Creek and went to Augusta with his family for protection during hostilities, while he, Daniel McKie, was in the field with the partisans of his section. The tradition is that he was a fearless fighter, though once captured by the Tories and condemned to die on the gallows extemporized by placing a grape vine over a swinging limb on a neighboring tree and around his neck, mounted on his horse, which was to be whipped out from under him. Fortunately, another gang came up with one in authority who knew the prisoner, and ordered him cut down and released. They had been friends before hostilities. After the cessation of hostilities this patriot left Augusta and settled on Stevens' Creek, five miles west of Martintown, where some of his descendants still live." You will excuse this mention, as the family has since filled a very humble place in the history of Edgefield, being tillers of the soil, fond of retirement—almost to seclusion—and never seeking place or preferment, and often shunning both. The name is little known beyond the limits of their immediate neighborhood. Thomas J. McKie, M. D., was surgeon of the Tenth Regiment South Carolina Volunteers. True, these lands are, and have been, in their possession during three generations; but that seems to be a peculiar characteristic with the inhabitants of this strip of country. The Craftons have been here for generations, the Meriwethers, the Nixons, and the Middletons, with others, have held their forefathers' lands with a tenacity and fixedness not observed in other sections. The Nixons have a most honorable record. The father came here and settled near Clark's Hill (named from a blacksmith who had a shop and a tract of land just below), the site of the depot now bearing that name. Mr. Thomas Nixon, called Esquire Nixon, was a public-spirited citizen, as well as a useful one. He began here as a school teacher and farmer. Was a superintendent of public works and represented Edgefield District in the Legislature. He died in the prime of life, having contracted, as was then supposed, a fever from a brother-in-law who had recently returned from Charleston, where yellow fever was then epidemic—suffering a similar affection.

When war with Mexico was declared, and the famous Palmetto Regiment was being made up, two of Thomas Nixon's sons, Jefferson P. and Thomas, volunteered along with Wm. E. Middleton, son of Major John Middleton, and Joseph Meriwether, since Auditor for Edgefield County, and son of Thos. Meriwether, one of the founders of Bethlehem Baptist Church, joined Captain Preston S. Brooks' company, which formed part of that regiment. Thomas died at or near Vera Cruz. Jefferson P. went through to the City of Mexico, distinguishing himself for gallantry on many fields, and especially at Chapultepec, where he behaved with such conspicuous bravery as to gain promotion, and after returning to his home, where the Hon. G. D. Tillman now lives, a silver pitcher, suitably engraved, was given him as an acknowledgment of the high appreciation accorded him by his fellow-citizens to his deeds of glory.

The Tillman family, the name of which occupies so conspicuous a place in State records of to-day, does not belong properly to this locality. The father of the two prominent representatives of the family to-day lived on Chavis' Creek, on the old Stage road leading from Edgefield Court House to Hamburg.

G. D. Tillman, the Congressman, now living at Clark's Hill, came here after his marriage to Miss Margaret Jones, a lady of wealth, whose parents resided two miles above Clark's Hill and owned extensive tracts of land and numerous slaves.

Middleton, a name familiar to the history of the country, is also linked intimately with the annals of the west side of Edge-field. It has been suggested that the land tenure idea which has prevailed so uniformly in this locality is due to the fact that its settlers came chiefly from Maryland and Virginia strongly imbued with ideas which cling to their descendants. The Middletons illustrated this. Hugh Middleton came here from Maryland and bought large bodies of land, and small ones as well—the custom in those days being to exchange lands for cattle. A man with small holdings and desirous of "going west," would trade forty, eighty, or more acres of land, which he cared not to occupy, for a cow and calf, which he would take with him. Thus he, Mr. Middleton, widely extended his possessions, having much cattle and a goodly number, nearly a hundred slaves.

He settled near the Savannah River, three miles southwest from Clark's Hill depot, where his remains now lie buried. Mention is made of him in the history of the country and par-ticularly how he defeated a body of the enemy at Briar Creek. His son John, Major Middleton, was also a distinguished man of this community. He in early life went to the African coast and brought back a number of natives, some of whom lived out their days in the possession of his sons. He suffered ship-wreck on the home voyage during which he took a distaste to rice, upon which he lived for a long while, and could never after be induced to eat rice. He was a most upright and honest man; his decision of a matter between neighbors was received without question. He also represented his people in the Legislature. He died at a ripe old age, about 84, honored and respected by all.

At one time the Wares were large landholders of this section. Captain Robert Ware had a then elegant residence near Wood-lawn, say four hundred yards distant, on an eminence, perhaps the highest in this section, where he must have lived in ease and elegance if not in luxury. Large orchards, brick walks, a distillery and other evidences of wealth and prosperity, were

noticeable not many years ago. This family, the males of it
at least, have died out and none here now bear the name.

John Pury, the founder of the ferry across the Savannah,
a mile below the present railroad bridge of the A. & K. Railroad, who lived on the opposite side of the river, was quite a
landholder in Edgefield. The importance of this highway may
be better appreciated when we learn that it opened a thorough-
fare by a shorter and more practical route to Augusta. Early
in the history of our country it became the accepted line to the
head of navigation on the Savannah for all the northern and
western portion of our State, and a large section of Western
North Carolina, besides many droves of horses, mules and, hogs,
from Kentucky and Tennessee, seeking a market in that portion
of the country tributary to Augusta. So heavy was this trade
and travel at one time that in the busy season of the year, the
Fall months, a string of wagons a quarter of a mile in length
might be seen on the river bank waiting their time to cross.
In this line of wagons might be found representatives of Kentucky, Tennessee, North Carolina, and every district in the
northern and western portions of our own State. Then it was
that Augusta supplied with salt, sugar, coffee, rice and almost
every other article of commerce, this vast interior section; and
it was transferred in road wagons, much of it finding its way
by this Ferry. At one time the mails were transported by
means of stages over this Pury's ferry route on to Willington,
in Abbeville District, near to which the distinguished McDuffie
had his Cherry Hill house. The opening of the Delaughter
bridge across Stevens' Creek, at a point two or three miles
above its mouth, was the means of turning a large portion of
this traffic to Hamburg, which was then a great cotton mart,
besides supplying its full quota of groceries to the up-country,
and correspondingly lessening the trade of Augusta, which the
opening of the Canal soon restored to her. The completion of
the A. & K. Road, after the building of the Greenville and
Columbia Railroad, has directed this trade to other points,
almost entirely broken up wagon travel and necessarily making
the once important highway—so important to Augusta's prosperity indeed, that the authorities in Augusta at one time
thought it worth while to lease and free this ferry, a neighborhood convenience. This property is still in the family.

In looking over old land papers many strange and since forgotten names appear. Besides this the now almost obliterated remains of old settlements are to be seen in many out of the way places all over this section of Edgefield. The names of Crookshank, Gardner, Stringer, Baker, Thomas, Boyd, McDaniel, (who kept a grog shop less than two hundred feet away from this spot), Groves, Carson, a Baptist preacher, Loya, another Baptist preacher, and many others once lived here.

About three miles south of Martintown and about two miles east of Stevens' Creek is a spot in the midst of a dense wood known as the Methodist meeting house.

On the dirt road, two miles below Clark's Hill depot, and one mile below Clark's Hill proper, is the site of perhaps the first Baptist, or perhaps any other church ever built in this neighborhood. It appears to have been founded in 1828, when Mr. Thomas Meriwether gave to that body five acres of land for the purpose of establishing a church. A few graves and fewer tombstones now alone mark the spot near where the building stood. Iconoclasts got hold of it and removed the church organization, called Bethlehem, to Clark's Hill, abandoning this almost sacred spot to the dead who lie buried beneath its soil.

The following letter throws some light from old times upon this particular section of which we are now writing:

POVERTY HILL, S. C., May 10th, 1893.

Thos. J. McKie, Woodlawn, S. C

DEAR SIR:—Yours of April 27th, to hand and contents duly noted. I have been told that Bussey was the founder of Anderson mill, not before 1780, or later than 1800. The road formerly crossed the Creek about one-fourth mile below the mill, and no doubt moved up on account of the mill. Some old land plats would give about the date or the time it was built.

Peter Day was the founder of Brigg's Mill and John Day of Mealing mill. George DeLaughter built on Reese shoals about 1815—moved to mouth of Sweet Water Creek about 1820. My father built a bridge across the creek just below the mouth of Sweet Water Creek about 1839 or '40—Free Ferry road and flat about 1830.

The oldest road was probably the River road, and leaves the Martintown road this side of Mr. Thomas McKie's and crossing Fox Creek near its mouth, via New Richmond, near Campbelltown, crossing Stevens' Creek near its mouth and up the river. This road was, no doubt, a military road, and can still be traced.

Carter's road passes near Currytown, via Boulware's Store—crosses the creek below the mill. This road is on the oldest land grants.

Martintown road on plats of 1754–1757 is marked "path to Augusta;" on later plats marked "road to Campbelltown;" and still later it is called "Martintown road" (1760).

Poverty Hill is said to have got its name from some soldiers of the Revolutionary War, who called there for something to eat, and failing to get anything, called it Poverty Hill.

New Richmond, probably named after Richmond, Va., was settled by Le Roy Hammond, from Virginia. I have been told that his land grant was given 1740. If this be so, it is probably the oldest land grant of this section.

Bussey settled the Market place; George DeLaughter, near your mill; Richard Pace, near Boulware's Store; John Hill, opposite Hardy Church; Enos Morgan, at W. H. Brigg's; Carson, at or near George Thurmond. It is said there was a Quaker settled in the forks of the creek, probably came from Quaker Springs, Ga., during the Indian War of 1757. Most all the parties I have named came from Virginia, and it can be said that this section of country was settled by parties from Virginia before the Indian War of 1757.

I remain yours truly,

J. P. DeLAUGHTER.

As regards the building of the Anderson mill, Dr. McKie writes me from Woodlawn, under date of May 14th, 1893:

Although I wrote you this morning about the Anderson mill, I venture to do so again, as I have since received a letter from Dr. Shaw, of Curryton, who learns from one of the family that it is most probable Mr. George Anderson built it at a period not definitely fixed. This man came from the Long Cane section to the Anderson place, and the record says his eldest son was born in 1757. From this it would seem possible that this mill antedates the Revolution.

Yours very truly,

Woodlawn.   THOS. J. McKIE.

PARKSVILLE.

Mention must be made of the lovely little town of Parksville on the Westside. This town which now, April, 1893, has about two hundred and fifty inhabitants, is situated on the Port Royal and Western Carolina Railroad, thirty-two miles above Augusta, and about the same distance from Greenwood. It has two churches, one Methodist and the other Baptist, both well attended during Sabbath services. At this time Rev. G. W. Bussey is pastor of the Baptist Church and Rev. B. O. Berry of the Methodist.

The Hon. W. J. Talbert has recently become a citizen. The town has a large and flourishing school of over one hundred scholars. The Principal is G. B. Toole, with the Misses Essie Jones and Lizzie Toole as assistants.

The people of the town were determined to be strictly temperate and sober, and by Act of Incorporation, the sale of intoxicating liquors is forbidden for ninety-nine years.

There are four stores, two conducted by Gilchrist, Harmon & Co., and one by L. F. Dorn. These do a general mercantile business. Then there is a drugstore kept by T. R. Whatley.

This town is certainly favorably situated to grow to be a place of considerable importance, as the Savannah River on one side is about a mile distant, and Big Stevens' Creek on the other not quite so far. Let the town spread itself, so as to fill up all the space between the two, which it can do very easily in the course of a few years.

REHOBOTH, &C.

There are other schools also on the Westside, which it may be well to mention in this connection. First, Rehoboth, which is now, April, 1893, under the care of that able and experienced teacher and veteran, Captain T. C. Morgan, This school is well attended and Captain Morgan is doing a good work.

Liberty Hill is taught by Professor Griffin; Whitetown is under the care of Miss Annie Seigler, and Dornville is kept by Professor Bussey. These schools are all admirably conducted. East Gray has three white schools, presided over by Professors Harting and Ouzts and Mrs. Faulkner.

On the Cambridge road, two miles below Kirksey's, there is

a new church building, named Springfield; belonging to the colored people, and which is, indeed, quite a credit to them. The pastor is the Rev. William Peterson. The dimensions of the house are 38 by 60 feet; and from floor to ceiling about 25 feet. The belfry is very pretty with its tall spire. The windows are about eight feet in height with Gothic tops. The whole cost of the building will be something over one thousand dollars, and speaks well for the enlightenment, enterprise and religious zeal of the colored people of that section of the country. It is a Baptist church.

SKIPPER'S GEORGIA AND THE DARK CORNER.

The following explanation of the origin of these names has been given to me in answer to inquiries I made. According to this tradition the name "Dark Corner" has a different origin from what I have heard. Which is the true one I cannot tell, but I believe the latter, as this comes from men born and reared and living in or near the region known as the Dark Corner. I do hope and believe that the name "Skipper's Georgia" did not originate as the tradition says. "The Annals of Newberry" shows no such name as Skipper, and I cannot believe that so great a fool was ever a native born in Newberry. Suppose we locate him in Laurens, somewhere above the line.

Skipper's Georgia, my informant says, is located below Scott's Ferry Road. Its name originated from a citizen of Newberry named Skipper, who stole a couple of horses in Newberry and was told that after he had crossed the second river he would be in Georgia. After crossing Big Stevens' Creek he exclaimed "thank God! I am in Georgia at last." A posse of men from Newberry was not far behind him and while grazing his stock between A. Sharpton's and the creek in that hilly country, the posse overtook him, some of whom he well knew. He refused to be arrested or even to give up the horses, saying he was in Georgia and not subject to Carolina laws; but he was overpowered and taken back to Newberry. He has not been heard from since, yet the hills below the Scott's Ferry road bear his name.

As to the "Dark Corner," the line commences just above the road leading to Scott's Ferry and extends up the river embracing all that territory between Stevens' Creek and the Savannah River, as far up as Little River, which empties into the Savannah in Abbeville County. Above said River is the Range, because, at my first recollection, it was a poor, barren country, inhabited mostly by wild beasts and very thinly settled.

The Dark Corner was first settled by Tuckers, Tompkins, Jennings, Blackwells, Pickets and Searles. "They organized a beat company and Tucker kept a bar-room. Our court house at that time was at Ninety-Six. There was a paper published at that place, which was the only one in this congressional district. Old Loudon Tucker was at Ninety-Six attending court and by accident saw one of the newspapers and the contents pleased him so much that he bought a dozen or more copies to distribute among his neighbors, believing he would be able to get them to subscribe to the paper—it was a weekly paper. There were no mail routes in the country at that time and Tucker's idea was to get as many subscribers as possible so that they might, by going by turns for the paper, lose as little time as possible.

Not a single member of the beat company would take the paper. After using all the persuasion and argumentative powers to no purpose he exclaimed, "how long shall we live in this d—d dark age and day!" Old man McKennie, well known to you, said that the Dark Corner was good enough for him, and would remain so if the people would only keep out books, newspapers and foreigners.

Dark then, but not now—now the most intelligent part of our county.

At Dorn's Mill, on Stevens' Creek, commences our Edgefield Range, taking in Liberty Hill, Rehoboth,—in fact, all that country between Stevens' and Turkey Creek. Below Turkey Creek is called Chota, after an Indian chief. Chota extends as far down as Martin town. Jeptha Sharpton, a descendant of Pocahontas, was born in Chota.

W. D. JENNINGS

To Dr. Thos. J. McKie.

AN OLD MEMORANDUM BOOK.

Old books, old papers, old documents, and relics of the past, of whatever kind, have always had great charms and attractions for me. Were I living in a country, or could I visit one in which the past is still present in the form of old buildings, or ruins of old buildings, and monuments to the dead, or libraries in which old books and old manuscripts are stored away for safe keeping, it seems to me that I could pass days, months, or even years, in looking over these things and calling into life the fading ghosts and memories of the past. But we have no antiquities in South Carolina. It has been only a little more than two hundred years since the first permanent settlement was made by white people on the territory of what is now South Carolina. Two hundred years! Why that was only yesterday. My own life covers one third of that period, and I have a clear and distinct recollection of many events that occurred sixty-five, or more, years ago. We have no antiquities, but letters and memorandum books that have stood the wear and tear of time for over a hundred years seem quite old. One such memorandum book has recently come into my hands—sent to me by a friend who had hopes that it would be of interest to me. It has given me great pleasure to look through and examine its contents. It was in use before the day of the adoption of the Spanish currency, when our money was still counted in pounds, shillings, and pence.

The book appears to have been used mostly as a book of receipts for money paid, though I find also a few entries of a different character. The book belonged originally to a Mr. James Read. Where he lived does not appear with certainty, but there is a clew in one of the receipts to the place in which he probably had his residence.

The oldest receipt is for 27 pounds, and bears date 18th November, 1771; the latest bears date May 2nd, 1782, and is for the sum of nine pounds, six shillings, and eight pence, Sterling; paid by Richard Guinn to John Dawson, in full for the balance of ninety bushels of corn and a barrel of rice.

The latest receipt for money paid by Mr. James Read bears date 8th July, 1777, for the sum of fifty pounds currency, being in part payment of his bond. [Signed.] R. O.
  Witness: WM. MATTLEY.

The book seems to have passed out of the ownership of Mr. James Read; whether by death, or failure in business, I know not. In one place I find the following, which I copy:

"Rece'd 16th March, 1775, five pounds, eighteen shillings, and 3 pence currency in full for a ballance due Mrs. Middleton for hoggs.

£5, 18, 3   [Signed.]   STEP: BULL."

When I came across and read this receipt I thought and wondered whether it could be possible that this Stephen Bull was the same Stephen Bull who was brother to Wm. Bull, one time Colonial Governor, and so remarkable for his ugliness. It is related of him that on one occasion, while walking in the street not far from his residence, he was met by a countryman, who, it appears, had never seen him before. As soon as the countryman met him and got a good sight of his face, he stopped short in front of him and stared at him in open-mouthed wonder. The Governor, being somewhat surprised, stopped also and said to him: "Well, my friend, what can I do for you?" The countryman, still staring and stammering a little, said: "Sir, where do you live? You are certainly the ugliest man I have ever seen in my life." The Governor, being of a very affable and good easy temper, laughed and good humoredly replied: "Wait, my friend, you just wait till you see my brother Stephen." Now, whether the Stephen Bull whose name appears signed to this receipt is the same Stephen Bull, brother to the Governor, I do not know.

There are three signed Nathl. Greene, but I do not suppose that he was General Greene of the Revolution. Two signed by Thomas Rutledge, one of which I copy: "Beaufort, April 8th, 1775, rec'd of Mr. James Reid fifteen pounds, 15, 7, currency, on account.

THO. RUTLEDGE.

Cash.....£10
Acc't....   5, 15s, 7d
_____

     £15, 15s, 7d

I find two signed Wm. McKie. On one of the pages, written in an elegant female hand, without date: "When this you see remember me though many miles you distant bee— Catherine D. Hammond."

My mind raises the question whether Catherine was of the Le Roy or Samuel Hammond family, but I get no reply. Catherine, or some other good woman, wrote also the following:

"I send the joys of earth away,
　Away ye tempters of the mind;
False as the smooth, deceitful sea,
　And empty as the whistling wind."

Again:

"I waited patient for the Lord,
　He bow'd to hear my cry;
He saw me resting on His word,
　And brought salvation nigh."

Again on another page:

"Why doth the man of riches grow
　In insolence and pride,
To see his wealth and honors flow
　With every rising tide?

"Why doth he treat the poor with scorn
　Made of the selfsame clay?
And boast as though his flesh were born
　Of better dust than they?"

The same hand writes on another page:

"Behold what wondrous grace
　The Father has bestowed
On sinners of a mortal race
　To call them sons of God!"

Again:

"Come, let us join our cheerful songs
　With angels 'round the throne—
Ten thousand thousand are their tongues,
　But all their joys are one."

And on the next page only the word "Catherine," with a flourish which I cannot copy.

The last verses written in this book are the following:

"I pass with melancholy state
By all these solemn heaps of fate;
And think—as soft and sad I tread
Above the venerable dead,
Time was like me—they life possess
And time will be—when I shall rest."

C. D. H.

She was a good woman who wrote these verses in this old memorandum book, and it is with a tender melancholy that I read and copy them here. Yes, Catherine, long ago you found rest.

I feel that I cannot part company with this old book without making a few more extracts, as it is altogether probable that L shall never see it again after returning it to the owner:

"Rece'd Dec. 24th, 1771, of James Read six pounds, five shillings in part for bread. MARY LINTON."

"Received 17th June, 1772, of Mr. James Read, fifty shillings currency in full for one month's hire my negro boy, named Joe. GEORGE BLAND."

"Rece'd 1 July, 1772, of Mr. James Read two pound four shilling & 3d in full for Beef & all demands to this day.
£2, 4, 3 ISAAC XARMENTOR."

"Received 14th Jan., 1777, of Mr. James Read the sum of fourteen pound five shillings currency, being in full for House Rent and all demands to this day.
£14, 5 WILLIAM DEVEANE."

Mr. James Read must have kept a hotel or house of public entertainment. The book passed out of his hands into others, and was used towards the close of its business career for entering of washing accounts.

"Wednesday, 8th April, Mr. Fowler came from Charleston. Sunday night, 12th" (year not given), "Mr. Smerdon came here. Saturday, 18th, begun to wash for Mr. Fowler;" then followed a long list of articles washed for Mr. Fowler, shirts, neck handkerchiefs, pocket ditto, stockings, waistcoats, breeches, &c. Then follows a similar list, but not so long, of articles washed for Mr. Smerdon.

And thus we find that all through life the practical and the poetic, the common-place and the ideal, go together, move together, stand together, side by side always. But, indeed, there is nothing common-place. Catherine, the refined and educated, the noble Christian woman, was a true sister to that one who did washing for Mr. Fowler and Mr. Smerdon. That woman, whose name is not given, who washed and did laundry work for Mr. Fowler and Mr. Smerdon, if she was a Christian, was also a daughter of the King. They both have found rest; whether together, whether they know each other, whether they have ever met, makes no difference. They know those whom they ought to know, and they have all things and such surroundings as is best for them.

"This book of receipts," writes Dr. Thos. J. McKie, under date of September 24th, 1893, "came into my hands with a lot of old books purchased at the sale of Mrs. Stephen Garrett, a very old widow woman, who lived on Horn's Creek near its mouth, where she owned a mill and plantation adjoining. This was more than 40 years ago."

XIV.

FRUIT HILL AND VICINITY.

For the facts in the following sketch of Fruit Hill I am indebted to Major Scott Allen:

Fruit Hill is situated 12 miles north of Edgefield Court House, and immediately on the direct road from Edgefield Court House to Newberry Court House. The country around Fruit Hill is level, but the drainage is good, from the fact that it is immediately on the ridge between the Savannah and the Saluda Rivers; in fact, in time of rain the water that falls on many „houses, that on, the East side runs to the Saluda and that on the West side to the Savannah.

The lands are naturally very productive, and lying so level they are susceptible of a very high state of cultivation. The best lands, when well cultivated, will readily yield one bale of cotton per acre, and will produce 25 to 40 bushels of corn per acre, and of oats 40 bushels. Pet patches in this immediate vicinity have produced as high as 4 bales of cotton, 80 bushels of corn, and 109 bushels of oats to the acre. But of course such yields require the most perfect preparation and cultivation and also excessive fertilization; but such are the facts.

The country around Fruit Hill was originally settled by the Allens, Goodwins, Richardsons, Culpeppers, Bakers, Hollingsworths, Harrises, Huskeys, Landrums, Nortons, and Hemslys.

The particular place and homestead known as Fruit Hill was settled by a man named Young Allen, from North Carolina. He married a Miss Richardson. He was no relation of the present owner of Fruit Hill. A daughter of Young Allen married Benjamin Frazier, and inherited the Fruit Hill place from Young Allen. Benjamin Frazier sold Fruit Hill to Major John C. Allen, and the place has remained in the possession of his immediate family to the present date, November, 1893.

Major John C. Allen was a son of Ossamus W. Allen, of Barnwell District. Major Allen married Hannah Coates, who brought him 12 children, namely, Ossamus W. Allen, Zulime G. Allen, Elizabeth E. Allen, Mary A., Joseph Duncan. John

R., James H., Sarah H., Fabian P., Margaret S., Walter
Scott, and Washington D. Allen. Major John C. Allen and
his sons Joseph D., John R., and Fabian P., all died with
typhoid fever in 1854.

Major John C. Allen was elected Major during the exciting
days of Nullification. He represented the District of Edgefield
in the Legislature in 1852 and 1853, and was a member at the
time of his death. He always took an active part in all public
matters from earliest manhood, and died in the full confidence
and esteen of his fellow-citizens. His widow lived many years
after his death. She died at the old homestead, Fruit Hill, in
1883, surrounded by her eight living children and many sorrowing friends. Truly it could be said of her that "none
knew her but to love her, none named her but to praise."

The oldest son, who was also the oldest child, Dr. Ossamus
W. Allen, graduated at the South Carolina College and afterwards at the State Medical College in Charleston, S. C., and
enjoyed a large and lucrative practice till his death. He
married Ellen Nicholson, of Edgefield District, and by said
marriage had four children. He entered the Confederate Army
in August, 1861, as first lieutenant, in which position he served
until prostrated with typhoid fever, in the winter of 1862,
when he resigned and returned home. He was wounded twice
in battle in Virginia—in the battle at Gaines' Mill—second
battle of Manassas—and at Sharpsburg, in Maryland. Two of
his children are living (November, 1893), Mrs. Kate Kinnaird
and Joseph D. Allen, serving his fourth term as Judge of Probate of Edgefield County.

Zulime G. Allen married William S. Smiley and is the
mother of eight Smiley children, five now living. Her husband,
W. S. Smiley, died in 1855, and she afterwards married Wm.
L. Stevens, and is the mother of two Stevens children, both
living.

Elizabeth E. Allen married Colonel John W. Tompkins.
Colonel Tompkins served with distinction in the war between the
States and died in 1887. His widow and six children survive.

Mary A. Allen married Benjamin F. Mays, who died in
1885 and left his widow and five children surviving. Benjamin
F. Mays was a good man. He made a good soldier during the
war. Was treasurer of the county in 1876—the first under the

Hampton Administration. He was also a leading member of the Horne's Creek Baptist Church and died in the full fellowship of his church and the confidence and esteem of the entire country.

James H. Allen married Martha Kinnaird, and they had seven children, five still living. The wife and mother died in 1885. James H. Allen entered the Confederate service as third lieutenant in 1861; was promoted to the captaincy on the field of battle at Gettysburg, Penn., for his distinguished bravery on the field. He served as captain until disabled by a gunshot wound at Riddle's Shop in Virginia in 1864. Since that date he is incapacitated for manual labor. He lives on his farm three miles west of Fruit Hill and enjoys the confidence of all who know him.

Sarah H. Allen married William E. Hobbs. He died from gunshot wounds received in battle at Resaca, Georgia, in 1864. Mrs. Hobbs afterwards married Arthur H. Collett. She is still living and has five children living, two by the first marriage and three by the last.

Margaret S. Allen married Benjamin Franklin Payne in 1862. He died in 1868, leaving three children. His widow afterward married Benjamin Jackson Stevens and by said marriage she had one daughter. She is now a widow and has four children living. (November, 1893). Her son, Joseph W. Payne, is a model young man, the support and mainstay of his widowed mother and three sisters, who are all devotedly attached to him, and he is also highly esteemed by all who have the happiness to be acquainted with him.

Washington D. Allen married Ella G. Mays, and has five children living. He entered the Confederate service as a private in Company B, Sixth South Carolina Cavalry, and served through the entire war and surrendered with Johnston's army in North Carolina in 1865. He was complimented on several occasions by the general commanding the brigade, and especially by his immediate commanding officers, for his untiring energy and determination, and his universal good humor and his willingness to discharge every duty imposed upon him. He has since the war filled positions of public trust with ability, and now lives on his farm one mile southwest from Fruit Hill.

W. Scott Allen, the present owner of Fruit Hill, was educated at the old field schools within five miles of Fruit Hill. He had prepared himself to enter the South Carolina College, when the war between the States came on. He gave up his books, donned the soldier's uniform, and entered the Confederate service as private in Company K, Fourteenth South Carolina Volunteers. He was severely wounded in the battle of Gaines' Mill, Va., in the right arm near the shoulder and slightly in the head. He was slightly wounded in the breast at Chancellorsville, but did not leave the field. He had his clothes completely riddled at Gettysburg, but did not get the skin scratched in the first day's fighting. On the third day at Gettysburg his gun-stock was shot entirely off at the small of the stock, but the shock did not even knock the gun out of his hand. He was highly complimented on both of these days by Colonel Abner Perrin, commanding the brigade. His company, K, commanded by Captain James H. Allen, his brother, went into the fight on the first day at Gettysburg with 39 men, rank and file, and 34 fell, killed and wounded, at the first fire from the enemy, and that, too, when the company had not fired a gun, for the orders were to take the work at the point of the bayonet, and they were taken as ordered, but at a fearful cost. In that charge company K lost some as gallant men as ever shouldered arms in any cause.

When General Lee decided to recross the river into Virginia after the battle of Sharpsburg, there was a call for volunteers for the "forlorn hope:" in other words for men to cover the retreat across the river. In the call it was distinctly stated that all who volunteered would most certainly be killed or captured, as they were expected to halt the line until the signal to move was given from the Virginia side of the river. Notwithstanding the great danger of death in the "forlorn hope," Scott Allen was one of the first to volunteer, and contrary to the general expectation, the entire company of volunteers, after doing some gallant fighting, successfully crossed the river and rejoined the command.

He was severely wounded through the face at Spottsylvania Court House, Va., in 1864, and in special orders by Colonel J. N. Brown of the Fourteenth Regiment, South Carolina Volunteers, was complimented for his distinguished conduct and bravery on the occasion, and was recommended to the Secretary of War for a commission. The Secretary of War appointed him a Second Lieutenant in the Confederate States Army, and the same day he was promoted Captain of Company K, Fourteenth Regiment, South Carolina Volunteers. After sufficiently recovering from his wound, he returned to Virginia, and took command of his company and commanded the same during all the trying scenes around Petersburg, Va. And at the surrender at Appomattox Court House, he commanded not only his own company, but also six other companies of the regiment, in all 35 men.

After the surrender he returned home and took charge of his mother's farm at Fruit Hill. In the spring of 1866 he married Frances E. Adams. By this marriage they have had eleven children, six of whom are living now (1893). He has aided greatly, and succeeded beyond his expectations, in building a fine school at Fruit Hill. His two daughters completed their education at the Greenville Female College. One son is at the Medical College in Augusta, Ga., and three boys are attending the Fruit Hill High School, of which Rev. William H. Simpson is Principal.

He was elected to the Legislature in 1876, and served two terms. Aided in the organization of the Democratic party in that year, and in the overthrow of the Republican party. He organized a rifle company, and all through that period of trouble had it ready for service and for any emergency that might arise. There is little doubt that his company was very useful in suppressing difficulties and preventing bloodshed. He is still living and enjoying the comforts of a happy home at Fruit Hill. There are four churches within five miles of his home—two Baptist and two Methodist.

Rocky Creek Church, the nearest, is Baptist, and was organized in 1831. Rev. Joseph Norris, pastor; John Cogburn, Esq., clerk. The pulpit has been filled from time to time by Revs. Norris, Watkins, Peterson, Norris, Bartley, Coover, McMillan, Carson, Bradford, and the present supply, Rev. William H. Simpson. The present membership is about one hundred. Great good has been done by this church, and under the present pastor the good influence promises to continue.

The other churches, Little Steven's Creek, Baptist; and Bethlehem and Gazzaway, Methodist, are also in a thriving condition, and are doing much good for the whole country.

XV.

CAPT. JAMES RYAN.

Captain James Ryan was a native of Virginia, but at an early age removed to South Carolina. He was one of the first settlers of Edgefield District—a pioneer in the wilderness—and was soon called into service as a soldier against the Cherokees. In the war of 1768 against that nation, he was appointed a Lieutenant in one of the companies and distinguished himself. He always volunteered in the most dangerous enterprises and was frequently engaged in hand to hand conflicts with the Indians. He was under Williamson, fighting against the Cherokees, when the Declaration of Independence was made in Charleston, August, 1776.

He took his stand upon the principles of that declaration, and never changed. He served as Captain under Le Roy Hammond, (Colonel) and was engaged in many bloody skirmishes of which there is no record. When the State was overrun in 1780, after the fall of Charleston, and was considered a conquered province, he, with many other true patriots, asked for his parole and took what is known as British protection. But when the British afterwards pronounced him a British subject, as a consequence of this act, and called upon him to bear arms against his countrymen, he refused, was arrested, and thrown into prison at Ninety-Six. From this place he was sent in irons with Captain James Butler, James Caldwell, Daniel Duff, and some others, to the provost prison in Charleston, where he was confined in the same cells with all sorts and descriptions of evil doers—British culprits. The prison was crowded—the weather hot—the temper of the parties not very amiable, and they soon began to quarrel and fight. Captain Ryan afterwards related that the Americans were beating their opponents soundly when assistance was sent to them from without. Ryan and his Whig companions were then placed on board a prison ship, which has always been regarded as a brief epitome, or condensed edition of hell. From this ship some were delivered by death, some were exchanged, and some few escaped. Captain Ryan was one of

these, but for some time he was not able to get out of the city.
At length one day he quarrelled with some soldiers in the
street.   After the soldiers left him and passed on, a lady who
had been listening called Captain Ryan to her door.   She,
being a good Whig and wishing to assist him to escape, advised him to go to a sentinel on the lines and pretend that he
was a rebel deserter—had been badly treated, and wished to
enlist under some British officer whom he knew at Monck's
Corner—an officer of reputation.   Ryan at once assumed the
character, and after a few visits to the sentinel he let him pass.
Ryan did not go to Monck's Corner, nor did he return to
Charleston, but made the best of his way to the home of
Colonel Thomas Taylor, an old friend and schoolmate.   Before
he reached Granby at the Congaree he was joined by three
others, brothers in misfortune.   There was neither flat nor
canoe in which they could cross, and two of the party could
not swim.   They made a raft, and placing upon it the two who
could not swim, Ryan and the other swam and towed them
over.   Colonel Taylor, who had just returned from a scouting
expedition, received Ryan with great kindness and loaned him
a horse to help him on his way home.   On the way, near the
Edisto, he unexpectedly met three men whom he believed to
be Tories.   These men stopped him and asked him who he
was.   He gave the name of Rambo, a well-known Tory in the
neighborhood; but Holley, one of the party, doubted the truth
of what he said.   They searched and found his commission.
Holley immediately seized his gun to shoot him, but Ryan,
with entire self-possession, asked him to wait a moment; and
then appealed to his feelings as a Christian and a man against
such doings.   Holley yielded, but took him to a Tory camp
not far off where he said he knew he would be put to death.
The Captain of the party, who was an old man, would not
permit them to kill him; but when Ryan left the camp, Holley
and a few others followed him until out of sight of those at the
camp, stripped off his coat, hat, and boots, took his horse and
dismissed him barefooted.   He got home, however, collected
some of his company, and returned to the Tory camp to look
for his horse and clothes.

The Tories were absent, but an old woman, the Captain's
wife, was there in great distress, who begged Ryan not to

injure her, but to give her some food. He immediately had a beef killed, cut up, and salted away for her to live upon. Soon after leaving the old woman, he fell in with the Tory party and captured Holley and a few others. Holley was put to death, but I believe no other.

While part of Lord Rawdon's army was on the retreat from Ninety-Six through the fork of Edisto, Captain Ryan, with his company of fifty ragged militia, resolved to attack the rear guard and capture their baggage. He sent all, except three or four, to make the attack. These three or four sounded their bugles and beat two or three drums, as though a much larger party were advancing to battle. The *ruse* succeeded. After a sharp skirmish the wagons were captured, with a good supply of arms, ammunition, and clothing. Every man was able to take something of a prize home to his family. The captured wagons were immediately burned and the Whigs dispersed. Unfortunately for their complete success, some of them overloaded themselves with plunder and with rum, especially rum, were overtaken, and captured. Ryan's men, who had gone from home almost destitute, returned to their families well armed, well clothed, well mounted, and in high spirits.

In the fall of 1782, while advancing upon a party of Tories in camp with great ardor, as he always did, he received a ball in his shoulder which he carried to his grave. Unable to proceed himself, he ordered his First Lieutenant, Wm. Butler, to lead on and continue the pursuit. This skirmish took place near Orangeburg, and was Captain Ryan's last battle, as his wound was too painful and dangerous for him to keep the field. He was carried home and took no more active part in the war, but he continued to issue orders and to plan operations against the Tories.

At the close of the war, he retired to his plantation on Horse Creek, where he remained, cultivating the soil, seeking no office, loved and respected by all who knew him. He was a man who never refused to face an enemy and never turned his back on a friend. He left a large and valuable estate, which was distributed among his relations and kinsfolk, as he had no children of his own.

LE ROY HAMMOND.

Le Roy and Samuel Hammond, two of the most active and energetic Whigs during the Revolution in Edgefield District, were both born in Richmond County, Virginia. Le Roy, a sketch of whom we will give first, was the son of John Hammond, who had married Miss Dobbins. The year of his birth is not given, nor is any mention made of his early life, education, and training. He married a Miss Tyler, and left Virginia about the year 1765, with his wife and one child. He began business as a merchant in Augusta, which was a town at the time about thirty years old, and a good place of business. Mr. Hammond remained in Augusta two or three years, when he removed over to South Carolina, to a place called Richmond, where he continued business as a merchant, and also kept a public ferry across the Savannah River. From this place he removed his residence to Snow Hill in Edgefield District, where he engaged in the tobacco trade and did much to promote and improve the culture of that noxious weed in South Carolina. At his warehouse at Cameltown, a short distance below his residence, the first year he only received twenty hogsheads of tobacco; the second year he received over one thousand. His business here was large and profitable.

Before the war he was a justice of the peace and captain of a militia company; and being a good surveyor, and a man of sound, practical sense and judgment, he had great influence. He was one of the first in Edgefield and, perhaps, in the State, to lay an embargo upon tea, by excluding it from use in his family on account of the arbitrary acts of the British Parliament. Tea had long been their favorite beverage.

The visit of Messrs. Drayton and Tennant to the up-country produced a profound sensation and tended to separate the people into two parties by causing them to declare themselves for or against the measures of the Revolutionary party. Browne, the Tory leader, became more openly hostile, and Drayton came from the Dutch Fork to see Hammond, and appealed to him for support, as his opinions were already well known. Tennant was then at Ninety-Six. To that place Hammond proceeded with Drayton to use his influence, which was great, in inducing the wavering and vacillating to sign the pledge of association.

Neighbor began to reproach neighbor, and the loyalists soon assumed a hostile attitude under the Cunninghams. They collected their forces at Ninety-Six, and Colonel Andrew Williamson, with about six hundred men, went to oppose them. Hammond was an officer under Williamson. In a few days a truce was made between the parties for twenty days, and the men disbanded and went home. In Williamson's expedition against the Cherokees in 1776, Le Roy Hammond played a very distinguished part. In fact, the success of the expedition was greatly due to him. When Williamson's army was ambuscaded and the prospect looked very gloomy—when Williamson's horse was killed under him—when Hammond's friend, Mr. Francis Salvador, of whom I shall have more to say after awhile, was killed and scalped by his side—when everything around was in the utmost confusion and victory seemed doubtful, it was then that Le Roy Hammond, with only twenty men of his own company, charged upon the Indians concealed in the thicket—charged with fixed bayonet— and when they broke from their cover and fled, he poured upon them such a deadly fire that they could not rally. Thus by the gallant conduct of Hammond the army was saved. And again, soon afterwards it was determined to cross the Seneca River and invade the Indian Nation. The officer who was ordered to lead the advance hesitated and evaded the duty. The men themselves shrank from the advance. Hammond volunteered to lead, and the movement was executed with gallantry and success. Hammond received promotion.

So complete was the defeat of the Cherokees that they were never afterwards troublesome. Many of them went down to Florida and became pensioners of the British, as their crops and all means of subsistence were almost entirely destroyed in this campaign.

In June, 1778, Colonel Hammond, with J. L. Gervais and George Galphin, was appointed by the Governor and Council, Commissioners to conciliate the Indian Nations. And in December, 1778, he was sent with George Galphin and Daniel McMurphy, by the Continental Congress, as Commissioners to the Upper and Lower Creeks, met them, had a friendly talk, and made peaceful arrangements with the young Tallassee King and other great men amongst the Creeks. These arrangements and treaties were preserved by Henry Laurens, President of the Continental Congress.

In 1779, Colonel Hammond was with his regiment and fought at the battle of Stono. In 1780, he co-operated with Clarke, and other Whigs, against the Tories and Indians in Georgia. In 1781, he was very active during the siege of Augusta; he with the infantry and Samuel Hammond with the cavalry. During this siege the war waged was one of the greatest barbarity. The Tory, Browne, who commanded at Augusta, with his Indian allies, put to death the prisoners taken with savage ferocity. And the Whig militia, it is altogether probable, were sometimes not much better. Captain William Martin, of the artillery, the oldest of seven brave brothers, was killed here. More will be said about these Martin brothers after awhile. Pickens, Clarke, Harden, and the two Hammonds pushed the siege with great vigor. After the capture of Granby, Lee joined them with his legion, and Browne soon afterwards surrendered. Pickens, Le Roy and Samuel Hammond then proceeded to Ninety Six to assist General Greene. When the siege of Ninety-Six was raised, the Hammonds were sent westwardly and northwestwardly to protect Greene on his retreat, by preventing annoyance from the Tories. From the mountains they were instructed to proceed eastwardly to the Congaree. Proceeding eastwardly they fell in with the rear of the British army under Colonel Cruger retreating from Ninety-six to Orangeburg, and captured some baggage and made several prisoners. Here Le Roy returned home; but he had scarcely reached his home when he was called out to aid General Greene in the battle of Eutaw. Near Granby he was met by a messenger from General Rutledge, at Camden, who required his presence there immediately. While he was at Camden the battle of Eutaw was fought, in which Colonel Samuel Hammond distinguished himself. From this period until the close of the war, he was engaged in scouting, but met no more British troops in regular battle array.

After the war he resumed business as a merchant in partnership with John Lewis Gervais, of Charleston, S. C. He was a member of the Legislature for many years, sometimes as Representative and sometimes as Senator. Of his character as a soldier, as a legislator, as a citizen, as a neighber, as a man, too much cannot be said in his praise. He was an Episcopalian in religion by education and practice. He died at his home in Edgefield, leaving only one descendant, a namesake, Le Roy Hammond. He also left but one son, Andrew Hammond. Some descendants of Colonel Le Roy Hammond are now living in Edgefield County. I hope they are as honorable, as brave, as true to the dictates of honor as ever their illustrious ancestor was.

SAMUEL HAMMOND.

There is not a name in Edgefield, nor in the state, that deserves to be remembered with more admiration and love for his heroic devotion to the cause of Independence than that of Samuel Hammond. He was born on the 21st of September, 1757, in Richmond County, Farnham's Parish, Virginia. He began his career of public service at an early age. In an expedition ordered out by Governor Dunmore against the Western Indians, he was a volunteer, and was in the desperate battle at the mouth of the Great Kenhawa River, fought by General Andrew Lewis, October 10th, 1774. When the troubles with the mother country began, he took the side of Independence—was made captain of a company of volunteers and was engaged in a battle at Great Bridge, near Norfolk, under Colonel Woodford, December, 1775. He also served in Pennsylvania and New Jersey, with the Virginia troops, under Colonel Mathews, General Maxwell and others. In 1778 he volunteered as aid to General Hand and with him went to Pittsburg. In January, 1779, he removed with his father's family to Edgefield District, and at once joined the army under General Lincoln, under orders of General McIntosh, who had superceded General Hand in Pennsylvania. The Virginia troops were about to return home as their eighteen months' term had expired; but Hammond remained with General Lincoln, as captain, that having been his rank in Virginia as General Hand's aid. On the second of February he was ordered by General Williamson to raise a company of mounted volunteers to be attached to Le Roy Hammond's regiment. He did so, and on the 3d of March, 1779, he was commissioned by Governor Rutledge captain of company, and continued in that service until the surrender of Lincoln in May, 1780, was known in the upper country. Before the fall of Charleston, during Prevost's invasion, he had fought at the battle of Stono, under Colonels Henderson and Malmedy. At the seige of Savannah, these officers with their men made a gallant attack upon the left of the British lines. After the seige of Savannah he continued under General Williamson until the surrender of General Lincoln at Charlestown, when Williamson with a great many other Whigs, accepted British protection as paroled prisoners; but Samuel Hammond did not.

General Williamson was at Augusta with a few South Carolina militia when Charlestown was surrendered. Governor Howley, of Georgia, Colonel Clary, of Georgia, Colonel Dooly and several other officers, continental and militia, held a conference which Williamson attended. The convention entered into and agreed upon by the British and the American commander at Charlestown, was presented by Williamson and was read by one of the governor's secretaries. Various plans were discussed, but nothing definite was agreed upon. Governor Howley determined to retreat northward with such State papers as he could carry away, and Williamson determined to discharge the few South Carolina militia then at Augusta, and return to Whitehall, near Ninety-Six. Colonels Dooly and Clarke promised Williamson to co-operate with him in any plan that might be adopted by the council at Whitehall for the defence of the lower part of the two States; or to retire with him to the North, if that should be the determination. These officers then retired to Wilkes County, Ga., and Williamson to Whitehall. Many of his officers were there assembled, and Samuel Hammond had high hopes, before the council met, that they would determine to move, without loss of time, northward, with all the forces they had assembled; to keep together; to increase their numbers; and to be ready, at all times, for offensive or defensive operations, until assistance could come from the main army.

General Williamson had, then and there, three companies of regular infantry, raised by the State and enlisted for three years or the war. The officers were good; the troops well trained. Besides these there were present one hundred and fifty or two hundred unorganized men. Colonel Andrew Pickens, with his force—number not given—was halted about three miles below Ninety-Six. This was the situation when the council met. General Williamson read the capitulation of Charlestown; made some comments; advised keeping together and retreating; but said that he would be governed by the determination a majority of the council should adopt. Samuel Hammond says that he was struck dumb on finding that not more than one officer of the staff, one field officer, and four or five captains were opposed to an immediate acceptance of the terms stipulated for the militia of the State by the Convention at Charlestown. It was now proposed and carried, to send a flag at once to Colonel Parris to notify him of their conclusion, and to settle the time, place, and manner of surrender. Still Williamson persevered and again addressed the council and expressed a wish for a different conclusion; and proposed to ride, with any number of the officers present, to Colonel Pickens' camp—a few miles distant—stating that he wished to consult with him and to address the men of his command. This was agreed to. Williamson talked with Pickens. The troops were then drawn up in square, all mounted. Williamson then addressed them in spirited terms, stating that with his men alone he could drive all the British then in the District without difficulty. He then caused the capitulation of Charlestown to be read. He again addressed them, and told them that they could safely retreat, and that he was sure they could soon return with force sufficient to keep the enemy confined to Charlestown. He told them what they had already done, and what he hoped they would do; but he left it to themselves to say what they would do. He concluded by putting the question to vote, and said: 'My fellow citizens, all of you who are for going with me on a retreat with arms in our hands, will hold up your hands; and all who are for staying and accepting the terms made for you by General Lincoln will stand as you are.' Two officers, Captain McCall and Captain McLidle, and three or four privates, held up their hands; all others stood as they were. He then put the question again with the same result.

Samuel Hammond, who was present at this conference, rode back with Williamson and his staff to Whitehall. That evening, in company with Bennett Crofton, adjutant of one of the regiments, he left Whitehall, determined to make their retreat and not acquiesce in the decision just arrived at.

At this point Williamson disappears from history, and nothing, or little more is said of him, until he is captured by Colonel Hayne near Charlestown. The place of his retirement, after he left Whitehall, was never spoken of. The time and place of his death are unknown. He died an obscure, heart-broken, poor man. He was not a traitor. Let that word cease to be applied to his name. He never bore arms against his country. He never received a British commission. He never received any British gold. He lived the balance of his days in obscurity and died poor. He was not a great man. He was not a heroic character, but a weak one. It was very unfortunate, both for himself and the country, that he had the chief command in the up-country at that time. That place should have been held by Le Roy Hammond, his brother-in-law, (they married sisters, the Misses Tyler, of Virginia,) who was of a more heroic mould. His success in the Cherokee war was due mainly to the courage and skill of Le Roy Hammond. And it is worthy of note that Colonel Hammond does not blame him for the course he took. Samuel Hammond was better fitted by nature for the chief command at Ninety-Six at that time than either Le Roy Hammond or Williamson; but he was too young.

Samuel Hammond and Bennett Crofton raised a company of seventy-six men, determined to seek assistance, or to die fighting as they were. Over half these men withdrew from Hammond in a short time and hid out; but they were afterwards captured by the British and sent to prison where many of them died. Hammond and thirty-two escaped to North Carolina. Concealing themselves all day and traveling all night, they passed Saluda and Bush River, and were kinkly supplied by T. Harvey and Charles Moore, but still they could hear of no party of Whigs whom they could join. Near the foot of the mountains they came to the home of Calvin Jones, a good Whig. He was absent and Mrs. Jones was in great trouble, as she had ben ill-treated that day and her house plundered by a party of Tories who were on their way to the British army. They had taken the clothing of her children, her side-saddle, and wantonly destroyed what they could not carry away. Mrs.

Jones told Hammond that they were seventy or eighty in number. Hammond's little band, thirty-five in all, determined to follow and chastise them. Mrs. Jones sent her little boy, a lad twelve or fourteen years of age, to guide and aid them in the pursuit. He very gladly joined them. They followed the Tory trail and overtook them next morning when they were at breakfast. Hammond and his men immediately charged, and they were in the midst of the Tory camp before they were aware of their approach. All the enemies' arms were taken, —four were killed and eleven made prisoners—these were released on parole. Mrs. Jones' valuables were all restored to her and she gladly supplied the Whigs with all refreshments in her power. They went on their way rejoicing, with a number of captured horses, and a fine supply of ammunition and provisions.

A day or two after this, while broiling their bacon and eating parched corn for bread, they heard the sound of horses' feet in a brisk march coming towards them. They had come within reach of the guns before they were discovered. On being hailed they answered, "Friends of America." "So are we, but let us know you. Men, stand to your arms." So they stood, both parties with their guns pointed at each other. Captain Edward Hampton, from the other party, advanced with a flag. He was well known and received a cordial welcome from all of Hammond's men. Both parties, actuated by the same motives, and moving in the same direction, were now happily united. Moving on together they soon came upon the trail of a party as numerous as their own, whom they supposed to be enemies. They determined to attack them. Hastening on they soon discovered a horse standing in the trail, a man lying on the ground fast asleep, but holding to the bridle. They surrounded him and hailed him, when he sprang up and boldly replied, "Friend to America, if I die for it!" His name was Harris, and he said he belonged to Colonel G. Clarke's command, which was not far ahead. He said he was obliged to sleep, but was going on as soon as he took a nap. They joined Clarke the same evening and they now numbered over two hundred men. They moved on into North Carolina. Then they learned of other parties, who had left South Carolina moved by the same impulse as themselues: Sumter's, Williams' and Brandon's. They sent expresses to all these to let them know of their arrival and intentions. They were here joined by Captains McCall and Liddle of Colonel Pickens' Regiment with a small detachment. Pickens, himself, had laid down his arms, but he soon afterwards resumed them, when called upon by the British to bear arms against his countrymen.

Samuel Hammond was in active service from the beginning of the trouble until the evacuation of Charleston in December, 1782. His rank was that of Major. He was in the battle of Musgrove's Mills, from which place, having heard of the defeat of both Generals Gates and Sumter, he moved rapidly to Charlotte, N. C. At Charlotte the prisoners taken from the British were delivered to him and conducted to Hillsboro. At Hillsboro he collected all the stragglers and refugees from Le Roy Hammond's Regiment, and others who might come into service. At Salisbury he formed a company and advertised for recruits; and collected a number, who formed part of Williams' command at King's Mountain, in which battle some were killed and some severely wounded. After the battle of King's Mountain he was joined by some from Ninety-Six, and with all the men under his command he marched into North Carolina, where he acted a short while under Colonel Davis. He was at the battle of Blackstocks with Sumter—he had a fight at Long Cane, near Ninety-Six. In the battle of Cowpens, on the 17th of June, 1781, he commanded, as Major, the left of the front line. From this time till the battle of Eutaw, he was actively engaged as a partisan. At the battle of Eutaw, on the 8th of September, he had the good fortune to distinguish himself.

After the war he settled in Savannah; and in Georgia he was honored with several important posts. He was Colonel in the war against the Creeks on the border; member of the Legislature; elected to United States Congress in 1802. In 1805, he was appointed by President Jefferson Military and Civil Governor of Upper Louisiana (Missouri), where he remained until 1824. In 1824, he returned to South Carolina, where he received a warm welcome; and in 1827, was elected Surveyor-General; and in 1831, Secretary of State. In 1835, being then old and infirm, he retired to his Varello farm, near Hamburg, S. C., at which place he continued to reside until his death.

He died on the 11th of September, 1842, in the 87th year of his age. He died on Sunday.

On Monday, the 12th, the military of Hamburg were joined by those of Augusta, comprising the Clinck Riflemen and the Augusta Artillery Guard, all under the command of Samuel C. Wilson; together with the Masonic Lodges of Hamburg and Augusta, and the citizens of both places, formed a procession at the corner of Covington and Market streets, Joseph E. Gladding acting as marshal. Minute guns were fired from the site of his old fort on Shultz's Hill by the artillery, while the procession followed the body of the deceased Veteran, with the solemn sounds of the muffled drums. When they arrived at the family burial ground, above Campbellton, the remains were lowered into the vault with Masonic honors, and a volley fired over it by the escorting infantry.

"It is remarkable," says his biographer, "that although so much of his early life was familiarized with battles and bloodshed, he preserved his natural gentleness and suavity of manner to the last—enlivening every circle where he went with his cheerful sallies of good humor." Dr. A. S. Hammond is authority for the foregoing facts in the life of his father.

In this sketch of Samuel Hammond I have left out many things that would have given me great pleasure to insert; but I fear that this history will grow to too great a size before I complete it. It is very pleasant to write of such men as Samuel Hammond, and of many others of Edgefield, who have lived noble lives and played honorable parts upon the stage of being. The writer is a native of Edgefield, and as this work progresses he begins to feel that he has good ground to be proud of the fact. It is true, however, that many dark deeds have been done upon Edgefield soil—deeds of violence and blood. The descendants of Cain are to be found in all parts of the world.

LE ROY AND SAMUEL HAMMOND.

The following additional facts in the lives of Le Roy Hammond and his nephew Samuel Hammond, and the descendants of Le Roy Hammond, were communicated to me by the two brothers, C. M. and E. W. Hammond. They write from Hamburg, S. C., under date of September 25, 1892:

The first information we have of the family of Hammond is that of Colonel Le Roy Hammond, who came from Virginia in the year or about the year 1765. He married a Miss Tyler, a near relative of President Tyler. He lived in Augusta a few years, then moved to South Carolina, on the Savannah River, seven miles above Augusta, and named his place New Richmond in memory of his old home. He built an imposing house for these days; the lumber was all sawed by hand, a *whip saw* being used. The bricks for the chimneys, and the nails, which were wrought, were made on the plantation. The brick-layers and plasterers, thirty in number, were also brought from Europe to complete the house. This house is now standing and is in very good repair; and is in possession of Major Andrew J. Hammond's family, who was a grandson of Colonel Le Roy Hammond.

Colonel Le Roy Hammond established a trading post on the Savannah River, buying skins, furs, &c., from the Indians, giving in exchange such things as they needed. These supplies were brought from Charleston up the Savannah by pole boats.

He died at Snow Hill, near New Richmond in 1790. He left one son, Le Roy, who was a captain in the Revolution at sixteen years of age. It is related that, in one of the skirmishes in which he was engaged, his cousin Colonel Samuel Hammond captured a number of Tories and one of them having a pistol concealed when in the act of firing on him (the colonel) Captain Hammond galloped up and cut his head in half, each half falling on his shoulders, one on one shoulder, and one on the other. The sword with which he accomplished this feat was made in a blacksmith shop to order, and has the name of the maker, Harvey, engraved thereon. This sword, with many hacks in it, showing the active service in which Captain Hammond was engaged, also his pistols, which are flint and steel with brass barrels, handsomely mounted in silver with coat of arms of an Englishman, from whom they were taken in an engagement, are now in the possession of the descendants of Captain Andrew J. Hammond.

During the Revolution a notorious character, Davis, a Tory and robber, was captured at Cherokee Ponds, in Edgefield County, S. C. It fell to the lot of Captain Hammond to kill him. One of these pistols was used on the occasion.

At one time while hunting in Georgia he lost his way and entered the camp of hostile Indians. They all sprang to their feet drawing their bows and tomahawks, ready to kill him. He not knowing their language was entirely at their mercy. He called the name of Le Roy Hammond, and such was the respect and veneration in which the name and good deeds of his father was held, of one accord they took him in their camp, made him presents and fed him and sent him on his way rejoicing. Captain Hammond, after the war, was a colonel in the militia. A large fortune was left to him by his father, most of which he spent in a most charitable manner, giving and helping all who stood in need of assistance. Of this fortune there remains to his descendants, the children of Andrew J. Hammond, the valuable lands on the Savannah River and the old Homestead, New Richmond: Captain Le Roy Hammond left a daughter, Julia, who married Charles Hammond, a planter and merchant, of Hamburg, S. C.

Andrew J. Hammond, his son, was born October 8th, 1814, and was reared by his mother at the old homestead, New Richmond. Mrs. Hammond survived her husband fifty-four years, and was noted throughout Edgefield for her fine business habits, strong intellect, great charity, and goodness of heart. All these fine traits of character were transmitted to her son, Andrew J. Hammond. He was educated at the then noted schools of Pendleton, S. C. In 1841, he married Elizabeth Butler, the only daughter of the Honorable Sampson H. Butler. For many years he was Captain of the Edgefield Hussars. He was a member of the Legislature for several years, and was a member of the Secession Convention in 1860. Captain A. J. Hammond retired from political life, but at the breaking out of the late Civil War between the States he was elected Major of the Twenty-fourth Regiment of South Carolina Volunteers, where he served with bravery and distinction until prostrated with fever and rheumatism, which confined him to his home until near the close of the war, when he was assigned a position on the staff of General A. R. Wright.

Major Hammond was a patriot, a Christian, and a gentleman; and was universally honored, loved, and respected by all who knew him. He died December 19th, 1882. His son, who bore the honored name of Le Roy, and who gave great promise of a noble and useful life, died in early manhood in the year 1882. Major Hammond's only surviving sons are Edgar and Charles, who, the writer of this history has reason to believe, inherit the courage, the strength of character and noble attributes of their illustrious ancestors. They reside on the lands bequeathed by their great-grandfather, Colonel Le Roy Hammond.

XVI.

PICKENS.

We group together the three Pickens, General Andrew, of the Revolutton; his son Andrew, and the late F. W. Pickens, Governor of South Carolina. We will take the last first. Governor Francis W. Pickens was not a native of Edgefield, but he lived so many years of his life in Edgefield District that we can well lay claim to him as one of Edgefield's sons. He was born in Pendleton District, in that part which is now Oconee County. His father, Andrew Pickens, moved to Alabama in 1819, and Francis was first sent to Athens College, in Georgia, and afterwards to the South Carolina College, from which institution he graduated with a high reputation for talents, honor, and energy. Mr. John C. Calhoun, who was his relation, regarded him as the most promising young man in the State at that time. He read law at Edgefield, was admitted to the bar, and was soon afterwards elected a member of the Legislature. He succeeded Mr. McDuffie in Congress, where he established a high character as a statesman and as a debater. He resigned his seat in Congress and was elected to the State Senate, where he served several sessions. He was then appointed by President Buchanan Minister to Russia. After his return home he was elected Governor of the State, just before Secession and the breaking out of the great Civil War. After the war he was a member of the State Conven-tion, which met in 1865, while B. F. Perry was Provisional Governor. This was his last public service to the State. He was married three times and left children, daughters, by each marriage; but no son to transmit his name to posterity. He was proud of his ancestry, and had reason to be.

General Andrew Pickens, grandfather of Francis W., was a native of Pennsylvania, but moved to South Carolina some years before the Revolution. From the beginning of the troubles he was an ardent supporter of Independence, and was engaged in active service in the field during nearly the whole of the war. There was a little while, after the fall of Charles-ton and the surrender of General Lincoln, when the whole upper country seemed paralyzed, in which he was quiescent as a paroled prisoner. When ordered by the British authorities to take up arms, in violation of his parole, against his countrymen, he immediately resumed his arms, and took the field in their defence. He fought at Augusta and received the surrender of that place; he fought at Ninety-Six, and was often before the celebrated Star Redoubt. A brother of his was killed there; another brother was taken prisoner, and delivered to the Tories—but, indeed, all the garrison were Tories—who took him over into Georgia and gave him to the Indians, who burned him to death on a pile of lightwood. General Pickens had chief command and gained the glorious victory over the Tory, Colonel Boyd, at Kettle Creek; he had a command at Cowpens, and gave General Morgan great assistance in gaining that victory; he fought Colonel Pyle, on Ham River, N. C., and destroyed his command of three hundred men; he was shot from his horse by a musket ball at the battle of Eutaw, and was picked up by the soldiers as dead, but he soon recovered. These and other services to the State and country mark him as one of the most active, energetic, and useful men of the time. He sat in the first county court ever held at the old Black House, near Abbeville Court House. His son Andrew, when a child, drew the first jury ever impaneled in Abbeville District after Independence. It is a fact worthy of honorable mention in his career that, when General Davidson, of North Carolina, died the brigade, which was commanded by him from the Mecklenburg section, elected General Pickens to command them; so that at that time he was a General in both States. It is also a fact in his career that he never received any pay for his services.

He was elected Representative in the United States Congress in the year 1793. He then resigned his commission of Major General in the State Militia, and recommended the appointment of William Butler. The appointment was made, and about this time a son was born to General Butler, whom he named Andrew Pickens Butler, as a graceful and grateful compliment to General Pickens.

Andrew Pickens, son of General Andrew Pickens of the Revolution, was a colonel commanding a regiment on the Canadian frontier during the war of 1812. In 1817 he was elected

Governor of the State, but soon afterwards moved to Alabama (1819.)

Besides the services of General Pickens, already mentioned, he rendered others to the country which should not be omitted. He held the treaty of Hopewell with the Cherokee Indians, by which all the western part of South Carolina was obtained; he was one of the commissioners appointed by President Jefferson to run the line between Georgia and Tennessee; and also the line between Georgia and South Carolina. He held the treaty of Milledgeville; that of Huntsville, and of Natches with the Indians; and was one of the first white men to pass down the Cumberland River, and was often shot at by the savages on the banks. In fact he was one of the most active and useful men of the whole South during the period of the Revolution and the year following. His home was never at any time in Edgefield; but he was of Ninety-Six and we have a right to claim him as our own through his illustrious grandson, F. W. Pickens, whose home for many years was at Edgefield.

CAPTAIN RICHARD JOHNSON.

Whether Captain Richard Johnson was born in Edgefield or not, is not known. His father came from Virginia and settled near Campbellton, on the Savannah River. Richard was about eighteen years old at the time of the Declaration of Independence. He took that side at the first and clung to it without wavering until the close. He was a captain in Samuel Hammond's cavalry. He had one great quality, which always inspired his comrades with confidence—coolness in time of danger. As an instance of his coolness and readiness it is related of him that at Eutaw, in retreating before the enemy, as he passed a cannon, he stopped and spiked it with a nail which he carried in his pocket. He was the man for the occasion, and he was always ready. Cunningham, on his return to the low country, after his celebrated raid in 1781, while feeding one day at the lower Fork of Little Saluda, his force at the time consisting of about one hundred and fifty men, suddenly saw Hammond appear on the opposite side with about seventy men. Hammond finding the odds so much against him, determined not to cross then, but to follow and harrass them until he received reenforcements. Captain Johnson wanted to cross and attack at once, and said if thirty men would volunteer and go with him he would cross and make the attack.   Thirty men *did* volunteer and among the number was Zachary Smith Brooks, grandfather of Preston S. Brooks. Hammond interfered and forbade the movement; placed himself in the way and gave a peremptory order to halt.   Hammond was right.   It would have been madness for thirty men to attack one hundred and fifty under Bloody Bill.   The next day General Pickens came up with them and the pursuit was continued as far as Orangeburg.

Johnson received high praise for his conduct.   And the bold spirit he exhibited on this and on all occasions, made him very popular.

In 1806 he was elected to the Legislature and continued to be a member of that body nearly all the remainder of his life. He died in 1817 at his residence in Edgefield.   He was opposed to the establishment of the South Carolina College; but after he saw the good resulting from it he frankly acknowledged his error.   He left a handsome fortune, but no children to inherit it.

MICHAEL WATSON.

Michael Watson's first essay in arms with the militia of South Carolina was in 1762, in the expedition against the Cherokee Indians led by Colonel Grant of the regular army. And after that he was found very forward, brave, and efficient in opposition to the lawless banditti in 1767 and 1768.   I find no mention of the time when Michael Watson's father settled in Edgefield, but he must have been amongst the first in that section of the country.   At that time there were no courts nearer than Charlestown.   Edgefield, or rather Ninety-Six, for Edgefield was not known until a good many years afterwards, was filling up very rapidly with people from 1760 to 1770, not only with good industrious settlers, but with a great many who were not so.

The peace of 1763 turned loose a great many soldiers on both sides of the Atlantic, who had been rendered unfit for the arts of peace, and who sought to live by preying upon the property of others.   Many of these sought refuge in the District of Ninety-Six as a secure asylum, and as a good field for their operations, as there were no courts nearer than Charlestown, which was a hundred and fifty or two hundred miles away. For peaceable, industrious citizens to carry offenders such a distance for trial and punishment, imposed upon them a burden much too great for them to bear. To lift this burden, or to avoid it, they organized themselves into bands of Regulators, so that when offenders were caught they could be dealt with at home. Such organizations may, and do, work well for awhile in extreme cases; but they soon fall off from the high plane of established law and order, and degenerate into mere instruments for the gratification of personal revenge. In this case much good was done, and the Regulators succeeded in their object and purpose. The attention of the authorities of the Province was called to the deplorable condition of affairs in the up country, and seven additional courts were established in different parts of the Province; one of which was at Camden; one at Orangeburg; and one at Ninety-Six. But before these courts were established we find that in 1767 a band of marauders made an inroad among the neighbors of Michael Watson on the Ridge, and threatened the life of his father. Michael, William, and their father, with two other men, pursued them about thirty miles. When they overtook them they found them lodged in a house in which they had taken shelter. The Watson party advanced and were fired upon by those inside. Old Mr. Watson, William, and one other were instantly killed. Michael was wounded, but he and the other survivor rushed into the house before those inside could reload their guns. Michael killed two of them; his friend, whose name is not known, wounded another, but the survivors made their escape. Some of them were afterwards captured and taken to Charlestown and tried.

November 3d, 1767, nine persons were convicted of plunder, horsestealing, and murder. One Ezekiel Tyrrel also was convicted of burning Watson's corn crib, and was sentenced to be hung June 1st, 1768. The troubles grew worse and worse until the marauders embodied under Colonel Scovial, who had friends at court, paraded under arms and made ready for battle. This brought matters to a crisis. The matter was laid before the Governor and Council, and soon afterwards the courts were established, and regularly held for the trial of all offenders by judge and jury.

When the Revolutionary War began Watson was already well known for his courage and patriotism. In the war against the Cherokees, in 1776, he rendered very efficient service at Little River, when the division was in some confusion, by collecting a chosen band and charging the Indians, driving them back and so saving the division. After the fall of Charlestown, and the British and Tories became dominant in the up country, on one occasion a party surrounded his house at night while he was in bed. He heard them talking at one end of the house about the mode of attack. He did not stay long upon the order of his going, but went at once, and seizing his gun he ran out of the door at the other end of the house, and escaped to the woods about fifty yards distant. He then began to call out, as if to collect a body of men on guard: "Here they are! Come on, boys! Charge!" He then fired off his gun. The Tories were frightened and somewhat disgusted, and left speedily.

At another time his house was surrounded in the open day, when he was alone with his family. He leaped out through a window and ran for the woods. The enemy fired at him as long as he was in sight, but he escaped unhurt, though his clothes had several bullet holes through them. Afterwards a Tory Colonel, Kin Williams, came to his plantation with three hundred men, each with a green oak leaf in his hat. Watson was not at home at the time, or he would probably have been killed. They burned every house on the place; killed every hog and cow, and all the poultry, and either destroyed or carried away all the provisions. With the assistance of his neighbors, he made another home about eight miles away, but he was still frequently disturbed. On one occasion a man named Hartley undertook to carry off the only horse he had left. Watson was then at home and was too much for Hartley. He fired upon him, wounded him in the arm, and took him prisoner; made him go home with him, dressed his wound, and treated him with the greatest kindness. Such kind treatment from Watson and his family had so good an effect upon Hartley that he left the Tories, became a good Whig, and served under Watson. Often after the war he was heard to relate these facts.

Watson's career was brought to a close a short time before

the close of the war. In May, 1782, hearing of a body of
Tories in Dean's Swamp, near Orangeburg, Watson and William Butler determined to attack them.   Watson's men were
mounted, armed with rifles and muskets; Butler's were cavalry,
armed with pistols and cutlasses.   These Tories were commanded by Bloody Bill Cunningham, and in hopes to be able
to surprise them, Watson and Butler ma'ched with great
rapidity.   On the way they captured a disaffected man, named
Hutton; but he made his escape, and gave the Tories warning
just before they reached the camp.   As soon as his escape was
known Watson wanted to stop the advance, but Butler was for
pushing forward.   Butler's wish prevailed; and as they advanced they saw two men who seemed to be trying to hide.
Butler, Watson, and Sergeant Vardel rode forward to capture
them.   Watson then discovered that they were only a decoy,
and warned the others, but too late.   The Tories, seeing that
they were discovered, fired upon the Whigs and brought down
Watson, Vardel, and several others.   Butler brought off the
wounded men, but now found that the infantry had very little
ammunition left, and that the Tories, twice the number of the
Whigs, were advancing upon them.   He immediately made
John Corley, a brave and gallant youth, his First Lieutenant;
and they charged so hotly upon the enemy's lines that they
were thrown into confusion.   The whigs pressed upon them so
fiercely and used their broad swords so rapidly that they could
not rally, and sought safety in the swamp.   As the Whigs
returned from the chase they found Vardel alive, but he expired
in the effort to wave his hand and to shout "hurra!"   They
buried him on the field.   Watson was carried to Orangeburg.
He was alive when they reached that place, but he died soon
afterwards, and was buried in that village with military
honors.

Shall we relate a little story of this battle? A smart young
man, name not given, was very anxious to distinguish himself, never having been in battle.   He sought the office of
Lieutenant and was elected.   Mounted on a beautiful filly, he
advanced bravely to the attack.   When they found the enemy
and dismounted to make the attack, he dismounted also,
hitched his horse and advanced on foot with the others.   When
the Tories rose and poured in their fire, seeing the number

that fell besides Captain Watson, the young man could not stand it; his courage evaporated; he turned and fled, and, for-getting his fine filly, never stopped until he reached home, spreading the report that all the party had been killed except himself. The horse was saved by those who brought off the wounded. When they reached Orangeburg the owner of the filly never making any claim, she was sold and the money she brought was expended in rum and other refreshments. Some others of Watson's men also ran off—names not known. I am not much inclined to blame anybody for running out of danger when he can save his bacon by it. Discretion is the better part of valor, always.

FRANCIS SALVADOR.

In a history of Edgefield, it is due to Mr. Salvador, whose name appears in every history of the State, that something should be said of him more than the mere casual mention of his name. He was the intimate friend of Colonel Le Roy Hammond. He was killed in the second battle of the war with the Cherokees in 1776, and his death was much lamented. He was highly accomplished, honorable, and generous. He was a native of England, but of Hebrew parents and a Hebrew in religion. He inherited a large fortune from his father, Jacob Salvador, which he increased by marriage. He came to South Carolina in the year 1774, with his friend, Mr Richard A. Rafeloy, purchased negroes, and a large tract of land in Ninety-Six District, and lived honored and respected. He became a member of the General Assembly, and was warmly attached to the cause of Independence. He was the first man killed in the battle. He was wounded twice—was scalped and died in less than an hour, unconscious of the barbarous act.

THE MARTINS.

The family of Martins in Edgefield were remarkable during the Revolution for being united in the cause of Independence. They were all Whigs and brave men. There were seven brothers, and all took active parts and all made good soldiers. All survived the war, except one, William, who was the oldest. He was Captain of Artillery, and was killed at the siege of Augusta. He was one of the oldest captains in the service.

These brothers were named William, Bartley, James, John, Edmund, Marshall, and Matthew. Matthew was alive in 1846, living in Tennessee; he died near the close of that year. The wives of these men were about as good and true soldiers as their husbands, if the following story be correct, of which there is no doubt:

Learning that important despatches were sent up the country by the enemy, Mrs. William and Mrs. Bartley Martin determined to waylay the courier and capture the papers. They dressed themselves in their husbands' clothes, (perhaps they were in the habit of wearing the breeches any how), took positiou near the road where the express must pass. Directly the courier appeared with a guard of two British officers. As they came up the young women presented their muskets and demanded their instant surrender. The officers, panic stricken, surrendered and were paroled at once. The ladies then took the despatches, hastened home through the woods and without loss of time sent their prize to General Greene. The officers soon appeared on their return and asked for accommodation as travellers. This was granted. Mrs. Martin asked how it was that they returned so soon? They told her that they had been taken prisoner by two rebel boys; and they showed her their paroles. The ladies rallied them and asked if they were not armed. They said yes; but were so surprised that they could not use their arms. Mrs. Martin allowed them to depart next morning without letting them know who their captors were. These Martins were of Martintown, on the Sayannah side of Edgefield. A more extended account of this family will be given.

CUNNINGHAM AND HAMMOND.

One purpose of Cunningham when he made his celebrated raid into the up-country in 1781, was the capture of Samuel Hammond, whom he expected to find at Anderson's Mills, on the Saluda, near Island Ford, as he heard he was then stationed at that place. Hammond was not there when Cunningham passed. From Cloud's Creek to Anderson's Mills his path was one of fire and blood. He crossed Saluda at Island Ford, went on to Hays' station, in the lower edge of Laurens, and put Colonel Hays and all his command to the sword.

MRS. CRUGER AT NINETY-SIX.

The following anecdotes of the residence of Mrs. Cruger at Ninety-Six may not be without interest to the readers of this book:

While the British occupied Ninety-Six the family of the commandant, Colonel Cruger, was staying at the house of Colonel James Mayson, which was about three miles from the town. Mayson was a man of family with several lovely, lively daughters. The officers of the garrison would frequently call and spend the evening there, and it sometimes happened that some of the rebels would also visit there and if they met any British officers all passed off pleasantly, as they regarded Colonel Mayson's home as neutral ground. Suddenly one day a cannonade is heard at Ninety-Six, and the ladies soon learned that General Greene's forces had attacked the Star battery. The ladies, in great alarm, immediately began collecting their movable values, jewelry, &c., and Mrs. Cruger sewing up her guineas in belts, so that she could secure them about her person. A young lady, afterwards the wife of General William Butler, says she assisted Mrs. Cruger in sewing up her guineas. The other ladies, very probably, had no guineas to hide. They had scarcely finished their work and completed their preparations for a speedy departure, when a number of armed men in American uniform, marched into the enclosure. The ladies were much alarmed, but the commanding officer advanced and asked to speak with any one of the family. He stated that he had been as sent guard to protect Mrs. Cruger and the family, and that they need be under no apprehension, and that the guard would remain as long as necessary. This attention was very well and thankfully received by Mrs. Cruger, Colonel Cruger and all his officers. When the siege was raised the guard was withdrawn, and when they parted Mrs. Cruger gave the officer commanding two guineas.

Mrs. Butler also relates that soon after this, when she had returned home to the house of her stepfather, Mr. Savage, near Saluda Old Town, she first saw William Butler, her future husband. A handsome young officer, with a rose cockade in his hat, rode up to the house alone and inquired if any persons had been there who might be stragglers from the American army; if they had taken anything away, and in what direction they had gone. Mrs. Butler told him they had taken nothing from the house but that they had gone in a direction which led her to believe that their purpose was to steal their horses. The lieutenant then gave a signal and he was soon joined by his men. They pursued; saved the horses; captured the stragglers and took them safely into camp.

Only a little while before this occurred, a young Virginia officer, named Wade, who had been badly wounded in a skirmish with some of Lord Rawdon's troops near the "Old Town," and had fallen from his horse, was brought into the house. While all were anxious and solicitous about his welfare, he thought only of his horse, and all he could say was, "Don't let them carry off my horse."

MRS. DILLARD AND MRS. THOMAS.

These ladies were not of Edgefield, but inasmuch as Colonel Samuel Hammond, who *was* of Edgefield, in his notes of the Battle of Cedar Springs, in Spartanburg District, relates the story, and I feel sure that it is not out of place here. Colonel Hammond says:

"Mrs. Dillard, who had given our party milk and potatoes the day before this battle, stated that Ferguson and Dunlap, with their party of Tories came there on the next evening. They inquired after Clarke's party, their numbers, &c., &c., and she gave them as little information as possible. They ordered her to prepare supper with despatch; and while she was so employed, she heard one of the Tory officers tell Ferguson that he had just been informed that the rebels under Clarke were to camp that night at the Green, or Cedar Springs. It was immediately resolved to attack them that night, and Mrs. Dillard's husband being with Clarke, she resolved to give them notice of it. As soon as she could set out the supper she slipped off to the stable, bridled a young horse, and, without a saddle, galloped off to apprise Clarke of his danger; under an impression that the enemy were too numerous to justify battle with them. She arrived just in time, for Dunlap had been sent forward by Ferguson, with orders to attack and detain us until he should come up with the remainder. Dunlap had advanced rapidly and charged soon after we had paraded and were ready for his reception. The lady returned home in safety and deserves well of her country.

"The credit of giving this seasonable notice to the Americans has also been claimed for Mrs. Thomas, the heroic mother of Colonel J. Thomas, jun., and no doubt with reason—they both did it. With such patriotic matrons and with a peasantry who refused to take protection, or acknowledge submission to the British forces, well may this District be designated as Spartan-burg."

Mrs. Thomas rode sixty miles to give Colonel Clarke the information. The foregoing should have appeared in the Sketch of Samuel Hammond and his Services, but was over-looked and inadvertently left out.

PICKENS AND WILLIAMSON.

After the battle of Guilford Court House, N. C., March 25, 1781, General Greene determined to return to South Carolina, and detached Major Samuel Hammond of South Carolina, and Major James Jackson of Georgia, from his army with orders to penetrate to the Savannah River and open communication with friends of Independence on both sides, in order that he might receive support in his progress through. When they came into Ninety-Six District, they sent for Generals Williamson and Pickens, the most influential men in that part of the country. They both attended the call and were invited by Hammond and Jackson to unite with them in carrying out General Greene's views. They stated that that they were prisoners on parole, on the terms of the surrender in Charleston, and although these terms had been violated as to some who had been ordered out by the British, yet, as to themselves, the terms had not been violated, and they did not feel justified in breaking their parole. The British Commander soon received information of the arrival of the Americans in the District, and at once issued the order calling upon and requiring Andrew Williamson and Andrew Pickens to enter upon active service in support of the Royal authority. Pickens immediately joined his countrymen in arms and ever after was a gallant and efficient leader. Williamson submitted; and after awhile left the District of Ninety-Six; retired to the neighborhood of Charleston, and always after remained within the British lines; but never, as far as is known, bore arms against his countrymen.

FORT GALPHIN—GEORGE GALPHIN.

On the arrival of Colonel Lee at Augusta, during the siege of that place, after the capture of Fort Granby, he sent down Captain Rudolph with his regulars to assist in the siege of Fort Galphin. The fort was soon taken. The capitulation was signed by Captain Rudolph. This capture was of great importance to the American cause. A large amount of arms and military stores, blankets, clothing, small arms, ammunition, salt, and hospital stores were captured in the fort and in the boats on the river—all of immense value to the Americans. Without this seasonable supply it is doubtful whether Fort Cornwallis could have been taken.

Fort Galphin was on Silver Bluff, the property afterwards of Governor James H. Hammond and his descendants, at that time owned by George Galphin, whose dreaming match with the Indian Chief will be given. Mr. Galphin, Assistant Superintendent of Indian affairs, was a devoted friend to the American cause, and by his influence with the Indians much bloodshed was prevented. He also frequently assisted the Americans in their wants—general as well as individual—with his fortune; which was large.

XVII.

NORRIS TOWNSHIP.

The history of Norris Township is here given as it is related by Mr. John M. Norris, who, in November, 1891, was in his seventy-fifth year, and who was born and raised in the township, and has resided all his life within a mile of where his father and grandfather lived and died.

Norris Township lies in the eastern border of the county and embraces a considerable portion of the famous Ridge Plateau, from the Lexington County line west to Ward Township, a distance of ten or twelve miles, and extends northwest to the Rhinehart and Mobley Townships, and embraces within its area Cloud's Creek, West Creek, and Norris Greek, all three of which have their source on the .Ridge and flow in a northwest direction. This section of our county cannot better be described than in the words of Professor Morse in his Universal Geography. He says: "The Ridge is a remarkable elevated belt of land extending from the Savannah to Bush River. It is a fine, healthy belt of land, well watered and of good soil. The Edistos have their rise on this Ridge, as well as creeks running into the Saluda. These waters interlock, and the traveler on the old Ridge Road crosses branches alternately running in opposite directions. As you advance northwest from the summit of the Ridge, commences a country exactly resembling the Northern States, or like Devonshire in England or Langudoc in France. The hills and vales, with all their verdure and variegated beauty, present themselves to the eye. Here heaven has bestowed its blessings with a most bounteous hand. The air is temperate and healthful. It is well watered, and the fertility of the soil is equal to every vegetable production."

This description by Professor Morse was intended for all the up country as well as Norris Township. Many changes have been made since that was written. The beautiful and majestic forests have dwindled away. Only here and there a small copse of the original woods is to be seen. The verdure and variegated beauty do not gladden the eye as of old. The hills and vales have been dispossessed of much of their fertile soil by improper husbandry. Gullies and barren hills, like the wrinkles of old age, bear witness to the fact.

Among the earliest settlers of the township was William Norris, grandfather of Mr. John M. Norris, who came from Pennsylvania, and settled on West Creek about the year 1750, and died in 1780. About the same time William Sawyer settled in the same neighborhood. Then Busheys, Bateses, Longs, Padgetts, Whittles, Yarboroughs, Smiths, Warrens, and others, on the eastern portion of the township; while on the Ridge and western side were the Watsons, Simpkinses, Perrys, Asbills, Holstons, Burtons, Reynoldses, and Williamses, with the Bodies, Herlongs, DeLoaches, and many others, whose names cannot be recalled at present.

William Norris was of the Quaker persuasion. He left three sons, Nathan, William, and Stephen, and also several daughters. All these lived long and useful lives. The wife of William Norris was Agnes Federick, a woman of remarkable qualities. By the death of her husband she was left alone, to take care of and to raise and train her children. Her training was so excellent that it is said that neither one of them was ever known to use profane language. Nathan, the oldest, was the patriarch of the Norris family. His education was imperfect, but he had a clear and strong mind. Benevolence supplied his strongest incentive of action, and the serving of others seemed to have been his favorite mode of serving himself. His public spirit manifested itself throughout his whole life by self-sacrifice and deeds of kindness. If he had any fault to be complained of, it was on the side of mercy. He was eminently a man of mercy and of peace. He exercised more leniency towards his slaves, and he had a goodly number of them, than perhaps any man in Edgefield County. During the greater part of his life he served as Justice of Peace, County Commissioner, &c. While inheriting from his father some of the Quaker spirit, he was a Baptist, and contributed more to the building and maintaining of the old West Creek Baptist Church, of which he was a member, than any one of the other members. In a large degree he was given to hospitality. He was kind and charitable to the poor, and was beloved and respected by all who knew him.

The Watson family have descended from Michael Watson,

who was killed in the old War of Independence, and of whom
a biographical sketch is elsewhere given. His descendants
have been prominent in this township and in the county, and
have been honored by the people of Edgefield. Major Tillman
Watson, than whom none of the Watson family ever stood
higher, was a man of sterling qualities. Although his education was limited, yet his sense of justice, his patriotism, his
integrity, and his clear, good sense caused him to be respected
and promoted by the people of Edgefield County, who often
bestowed upon him the honors he deserved by sending him to
represent them in the Legislature, sometimes in the Senate and
sometimes in the House.

The Holston family of this township descended from Moses
Holston, Sr., who died about the year 1838. He had a number of sons and daughters who settled in the township, and
who, at one time, owned and cultivated a considerable portion
of the best lands. They were remarkably successful as cotton
planters, and continued buying land and slaves with the produce of their cotton fields. No one of them was more successful than Wade Holston, who was the youngest son of Moses,
Sr. Before the War of Secession he owned a large number of
slaves and several thousand acres of land. He was ambitious
to succeed, and he usually did succeed in all he undertook.
He represented the county in the Legislature for awhile. The
greater part of his property was accumulated by industry and
perseverance.

The William Sawyer, who was cotemporary with William
Norris, Sr., is the head of all the Sawyers of this section of
Edgefield. He had a son named Ansel Sawyer, who was
killed with Captain James.Butler at the massacre on Lick
Creek in time of the Revolution. He was only 17 or 18 years
of age. He was horribly mutilated, having been chopped to
pieces by the Tories with their swords. He was carried home
from the battle ground on a ground slide by an old negro slave
named Beister, who belonged to the widow of William Norris,
Sr. William Norris, her son, a lad at the time, was an eye
witness, and gave the facts as here stated to his son, John M.
Norris.

In reading and writing history, I often pause and ask myself whether men are not already devils, and this world a bit

of hell set apart for their temporary residence and habitation; a world of probation to see whether any of them can ever be restored to that better condition from which they all fell.

On the waters of West Creek, in a shady grove near a purling spring, stands the old West Creek Baptist Church, which took its name from the creek on which it is situated. It was constituted in 1790. Old men relate that long before this church was regularly constituted a rude house of worship existed at the same place, and that services were occasionally held here. This old church has gone through many vicissitudes, but at present it is in a flourishing condition. It is the mother of several other Baptist Churches in Edgefield, of some also in Lexington. One of these is Bethel Church, on the Ridge, from which sprang the Ridge Spring Baptist Church. All three of these churches have flourished under various pastors, and have largely contributed and exercised an influence for good in the township.

The old Methodist Church, Providence, situated on Cloud's Creek, was also constituted very early. The Boddys, Herlongs, Bouknights, Mitchells, and other families were prominent in building up and sustaining Methodism in this section. Their descendants are following in their footsteps, and are faithfully doing the same work in which their fathers were engaged.

In this township are found immense quantities of granite rock, both the Poaphoritic and Syenitic. Excellent millstones are being dressed and shipped to all parts of the State by E. W. McLenna, the energetic and enterprising editor and proprietor of the Johnston Monitor. These beds of Syenitic granite are inexhaustible. The stone is of fine grain and capable of a high polish, which qualities make it very suitable for monuments, tombstones, &c. These quarries are near the C., C. & A. Railroad, and can supply building material for all time; clays for the making of excellent brick abound.

The present inhabitants of the township are mostly native and to the manner born, descendants of the original settlers. In common with all other parts of the country, Norris Township bore its share of the sacrifices made for the Lost Cause, in sending its sons to the war, a large portion of whom never returned, and are buried far from home, resting in soldiers' graves by the wayside; or in some cemetery with no headstone to mark the spot. They suffered much also in the loss of property, and endured all the hardships incident to the great changes produced by the war and by the reconstructive process.

The C., C. & A. Railroad runs through this township, along the old Ridge Road, and has been the cause of many and great changes. Three towns have sprung up like magic within the boundaries of this township, Batesburg, Ridge Spring, and Monetta. Batesburg is a little over the line in Lexington County, but a considerable slip of Edgefield territory is within the corporate limits, and the greater part of its trade is drawn from Edgefield County. Batesburg is a flourishing town, with some twenty stores, two banks, two colleges, two churches, Baptist and Methodist. It is a considerable place of trade.

Ridge Spring is named after the Ridge on which it is situated, and the bold, unfailing spring that gushes out of the earth in the very midst of the town. This spring is the source of Cloud's Creek. This is a beautiful town for situation, occupying as it does the original home of the Watsons. R. B. Watson, Esq., a grandson of Elijah Watson, Sr., is now living (1891) in the house in which his grandfather lived and died.

Monetta is a small place on the railroad between Ridge Spring and Batesburg, and has sprung up since 1885.

In the earlier times in this section the facilities for getting an education were very poor. Old field schools, and they with rather incompetent teachers, were the only chance, with some rare exceptions. In 1826, John Knox established a school near the Lexington line, which perhaps did more in educating the people in this section than any other school has done. He was a classical scholar and continued this school a number of years. It was well patronized by all in reach, and many from different parts of the county and State received their education at this school. Since the war schools, academies, and colleges have been established for the complete and thorough education of all the children.

In complimenting the godly mothers and wives and daughters of this section of our county, it is but just to say that there is at least as great a number of industrious, discreet, amiable, gentle, and handsome women here in proportion to the number of inhabitants, as in any other section of the county or State.

Many might be mentioned by name, and their deeds might be recorded here; but as it is a lovely and adorable trait in woman to shun notoriety, and to modestly and faithfully fill her sphere of usefulness, we will desist. But if all were written that might be truthfully written in her behalf, even in the narrow bounds of this township, it would fill many volumes.

"Full many a gem of purest ray serene,
  The dark, unfathomed caves of ocean bear;
Full many a flower is born to blush unseen,
  And waste its sweetness on the desert air."

Slaves were introduced into this township at an early period in its history. And cotton, the great staple of the South, was and still is the chief article of cultivation. The climate is mild and genial; the soil is good; the people are religious and industrions; and, notwithstanding the great disadvantages of unjust and unequal legislation and taxation, under which the producers of the wealth of the country labor, the inhabitants of Norris Township, as a rule, are prosperous and happy.

XVIII.

Biographical sketches of some distinguished natives of Edge-field, who lived and died elsewhere are here given.'

REV. ALEXANDER TRAVIS.

I am indebted to the History of Conecuh County, Alabama, by the Rev. B. F. Riley, for the information contained in this section.

Rev. Alexander Travis was born in Edgefield County, S. C., on August 23rd, 1790. Reared on a farm, he was inured to work and hard service, and in this manner was made better fitted to perform the duties and undergo the labors which awaited him in the latter half of his life. His school education was quite limited, being confined to an imperfect training in the rudiments of English. Being a man of strong mind and retentive memory, he learned much by observation, and soon held a respectable position amongst men, as a man of thought and action. He was tall and dignified, and by the gravity of his manner commanded the respect of all who knew him. He was converted in 1809, and baptized into Addiel Church, in South Carolina. (Where is this church?) In 1810 he was licensed to preach, and was ordained in 1813. He became pastor of several churches, and so remained until 1817, when he removed to Alabama.

He located near Evergreen, in Conecuh County, where he resided until his death. He was devoted to the Master's work, and gathered, as he could, a batch of hearers from Sunday to Sunday, to preach to them the riches of Christ. He did not preach in vain. He soon collected enough of converts, with those who had before been members of Baptist Churches, to form a church near his home. This was done in 1818. His labors were not confined to this section, but in all directions he worked for the building of other churches. His first was the old Beulah Church between Sparta and Brooklyn. From this as a central point, his labors radiated in all directions. Often he would take long journeys on foot, leaving home frequently on Friday morning in order to meet his appointments at a distance. Often the streams were swollen so much that he was compelled to swim across. During the week he was an earnest, persistent student. His library was a plain English Bible, over which he pored by the aid of blazing pine knots, after his day's labors in the field. Through his exertions, which knew no wavering nor faltering, thriving churches were established in different parts of the county, and some in districts quite remote from others. His zeal and ability were so great and eminent that he remained in charge of several of these churches as long as he lived. Of the Beulah Church, the one he first organized, he was pastor thirty-five years; of Bellville, thirty-two. Between Burnt corn and Evergreen, in the Higdon settlement, a large and flourishing interest was established by him. By reason of his great parliamentary ability, he was chosen Moderator of the Bethlehem Association for more than twenty sessions in succession, and because of his earnest support of the cause of education, he was made the first Chairman of the Board of Trustees of the Evergreen Academy, for many years together. So evenly balanced were all his powers, that he was most admirably fitted for the work assigned him by providence in a pioneer region.

Elder Travis died in 1852, at his old home, where he had lived full thirty-five years. His death was a public calamity, and was universally lamented. He was a good man, and in many respects a great one. He was true to his principles and convictions of truth and right, and never shrank from their defence. Yet he was a meek man, as brave and good men always are.

At the pulpit end of old Beulah Church may be seen to-day by the passer-by, a plain marble shaft, which marks the resting place of this sainted pioneer and hero.

NICHOLAS STALLWORTH, SR.

If I mistake not the name Stallworth is still an honored one in Edgefield County.

Nicholas Stallworth, Sr., was born in Edgefield District, on April 25th, 1777. He moved from Edgefield to Clarke County, Alabama, in the year 1817, but remained there only one year. In 1818, with several others, he removed to the east side of the Alabama River, after the troubles with the Indians had

subsided. He made his home four miles southeast of Evergreen, on the Evergreen and Brooklyn public road, where he
continued to reside until his death, in 1836.

Mr. Stallworth was well fitted by nature to brave the perils
of a pioneer country. With robust frame, determined will,
and unlimited energy, combined with business tact and shrewd-
ness, he rapidly accumulated a handsome fortune, and became
one of the wealthiest men in the county. He was the ancestor
of quite a number of descendants, some of whom attained
marked distinction.

NICHOLAS STALLWORTH, JR.

Prominent among the first generation of young men reared
in Conecuh, was Nicholas Stallworth, Jr. He was born in
Edgefield District, February 21st, 1810. When he was only
eight years of age he was brought with the remainder of his
father's family to Alabama.

He was married to Miss Martha Travis, eldest daughter of
Rev. Alexander Travis. The result of this union was seven
children, among whom were Robert P. Stallworth and Frank
M. Stallworth, of Falls County, Texas; Major Nick Stallworth, late of Hilliard's Legion; and Mrs. Barnett, the wife of
Honorable Samuel A. Barnett, of Mobile. Mrs. Barnett is
dead.

Reared at a time and in a community where few schools
existed, Mr. Stallworth had to depend almost entirely upon
self-training. He lacked none of the virtues of a sterling
citizen. Hospitable, liberal, and public spirited, he was quite
popular. Without himself seeking the position, he was at one
time made Circuit Clerk of Conecuh County. When, in 1850,
the office of Judge of Probate was made elective, he warmly
espoused the candidacy of A. D. Cary. As early as 1838 Mr.
Stallworth foresaw the struggle which reached its bloody cul-
mination in 1861. The tendency of existing political issues
caused him to predict the dismemberment of the Union, and
the probable abolition of slavery. Mr. Stallworth died in 1853,
in the prime of manhood. He left descendants, sons, J. A.
Stallworth and young Nick Stallworth, who were an honor to
their ancestry and to Edgefield.

WILLIAM BARRETT TRAVIS, THE HERO OF THE ALAMO.

William Barrett Travis was born in Edgefield District, S. C., August 9th, 1809, within four miles of Red Bank Church. He was the son of Mark Travis, Sr., who was a brother of Rev. Alexander Travis, already noticed. The family moved to Conecuh in 1818. Young Travis was as well educated as the times and country could afford. At maturity he studied for the bar at Claiborne, under the Honorable James Dellett. Quite early in the year 1835 he bade farewell to his quiet home in South Alabama and removed to Texas. The province was then in a state of seething excitement. Santa Anna was Governor, President or Dictator of the Republic of Mexico, of which Texas formed a part, and was doing his utmost to destroy the Federal system and to consolidate all power in the central government at the capitol city. Against this movement the Texans warmly protested. Young and ardent, and just from the United States, Mr. Travis naturally sympathized in feeling with the Texans. Early in the beginning of hostilities we find him a chosen and willing leader. When the war actually began and Santa Anna invaded Texas at the head of four thousand men and marched upon San Antonio in the beginning of 1836, we find Colonel W. B. Travis in command at this point. Santa Anna's advanced columns reached the heights of the Alazan, which overlooked the city of San Antonio, on the 22d of February. Colonel Travis had only one hundred and forty-four men, and with these he retired into the Alamo. As soon as Santa Anna occupied the city he demanded the surrender of the garrison. The demand was responded to by a cannon shot, for Colonel Travis knew too well the treacherous nature of his foe, and he believed that a surrender would be followed by a massacre. There were fourteen cannon in the Fort, but only a small supply of powder.

Immediately after receiving the answer to his summons for surrender, Santa Anna ran up a blood-red flag, proclaiming "No Quarter"! On the 24th of February couriers were sent by Travis to San Felipe and Goliad for assistance. The Mexicans steadily bombarded the fort without effect. Early in the morning of the 25th, the Mexicans brought into play all their available guns. Towards noon Santa Anna left his head-quarters and gave his personal supervision to the aim of the gunners.

At every opportunity, when screened from view, he advanced and planted his guns nearer the fort. On the night of the 25th the Texans made a sally into the town and burned some houses that were near the fort. The next morning there was a brisk skirmish without any decisive result. The number of Mexicans was now increased and Santa Anna made great efforts to cut off the supply of water from the garrison. In this he completely failed. Again at night Travis' men made another sortie and burnt some houses. Meantime the Mexicans kept up the bombardment for several days together, incessantly, but without any serious result.

On the second of March the garrison received a re-inforcement of thirty-two citizen soldiers, who had fought their way through the ranks of the enemy. These were commanded by Captain John W. Smith, of Gonzales. On the third, Colonel Travis sent a courier with a message to the State Convention then in session at Washington. The message was to the following purport: "I am still here, in fine spirits and well to do. With one hundred and forty-five men I have held this place ten days against a force variously estimated at from 1,500 to 6,000; and I shall continue to hold it until I get relief from my countrymen, or I will perish in its defence. We have had a shower of cannon balls continuously falling among us the whole time, yet none of us have fallen. We have been miraculously preserved."

During that day, Colonel Bonham, who had been sent to Goliad to secure re-inforcements, returned and gave his assistance once more to the defence of the fort. That night the Texans again made a sally but effected nothing. The Mexicans continued heavy firing, but the defenders of the fort fired but seldom, as their ammunition was scarce. The fourth of March wore heavily away without change in the situation; but the beseiged knew that, unless some great and miraculous assistance came to them, they were doomed to a speedy and bloody death. Santa Anna grew tired of the seige and urged upon the council of officers, which he had called, the necessity of making a speedy assault. They wanted to wait until the arrival of the heavy seige guns. He chafed under the delay and finally his wish prevailed. The fort was stormed. The attack was made from different directions, by four columns under the leadership of his most experienced officers. Each column was provided with every thing necessary; ladders, pick-axes, crow-bars, &c. The attack was ordered for midnight; but delays always occur, and it was not until precisely at four o'clock on the morning of March 6th, the thirteenth day of the seige, that the bugle sounded the advance along the whole Mexican line. The garrison, feeling the movement, leaped to their guns and poured upon their assailants a storm of lead and iron. Before the fire of the Texans the three columns, on the north, west, and east, staggered and swung back. Some confusion was produced, but the solid mass rallied under their officers and renewed the assault. This time they broke through the wall into the yard running round the fort. At about the same time the column from the South made a breach in the wall and took one of the guns. This cannon was commanded by Colonel Travis himself, and it is supposed that he was killed early in the action, as he was found dead near the gun. The Mexicans turned this gun against the last stronghold and dislodged the Texans, who took refuge in the different buildings. Then began a deadly, close conflict. Each building was a separate battle ground. Each Texan knew that his own death was certain, and he resolved to have as many as possible of the enemy to bear him company to the shades. The heroic Crockett, knowing that death was inevitable, struck down his enemies until, when his own dead body was found, it was in the centre of a circling heap of dead Mexicans. Colonel Bowie was lying on his bed in the last stage of consumption; but as the enemy rushed into his room, he shot and killed seven of the foe before he, himself, was killed.

The details of the horrid massacre need not be repeated here, even if they could be given. The bodies of the Texans were collected into heaps and burned. A year later Colonel John N. Seguin superintended the collection and proper interment of the bones of these heroes.

As you enter the capitol at Austin, you see a monument bearing this inscription: "Thermopylæ had its messenger of defeat. The Alamo had none."

Thus died the brilliant and the brave Colonel William Barrett Travis. Bonham and Bowie, sons of Edgefield as well as

Travis, went with him on the same dark journey. And Crockett was not far away.

"Disturb not their slumbers, let the heroes here sleep
'Neath the boughs of the willows that over them weep!
Their arms are unnerved, but their deeds remain bright
As the stars in the dark-vaulted heaven at night!

O, wake not these heroes! their battles are o'er!
Let them rest undisturbed on Antonio's fair shore!
On the river's green border as flowery dressed,
With the hearts they loved fondly let the heroes here rest!"

MARK BUTLER TRAVIS.

Mark Butler Travis was not a son, but a grandson of Edge-field, and deserves a place in the history of the county, as he was with the Palmetto Regiment, a member of it, in the war with Mexico. His life was one of chivalrous heroism and devotion to his country. He was born in the neighborhood of Old Town, Alabama, on May 18, 1827. He was very apt in the acquisition of knowledge. Having read medicine he left home to attend a course of lectures in a distant State, being at the time only seventeen years of age. While on the way to college he met up with the famous Palmetto Regiment on the way to join General Scott in Mexico. He at once determined to enlist in the Regiment and go with them to Mexico. This he did, and shared with the members of that Regiment the glories of Contreras and Cherubusco. At Cherubusco he received a wound in the head, which prevented his being with the Regiment when they entered the capitol city. He recovered from his wound, rejoined his comrades, and served through the remainder of the war. After his return home he was made colonel and then general of militia. He was also elected Clerk of the Court for four successive terms. When the war of Secession came on he was one of the first to respond to the call to arms. He enlisted in the Conecuh Guards; was made second lieutenant and went with the company to Virginia.

At the battle of Bull Run, or First Manassas, the gallant Colonel Jones of the Fourth Alabama Regiment was killed. To this regiment the Conecuh Guards belonged. At the time of Colonel Jones' death the situation was such that the whole regiment seemed threatened with destruction. Becoming cognizant of the fact, a panic seemed inevitable, and the men began to turn their feet and faces towards the rear. Seeing the situation, Lieutenant Travis tried to stop the flight of the regiment, and stood with brandished sword before the retreating columns and begged them not to run. While thus exerting himself he was suddenly confronted by a burly Teuton, whose glaring eyes, open mouth, and dilated nostrils showed that he was a victim of stupendous fright, and when he saw the efforts of Travis to check the flight, he exclaimed: "O, mine friendt, my life is too schweet!" The Lieutenant, finding his efforts to stay the flight vain, concluded that discretion was the better part of valor, and sought a more secure position. He had on a very heavy pair of boots, so that he could not make very good time, but as he ran somewhat hastily past Dr. Taliaferro, the doctor called out to him: "Lieutenant, you had better look out, or Barnum will have those boots in his museum before night."

Lieutenant Travis was honorably discharged from service on account of failing health and disability to perform the duties of a soldier before the close of the war, and died at his home of pneumonia in 1864. There were combined in his character many elements of true nobility.

COLONEL P. D. BOWLES.

Pinckney Downey Bowles is a native of South Carolina, and was born in Edgefield District, date of birth I do not know, but even at this date, 1891, he is not an old man. He read law with General Sam. McGowan. He received his educational training at the Citadel, in Charleston, and at the University of Virginia. He went to Alabama in 1859, and into the office of Honorable James A. Stallworth, whose father also was a native of Edgefield. He remained in Mr. Stallworth's office until the beginning of the war. In 1860 he was elected Colonel of the Twenty-eighth Alabama Militia, and Second Lieutenant in the Conecuh Guards. In January, 1861, he went with his company to Pensacola, Florida. When they returned home, upon re-organization, he was elected Captain and went as such with the company to Virginia. He soon became Colonel of the regiment, and was its brave and faithful commander during almost the whole of the war. He led his regiment into nearly all the battles fought in Virginia. They fought at the First Battle of Manassas, under General Bee. They were in the battles of Seven Pines, Cold Harbor, Malvern Hill, Second Manassas, Boonesboro, Sharpsburg, Fredericksburg, and Suffolk. They were in the invasion of Pennsylvania and in the awful conflict at Gettysburg. They went with Longstreet to reinforce Bragg in North Georgia, returned by Knoxville through East Tennessee, rejoined the army of Virginia, and fought in the battles of the Wilderness and Spottsylvania. Again, they were engaged at Second Cold Harbor, and lay for ten months behind the defences of Petersburg, sharing in all the movements and assaults of that period. At last crippled, broken, depleted by death and wounds and sickness, they, the remnant of the Regiment, Fourth Alabama, surrendered at Appomattox two hundred and two men. Throughout all this period Colonel Bowles was always at the head of his regiment, with only one respite for a little while, in February, 1863, when he went home to be married to Miss Stearns, daughter of Judge Stearns. Towards the close of the war he was acting as Brigadier, having command of five regiments; though, in fact, he never received a commission as Brigadier.

When he returned home he had fifty cents in his pocket, but he immediately resumed the practice of the law and did well. In 1866 he was elected County Solicitor for Conecuh County, which position he held for a long time. His home was at Evergreen in 1881. Whether he is now living, 1891, I do not know.

XIX.

We may as well continue our biographical sketches of the eminent men of Edgefield at this place, but we will study some of the eminent civilians of the county, as the heart grows weary when it dwells too long upon the deeds of fighting heroes and fields of blood. The names of the men of whom we now propose to write will not be taken in exact chronological order; but that will make no difference in detached historical sketches. When we are through with these biographies, the idea then is to make the narrative more continuous until after the close of the War of Secession.

We will take up first on the roll of illustrious civilians the name of Andrew Pickens Butler, who has already been briefly mentioned in a notice of his father, General William Butler. Judge Butler was born on the 19th of November, 1796, and died the 25th of May, 1857. He was educated first in the primary schools in the neighborhood where he was born. He then went to the celebrated Willington School, in Abbeville District, kept by the great teacher, Dr. Waddell. In December, 1817, he graduated from the South Carolina College. He then read law and was admitted to practice in December, 1818. He first settled in Columbia; but after the death of his brother George, he removed to Edgefield, and there, in partnership first with General Waddy Thompson and afterwards with Nathan L. Griffin, he had a lucrative practice. He had also a large practice at Orangeburg, Barnwell, and Newberry. In 1824 he became one of the aides of Governor Manning, and as such, was one of the brilliant *cortege* which attended General Lafayette on his visit to the State in 1825. From 1824 to the close of 1833, he was in the House of Representatives, or in the Senate, from Edgefield. He was one of the committee in 1827–28 charged to inquire whether Judge James should be removed from the bench. Judge James was an old Revolutionary soldier, and the charge against him was incompetency arising from the excessive use of intoxicating drinks. He was found guilty and removed from the bench; but the Senate and the whole House were in tears when the sentence was pronounced.

In 1833 Butler was elected one of the Circuit Judges, and held his first court in Charleston, in January, 1834. He was made Judge to fill the vacancy occasioned by the death of Judge W. D. Martin. He was elected to the United States Senate in 1846, having filled the office of Judge for thirteen years. In the year 1847, on a trip by steamer from Charleston to Wilmington, there came an awful storm, and while it raged with tremendous violence, the vessel became an unmanageable hulk. The captain gave up as lost. This fact was communicated to Judge Butler, when he desired that the passengers and all on board should be called forward. He then stated to them the sad fate which appeared to be the inevitable doom of all, and desired that each and every one should be made known to one another, so that if ever any one reached the land, he, she, or they might state the fate of the others. An elderly negro woman, the stewardess, then said: "Old Marster, this is no time for introductions, you had better pray." He said: "I cannot, but, old lady, if you can pray, do so." She instantly knelt down and poured out a fervent prayer. Almost as soon as she ceased the lights from the steamer sent out from Wilmington in search of them, as they were twenty-four hours over time, were seen bearing down to the rescue. The boat and all were saved. His sister, Mrs. Thompson, who was a member of the Baptist Church, remarked to the Judge, after he had narrated the circumstances to her: "Brother Pickens, it was that old woman's prayer which saved you."

Judge Butler began his duties as Senator in 1847, and was continued Senator until the close of the extra session in March, 1857, when he returned home in ill health, lingered until the May following, when he died.

Judge O'Neall, in his "Sketches of the Bench and Bar of South Carolina," 1859, closes his notice of Judge Butler in these words: "In 1850, when Secession burst upon South Carolina, Judge Butler did not favor it—he was for a Southern Congress; and, in 1851 and 1852, he met the issue and South Carolina sustained him."

Judge Butler was married twice. His first wife, Susan Ann Simkins, the second daughter of Colonel Eldred Simkins, in a few months after her marriage, he followed to the tomb. His second wife, Miss Harriet Hayne, the daughter of Wm. Edward Hayne, Esq., of Charleston, he, soon after the birth of their only child, Mrs. Haigood, of Barnwell, saw languish and die. He ever after lived a widower. His mother and sister took charge of his lonely child. At his house was seen the venerable face of his mother as its mistress—her unexampled fortitude and cheerfulness sustained him in the dark hours of sorrow for the loss of wife, brothers, and sister.

But I must pause. You all, my readers, knew Judge Butler. You have often joined in his merry laugh—you all remember his florid face, his head of snow, his dancing eyes, and his manly form. But you do not all know that which distinguished him more than most men, *his kind heart.* No man was ever more devoted than he was to his mother, his child, his sister, and brothers—no one ever was a truer friend. Distress never sought him in vain. He despised a mean action, and the rod of cruelty and oppression he was ever ready to turn aside. He pitied more than he despised his enemies. He was a just, honest, good man in all the relations of private life. In public life he aimed to do right, and he sustained his purposes by well directed actions and words. He was not what may be called an eloquent man, but he thought right, and he spoke as he thought. Sometimes, and indeed often, he gave utterance to sublime thoughts in impassioned eloquence.

This able servant of the people is no more! He has been called away when few were prepared for it. His well spent life will be his epitaph, and entitles him to live in the memories of us all.

> "Statesman, yet friend to truth! Of soul sincere;
> In action faithful, and in honor clear;
> Who broke no promise, served no private end;
> Who gained no title, and who lost no friend.
> Ennobled by himself, by all approved;
> Praised, wept, and honored by *him* he loved "

The compiler of this history may here be permitted to say that he sometimes met Judge Butler, and once had the honor to give him the address of welcome at a public dinner prepared in his honor at Mount Enon, a place midway between the birth place of his mother on Saluda, and his own ancestral home on Big Creek. This was in the year 1854. He was then Senator, and the dinner and reception were tendered him by his old friends and neighbors.   •

JOHN F. GRIMKE.

John F. Grimke was a Revolutionary soldier and officer. He was born December 16th, 1752; died at Long Branch, N. J., August 9th, 1819. Mr. Grimke was made one of the Law Judges, March 20th, 1783. He was a member of the Legislature at the time and Speaker of the House of Representatives from March, 1785, to March, 1786, there being at that time no hindrance, either by law or custom, to a person's holding these two offices at the same time. He was not popular as a Judge, nor, perhaps, as a man, as he was of a stern, unbending, unsocial, uncompromising character.

The following incident is given because the facts occurred at Edgefield Court House. I quote from Judge O'Neall's "Bench and Bar":

"In the spring of 1815 I first attended Edgefield Court. The dockets were enormous. My late friend, Solicitor Starke, presented forty bills of indictment for every grade of offence, from assault and battery to murder. Thirty-nine were found true. Many convictions followed. One of the Edgefield rowdies of the time looking on at the scene, swore it was no place for him. 'For,' said he, 'Starke holds and Grimke skins.' Upon the issue docket there were more than two hundred cases. In the second week of the term, the late General Glascock proposed to give a dinner to the Judge and Bar. A civil action for assault and battery was to be tried; there were seven speeches to be made, one for the plaintiff and six for the defendant, (for at that time the rule did not exist which limits two speeches to a side). It was well known that if they all spoke as long as they could that the dinner could not be ate. It was therefore proposed and agreed that each of the lawyers for the defendant should speak fifteen minutes by the Judge's watch. It was accordingly laid down, and as each progressed to the limit, the Judge said: 'Your time is out,' and he ceased. At last, Mr. Bacon, who was closing for the defendant, and who was blessed with as fine an elocution as I ever heard, had scarcely finished his exordium, when the Judge said: 'Mr. Bacon, your time is out.' Mr. Bacon, instead of yielding, as good taste would have directed; said: 'I claim the right which every citizen has to be heard by his counsel.' 'Very well,' said the Judge, 'we will leave it to the jury.' A stout man rose and said: "May it please your Honor, we have been tired of their clack for this hour.' This ended the contest."

Solicitor Robert Starke, born near Petersburg, Virginia, January 10th, 1762, mentioned above, though never residing in Edgefield, yet was Solicitor of the Southern Circuit, of which Edgefield formed a part, from December, 1806, to December, 1820. He was an able lawyer, and in his office, a terror to evil doers.

JUDGE RICHARD GANTT.

This good man, good lawyer, and merciful and just Judge, once made his home and practiced law at Edgefield Court House. He was born in Prince George County, Maryland, August 2nd, 1767, and died October 18th, 1850. He married Miss Sarah Allen in Augusta, Ga., about the year 1794, he having resided in Georgia two or three years previous to the marriage. His estimable wife died November 17th, 1848, a little less than two years before his own death. Few couples are so blest as to live a greater number of years together. He was admitted to practice in Charleston, S. C., in 1794, and settled at Edgefield the same year. His eldest son, Thomas J., was born at Edgefield in 1795. He was eminently successful as a lawyer. He was elected Clerk of the House of Representatives in 1804, which position he held until 1818, when he was elected Judge. Generally as Judge he leaned to mercy's side, and was disposed to favor prisoners—except in cases of homicide accompanied with circumstances of cruelty, when his whole nature revolted and carried him against the prisoner. He resigned as Judge in 1841, and the Legislature presented him with a year's salary. Very complimentary resolutions were passed on the occasion, moved by Mr. Albert Rhett, in the House, and agreed to by the Senate.

JUDGE WILLIAM D. MARTIN.

William D. Martin, of the Martins of Martintown, was born at Martintown, in Edgefield County, on the 2nd of October, 1789. He received a good academical education and read law

at Edgefield wit'n Mr. Edmund Bacon, by whose assistance he
was enabled to attend a course of Law Lectures at Litchfield,
Connecticut. He married at Edgefield Court House on the
28th day of May, 1811, Miss Henrietta Williamson, the
daughter of Dr. Peter Williamson, a distinguished physician,
and who had been a Revolutionary soldier. He was admitted
to the Bar the 27th of November following, and became the
partner of Mr. Edmund Bacon, and the principal management
of a large and lucrative practice fell into his hands. In a few
years he removed to Coosawhatchie, and was elected a member
of the House of Representatives from St. Luke's Parish, in
1816. After the death of Benjamin C. Yancey, Chairman of
the Judiciary Committee of the House, Mr. Martin, in 1818,
was elected Chairman by the committee. He was elected
Clerk of the Senate November 23rd, 1818, which office he
filled until 1826—eight years—when he was sent as a Representative to Congress. His wife died July 13th, 1824, leaving
four children. After her death he removed to Barnwell.
After he was sent to Congress he married the second time,
choosing for his companion Miss Dorsey, daughter of Judge
Dorsey, of the Supreme Bench of Maryland. In December,
1830, he was elected one of the Circuit Court Law Judges,
when he removed to Columbia, in which city he made his
home until his death, which occurred on the 16th of November, 1833. On his way home from court at Harry Fall, term
of 1833, he retired to rest at Jones' Hotel, in Charleston, and
the next morning he was found dead.

He was a good judge of law, and his decisions, many of
which were reviewed by the Court of Appeals, generally
received the approbation of that court. A larger account of the
Martin family will be given before we close.

JUDGE EPHRAIM RAMSAY.

Mr. Ramsay was an eloquent and distinguished lawyer
residing at Ninety-Six, when on the 19th of December, 1799,
he was elected Judge. He served as Judge something less
than two years, dying in 1801. He died at Silver Bluff, in
Beech Island, a place afterwards owned by Governor James H.
Hammond. This place he had bought in company with his
brother-in-law, Major Charles Goodwyn. Mr. Goodwyn and

himself married sisters, the daughters of General Andrew Williamson, of Ninety-Six.

They bought Silver Bluff from Thomas Galphin, son of the celebrated Indian trader, George Galphin, who was so successful in outdreaming an Indian Chief, with whom he had many dealings. Silver Bluff was his great trading station, at which he lived and died. He built there the first brick house ever built in the back country. It was used as a fort during the Revolutionary War, and was sometimes in the hands of one party and sometimes in the hands of the other. Its gables showed for nearly a hundred years, and perhaps show yet, the holes of a cannon ball shot clear through. In this house Judge Ramsay died; but no stone marks his resting place, and the identical spot where he lies cannot be pointed out, though the graveyard itself is still known.

It was at this place that George Galphin, the great Indian trader, was visited by one of the principal Indian Chiefs from beyond the Savannah, when that dreaming match took place, in which the Chief was so badly beaten. Next morning after the Chief's arrival on a friendly visit, as he and Mr. Galphin were walking around and looking at the buildings, improvements, and the landscape generally, the Chief suddenly stood still, and looking at Mr. Galphin, said: "Mr. Galphin, me dream last night." "And what did my red brother dream?" "Me dream you give me a fine rifle." "If you dream it, you must have it," and the rifle was handed over at once. Next morning, as they were walking around again, Mr. Galphin suddenly said to the Chief: "I dreamed last night." "What you dream?" "I dreamed you gave me your fine Chickasaw stallion." "If you dream um, you must have um;" and the horse was given to Mr. Galphin. The next morning it was the Chief's turn, and he said: "I dream last night." "And what did my red brother dream last night?" "I dream you gave me the red coat you wear and much calico." "If you dream it, you must have it;" and the coat and calico were handed over to the Chief. Next morning it was Mr. Galphin's turn: "I dreamed last night," he said to the Indian, "a very beautiful and wonderful and most delightful dream; O, it was so happy." "What my white brother dream now?" said the somewhat astonished Chief. "I dreamed you gave me ten miles around the Ogeechee Old Town " "Wugh!" said the Chief, who by this time was becoming very much disgusted with the game of dreaming, as he was decidedly getting the worst of it. "Wugh! if you dream um, you must have um, but I dream with you no more." Poor fellows! they have dreamed all their lands away, and the happy hunting grounds of the West, of which they also once so fondly dreamed, have vanished with their homes in the East.

JAMES J. CALDWELL.

This very able and excellent man made his home at Edgefield during the year 1819, as teacher and principal of the Edgefield Academy. He was a native of Newberry, and was prepared for the South Carolina College at the celebrated Mount Bethel Academy, then under the care of Mr. Elisha Hammond, father of Governor James H. Hammond. He entered the Junior Class of South Carolina College in December, 1815, and graduated in 1817. After teaching one year at Edgefield he returned to Newberry and read law with Judge O'Neall, who was then in practice at that place. He was admitted to the bar in 1821; in 1830 he was sent to the Legislature; in 1835 he was elected Solicitor, the duties of which office he discharged until 1846, when he was elected Chancellor in place of Chancellor Johnson, who was elected Governor. Some years before he was elected Chancellor he had removed to Columbia, in which city he died in the early part of March, 1850, in the fifty-second year of his age.

This writer never knew Chancellor Caldwell, but he was very highly esteemed by his father, who was a school-mate of his for a time at Mount Bethel; and he, too, completed his academical course of study and also his school life at that academy, in May, 1815. The present writer has now in his possession, in the handwrite of Mr. Elisha Hammond, the certificate, dated May 6th, 1815, of the proficiency of John Chapman in surveying, which branch of mathematics he had made a special study, in order to prepare himself for the duties of a surveyor.

I never saw Chancellor Caldwell, but I knew his son, Howard H. Caldwell, who died too soon; and I have long known another son, J. F. J. Caldwell, whom I am glad to have on my list of friends. His contribution to the history of the late war I consider very valuable.

JOHN S. JETER, SOLICITOR.

Mr. Jeter was born about seven miles south of Edgefield Court House, on the 20th of June, 1779. Edgefield was then part of the District of Ninety-Six. He was educated at Dr. Waddell's School at Willington, in Abbeville County. He read law with Abram J. Dozier, at Cambridge, and was admitted to practice in Columbia in 1811. He practiced at Edgefield with good success. In 1814 he was married to Miss Sabra Simkins, daughter of John Simkins, Esq. In December, 1824, he was elected Solicitor of the Southern Circuit, and in 1820 he was re-elected. In December, 1828, the State was divided into five instead of six circuits, and Edgefield and Newberry, which were part of the Southern Circuit, were thrown into the Western, of which Mr. Earle was Solicitor, and Mr. Jeter's solicitorship ceased.

He was a good Solicitor, making no fuss nor parade, but working faithfully for the dispatch of business. He served as a member of the House of Representatives, and was elected Senator in 1838, and again in 1841. At the next election, in 1846, he was not a candidate, and Nathan L. Griffin was elected to succeed him.

He died April 14th, 1847. Two daughters survived, one Sarah, wife of Mr. Harris, who removed to Columbia; and Caroline, the wife of Rev. Mr. Walker, a minister in the Episcopal Church.

EDMUND BACON.

Edmund Bacon, one of the most brilliant members of the Bar Edgefield ever had, was a native of Georgia, born at Augusta on the 17th of April, 1776. His father was a Virginian, but he had removed to Georgia sometime before the great struggle between the colonies and the mother country began. He was left an orphan at an early age by the death of his father; but his guardian, General Glascock, who was also his brother-in-law, did not neglect his duty, but placed him at one of the best schools in the State, and afterwards at the first academy in Augusta. His taste led him to the study of the ancient classics, to letters and to polite learning, with a de-

cided repugnance to the study of a profession.   In this he was
encouraged, perhaps unwisely, by his guardian, as his fortune
was not very large.   But a circumstance, altogether unlooked
for and unexpected, caused him to choose the profession of the
law as his calling for life.   Early in the year 1791 General
Washington took his Southern tour, and in May paid a visit
to Augusta.   All the beauty and chivalry of the city was
collected to receive and honor the hero.   Mr. Bacon, young as
he was, only about fifteen, was chosen by the academy of
which he was a member, to give the address of welcome on
the occasion.   This delicate and honorable task was so well
performed that it attracted the special notice and attention of
the great man, and induced him to give the youthful orator a
handsome present of several law books.   This decided his
future calling, and with the consent of his guardian he entered
the then celebrated Law School of Litchfield, Connecticut,
where he industriously applied himself and graduated with
honor.

After graduation he settled at Savannah, in which city he
was very successful.   He was here induced to undertake the
management and settlement of the estate of General Greene.
This labor he did well; but his health, which had begun to
fail before, had by this time failed so much that he thought it
prudent to retire, at least for a time, from his profession.   To
this end he purchased a plantation on Beech Island, on the
Savannah river, in which pleasant spot he hoped to regain his
health and pass his time in those literary pursuits, which were
most congenial to his tastes.   This dream was rudely broken
and dispelled.   His house was destroyed by fire; his farming interests were neglected by his overseer, who was the only gainer
by his farming investment.   He was compelled to resume the
practice of the law.   This he did at Edgefield Court House.
He here built him a handsome dwelling house, into which he
moved, but which he did not occupy a great while before it
too was consumed by fire.   In this fire he lost his whole
library, including the books which had been presented to him
by Washington.   It was also with great difficulty that his
infant child was saved from the conflagration.   He rebuilt
near the same place, resumed the practice of his profession and
soon became eminent at the bar.

He was married to Eliza Fox at Augusta, Ga., January 29, 1797. He left at his death four children, John, Edmund, Sarah, and Thomas. Thomas, who was so long Clerk of the Court at Edgefield, is the only one this writer ever knew.

Dr. Laborde once a Professor in the South Carolina College thus writes of Mr. Bacon: "Between the years 1822 and 1825 I was a law student in the office of Messrs Simkins and McDuffie; and Mr. Bacon being there in the practice of his profession, it was my fortune to witness the happiest efforts which he made during this period at the Bar of Edgefield. * * His natural endowments were extraordinary. His person was commanding, his face and head uncommonly fine, his voice chorded musical, and of wonderful power. His style of speaking was highly finished, and I think I am justified in saying, that, as a model of graceful and eloquent elocution, the Edgefield Bar cannot present another entitled to equal praise. Let it not be supposed, however, that his merit was that of a mere rhetorician. When the occasion demanded it, no one exhibited a livelier sensibility or a deeper feeling; or was more apt to awaken a sympathetic emotion in the bosoms of others.

"I remember when quite a boy that I was much moved by a speech from him in behalf of a man who was on trial for his life. His whole soul seemed melted by compassion—the tears were flowing freely down his face, and he urged the acquital of the unfortunate man, with a natural earnestness and eloquence which touched every heart. His appeals to the sympathies of the jury were those of a man who was pleading for his own life; and when, after sketching most touchingly, the picture of human passion and infirmity, the sad heritage of the man—he called upon every member of the jury to adopt for himself the sentiment of the Universal Prayer.

'Teach me to feel another's woe,
To hide the fault I see,
That mercy I to others show,
That mercy show to me.'

"The effect was electric, and all could see that the prisoner was soon to be restored to his family and friends."

JOHN DUNLAP.

He was admitted to the Bar in Charleston, January 26th, 1795. His home was at Ninety-Six, but he practiced at Edgefield and in all the adjoining counties. His reputation as an advocate was very fine, but his life was short. He married Miss Anne Gedder of Charleston. He died and left no children.

His brother, Major William Dunlap, of Laurens, was one of Colonel Hays' party who were captured by Major William Cunningham in his celebrated bloody raid in October, 1781, when Hays and the most of his party were put to death. William Dunlap was spared, and when discharged by Cunningham the next morning at Odell's Mills on Beaver Dam Creek, he was covered with the blood and brains of his slain companions.

ABRAHAM GILES DOZIER

Was another of those old-time lawyers whose home was at Ninety-Six, but who practiced at Edgefield and in the adjoining districts. He was admitted to the Bar in 1798. He had a large practice at Edgefield, and was very successful. He died at his home at Ninety-Six of the great epidemic in 1816, which killed so many, at least one-tenth of the whole population of Edgefield, Abbeville, Newberry, and Laurens. Ninety-Six, as the most of my readers well know, was a place of great importance in the early days of the settlement of the middle and upper country, and was the capital and county seat of a large territory of country previous to the Revolution and down to the year 1785, when the district was divided. It was the centre of rich farming lands, and men most eminent for intelligence and learning in the upper country, naturally made Ninety-Six a social centre. Hence we find it for a good many years after the Revolution the home of some of the leading men of the State.

CHARLES GOODWYN

Was another lawyer of the early times who made his home at Ninety-Six. He was an Englishman, and was admitted to the bar in Charleston, May 28th, 1784. He practiced much in the county courts and was very successful. He married one of the daughters of General Andrew Williamson. Judge

Ephraim Ramsay, of Ninety-Six, married General Williamson's other daughter, and he and Mr. Goodwyn together bought Silver Bluff, on Beech Island, an unfortunate speculation, as the debt they made in buying it was too heavy for them to carry. Mr. Goodwyn left descendants in Edgefield, and some are still living in the town and county.

JOHN S. GLASCOCK

Was born near Augusta, Ga., April 18th, 1788, of Virginia extraction—read law at Edgefield under Edmund Bacon, and was admitted to practice in 1811. Previous to his admission to practice law he married in 1810 Miss Eliza Simkins, daughter of John Simkins, Esq. He was a member of the House of Representatives—elected first in 1820 and again in 1822. At the time of his death in 1822, he was State Senator and Major General of the First Division of South Carolina Militia. He was very successful as a lawyer, and was a very genial and popular man. His death was caused by a wound through the hand from the accidental discharge of a gun while hunting game. This produced lockjaw, which resulted in death. He was an ardent lover of field sports and of the fox chase. Dr. Laborde says of him that "he rode the noblest horse in the upper country, and his large pack of fox dogs would excite the envy of an English nobleman." Dr. Laborde says he saw him die—"he was dying of lockjaw and his lovely wife was near by in the last stage of consumption. Their weeping little ones were around them, and it was apparent that in a few short days of fleeting hours both parents were to be committed to the tomb and their happy home made desolate. And so it was. They died within the same week, and their bodies were buried in the Baptist Church yard of the village. The house passed into the hands of strangers, the children were distributed among their relations, and he who but a short time before, filled so large a space in the community of that intelligent district, like the whole family of the dead, (with fewest exceptions) soon ceased to be remembered."

NATHAN LIPSCOMB GRIFFIN.

Though not a native of Edgefield, yet Mr. Griffin lived at the Court House all his active business life, and was identified with the growth and prosperity of the town and county. He

was born in Abbeville County, near White Hall, February
9th, 1803.   He began the reading of law in the office of Judge
Whitner at Ninety-Six, but in 1823 he removed to Edgefield
and completed his studies with A. P. Butler.   He was admitted to practice in the fall of 1824, and immediately opened an
office at Edgefield.   In May, 1825, he was married to Miss
Anna Butler, daughter of Stanmore Butler, Esq.   In 1826 he
became a partner of A. P. Butler, and continued with him
until Mr. Butler was elected one of the Law Judges of the
State.   He soon afterwards formed a partnership with Mr.
Armisted Burt, which partnership was discontinned by
Mr. Burt's election to the Congress of the United States.
This was the last of his partnerships.   Ever afterwards he
practiced alone, and became an eminently successful lawyer.
Never remarkable for eloquence or brilliance of elocution, he
was a hardworking, studious, and industrious lawyer.   In 1838
he was elected to the House of Representatives.   In 1846 he
was elected Senator, and in 1850 he was re-elected.   He united
with the Baptist Church in 1831; and was an earnest Christian
and ardent teetotaller for many years.   He was a man of
whom it may be truthfully said that he faithfully discharged
every duty of life in every sphere to which he was called.

He died on 16th February, 1853, having just passed by one
week into his fifty-first year.   He left a widow and eight
children.

GEORGE McDUFFIE.

This great man was a native of Georgia.   His father was
John McDuffie, a poor, hard working man, and a blacksmith
by trade and occupation.   The date of Mr. McDuffie's birth I
am not able to give, but it was about or sometime during the
year 1788.   He first started in life as a clerk in the store of
Mr. James Calhoun, in Augusta, Ga.   This gentleman soon
noticed that he was a lad of remarkable ability, and he mentioned the fact to his brother, William Calhoun, of Abbeville.
Mr. William Calhoun soon afterwards proposed to board and
educate him at the then celebrated school at Willington, kept
by Dr. Waddell.   He accordingly took him into his own
family and sent him to the school, in the near neighborhood of
which he lived.   At this school McDuffie soon went ahead of

all competition, and was quickly prepared for college. He entered the Junior Class of the South Carolina College in December, 1811, and was very soon recognized as the first man in it.

After his graduation he read law from December, 1813, to May, 1814, when he was admitted to practice in both law and equity. A very short course of reading truly; and there is little wonder that he did nothing at Pendleton, at which place he first settled. In December, 1814, he was a candidate for Solicitor of the Western Circuit, but he was not elected. Soon after this he became a partner of Eldred Simkins, Esq., at Edgefield Court House. Mr. Simkins had a large practice and a good library. By this fortunate connection, McDuffie's rise was rapid, so rapid as to be without parallel. By Mr. Simkins he was introduced into the best society. In a celebrated case at Abbeville, called the James Land case, he was successful, and in the Court of Appeals he showed that he was able to grasp and understand the most involved intricacies of law. The people of Edgefield elected him to the Legislature in October, 1818, and in that sphere of action he showed his 'great abilities, both as an orator and as a man of business. The same year he was elected one of the trustees of the South Carolina College. In October, 1820, the people of Edgefield and Abbeville elected him as their Representative in Congress. Here he showed his great abilities as an orator and debater. During nearly the whole time of his service as a member of Congress the protective tariff was the great subject of debate, and convulsed not only the halls of Congress, but the whole country from end to end. Mr. McDuffie was an ardent nullifier, and threw himself into the thick of the fight with his whole soul. He favored the Ordinance of Nullification as passed by the Convention of South Carolina. The storm was lulled after awhile by the introduction of Mr. Clay's compromise measures, to which McDuffie gave a reluctant assent.

In December, 1834, he was elected Governor of the State, and while Governor, as President of the Board of Trustees of the South Carolina College, he did much to raise that institution from a languishing to a prosperous condition. At the expiration of his term as Governar he retired to private life, which retirement he was permitted to enjoy for about six years. He was then, in 1842, elected to the Senate of the United States. At this time his health was very feeble, but he was still able to do good service as Senator, especially in the advocacy of the annexation of Texas. At the close of the session of 1846 he resigned his seat, feeling that his health was too bad for him to try to serve any longer. He lingered a few years, until the spring of 1851, when he passed away.

Mr. McDuffie married, in 1829, Miss Singleton, who left him a widower with one child, a daughter, in 1830. This daughter afterwards became the wife of Wade Hampton.

About the year 1820, Mr. McDuffie unfortunately became involved in a duel with Colonel Cumming, in which he was wounded, and from which wound he never entirely recovered, though he lived for thirty years after it was received.

The protective tariff, for the suppression of which he fought so long and well, still rules the country, in spite of its unconstitutionality; in spite of the fact that it is a great wrong to the cultivators of the soil; and in spite of the fact that it is robbery to tax one industry and make it pay for the support of another. The great American system is one of the strongest evidences possible to be produced of the corrupting and debasing influence of money. The *love* of money *is* the root of all evil.

XX.

THOMAS H. POPE.

Mr. Pope was born in Edgefield, but passed the latter part of his life and the most active business part in the County of Newberry, though he never entirely deserted Edgefield. He was the eldest son of Sampson Pope and his wife, Sarah Strother, Virginians by family descent, and was born November 12th, 1803. He was educated mainly in his native county, but, for a short time, was in Yale College. He read law with Judge O'Neall; was admitted to practice in 1825, and first settled at Edgefield Court House. In January, 1830, he was married to Miss Harrington, the second daughter of Young John Harrington, of Newberry, and in 1832 he moved to that place.

He was very successful as a lawyer and had a large and lucrative practice. He never neglected the business interests of a client, but made a client's business his own.

He was elected Commissioner in Equity in 1836. He served until 1840, when he resigned. In 1840 he was elected to the Legislature as Representative—served two years. He was opposed to the Bank of the State; was a warm and earnest friend of the Greenville and Columbia Railroad, the charter of which he did much to secure. His life was very busy, active, and useful. He died of typhoid pneumonia on February 4th, 1851, in his 48th year. He left surviving him several sons and one daughter. Of his sons three are now living—Young John, an eminent lawyer and Attorney General of the State—Associate Justice, has been State Senator; Sampson, practicing physician at Newberry and Clerk of the Senate; David Strother, physician at the Penitentiary. The daughter is still living (1891).

It would make this work too large, were I to say all that might be said, and all that I would be glad to say of the many worthy men and women that must be mentioned. Sometimes it is very difficult to condense, and to give at the same time, a vivid and life-like picture of persons, places, and events. Let the reader, then, accept this apology once for all, for any

meagerness he may find in any sketches in this book.   Many
persons of whom I write and shall write are friends, relatives,
and connections.   Many, in both Edgefield and Newberry, are
relations and connections, and all are friends, I hope

ELDRED SIMKINS.

There are few names that shine with a purer and better
lustre; and few more deserving of honor by the people of
Edgefield and of the State than that of Simkins.

Arthur Simkins, the father of Eldred, was one of the earliest
settlers in Edgefield District.   He came from the Eastern
Shore of Virginia and first went to the region of the Santee,
but becoming dissatisfied in a short time with that region, he
went on to the less frequented forest of the Savannah side of
the State.   After several years of observation he settled on
Log Creek.   The place he settled was known for a long time,
and may be still remembered by some older person as the
"Cedar Fields."   The writer of this has a feeling that many
years ago he heard the place spoken of by that name.   It was
at the Cedar Fields that Arthur Simkins lived and died.   He
was County Judge under the old system and was regarded by
all who knew him as a man of sterling worth, and as a model
of honesty and uprightness.

When the Revolution broke out and the war for Independence began he took the side of Independence, and at an early
period of the war the Tories burned his dwelling house, then
one of the few large houses in the up-country, besides harrow-
ing and harrassing him in every other way incident to a state
of civil war

After the war he was a member of the General Assembly
and of the Convention which had been called to consider the
adoption of the Constitution of the United States.   He voted
against the adoption, as did nearly all the delegates from
Ninety-Six District.   The Act passed by the Legislature for
calling the Convention to consider the adoption of the Constitution of the United States was very nearly defeated.   General
Sumter and General Pickens were both opposed to the Constitution on the ground that it took too much power from the
State and made the General Government too consolidated.
Arthur Simkins agreed with them.

Mr. Simkins remained a member of the General Assembly for many years. He died in 1826, wealthy, honored, and respected, having done his duty as a man and citizen.

Eldred Simkins was the youngest son of Arthur, and was born during the Revolutionary war, August 29th, 1779. It is said that he was sent at an early age to the famous Academy of Dr. Moses Waddell, at Willington in the County or District of Abbeville, where he was thoroughly taught in all the fundamental branches of education and became a proficient in studies of a higher grade, especially Latin; that then he was sent to the Law School at Litchfield, Connecticut, where he remained more than three years; afterwards read law under Chancellor DeSaussure in Charleston, and was admitted to practice law in Charleston, May 7th, 1805. There is surely an error, or errors, in these statements somewhere. The school at Willington was not established until the year 1804. Dr. Waddell had been a teacher for some years, and had acquired a great reputation as a teacher at Appling, in the State of Georgia, and also at Vienna in Abbeville County, before the establishment of the school at Willington, and it must have been at one of these places that Mr. Simkins was his pupil, for that he was the pupil of Dr. Waddell is, I suppose, a well established fact.

Soon after his admission to the Bar he began his professional life at Edgefield. His practice soon became large and valuable, as he prepared his cases with great care and was a thorough practical business man.

In April, 1807, he married Eliza Hannah Smith, daughter of Benijah Smith, and grand-daughter of Elijah Clarke, so celebrated during the Revolutionary war. Colonel Pickens describes her as a "beautiful woman, the sweetest and most intertaining lady I ever saw in any society." Eldred Simkins was more than once sent to the Legislature from Edgefield.

In 1816, when Mr. Calhoun became a member of President Monroe's Cabinet, Mr. Simkins was elected to Congress. Mr. Edmund Bacon and General William Butler were also candidates for Congress at the same election. Mr. Simkins was in Congress four years; was an active and useful member, and, especially distinguished himself in a speech he made on the Missouri Compromise bill. At the end of four years' service he declined a re-election in favor of his friend and law partner, George McDuffie. After the election of Mr. McDuffie to Congress Mr. Simkins took as his law partner Mr. Ford, who, after a while, abandoned the law, became an Episcopal minister and pastor of a church in Augusta, Ga. In 1830 Mr. Simkins formed a partnership with Colonel F. W. Pickens, from which time he no longer attended closely to the business of his profession. He died in 1832. In 1859 his daughters were all dead, none leaving children except Mrs. Pickens. Three sons were then living, but they, too, have long since passed away. Arthur was for many years the genial and popular editor of the Edgefield Advertiser. Clarke this writer knew for a little while at Mount Enou Academy, as far back as the year 1835, with many other Edgefield youths. John, Lieutenant Colonel of his Regiment, died a heroic death at Battery Wagner, on Morris Island, on the night of July 18th, 1863. At about 9 o'clock he fell, pierced by a minnie ball through the right lung. His name with a brief sketch appears in the Annals of Newberry.

I transcribe it here, for John C. Simkins belonged to both Edgefield and Newberry.

LIEUTENANT COLONEL JOHN C. SIMKINS,

Whose name appears upon the Monument at Newberry, as one of the fallen soldiers of that county, was a son of Honorable Eldred Simkins, and was born at Edgefield Court House on the 11th day of March, 1827. He attended school at Edgefield and at Greenwood, S. C. He was not a graduate of any college or university; but, instead of continuing his studies at school, though only about eighteen years of age at the commencement of the Mexican War, he volunteered as a private in Captain Brooks' Company "D," of the Palmetto Regiment. During the campaign he was transferred to the Twelfth United States Regular Infantry, and, as captain in that regiment, distinguished himself at the battle of Churubusco, where he received two wounds. He was recommended to the government for a brevet "for gallant and meritorious conduct." At the close of the Mexican War he returned to civil life, that of a planter. In 1850 he married Rosalie, daughter of Judge Wardlaw, of Abbeville, and continued to live in Edgefield

District until about a year before the war between the States, when he bought from the Chappells a plantation in Newberry District on the Saluda River, about a mile above Chappells Depot. This plantation is part of what is known as Maxwell's Neck.

As soon as the State seceded and it was known that war was inevitable, he was amongst the first to offer his services to Governor Pickens. He was immediately appointed Captain in the First South Carolina Regular Infantry. His regiment was employed largely as artillery. As commander of Battery Bee, on Sullivan's Island, he did good service in the repulse of the iron-clads in the naval attack on Charleston, April 7th, 1863, when the Keokuk was sunk.

By successive promotions, he became Lieutenant Colonel of his regiment. On the 16th of July, 1863, he, with three companies of the regiment, Captains Haskell, Adams, and Tatum, was ordered to Battery Wagner, our advance post on Morris Island. Here he acted as Chief of Artillery, and he and his devoted little band, without rest or sleep, stood under a terrific bombardment until the night of July 18th, 1863, when the enemy, in overwhelming numbers, landed and assaulted the works. They were repulsed with heavy loss. In that night assault, at about 9 o'clock, Colonel Simkins fell pierced through the right lung by a minnie ball. Captains Haskell and Tatum were also killed during that engagement, and Captain Adams was severely wounded. Colonel Simkins was 36 years old at the time of his death, and left a widow, four sons, and a daughter surviving. His widow died in 1891.

In his official relation, Colonel Simkins was strict, but just. A born soldier, he was devoted to his profession. Although a good disciplinarian, he was respected and beloved by his comrades. He was very modest and retiring, but warm-hearted, frank, and true. His purity of heart was shown in his exceeding fondness for children, whose company he would seek.

CHARLES MARTIN GRAY.

The following instructive biography has been placed in my hands as good material for the history of Edgefield. I do not think any reader will be sorry to find it here. I have been informed that it was written by Joseph Abney, Esq

Charles Martin Gray was born at Edgefield Court House, South Carolina, on the 3rd of December, A. D. 1800, and was named after Charles Martin, a chivalrous and distinguished lawyer of his day.' He was the son of John Gray, Jr., for many years a merchant at that place, and of Ridley M. Mims, daughter of Drury Mims, who was supposed to be well tinctured with native American blood, his father having been descended from that stock, and his mother from the English. Drury Mims, during the War of the Revolution, was an ardent Whig and a daring soldier. John Gray, Jr., the father of Charles M. Gray, was a Scotchman of full blood, born in Edinburg, but immigrated to this country with his father, John Gray, Sr., when a small boy. He had a large family by his marriage with Ridley M. Mims, no less than eleven in number, and of those who lived to the years of maturity, only three were boys. All of his daughters had the happiness to contract marriage with industrious, honorable, and thrifty men— one of them, Elizabeth, marrying Dr. Chamberlain H. Goodwin, the son of Charles Goodwin, a lawyer of eminence at Old Cambridge, and the grandson, on the mother's side, of General Williamson, of Revolutionary fame.

Charles M. Gray was bound out at the age of thirteen years to one Mr. Pugh, of Augusta, Georgia, for seven years, as an apprentice at the trade of Fancy and Windsor Chair-making. But the war having broken out between Great Britain and America about this time, and the young apprentice having the keenest military propensities, and the most ardent thirst for distinction as a soldier, as well as a natural love for the exciting adventures of a soldier's life, while one Captain Musgrove was raising a volunteer company in the city of Augusta to march to the defence of Savannah, bade adieu as he supposed forever to fancy chair-making, attached himself to the command of the gallant captain, and hastened off to rekindle his military zeal and his love for glory, at the grave of Greene, and at the Monument of Pulaski. But avarice in some is stronger than the love of renown, or even the love of country. Mr. Pugh went in pursuit of this strippling warrior, and overtaking him at the Oglethorpe Barracks, reclaimed him as his property, and carried him back dejected and crest-fallen to Augusta, where he remained busily plying his trade, until his master, about a year afterwards, having failed in business, he was set at large, and permitted to control his own actions. In obedience to his natural proclivities, he again enlisted in the army, but this time in the regular army, under Major James E. Dinkins. His father hearing of it, hastened to the city, and, by virtue of his parental authority, recognized by the United States, sued out a writ of *habeas corpus* against Dinkins, and having returned his enlistment bounty, demanded and obtained his truant son, on the ground that he was a minor and under the proper military age. His father then took him home and entered him at school to Mr. Armstrong, famous in his day as a teacher, and then employed as Principal of the Edgefield Male Academy. But all the aspirations of our hero were for the army, and the din of musketry was more pleasing to his imagination than the noise and clatter of the school room. His father having become perfectly aware of the bent of his son's mind, on the 24th day of April, A. D. 1819, suffered him to re-enlist under Brevet Major David E. Twiggs, who was then in Augusta on recruiting service. He was assigned to Company A, Seventh Regiment, United States Army, and continued a member, first and last, ten years. The term of second enlistment of five years having expired, he was honorably discharged, and made his way home on foot, which he reached after traveling alone, camping out at night and cooking his own meals, for thirty-four days, in which time he walked a distance of nine hundred miles.

Long years of service in the army utterly unfitted him for the life of a civilian, and for many years he was too much addicted to indulgence in artificial stimulants to be prosperous. This bad habit too freely indulged during his enlistment, most likely deprived him of all chance of promotion. Many amusing instances might be related in illustrating the ingenuity displayed in procuring the desired stimulant, did space permit. But one or two, as related by the old soldier himself, will suffice: "On one occasion Major Twiggs commanded a party of twenty-four men, who were borne in the gallant vessel called the 'Support;' but it happened that myself constituted one of the number. Before starting out on my journey, I had been well schooled by my chum, George Riley, and among other commands was enjoined to procure for my mess a boun-

tiful supply of good liquor from John Cosby, the famous sutler
of Fort Gadsden. But I lacked that great desideratum, the
money, which was the 'sine qua non' with a soldier of our
command, who was to procure supplies and luxuries from the
sutler of a different corps. Genius then must supply the place
of gold and silver; and George Riley and myself, his hopeful
pupil, had no lack of that. The latter was dressed in the
ordinary uniform of a soldier, and had an overcoat supplied
with several more than the usual number of pockets. In each
of these was deposited a trusty 'big bellied bottle'. One of
them was filled with water, and another of the exact form and
dimensions was entirely empty. When the gallant vessel ar-
rives at Fort Gadsden, I approached the sutler, handed him
the empty bottle, and requested him to fill it, which was done
in a trice. It is then carefully stowed away in my pocket; but
poor soldier as I was, I had no money, and beg for a little
credit. The hard-hearted sutler, having had many such appli-
cations made to him before, peremptorily refused to credit, and
demanded the bottle of whiskey to be returned. Without a
moment's hesitation, it is done to all appearances, and with an
indignant imprecation; but, by an easy slight of hand, the
vessel containing the water is handed to the incorrigible John
C., Esq. It is emptied into the cask and returned to me to
my apparent disappointment and chagrin. But the trick was
too good not to be improved, and the same good bottles were
passed again and again to different members of the detail, who
all rejoiced in their own success as often as they tried the expe-
riment, until we had obtained excellent whiskey enough to
sustain my mess and colleagues in a royal spree.

"Major Twiggs, who was then opposed to drinking in his
command, observing me on my return from the direction of
the sutler's, called me to him and ordered me to display my
bottle. With an air of innocence I handed him the empty bottle,
when he immediately excused me, uttering at the same time
the direst imprecations of what he had done, had it contained
whiskey.

"Not long after the return of this party from the bay to
Fort Scott I approached my commanding officer, Major
Twiggs, for permission to purchase of the sutler a bottle of
whiskey, without stating the size. The application was

granted, and the needful order countersigned. On the faith thereof I hastened to the sutler's with a bottle I had previously obtained from the Surgeon or Apothecary, which, having been used to hold acids and medicines in large quantities, was capable of containing at least one or more gallons of liquor. It was, at any rate, bottle-shaped, and I had so thoroughly studied my superior that I well knew no punishment would result from the kind of prank I was about to practice. When I had procured the liquor, therefore, I made no secret of it, but slinging the huge vessel on my shoulder, passed directly by the quarters of Major Twiggs. When the latter beheld me as he walked to and fro along his little piazza he called me to him and demanded of me the authority I had for purchasing so much whiskey, and received the answer that it was derived directly from him, as could be attested by the written order itself. He then turned to Lieutenant Pierce M. Butler, who was promenading with him and inquired if Edgefield was composed of such men as Charles Martin Gray. Receiving an affirmative reply, he good humoredly said that he knew the devil must have his headquarters there, and beckoned me to go on.''

Charles M. Gray was happily married to Ann Green on the 3rd of September, 1841. He had previously foresworn his favorite beverage and had become an industrious and temperate citizen. He had as much business as he could attend to as Deputy Sheriff and as constable for one or more Magistrates, and earned not only money enough to subsist his family, but to pay all of his debts. He was elected door-keeper of the House of Representatives, and held the position until the inauguration of negro rule, a period of about twelve years.

There was one incident in the married life of the old soldier, which we think proper to allow him to relate: "A great chicken fight was to take place in Augusta—the Edgefield boys were pitted against those of Augusta, and I had an invincible disposition to take part in the sport—it suited my mind and temper. I was fond of game chickens and my wife had assisted me in raising a beautiful flock. My better half disapproved of my designs, but seemed to have a promonition that I would not be a gainer. I determined, though, to carry out my own purposes. I had in my pocket one hundred and fifty dollars. I went to the cock fight and lost it all. Returning home late at night I found madam discontented indeed, and indisposed even to give me a word of welcome. The old soldier returned in me at once. I had reserved from the wreck three silver dollars. I therefore went to the sideboard and counted these three dollars over and over again, with my back to my spouse until they amounted to the sum of three hundred and fifty dollars. Madam hearing all this could not be insensible to the claims of one, who, in the conflicts with fortune, had been so happy as to secure so much for her comfort. She then, for the first time, moved herself in the bed and called out to her dear husband that the old blue hen he had left setting had hatched twelve of the prettiest chickens he ever beheld. Upon this she rose from her bed and by sunrise procured for me one of the best breakfasts I had ever tasted before."

Charles M. Gray, by his marriage with Ann Green, had four sons and three daughters. One of his sons entered the Confederate Army at the age of 14 years and died of a disease contracted in service. Two others received desperate wounds in sustaining the "Lost Cause." Charles M. Gray, Jr., better known as Scout Gray, of Longstreet's Corps, was wounded seven times in battle, still lives at Edgefield Court House. He bears great resemblance to "Buffalo Bill."

Before we conclude this memoirs it is proper to remark that Charles M. Gray enlisted in the 7th Regiment from South Carolina in the war between the States—was made colorbearer and bore the Southern Cross throughout the whole of those desperate, bloody, and glorious combats, beginning at Bull Run and culminating at Manassas. But age and imfirmities admonished him that he must quit the service forever and bid farewell to "the drum, the shrill-sounding fife, and all the pride, pomp, and circumstance of glorious war," and receiving accordingly an honorable discharge, he retired to the bosom of his family.

A few years after the war he died at the age of three score and ten years.

XXI

WAR OF 1812 – SEMINOLE.

There are other Biographical sketches to be given, and which must be given to make the records complete, but we will desist for the present and resume the more direct historical narrative for a little while. History and Biography, however, are so interblended that they cannot be completely separated. The only difference is that in Biography the individual is made prominent and events become subordinate: while in history the cases are reversed.

Perhaps enough has already been said, incidentally, of the war of 1812, in the Biographical sketches of prominent men. General William Butler, Samuel Mays, and Colonel George Butler were most prominent. Thornton Coleman, an elder brother of Rev. Jones W. Coleman, held a Captain's commission in that war. The reader, however, understands that though troops were called out, that is the militia, and stationed on the coast, yet they were never actually engaged in battle. John, Joseph, and Jesse Edwards were in that war, and John Bledsoe, Henry Trotter, William Riley, and Isaac Riley.

Incidentally, too, enough has already been written of the stormy period of nullification and of the prominent actors of that time. Edgefield was a nullifier and was in hearty sympathy with the Act of the Convention nullifying the unjust tariff laws of Congress.

To the war against the Seminole Indians in Florida, three companies of infantry and one of cavalry volunteered from Edgefield. I may be able to give in the conclusion of this work a list of all the volunteers to Florida, as well as of those who served in the war with Mexico, and also in the late war of Secession, with the casualties incident to each individual. At present I can recall the name of James Edwards, a member of the company commanded by Captain David Denny, which went from the Tenth South Carolina Militia. There was also William Abney, who had vowed to whip, on sight, Charles K. Johnson, who, he supposed had wrongfully treated his son,

Henderson, at Mount Enon School, when he was a pupil of Mr. Johnson. After the threshing Mr. Abney and Mr. Johnson had never met until they met in Florida as soldiers and comrades in the same army. So far from threshing Mr. Johnson, Abney, when he came to know him, fell in love with him and was ever afterwards one of his warmest friends and admirers.

The company from the Seventh Militia Regiment was commanded by Captain James Jones, who was afterwards a General in the Militia. Milledge L. Bonham was Orderly Sergeant in Jones' company. The company from the Ninth Regiment was commanded by Captain Jefferson Hibler. Captain Hibler was afterwards Colonel in the Militia. Hibler Township, in the upper part of Edgefield, as I have been informed, was named in his honor. The company of cavalry was commanded by Captain Sibley, who, I think, was of Hamburg, as the members of the company were mostly from Hamburg and vicinity.

The following episode of the Seminole war I condense from an article by Rev. Wm. M. Wood in the Southern Christian Advocate of November 20th, 1890.

Mr. Peurifoy's father was from North Carolina. He moved to Putnam County, Georgia, where Tilman Dixon Peurifoy was born, January 21st, 1809. At nineteen years of age he was admitted to the Georgia Conference, having been converted at the age of fifteen. He was married when a young man to Miss Louisa Ann Bird, daughter of Captain Daniel Bird, of Edgefield, S. C. After a few years he moved to Florida and settled in Jefferson County in 1833. The war with the Seminoles was then going on, but from the place of his settlement the nearest Indians were a hundred miles distant, and no apprehensions of danger were felt by him or by any one in that section. Mr. Peurifoy was frequently absent for a long time attending to his preaching appointments. It was during one of these absences, and he was sixty miles distant attending Quartely Conference, when the attack, so disastrous and terrible, was made upon his home. It was on Sunday, April 1st, 1836; Mrs. Peurifoy was lying quietly and happily upon her bed reading that comforting book, "Heavenly Recognition," when the door was suddenly opened almost without noise, and a tall Indian, in feathers and war paint, quietly entered the room. The house, which was a double log cabin, with a wide passage between, had been surrounded quietly by a party of fifty or sixty Indians. A negro girl about twelve years of age, who was in the room with Mrs. Peurifoy, quickly understood the situation and tried to make her escape. She immediately darted out of the room between the Indian's legs as he stood for a moment in the door. She made her escape, but was fearfully wounded in the effort. She was still living near Augusta at the close of the year 1890, and may be living even now, 1891.

Before Mrs. Peurifoy swooned away she remembered seeing the savage kill her daughter, Elisabeth. The fate of her little boy she did not know. When she revived and came to herself she found the room full of Indians, and they were hurriedly eating the ham and potatoes and what other food they were able to find. Hoping that she would not be observed she made a great effort to escape. She was able to get out of the house and had reached the ground when she was shot and the bullet pierced her shoulder blade. Almost at the same time another bullet struck her thigh and she fell forward on her face. The savages then surrounded her, stabbed her in the back and cut her person fearfully. They cut her throat, but a shawl or handkerchief about her neck and shoulders saved her from death. They then beat her over the head with a light-wood knot, but unconsciously she raised her right arm to protect her head, and that was terribly bruised and broken. They did not scalp her. She became unconscious, and they left her for dead. When she came to herself again the savages were plundering the house and setting it on fire. She then crawled towards the kitchen, hoping that her cook, who had nursed her when she was a baby, might be able to help her. The cook herself was dying from wounds she had received, and could only spread her handkerchief on the ground for her mistress to lie on, when she quietly passed away.

After this, suffering from intolerable thirst, Mrs. Peurifoy dragged herself to a swamp or pond three quarters of a mile distant, where she was able to get some water to assuage her thirst. Here she lay that night, and until sunset next day, when she was found by the searching parties. Her father, who lived only a few miles distant, was with the searchers; and he, it seems, had a presentiment that she was still living, and would be found alive. The charred remains of the two children, Elisabeth and Lovick Pierce, were found in the ruins of the building. Mr. Peurifoy, on his return from Conference, was within twenty miles of home before he received any intimation of the terrible disaster. Upon sheets Mrs. Peurifoy was carried to her father's, near Monticello, Florida. For many weeks she breathed through several of her wounds, and for months she could only be moved and turned upon sheets. After these terrible events they removed to Georgia, and in 1849, came to Edgefield County and settled near Butler Church, where Mr. Peurifoy died June 3rd, 1872, and Mrs. Peurifoy, July 5th, 1878.

Three negroes, besides the cook already mentioned were killed in a house which was used for a church. One woman, who fought them to the last, was killed by having her head beaten to pieces with a lightwood knot. Her baby was saved by the door being thrown down in the scuffle and falling over the cradle in which the baby lay. This child was alive in 1890.

Mr. and Mrs. Peurifoy left several children; Eliza, who married Mr. Yarbrough, and Hon. D. B. Peurifoy, named after his grandfather, Captain David Bird. D. B. Peurifoy, familiarly called "Dan," by his friends, has been a member of the Legislature, but declined to be a candidate in 1890.

Thomas Bird, whom I knew at school, and who, I thought was a young man of very lovely character, was, if I mistake not, a son of Captain David Bird, and brother to Mrs. T. D. Peurifoy.

In making the statement that Pierce M. Butler was a Brigadier General during the Seminole war, I write from the recollection of my readings of history, without having books or any authorities to refer to just at this moment. But, whether he was Brigadier General or not at any time while that war lasted, he was inaugurated Governor of South Carolina, November, 1836, and was Governor two years; and a few years thereafter served with distinction in the war with Mexico, as Colonel of the Palmetto Regiment, and was killed at the battle of Churubusco.

In that war with Mexico, which was brought about by the annexation of Texas to the United States, Mexico never having acknowledged the independence of that State, but instead, had always claimed it as an integral portion of the territory of itself, the company from Edgefield, known as the Ninety-Six Boys, was commanded by Preston S. Brooks as Captain, having for Lieutenants W. C. Moragne and Joseph Abney; and was Joseph Culbreath also one, or was he First Sergeant? Milledge L. Bonham was a Colonel in this war, but in another regiment. Joseph Culbreath went as a private in Captain Williams' Company from Newberry—returned as Lieutenant.

Giles Chapman, the elder brother of the writer, was living in Indiana when the war with Mexico came on, and in that State he volunteered and was a member of the Second Indiana Regiment, under General Zachary Taylor. He was killed in the battle of Buena Vista, where General Taylor gained his great victory which made him President of the United States. In some movements of that part of the army, the retreat of the Second Regiment from the field, a wounded comrade of my brother, unable to keep up with his company, had been left behind. The Mexican lancers were scouring the field, killing all the wounded and stragglers, though at the time they were at some distance from that part of the field. Giles and another soldier determined to return and bring off their wounded comrade, if possible. They were warned against making the attempt, that it would be going to meet almost certain death without accomplishing their purpose. Their reply was that they would make the attempt even if they lost their own lives—that they could not see a comrade butchered before their own eyes without, at least, trying to save him; and if they could not save him, they would die with him. They went; they tried to save their friend, but failed, and all three were killed. Giles Chapman was a native of Edgefield. His name does not appear on the roll of the Palmetto Regiment, nor has it ever appeared in the Records of Edgefield County. It appears in the History of the Mexican War as a member of a regiment of another State, but he was of Edgefield, S. C., and as brave and fearless on the field of battle, and everywhere else, as ever human nature grows to be.

Before this book is closed and finally dismissed from the hands of the writer, it is his purpose to give a list of all the men engaged in these wars, with the ranks, casualties, &c.; so we will proceed with the general narrative of events as fully as we can, without making the work too large, which I fear will be done.

XXII.

THE TILLMAN FAMILY.

We have seen that Captain James Ryan came from Virginia and was one of the earliest settlers of Edgefield; and we might suppose from the name he bears that Benjamin Ryan Tillman, at this time Governor of South Carolina, was a relative or connection of the Ryan family. But such is not the case. The Tillmans came from Maryland or Delaware and settled on the southern side of Edgefield towards Hamburg. The father of the Governor once lived on the road leading from the Pine House to Hamburg, nine miles from the latter place. Benjamin Ryan was born thirteen miles north of Augusta in Merriwether Township. The name Benjamin Ryan was given to him through the great respect his father had to the Ryan family, and not from any blood relationship or connection with that family.

When George D. Tillman first went to Edgefield Court House to live and to practice law, he made himself very unpopular in the town, whatever he may be now, and had many enemies. What he was, or is, I know not, for my acquaintance with him personally is nothing. When the quarrel occurred, that is its date, I do not know, but he once had a serious difficulty with General John R. Wever and gave him a dangerous pistol wound in the side. Some time after that he killed a man named Henry Christian. He fled the country and went to Central America, where he joined General Walker, of Filibuster fame, was wounded, and taken prisoner, but was released after promising not to meddle any more with the institutions or government of that country. He then returned home, was tried at Edgefield for murder, found guilty of manslaughter, and sentenced to two years imprisonment in the District Jail, which penalty he suffered. After the War of Secession he was a member of the Constitutional Convention, which met in Columbia in 1865. In a book, "The South Since the War," published in 1866, the writer of that book thus speaks of Mr. Tillman as he appeared in that convention:

"George D. Tillman, a man of immense frame and very considerable abilities, genial and offhand, who has lived in South America and California, and now hails from Edgefield District, who has served six years in the State Legislature for honor, and two years in the State Penitentiary for manslaughter, (South Carolina had no Penitentiary at that time,) who quotes philosophy from DeTocqueville, and historical maxims from Gibbon—the man who makes friends with everybody, and at whom, the gentlemen, so called, of the low country, affect to sneer, is a genuine Red Republican in his disregard of what is called ancient rights and privileges. Sitting with great blue-gray eyes, that seem always half asleep, he is always alert and wide awake, slouching along with a rolling gait, he is careful and earnest; utterly wanting in the power of oratory or rhetoric, he has made more points than any other member of the Convention, and has carried all of them but one, and that of minor importance. He is the leader of the advance line of the up-country, delegated, not so much by any election as by the inherent force of necessity, for he fights independently, and leaves them no choice but to follow. He is fairly entitled to the honors of the day in the open field fight against the Conner resolution; and has been from the first the restless and untiring and self-possessed and good humored enemy of the parish system, or to use his own phrase, the Chinese conservatism of Charleston. His object has been, and still is, to cripple the power of the low-country in every possible way. He will take no bond of fate, but builds his walls of offence and defence in the constitution itself.

"On the tenth day Tillman smote the routed enemy once more; he called it reaping the 'first fruits of victory.' His blow came in the form of an amendment to the Constitution, providing that after 1869 no district in the State shall have more than twelve Representatives. This was aimed at the city of Charleston, which now has twenty. The low country was exhausted and the amendment was adopted after a brief debate by 61 to 43."

Another estimate of Honorable G. D. Tillman, written twenty-five years after the publication of the 'South Since the War.' This, too, is the estimate of a Northern man, Amos J. Cummings. At the time of the writing Mr. Tillman was Chairman of the Committee on Patents, and the writer says of him:

"He is quaint and honest and makes speeches that touch the marrow. In appearance he somewhat resembles Horace Greeley. But there is a manly ring to his voice, as well as virility in his arguments. Once convinced that he is right, neither persuasion nor force can drive him from his position. He is a brother of the Governor of the Palmetto State, and has all his brother's characteristics. No man uses the Southern dialect more penetratingly. Detecting jobbery in legislation, he flies at it like a bulldog, and there is nothing left of it when he gets through with it.

"Mr. Tillman was 65 years old last August, (1891). Born in South Carolina, he received an academical education in Georgia. He afterward entered Harvard, but did not graduate. He studied law, and was admitted to the Bar in 1848. He served as a private in the ——— South Carolina Infantry and in the Second Regiment of Artillery. After the war he became a cotton planter. In the ante-bellum days he had been a member of the State Legislature. He was elected to the State Constitutional Convention under the reconstruction proclamation of President Johnson. Afterward he became State Senator under the new Constitution. He was a candidate for the Forty-fifth Congress, and unsuccessfully contested the seat of Robert Smalls. The Committee on Elections reported in favor of vacating the election, but the House failed to act on the report.

"This is Mr. Tillman's seventh term. In the Forty-seventh Congress he first took his seat. J. Warren Keifer was elected Speaker and Mr. Tillman was ousted to make room again for General Smalls. Mr. Tillman was a member of the Committee on Patents in the Fiftieth and Fifty-first Congress. It is safe to say that no patent will ever be renewed while he is Chairman of that Committee. He usually makes two or three speeches each session, and they are speeches that command, not only the attention, but the admiration of the House. He belongs to the old school of statesmen, now almost extinct.

"South Carolina may well be proud of him."

He was a candidate for re-election in 1892 and was beaten by W. J. Talbert, a native and citizen of his own county, Edgefield.

This generation is retiring all its old sevrants, whether

wisely or not it is impossible to say—not for this historian to say.

The progress of events recently has made it necessary to write more fully of B. R. Tillman. In 1890 he was elected Governor of the State; in 1892 he was re-elected; in 1894 he was elected to the Senate of the United States to succeed General M. C. Butler, who was retired to private life.

Whatever may be said of B. R. Tillman for or against, he is certainly one of the most remarkable men the County of Edgefield—I might say the State has ever produced. Without any preliminary political training whatever, never even having held any office except that of Captain of a cavalry company to which he was elected in 1882, he passed at one bound to the position of Governor of the State. From Governor he was elected to the United States Senate. By the Democratic Convention which was held in Columbia in May, 1896, he was endorsed as a candidate for President of the United States, that is for his name to go before the General Democratic Convention to be held in Chicago. He stands squarely for the free coinage of silver, according to the old standard of value of 16 to 1, as compared with gold.

Mr. Tillman has the great power of binding his friends to him as with hooks of steel, and of making his enemies hate him. He seems to be fond of political battles and wants no one to be indifferent.

W. B. DORN.

Mr. William B. Dorn was once a noted man of this section. He discovered a gold mine, which, for a number of years, was very productive. If ever mortal man had the gold fever, mania it might well be called in his case, he was one. For years and years before he made any discoveries worth notice, he was a patient and untiring seeker, sinking money all the time in fruitless and unprofitable digging. At last his labors were crowned with success, and he became a wealthy man. The first year's work that paid produced about ten thousand dollars. I heard his partner, Mr. Bell, I think his name was, describe how it was that they came to sink the first paying shaft. He said that they were heart-weary; had been digging and prospecting and finding not enough to make it pay, and had about come to the conclusion to give it up and dig no more, but thought they would make one more effort and dig wherever the axe, which Mr. Bell carried in his hand, might fall after throwing; and if that digging failed they would try no more. Taking the axe by the end of the handle Mr. Bell whirled it around his head two or three(times and let it fly with all his might. They dug where it struck the ground and their success was assured.

Mr. Dorn became very wealthy, worth, perhaps, a million dollars; married a beautiful young wife and was elected to the Legislature. He died about ten years after the war at about eighty years of age. At the time of his death he was not rich.

THE EDWARDSES—ADDITIONAL.

Joseph Edwards, the great-grandfather of J. C. Edwards, was a native of Wales and emigrated to Maryland and lived in the old town of Benedict at the mouth of the Patuxent River.

His son, Jared Edwards, first married Susan Porter, of Virginia, who bore him four sons, John, Joseph, Jesse, and Stephen, who, all removed to Alabama soon after the war of 1812. Jared Edwards, the grand-father of J. C., came to Edgefield in 1805, and there married for his second wife Rebecca Bell, who, also bore him four sons, William, Benjamin, James, and Isaac. James never married. Jared Edwards was born in the year 1746 and died January 31st, 1832. John Crowder Edwards, who gives me this information, is the third son of Benjamin Edwards.

Rev. Zedekiah Watkins, whose name has already been mentioned, was born October 15th, 1791, and died September 25th, 1867. He was converted at the age of 15, and was ordained by John Landrum and Carson Howell, October 15th, 1826.

XXIII.

KANSAS TROUBLES—SECESSION.

Having brought this history down to a period immediately preceding Secession and the war following, it becomes necessary to write of the events leading to that decisive act, an act the most momentous in the history of the world since the advent of Christ.

The student of United States history does not need to be informed that from the very beginning the union between the States was not altogether as cordial as it might have been. Absolute cordiality was wanting long before the Republican-Abolition party came into being, long before the lawfulness of the institution of slavery was called in question by any person in any part of the country. There were extreme State Rights men at the first before the Constitution was adopted and the Union formed. Of these the leaders were Jefferson and Patrick Henry in Virginia, and we háve already seen that some of the ablest men in South Carolina voted against the adoption of the Constitution, because it took away from the States and gave to the central government too much power. There were also extreme Centralists, or Federalists, as they were then called, at the first. Conspicuous amongst these were Alexander Hamilton and John Adams. Washington, himself, belonged to that party. These conflicting views resulted in a compromise out of which was born the Federal Constitution, as it was when it became part of the organic law of the States. Union of some sort, and a closer union than was made by the old Articles of Confederation, was found to be absolutely necessary, if the States continued to live under one general government. So the Constitution was adopted as a compromise between conflicting views and opinions. It never was entirely satisfactory to anybody. But something had to be done, or chaos would come again. It is due to truth to say that this great instrument, the result of the deliberations of the wisest men of the country and of the age, was only a compromise of conflicting views and wishes to prevent other and greater evils. And like all other compromises, it was not able to stand the day of extreme trial and pressure. Long ago a writer in Harper's Monthly or Weekly said that all written constitutions become mere waste paper when they stand in the way of the advance or evolution of great ideas. In our country the seeds of discord existed in the minds, habits, and modes of thought and life of the people of the different sections, even from the first. Owing to a difference of the produce of the lands, and the means by which those lands were cultivated, the men of the South were naturally more baronial and lordly in their manner and habits. They were also better statesmen, and their influence predominated for many years in the councils of the nation, during the War of the Revolution, before the adoption of the Constitution, and for many years following the adoption. Mr. Jefferson, the greatest statesman this country has ever produced, seemed to care but little for the nation, but took great pride and glory in the freedom and independence of the States. His policy ruled for many years, and the influence of Southern statesmen was paramount, until, I am forced to believe, a deep-seated feeling of hatred for the South and the Southern people grew out of, supplanted, and took the place of that of jealousy, which had existed from the first in the minds of the leaders of Northern thought. The dislike found full expression and hearty satisfaction in the formation of the Abolition and Free Soil parties.

The Abolition party, pure and simple, was almost a dead failure. Its leaders were not wise. They aimed at that which, it was too plainly manifest, was entirely beyond their jurisdiction to meddle with, and out of their power to accomplish in a direct mode of attack. The feeling of the Abolition party at last became embodied in, and found triumphant expression through the Free Soil party. The life and animating spirit of that party was to prevent the admission of any more States holding slaves into the Union. This, it was very easy to persuade themselves, that they had a right to do legally under the Constitution. Their standpoint was that all the territorial soil then belonging to the United States, or henceforth to be acquired by them, shall be owned by free men, and shall be cultivated by free men only. No more extension of slavery into the free territory of the United States. No more slave States.

The hatred and bitter feeling engendered and fostered by the discussion of this subject, in and out of Congress, continued for many years, and grew and increased in intensity, until at last they were quenched in blood—if they have been quenched. After many years of weary and bitter agitation the so-called compromise measures on the admission of Missouri were introduced and passed. Mr. Clay, of Kentucky, aided by his great influence in having Missouri admitted as a slave State, but with the proviso that thereafter no State holding slaves should be admitted North of 36° 30', which was the Northern boundary of that State. Missouri was admitted in the year 1821.

For years the discussion on the restriction of slavery had been very bitter. The Missouri Compromise did not stop the discussion nor the strife, though the tariff question for a time held the attention of the people and kept their feelings at white heat. That agitation reached its climax in South Carolina when the Convention of the People of the State, on the 17th of December, 1832, passed an ordinance nullifying the tariff laws of Congress. Again compromise measures were resorted to which stilled the agitation and averted a conflict. Jackson was then President and would have made short work with the job of suppressing nullification in South Carolina, if Congress had not taken speedy action.

In the meantime the discussion of the slavery question never ceased. This writer is no longer a young man, having been born in 1821, the year of the admission of Missouri into the Union; and, looking back over a somewhat long life, he does not remember the time when the country had a calm and settled peace with any prospect of long continuance. Nullification, the Seminole War, the threatened War with France about the same time, the War with Mexico, the continued agitation of the slavery question, Secession, the War of Secession, the terrible period of reconstruction, and now the great danger of plutocracy grasping and swallowing into its voracious and capacious maw all the liberties and possessions of the toiling people, through the operation of the tariff and land monopolies, with the discussions of other great questions, all show that the end is not yet, and that a calm and enduring peace is not to be found in a world where moral evil has its fixed seat and firm abiding place. The suppression of evil, without its eradication, is only introducing order into hell.

The compromise on the tariff settled nothing. The protective tariff continued and became the settled policy of the country, in spite of the fact that in its very nature it is robbery. The agitation of the slavery question continued, and was intensified whenever a new State applied for admission. By the War with Mexico, to which Mr. Calhoun was opposed, because he saw with clear vision that territory would be acquired, and that the States would quarrel over it, like a parcel of hungry dogs over a bone, a large quantity of territory, many millions of miles in extent, was added to the landed domain of the Union, and the question immediately arose whether any of that territory should be made into slave States. A few years after the close of that war the act of 1850 was passed, by which the Missouri Compromise of 1820 was repealed, and the whole territorial domain of the United States was thrown open to settlers from all the States; and they were permitted to carry their property of all kinds, slaves as well as other into any territory wherever they might choose to go or settle· and when the time arrived for the formation of State Constitutions the people might allow or prohibit slavery as they chose. This was a measure of Mr. Clay's, and it made him more popular than he ever had been before. It was thought to have been the crowning and most glorious act of his life. He hoped, the people hoped, and the whole country hoped for a long-continued peace, and that an era of good feeling and of good will had come to stay. Mr. Clay did not live long enough to see the dissipation of these hopes. He died in the fullness of his fame, and content.

For a little while, a very little while, these hopes seemed likely to be realized. They were soon dispelled. They were, indeed, a dream baseless and insubstantial. The very fact that all the territories, North and South, without regard to degrees of latitude, were open to all settlers alike, very soon roused in the minds of the people of the different parties, pro and anti slavery, the intense and inextinguishable desire to fill up the new domains, each with settlers of its own sort. The fires of sectional strife soon raged hotter and fiercer than ever. Emigrant aid societies were formed North, in which Bibles and

rifles played a prominent part.   They were also formed in the
South, in which pistols, perhaps, played a more prominent
part than either Bibles or rifles.

Kansas became the first battle ground for settlers from the
opposing parties.   Indeed it was there that the great Civil
War began.   It was there that the celebrated John Brown,
who was afterwards hanged for his armed invasion of Virginia
and his attempt to excite an insurrection in that State, first
became conspicuous as a public character, and whose soul is
said to be still marching on.   May God in His mercy soon give
it rest.   Kansas became the first battle ground, because it was
the first territory to apply for admission as a State under the
new order of things.   Emigration societies were formed all over
the Union for the purpose of aiding settlers to gain a foothold
in that new region in order to shape its future character and
destiny as a pro or anti slavery State.

Edgefield was not backward in this work.   Edgefield is
never backward when live men are wanted to push on any
work.   The District did its part, but how many went to
Kansas, and how many, if any, became actual settlers, my
information on this point is too defective to allow me to speak
with certainty.   It was in Kansas that the great Civil War
began, but that territory was not admitted as a State until
after Secession was an accomplished fact.

The two great parties that then divided the people of the
United States, as they yet divide them, were known as the
Democratic and the Republican; the one State rights, believing
in the Strict construction of the Constitution; the other national in character, in all its proclivities, doctrines, and ten-
dencies.   By a strange infatuation, which can in no otherwise
be accounted for than by the old saying that whom the gods
wish to destroy they first make mad, the Democratic party,
which had a majority, both of the people and the States, instead of uniting their forces upon one man for President and
one for Vice-President, had three sets of candidates in the
field at the election in 1860, and the result of the contest was,
of course, the election of Mr. Lincoln, the Republican candidate.   But, even had the Democratic party at that election
succeeded in electing, both President and Vice-President, as
they might have done if they had had only one set of candi-

dates, it would only have prolonged the struggle without, in the end, producing a different result.

It appears to have been the fixed determination of the people of South Carolina, whatever it may have been in other Southern States, to withdraw from the Union should the Republican party succeed in electing the President, and get control of the government of the United States. Under the dominion of the Republican party we had no hopes of being able to preserve our equality in the Union for any length of time and thought it better to part company and go our own way and let them go theirs. Acting according to this resolution, without waiting even to try Mr. Lincoln and see whether he would be false or true to his oath of office, a convention of the people was called soon after the result of the election was known. The Act of the Legislature calling the convention was ratified on the 13th day of November, 1860, and the delegates from the several election Districts of the State assembled in the Baptist Church, in the town of Columbia, at twelve o'clock m., on the 17th day of December, 1860. The day was Monday.

The delegates from Edgefield were Francis Hugh Wardlaw R. G. M. Dunovant, James Parsons Carroll, William Gregg, Andrew J. Hammond, James Tomkins, James C. Smyley.

The convention having assembled on motion of Mr. James H. Adams, of Richland, Mr. D. F. Jameson, from Barnwell, was called to the Chair. Mr. Jameson was afterwards elected permanent President of the Convention. As part of the history of that momentous time I deem it but proper to give the address of Mr. Jameson when called to the Chair

He said: "Gentleman, we have met here under circumstances more solemn than any of us have ever been placed in before. No one, it seems to me, is duly impressed with the magnitude, who does not, at the same time, feel, that he is about to enter upon the gravest and most solemn act which has fallen to the lot of this generation to accomplish. It is no less than our fixed determination to throw off a government to which we have been accustomed, and to provide new safeguards for our future security. If anything has been decided by the elections which sent us here, it is that South Carolina must dissolve her connection with the confederacy as speedily as possible.

"In the progress of this movement we have two great dangers to fear—overtures from without and precipitation within. I trust the door is now forever closed to all further connection with our northern confederates; for, what guarantees can they offer us more strictly guarded, or under higher sanctions, than the present written compact between us. And did that sacred instrument protect us from the jealousy and aggressions of the North, commenced forty years ago, which resulted in the Missouri Compromise?

"Did the Constitution protect us from the cupidity of the Northern people, who, for thirty-five years, have imposed the burden of supporting the General Government chiefly on the industry of the South? Did it save us from abolition petitions designed to annoy and insult us, in the very halls of our Federal Congress? Did it enable us to obtain a single foot of the soil acquired in the war with Mexico, where the South furnished three-fourths of the money, two-thirds of the men, and four-fifths of the graves? Did it oppose any obstacle to the erection of California into a free-soil state without any previous territorial existence; without any defined boundaries, or any census of her population? Did it throw any protection around the Southern settlers of Kansas, when the soil of that territory was invaded by emissaries of Emigrant Aid Societies in a crusade preached from Northern pulpits, when church men and women contributed Sharp's Rifles and Colt's Revolvers to swell the butchery of Southern men? And has not that Constitution been trodden under foot by almost every Northern State in their ordinances nullifying all laws made for the recovery of fugitive slaves, by which untold millions of property have been lost to the South?

"Let us be no longer duped by paper securities. Written constitutions are worthless, unless they are written at the same time, in the hearts, and founded on the interests of a people; and as there is no common bond of sympathy or interest between the North and the South, all efforts to preserve this Union, will not only be fruitless, but fatal to the less numerous section. The other danger to which I referred may arise from too great impatience on the part of our people to precipitate the issue, in not waiting until they can strike with the authority of law.

"At the moment of inaugurating a great movement, like the present, I trust that we will go forward and not be diverted from our purpose by influences from without. In the outset of this movement I can offer you no other motto than Danton's at the commencement of the French Revolution: To dare! and again to dare! and without end to dare!''

Three days thereafter on the 20th of December, 1860, the Ordinance of Secession was passed by the Convention without a single dissenting voice. The Ordinance was as follows:

AN ORDINANCE

"To dissolve the Union between the State of South Carolina and other States united with her under the compact entitled 'The Constitution of the United States of America.'

"*We, the people of the State of South Carolina, in Convention assembled, do declare and ordain, and it is hereby declared and ordained;*

"That the Ordinance adopted by us in Convention, on the twenty-third day of May, in the year of our Lord one thousand seven hundred and eighty-eight, whereby the Constitution of the United States of America was ratified, and also all acts and parts of acts of the General Assembly of this State, ratifying amendments of the said Constitution, are hereby repealed; and that the Union now subsisting between South Carolina and other States, under the name of the United States of America, is hereby dissolved.''

On the question being put, "Will the Convention adopt the Ordinance?" it passed in the affirmative. Yeas, 169; nays, none.

So the great and decisive act of Secession was accomplished; that act which brought a terrible and bloody war of four years' duration; hastened that end from which we had so long shrunk; completely changed our institutions; paved the way for other changes, which are now in rapid process of development, and the end of which no man can see. The position in which we, the people of Edgefield and of the State, find ourselves to-day is one which would have been utterly impossible under the old order of things. Whether the changes which are now so rapidly moving on, not only in South Carolina, but in the whole country, are to bring about a better state of things,

or whether they will ultimately end in disastrous wreck and
ruin to the whole country, it is impossible for the wisest statesman to foresee and predict with certainty. Whatever the *end*
may be, this we know that men in their selfish and evil blindness are sure to bring disasters upon themselves as they are,
because they do not aim at what is right, but at that which
they think will be gainful to themselves, whether right or
wrong. Little did the Convention of 1860 dream of the events
of the next four years! They thought the people of the North
would not fight; that they loved money too well to think of
going to war to make a coercive union, and that the experi-
ment would be entirely too costly. Or, even supposing that
they should resort to arms to preserve the Union, we felt that
we could whip them, and that after a few well-fought battles,
in which they would be sure to get the worst of it, they would
be glad to make peace, and to let us go our own separate ways
without further molestation.

There was no opposition in Edgefield to the action of the
Convention, and the vote of their delegates was heartily endorsed by almost everybody. When the act of Secession was
consummated great enthusiasm was felt and manifested everywhere, and preparations for war began to be made in all parts
of the district. We have already briefly noticed the enthusiasm manifested at Mount Willing. As it was there, so it was
in all parts of the county. The war drums beat and volunteer
campanies began to be formed at an early day. Meantime,
however, efforts were made by South Carolina and by the
Confederate government, which was soon formed by the Secession of other States from the old Union, to make a peaceful
solution of the existing difficulties without resorting to the
terrible arbitrament of arms. These efforts were all in vain.
Mr. Buchanan and the authorities of the United States government could not receive the commissioners sent on to Washington in any other manner than as private gentlemen. They
had no power nor authority to treat with them, or to make
any arrangement looking to or recognizing the fact of the dissolution of the existing Union. Our commissioners effected
nothing; and preparations for war went on all over the State.
Companies were formed and moved to Charleston. Fort
Sumter was invested and batteries were erected on Morris

Island, manned by cadets from the South Carolina Military Academy and commanded by Major P. F. Stevens. Fort Sumter was thus invested to prevent re-enforcements, or supplies of any kind from being sent to Major Anderson, who commanded there, and not for the purpose, as yet, of making an attack upon the fort. On the 9th of January, 1861, just twenty-nine days after the passage of the Ordinance of Secession, the Star of the West, a light ocean steamer, made an effort to pass the batteries with supplies for Fort Sumter. She was fired into, when she retired and did not again try to pass.

All efforts at negotiation having failed, and at this time it being well known to the Confederate authorities that it was the fixed purpose of the United States government to re-enforce Fort Sumter, an attack was determined on. Accordingly, General Beauregard, who then had command of the Confederate forces at Charleston, was instructed to demand its surrender, and if the demand was not complied with, to proceed at once to attack. On the 11th of April, 1861, he made the demand. The demand was replied to in the negative, and at half past four A. M. on the next day, the firing began. The bombardment of the fort continued steadily for thirty-two hours, when Major Anderson surrendered. No one was killed on either side in this memorable contest. At this time General Beauregard had under his command about six thousand Confederate troops, a part of whom, one regiment, commanded by Colonel Maxcy Gregg, of Columbia, was from South Carolina. There were two companies from Edgefield, one led by Cicero Adams and the other by Captain Robert Merriwether.

XXIV.

The larger number of volunteers from Edgefield were embodied in the Seventh and Nineteenth Regiments. The Seventh South Carolina was organized at Camp Butler, on the 15th of April, 1861, to serve for twelve months. Thomas G. Bacon was elected Colonel; Robert Fair, Lieutenant Colonel; and Emmet Seibles, Major. This regiment was among the first to go to Virginia. It was formed into a brigade with the Second, Third, and Eighth South Carolina, and placed under General Bonham as Brigadier, and always occupied the advanced position of our army around Centreville. In the movement from Fairfax to Bull Run, and before the battles of the 18th and 21st of July, this brigade covered the rear. During these battles the Seventh and Third were not engaged, though under artillery fire. The Second and Eighth were engaged. Soon after this General Bonham resigned, having been elected to the Confederate Congress, and J. B. Kershaw was appointed Brigadier, a position he honorably filled to the close of the war. At the expiration of the twelve months for which the Seventh had enlisted, a reorganization became necessary—a reorganization and enlistment for the war.

On the 12th of May, 1862, the reorganization was effected and D. Wyatt Aiken, of Abbeville, was elected Colonel; Dr. Elbert Bland, of Edgefield, Lieutenant Colonel; and White, Major. At the battle of Sharpsburg, Colonel Aiken was shot through the lungs and disabled for the war, when the command devolved upon Lieutenant Colonel Bland; and by the death of Major White, John S. Hard, of Graniteville, senior Captain, became Major. Colonel Bland and Major Hard were both killed at the battle of Chickamauga. Colonel Bland had served as Assistant Surgeon during the Mexican War. Although Major Hard was the senior Captain of the regiment, was a married man and had left at home several children, yet such was his youthful appearance that he was known as the boy soldier of the regiment. Captain William Clark, of Saluda, near Chappell's Ferry; Captain John W. Kemp, of Mountain Creek, and Lieutenant A. T. Traylor, of Liberty

Hill, were all officers of merit in the Seventh Regiment, and were all killed in battle. Lieutenants J. B. Bouknight, W. J. Denny, J. M. Daniel, and W. A. Rutland were also members of this regiment.

The Nineteenth Regiment was never sent to Virginia, but was attached to the Western Army, and all its service was under Bragg, Johnston, and Hood, and other generals commanding in that department. William C. Moragne, a lawyer from Edgefield, who had served as Lieutenant in the Palmetto Regiment during the War with Mexico, was first Colonel of the Nineteenth, but he died soon after the war began, and was succeeded by A. J. Lythgoe, of Abbeville. Colonel Lythgoe and Major John A. Crowder, of this regiment, were both killed in battle. After Colonel Lythgoe's death Lieutenant Colonel John P. Shaw had command until he was wounded and taken prisoner at Franklin, Tennessee; that "dearest victory of the war," as Mr. Caldwell, in his History of McGowan's Brigade, well calls it. Colonel Shaw was succeeded in command by Captain Thomas W. Getsen. Captain W. S. Peterson, of Big Creek, who was killed at Atlanta; Captain William Norris, from near Batesburg; and Captain John C. Shaw, of Curryton, all belonged to the Nineteenth Regiment; as also Sergeant Thomas Chapman, (mortally wounded at Atlanta) Levi Crouch, Hiram Holstein, Lieutenants; and Lieutenant John C. Wheeler, Color-Bearer, killed at Atlanta. At the close of the war Robert Merriwether was Major, and he, with some others, shamed and disgusted with the conclusion of the struggle, and being rather hopeless of the future of our part of the country, emigrated to Brazil.

Major John Blocker, of Blocker Township, and Captain R. W. Tomkins, of the Hampton Legion, were killed during the war. Colonel Twiggs, afterwards killed by Mr. Robert Butler, and Colonel Thomas G. Lamar, were quite prominent, active and dfficient soldiers and officers. Captain James Tillman, brother of B. R. Tillman; Captain W. F. Trescott, Captain James J. Gregg, of Graniteville, and Major B. E. Nicholson, all good soldiers, have died since the war. The foregoing names will all appear again with many others, all that can be obtained, in the rolls to be inserted at the close of the book.

It was while Colonel Shaw was in command of the Nineteenth Regiment that this writer became a member of it, in Captain W. S. Peterson's company. Captain Peterson was at home at the time on recruiting service, his company having been, temporarily, consolidated with that of Captain Chatham, who was left in command. This was while the army was in winter quarters at Dalton, Georgia, in command of which General Joseph E. Johnston had been recently placed. A six months term of service had just expired of the Second Regiment of State troops under Colonel William Fort, stationed at Pocotaligo and forming part of the brigade of Brigadier General Walker, who had been promoted from Colonel to Brigadier for his skillful defence of the place and successful repulse of the enemy at that point. At Pocotaligo I saw many men from Edgefield, some of whom had seen a good deal of service before. Captain Ira Cromley, Geo. D. Huiett, C. L. Refo, Lemuel Salter, who had been through the Kentucky campaign under Bragg—and others. I afterwards met Salter at Dalton, and after the campaign opened, one Friday night a short time before I was wounded, we stood, or rather lay all night together on picket duty, where we were fired at all night long by a picket on the other side. There is no danger of being shot now for sleeping on post then, but I slept some that night and was asleep when the officer of the day, or rather night, passed. My companion was awake and did not even nod the whole night.

It was very pleasant to leave the low-country about Pocotaligo, the low-lands all flooded with water, and go to the hilly uplands above Dalton in the neighborhood of the mountains. It was while we were in winter quarters at this place that I joined in the last game of snow-balling I have ever had. When the snow-balling began I had no thought of taking any part—only wanted to look on a while. It was brigade against brigade, division against division, I do not remember which, but I think division against division, as there seemed to be many thousands engaged. It was a fine spectacle and fine fun to the participants. This writer got the worst of the fight, just as he has got the worst of it in all the battles of life. But when overcome he was kindly treated by his captors and sent back to his temporary home without having suffered any detriment.

Shortly before the opening of the campaign of 1864, that is before active operations began, one bleak windy day in March, not very cold, but awfully disagreeable, there was a grand review and inspection of the whole army. This is the only time that I ever saw General Johnston. I saw Hindman and Hood and some others frequently, but I think that.at this general review is the only time I ever saw our general-in-chief. At this review we had something less than 48,000 men under arms—rations were issued to about that number. Over beyond the mountains above Dalton Sherman had a force of 150,000. During the whole campaign until General Johntson was relieved of the command, the disparity between the two armies remained about the same. And yet under these circumstances positive orders were sent down from the ruling powers of the Confederacy at Richmond that we must go forward; that General Johnston must make a forward movement. Undoubtedly he could have made a forward movement; he could have abandoned his position at Dalton; moved South and Westward, and perhaps have flanked Sherman and gone into Tennessee, as Hood did afterwards. He could not have made a movement more pleasing to Sherman. But it is too late to discuss now what might have been done; it is the business of the historian to relate what was done.

When active operations began we entrenched ourselves above Dalton to oppose the forward movement of Sherman. That General was far too wary and wise to make a direct attack upon us in our entrenched position. He knew that he could not carry it. He felt it. He knew where its strong points were, and he knew that, with ten times the number of men he had with him, he could not break General Johnston's lines by any direct attack. He did not make the attempt. He knew, however, that his army far outnumbered Johnston's and that he could increase his numbers by drawing on other divisions in the North and West, and he knew that Johnston had almost literally nowhere to draw from, as many thousand men too old for military service and many thousand boys too young were already in the ranks. These facts were as well known to Sherman as they were to us, and therefore he knew that it was utterly impossible for General Johnston to prevent a flank movement. Flank he did, and General Johnston was drawn out of his stronghold at Dalton and made to move to Resaca, where the first fighting of the campaign was done.

The reader of this history will please pardon the writer if a little personal narrative here and elsewhere mingles with the story, for when one has been an actor in the scenes and incidents he undertakes to narrate and describe it is almost impossible to keep the personality of the first person from intruding itself.

When active operations began and permanent camp was broken up for good, this writer, with a few others, was detailed to go with the wagons and superintend the cooking which was done by colored servants belonging to officers and soldiers of the regiment. This detail was not agreeable to the feelings of the writer and he expressed as much to the Sergeant who brought him the detail. This the Sergeant reported to the Captain, who sent for the writer to appear before him. The Captain explained that it was necessary for some one to go, in whom they had confidence, and who was not a very able bodied man. "Very well," was the reply, "I will go, of course. It is a soldier's duty to go wherever he is ordered, but if I do not like it I am coming back here and report to you." He said all right and I took my detail from Assistant Adjutant General Dean and left for the rear. This Captain was Captain Chatham, a young man from Abbeville, who was well liked as an officer and as a man. He was afterwards mortally wounded by the same ball that wounded me and permanently disabled me as a soldier. If every gun fired by the enemy had been as fatal to our ranks the Confederate army would soon have been nowhere. I remained with the wagons about ten days, having really a very comfortable time, though slightly exposed to the fire of the enemy for a little while at Resaca. All the while that I was with the wagons it seemed as though I was out of place and that a burden was pressing upon me which grew heavier every day, and that I must go back to my company to get rid of a weight which was becoming well nigh intolerable. So one pleasant afternoon about the middle of May I spoke to Captain Sullivan, of Edgefield, Quarter-Master, and told him that I wanted to go back to my company. "Well," he said in that quiet, easy way habitual with him, "you may as well go." The burden was lifted at once and I felt that I was going home. I took my knapsack and haversack, and in an hour's time reported to Captain Chatham and took my place in line. I found them in line of battle at the time; but, indeed, they were always, or nearly always in line of battle from the beginning of that campaign to its close. A few days after this the feeling came upon me that I would be wounded soon, but that it would not kill me. I mentioned it to my brother, Sergeant Chapman, who was with me; mentioned it several times. He said that he had never felt any such sensations in all his three years' experience of the war. Every day for a week or ten days before the time arrived I could feel the fatal moment drawing nearer and nearer, as sensibly as the eye can perceive any object moving before it. At last on Sunday night, the night of the 29th of May, 1864, it came. On Saturday the 28th Granberry's Texas brigade had a sharp encounter with the enemy. Manigault's brigade relieved them and took their position, and all day Sunday we lay in presence of the enemy near enough to hear a loud voice speaking across the intervening distance. While lving here I said to my brother, "Thomas, I'll get it soon, but it won't kill me." At about two or half past two that night as we were all lying down in line—some firing going on all the time—suddenly—it seemed to me quite near—a gun fired. The ball came diagonally across the line, passed through my right leg just above the ankle, tearing out the smaller bone, as I was lying on my left side; struck Captain Chatham near the pit of the stomach and lodged in his bowels. My first words spoken after I received the wound were: "Boys, I've got it;" the next, "O Lord, how it hurts!" I got up and tried to walk, but could not touch the right foot to the ground, but stood on the left, supported by the gun. Sergeant Mathis or Matthews, then said to me: "Mr. Chapman, lie down." I replied: "Take me to the rear." I knew that I was done for for that time. Billie Reese with his litter then came up. I was placed very carefully upon it and borne off. I asked Billy about my gun and told him that I wanted it properly taken care of and sent to the ammunition or arsenal wagon. "O," he says, "damn your gun we are after taking care of you now." Captain Chatham and myself were both carried back together to a little house somewhere.

At this little house, just before I was lifted into the wagon to be transported to Marietta, I saw Captain W. S. Peterson for the last time. He had a few days before returned from re-cruiting service and immediately resumed command of his company. He was afterwards killed at Atlanta in one of Hood's fool-hardy efforts to carry Sherman's works by storm. Captain Chatham was alive when I left him, but he died that evening or night.

A few days before I was wounded and my military service—service in the field—closed forever, we had a fight at New Hope Church. As we marched down the road towards the church, which was quite near, taking note of what a clean, pleasant place it was, I remarked to my comrades: "Boys, this would be a mighty pretty place for a fight." Soon we were halted and marched down to the right in the woods, and began to throw up breastworks. A sharp engagement soon ensued, in which the Federals engaged were severely pun-ished. Our brigade was not actually engaged, though it was under fire. The Federals called this engagement the "Battle of Pumpkin Vine Creek;" we called it the "Battle of New Hope Church." I suppose there was a pumpkin vine creek somewhere about. Long after the war a monument was erected to commemorate the career of some New York Regi-ment, and engraved upon it were the names of all the battles in which the regiment had been engaged during the war, with the losses sustained in each. The getters up of the monument were very well pleased with the whole concern, until they came to Pumpkin Vine Creek, in which battle the regiment had sustained very heavy loss, heavier, indeed, than it had sustained in any other battle. But Pumpkin Vine Creek! They could not stand the name! The idea of suffering so much at Pumpkin Vine Creek! They could not stand it. At length they happily discovered that the Confederates had given the name of the Battle of New Hope Church to this en-gagement. This name was adopted and the monument stands with the name of New Hope Church engraved upon it.

From Marietta I was carried to Atlanta and placed in Gilmer Hospital, which was in charge of Dr. Michel, of Char-leston. My ward was under Dr. Rutherford, of Kentucky, a kind-hearted, good man, to whom I am under many obligations for courtesies shown in bringing me books, and in other ways. Books! Books! How hungry I was for books! What a glorious time I dreamed of having when I could get home and find myself amongst my books once more! In hospital I devoured everything in the shape of books that I could get hold of. Some kind lady brought the life of Daniel Webster; and some one gave me a copy of Young's Night Thoughts. That is a grand book. Though over two hundred years old, it is as fresh and good to-day as it was when it was first published. From that book more pithy sayings have gone into the common English speech, and have become the property of the thought and language of the people than from any other printed in the English language, except the Bible, and that is not originally an English book.

The hospitals remained at Atlanta until the approach of the combatants necessitated a removal to Forsyth.

Here I must be permitted to correct a statement made by General Howard in his account of this campaign. He says it rained almost incessantly during the month of May. In fact it rained very little during May; but it rained day and night during June. All through the month of June, 1864, I was lying on my back in the hospital tent, listening to the wearisome clang of iron and machinery at the Confederate workshops, which were not far off, and watching the steady down pour of rain. It was June and not May, General Howard, during which there was a steady down pour of rain almost without cessation. There was, however, one tremendous fall of rain in the early part of the night of the 9th of May, to which I was exposed. And that was very nearly all the rain that fell during May; but through June it fell day and night, nearly all the time.

On the 10th of August I received a furlough for sixty days. The hospital was then at Forsyth. From Forsyth we had to go to Macon, at which place we were delayed just 23 hours. At Macon we saw Stoneman and his raiders, who had recently been captured and were then about to take the train for Charleston. They were an insolent looking set of fellows, and their appearance, deportment, and general manner inspired this writer with no worse feeling than a very natural and laudable desire to kick them. From Augusta we had to pass through Branchville, Orangeburg, and Columbia on the way home. I had heard of the good deeds of that noble lady, Mrs. Rowe, and at Orangeburg I was so happy as to see her come on board with baskets of provisions for the hungry soldiers. Being convalescent after a sojourn in hospital of a little over ten weeks, I was always hungry. As soon as I saw Mrs. Rowe's benevolent face I smiled and bowed to her. She came to me at once, opened her basket, and gave me to eat until I was ashamed to eat any more, and thought that I must leave something for some other sufferer. That night I slept at the Wayside Hospital, in Columbia, not the Ladies' Hospital, and left more hungry in the morning than when I arrived there at night. On the 13th of August I arrived at home safe, and found all well and at peace. The clang of arms was not heard in that section, (Mount Enon) though some small part of the Confederate Army, cavalry, camped for a day and night only a few miles away. The Federal Cavalry that did so much devilment in the lower part of Edgefield and Newberry, did not come nearer than thirty miles of us. I laid aside the weapons of carnal warfare forever, and when the time comes to go to my eternal home, I think I can say with truth, that, whatever my feelings may have been and are towards the Yankees, I have never killed nor hurt one of them.

But I have written enough, and more than enough, the reader may very properly think of my own personal adventures during the comparatively short time in which I was in the field, though the whole term of my service was over eighteen months. My excuse must be that as men grow old they become garrulous.

XXV.

THE SEVENTH REGIMENT.

As already stated the volunteers from Edgefield were mostly embodied in the Nineteenth and Seventh Regiments. Those in the Nineteenth went West and were in all the campaigns and battles in Kentucky, Tennessee, Alabama, Mississippi, and elsewhere disastrous or fortunate; and those who endured or survived so long were with Johnston at the final surrender. Some were in the Twenty-fourth which also went West. Those in the Seventh were early sent to Virginia and shared in all the glories and disasters that befell Lee's veterans from the first fight at Bull Run to the closing scenes around Richmond and the falling of the curtain at Appomattox.

The story of that regiment as told by one who was in it and part of it, almost from the first until very nearly the close now lies before me, and from it I propose to condense briefly and relate its history. It was organized at Camp Butler, S. C., April 15th, 1861, to serve for twelve months; Thomas G. Bacon, Colonel; Robert Fair, Lieutenant Colonel; Emmet Seibles, Major. It was amongst the first to go to Virginia and with the Second, Third, and Eighth it formed a brigade under M. L. Bonham, afterwards under J. B. Kershaw. This regiment was not engaged at the battle of Bull Run, First Manassas, though under artillery fire. The writer of the sketch, from which we draw, enlisted for the war in a re-enlisted company (M), of which E. Jerry Goggans was elected Captain on the 24th of March, 1862, and joined the regiment on the Peninsula. On the Peninsula they were under command of General J. B. Magruder until the arrival of General J. E. Johnston. They were near, but not engaged in the battle of Williamsburg. On the 12th of May, 1862, the regiment was re-organized. At an election for field officers held on the 13th, D. Wyatt Aiken was elected Colonel; Elbert Bland, Lieutenant Colonel; and —— White, Major. This regiment was in all the campaigns of the Peninsula and around Richmond under Magruder and Johnston and Lee. They were in the desperate conflict at Malvern Hill, where Lieutenant J. R. Bouknight was killed

They were in the invasion of Maryland, fording the Potomac where it was about 400 yards wide. Some soldiers stripped naked in order to keep their clothes dry; most of them only pulling off their pants and drawers, keeping on their shirts; some only rolled up their breeches, and these got their clothes wet, as the water came up higher than they could roll their breeches.

In Maryland they met many friends and some foes. The friends would smile and wave their handkerchiefs, and a smile from a lovely girl was very charming. The enemies would close their doors as the Confederates passed, grin and make faces at them through the windows. As they passed Frederick City great demonstrations were made by both friends and foes—some ladies brought pails of water; some milk, some bread, some waved handkerchiefs, and Confederate flags, while others waved Union flags from the windows and held their noses as the Southerners passed. "A Georgia Major, inspired by the occasion and by liquor was riding along the lines and speaking. He was calling the attention of the citizens to the grand, invincible army of the South. As he passed Kershaw's brigade he said: 'I'm a Georgian, but I give to South Carolina the honor of beginning this struggle for liberty?' We cheered him and he passed on."

This regiment was at the taking of Harper's Ferry and played an important part in that enterprise. They were at the battle of Sharpsburg, where Colonel Aiken fell, shot through the lungs, and the regiment lost 169 killed and wounded, being half that went into action. Company M lost 17 killed and wounded out of 29 that were present on the field of battle. Major White was killed in this battle. After crossing the Potomac at Winchester on the return from Maryland after the battle of Sharpsburg, Lieutenant Colonel Bland took command of the regiment. He had been wounded at Savage Station and was not at Sharpsburg. J. S. Hard, senior Captain, became Major. He was afterwards killed at Chickamauga.

I am tempted to give here large extracts from this Diary of Sergeant J. J. McDaniel, of company M, as personal narratives always have great charms for me; but I am compelled to forego that pleasure. I yield, however, to the temptation to give a description of "winter quarters."

"The Seventh Regiment remained encamped near Fredericksburg from the time of the battle of the 13th of December till the
10th of January, 1863. On that day McLaw's Division moved
back some six miles from town, where we could obtain wood
plentifully. For where a division encamps during the winter
in a cold climate, it takes but a little while to clear large
fields, leaving not a tree, where so lately waved a large forest.
Our brigade was placed in the midst of a dense forest, the
regiments composing it being crowded together closer than
usual. Here we went regularly into winter quarters, and I
will describe here the appearance of some of our quarters.
With the exception of a very few officers we had no wall
tents; but a simple fly, which is a piece of canvass stretched
across a ridge pole, generally raised on two forks as high as
you could reach, so as to be convenient to hang up articles.
We often run our waist belts around the pole, buckling them for
a 'rack,' or swing for our guns, and these in their turn serving
to hang clothes upon and other articles of camp equipage. The
ends of the canvass we pegged to the ground on each side,
some six or seven feet from the upright forks, leaving the
tent open at both ends, with but little inside. To obviate this
inconvenience most of the messes built log pens 3 or 4 feet
high, and put the fly on top of this pen, which, when daubed
with mud, formed an excellent wall to exclude the rigor of
the winter. To complete the tent a chimney must now be
built. This is first made of sticks and afterwards daubed with
mud. Many being too lazy to build their chimney high
enough with sticks, obtained empty flour barrels, which they
set on top to lengthen out the funnel. These generally burnt
up, as they could not be daubed or plastered with mud to
shield them. It was no uncommon thing to hear a passer-by
cry out to the inmates, 'Your barrel is on fire.' But there are
other kinds of tents or quarters which some build without any
canvass. These resemble the roof of a house, and are made by
leaning poles or boards against the ridge pole at an angle of
about 45 degrees, and covering these with leaves and dirt, form
a very warm tent. Others again, when they are camped on
the side of a hill, cut out a tent in the side of the hill, making
solid walls of earth, and thus literally, Esquimaux fashion,
burrowing under ground. These excel all others in warmth.

"The next question after the tent is finished is how shall we sleep? for it is unhealthy to sleep on the ground, with nothing but your bedding under you, though some do it. The plan generally adopted is to drive up four forks some 2 feet high, form a scaffold, and cover this with small poles, upon which make your bed. This seems pretty rough at first, as soldiers don't have bedding enough to make the poles soft, yet in a few nights they would not exchange them for feather beds.

"The amusements and employments of our soldiers while in winter quarters were various. The inclemency of the weather during this winter in Virginia, was such that for weeks we did not drill. There were many heavy falls of snow, generally followed by rain. Two or three days after a heavy fall of snow the country for miles around would be full of soldiers hunting rabbits. When they would get on one's track in the snow, they would be almost sure to 'jump' him, and then he was almost sure to be caught, for, hindered on one hand by the deep snow, and, headed on all sides by soldiers, he was soon captured. I have known some exciting races.

"Another great sport was snow balling. Frequently when you showed your head outside of your tent you would be saluted with a volley of snow balls, and if you were not disposed to join in the fight your best policy would be to double-quick out of danger. I have frequently seen one regiment arrayed against another in these snow ball battles, led by their respective officers. In fact, I have seen two brigades meet in these bloodless contests, each man having a haversack full of ready-made snow balls. In such a battle the air is white with the flying missiles, darting sportively through the contending ranks.

"Other favorite sports were the various games of town ball. But I am sorry to say that many spent most of their time at cards, playing and betting on games of chance. I have known soldiers paid off 2 or 3 months' wages, and before night lose it all gambling. How much more profitably it would be to them to spend their time in reading some religious book or tract, and then save their money, character, and morals.

"Nothing of an exciting nature occurred for some time to break the dull monotony of camp life in winter quarters. We received a daily mail from Richmond, together with the daily papers, which served as a source of instruction and a means of employing profitably much of our time. The 'Dispatch,' 'Whig,' 'Examiner,' and 'Sentinel' were eagerly sought to learn the latest news. We paid for each of these papers mostly 15 cents, sometimes less and frequently more. We sometimes formed clubs of eight or ten, which would enable the club to read all the dailies at a small cost to each member. The Illustrated Southern News was the favorite weekly, in which we received a likeness and history weekly of some of our distinguished generals. We also received a great many religious papers and tracts, sent by the various religious associations for that purpose throughout the Confederacy. These, like bread cast upon the waters, will doubtless be gathered after many days. Their fruits in part were seen in the revivals which followed in the spring. . . . Our camp had the appearance of a busy workshop on cold winter evenings. You could see the soldiers coming and going in all directions, carrying wood for the night, and the sound of many axes resounded throughout the camp.

"Our regiment picketed at Fredericksburg. When it came our turn to go we would stay a week and quarter in the houses around the town. We picketed up the river, near a mile above town, opposite Falmouth, a small place on the north bank of the Rappahannock. The Yankees were stationed on that bank and we on the south. By agreement the pickets did not fire at each other across the river near Fredericksburg. For awhile they exchanged papers, and the Yankees would swap coffee for tobacco. The means by which this traffic was conducted was a very small boat into which they put the articles, and then arranging sails it was carried over by the winds. The Yankee officers captured one that some of ours sent over called the 'Body Louse'. They stated in their account of it that they would send it to Washington to be placed in the patent office as a curiosity."

But winter quarters passed away; and the campaign of 1863, with all its battles and bloodshed, began about the middle of April. In May of this year was fought the battle of Chancellorsville, where Stonewall Jackson was killed, a loss from which the Confederacy never recovered. The writer of the Diary from which we are reading says: "Chancellorsville,

which consisted of a large house used as a hotel and latterly
as a female boarding school, was all in flames when he saw it.
It had been set on fire by our shells. This was Hooker's
headquarters, and report says that while leaning against a
piazza post it was knocked down by a cannon ball, precipi-
tating him to the ground. He villianously retained several
ladies in the house, saying to them that General Lee would
not fire on the house while they were in it. The Richmond
Dispatch gave the names of the ladies, and a full account of
it. They plead with the brutal coward, telling him that
General Lee would not sacrifice a victory for the sake of a
few ladies—that there was too much at stake—the cause of
the entire Confederacy. Yet he would not let them go till the
house was in flames, and then he had to move his own carcass
to a safer place.'' Some wounded soldiers were burned to
death in the house, and many in the woods which took fire
from Jackson's artillery.

It would be a pleasure to give the sergeant's account of this
battle in full, and of the march of the army into Pennsylvania
and of the battle of Gettysburg, but want of space forbids.

The writer of the Diary was wounded at Gettysburg—shot
clear through the body, the ball passing through the lungs.
As soon as he was able to travel he was sent home, leaving
the army on the 2nd of July, 1863. He returned to it again,
arriving there on the 19th of July, 1864, having been absent a
little over one year. His Diary contains an account of the
movements of the army and of the battles in which his regiments were engaged during his absence. After his return he
served faithfully, continuing his record until the 28th of
December, 1864, when he was honorably discharged from the
army on account of his wound, which, it was considered, entirely disabled him for further military service. He left
Richmond on the 29th of December, 1864, and arrived at
home on Monday, the 2nd of January, 1865. Having been
wounded at Gettysburg, he was not with his regiment when it
was sent to the assistance of Bragg at Chickamauga, nor
when it passed through Middle and East Tennessee on the
return to Virginia.

The Diary is well written, and could it be printed and published, it would make a valuable contribution to the history of

the war. It portrays faithfully the spirit which animated the men in the ranks.

But perhaps enough has been written in this book about the war. In that time of fiery trial, as far as is known to this writer, Edgefield did her part nobly and well.

We will go back for a little while to an earlier period in our history and give a brief account of one of the dead towns of Edgefield and its father and builder.

We will give first, however, the following papers from the Edgefield Advertiser of July 31st, 1861, and June 11th, 1862·

SOLDIERS' RELIEF ASSOCIATION.

A meeting of the ladies of Edgefield and its vicinity was held at the Masonic Hall on Monday morning at 10 o'clock. The meeting was called to order and Mrs. J. A. Bland was called to the Chair. After stating the object of the meeting the following preamble and resolutions were offered by Mrs. Captain Bland and unanimously adopted:

WHEREAS, As our country is involved in all the turmoil and strife of horrid war, and all that is dear to us is at stake.

Resolved, That we, the ladies of Edgefield, do desire to aid our brave and suffering soldiers, so far as it is in the province of woman to do.

Resolved, 2nd. That we form ourselves into a Soldiers' Relief Association.

Resolved, 3rd. That the object of this Association shall be the procuring and making of all articles necessary for the comfort of all the troops without discrimination who represent Edgefield.

Resolved, 4th. That each lady on paying the sum of one dollar, or its equivalent, shall become a member of the Association, and entitled to all privileges.

Resolved, 5th. That a committee be appointed to nominate officers for the Association.

Resolved, 6th. That the officers consist of a President, Vice-President, Secretary, Treasurer, and twelve Directors.

A committee was appointed and the following officers nominated and unanimously elected:

President—Mrs. M. L. Bonham.

Vice-President—Mrs. J. A. Bland.

Secretary—Mrs. R. H. Mims.

Treasurer—Mrs. Joseph Abney.

Directresses—Mrs. N. L. Griffin, Mrs. William P. Butler, Mrs. H. R. Spann, Mrs. E. Bland, Mrs. Mary Miles, Mrs.

John Maloy, Mrs. John Huiet, Mrs. Henry T. Wright, Mrs.
Lewis Jones, Mrs. A. G. Teague, and Miss Cornelia Jones.
The meeting then adjourned to meet once a week.

PRESENTATION OF A FLAG TO THE HOLCOMBE LEGION.

Mrs. Pickens, whose maiden name this Legion bears, has
presented them with a beautiful flag and a beautiful letter
accompanying it, as follows:

Officers and Soldiers of the Holcombe Legion:

I can find no words with which to thank your gallant
Colonel for the compliment he has paid me, in giving to his
noble command the name I once bore; but I trust the presentation of this standard may in some small measure testify my
deep appreciation of the honor conferred upon me. In seeking to render this ensign worthy of your valor and devotion, I
have placed first among its devices the armorials of your beloved State, the glorious palmetto and crescent, emblems consecrated to noble daring and high resolve, for they waved in
our harbor when Carolina stood alone in this momentous
contest, and floated over that heroic battery which threw its
steady and victorious fire into the arrogant "Star of the West."
I remember with pride that your commander, Colonel Stevens,
had charge of that battery, and thus early in the war established a claim to Carolina's grateful remembrance. While I
give into your honorable keeping the spotless escutcheon of
your State, I look with eager confidence toward that future,
when your heroism shall achieve for it a new lustre and renown.

The dates inscribed 1776 and 1860 are eloquent with mean-
ing. The first commemorates our disenthralment from a
foreign foe, the second speaks to you of that glad hour when
we threw off the tyranny of domestic wrong, and welcomed
the new birth of a higher freedom. If I have reversed the
Palmetto with the Lone Star of the "Imperial State of Texas,"
if I have thus sought to associate on your battleflag the two
devices which share the devotion of my own heart, you will
not blame me; you will remember the bloody struggle, the
Spartan endurance, the indomitable courage by which she won
her right to honor and independence; and the chivalric, heroic
blood of South Carolina which flowed at the Alamo will, to

the last day, challenge an admiring tribute from every son of her soil. I feel assured that the noble motto inscribed on this banner, "It is for the brave to die, but not to surrender"— is but the expression of the spirit which animates the breast of every soldier in your midst. Patriotism ranks with us, as with the ancients, first among virtues, and life is only worth keeping that we may perform the duties belonging to it.

> "Death comes but once to all,
> Then how can man die better,
> Than facing fearful odds
> For the ashes of his fathers,
> And the temple of his gods."

And now I cannot resist telling you how anxiously I will follow your every movement; what pride I will feel in your moments of victory and success; and I will grieve if reverses befall you. I earnestly pray that God will keep each one of you in His charge, and that the fortune of war may give you all you require, an opportunity to show yourselves a legion of heroes. LUCY HOLCOMBE PICKENS.

XXVI.

HAMBURG.

Hamburg and its founder have already been mentioned in these pages, but the following account, which is copied verbatim from the Atlanta Journal, and for the exact accuracy of which this writer is not responsible, but which he believes to be very nearly correct, gives some particulars of interest which ought to be included in a history of Edgefield:

" 'The dead towns of Georgia' have been the subject of a work of great interest and unusual merit, but as far as is known, 'the dead towns of South Carolina' have not been touched upon.

"Mr. William C. Sibley, President of the Sibley Mills of Augusta, and a citizen that the Electric City prizes as one of its most valued, was in Atlanta Thursday night. (This was in June or July, 1891.) He was in a reminiscent strain, and told me some facts about the history of Hamburg, the desolate city now populated by from one hundred to one hundred and fifty lazy vagrant negroes, just across the river from Augusta.

"He knew it when it was the centre of commerce for four States, when hundreds upon hundreds of wagons each day from Georgia, Upper and Lower South Carolina, North Carolina, and Tennessee would roll into its streets loaded down with articles of commerce.

"Along in the early thirties Augusta had an old German citizen by the name of Schultz. The city was at that time a trading centre for hundreds of miles of the sourrounding country. Schultz was one of the wealthiest citizens. He erected and owned three brick buildings on the north side of Broad street, just below the monument, which are standing until this day.

"They were known as the Bridge Bank buildings, because, presumably, was a bank located there which was run by old man Schultz and McKinney. Schultz also owned the bridge that spanned the Savannah and connected Georgia and South Carolina.

"The bank failed, as it owed money to Augusta; through

some lawsuit the city managed to get possession of the bridge. This angered Schultz, and in a fit of pique he vowed that he would kill Augusta's trade and build up Hamburg. He went before the South Carolina Legislature, and on the strength of his representations of the feasibility of establishing direct trade between Hamburg, S. C., and Hamburg, Germany, borrowed $50,000.

"This was in the year '32' and in one night, where the night before there was a howling wilderness, Schultz had up the fronts of a row of houses. It was the terminus of the South Carolina railroad, the first railroad of a hundred miles in length that the world ever saw, and was on the side of the Savannah river where the channel was the deepest.

"Hamburg grew to be the most important trading town in the interior of South Carolina, and its business continually increased till 1848. 'When I first went there,' said Mr. Sibley, 'Hamburg received 70,000 cales of cotton, the remarkable part of which was that 60,000 of them were in on wagons.'

"'To show you what a town Hamburg was at that time,' Mr. Sibley continued, 'the city built a plank road from Hamburg to Edgefield, a distance of twenty-six miles. Along about November and December the streets would be so crowded with the wagons of the country people from four States that frequently people would have to walk four or five blocks before finding a place to cross.

"'On the outskirts of the city the wagoners would strike their tents, and frequently there would be as many as five or six hundred of them in compact at a time. The road going and coming for a distance of five or six miles would be literally jammed up with wagons, rendering it almost impossible to make more than a mile an hour.

"'Old Schultz was a genius,' said Mr. Sibley, smilingly, 'and, like a good many other men of profound brain, wouldn't pay his debts. He was the most plausible of talkers and the most industrious of workers. He had Hamburg laid out in beautiful streets and Schultz's Hill was a park of great beauty.'

"A great many of these improvements were made with the $50,000 which Schultz borrowed from the South Carolina Legislature, and which, by the way, he never paid back. Schultz came very near owing everybody he came in contact with, and invariably failed to pay them. One day he had about twenty Irishmen at work in front of his store and one of his creditors told him, 'Mr. Schultz, I don't see how you can afford to hire these men when you owe me and everybody else.' 'Well sir,' said the German, 'I sacrifice my private interests to the public good.'

"There were two causes for Hamburg's downfall. One of them was the building of the Greenville and Columbia Railroad and the other the cutting of the first Augusta canal.

"It was the first intention of the railroad builders to make Hamburg one of the termini of the railroad, and they offered to do so if Hamburg would make a subscription of $50,000, but in those days there was great prejudice against railroads, and the citizens of Hamburg were afraid that it would take away their wagon trade, so the road was built to Greenville, and fully one-half of Hamburg's trade was taken away.

"Then Augusta got Hamburg's cotton that used to come from up the river, because coming down the canal took away the great danger of shooting the rapids. Hamburg gradually grew from bad to worse, and finally, about the time of the war, its sole population was composed of negroes.

"Now it is nothing but almost a howling wilderness. Where once the busy merchant sold his wares a lazy negro skulks; where fine residences, that beatiful Southern women graced, once stood, now negro ramshackles, with dirty pickaninnies playing on the porch, are to be seen. The well-kept streets are a mass of weeds, and Schultz's beautiful park, under whose trees many beautiful tales of love have been told, is now the resort of negro pic-nickers.

"The town has been through riots and fires, and no house that has burned up or blown down has ever been replaced.

"Hamburg is surely an evidence of what narrow-minded, illiberal citizens can do. It now serves but one purpose. It is the battle ground for game cocks and bull dogs.

J. C. S."

Let the people of Edgefield congratulate themselves that Hamburg is no longer in their County.

The following additional information in regard to Mr. Schultz was derived from another source: Mr. Schultz, the founder of Hamburg, was a native of Hamburg in Germany. When about nineteen years of age he was taken prisoner by Bonaparte and released upon the promise of not bearing arms any more against the French, which he violated and was re-captured. Napoleon, not caring to put a mere boy to death, gave him liberty to emigrate to America. He came to Augusta and first followed boating to Savannah. After Augusta took possession of his bridge Mr. Schultz then went before the Legislature of South Carolina and promised, if they would help him, to build a town that would rival Augusta. The State must have failed to fulfill some of its promises, for after Schultz was ruined he was often seen in Columbia during the sessions of the Legislature with his long overcoat dangling around his heels and the mark of Cain upon his brow. After Augusta took possession of his bridge he built a toll gate on the Carolina side and collected his tolls from there. When the courts decided the case against him Mr. Schultz tried to commit suicide by firing a pistol in his mouth, but the bullet came out at his forehead, greatly disfiguring his face.''

Whether the State failed to keep any of its promises to Mr. Schultz or not, is not known to this writer, most probably not; but he was involved in a long lawsuit about his bridge, in which he was loser and he sank the State's $50,000. Hamburg was built as promised, and did for some years an immense business.

We have already seen that, in the early settlement of this country, some years before the founding and building of Augusta, on the site afterwards occupied by the town of Hamburg, was an important trading station, at which, for many years, a large business was carried on with the Indians up the river all the way to the mountains and beyond. Fort Moore was erected at that place for the protection of the trade. The building of Augusta, which town flourished and grew rapidly, drew off the trade from the Carolina side, and made the station insignificant as a trading post. Three-fourths of a century passed and Hamburg came into being through the energy of Mr. Schultz; lived and flourished, and became the focus of a great trade for many years; but it finally decayed and died through the force of the influences already mentioned, the cutting of the Augusta canal and the building of the Green-

ville and Columbia Railroad. Thus twice in the history of
the country has Augusta been largely instrumental in divert-
ing trade from the Carolina side and destroying the germ of a
city on the opposite side of the Savannah River.

Many years ago, going into Hamburg with wagons loaded
with cotton, we camped a short distance back on the uplands
on the Edgefield side, so that we could get into market as early
as possible. The sun rose clear and was shining bright and
clear in the uplands, but as we drove on we found the whole
valley of the river covered with a dense fog, and on that fog
was clearly and distinctly defined a white solar rainbow—no
colors. I saw the same, or a similar phenomenon, once on the
fog over the river as I walked down from Columbia to the
depot to take the cars for Newberry. In both cases the bow
was well defined and very distinct, white without colors,
having the same appearance as a lunar rainbow. The white
solar rainbow appears upon a dense fog; the lunar rainbow
upon falling rain. While writing the above a perfect solar
spectrum, with all the colors that an analysis of the sunlight
gives, has formed itself upon the floor of the room. A broken
piece of glass resting with one edge upon the window sill
outside, the upper edge leaning against the window pane
touches it in such a manner as to act like a prism forming a
perfect spectrum upon the floor with all the colors beautiful
and bright. (January 14th, 1892).

To what has already been written of Hamburg must be
added that by Act of the Legislature, passed December 17th,
1813, Henry Schultz and Lewis Cooper were authorized to
build a toll bridge across the Savannah River so as to connect
the two places, Augusta and Hamburg. The bridge was
already in process of erection when the Act was passed. This
bridge was re-chartered December 18th, 1830.

Inspection and warehouse for tobacco authorized to be
erected December 20th, 1821, on the same day lands and slaves,
and indeed all property in the town, by Act of the Legislature
were declared exempt from taxation for five years. The town
was incorporated December 19th, 1827.

The Bank of the State was authorized to establish a branch
at Hamburg December 18th, 1830, and in December 1832
the Solicitor was authorized to convey the State's interest

in Hamburg to Henry Schultz. The town was incorporated a second time, December 19th, 1835, and charter amended in 1837. The Bank of Hamburg chartered December 21, 1823, charter amended December 19th, 1835, and again December 21st, 1836.

There is a story or tradition connected with the history of Hamburg that, with propriety, might be related here, as it was a source of great amusement when it was first told. Doubtless there are many persons now living in the County of Edgefield who never have heard the expression: "The Gyascutus has broke loose." This, like many other slang phrases, such as "That's what's the matter with Hannah," had a great run for awhile, but suddenly died and dropped out of circulation, and passed into that dead region of limbo, where all unrealities are sure to go at some time.

The phrase had its being and birth as follows: Just after the close of the War with Mexico some volunteers from Virginia or North Carolina, who were under General Taylor in the army of the Rio Grande, undertook to make their way home on foot from Texas or from New Orleans. In all that Western country there were few, in fact, I believe no railroads at that time. They found travelling on foot very pleasant, as the weather was good, and they were soldiers and used to foot wear. When they reached Hamburg they found that they were short of funds, in fact, about out, with barely enough to carry them another day's journey. In this extremity they were compelled to resort to some very energetic measures to raise the wind. A caucus to consider ways and means was held, and they came to the conclusion that a tax to defray expenses must be levied upon the citizens of Hamburg and Augusta, and as many of the inhabitants of the adjoining country in Carolina and Georgia as they could reach. Accordingly they spent a day in Hamburg making preparations. They hired a large hall, gave out that they would have on exhibition there for one night, and for one night only, a very large, strange, and furious animal, such an one as had never been heard of nor seen in that part of the world before. They had caught it, they said, somewhere in the wilderness of the Mississippi swamps, one night when it invaded their camp. It had devoured two of their number and was in the act of

swallowing the third, a very large man, when the survivors
succeeded in lassoing the monster and binding it so strongly
that it could not move.   They had it firmly fastened in a
large car, or van, drawn by four of the strongest horses.   The
car would cross the Augusta bridge about 4 o'clock in the
afternoon and drive into town in good season to have all ready
for the show, which would open about 8 o'clock in the evening.   Of course there was great curiosity to see this wonderful
beast.   The news spread like wild fire over town and country,
and long before night the streets of Hamburg were packed and
jammed.   Such a crowd was never seen in that town before,
never has been since, and very probably will never be seen
there again.

Sure enough, about 4 in the afternoon the car made its appearance in Augusta in the street leading to the bridge, preceded by a single man on foot, making the air ring with the
shrill notes of a fife, playing the tune, "See, the conquering
hero comes."

In due time the car drove to the hall and drove into a closed
and covered shed in the rear; and the announcement was made
that at eight precisely the front door would be opened to the
anxious crowd for admission to see this greatest of curiosities
the world had ever produced.   In the mean time two men at
the door were kept busy selling tickets of admission to the
show.   The price was one dollar each.

The earth rolled on, the sun sank and set, and eight o'clock
came.   The door was opened and the crowd began to pour in.
The hall was well lighted, but there were very few seats.
But this made no difference, as there were no ladies present—
this strange, fierce animal not being considered altogether
proper for ladies to see.   Over the far end of the hall a curtain appeared to hang, on which was depicted a likeness of the
most uncouth creature ever seen, or that any imagination ever
conceived.   This was said to be a good likeness of the Gyascutus, which was the name of the monster supposed to be hidden in the rear.   The hall was soon packed tight, but the
large windows were open to the cool night air, so that there
was no danger of suffocation.   As the moment drew near for
the curtain to rise, so that the many eyes of the crowd might
see this greatest of the world's curiosities, suddenly a deep

growl was heard behind the curtain. This was succeeded by an awful roar, followed by a succession of screaming shrieks and hisses, more terrifying than any the lions and tigers and all the beasts of the jungle ever made. To say that the crowd was startled is saying nothing. Many began to move towards the door, some towards the windows, and not too soon, for suddenly a mighty uproar and noise of breaking and crashing timbers was heard, and the climax was reached when the show man, who was near the far end of the hall, cried out with a loud voice: "The Gyascutus is broke loose! The Gyascutus is broke loose!" You better believe the crowd dispersed speedily. In a short time, not only the hall, but the streets of Hamburg were almost entirely deserted. Some never stopped running until they were safe in Augusta. Some thought they could clear the Savannah at a leap, tried it, and landed safe in the mud on the Carolina side. In a little while the tumult subsided, and the night that followed was the quietest ever known in that part of the country.

In the morning an investigation was had; no damage was found done to the building, but in the rear the very ghost, and a dilapidated one, of a wagon or car was standing solitary and alone a broken wreck; the four fine horses had vanished and were very quietly standing in their stalls in Augusta and eating their oats; the Gyascutus had indeed broken loose and was never seen nor heard of any more, nor were those returned soldiers from the War with Mexico ever seen or found. They left with their pockets full of money, and were far away when the morning broke. Who were they? Perhaps some of Hamburg's own sons with some of the boys of Augusta on a lark.

Ah, old men, contemporaries of this present writer, do you feel sometimes, as he does, that there is no longer any fun in the world? Or is the world what it was then, and has the spirit of fun only evaporated from us? Does the Gyascutus ever break loose now?

XXVII.

FRANCIS HUGH WARDLAW

Member of the Secession Convention and one of the signers of the Ordinance of Secession.

Francis H. Wardlaw, son of James Wardlaw and Hannah Clarke Wardlaw, was born at Abbeville Court House, S. C., December 16th, 1800; was baptized by Rev. Robert P. Wilson, of the Presbyterian Church; went to the common English schools of Abbeville, taught by Francis Walker, William Sadler, Flinn, Clary, Hooper, James Curry, and Thomas Fulton. In 1812 he went to Willington, in Abbeville District, and there attended for two years Dr. Waddell's famous Classical Academy. He spent the year 1815 at home at Abbeville Court House, in studying arithmetic, algebra, trigonometry, and surveying, under Captain William Robertson, and in writing in the Clerk's office under his father, then Clerk of the Court for Abbeville District. He entered the South Carolina College April 13th, 1816, and graduated with first honor of his class in December, 1818. Read law in the office of A. Bowie, Esq., at Abbeville Court House, and was admitted to practice law at Charleston, January, 1822, and equity at Columbia, May, 1822. He settled at Edgefield near the end of February, 1822, and practiced law there in partnership with Whitfield Brooks until the fall of 1825; with William Garrett from 1826 to 1828; with D. L. Wardlaw from 1831 to 1841, and with William C. Morange from 1841 to 1846; was editor of a newspaper at Edgefield from March, 1829, to the spring of 1832; elected to the State Convention from Edgefield in 1832, and to the House of Representatives of South Carolina Legislature in 1834 and 1838; was partner of R. H. Spann's in 1850; was elected Chancellor December 3rd, 1850, and Judge in the Court of Appeals December 21st, 1859; delegate from Edgefield in the conventions of 1852 and 1860, being one of only four or five persons who were members of all three conventions above mentioned; 1832, 1852, and 1860.

He was married at "Airville" near Hamburg, in Edgefield District, Wednesday evening, April 22nd, 1835, to Ann

Gresham Lamar, daughter of Thomas Gresham Lamar and Martha Leland Cary, by Rev. Henry Reid, Presbyterian minister from Augusta. By this union he had seven children, three of whom died young. One son, Lieutenant T. Lamar Wardlaw, was killed at Fort Moultrie, July 17th, 1862, another son, Francis H. Wardlaw, died December 5th, 1887, at Edgefield where he was practicing law. One son and one daughter only are now living, Mrs. J. W. Hill, of Edgefield, and J. Lewis Wardlaw, of Fairfield County. Chancellor Wardlaw died at Columbia in the house of Major Theodore Stark, May 29th, 1861, and was buried at Edgefield Court House, South Carolina.

As a lawyer and judge of law I have heard this related of him: A decision of his was once quoted in a court at Westminister, the opposing counsel ridiculed the idea of resorting to South Carolina law as a precedent for England or English courts, whereupon the presiding Judge remarked that the decision in question was worthy of the highest respect and would do honor to the courts of any country.

JOHN E. BACON.

The writer of this history is indebted to Frank Leslie's illustrated newspaper and to Appleton's Biography for the following notice of Honorable John E. Bacon. Mr. Bacon, recently minister from the United States to Uruguay and Paraguay, was born at Edgefield, S. C., and is now between fifty-five and sixty years of age. (January, 1892) His family have been identified with the State of his birth from its earliest history, and members of it have enjoyed many offices of honor and trust. He was graduated with distinction at the South Carolina College in 1852, and was admitted to the Bar in 1854. He was sent to St. Petersburg as Secretary of Legation, and married there the youngest daughter of ex-Governor Pickens, then the Minister at that Court. He is an accomplished linguist, speaking French, Spanish, Italian, and Russian.

Mr. Bacon entered the Confederate Army in 1861, at the commencement of the war and served throughout the struggle, reaching the rank of Major. After the war, finding himself completely impoverished, he returned to the practice of his profession and was soon in the enjoyment of an unusually

ßarge and lucrative business.   In 1867 he was elected District
Judge for the District of Edgefield, and presided regularly
until deposed by the Federal Commander, and a "Military
Judge" was put in his place.   In 1872 he removed to Columbia, where he has ever since resided.   In that year he was
elected President of the largest Democratic Club in the city,
and was re-elected four consecutive times.   During this period
he was also a member and Secretary of the State Democratic
Executive Committee, and also a member of the County Executive Committee.

In 1878 Judge Bacon was sent to the Legislature for the
purpose of reopening the South Carolina College.   He was
made Chairman of the Committee on Education, and, by the
aid of his able colleagues and other experienced members, the
measure was put through, after a severe struggle, the bill
passing the Senate by the vote only of the distinguished President of that body.   Judge Bacon regards his connection with
the re-establishment of this college on a solid basis—whereby
the young men of the State can get a first class collegiate education for about the third of the cost of *ante-bellum* days—
with greater pride and satisfaction than any, indeed, all of the
acts of his life.

In 1884 Judge Bacon was elected a member of the State
Convention for the nomination of delegates to the National
Democratic Convention at Chicago and of Pesidential electors
and was himself nominated an elector and elected .

In 1885 he was appointed United States Minister by President Cleveland, at Montevideo, and in 1887 his salary was
almost doubled in consideration of able and meritorious services.   Upon the election of President Harrison he resigned
his office and returned to Columbia, where he died in the early
part of the year 1897.

JOSEPH ABNEY.

Joseph Abney was a native of Edgefield District, of the
Saluda side, and was born December 2nd, 1819, near the river
not far above what is now Herbert's Ferry, then Lorick's.
His father was John Abney, his mother Agatha Griffith.   His
mother was his father's second wife.   His father's father was
a Virginian, and among the first comers to that section of

country. His mother's people were of Welsh descent. The education of Joseph Abney was as good as it was possible for him to get in the schools and academies of the country. His father died when he was only three or four years old, and his mother married again, a Mr. Cadaway Clark, a kind, good man, who treated his step-sons, Joseph and John, with great kindness. Joseph Abney was not a graduate of a college, but he was a fairly good classical scholar and mathematician. He was a hard and diligent student and a natural orator. His command of language was so great, and he so far surpassed the other boys at school as a speaker, that he received the name of the orator, which he really deserved. After his education was completed as far as his limited means enabled him to carry it, he taught school to acquire money upon which to live while reading law, having chosen that profession as his business for life. He was quite successful as a teacher, winning the love and respect of his pupils. He read law at Abbeville in the office of Mr. Perrin, and had for a companion in his studies, a young man, who afterwards became eminent as a lawyer, as a soldier, and as a Judge—Samuel McGowan. He was admitted to practice law in Columbia in the year 1842; the same year and place in which his friend and companion, Samuel McGowan, was admitted. Henry R. Spann, another Edgefield lawyer, was admitted the same year.

After Mr. Abney was admitted he located at Edgefield Court House, the county seat of his native District. As a lawyer he was quite successful, building up a good and lucrative practice, which he held through life. When the war with Mexico came on, after the annexation of Texas, he volunteered, was elected Lieutenant, and served in the Palmetto Regiment as such until the close of the war. In the city of Mexico he was attacked by an enemy which was more fatal to our soldiers than the bullets of the Mexicans had ever been—the dysentery. He lay prostrated for many days, seemingly at the point of death, unconscious part of the time, and weak and helpless as a babe. He attributed his recovery to the faithful and careful nursing and attention of a good Catholic Priest, who sat by him for many hours at a time with his finger on the pulse of his wrist, administering ice. The good Priest graduated the quantity of ice given by the strength and rapidity of the pulse beats. If he felt the pulse growing too weak he would leave off the ice for awhile, and then when the fever rose to too great a height he would give the ice again.   In this way, and by careful nursing, the patient slowly won his way from the shadow of death back to life again.

After the war Mr. Abney returned to his home in Edgefield, and resumed the practice of the law.   A few years before the war he married Miss Susan Miller, a beautiful and accomplished woman, a lovely and amiable wife.   In the late war between the States he was again a volunteer in the service of the Confederate States, in which he held the rank of Major.

He died a few years after the war at his home at Edgefield, leaving a widow and two daughters surviving him.   His widow, a few years after his death, married T. S. Arthur, a lawyer of Greenville, who afterwards settled at Lexington, where she has since died.

Mr. Abney left no sons; there were two, Paul and Charles, born.   His daughter Agatha, who married Rev. Mr. Woodson, is living at their home in Edgefield where her father died. His daughter Eleanor is not living, not living in this world, but is, we hope, with her father and mother in a better. Sophie died young.

JOSEPH ABNEY—ADDITIONAL.

He was Second Lieutenant in the Palmetto Regiment, commanded by Colonel Pierce Butler, during the War with Mexico, and was severely wounded at the battle of Cherubusco.   Lieutenant Sumter was also wounded in the same battle, and though they were both wounded early in the engagement, yet they continued with their companies until the last shots were fired.

In the War of Secession Joseph Abney was appointed Major in the Provisional Army of the Confederate States, and was placed in command of the Second Battalion of South Carolina Sharpshooters of three companies, commanded by Captains ReO. Chisolm, Joseph Blythe Allston, and Henry Buist.   Appointed July, 1862.

This battalion was united with the Charleston Battalion under Lieutenant Colonel P. C. Gaillard, and formed the Twenty-seventh South Carolina Infantry.   Major Abney was in all the battles around Petersburg, until he was wounded at Drury's Bluff, in the attack by Beauregard on Butler. The Twenty-seventh South Carolina Infantry was in Johnson Hagood's Brigade, in the division of Major General Hoke, of North Carolina, Longstreet's corps.

He died at his home in Edgefield, at the Court House, in the year 1869.

From the Edgefield Advertiser, February 12th, 1862, I glean the following list of officers of the Twenty-Second Regiment, South Carolina Volunteers:

Colonel—Joseph Abney, of Edgefield.

Lieutenant Colonel—S. D. Goodlet, Spartanburg.

Major—T. C. Watkins, Anderson.

Quarter Master—G. A. Taylor.

Commissary—W. C. Hillhouse.

Adjutant—P. B. Crocker.

Surgeon—Not yet appointed.

Assistant Surgeon—John B. Abney.

Sergeant Major—George B. Lake.

Assistant Quarter Master—J. Haltiwanger.

Assistant Commissary—C. A. Barry.

LIST OF COMPANIES.

Company A—Captain, Cicero Adams, Edgefield.

Company B—Captain, J. Wheeler, Spartanburg.

Company C—Captain, W. W. Hendrix, Spartanburg.

Company D—Captain, ——— O'Connell, Pickens.

Company E—Captain, M. Hilton, Lancaster.

Company F—Captain, J. M. Stewart, Pickens.

Company G—Captain, James Orr, Anderson.

Company H—Captain, Jeff. Barton, Greenville.

Company I—Captain, H. Millhouse, Lexington.

Company K—Captain, M. S. Messer, Pickens.

From the Edgefield Advertiser of June 4th, 1862:

"We understand that Colonel Joseph Abney, late of the Twenty-second South Carolina Regiment, has received the appointment of Major of Sharpshooters from General Pemberton. He goes to superintend the organization of the new corps."

JOSEPH QUATTLEBAUM.

It is impossible for the compiler of this history to give even the very briefest biographical sketch of all the worthy dead of Edgefield, who lived as private citizens. But now and then there are some so worthy or so remarkable for some characteristic, that it were a pity to pass them by without some record. Among such may be numbered Dr. Joseph Quattlebaum, of Ridge Spring, who has been justly mentioned as an old time Southern gentleman. He d:ed on the 6th of January, 1892, leaving a widow and seven children. One of his daughters, Mrs. Edwards, a lovely, amiable, and accomplished lady, lived with her husband at Newberry for a few years, but returned to Ridge Spring, where they were living at the time of Dr. Quattlebaum's death.

Dr. Quattlebaum was a native of Lexington County, but lived for a long time at Ridge Spring. He was a good man, genial and warmhearted, and a Christian. He was a loyal friend, steadfast, and true; chivalrous, hospitable, and generous. He was emphatically good company, being gentle and genial, and of unfailing humor and good nature. This writer met him a few times in the latter part of his life, and was much drawn to him.

WILLIAM WALKER.

Few men reach, and few can hope to reach, the great age of Mr. William Walker, who died on Friday, the 15th of January, 1892, at the age of ninety years. He was a life-long and very earnest Methodist. If he could have written the recollections of his lifetime what a book he might have made. He could have given us distinct recollections for eighty years and a little more. He could have carried us back to the year 1810. He could have carried us through all the intervening years and told us many items of interest of both public and private history. How much is included in the words, "He was a life-long and very earnest Methodist." Four score and ten, and the larger number of those years spent in the love and service of God.

He died at his old home five miles north of Edgefield, and was buried near thereby on Saturday, the day following his death.

XXVIII.

AFTER THE WAR—RECONSTRUCTION.

In a book from which a brief quotation has already been made, entitled "The South Since the War," by Sidney Andrews, published in 1866, there is something said of the negro situation, which it may be well to quote before we enter upon the history of reconstruction. The writer says (he writes in Orangeburg): "The district above this, Edgefield, has also an undesirable name. At Columbia I heard two delegates speaking of affairs therein. They admitted that many negroes had been beaten to death during the summer, and said the planters were very slow in discovering what emancipation meant. Among the negroes whom I met at Orangeburg was one from Edgefield, who showed me a back not yet healed from a severe whipping given him in August." (This story may be true, for this writer knew a negro man in Edgefield, he is living yet, knew him from his birth, and he never was whipped in all his life while a slave, but who was very severely beaten, for what offense, if any, is not known to the writer, some time during the year following the close of the war.)

The same author, Mr. Sidney Andrews, thus writes of the military murder of Calvin Crozier at Newberry· "In Newberry District a case has recently occurred, in which the negroes took justice into their own hands. It appears that in a car which was standing on the track, were three or four women and two Rebel soldiers—one of them a Texan. A negro Sergeant had occasion to enter the car and was roughly ordered out by the Texan. He responded to the effect that he knew his own business and should mind it. The two Rebel soldiers thereupon seized him and undertook to thrust him out. He resisted and the Texan stabbed him, inflicting what was supposed to be a mortal wound. In an hour the two Rebels were caught by the negro soldiers of the regiment to which the Sergeant belonged, and in three hours more the Texan had been tried by drum-head court martial, shot and buried. The other Confederate escaped while they were taking him up for trial, and will not be retaken."

A few more extracts must be made from this amusing book. Of education the writer says: "Education never was general in the State, and for the last two or three years it has been almost entirely neglected. The ignorance of the great body of the whites is a fact that will astonish anybody conversant with the middle classes of the North. Travel where you will, and that sure indication of modern civilization, the school house is not to be found. Outside half a dozen of the larger towns I have not seen a dozen in over six hundred miles of travel. A few persons express the hope that the Legislature will do something to set the college once more at work; but, generally speaking, the indifference of the masses to the whole subject of education is as startling as it is painful."

Of the language used by the common people he says: "A South Carolinian never thinks or guesses, but 'lows or reckons. He hasn't got no use for a Yankee no how, and thinks him a no count fellow, or a low down trifling cuss of whom he would like to get shet, and he will feel obligated to you if you will help him out of his ill-fortunate situation; and dog-gone you, as you are not an ill-conditioned man, and as he refugeed from the Yankees he will take a little whiskey with you, dry so."

Is it possible for a stranger, or for one unfriendly, to tell, or even to see the truth about others? Sympathy is a great quickener and enlightener of the intellect. The statement above quoted in regard to education is entirely false. The writer of this history was born and reared in the country, many miles from any city; at least a dozen miles from the nearest county seat of any county; twenty-six miles from the county seat of his own county; four miles from the post office, with only a weekly mail, which was carried by a rider on horse-back—and yet there were schools every year open the year round for instruction in all the elementary branches of an English education. In 1835 there was an academy or high school founded at Mount Enon, remote from any town, city, or village, in which a good classical education could be had, as the school had for its principal and head-master one who was a fine scholar, a graduate of Yale College and a native of the county in which the school was. Schools in the same neighborhood were kept open and in active operation during the

whole war.   There is no reason to believe that this part of the
State was more highly favored than others.

As to the military murder of the Taxan soldier at Newberry,
for it was indeed and in truth a murder, it was not shown, nor
could it be shown at the drum-head court martial that he had
acted in an unjustifiable manner.   The ladies in the car were
under his protection and the negro Sergeant was an intruder,
and being an intruder Crozier had certainly the right to put
him out if he could, since he would not go without it.   Calvin
Crozier was a hero, and his death was one of the finest instances
of self-sacrifice of which I have ever heard or read.   It was
some time after the difficulty was over before any arrest was
made, and then the colored soldiers arrested the wrong man, a
man who knew nothing of the difficulty and was not present
when it occurred—an employee of the railroad.   They were
about to deal with him summarily when Calvin Crozier, the
Texan, who had stabbed the negro, who was then at large,
unrecognized and might have escaped entirely free, voluntarily
made himself known as the man and surrendered himself to
certain death to prevent another, and that other a stranger,
from suffering for what he had done.   To the honor of Prince
Rivers, who was an officer at the time in that colored regiment, and who was afterwards somewhat well known at Edgefield, be it said that he wanted to save, and tried to save
Crozier from the doom that awaited him.   The people of Newberry have honored themselves in erecting a monument to the
memory of Calvin Crozier.

The author of "The South Since the War" seems to have
been very fortunate in making acquaintance with the rude and
unlettered wherever he went.   He must have taken special
pleasure in talking to all the "ornery cusses" he could find in
the country or on the road.   Let it be hoped that he found
some improvement on his second visit, if he ever came again,
and that he found better fare at some stopping places than he
did at the hotel in Orangeburg in 1866.

CONTEST BETWEEN THE LEGISLATURE AND GOVERNOR.

In the third volume of the Statutes at Large, page 273, it is
stated that there were no Acts of the Assembly for the year,
1728, 1729, and 1730, but there is no cause nor reason given

as an explanation of the fact. The Legislature was often in
session during that time, and the explanation of the fact that
no laws were passed, is that there was no harmony between
the Governor and the Assembly, and it was found impossible
for them to work in harness together. The Governor, throughout the contest, felt in duty bound to uphold the royal prerogative, which, as he thought, was continually encroached
upon by the Assembly. During this period Arthur Middleton
was Governor, and, as the historian of that period says, "the
encroaching disposition of the recently successful people forced
him to raise the barrier of the 'royal prerogative' so high that
his head was hid behind it." Both the Governor and the
Assembly were true to the principles each thought right, both
were loyal. It was the beginning of the contest between
Royalty and Republicanism, which finally culminated in the
triumph of the latter.

RECONSTRUCTION.

We will now proceed to give as briefly and succinctly as possible, at the same time with satisfactory fulness, a narrative of
the troublous times of re-construction. The years immediately
following the close of the war, were, in some respects, the
gloomiest and most trying we have ever experienced. We
hoped for awhile that the restoration of the Union and the
return to a settled and well-established Order might not be so
very difficult. These hopes were rudely dispelled and several
years of misrule and partial anarchy under military despotism
had to be gone through before the return of a settled peace. It
is no pleasure to the historian to write of this time. In truth
there are many things which the historian finds it necessary to
record, which fill him with sadness, and which he would gladly
pass over in silence, but he cannot. History is but the record
of the acts of men and women as they pass across the stage of
life, and it is for them to see that they act their parts well and
give the pen of the scribe something pleasant to record. We
today are making history. Since this writer began the History
of Edgefield in January, 1891, the whirligig of time has
wrought many changes, and many men, the puppets of the
hour, have cut many fantastic tricks before high heaven.

At the close of the war A. G. Magrath was Governor. The

State was conquered, and prostrate, and helpless at the feet of the conquerors. What next? was the question in the minds of all. The ancient institutions of the State were overthrown. The State had no status, because she had no existence. For the time being South Carolina was dead. Could she ever revive and live again?

The years immediately following the war were not pleasant; and we who had lived through it and remembered with what glorious anticipation of success and independence we entered into it, could not help but feel rather gloomy forebodings when we faced the future.

For a moment, however, there was a gleam of light, and we were cheered; but that rift in the cloud soon closed, and the darkness was indeed visible, for we could see nothing else. In looking back and reviewing the ten years immediately following the conclusion of the war, it is often a matter of wonder and surprise to the writer that the people were not more demoralized and desperate than they were, though they were bad enough, worse than we wish ever to see them again.

Soon after the close of the war, Andrew Johnson, Vice-President, having become President by the assassination of Mr. Lincoln, sent for Benjamin F. Perry, of Greenville, an able man, a man who had the respect and confidence of all classes, and who had always been known and recognized as a consistent and loyal Union man, to confer with him on the measures to be adopted for the restoration of South Carolina to her true position as one of the organic parts and members of the Union. Mr. Perry was urged by his friends and by the people to accept the invitation, as it was regarded as an earnest of the President's good feeling towards the South and the State. He accordingly went to Washington, where he was received and treated with the greatest respect and consideration. He received the appointment of Provisional Governor of the State, and immediately went to work upon the basis agreed upon by the President, and other prominent Northern men, for the reconstruction of the State. Increased confidence in the future was immediately felt all over the State by the appointment of Mr. Perry. He issued an ably written proclamation, which was received with enthusiasm by all, and a hope of rescue from what seemed absolute ruin was fondly cherished. Civil government was restored; a Constitutional Convention of the people was called; the State was reorganized by the adoption of a Constitution, which, it was hoped, could not be offensive to any. Of that Convention the members from Edgefield were: Francis W. Pickens, George D. Tillman, and ————————.

On the 18th of October, 1865, a Governor of the State and members of the Legislature were elected. The members from Edgefield were: Luke Culbreath, Dr. John Landrum, Thomas Jones, M. L. Bonham, M. W. Gary, John E. Bacon, and M. C. Butler; G. D. Tillman, Senator. James L. Orr, one of the ablest and most eminent men in the State, was elected Governor. Senators and members of the House of Representatives were elected to the Congress at Washington. F. W. Pickens elected United States Senator.

So far all seemed well, as if we were about to drop down into the old grooves and move on as we did before the war. This was not to be for some years. Under the new Constitution and reorganization of the State, the courts were also reorganized, and district courts were established for the trial of minor causes and offences. Of this court at Edgefield, John E. Bacon, Esq., was made Judge.

Unfortunately, the Legislature, at the session of 1865, passed an act known as the Black Code, which discriminated between the whites and blacks as citizens, separating them in the courts; in fact, giving them different courts, and not recognizing their citizenship in all respects as equal to that of the whites.

Whether this action of the Legislature was used as a pretext, or whether Congress and the Northern people would have acted as they did in any case, is mere matter of conjecture. Be this as it may, a change soon came over the spirit of their dream, and the political sky grew cloudy. The Senators and Representatives elected to Congress were not permitted to take their seats. Several amendments to the Constitution of the United States were made. Military government was established in the State, with General Sickles as Commandant, afterwards General Canby, who, under the reconstruction acts of Congress, ordered an election of delegates to a Constitutional Convention to be held, and the Convention to meet on the 14th day of January, 1868. The delegates to this Convention from Edgefield were: Frank Arnim, R. B. Elliott. Davis Harris, P. R. Rivers, John Mobley, and John Bonum. This Convention was in session two months, and framed the Constitution to meet the requirements of the Constitution of the United States, and under that Constitution we now live. The State was, in all respects, reconstructed before it could be recognized as a member of the Federal Union. Under this new Constitution an election was held for Governor and for a full set of State officers. Robert K. Scott, of Ohio, was elected Governor. He was inaugurated July 9th, 1868.

From the time of the inauguration of Governor Orr, in 1865, to the inauguration of Governor Scott, July 9th, 1868, the State presented the singular spectacle of a dual government, both civil and military. The military was on top, and the civil government all the way through, from Governor down to Magistrate, was only permitted the management and administration of those affairs with which the military authorities did not care to be bothered.

Governor Orr had certainly a very trying time. He was allowed to retain his position as Governor, not as constitutional and because elected by the people, but as provisional, until the completion of reconstruction and the election of a Governor. His position was surrounded with difficulties from which he was glad to be relieved by the election and inauguration of a successor.

With the inauguration and installation of Governor Scott, the military government of the State ceased, and the United States troops were withdrawn. The State was then declared to be reconstructed and restored to its place in the Union. Yes, South Carolina is in the Union again, but it is not the South Carolina that we knew before the war. No vestige of that old State remains. Whether the South Carolina of the future will be better than of the past, the future only can tell.

The Senators and Representatives in Congress, elected under the reconstruction acts and under the new Constitution of the State, were permitted to take their seats, and since that time the State has not been without its due representation in Congress.

Such is a brief general view of reconstruction, which covers a period of a little over three years. There were incidents occurring in Edgefield during that period, and after, especially until 1876, which ought to receive a more particular attention.

In closing this general view of reconstruction, it may be as well to state that General Scott was re-elected Governor in 1870, and that his administration was a very unsettled and unhappy one. In 1871 the new County of Aiken was made and established by cutting off parts of the Counties of Barnwell, Edgefield, and Lexington. Edgefield supplied a considerable part of the territory, giving Hamburg and Beach Island. The county seat of the new county is at Aiken, a railroad town, which was very near the line between Barnwell and Edgefield, but in Barnwell. Many, many years ago this writer passed a night at Aiken, when the inclined plane was still there and the trains of cars were brought up and lowered by means of an immense cable and stationary engine, one train of cars passing down as another came up. I stood at the top of the incline and watched the ascent and descent. I think Mr. Marsh was the landlord of the hotel at which I stopped. One name over a store door attracted my particular attention, as I had never seen it before, nor have I ever seen it since. It was Eugene Durbec. What kind of business he was engaged in I did not know, only that it was a mercantile business of some kind. I have heard that Aiken was once pretty well burnt out by some persons trying to burn out a yellow-jacket's nest.

The latter part of the year 1865 was a very trying time for the people of Edgefield, as well as for all other parts of the South. Negro troops were placed at the Court House, apparently to humiliate and mortify the old masters and rulers of the country. The pretext was to keep the peace and ensure protection to the lately emancipated. White troops would not have been nearly so disagreeable. This writer, at that time, all through the year 1865, was living twenty-five miles from the Court House and never saw a negro soldier at any time, only heard of them and knew of the great disintegration of the old order of things that was taking place all around. During that and the following year it was as though the foundations of the great deep were broken up. The following anecdote will give the young reader of this day a faint idea of the condition of the country at that time. For the proper protection of the late slaves it was required that all contracts for labor were to be made in writing and before the proper officers duly authorized to make the same. On one occasion a spirited old lady got a gentleman to go with her to the Court House to get the officer to sign a contract between her and her former slaves. When they came to the office the negro guard stationed at the door said the ladies could enter, but men could not. After the lady had gone in she was asked by the officers what she would have, when she angrily replied that she had a gentleman along to help attend to her business, but an old negro at the door would not allow him to come in. It is needless to say that her business was promptly and with dispatch attended to.

From semi-military rule in 1865–66–67, the State passed under Radical rule in 1868 when the military were withdrawn. A Radical Legislature was elected in 1868, the old-time Democrats having no showing whatever in Edgefield. Frank Arnim, a second-hand Prussian, (why second-hand is not so clear) of Hamburg, was elected to the State Senate, and four negroes and one white man were sent to the House. This white man also lived in Hamburg. R. B. Elliott and Prince Rivers, two of the colored members, had both served in the Union army. At the next election for Senator, Lawrence Cain, a native negro raised near Old Cambridge, was elected in Arnim's place. Is this Lawrence Cain the Daddy Cain, who was also a Methodist preacher? I heard him preach once, and also heard him make a political speech, and I must say that his political speaking was much better than his preaching. Going into politics will spoil any preacher, black or white.

R. B. Elliott was afterwards elected to Congress, and Rivers, who was known as the "Black Prince," was appointed a Major-General in the State Militia. After 1876, he obtained employment in his old occupation of carriage driver, and died at Aiken in 1888. He was not by any means a bad specimen of humanity.

In 1870 an effort was made by all conservative men and well-wishers of the State to make, if possible, some reform in the administration of affairs. To this end what is known as the Reform Movement was inaugurated and a Reform ticket

for all offices, State and County, was nominated, having on it
conservative and influential colored men, who, it was hoped,
would command influence sufficient to defeat the extreme
Radical party. This writer living in Newberry voted the
ticket nominated in that County, though he doubted very
much the expediency of the movement. General M. C. Butler
ran for Lieutenant Governor on the Reform ticket. The Re-
formers were very badly beaten. About this time a taxpayer's
convention was held to memorialise Congress on the miserable
condition of affairs in the State. Congress took no action, but
this writer believes that good was done by the movement, as
the attention of Congress, of the United States and of the
world was thereby drawn to a state of affairs, which was a
shame and a disgrace to the whole country and the Radical
party was checked in their career. George D. Tillman and
General M. W. Gary both opposed this plan, on the ground
that it would not only lower the dignity of the people, but
that it would end in failure. It apparently ended in failure,
but really it did not.

In 1874 Governor Moses, who, it will be remembered, was
private Secretary of General Pickens when the troubles began, and was, during the war in 1863–54, stationed at Edgefield as enrolling officer of the Confederate States, issued arms
to a half dozen colored companies in the county—volunteer
militia companies; for what purpose it was hard to say; devilment I reckon. In August of this year a riot occurred at Ridge
Spring, and another later on, on the Savannah. Ned Tennant, a colored man, the instigator of the last mentioned
trouble, was rewarded with the office of County Commissioner.
He then removed to the Court House where he soon afterwards
died.

In 1875 there occurred in the county several violent and
destructive storms and tornadoes, by which much damage was
done; several persons were killed, many were crippled; trees
were uprooted and houses blown and torn to pieces. To go
back, for a moment, a good many years. The 9th day of
March, 1855, thirty-seven years ago today lacking one week,
was the fieriest day this writer ever saw. From about midday
until night, when the wind lulled, the whole country, that is
the wooded country, from the mountains to the seaboard was

in a blaze. In that great fire many houses in Edgefield were reduced to ashes and much fencing was destroyed.

In 1876, just one hundred years after the Declaration of Independence, affairs became so bad that the great crisis could no longer be deferred. The State had gone from bad to worse, and in that year Edgefield fairly and squarely took the bull by the horns, and with the help of the other parts of the State, he was throttled. Candidates were selected in June, and the riots in Hamburg filled the white people of the county with enthusiasm. Hamburg had been infested so long and so terribly with thieves, and with harlots of the baser sort, that wagoners, had ceased to camp within eight or ten miles of the place, for fear of being robbed. It was reported, but it is to be hoped that the report was not true, that negro thieves desecrated graveyards in search of plunder.

On the 4th of July a colored company, commanded by Captain Dock Adams, refused to permit white men to pass through the town along the public road. A quarrel took place, and General M. C. Butler was sent for to organize and lead the whites. B. R. Tillman, afterwards Governor, was an active participant in this riot. Captain Adams, with his forces, retired to a large brick building owned by Mr. Sibley, and ordered his men to shoot their opponents from the windows. A young man named Merriwether was killed. A cannon was then loaded with grapeshot and discharged at the house. This drove the negroes into the cellar, where they surrendered. It is said that after night Allen T. Attaway, a mulatto giant, and five others, were taken into a cornfield and dealt with summarily. The Radicals say that the tongue of Attaway, which had been used so badly, was cut out. Of the truth of this statement this deponent saith not.

In August of this year Chamberlain, who, by the way, was by far the best Radical Governor of them all, and not such a bad fellow, with a host of friends and backers, came to the court house on an electioneering tour. Here he was met by Gary, Butler, and the crowd, and vanquished, fairly or unfairly, and driven from the field. The platform upon which he stood, and upon which he hoped to gain a great and signal victory, was not firmly enough joined and fastened together to hold the discordant materials that sought a place upon it; or it had not planks enough, or was not broad enough; something was the matter, and it went to pieces and would hold nobody, not even the Governor.   The result of the contest was General Hampton was elected Governor, and in Edgefield the old Democratic party had a majority of several thousand.   General Gary managed this election with great skill and success, and carried the election triumphantly, notwithstanding the presence of United States soldiers at the court house the whole time.   After this election and the expiration of his term of service in the Legislature (Senate), General Gary never took any further part in political life; but indeed he lived only a short time after his term expired.   He died April 9th, 1881. General Gary's influence in Edgefield was very great, and it is felt very strongly in all the political agitations and movements to this day.   He was succeeded by James Callison, a gentleman of Irish descent.

W. J. Talbert, late Superintendent of the Penitentiary, 1893, now member of Congress, was the next State Senator succeeding Callison.   In 1883 W. J. Ready was elected State Senator, defeating W. J. Talbert.   Ready died January 16th, 1891, and Dr. W. H. Timmerman succeeded him as State Senator.   In 1896 Dr. W. H. Timmerman was elected State Treasurer, and Mr. J. M. Gaines was elected State senator.

XXIV.

DR. JOHN LANDRUM.

This good man, who died on Sunday morning, January 31st, 1892, was born in the lower part of the county, in the old Wells and Vaucluse section, where the Landrums, in the earliest days of Edgefield, were people of means, of intellectual ability, and of decided influence for good. Dr. Landrum lived to the advanced age of eighty-seven years. His body had become feeble, but his intellect remained keen and bright. He was a man of eager and grasping mind, and had enjoyed every advantage of education. He was a graduate of the South Carolina College; and from the time of his graduation all through life he kept up an intimate acquaintance with the Greek and Latin writers.

He died at the house of his daughter, Mrs. M. H. Mims, who had been only recently widowed; and was buried at Stevens' Creek Church, near his old home and by the side of children long gone before. His widow and two daughters survive him. His daughters both live at Edgefield, and are Mrs. M. H. Mims and Mrs. James A. Holland.

COLONEL JAMES C. SMYLEY.

Colonel James C. Smyley was born at Meeting Street, in Edgefield County, in 1820, and died in 1872. His mother was a sister of Marmaduke Coates, of Newberry, S. C. He held no office during his life, except that of Colonel of Militia, and the very important position of delegate to the Secession Convention. He, with all the other members of that body, signed the Ordinance of Secession.

He was a planter by business and occupation, and enjoyed the respect and confidence of the people. His wife was Catherine Watson, of Ridge Spring, S. C.

COLONEL JAMES P. CARROLL.

Colonel Carroll was born in the city of Charleston, but from early boyhood his home was in Edgefield. After his graduation from the South Carolina College he read law, and was admitted to practice in Columbia in 1830. He became a distinguished lawyer at Edgefield, though it is said that business came to him very slowly, and that he waited long for his first fee. But his labor and patience were crowned with success, and few lawyers at Edgefield ever stood higher in the profession than he did.

He represented Edgefield in both branches of the Legislature—sometimes in the Senate and sometimes in the House of Representatives. He was a member of the Convention of 1860, and signed the Ordinance of Secession. He died in 1883, aged about 75 years.

He was one of the Chancellors, or Equity Judges, of the State, and filled that position with honor and dignity. He had a clear, logical, and discriminating mind—impartial and just in his temper and character.

GENERAL R. G. M. DUNOVANT.

This gentleman was a native of Chester County. He graduated from the South Carolina College. After his graduation he read medicine and moved to Texas, in which State he practiced his profession until the breaking out of the War with Mexico, when he returned to Chester, raised a company for the war, and was elected Captain—was promoted to the rank of Lieutenant Colonel, which position he was holding when the war closed. He has represented Edgefield in the Legislature; was a member of the Convention of 1860 from that county, and signed the Ordinance of Secession.

During the War of Secession he held the rank of Colonel in the Confederate service. Since the war he has lived in retirement at his home in the town of Edgefield.

Not long after the War with Mexico he married a sister of Hon. P. S. Brooks. He is still living (February, 1892,) and is about seventy years of age. Born May 18th, 1821.

ANDREW J. HAMMOND,

One of the signers of the Ordinance of Secession, was a worthy descendant of Colonel Samuel Hammond, of the Revolution, one of the bravest and truest men of that day. Andrew Hammond was a planter, and never, I believe, aspired to any political office, nor sought any political honor; but, enjoying the confidence of the people who knew him, (his home was not far from Hamburg, on the Savannah side of the county,) he was elected a member of the Convention of 1860. At one time he represented Edgefield in the Legislature.

During the War between the States he held the rank of Major in the Confederate service. He married Elizabeth Butler, who survives him.

COLONEL JAMES TOMKINS.

This gentleman was a planter on the Savannah side of the District, in the neighborhood of Modoc, in that part of Edgefield known as the Dark Corner. He was born June 28th, 1793, and died May 9th, 1864. He was happily married on the 3rd of February, 1819, to Mrs. Jennings, widow of William Jennings. The maiden name of Mrs. Jennings Tomkins was Huldah Hill, born December 28th, 1796, and died July 4th, 1868.

Colonel Tomkins, though not a very ambitious man, yet was one of considerable influence and ability. He had the honor of being elected to the Legislature; and in that supreme hour, when that last desperate struggle was made to place upon an impregnable basis our old and cherished doctrine of State Rights, as one of the Representative men of Edgefield, he was called to meet with others from different parts of the State in that heroic Convention which has become forever historic, to consult together and to see, in that dark hour, that the State should receive no detriment. He and they did their duty, or what they conceived to be such. It is not possible for any man to do more.

PRESTON S. BROOKS.

P. S. Brooks, son of Colonel Whitfield Brooks, and grandson of Colonel Z. S. Brooks, of Big Creek, celebrated for his bravery and daring as a Whig in the Revolution, was born at Edgefield Court House, August 6th, 1819, and died in Washington city while a member of Congress in 1856, only a few months over thirty-seven years of age. After the close of the Mexican war, through which he served as Captain of a company raised at Edgefield in the Palmetto Regiment, he was elected to the Legislature, where he served one term, and was then elected as Representative to Congress. He was a lawyer by profession, but practiced only a little while. He was a farmer and made his home in the country in the upper part of the District, not far from Ninety-Six, near which place his mother lived.

He was educated at Mount Enon, Willington, and the South Carolina College. This writer knew him well at Mount Enon and all through his public life. He was always a conspicuous figure. He died young. Had he lived it is impossible to say what he would have been.

It is hoped that this writer will be pardoned for making mention here that at Mount Eunon he formed a life-long acquaintance and friendship with James C. Brooks, a brother, younger by a few years than Preston, and not far from the same age of this writer.

WILLIAM GREGG.

Mr. Gregg was born 2nd of February, 1800, in Monangahela County, West Virginia. He established himself as a merchant in Columbia, S. C., about the year 1827, and was married to Marina Jones, daughter of Colonel Mathias Jones, of Edgefield. In 1838 he removed to Charleston and resumed his former business with the Hayden brothers, who were jewelers. Gregg, Hayden & Co. were known throughout the South as extensive importing merchants. After hard work he obtained in 1845 a charter for the Graniteville Factory, with a capital of $300,000. His time was almost entirely devoted to the interests of the factory. He built churches, established schools, and endeavored, in every way, to elevate the employees of the factory in morals, intelligence, and in the true dignity of life.

He was a member of the Convention of 1860, and, with the other members of that Convention, signed the Ordinance of Secession. He died September 12th, 1867, and was buried in Magnolia Cemetery near Charleston, S. C. His was certainly a very honorable and useful life. He who gives employment to others and deals justly by them, and tries to make them self-respecting men and women does not live in vain.

COLONEL JAMES B. GRIFFIN.

This gentleman, who died at Fort Worth, Texas, on the 25th day of June, 1881, was the son of Mr. James Griffin, who lived about three miles from the village of Edgefield. Inheriting a large estate from his father, who was quite wealthy, and having no political ambition he was quietly pursuing his avocation of planter when our sectional strife culminated in secession and war. For some years he had been holding a commission in the militia and was Brigadier General of cavalry when the State seceded. When Colonel Hampton received permission from the Confederate government to organize a legion, including in it four companies of cavalry, Colonel Griffin was selected to command that part of the legion with the rank of Major. In June 1861 the Hampton Legion moved to Virginia and the cavalry was sent to the camp of instruction at Hanover.

On the 19th of July the infantry of the legion was ordered to Manassas and was engaged in the battle of Bull Run. In that battle Lieutenant Colonel Johnson was killed and the legion lost an able officer. After the death of Colonel Johnson Major Griffin was promoted to Lieutenant Colonel and transferred to the infantry. The cavalry had taken no part in the battle of Bull Run, and it made the infantry feel a little sore that a cavalry officer, who had had no part in the fight, should be put in command of them in place of their Lieutenant Colonel, who had been killed in battle.

However, the time came after awhile in which Colonel Griffin showed that he was worthy of the position which he held. In the march to Yorktown, in the retreat from Yorktown, in the skirmish at West Point, in the battle of Seven Pines, in which the legion was hotly engaged, he showed what stuff he was made of, and his coolness and bravery won the hearty admiration of the whole command. He came out of that battle with a popularity as great, it may be, as that of any of the officers of the legion. But it was too late to make up to him what he had already lost.

On the re-organization of the army in 1862, under the conscript Act, Colonel Griffin was not elected. His career in Virginia closed and he returned home. On his return to the State he was very soon assigned to duty in the Regiment of State Troops, commanded by Colonel Thomas G. Bacon, with the rank of Lieutenant Colonel. In this service he continued until the close of the war when his regiment was discharged at Spartanburg and he returned home.

After the war he removed to Texas, where he was doing

fairly well in the effort to repair his shattered fortunes, when he was cut off by death.

Colonel Griffin had one sister, who first married Diomed Hollingsworth, and after his death she became the wife of Dr. William H. Harrington, of Newberry. They, too, have passed over the line.

GENERAL MARTIN W. GARY

Was a son of Dr. Thomas R. Gary, of Cokesbury, Abbeville County, S. C. His grand-father, Captain Jesse Gary, lived and died in Newberry County. Captain Jesse Gary was one of eight sons of Thomas Gary and his wife, Rebecca Jones. General Gary's mother was Mary Ann Porter, a descendant of a brother of John Witherspoon, who signed the Declaration of Independence, and who was for many years President of Princeton College, New Jersey.

Judge Ernest Gary is a son of Dr. F. F. Gary, of Abbeville, a brother of General Gary, and John Gary Evans' mother, who married General N. G. Evans, was a sister of General Gary.

COLONEL W. C. MORAGNE.

The following biographical sketch of Colonel W. C. Moragne has been very kindly written for me by Colonel H. W. Addison, his friend and partner in law:

"EDGEFIELD, S. C., February 6th, 1893.

Mr. John Chapman,

DEAR SIR: You ask me to give you a brief sketch of the life of the late Colonel William C. Moragne of this place.

"Of his early life, I personally, know nothing. His ancestors were French Huguenots, and were banished under the Edict of Nantes by Louis XIV, King of France, and settled in Abbeville County, near Bordeaux, on the Savannah River. There, and I think, in Charleston, he delivered orations upon the Huguenots and their descendants, with their trials, sufferings and heroism.

"He finished his collegiate education at Gottingen, Germany, and while there seemed to have thoroughly imbibed a taste for German and French literature: to have a great admiration for Schiller, Humboldt, and Goethe—Voltaire, Moliere, and others.

"Moragne and a brother, John, enlisted for the war against Mexico. The latter fell, gallantly fighting at the battle of Chapultepec, or at the Capital City. I do not know the date of Colonel Moragne's promotion to Captaincy in the war; that he bore himself with great courage was well known; he suffered much and long from sickness before his return home.

I became intimately connected with him on my return from the University of Virginia, about 1855, when I began reading law under him; and, in 1856, I formed a partnership with him, which continued most pleasantly and profitably till the breaking out of our Civil War in 1861. During this relationship I met him almost daily, and was in immediate personal contact with him. He was of fine form, well proportioned, about six feet high, and with an aquiline nose, brownish hair.

"His manner was by no means familiar, but rather the contrary to those not familiar with him; yet his extremely polite, agreeable, and interesting conversation grew upon acquaintance and ended by the firmest and most durable friendship.

"He did not believe in acquiring professional business by personal popularity, nor maintained thereby, but by true ability and merit—these the result only of a good and liberal education, followed up by hard and laborious application to the profession. While he admitted that the law was a jealous mistress, he thought she fully admitted the devotees of all liberal arts to her shrine; and that no person should attempt the law without years of laborious application to study, with a general information in history and literature. He had a contempt for the quillets of the law and a disgust for its chicanery. He would under no circumstances resort to improper means to gain a case. At the time I began the law with him he was one of the rising members of the Bar, studious and painstaking, ambitious and in the bloom of manhood. At the beginning of the war he had worked himself up to the very foremost of the front rank of his profession here, as will be seen by the records and the decisions of our Supreme Court.

"He was at all times genial, pleasant, instructive, though never obtrusive, ever liberal, and at all times the highest type of an educated gentleman. Politically he was a strict constructionist of the Constitution—wrote many articles for the Charleston Mercury and pamphlets on national issues. And,

though they differed widely in politics, vet he was a warm
admirer of the political antipodes, Calhoun and Petigru.

"He married about 185– Miss Emma Butler, daughter of
James M. Butler, a beautiful and eloquent lady, to whom he
was a loving and devoted husband. She lived but a few
years, leaving a son, a pledge of their mutual love, who
resides in Florida, near his distinguished uncle, Dr. Moragne.

"Colonel Moragne at the beginning of the late war was aide to
General M. L. Bonham at the battle of Bull Run. Soon after
this he returned home and organized the Nineteenth South
Carolina Regiment, of which he became the Colonel. Soon
after this his health failed him and he returned to his beautiful
home at Edgefield, where he died loved by many, and held in
the highest respect by all for his pure life, a beautiful example
to all young men."

The following additional particulars were communicated by
H. A. Lee, Esq., of Abbeville, in a letter to Colonel H. W.
Addison:

"I regret that I am able to add so few facts to what you
already have in regard to the late Wm. C. Morange, Esq. He
was admitted to the Bar in 1844, two years before I came to
Abbeville, and as he established himself at Edgefield, attending only to an occasional case here, I saw but little of him.

"His brother, John B. Moragne, who came to the Bar
about the same time, practiced here until he went to Mexico
in Captain Marshall's Company as First Lieutenant, and after
attracting the notice of General Scott as 'the gallant West
Pointer of the Palmetto Regiment,' was killed in the storming
of the city.

"W. C. Moragne, Esq., was of French ancestry, and his
father and mother were descendants of those French refugees,
who, under the lead of the Rev. Pierre Gilbert, settled at
Bordeaux, Abbeville County, in 1765, on the concluding of
the Treaty of Paris. They were a distinct offshoot from those
Huguenots who fled from France upon the revocation
of the Edict of Nantes by Louis XIV, and who settled, many of
them, in Charleston and vicinity, and who have done so much
to illustrate the past history of the State.

"His brothers were John B., Isaac, and Nathaniel; and his
sisters Mrs. Davis, of Abbeville, the author of an interesting

Revolutionary story; Mrs. Fleming, of Augusta, and Miss Louisa, who died unmarried. I knew them all, and visited at the family homestead and can testify to the cultivation and refinement of the home circle. They were a talented family, and, as in many other instances, derived their best qualities of mind and heart from the mother.

"He graduated at the South Carolina College with honors, and then went to Europe, where he spent a year or so, and settled at Edgefield for the practice of law.

"In 1852 he delivered the address to the students of the Clear Spring Academy. His subject, I think, was 'Public Speaking.' In 1854 he delivered an address before the Christian Association of Abbeville on the 'Statesman,' and in 1855 he made the Centennial Address to the French of Bordeaux, copies of which exist in pamphlet form. He doubtless delivered other addresses.

"In 1861 he was volunteer aide to General Bonham, at the First Manassas. In 1862 he was elected Colonel of the Nineteenth South Carolina Regiment, but on account of ill health was forced to resign. He was a close student, a well read lawyer, and an accomplished scholar. He was a good French and German scholar, and had devoted much attention to the *Belles Lettres*. He was a forcible and pleasing speaker. He was a man of the highest character, and was respected by all who knew him for his sterling integrity and many noble traits of mind and heart."

XXV.

THE BLOCKER FAMILY.

The Blocker family, which is one of the oldest in Edgefield County, is of Prussian origin. The name was originally Blucher. Michael Blocker was the first of the family who come from Prussia; and, after living here a few years, he sent his only son, John, back to the fatherland for others of his countrymen. John on his return to this country brought over with him a number of families and planted quite a large colony on lands which had been granted to him by the King.

John Blocker was a man of learning, and being made a Magistrate, used his position for the good of his neighbors. Being himself a man of peace, he became a peacemaker, and sought to allay strife whenever it was possible to do so. He was much beloved, and was called upon at all times for advice from these honest, respectable, good people which made the colony prosperous and happy—some of them filling very important positions in the county.

The children of John Blocker were seven sons and one daughter. They were high-toned, enterprising men, marrying ladies of culture. Most of their children received their education at the once celebrated Blocker Academy.

James, the eldest son of John Blocker, was the first man that entered into the mercantile business in the town or village of Edgefield. He married Miss Isabel Morrison, of Charleston. She was a highly accomplished and educated lady, and by her beautiful Christian life made her home a resort of the refined and intellectual of that day.

Mr. John Blocker, another son, married Miss Mary Johnston and built the stately home at Cedar Grove, now, 1893, owned by Colonel Robert Hughes. He afterwards moved West, accompanied by Colonel Abner Blocker, who married Miss Amelia Clifton, and at her death married Sarah Kennerly. General Jesse Blocker and Michael Blocker married sisters, the Misses Malone. Major Bartley Blocker, the sixth son, married a sister of Colonel Whitfield Brooks. David, the other one of the seven sons, seems not to have married, as I find no mention made of it.

Bartley, David, James, and Jesse are interred in the Blocker Cemetery with the preceding generation of the family.

The Blocker settlement, as it was called in its palmy days, will long be remembered for the kindness and generosity of its hosts and its pleasurable enjoyments, for there reigned peace, and plenty.

The only daughter, sister to the seven brothers just mentioned, married Dr. Bejamin Winn. They, too, moved West. The sister, as well as the brothers who went West, prospered. They have numerous descendants, some of whom fill prominent positions.

Young John Blocker, grand-son of Bartley, is the only one of the name now living in Edgefield County. He is Captain of the Edgefield Rifles. He is a decendant of the celebrated Emily Geiger, General Greene's Courier to General Sumter, and the Heroine of Newberry in the old Revolutionary War.

Emily Geiger has other descendants now, 1893, living in Edgefield County. After the war she married a planter named Threewits—moved down the country and lived and died at Granby. Miss Elizabeth Threwitts, a daughter of, or a grand-daughter of Emily Geiger, married John Nicholson, brother to Benjamin. Her son Benjamin Nicholson was Clerk of the Court at the time of his death. Her sons, Albert, John, and Joseph are now, February, 1893, living. Joseph is Probate Judge. One daughter, Mrs. Emma Blocker, is also living. One daughter, who married Dr. Allen is no longer living. Miss Sophie Nicholson should be mentioned, also as a descendant of Emily Gieger, and there may be others.

From the Advertiser, July 31st, 1873, Biographical—Copied by John R. Abney, Esq..

DEATH OF AN AGED AND REMARKABLE LADY.

On Sunday last, there expired, at her ancient home on Turkey Creek, in our District, a woman whose birth, gifts, and character caused her to stand out always prominently from the mass. This was Mrs. Isabella M. Blocker, relict of James Blocker, Esq., deceased many years since. Mrs. Blocker was the only child of James and Anna Berwick Morri-

s)n, native Scotch people, of high standing and great culture,
who lived and died, many years ago, in Charleston. She was
also a grand niece of James Beattie, the famous Scotch poet.
Born, educated, and married in Charleston, this lady had
every advantage of the day in which she grew up. She was
an accomplished pianiste, a fine French scholar, and her home
was tastefully adorned with the fruits of her own pencil and
brush. And with all this and through all good and evil and
through long years of pain and suffering, in fact, through
every day and hour of her life she was the pure, humble,
earnest child of God.

Mrs. Blocker would have completed her 80th year on the
31st instant. She leaves three daughters, Mrs. Felix Lake,
Sr., Mrs. John Lake, and Mrs. Dr. Abney, and numerous grand
and great-grandchildren. Her remains were interred on Monday last in the old Blocker burying ground, two miles from
her home.

Edgefield Advertiser, June 8th, 1864, copied by John R.
Abney, Esq.:

WOUNDED OFFICERS.

Major Joseph Abney, of the Twenty-Seventh South Carolina
Volunteers, wounded in the fight at Drewry's Bluff on the
16th ult., has arrived at his home in our town. We have
been to see this gallant soldier, who is unable to be out, and
find him with not only a considerable "spot of tragedy" on
his right side, but suffering in general health, and looking
worn and weary. His wound, which though not dangerous, is
very severe, appears to be doing well, however, and we earnestly hope the comforts and endearments of home may soon
restore him to his usual vigor and usefulness. He pays the
highest meed of praise to the gallantry and military capacity
to General D. H. Hill, who, he seems to think, has been the
real leader in the late successful military operations in Ches-
terfield County.

Edgefield Advertiser, August 1st, 1866, copied by John R.
Abney, Esq.:

JOHN B. ABNEY

Departed this life, at the residence of his parents, in the village of Edgefield, on the 30th of June, 1866, and in the 21st year of his age, John Bay Abney, the last son of Dr. M. W. and Caroline Seabrook Abney.

The deceased entered the service of the Confederate States early in the war, first, in the Regiment commanded by Colonel Abney, and then in the Cavalry Regiment commanded by Colonel Aiken, and was discharged from each, on the Surgeon's certificate of disability. As soon, however, as his health was a little restored, true to the spirit and traditions of his race, he hastened to rejoin the army, in the Battalion of Sharp Shooters, commanded by his uncle, Major Joseph Abney, to which also was attached his brother-in-law, the lamented Pickens Butler Watts. He served in this corps, as Hospital Steward, until it was amalgamated with the Charleston Battalion, and the two were constituted the Twenty-Seventh South Carolina Infantry. Being then appointed Sergeant of his Company, he soon participated in the action of Walthall Junction, which was fought in May 1864. At one period of the battle, being much exposed, his company faltered when ordered to advance, and he, the youngest of its members, moved forward to the onset, and by his noble example re-established the courage and confidence of his comrades. For this brilliant conduct on his first field, he was recommended for promotion, whilst his brother-in-law Watts was alike commended for equally conspicious behavior. In all the first actions around Petersburg, he bore a manly part, though suffering all the while, from disease, which had even then fastened itself upon his system. On the terrible 24th of June, when Hagood's glorious Brigade displayed so much heroism, and shed so much blood, in carrying, as skirmishers, the rifle pits of the enemy, Sergeants Abney and Watts, in the absence of commanding officers, were each appointed by General Hagood, Lieutenants, *pro tempore*, in compliment to their skill and gallantry, and assigned to the command of companies. Sergeant Watts, in an almost hand to hand conflict with the foe, fell like a hero on their bristling ramparts. Sergeant Abney, more fortunate for the time, carried with his company, and the company on his right or left, which had lost its commander, the extreme right of the enemy's lines resting on the Appomattox, and after holding it for some time, actually bore off twenty-five or thirty prisoners, in triumph. The demeanor of our troops, on this part of the line, elicited from General Lee, who was a beholder from the other side of the river, the warmest encomiums. But in the next disastrous engagement of General Hagood's, on the Weldon Road, John Abney, along with many others, was captured, and carried a prisoner to Point Lookout, the disease of the kidneys, under which he had been suffering for years, became aggravated by privation and exposure and on his release, he returned home, but to linger and to die.

But in his death, he has left us the same example of heroic endurance, of Christian fortitude, and Christian hope, that illustrated the higher portion of his youthful existence. Amid his long protracted sufferings, he never repined—never complained at the dispensations of Providence. His whole life was marked by filial devotion, and was free from guile, and as he had lived without reproach, he died without fear.

This family has been truly afflicted by the scourge of war. Their oldest son, Joseph Abney, who was a pattern of every virtue, after passing through all the earlier battles and campaigns, with little injury to his person, and after winning a name for courage and intrepidity, that would have done honor to the proudest soldier in the army of Virginia, perished, in the front ranks of his company, on the bloody field of Sharpsburg. Then the chivalrous high-souled Watts followed in his track of glory; and John B. Abney, the last, the only son, and because the last, the best beloved, is now summoned to heaven to join his immortal brothers, "Where the wicked cease from troubling, and the weary are at rest."   J. A.

Edgefield Advertiser, October 21st, 1846, copied by John R. Abney, Esq.:

MARK MADISON ABNEY.

(Communicated.)

Mark Madison Abney is numbered with the dead. His pure and meek spirit has ascended to mingle with "the spirits of just men made perfect."

This excellent man and good minister of Jesus was born on

the 8th December, 1808, and died on the 29th September, in the present year, 1846. From his youth he was remarkable for his orderly, moral deportment; and at an early period put on Christ in baptism. In the prosecution of his studies for the ministry, he availed himself of the advantages of the Furman Theological Institution, and soon took a high rank in the ministry of the Word. Endowed with a strong and vigorous mind, he applied himself with patient and persevering atten- tion to the study of the Bible. In this course, which he strictly pursued, he was enabled to enrich his sermons with an abundant and judicious store of the Bible truth. Not satisfied with the mere surface of things, he penetrated into the depths of heavenly wisdom, and drew thence that profound knowledge of its principles and their just application, with which he de- lighted, improved, and instructed his hearers. Deeply im- pressed with the solemn responsibilities of the ministerial office, he performed its duties most faithfully. He daubed his people with no untempered mortar, but cried aloud, and spared not, preaching Jesus, "warning every man and teaching every man, that he might present every man perfect in Christ Jesus." He was eminently "set for the defence of the Gospel;" for stopping the mouths of gainsayers, and for put- ting to silence the ignorance of foolish men. The favorite subject of his ministrations was the inculcation of practical godliness on Evangelical principles. He delighted, therefore, to enlarge upon the duty and privilege of giving the heart to God. The desolations of Zion deeply affected him. He mourned and prayed over the coldness, the wide spread cold- ness of her sons and daughters, and labored much and faith- fully to allure them to greater spirituality and conformity to Christ. The life of this devoted servant of the Lord was in accordance with his preaching, and his death was both. For, he lived the life, and died the death, of the righteous.

His last sermon was preached a few days only before his death, and under a presentiment that it would close his min- isterial course on earth. At its commencement a peculiar feeling of humbleness of mind came over him, accompanied with enlarged manifestations of the divine majesty and good- ness. These filled his soul with heavenly joy, and imparted to his manner unusual animation. The Scriptures came to his recollection with readiness, and a spiritual unction bedewed his whole discourse. He preached as a dying man to dying men. The feelings of the audience were in unison with those of the preacher, and a holy influence seemed to pervade the whole audience.

He returned to his family under the pressure of sickness, which the skill of the physician could not remove. For this dear and honored servant, having fought a good fight, finished his course, and kept the battle, was now to be called up higher to receive his reward.

During his illness he spoke affectionately and faithfully to those around him, with the calm and firm confidence of one who knew "in whom he believed," and to whom he had committed that which he knew would be kept in safety against that day. Assembling his family around him on the day of his decease, he bade them an affectionate farewell, and commended them to the care of the orphan's Father and the widow's God and husband, and then betaking himself to holy converse with his Lord, he lifted up his heart in fervent prayer, and reiterating the word amen, fell sweetly asleep in Jesus.

The death of such a man, at such a time, is no ordinary loss, may its voice be heard by the churches, and especially those to whom he ministered. May we all have our loins girded about, and our lamps trimmed and burning, awaiting the call of our Divine Master.

Our departed brother has left a widow and three children, with an aged mother, brothers and sisters, and a large number of brethren and friends to mourn his loss.

In the preparation of this article the writer takes a melancholy pleasure in making it short and plain, according to the dying wish of its dear and honored subject. It is now closed with this incident. A brother, having heard the deceased express his determination to read the New Testament through once a month, bought a pocket volume to present to him. But death prevented the execution of the benevolent design. May it fall into the hands of one who will execute the purpose of him for whom it was intended, but now needs it no more.

CAPTAIN JAMES POPE BEAN

A grandson of Rev. Mark Abney, was elected a member of the House of Representatives from Edgefield County in 1888; was private secretary to Governor Tillman in 1890, and was appointed a member of the commission for the new County of Saluda by the Constitutional Convention of 1895. Captain Bean was happily married in 1890 to Miss W. Bessie Ready, a daughter of Honorable Wm. J. Ready, and a grand-daughter of Dr. John C. Ready, a sketch of whom is given elsewhere in this book.

Edgefield Advertiser, October 21st, 1868, copied by John R. Abney, Esq.:

DEATH OF MAJOR CICERO ADAMS.

Major Cicero Adams, the gallant soldier, who, in the late war, led forth the first company from Edgefield and from South Carolina, is no more. Since the close of the war he has dwelt, in high honor and esteem, at Bamberg, on the South Carolina Railroad, where he departed this life on the 2nd inst., aged thirty-four. Major Adams spent his early manhood in our midst, and married a daughter of one of our most honored families. Troops of friends will cherish the memory of this generous comrade and noble soldier

Edgefield Advertiser, January 11th, 1865, copied by John R. Abney, Esq.:

JOSEPH MATTHEW ABNEY,

Whose untimely death we now come to notice, was the elder son of Caroline S. and Dr. M. W. Abney, (late Surgeon P. A. C. S.,) and fell mortally wounded at the battle of Sharpsburg, Maryland, on the 17th of September, 1862, in the twenty-first year of his age.

No public announcement has until now been made of the sad event, owing to the uncertainty in which his fate has hitherto been enveloped. And even to this day and hour his family and relatives are in a painful state of incertitude whether he breathed his last while

"The stream of slaughter from that place of blood
Spread o'er the tainted sky,"

or the vital spark of his youthful life was extinguished in the noisome wards of a Northern hospital. However this may be,

no doubt any longer lingers, even in the minds of the most
hopeful, of his having perished in fighting in the battles of the
South, and here to-day it is our proud, albeit mournful, privilege to add his name to Carolina's Roll of Honor.

Young Abney first entered the lists as a soldier with the
"Edgefield Riflemen," in Jannaay, 1861.   After some months
of service on Sullivan's and Morris' Islands, he volunteered to
go with the First Regiment to Virginia under Colonel Gregg.
Having served out his time in the First Regiment, he came
home, where he had arrived but a few days before his life was
threatened by a severe attack of typhoid fever.   This danger
escaped, he returned to Virginia, and enrolled himself as a
member of Captain Bland's Company of the famous Seventh
Regiment, with which he did most loyal service, having been
on every campaign and in every action in which that band of
scarred Veterans was represented from the Manassas retreat,
and the battle before Richmond to that of Sharpsburg, where
he received his fatal wound.

In a letter to his father on the morning before the battle he
avowed that he was prepared and willing for any sacrifice.
The lamented Hard, in a letter to his mother in answer to inquiries concerning his fate, paid the following high and well
deserved testimonial to his gallantry on that occasion, and at
the same time limned a picture of his condition when last seen
on that gory field, which might well melt a heart of stone.
He says: "It affords me a melancholy pleasure to give you
such a slight information concerning him as I possess, and to
testify to the gallant manner in which he conducted himself
upon the field on which he was wounded.   On the 17th of
September we engaged the enemy at Sharpsburg, Maryland.
In making a desperate, but unsuccessful charge upon one of
the enemy's batteries, many of our men fell, and amongst
them, near to the guns, your son was shot down.   I saw him
as we fell back.   He called to me as I passed him, and asked
me if I could give him a drink of water from my canteen, say-
in at the same time: 'I am wounded in the leg.'   I paused a
moment to glance at him, but having no water, being unable
to render him any assistance, and being left in command of
my regiment, I passed on to a point at which we were ordered
to rally.   *   *   *   In my association with your son, I had

learned to regard him as high-toned, gallant, honorable. He won the affections of his companions, and the respect of all who knew him.''

Colonel Joseph Abney, in a letter to his father concerning his death condoles with him in the following beautiful and pathetic terms: ''He was the most trust-worthy and reliable young man of all my kindred and of all my acquaintance, and he had the highest place in my esteem and in my warm affections. His image can never be effaced from my heart, and if he is fallen, the loss to me is irreparable, for he stood to me in the same relation as son. He had so much honor, so much gentleness, and so much manhood that when disgusted with the vices and wickedness of other young men, to him, I could always turn with pride and inexpressible relief, as from a barren waste, to a meadow rich and green with all that can delight the eye or satisfy the soul of man. He was, in a great measure, my own pupil, and he was a comely scion that grew up under the training and trimming of my own hands, and he promised to be the honor and glory of his family and of all that loved him. Your grief can scarcely exceed my own. The occasion is one, which, but for his triumphant and glorious disappearance, and the bright companionship he had along might fill a community with sadness, depression and gloom.''

The writer of this tribute believes that he could not do more loving justice to the noble youth who forms the subject of the above glowing encomium than by presenting similar extracts from other condolatory letters to his bereaved parents, as showing what profound regret was felt at the loss of one so young, so promising, and so true. But he trusts that those already given will sufficiently evidence that he was a young man of no ordinary mould, and that, if his life had been spared, he would have been a most useful, exemplary, and honored member of society.

His life was as blameless and irreproachable, as his exit was glorious and triumphant, and the memory of the great sacrifice he has made for his country and the loved ones at home should be preserved as sacredly as the vestals guarded the chosen fire of the Gods. He lies dead upon the field of glory, but as to ''a thing ensky'd and sainted'' we speak farewell to his honored shade.   W. H. A.

Edgefield Advertiser, February 10th, 1870, copied by John R. Abney, Esq.:

DEATH OF COLONEL JOSEPH ABNEY.

Suddenly and unexpectedly, we are called to mourn the loss of a much valued and beloved citizen. Colonel Joseph Abney died at his residence in the town of Edgefield, on Wednesday night, the 2nd instant, after an illness of only ten hours, a victim of the prevailing epidemic, Meningetis, as pronounced by his brother, Dr. M. W. Abney, the attending physician. He died in the prime of manhood, at the age of forty-eight, leaving a wife and three children.

Bravely, honestly, and efficiently, he fought the battle of life, as he fought for the honor, interest, and glory of his country. Educated, he became an accomplished scholar, lawyer, and soldier. His civil triumphs in popular assemblies, in the Legislature and in the forum, as well as laurels won in war, make up the sum of a reputation, of which his family, his friends, and his native Carolina are justly proud. But although he received the plaudits of his country, for services rendered in peace and in war; while every battle ground from Vera Cruz to the Garita de Belin, of Mexico, and his blood shed on the field of Churubusco; and later in life, at Drury's Bluff, in our last war, attest his devotion and skill as a warrior, he has left behind a monument to his fame, not less to be appreciated in the memory and gratitude of care-worn poverty, which, with a ready hand, prompted by Christian Charity, he never failed to alleviate; and the poor will bless him, in their sorrow for his departure. But he is gone! And it is a consolation to believe, that he has entered into his eternal rest, as a Christian and an heir of Salvation.

Edgefield Advertiser, January 11th, 1865, copied by John R. Abney, Esq.:

PICKENS B. WATTS—IN MEMORIAM.

The martial deeds and chivalrous feats, "fit for song and story," of our glorious Southern heroes, illustrated on many a hard-fought field in this our unequal contest for national independence, are deeply furrowed and embalmed in the memories of a grateful people. The treasure of their blood has enriched the verdant plains, hillsides, and valleys of our country's soil, and the brooks and rivulets, as they murmur over them, blush blood-red at the barbarities and iniquities of a worse than Scythian foe. But the blood of those who have thus nobly immolated themselves on the altars of their country will ever be cherished and sanctified as the precious ransom of our liberties. In the future days of the republic, those classic battle grounds will become so many Mecca-shrines to which our ardent and peerless youth will emulously flock as pilgrims to imbibe from the relics of the illustrious dead the exalted lessons of patriotism, devotion, and virtue. The historian of this war, perchance, will deem that he has discharged his obligation to posterity when his stylus has inscribed on the historic scroll the name of each "Captain, or Colonel, or Knight-at arms" who has figured in the eventful story, the successes he has achieved, and his vivats of popular applause. But it will be the legacy of the faithful chronicler to fill up the chasm left by the more ambitious historian and "set down with gold on lasting pillars" the names and unhonored laurels of those warrior-heroes who, though holding subordinate stations in the military arena, nevertheless dealt doughty blows, and performed prodigies of valour, in delivering their country from the galling yoke of servitude. And here offer we up the meed —a tearful and grief-wrung tribute to the manes of two devoted martyrs who have thus poured out the rich spilth of their heart's best blood as a libation to the goddess of Liberty.

"The king of shadows loves a shining mark."

Never were the words of seer or poet more strikingly confirmed than in the death of First Sergeant Pickens Butler Watts, Company F, Twenty-Seventh Regiment South Carolina Volunteers, who fell near Petersburg, Va., on the 24th of June, 1864, while in command of a company charging the enemy's work. He was the son of Mary S. Watts, deceased, and Richard Watts, Esq., of Saluda, Laurens District, and was 32 years of age when the silver cord of his life was loosed forever.

Immediately after the ratification of the Ordinance of Secession by the State Convention on the memorable 20th of December, 1860, Sergeant Watts attached himself to a company of minute men, the "Rhett Guards," raised at Newberry Court House by Captain Whit Walker. This fine Company

shortly afterwards tendered its services to Governor Pickens,
and was ordered to report to Colonel Maxcy Gregg on Sullivan's Island, which it did early in January, 1861, and composed a part of that chosen phalanx, known as the First Regiment of South Carolina Volunteers. The operations of this
Regiment on Sullivan's and Morris' Islands, and its subsequent
brilliant career in Virginia are already "familiar as household
words."

On a few weeks before the Regiment's term of enlistment
expired, Sergeant Watts had led to the bridal altar one of
Edgefield's most lovely and accomplished daughters. Of
strong attachments and of an ardent and loving temperament,
he was not insensible to the claims of conjugal affection, or
the endearing charms and influences of home and family. But,
glowing with patriotic ardour, he felt that the claim of his
country was paramount to every other consideration. Accordingly, in the fall of 1861, he joined the "Edgefield Blues,"
a Company raised by Captain Joseph Abney, and which subsequently became Company A, of the Twenty-Second Regiment, South Carolina Volunteers, a Regiment of twelve
month's troops, of which Captain Abney was elected the
Colonel. At the re-organization of this Regiment Colonel
Abney failed to be re-elected. A special Act of Congress,
however, passed about this time, provided for the organization
of Battalions of Sharpshooters in the different States, the
materials for which were to be eliminated from the various
Brigades and Regiments already in service. Colonel Abney
was nominated and appointed by Major General Pemberton to
organize and assume command of one of these Battalions.
Sergeant Watts obtained a transfer to Major Abney's Battalion
in the month of July, 1862, and was appointed Orderly
Sergeant of Company B, commanded by Jos. Blythe Allston.

The First Battalion of South Carolina Sharpshooters will
long be remembered for its faultless discipline and the excel-
lence and maturity of its drill. It is unnecessary to enumerate
here the valuable services rendered by that picked corps at
Grahamville, Bee's Creek, Coosawhatchie, Pocotaligo, Com-
bahee Ferry, Johns', Wadmalaw, and James' Islands, and
Winyaw Bay near Georgetown. But it was at Pocotaligo, on
the 22nd October, 1862, that the Company to which Sergeant

Watts belonged particularly distinguished itself. It there evoked the unqualified "well-done" from General "Liveoak" Walker for its gallant behaviour, all three of the commissioned officers present, having been wounded in that engagement.

After a separate existence of about sixteen months, Major Abney's Battalion was amalgamated with the Charleston Battalion, Lieutenant Colonel P. C. Gaillard forming the Twenty-Seventh Regiment, South Carolina Volunteers, Hagood's Brigade. Towards the close of April 1864, this splendid Brigade was ordered to Petersburg, Va., and there it won golden opinions and imperishable renown in all those brilliant and bloody encounters, which rendered its name no less a terror to the foe, than a pride to the gallant State which sent it forth on its errands to avenge the blood of her fallen children. In all of those sanguinary conflicts, Sergeant Watts bore a conspicuous part. The official reports of those battles announce him as having been engaged with distinction at Walthall Junction, Drewry's Bluff, Bermuda Hundreds, and Cold Harbor.

On the fatal 24th of June, he was acting as Lieutenant and commanding a company, which with clarion-voice he was cheering forward, leading the way himself, in a desperate assault on the entrenched position of the enemy. He had just gained the enemy's works, and was still encouraging his comrades, when his brain was pierced by a hostile bullet, killing him instantly.

Thus has passed away from us this earnest, impassioned, and intrepid spirit. His officers and fellow-soldiers, as well as his family and friends, fondly cherished the hope that he was a captive, and would soon be restored to them by the usual mode of exchange. But an officer of high rank, and who had read his character well, concluded with more discernment when he declared that "he was too brave a man ever to allow himself to be taken alive."

In thus attempting a brief sketch of his not uneventful military career perhaps as much has been said as will be required to establish his shining qualities as a soldier. He was ever

"Ready to do what a hero can,
    Wall to sap, or river to ford,
Cannon to front, or foe to pursue,
    Still ready to do, and sworn to be true,
    As a man and a patriot can."

In a private and social aspect, the character of Sergeant
Watts needs no eulogium.   His amenity, openness, and access-
ibility were esteemed traits which elevated him high in the
social scale and made him a most welcome companion to all
with whom he mingled.

"He was one,
    The truest manner'd, ——— ——
Half all men's hearts were his."

He possessed in a degree rarely acquired the happy faculty
of unbending himself to the young and ingratiating their
affections.   Even his faults were of that peculiar mitigating
class which are supposed to have a leaning to the side of
virtue.   Over his noble and fearless soul a dishonorable purpose never flapped its raven wing.   Stern, resolute, and
inflexible in all matters of duty, he was yet engaging in his
address, and mild, winning, and conciliating in his intercourse
with all.

"His life was gentle: and the elements,
    So mixed in him, that nature might stand up,
And say to all the world, this was a man!"

Edgefield Advertiser, February 24th, 1870:

JOSEPH ABNEY.

Colonel Carey W. Styles, of the Albany (Ga) News, after
copying our announcement of the death of Colonel Joseph
Abney, adds an eloquent and feeling tribute to the memory of
the deceased as follows: "We knew him well—messed with
him through Scott's Mexican Campaign, slept in the same
tent, and fought by his side—and in all the relations of companion, messmate, officer, and soldier, he was kind, generous,
courteous, and brave.   He possessed exalted character, and a
sense of honor as pure and lofty as the knightliest champion
that e'er bore a prize from the lists.   We esteemed him for his
manly contest with the ills that flesh is heir to; admired him
for a noble courage that ever dared misfortune and danger

with nerveless inflexibility; loved him for his social and companionable virtues, and mourn him as a friend gone to that undiscovered country from whose bourne no traveler returns."

JOSEPH HADDON,

An Englishman, who died in the early part of the year 1896, in Abbeville County, deserves to have his name mentioned in the history of Edgefield. Indeed, it would not have been out of place in the history of the State, as he was the first engineer who ever run a locomotive on any railroad in the State. When the South Carolina Railroad from Charleston to Hamburg was building it is said that he came over from England with the locomotive that was first put upon that road, and that he helped in the making of it. Whether the story is true this writer has no means of knowing, but it is altogether probable that the honor belongs to Joe Haddon. If I am not mistaken, he and his wife once lived at Mount Enon in a house built by Dr. J. C. Ready. I used to meet him occasionally when my home was in that part of Edgefield District which is now Saluda County.

Mr. Haddon was at an advanced age at the time of his death.

THE OUZTS SETTLEMENT.

Near Meeting Street, about ten miles north of Edgefield Court House, is a settlement which has been, and is yet known as the Dutch Settlement. It embraces a scope of country about ten miles square. The founder of this settlement, Peter Ouzts, came direct from Germany with his father, Dietereig Ouzts, before the Revolutionary War, in 1769, and was a brave soldier in that war. He was in many battles and was severely wounded several times. He was only twelve years old when he landed in America. His mother died aboard ship, was buried at sea, and he was left alone with only his father to care for him.

Mr. Dietereig Ouzts lived near the River Rhine, in Germany, and sailed from Hamburg for this country. After the Revolution he married again and became the father of three other sons, Mike and Jacob, of Newberry County, and Martin, of Edgefield. All married and reared families.

Peter grew to manhood, wooed and won Miss Elizabeth

Harling, and they became the happy parents of a large family of children, thirteen sons and two daughters. One son and one daughter died in youth, the others married and succeeded well in farming. As each one married off he was set up in life with a farm of several hundred acres, cut off from the home tract, and was given stock and supplies sufficient for a year, and then left to carve out his own fortune. Tobacco was the principal money crop at that time, and plenty of provisions were raised on the farms for home consumption. These sturdy people were very quiet and were contented with the enjoyments of home life, caring nothing for the excitements of town and city life. Peter Ouzts' sons were named David John, Henry, Martin, Aaron, Jacob, Abram, Isaac, Peter, Daniel, and Benjamin. The daughter married Daniel George.

Mr. Peter Ouzts, the patriarch of the settlement, lived to the age of 77 years, long enough to see all his children married and settled in life, except one or two of the younger ones, who married soon after his death. Nearly all the children of the older generations were boys, and hence the numerous descendants of Mr. Peter Ouzts are easily traced. In 1880 there were nearly one thousand (940) descendants of Mr. Peter Ouzts, and nearly all of them were living in Edgefield County. In the War of Secession this family furnished as many boys, thirteen, to uphold the "Lost Cause" as any family in the State, and no truer nor braver people were ever found in battle. Some lost arms and legs and some their lives upon the battle field. Five were killed.

The name Ouzts is Americanized. In Germany it is Uzt, and to make it more complete the letters O and S are prefixed and affixed, but whether the name was improved by the change is yet a debateable question. It was once spelled "Utes,," in the year 1800. In the year 1819 the present form was used. Since the war, and with its various changes, this family and their descendants have become greatly scattered. Dr. B. F. Ouzts, son of one of the original twelve brothers, is living in Texas, and for several years has been a member of the city council in the town in which he lives. He is an able physician; in business has been very successful, and has acquired considerable property.

W. H. Ouzts, the oldest son of Daniel Ouzts, is now (1892) Sheriff of Edgefield County. The duties of this office are, and have been, faithfully and impartially discharged by him. That he is one of the most popular men in the county, and that he has faithfully discharged the duties of the office, is proven by the fact that he is now serving his third term, making twelve years during which he has held the office. Mr. Benjamin Ouzts, the youngest son of Peter Ouzts, is still living in his father's old house. The house, however, has been moved about a mile from the original site. Mr. Ouzts has amassed considerable property, and is still as persevering as ever, although he is nearly three-score. Mr. D. T. Ouzts, son of Benjamin Ouzts, is the present popular and efficient Cashier of the Bank of Johnston.

Dr. W. D. Ouzts, grandson of Isaac Ouzts, the third next to the youngest of the orignal brothers, is an able and prominent physician of Edgefield. Mr. James W. Ouzts, grandson of Daniel Ouzts, is a civil engineer in Alabama. He has acquired some very valuable property in the Southwestern States. Mr. Daniel A. G. Ouzts, the youngest son of Daniel Ouzts by his second wife, Miss Martha Hill Lowery, a distant cousin of President George Washington, is at this writing, May, 1892, with Pelzer, Rodgers & Co., of Charleston, S. C. He was in the South Carolina College, but left without graduation to edit and take charge of the management of the Edgefield Chronicle, of which he was owner while in college.

XXVI.

CHURCHES—METHODIST.

In Shipp's History of Methodism in South Carolina, which is my authority for what I write of Methodism in Edgefield, no dates are given of the establishing or building of the different houses of worship in the various localities, nor of the formation of Circuits and Districts. The book is very valnable as a history of the movements, lives, and labors of the preachers engaged in the work, but in other respects it is quite defective—leaves the general reader in the dark as to what part of the State Saluda Circuit is, or Butler Circuit, indeed, as to the location of any circuit or meeting house. As a rule, the names of the churches or meeting houses, are never given.

The earliest notice I find of Methodist preaching at Edgefield Court House was in May 1790. Beverly Allen, the minister, writing to Mr. Wesley, says: "May 8th I attended a quarterly meeting on Saluda. The first day there was a considerable work among the people, but on the second we had a large, attentive congregation, to whom I spoke freely. All were still and attended to what I said, till, toward the close of the sermon, when the word caused a trembling and a weeping in the whole assembly. Soon after they cried for mercy, and the poor, distressed creatures fell on their knees beseeching us to pray for them, which we did. Some found mercy and peace to their souls, and others were under deep distress. On my way the day following I preached in Edgefield Court House to a very considerable number of attentive people, to whom I declared the oath of God, that he has no pleasure in the death of a sinner. Towards the conclusion, one woman, sitting on a lofty seat, dropped to the floor, and soon after a number of others came and fell on their knees, crying for mercy, and several found deliverance."

This Beverly Allen was ordained at the First Conference held at Green Hill, N. C., beginning April 20th, 1785. For a few years he was a great preacher, a traveling companion of the Bishop Asbury, and a correspondent of Mr. Wesley. In 1792 his name stands in the Minutes as "expelled." He engaged in mercantile business in Augusta; got into difficulties and killed Major Forsyth, the United States Marshal, while attempting to arrest him for debt. He fled, but was captured and imprisoned in Elbert County, Ga., but was soon released by his friends, who charitably supposed him to be insane. He then buried himself in the wilds of Kentucky, where he practiced medicine. Rev. Peter Cartwright, D. D., says of him "After killing the Sheriff he fled from the country to escape justice, and settled in Logan County, Kentucky, then called 'Rogue's Harbor.' His family followed him, and here he practiced medicine. To ease a troubled conscience he drank in the doctrine of Universalism, but he lived and died a great friend to the Methodist Church" This writer has learned from his reading that some as holy and saintly men as ever lived were believers in the doctrine of Universal Salvation; and others as saintly and pure as it is possible for human nature to be, were devout members of the Roman Church, that church, which we Protestants are so prone to regard as the mother of harlots and of all abominations. The truth is, the Holy Spirit of God touches, quickens, and regenerates every one who desires the divine life, be his religious faith what it may, without regard to his intellectual perception of dogmatic truth.

As far back as 1785 and 1786 the preachers penetrated the country up the principal rivers. Saluda is not named, but Broad River is, and Broad River Circuit was formed, which embraced part of Newberry. George Daugherty, a native of Newberry District, came to Saluda District as Presiding Elder in 1802. We find that in 1791 Dr. Coke preached at Ninety-Six on his return from a Conference in Wilkes County, Ga. I must note here that the celebrated Lorenzo Dow wandered into the wilderness of the Tombigbee River in 1803 and 1804, and preached the first Protestant sermon on the soil of Alabama. On his return North he passed through Edgefield, preached at the Court House and at Abney's Meeting House on the Saluda River, near Higgins' Ferry.

Joseph Moore, who closed his active life in the ministry in Edgefield on the Saluda Circuit in the year 1833, though he lived until the 14th of February, 1851, dying in his 85th year, was born in Virginia in 1767. He was about 65 years in the active and efficient ministry of 'the Gospel. I have a sermon of his showing the difference between the foreknowledge and the decrees of God, which was printed at the N. A. Gazette Office, Augusta, Georgia, in 1833, and, I suppose, was preached to his people some time that same year; though it is not stated when nor where nor on what occasion the sermon was delivered, except that it was at a particular request.

Joseph Moore was born in Virginia in 1767. In his childhood his parents moved to Rutherford County, N. C. He was licensed to preach in his 19th year. Five years afterwards he was admitted to traveling connection and became one of the pioneers of Methodism. He preached in North Carolina, South Carolina, and in Virginia. In 1806 he was located at his own request. In 1826 he rejoined the South Carolina Conference and continued laboring until 1834.

Nicholas Walters was born in Maryland, November 20th, 1739,—received on probation in 1776, and, besides the labors bestowed on Maryland and Virginia, he traveled the Union, Saluda and Broad River Circuits in the South Carolina Conference, and was stationed in Charleston in 1804, where he died of yellow fever on the 10th of August of that year, in the 65th year of his age. His youngest brother, William Walters, was the first American preacher who entered the traveling connection.

Coleman Carlisle joined the itinerancy in 1792, and was sent to Broad River Circuit. In 1802 he was sent to Saluda. "I have known him," says Mr. Travis, "after returning home from preaching several miles distant, after supper to take the same horse (he had but one) and plow with him by moonlight until nearly midnight, and then go off next morning to his appointment. He neither owned nor hired servants." He was a very popular preacher, and when local was sent for, far and near, to preach funeral sermons. For these labors he received no compensation. He has two grandsons living in Newberry County, M. A. Carlisle, Esq., a lawyer practicing at Newberry Court House and Dr. R. C. Carlisle, a physician practicng in the County.

In 1797 George Clark had charge of the Saluda Circuit. From 1802 to 1804 George Daugherty was Presiding Elder of the Saluda District. Of Mr. Daugherty something more must be said than that he was Presiding Elder of Saluda District. He was a great preacher and a remarkable man. He was born in 1772 in Newberry District near the Lexington line. He began life as a teacher in the fork of Saluda and Broad Rivers, boarding with a Mr. Reamy. In December 1797 he went down with George Clark, who had charge of the Saluda Circuit, as an applicant for admission into the traveling connection. Conference met in Charleston January 1st, 1798. He was received and appointed to a circuit. His career as a preacher was not long, but very active and useful. In 1807 he attended the last conference in which his voice was ever heard on earth. At this conference he brought forward and triumphantly carried the resolution which fixed the sentiment of the South Carolina Conference true to duty for all time to come. "If any preacher shall desert his station through fear in time of sickness or danger, the conference shall never employ that man again." A noble resolution.

The following anecdotes are given as incidents in his own personal history, and also as illustrating the spirit of the times and the state of society at the period of his active career. He lived at a time when the public, especially that of Charleston, was easily excited on the subject of slavery, and Methodist preachers were objects of suspicion and dislike. This arose from the insane zeal of some of the early preachers on that subject. The course of Dr. Coke had been influential in producing this state of feeling. It is not strange, therefore, that a few injudicious remarks made in one of the Charleston churches by a transient Methodist preacher should have produced some excitement. A company of young men went to the Methodist meeting house, determined to give the offending preacher a taste of mob law; but they mistook their man, and, seizing Mr. Daugherty, they dragged him to the pump and pumped water upon him until he was nearly dead. He would probably have been pumped to death had he not been rescued by a heroic woman. Mrs. Kugley, seeing his predicament, and the great danger in which he was, rushed through the mob, and, gathering up her gown, stuffed it into the spout of the pump and stopped the flow of water. The mob then let Mr. Daugherty go, and Mrs. Kugley took him to a place of safety and had him properly cared for. It is probable that he never entirely recovered from the injury thus received.

Another incident, illustrative of Mr. Daugherty's power as a preacher, must be given. At a camp-meeting held in Darlingtou District, in 1805, the assembled rowdies perpetrated enormities over which it is necessary, even at this distant day, to draw a veil. On Sunday the crowd of rowdies was very large, and while roving about through the pine forest which surrounded the camp, it came to pass while Rev. James Jenkins was preaching that a lady in the congregation began to praise God aloud. From every point of the compass the rowdies came thundering into camp with the tramp of a herd of buffaloes, thus producing a scene of wild confusion. By this time the lady had become quiet, and the time had come for Mr. Daugherty to launch a thunderbolt. He rose and said: "I desire very much to engage your attention for a short time, and as I am aware of your impatience, I propose, as a sort of compromise with you, to waive all the introductory services and proceed directly to my discourse." He then announced for his text Mark 5:13, "And the herd ran violently down a steep place into the sea, and were choked." He first spoke of the wiles of satan, showing that he was willing to be anything and to do anything so that he could lead his victims astray. He then considered the text in the order of the thoughts which it suggests: First, the herd into which the devils went; second, the drivers, and third, the market. He swept along his pathway like a blazing comet, drawing such life-like pictures of vice and diabolical intrigue that the miserable creatures before him seemed spell-bound; though they were all standing, scarcely a man among them broke ranks. When he reached his imaginary market with them, the end of an abandoned life, of a dark and soul-destroying course of wickedness, the picture took on such an appalling hue that an involuntary shudder came manifestly over the vast audience; they seemed actually to see them, in successive columns, disappearing from mortal view and sinking into the everlasting abyss. The most stout-hearted sinners present seemed overwhelmed with amazement, and when the preacher closed they left in wild confusion, and were soon en route for home.

Never, perhaps, was effort made under similar circumstances that equalled this. It was pertinent, awful, loving, scathing, and unique. It was the attack of a master-mind in a last resort, and was entirely successful.

From 1807 to 1810 Lewis Myers was Presiding Elder of the Saluda District. He was born at Indian Fields, in Colleton District, S. C., May 7th, 1775, and died on the 16th of November, 1851.

In 1810 Reddick Pierce was Presiding Elder, and John R. Coburn rode Saluda Circuit in 1831. In 1842 and 1843 Samuel Dunwoody rode a circuit in Edgefield, where I used to see him frequently. Zoar, then called Persimmon Creek, was one of his churches, where I sometimes heard him preach. Many anecdotes used to be told of his oddities. His son Samuel I knew well for many years, and loved him for his truth and purity of character. His death was tragic. He was night watchman at the railroad depot at Newberry, a few years after the war. One night while on duty he was murdered by some persons who wished to plunder, and the next morning his mutilated body was found lying on the ground near the depot. He died at the post of duty—murdered.

John Tarrant, born in Virginia, joined the South Carolina Conference in 1809; was at Edgefield as pastor in 1841. He died April 1st, 1849, in his 65th year.

In 1841–44 Nicholas Talley was Presiding Elder of Cokesbury District, of which, I believe, Edgefield is part. Joel Wilson Townsend was born in Marlboro District, January 19th, 1800; was converted in 1819; admitted to conference February, 1823; was on Saluda Circuit 1831–32; at Edgefield 1837–38; superannuated in 1844, and settled at Cokesbury, where he died May 14th, 1880, while his son was conducting family worship.

John R. Picket was at Edgefield in 1858 and in 1859. In 1860 and 1861 he was at Butler, in the same county. Mr. Picket was born in Fairfield County, April 2nd, 1814; converted in 1831; entered the conference on trial February, 1835. He died at his home in Chester, March 15th, 1870.

This sketch of the history of Methodism in Edgefield is very meager and imperfect, but Shipp's History of Methodism in South Carolina, upon which the writer has relied for his information, confines itself, almost exclusively, to the lives and labors of the preachers engaged in the work. It does not tell when the church was established at Edgefield, nor, indeed, at any other place in the county, nor when the meeting houses were built, and seldom gives the names of any.

Since the foregoing was written I have received the following information in regard to the history of this church in Edgefield:

Saluda Circuit was the name given probably to the first charge ever organized by the Methodists in Edgefield, while yet, perhaps, it was a part of Ninety-Six District. In 1834 the name was changed from Saluda Circuit to Edgefield Circuit. The Saluda Circuit in 1830 embraced the following named churches or places of worship: Mount Lebanon, Republican, Martin Town, Langley's, Nixon's, Swamp, Moore's, Rehoboth, Providence, Bethel, Reedy Creek, Mile's, Bethany, Spring Hill, Court House, Pine Grove, Gassaway, Persimmon Creek, Cockran's, Kenny's, Spann's, and Sleepy Creek.

Persimmon Creek is now known as Zoar, and the name of Sleepy Creek has been changed to McKendree. Pine Grove has been abandoned, and some of the others have either acquired new names or been abandoned. Langley's was cut off with the territory which forms part of Aiken County. The amount raised by these churches for ministerial support in that year (1830) was $372.62½.

The Methodist have kept pace with other denominations in church building and increase of membership. The amount of money raised for ministerial support and for benevolent purposes in recent years, is in striking contrast with that formerly given for such purposes.

In 1893 there were thirty Methodist houses of worship in Edgefield County, with an aggregate white membership of 2,823. These churches paid for ministerial support that year the sum of $5,647.40, and the sum of $1,684.35 for benevolent and other purposes. The total valuation of church property then amounted to $33,300.

Edgefield Circuit, formerly Saluda, used to require about four weeks for the preacher in charge to make the rounds of his appointments. From time to time the circuit has been divided and sub-divided until now there are nine circuits and parts of circuits carved from it. The following are the names of these circuits and the churches composing them: Parksville

Circuit with five churches: Parksville, St. Paul, Barr's Chapel, Modoc, and Dothem.

North Edgefield Circuit with four churches: Rehoboth, Bethel, Mt. Vernon, and Mt. Carmel.

Saluda Circuit with four churches: Emory, Butler, Zoar, and Bethany.

Edgefield Circuit has three churches: Edgefield, Trenton, and McKendree.

Johnston Circuit has three churches: Johnston, Harmony, and Spann's.

Butler Circuit has four churches: Bethlehem, Gassaway, Shiloh, and Traywick.

Batesburg Circuit has two Edgefield churches: Ridge Spring and Providence.

Leesville Circuit has three Edgefield churches: Nazareth, Rehoboth, and Clyde.

Ninety-Six Circuit has two Edgefield churches: Kinard's and Mt. Lebanon.

Mr. William Griffith, whom the writer of this history knew well for a great many years, claimed for Zoar as being the oldest place of worship in the County. That before the Revolution a log church was built where the present church stands. In that war a British squadron of cavalry camped there for a short time. The present writer was born in a house which stood on the old Ninety-Six road which was a few miles nearer Saluda than Zoar, and near that road on a hill side by Tosta Creek he found, when a boy, the barrel of a pistol, which certainly had once been finely mounted, as there were still to be seen on the barrel, or sticking to it, some scraps of gold. The barrel was kept for a number of years, but no special care being taken of it, it was finally lost, never to be found again.

At a Quarterly Church Conference held at Zoar some years before Mr. Griffith's death, the question of breaking up and discarding this church was being debated, and Mr. Griffith's residence being very near and he hearing of what was going on went down and opposed the proposition. In an earnest speech he pleaded for the church, and as related above, stated in regard to the age of the church. He said, rather than see the house pulled down and the graves of the dead neglected, he would keep them up at his own expense. Mr. Griffith was able to carry his point and the church was retained, for which this writer is glad, as at that house and also at Bethany when it was still a log house, he sometimes met the brethren and sisters at love feasts and class meetings.

Mr. Griffith once made a trip to Philadelphia with a wagon and team and brought back a load of goods for some Edgefield merchant. At that time such trips were not unusual. This was one of the inconveniences growing out of that war with Great Britian known as the War of 1812.

The land on which Bethany is built was donated by Reuben Blalock in 1809. The first house built was of logs. Mr. Blalock's remains are buried at this church.

XXVII.

THE PRESBYTERIAN CHURCH.

Edgefield was one of the three counties in the State of South Carolina, Lexington and Georgetown being the other two, which never, until 1877, had a Presbyterian Church in its bounds. This is somewhat remarkable when we consider the fact that the adjoining County of Abbeville is one of the great strongholds of Presbyterianism in the State. Abbeville, however, was settled by large colonies of Scotch-Irish and Huguenots, who brought their religion with them, whilst no such colonies of Presbyterians located in Edgefield.

An effort was made before the War of Secession to establish a Presbyterian Church at the county seat, and a handsome sum was subscribed for the erection of a house of worship; but the war suspended the efforts in that direction. When the war was over many of the friends of the church were dead upon the field of battle and others were so dispirited that no further attempts were made till more than ten years had passed after the restoration of peace.

For a long time Mrs. J. W. Hill, then Miss Mattie Wardlaw, was the only Presbyterian in the county. She held her membership in Augusta, Ga. In spite of her loneliness and the solicitations of friends to unite with other denominations, she clung to the faith of her fathers in the hope of establishing a church of like faith in which she could feel more at home. At length her fidelity and patience were rewarded and she became, under Providence, the mother of Presbyterianism in the county. As soon as one or two more were located in the county a petition was forwarded to South Carolina Presbytery, asking for an occasional ministerial visit, looking to the organization of a church. Finally a committee of South Carolina Presbytery was appointed. The committee consisted of Revs. J. L. Martin, D. D., R. A. Fair, W. F. Pearson, and Elders Thomas Thomson and Robert Wardlaw, who met at Edgefield Court House and organized the church, May 20th, 1877, which adopted the name "Edgefield Presbyterian Church." The organization was made after much hesitation,

many misgivings and earnest prayers, for only four persons were
found ready to enroll themselves as its membership.   Their
names will be always held in honor by the church as examples
of faith.   Each one of the four is living at this date, May
1892, and in active connection with that church; their names
are Mr. S. H. Manget, Mrs. J. W. Hill, Mrs. R. S. Anderson,
and Miss Etta Rainsford, now Mrs. J. B. Norris.   Mr. S. H.
Manget was elected, ordained, and installed its first ruling
elder, and was for a long time its only officer.

The new church was for several years supplied with preaching and sustained jointly by Charleston and South Carolina
Presbyteries, as the C., C. & A. Railroad running through the
county was the dividing line between them.   Preaching was
maintained at Edgefield Court House, Trenton, and Johnston
as "stations" in the bounds of the church of four members.
This was, however, necessary, as several Presbyterians had
located in Trenton and Johnston.   The Edgefield Presbyterian
Church was considered to cover the territory of the entire
county.

In May, 1880, Rev. S. L. Morris visited it by invitation and
held a meeting at Trenton, which resulted in ten additions to
its membership.   It was this visit which introduced to the
church its first paster, and enlisted the interest of Rev. S. L.
Morris in the church.   The following year the supply system
terminated, and the church unanimously called Rev. S. L.
Morris as its pastor.   He was already in charge of Walhalla, a
flourishing church, and so left the matter entirely in the hands
of Presbytery, whether to accept or not.   After debating the
matter a whole day, it was decided by a two-third vote to send
him to Edgefield.   He began his labors in May, 1882, as
pastor, but was not installed until August 20th, 1882.

At the beginning of his pastorate the membership of the
church was about thirty, and a house of worship had been
erected at Trenton and dedicated in December, 1881.   Rev.
J. L. Martin, D. D., preaching the dedicatory sermon.

The first thing Rev. S. L. Morris did after his installation
as pastor, was to establish a fourth preaching station, at the
invitation of Mr. B. R. Tillman and his sisters, at the
"Pavilion" of the "Hussars," near the residence of Mr. Tillman.   The next in order was the erection of a church build-

ing at Johnston, which was dedicated in June, 1883, by Rev. J. L. Girardeau, D. D. This was quickly followed by a neat church building near Mr. B. R. Tillman's and upon the Till man property, which was dedicated in November, 1883, by Rev. J. L. Girardeau, D. D. The fourth and last building was erected at Edgefield Court House and dedicated May, 1885, by Rev. J. L. Girardeau, D. D., about eight years from the formation of the church of four members at Edgefield. These four church buildings in the county cost about seven thousand dollars. A very good showing for eight years' work, starting with only four members.

As yet, there was only one organization, the church preferring to hold together until it felt strong enough to separate into four. After preaching seven and a half years the pastoral relation between Mr. Morris and the church was dissolved in October, 1889, in order that he might accept a call to Macon, Ga. During his pastorate Mr. Morris preached at two stations every Sabbath, riding on an average twenty miles each trip, making about a thousand miles a year. He received 130 : sons into the Edgefield Church, and baptized 6; ' vine church with a membership of 120. When his pastorate began there were 30.

Upon the dissolution of this pastoral relation, the church was without a pastor nearly a year before they could agree upon one. Finally they called Rev. J. M. Plowden, who has at the date of this writing, May, 1892, been among them acceptably for about eighteen months. Under his administration a manse has been built, and Johnston and Trenton, in 1891, was organized into separate churches. This gives three fully organized churches in the county, with Highview still as preaching station.

Among the most prominent members are the original four, Mr. S. H. Manget, Mrs. J. W. Hill, Mrs. R. S. Anderson, and Mrs. J. B. Norris; also Dr. J. W. Hill, W. E. Lynch, O. F. Cheatham, Dr. James H. DeVore, John K. Allen, B. B. Hughes, E. M. Hix, Dr. D. B. Frantis, Mrs. B. R. Tillman, Mrs. F. T. Simpson, Mrs. G. W. Wise, Mrs. J. M. Wise, Mrs. T. J. Teague, Mrs. Jno. Roper, and many of the most promising young people of the county. The progress of this church is quite wonderful, and its future is bright with promise.

Rev. S. L. Morris, the first pastor, was born in Abbeville County, S. C., December 25th, 1854. He joined Hopewell Church November 21st, 1868; graduated at Erskine College June 25th, 1873; graduated at the Theological Seminary, Columbia, S. C., May 10th, 1876; pastor at Walhalla from May, 1876, to May, 1882; pastor at Edgefield from May, 1882, to October, 1889; Stated Clerk of South Carolina Presbytery from October, 1878, to October, 1889; represented South Carolina Presbytery in the General Assembly of 1880, at Charleston, S. C., and 1887 at St. Louis, Missouri; director of Columbia Seminary from 1885 to 1887; installed pastor of Tatnall Square Presbyterian Church, at Macon, Ga., January 1st, 1890. From this brief summing up the reader will see that Mr. Morris has not led an idle life, but that on the contrary he has been an indefatigable worker.

LUTHERAN—ST. MARK'S.

The oldest Lutheran Church in Edgefield County—there are only six in all, as originally, very few Germans or Dutch, and no Scandanavians, settled in that part of the country—is Saint Mark's, not far from Big Saluda. During the early part of the Nineteenth century, from 1800 to 1810, several families from Newberry settled in the neighborhood. These were visited by Rev. Wertz, who held services in private houses and preached in both the German and English languages. In a few years after the Synod of South Carolina was organized—which was in January, 1824, and the first meeting was held November 14th, 1824,—the Rev. J. D. Sheck was employed as missionary. During his mission he visited the congregations, and towards the close of the year 1828 a house of worship was built, which was very small. Rev. G. Dreher first had charge. He was succeeded by Rev. Schwartz, who soon died, and after his death Revs. Herman Aull and Sheppard served them. During Mr. Sheppard's services the membership increased so much that it was necessary to enlarge the building, which was done in 1841. Revs. Bauknight and Sheppard then served them, but in a short time, that is in a few years, Mr. Sheppard moved to Mississippi.

Mr. Sheppard did one service while pastor here, and if all other services and duties done and performed by him resulted as happily as this, he has reason to congratulate himself. On the evening of May 1st, 1845, he officiated as clergyman at the marriage of this writer to her whom he had chosen as his companion for life. A happy union of over forty years duration, which was dissolved only by death.

In 1856 a new house was built not far from the old one and was dedicated in 1857, by Revs. Berley and Bouknight. Mr. Bouknight continued pastor until 1868, when he was succeeded by Revs. Hawkins and Sligh. After this time the membership became considerably reduced by the removal of several families to other localities. Some moved and settled in Sumter County, Georgia, where the Rev. J. P. Margart organized and built a church.

Synod held meetings at St. Marks in 1842, 1852, and 1866, the Nineteenth, Twenty-Ninth, and Forty-Second Sessions.

MOUNT CALVARY,

The next oldest, and very near the same age, is Mount Calvary. In 1827 the Revs. J. D. Sheck and Jacob Wingard visited this locality as missionaries, when it was determined that a building be erected in which to worship. In 1828 a small log house was built, in which services were held in the early part of the year 1829. In February, 1830, a society was organized and the house was dedicated by Revs. W. D. Strobel and J. G. Schwartz. The church was supplied by them for some time, and afterwards by Revs. Moser and Aull. In 1835 Rev. L. Bedenbaugh took charge and the congregation increased in numbers so much that it was found necessary to build a larger house. A new one was accordingly commenced and built, but in a different locality. This house was completed and dedicated in July 1837, the services being conducted by Revs. Moser, Haltiwanger, and E. Caughman. The congregations were served successively by E. Caughman, S. Bouknight, and B. Kreps. Synod held its Thirty-Third Session at this church in 1856.

TRINITY.

In the year 1835 a number of Lutherans from Newberry settled in this locality and formed a society. These were occasionally visited by Rev. Haltiwanger, Sr., when, through his exertions a committee was appointed, consisting of Messrs.

Jacob Haltiwanger, John M. Witt, and John Glaze to have a house of worship built. They, without delay, commenced the duty and the house was built at a cost of $417. It is situated on the Chapel Ferry Road, near the 43rd mile post from Hamburg, S. C. On the third Sunday in August, 1835, the building was dedicated as a house of worship by Rev. John C. Hope, with but eight regular communicants as members of the church there at that time. The number increased to over fifty as the year went by, and the church continues to have a good membership. This church has been served by Revs. Cloy, Sheppard, Rauch, Kistler, Lindler, Wertz, Whittle, Bouknight, Blackwelder, Moses, and P. Derrick.

Being isolated and distant from other Lutheran congregations, it labors under many disadvantages. This church has been served by other faithful pastors, besides those mentioned above, since their time.

GOOD HOPE.

Good Hope was organized about the year 1839. The building of a house, which was soon finished, was undertaken by the members of the church immediately after the organization. It was dedicated in April, 1840, by Rev. Margart. Mr. Cloy was first pastor. He was followed by Revs. Bauknight, Sheppard, Lindler, Caughman, Sheely, Hallman, and Bailey, and others since. At the formation of Pastorate No. 6, Mr. Wertz took charge; but he resigned in 1874 and took charge of Pastorate No. 3.

CORINTH.

This church is situated in the Fork of Big and Little Saluda Rivers. In 1842 a society was organized with twenty members. Not having a settled pastor, services were conducted by two pious laymen, Peter Hawkins and Martin Singley, in a school house and also under a brush arbor. A church was built as soon as possible and Rev. Sheppard became pastor. He was succeeded by Revs. Rauch, Metz, Bailey, Caughman, Hallman, Sligh, and P. Derrick. The corner-stone of a new church was laid on the fourth Sunday of October, 1871, and, soon after completion, the new building was dedicated in March, 1872. Rev. Edwin A. Bolles preached the dedication sermon, and Revs. Emanuel Caughman and P. Derrick were present and assisted in the services.

ST. JAMES', GRANITEVILLE.

In 1858, Rev. S. Bauknight began laboring at this place, assisted by Revs. Emanuel Caughman, A. W. Lindler, and J. N. Derrick. In 1860 the church was organized and received by the Synod. An effort was made in 1861 to build a house of worship, but the work progressed slowly. However, in 1862, the work had gone on so far as to enable the people to hold divine service in the house. It was then dedicated by Revs. Berley and J. N. Derrick, the latter remaining pastor for several years. There was little done during the war to complete the building. In 1865 Rev. B. Kreps took charge. He was succeeded by Rev. Emanuel Caughman in 1870, Mr. Caughman soon began soliciting subscriptions to complete the building, and in 1871 he had the satisfaction of knowing that his labors were not in vain. The house was finished and dedicated soon afterwards by Revs. J. Hawkins and P. Derrick. Mr. Caughman took charge as pastor, but soon resigned and Mr. Kreps became pastor. In 1873 the other church, which was in this connection, was removed by Synod into another pastorate, leaving this one standing alone. Rev. E. Dufford then took it in charge.

The foregoing are all the Lutheran churches in Edgefield County. These are all doing good work. Other pastors of late years have served them besides those mentioned. Rev. C. P. Boozer is pastor of some. He has served several years as a Representative in the Legislature from Edgefield County and re-elected in 1890. He was a Confederate soldier during the War of Secession, and lost an arm in the service. He is a native of Newberry County and a graduate of Newberry College.

XXVIII.

BAPTIST CHURCHES—RED BANK.

This church was constituted in 1784, under the ministry of Rev. John Thomas. Rev. Mr. Norris, who had been imprisoned at Ninety-Six for preaching non-resistance during the Revolutionary War, succeeded him. Abram Ferguson, a brother of the celebrated Colonel Ferguson, who was killed at the battle of King's Mountain, was deacon. Henry King, a very eloquent man, next served as pastor. His brother, Rev. Joseph King, had charge of the church at the beginning of the War of 1812, and was appointed Chaplain of Colonel George Butler's Regiment. The soldiers gave him the nick-name of "Cold Souse." Mumford Perryman, who had been clerk, died in 1820. He was the grandfather of General Perryman, of Texas, who was distinguished in the war between the States, and was, in 1891, one of the Judges of that State. The Perrymans and Travises were related. Colonel Wm. Travis, massacred at the Alamo, once belonged to Red Bank.

Rev. John Landrum preached here from 1812 to 1826. Mr. Landrum was a boy during the Revolution and lived near the Pine House. It is related that once while on his way to mill with a bag of corn on horseback, a mischievous Tory pushed the bag off and left him standing on the ground crying beside it. Years after the war this Tory returned to Edgefield on a visit; and then Mr. Landrum, no longer a little boy, but superior in strength to his old tormentor, would have beaten him well, had he not been prevented by his friends.

The leading members of Red Bank in 1826 were William Little, Pryor Dozier, Benjamin Culpepper, Eli House, and Zebulon Rudolph. At this time there were about twice as many women as men members of this church. Patty Bohler, (Boulware), a Rutherford by birth, Lucy Jones, and Sophia Bonham were model Christian women.

Rev. Basil Manly, father of Rev. Charles Manly, of Greenville, often preached at Red Bank at this period. Mr. Manly married a daughter of Zebulon Rudolph, who was clerk of this church for many years. Mr. Rudolph removed to Alabama, and Major William Daniel was elected clerk. Major Daniel is said to have been rather odd, but his oddities did not detract from his worth as a good man, and he was much esteemed. Rev. S. D. Worthington was pastor in 1833. Then Rev. Zedekiah Watkins. Rev. James F. Peterson took charge of the church in 1836 and was pastor 42 years. Red Bank enjoyed much prosperity during his long pastorship.

Thomas Bartley, the oldest member, and a Revolutionary soldier, died 16th September, 1854, aged 103 years. He had been an orderly member of the church for a long time. September 14th, 1856, Mrs. Rebecca Edwards died. Her son, William Edwards, who was an esteemed deacon, left eight sons. He had the satisfaction of seeing them all baptized at Red Bank before he died. John Mobley, the oldest deacon of Red Bank, died December 3rd, 1857. He was the father of Dr. W. S. Mobley. In 1869 109 persons were baptized at this place, and 84 the next year. Rev. James F. Peterson died June 10th, 1881. He was born in Newberry County, October 21st, 1796, and was baptized at Good Hope, in Edgefield, by Rev. Jones W. Coleman. Not long after his baptism he began to preach, and his preaching was attended with remarkable success. Mr. Peterson was a striking example of what men of moderate abilities and bearing can accomplish, when they are thoroughly consecrated and devoted to the work in which they are engaged. Rev. James Carson was pastor in 1891.

Thomas Bartley just mentioned as the oldest member and as a Revolutionary soldier was also a Baptist preacher and settled the place where Clyde's Chapel now stands—died at the age of 103. His son, Thomas Bartley, died at the age of 90 years near Johnston. He died in a large brick house built by Rev. Henry Herlong. He left surviving him among other children, Thomas Bartley and John Bartley. John Bartley lives on the farm where his father died. Mrs. Elisabeth Leppard was a member of Red Bank and died at the age of 106 years. A monument beside this church marks the last resting place of Rev. James F. Peterson.

DRY CREEK.

On March 5th, 1804, the brethren, John Landrum, Samuel Marsh, Henry King, and Thomas DeLoach, met at Dry Creek according to a call of Cloud's Creek Church and formed

themselves into a Presbytery to view the standing of the above
place for constitution. Their strength being approved the
church was constituted and Levi Kirkland was appointed
deacon. Rev. Thomas DeLoach did most of their preaching
from 1804 until 1820, and now fills an unknown, unmarked
grave in the churchyard. What a pity! He was the father
of the late Alison DeLoach, of Red Bank, and Mr. Thomas
DeLoach, who lived near Johnston. Since the death of Mr.
DeLoach Dry Creek has been remarkable for the short terms
of its pastors. Stanton S. Burdett, William B. Villard,
Prescott Bush, and John Windsor preached from 1820 to 1830.
The Cogburns, Barontons, Martins, Bushes, Rottens, Rabuns,
and Cachrofts were the principal members at this period.
February 26th, 1830, Rev. William Watkins was ordained at
Dry Creek by William B. Villard, Joseph Norris, and John
Windsor. He was called to serve as pastor shortly after. The
church was much reduced in 1832. February 2nd, 1834,
John Lott was elected clerk and the record began to be kept in
splendid order. William Watkins served as pastor until 1840,
when he returned to Orangeburg. He was succeeded by Rev.
James F. Peterson. Mr. Peterson serve1 two years. Then Rev.
Henry A. Williams had charge of the church until he was
succeeded by Rev. A. P. Norris in 1849. Then came the
short terms of Revs. A. B. Couch, Zedekiah Watkins, and
Mr. Merritt. Mr. Merritt was pastor during the War of
Secession. Dry Creek had reached the zenith of its prosperity.
The congregations were large and many of the church members were wealthy and noted for their culture and elegant
hospitality. Rev. George Bell, a local preacher, who belonged
to this church, did much of their preaching from 1840 until
1865. Mr. Bell was born at Mount Willing in May 1802 and
died near Batesburg in August 1881. Mr. Bell was an extraordinary man in many respects and was noted for his financial
ability—a rare quality in a minister of the Gospel. After the
war Captain J. W. Denny became clerk. Captain Denny died
in 1885 or 1886, and since his death Mr. P. B. Watson has
been clerk. Rev. Mr. Bradford was pastor in 1892.

Dry Creek has regained of late years much of its former
prosperity and now occupies a worthy position among the
churches.

SARDIS.

Sardis was constituted in 1804. Its record has been so imperfectly kept that at this date we can give no account of it for thirty years except by tradition. And the tradition is that William Ferguson was pastor from 1804 until the War of 1812. He first lived at the place where Mr. John McCarty was living in 1821, but after the death of his brother Abram he bought his plantation and moved to the place afterwards known as Denny's. Soon after this he retired from the ministry, took an interest in public affairs and became a politician.

The original place of worship at Sardis was a mile or two northwest of the present church on a little stream known as Cedar Creek. Rev. Henry King and his brother Joseph King both sometimes preached at Sardis, but Sardis and the county lost them by their emigration to Alabama.

David Peterson, an elder brother of Rev. James F. Peterson, was pastor about the year 1825. He was a native of Newberry. He married a widow Strother, sister of James Richardson, of Richardsonville, and mother of Major William A. Strother.

Robert Corley succeeded Mr. Peterson. Mr. Corley died in the prime of life and his funeral was preached by Richard Todd, at that time one of the most prominent ministers in the State. Rev. B. F. Corley is a son of Rev. Robert Corley.

Rev. Zedekiah Watkins was pastor in 1835 and Dr. R. G. Mayes, son of General Samuel Mayes, was clerk. Benjamin Etheredge and Nathaniel Corley were the ordained deacons. Miller, a slave belonging to Jacob B. Smith, and Abram, a servant of Rev. A. S. Dozier, were elected deacons or overseers of the colored members at the same time. No church has ever taken more interest in the spiritual welfare of the negroes than Sardis.

A host of good old Edgefield names are to be found on the roll of Sardis at this period, the Dennys, Etheredges, Edwards, Clarks, Matthews, Corleys, Longs, Hardys, Padgetts, Mayeses, Smiths, and Lamars all were members of this church.

Rev. Mark Abney succeeded Mr. Watkins as pastor, and then Henry A. Williams occupied the pulpit.

One cannot fail to be impressed with the small salaries these faithful old ministers received for their services, when several members of the church were worth, at a moderate estimate, over fifty thousand dollars each. Henry C. Bartley was pastor from 1850 to 1860, when the church called Rev. James F. Peterson who served until 1874.

Then Revs. Joab Edwards, N. N. Burton, Milton Norris, and M. D. Padgett followed each other in quick succession.

Colonel David Denny, who was elected clerk in 1842, died in 1879. J. B. Edwards, a pious and highly cultured young man, then filled the position. He died in a short time and J. B. Edwards was elected to succeed him. Rev. James A. Carson was pastor in 1891.

PHILIPPI.

Philippi is a member of "The Ridge" Baptist Association and is situated about five miles southeast of Johnston and about the same distance northeast of Trenton. This church was constituted in the year 1814. When first constituted it was located on Bull Branch about three miles South of the present site. Its membership at first was twenty-five, three of whom were negroes. Revs. Thomas DeLoach, Francis Walker, and John Landrum were the ministerial Presbytery that constituted the church. Who was first pastor is not now known, the record not showing but Thomas DeLoach, Prescott Bush, Benjamin Still, and Peter Galloway preached for the church at different times. Joshua Monk was the first clerk. David Foshee and Benjamin Medlock were ordained deacons in March 1816. Joshua Monk and Enock Phelps in July 1819 by Messrs Carson, Howell, Benjamin Still, and Prescott Bush. Jacob Whitehead and Joshua Monk, Zechariah Claxton, Samuel Posey, Anselm Cullam, Jesse Williams, E. W. Horne, C. A. Horne, William Howard, Jackson Holmes, and W. H. Timmerman have filled the position; the last name having served in that capacity continuously since 1862.

In September, 1823, the church membership numbered 21— a little less than when constituted. In 1829 William Bloodsworth and Zechariah Claxton were made deacons by a Presbytery composed of Revs. John Galloway and Peter Galloway. In 1833 William Johnson and Anselm Cullam were ordained deacons by Revs. Peter Galloway and Joseph Norris. Absalom Horne was made deacon in 1834 and given authority to exhort in public. Deacon William Johnson was ordained to the gospel ministry in August, 1835, and Deacon Absalom Horne in June 1842 by Revs. Joseph Norris, H. Prescott, and William Johnson. Ansel Devore, James A. Howard, William Toney, E. W. Horne, C. A. Horne, Malachi Cogburn, Hammond Cumbee, L. B. Smith, H. W. Jackson, Winfield Scott, T. H. Derrick, and J. O. Johnson have all served as deacons.

Rev. Peter Galloway is the first pastor of whom we have any record, though he was doubtless preceded by others. Rev. William Johnson was called in 1845, and served for several years. Since then the pastors have been H. A. Williams, Absalom Horne, Elijah W. Horne, Edward F. Kendall, James A. Woodward, Henry T. Bartley, Dr. William B. Shaw, W. T Hundley, and J. C. Brown, who has been serving the church for the last seven years. Elijah W. Horne was ordained to the ministry at Philippi in May 1857 by Revs. A. W. Asbill and Absalom Horne, and was pastor at the time of his death, January 2nd, 1883. He was stricken with paralysis at a Union Meeting at Ridge Spring on December 31st, 1882, while on the floor talking to the children on the subjects of death and the resurrection. He never spoke after he was stricken. He was a graduate of Furman University, and attended the Baptist Theological Seminary two years. He was a good preacher; an active, working Christian, and a patriotic citizen. If I mistake not, he was Captain of a company in the Nineteenth South Carolina Volunteers during the War of Secession. I was in a company in the same regiment and saw him sometimes and heard him mentioned as a good officer, a brave soldier and a pious man.

Revs. Hundley and Brown are the only two of Philippi's pastors living in 1891. Mr. Brown is a graduate of Mercer University. It is said that he preached without notes or manuscript before him—a practice which should be followed by all who stand in the pulpit to speak to the souls of men. Let the living Word be spoken by the living voice.

There is one incident in the history of this church, which, happily, is not common to all the churches. In 1855 a citizen of the community, who had been selling liquors under a license for several years near the church, was prevented from obtaining license after the expiration of that under which he was then selling. Whereupon, he, supposing that the church had no title to the land upon which the building stood, built a fence around the house with new rails and forbid entrance. He was, of course, prosecuted for the act, and after awhile was glad to compromise the matter by giving a warranty title to the church of two acres of land additional, and by paying all costs. Better still, he afterwards mended his ways and became a member of Philippi Church.

This church is situated in a thickly peopled section of country. The people are not wealthy, but they are better than being only wealthy in worldly goods—they are sober, industrious, and well to do in every respect.

BETHANY.

This church was constituted December 2nd, 1809, by Revs. Amos Dubose, Enoch Brazeal, and Robert Marsh, with eight members from Fellowship and Plum Branch Churches, viz.: Garrett Longmire, John Chiles, George Coleman, Elizabeth Barrett, Winnefor Ferr son, Francis Henderson, Francis Davidson, Abigail Jay. Rev. Amos Dubose was first pastor and served till the end of the year 1824. Larkin Cason was first clerk, serving until 1829. John Longmire was made deacon in 1816—the first recorded. There was a great revival in 1810. This revival was followed by a state of lukewarmness, as it appears from the records that only seven persons were baptized into the church from the close of 1810 to the first of 1829. The church then took on new life and had great revivals for several years. Many were added to the church by baptism, some of whom were negroes. For three years there were revivals each year, and they have continued at intervals to the present time.

This church united with the Edgefield Baptist Association in 1810. Rev. R. M. Todd was pastor from some time in 1825 to the end of 1831, with the exception of an interval from January to August, 1828, during which time a Rev. Mr. Roberts was pastor. The church licensed Henry Casper and Washington Belcher to preach in 1810, and ordained Henry Casper in 1811.

William Chiles was made clerk in 1829 and served to 1841. James M. Chiles was licensed to preach in 1830, and was ordained in 1832. At the same time John Chiles was ordained deacon. Rev. James M. Chiles became pastor in 1832, and served as such until the close of 1844. Under him the church prospered—had several great revivals—and also the Sunday school cause was revived. Littleton A. Brooks was ordained deacon in 1833. John Anderson was made clerk in 1841, served till 1845, and was succeeded by W. B. Brannan, who served to 1847. Richard P. Quarles was clerk from 1847 to 1850.

Rev. William Royal became pastor in 1845, and served until the close of the year 1848. During the year 1849 Rev. A. P. Norris was pastor the first Sunday and the day before in each month; Rev. James Shadrack fourth Sunday in each month.

In 1850 there was a new house of worship built at Shinburg muster ground, near Longmire's postoffice. The old meeting house, which was on the road from Edgefield Court House to Abbeville Court House, and about midway between Hard Labor and Cuffeetown Creeks, was sold and the church moved into the new house of worship. Rev. John Trapp was made pastor in 1850, and Rev. James Shadrack was ordained to the Gospel ministry the same year, and during the same year Joseph L. Talbert was made clerk.

Rev. John Trapp served as pastor to the close of 1874. Under his administration the church prospered—he was greatly beloved and was finally compelled to resign on account of age and infirmities incident thereto. Hezekiah Edwards and Peter Quattlebaum were made deacons in 1854. John G. Thornton was made deacon in 1863, and in the same year R. W. Seymour was ordained to preach, and called to preach one Sunday in each month, as an assistant to Rev. John Trapp, the regular pastor.

· The clerk of the church, Joseph L. Talbert, was killed on Maryland Heights at the capture of Harper's Ferry in 1862. George J. Sheppard was then made clerk, and served until 1869., when he and Orlando Sheppard were ordained deacons. W. H. Yeldell was made clerk, which position he still fills (1894). Rev. R. W. Seymour became pastor in 1875, and served until the end of 1877. Rev. A. G. Collier was called, and served as pastor 1878 and 1879. Rev. B. F. Miller served the years 1880, 1881, and 1882. Under Mr. Miller the church prospered, and many were added to the membership. J. T.

White and A. L. Bushnell were ordained deacons in 1882. Rev. J. K. Fant was pastor during the year 1883. Rev. B. F. Miller was again called, and served as pastor from June, 1884, to the end of 1885. The church ordained Rev. J. S. Manardis to the ministry in 1885.

Rev. J. S. Jordan was pastor during the years 1886 and 1887, and was very successful in his labors.

H. Q. Talbert, L. D. White, C. W. Burress, and W. A. Cheatham were ordained deacons in 1887.

The history of this church was sent me by J. T. White.

BETHEL.

The records prior to the year 1853 have been lost or mislaid, so that it is now impossible to give a complete history of this church. An imperfect sketch can only be given from the recollections of the older members.

Flat Rock, situate at Flat Rock, a large shoal of rock about four miles from Ridge and seven miles from the present site of Bethel, was the first Baptist Church in this section. There lived near here two or three families named Walker, who were Baptists, and one Fowler was a preacher. These, with a few other Baptists at a distance, (the country was thinly settled then,) formed a church, as near as I can learn, about the year 1805. A few years afterwards the Walkers, and some others who lived near, moved West, and the church languished. In 1820 Mr. Lambkin and a few others, who lived near where Bethel now (1892) is, and whose membership had previously been at Flat Rock, built a church at a place on the Columbia and Augusta public road, known as Double Branches, and christened it "Bethel." Whether this church was a continuance of Flat Rock, in the absence of records, is not known positively, but it is thought to be. At any rate, all the members of Flat Rock came to Bethel. This church has a noble record.

The first pastor was Cyrus Howel, whose name is still frequently mentioned by the oldest Christians. He was succeeded by such men as Revs. Brooker, Watkins, Asbill, Shaw, and others, whose names and memories are fondly cherished by a grateful and loving people.

The first church building was replaced by a handsome edifice in 1862.

From Bethel has sprung entirely the noble Ridge Church, and largely the Batesburg Church, and also the Bethlehem Church.

RICHLAND SPRING

Baptist Church was organized August 12th, 1859, under the ministry of Rev. H. T. Bartley.

The first deacons were Major Josiah Padgett and Mr. Luke Rodgers.

The pastors who have succeeded Mr. Bartley in charge of this church are: Rev. H. Jones, Rev. W. W. Burton, Rev. W. D. Padgett, and Rev. J. A. Carson.

I am not informed as to the number of the membership at this time, December, 1892.

DAMASCUS

Baptist Church is located in the northern part of Gray Township, one-half mile from the line dividing Edgefield from Abbeville, and between Phœnix postoffice and Gaines' post-office. Old Damascus Church stood about one mile north of the present church, in Abbeville County, near Phœnix, and previous to 1831 the house was used as a union meeting house by the Baptists, Methodists, and Presbyterians. In 1831 the Baptists organized a church with twelve members, and called Rev. James Chiles to the pastorate, who served the church until 1840, when he was succeeded by Rev. John Trapp, who served until 1856. During the later years of Rev. Trapp's pastorate the present church building was erected on a lot donated by Nathaniel Henderson. Since 1856 the church has been served by the following pastors: Rev. William P. Hill, 1857–1862; Rev. Basil Manly, Jr., 1863–1868; Rev. W. B. Jones, 1869–1873; Rev. R. M. Sanders, 1874; Rev. Jno. H. Dargan, 1875–1876; Rev. M. E. Broadus, 1877; Rev. J. S. Jordan, 1878–1890; Rev. Thomas Campbell, 1891; Rev. J. T. B. Anderson, 1892; Rev. J. L. Ouzts, 1893.

The following have served as clerks since the organization of the church: Dr. Thomas Lake, 1831–1838; Felix Lake, 1839; Elias Lake, 1840; Robert Turner, 1841; N. Henderson to 1868; W. H. Stallworth, 1869–1883; J. M. Gaines, 1884 1893.

Treasurers: S. J. Burnett, 1858; W. H. Stallworth, to

1868; George R. Caldwell, 1869–1876; J. H. Burnett, 1877–1878; A. C. Stallworth, 1879–1884; J. O. Watson, 1885–1893.

Deacons: Thomas Lake, 1831–187–; Russel Vaughn, 1832–1854; Felix Lake, 1839–1840; Elias Lake, 1841–1853; J. S. Burnett, 1856–1889; Johnson Sale; Willis Ross, 1863–1871; W. H. Stallworth, 1866–1893; George R. Caldwell, 1866–1887; J. H. Burnett, 1866–1893; H. B. Maxwell, 1878–1893; P. H. Adams, 1878–1893; J. S. Watson, 1885–1893; J. M. Gaines, 1885–1893; Z. P. Henderson, 1889–1893.

In 1866 the colored members withdrew from the church and formed Damascus Colored Church. They have a very neat church building standing about one-quarter mile from the white church.

In 1868 Damascus withdrew from the Edgefield Association to join other churches in the formation of the Abbeville Association and the first meeting of the new Association was held with Damascus Church in that year.

The church has had a steady and healthy growth and now numbers 118 members.

J. M. GAINES, Church Clerk.

JOHNSTON.

The church at Johnston was organized on the 21st day of February, 1875, in the Johnston Academy after preaching by Rev. W. A. Pearson.

The following are the names of the members who united in organizing the church at that time: Jesse M. Cogburn, Edward J. Mims, M. D., Benjamin S. Cogburn, Jeter W. Crim, Nathan G. Carwile, Augustus C. Mobley, Edward A. Mims, M. H. Mims, Mrs. Z. L. Carwile, Mrs. E. J. Mims, Mrs. A. C. Mobley, Mrs. W. L. Coleman, Sr., Mrs. Jesse M. Cogburn, Mrs. J. W. Crim, Miss S. C. Carwile, Mrs. W. S. Mobley, Miss P. E. Mims. Total, 18. Rev. Luther Broadus was pastor in 1875, Rev. W. J. Alexander, D. D., 1876–1877; Rev. Richard Furman, D. D., 1878–1879; Rev. W. T. Hundley, 1880, closing November 1892; Rev. W. E. Parish began his pastorate July 1st, 1893.

The church membership July 1893 numbered 175 and pays the pastor $750 and furnishes a parsonage rent free. The annual contributions of this church to missions, education, and other benevolent purposes are from $500 to $700. The church is in a healthy and growing condition.

EDGEFIELD.

This church was organized in 1823 with 23 members. Rev. Basil Manly, D. D., was first pastor; he also wrote the Constitution of the church. The deacons were A. B. McWhorter M. M. Mims.

Since the resignation of Dr. Manly to accept a call to the First Church in Charleston this church has had as pastors Rev. James A. Warren, 1827; Rev. W. B. Johnson, D. D., 1830–1852; Rev. J. M. Chiles, 1851; Rev. C. A. Raymond, 1853–1854; Rev. E. L. Whatley, 1855–1856; Rev. L. R. Gwaltney, 1858–1868; Rev. Luther Broaddus, 1869–1875; Rev. W. J. Alexander, 1876–1877; Rev. W. T. Hundley, 1878–1882; Rev. H. A. Whitman, 1882–1886; Rev. T. D. Clark, 1886–1888; Rev. G. L. Hunt, D. D., 1888–1890; Rev. I. N. Booth, 1891–1893.

In July 1893 the church, after the resignation of Mr. Booth again called Rev. L. R. Gwaltney, D. D., who accepted and began his work there September 1st of that year. The church was fortunate in securing the services of this eminent divine. He was much loved during his first pastorship and is an earnest worker in his Master's vineyard.

The following is a list of names of the constituent members of this church at the organization in 1823: Matthew Mims, Arthur Simkins, Sr., A. B. McWhorter, Henry Lowe, Abner Whatley, Wiley Melton, Patience Addison, Elisabeth Milton, Isabel A. Drysdale, Phyllis Whatley, Margaret Pixley, Ann Lane, Eliza A. Drysdale, Martha Mims, Sabra Jeter, E. M. McWhorter, Ridley Gray, Eliza Mims, the last survivors, Mary L. Drysdale, Bettie Tutt, Sarah Drake, Mary Tutt, Bethany Blease, Pudence Martin, Elizabeth Youngblood, Winfred Ferguson,

For this sketch I am indebted to Mr. J. Leslie Andrews, of Kirksey's, Edgefield County, S. C.

MOUNTAIN CREEK.

From the best information obtained, the record having been lost, this church was organized in 1798. A few years before

the church was organized a school was established and a school
house was built where the church now stands.

Rev. N. W. Hodges, a missionary employed by the Edgefield Association and laboring in its bounds, made an appointment to preach at this school house. He saw that it was a
prosperous neighborhood and had the prospect of becoming a
centre of influence. He went to work with zeal and energy
and for several years continued to preach in the school house.
In due time the fruits of his labor began to show. Quite a
number manifested a desire to unite with a Baptist church. A
few of the members of Little Stevens Creek Church joined the
brethren at the school house and organized a church. They
then went to work and built a log house in which to worship.

The church was not supplied regularly, but Mr. Hodges
continued to preach there occasionally. The church grew
rather slowly for some years, but in 1829 a revival was experienced by the little church and also through the neighborhood. Among the number converted was John Trapp, a
young man from Fairfield County, who was then teaching in
the neighborhood. He was a young man of great promise
and the church gave him all the encouragement possible. He
soon applied for license to preach, but he continued to teach
school also until 1833, when he was ordained to the ministry,
and laying aside all else, gave his whole life to preaching the
gospel. The church grew slowly, moving steadily on without
any special revival, until about the year 1840, when many
were converted and joined.

Needing a larger house the people now put up a good frame
building. About the same time, the year 1840, several members obtained letters of dismissal, moved about ten miles northwest and organized Damascus Baptist Church. Note this if
there should be nothing more said about Damascus.

The church grew and prospered until, in the year 1852,
there was a gracious revival, eighty new members being baptized and a number restored. Among those baptized was
Theophilus Williams, who was soon ordained to the ministry.
He lived only ten years after this.

At this time Mountain Creek was one of the strongest
churches in the northern part of the Association, the membership being (colored people were then included) over five

hundred. In 1856 a number of the members branched off and organized Olive Branch Baptist Church. Note this also?

In 1859 there was another revival, and sixty persons professed religion and were baptized.

During the Civil War the church suffered great loss in membership and financially. But in 1866 there was another great revival, and ninety-eight were baptized and five restored. This meeting lasted seventeen days and was conducted by Rev. John Trapp, who received some help from a Methodist minister living near the church.

Though beginning to feel the feebleness of age, Mr. Trapp continued to preach, when able, "without money and without price." He died August 27th, 1876, having been pastor continuously from 1834, with the exception of the years 1855 and 1856. He was succeeded by Rev. R. W. Seymour, who was pastor for four years.

Towards the close of Mr. Seymour's ministration the church had grown somewhat cold in the religious life; but in 1881 that earnest and zealous man, Rev. J. K. Fant, was called and accepted the call to the church. He had hard work to do, but his labors were blessed and he soon brought the members to realize the fact that they had work to do. He preached two Sabbaths each month, and Saturday before each fourth Sabbath. His salary was $300.00.

During Mr. Faut's term of service many changes were made. The old box pulpit was removed and a nice stand put in its place. Suitable furniture was provided, and a stove, and an organ, and other improvements were made. All this was largely the work of the women. They organized also a flourishing "Ladies' Aid Society." During the year the church gave to State Missions fifty dollars; thirty to Foreign Missions, and thirty to ministerial education. During this year, 1881, in August, a series of meetings were held, in which the pastor was assisted by Rev. H. C. Smart. A revival was had, eight backsliders were restored, and thirty-four were added to the church by baptism.

Mr. Fant was pastor four years, and during that time eleven were restored to fellowship and seventy-six were baptized. A Sunday-school was also established.

In February, 1885, Mr. Fant resigned the charge. He was

succeeded by Rev. J. F. McMillan, of North Carolina. During the eight months of this year, 1885, he gave all his time to the church at a salary of $500.00. Through 1886 and 1887 he gave his whole time. In 1888 two Sabbaths in each month.

The Sunday-school was reorganized in 1868, and did fairly good work under Superintendents D. A. J. Bell, J. W. Aiton, W. L. Durst, R. T. Strom, J. M. Rambo. In the spring of 1887 the Sunday-school was reorganized and worked with greater zeal than ever before, with J. Leslie Andrews superintendent. In 1887 the school contributed fifty-six dollars for missions, incidentals, &c., and increased in giving from year to year, till in the year 1890 one hundred and ten dollars were raised by the school.

In 1888 Mr. McMillan resigned the pastorate, and Rev. B. F. Miller was called. He accepted the call in January, 1890, and served the church two Sabbaths in each month, until April, 1891, when he was compelled to resign on account of ill health. After a long and painful illness he passed to a better world.

In July, 1891, Rev. J. T. B. Anderson, of Barnwell, was called. He remained pastor during that year. In January, 1892, the church called Rev. J. P. Mealing for two Sundays in each month. He served them during the year. At this time, 1893, Rev. J. L. Ouzts, of Mountain Creek, a graduate of Furman University, is preaching to the church. Through Mr. Fant's influence he was induced to study for the ministry.

BETHLEHEM.

This church was constituted October 14th, 1853, by a Presbytery consisting of the Revs. J. A. Carter and S. P. Getzen, with a membership of four males and eight females.

Rev. J. A. Carter was first pastor to May 24th, 1856, when Rev. P. F. Burgess was elected. Mr. Burgess served three years, when Rev. W. L. Hames was elected, May 22nd, 1858.

There was no conference from August 24th, 1861, to July 24th, 1864, at which time Rev. J. P. Mealing was elected. Mr. Mealing served the church until January 11th, 1885. Rev. J. A. Bell served from latter date for two years; Rev. J. L. Ouzts, during the year 1887; Rev. Wm. M. Verdery,

1888; Rev. E. W. Sammons, 1889 and 1890; Rev. G. H. Burton, 1891, 1892, and 1893.

Present membership of Bethlehem, sixteen males and eighteen females.

PLEASANT LANE.

This church was organized and dedicated as a Baptist Church in May, 1837, with but few members, but in course of time there was as many as 100 members, and was served by such ministers as Revs. Brunson, Z. Watkins, Abner Asbill, H. A. Williams, —— Getzen. Rev. Mark Abney was serving this church at the time of his death, "one of our very best ministers" and a near relation of the writer of this history. Rev. —— Asbill also was serving the church at the time of his death. All these men were faithful and good laborers—all have passed to their eternal rest.

At the close of the war the church membership was very small, and the white population around being very sparse, the land nearly all being owned by a few persons and tenanted by negroes, early in the year 1868 the members thought it best that they should dissolve Pleasant Lane and join other churches, which they did.

The church property was then claimed and recovered by the Landrum estate. It was then immediately sold to the colored Baptists to be used by them as a church. The church has, at this date, August, 1893, about one thousand members.

For this account of Pleasant Lane I am indebted to Mr. Lemuel Corley, communicated through Rev. G. A. Wright.

GOOD HOPE.

This church was constituted in the year 1804 by Henry King, Chesley Davis, and William Eddins. The membership was small.

The pastors have been Chesley Davis, William Still, —— Todd, David Peterson, James F. Peterson, Jones W. Coleman, —— Proffit, A. P. Norris, W. A. Gaines, N. N. Burton, J. F. McMillan, T. J. Rooke, and James A. Carson. There were possibly other pastors at short intervals.

Rev. James A. Carson is pastor this August, 1893, and the membership at this date is 289.

This information is furnished by L. Rice, C. C.

BIG STEPHEN'S CREEK.

From the best information we can get, the earlier records having been lost, this church was organized by Rev. Daniel Marshall as far back as 1769 or 1770, at any rate just before he established himself at Kiokee, across the river, which was in 1770. We find in Bolsford's Memoirs that he preached here in 1773, and there is no doubt that it was an established church at that time. There are no means now of ascertaining who was the first pastor. Like most churches of that day it was a long time from its organization to the time of having any regular supply. And like other churches, situated in neighborhoods of large plantations, where there were many negroes, its white membership was never large. Its present membership is made up in part of descendants of its earliest members.

In March, 1854, Rev. Ivesun L. Brooks was pastor and had been for several years. He was noted not only for his ability as a Gospel preacher, but for his learning and culture, and as an educator.

G. W. Medlock and Dr. Timmerman.

OLIVE BRANCH AND BOLD SPRING.

Olive Branch Church was organized in 1855, and dissolved in 1878.

Bold Spring was instituted in 1853, and is now, August 1st, 1893, a flourishing church of over 200 members.

By James Callison.

MOUNT LEBANON.

This church, sometimes called Sweet Water from a refreshing spring near by, was constituted in 10th month, 1832, and is situated near the line of Edgefield and Aiken Counties. Revs. Robert Carter and Thomas Morris were the first pastors. Brethren John Curry and John Clerrel were the first deacons, and John P. Banks first clerk of the church. Number of original members, 32; present number, 101. Present pastor, Rev. J. M. White, with a long line of intervening pastors, among them Joseph Morris, Samuel Getzen, Wm. B. Shaw, J. P. Mealing, and Thos. Walker.

By Dr. Timmerman.

XXIX.

RED HILL.

This church was constituted June 20th, 1835, by Elders Samuel Cartledge and William Watkins, with the following members: William Watkins, pastor; Reuben Johnson and Erasmus McDaniel, deacons; Levi McDaniel, clerk; members, Martin Rose, Sr., Frederick McDaniel, Wm. Roberts, Sr., Thos. Ford, Calvin Cox, Eady Rose, Judy Johnson, Henry Baugh, Anna McDaniel, Emilia McDaniel, Obedience McCary, Sealy Shinall, Caroline McDaniel, Elizabeth Holmes, Clarracy Roberts, Martha Cox, Orpha Forde, Lydia Parkman, Lucy Holmes, Elizabeth Collins, Patience Blalock—ten males, fourteen females. Not one of these is living at this date, September 5th, 1893.

July 18th, 1835, at the first conference, two were received by letter. August 15th, second conference, two were received by baptism and three by letter. February 20th, 1836, first dismissal by letter. September 17th, 1836, the first delegate was appointed to the Association, but no record as to where Association was held.

Rev. W. Watkins was pastor from June, 1835, to 1884. Discipline was strictly enforced during this time, and the membership increased very slowly.

Rev. James Morris was elected pastor in 1841. In 1842 a great revival is mentioned, but only one member was added to the church. Mr. Morris resigned in 1843 and Rev. D. D. Brunson was called. The same year Lewis Collins was elected clerk.

In 1845 there was a great revival. During the meeting the pastor, Rev. D. D. Brunson, was assisted by Revs. Getzen, Kennedy, Abney, and Hughs. At this time Clerk Lewis Collins was made a deacon, and Samuel Scott elected clerk.

Three were added to the church in 1846. In the fall of 1850 Rev. D. D. Brunson resigned, and Rev. David Bodie was elected pastor. In 1851 there was a protracted meeting of seven days in August, and several days again in September, at which 51 were added to the church by baptism, (and a large number of negroes,) but few of these are living to-day, September 5th, 1893. Protracted meetings were held in 1852, 1853, 1854; and in 1855 Rev. D. D. Brunson was again called to the church. William Holmes and E. Bartley were elected deacons, and Captain W. F. Prescott was made clerk.

Rev. S. P. Getzen was pastor the first half of 1856. (Was preaching until a pastor could be had.) Dr. T. M. Bailey filled the pulpit the remaining half of 1856 and the year 1857. Rev. Hams preached from 1857 to 1867—1867 W. B. Shaw was pastor to 1869. In 1869 Rev. G. W. Bussey was ordained, and preached '69 and '70; was again called for 1870 and 1871, but declined, and attended the Seminary at Greenville, S. C., and Rev. McCrackin filled in the time for two years. 1873 the first mention of a stipulated salary for the pastor. During the entire pastorate of Rev. Bussey large additions are recorded. 1877 Captain W. F. Presscott resigned clerk, serving 22 years; C. J. McDaniel made clerk 1877. W. L. McDaniel and R. M. Johnson were made deacons in 1878. In 1879 there were thirty-five new additions to the church. In 1882 H. W. Quarter, the present incumbent, was elected clerk.

Rev. E. W. Samons, pastor during 1886; Rev. J. L. Ouzts, pastor during 1887; Rev. J. J. Getsinger, pastor during 1888 and 1889. Rev. G. W. Bussey again the pastor in 1890, and is still the pastor at this time, September, 1893. The church has now a membership of 167. The number has but a very few times exceeded the present, never reaching more than 175 or 180.

Some changes and improvements have been made in the building, so that it is somewhat different from the original structure. It was ceiled and painted in 1882. An organ was bought in 1887, and in 1888 and 1889 the Ladies' Aid Society supplied new seats.

The church now needs a new building, the old one having served its time, is considerably decayed and is entirely too small for the accommodation of the congregations. At this writing, August 21st, 1893, a protracted meeting is in progress and promises to be very fruitful.

So much for Red Hill Church. There is also a fine school at Red Hill, known as Red Hill Academy. It is an old school having been in existence for a great many years, and it is at this time in a prosperous and flourishing condition.

This sketch of Red Hill Baptist Church has been kindly furnished by Wyatt H. Seigler, Cold Spring, S. C., through Dr. W. H. Timmerman.

RED OAK GROVE.

From information given by J. A. Prime, clerk, and forwarded to me by Hon. W. H. Timmerman, we learn that Red Oak Grove Church was constituted on the 15th day of February, 1812, by a Presbytery composed of Revs. Samuel Marsh, John Blackston and Samuel Cartledge as appointed by the church. The church was constituted with 28 members who brought letters from Antioch and Callahan, (now Parksville) Churches. First pastor was Elisha Palmer and Dempsey Bussey and A. Bush were first deacons. The former deacon belonged to the Antioch Church and lived 8 miles from the church and usually walked the distance and attended the conference meetings. He was the grandfather of the present pastor, Rev. G. W. Bussey, as well as one of the founders of Oak Grove Church. The church has undergone many changes, but there yet remains the works of our forefathers upon the old church book, which is sufficient proof that those who have gone before us loved their place of worship, and served Him, whose eye ever rests upon us in a way worthy of imitation.

The church has had for its pastors Palmer B. Carson, S. Cartledge, William Watkins, L. Furbry, S. P. Getsen, W. L. Hawes, and for the the last 24 years Brother G. W. Bussey, with the exception of one year when Rev. Eddie Walker preached for it.

This church began with 28 members. There have been at times as many as 200 members. At present it numbers amongst its membership the Griffins, Dorns, Whatleys, Timmermans, Busseys, Princes, Thurmonds, Hon. W. J. Talbert, and many other good men and women.

SALEM.

The Baptist Church of Salem is situated in the Northern portion of the county, known as the Saluda section, about 3 miles from Bouknight's—Herbert's Ferry. The church was constituted in 1800. This is as far as the records show, but tradition says that the church was in existence here prior to that date. It was a place of worship before the Revolutionary War. In the membership of that early date we find names still familiar in that section, viz.: Corleys, Kings, Colemans, Rileys, Wheelers, Havirds, Worthingtons, Merchants, Berrys, and Abneys.

Rev. Samuel Worthington, whose name we find among the earliest students of Furman University, when that Institution was located on the high hills of Santee, was received into the church in December 1824.

The first pastor is not known. The name of Rev. Henry King is the first appearing on the record as pastor. Mr. King and his wife were received by letter in 1810, and he was called at once as pastor. The pastors since Mr. King have been Revs. B. Still, D. Peterson, Robert Corley, Zedekiah Watkins, J. F. Peterson, J. W. Coleman, H. T. Bartley, and others until the present time. It is now supplied by Rev. M. D. Padgett.

In 1810 there were 90 members; in 1834 there were 109; in 1841, 83; in 1850, 52; from 1850 to 1867, 52; from 1867 to 1878 there was an increase of 10, showing 62 members in 1876. Since that time the membership has fallen off, so that now, in 1893, there are only 33. This reduction was caused by expulsions, deaths, and dismissals, but the principal cause was the advent of the Second Adventists into this section, many leaving and going into the new sect.

Since the war this church has been supplied by Rev. L. O'Neall, now dead, W. A. Gaines, Joab Edwards, N. G. Cooner, N. N. Burton, and others.

For some years this church has been aided in her work by the State Mission Board. The present church building was erected in 1837—has been since repaired and improved. House and other church property valued at $800.

In 1809 and in 1810, and again in 1832 there were great and glorious revivals in this church. Ah me! why not have another and now?

Pine Pleasant was organized or constituted about the year 1832 or 1833, and the house was built soon after. This was one of the fruits of that great religious wave that swept over the whole county about that time. The preachers at Pine Pleasant who took an active part in the revival there were N.

W. Hodges, Samuel Worthington,—Barnes, and—Chiles—
Dr. J. C. Ready was one of the converts and second pastor.
The church has been served since by Revs. Jones W. Coleman,
Watkins,—A. P. Norris at the close and during the war—
James Carson since the war, and others whose names I cannot
recall, as I write from memory. The church has sometimes
been without a pastor—sometimes quite low in feeling and in
membership, and sometimes quite zealous and healthy.

CHESTNUT OR CHESTNUT RIDGE.

This is an old church constituted by Revs. Robert Marsh,
Samuel Marsh, and John Bolger in 1809. The Culbreaths,
Scotch people, settled in that neighborhood in the year 1765.
The house of worship was built not long after the church was
constituted, it may be before, as the Culbreaths were religious
people and did not choose to remain destitute of the ministry
of the Word. The first deacons were Thomas Scurry, John
Culbreath, and Thomas Christian. There was a church once
on a hill near Mill Creek, Mine Creek, and near the Saluda
Old Town, (also a schoolhouse, where A. P. Butler went to
school when a boy,) but whether Chestnut Ridge took the
the place of this, drew off the membership, and this was permitted to go down, I cannot say. Be this as it may, Chestnut
Hill, or Chestnut Ridge, is one of the old churches of the
county, and has at this time a good membership and is in a
healthful condition. Some of the first and most prominent
members of this church were William Smith, Sr., William
Culbreath, Sr., William Marlow, Daniel Rodgers, Toliver
Towles, Daniel Butler, and James Maynard.

The church has been served as pastors by Revs. Mangum,
William Watkins, Jones W. Coleman, James F. Peterson, and
James Carson, nor is this all, but the records of the church are
so broken that it is impossible to do more than I have done.

Information given by the present clerk, Mr. Roton, 1894.

Rocky Creek and Little Stevens Creek are mentioned in
the sections on Fruit Hill, with same notice of their pastors
and present condition.

Mention is made also in that section of two Methodist
Churches, Bethlehem and Gazzaway.

ANTIOCH.

"Whereas on Saturday 24th of March, 1804, the Baptist Church at the Cross Roads appointed John Cogburn, Lewis Tillman, Stephen Norris, William Howel Smith, Floyd Mitchel, Barkley Martin, and John Huffman to form rules for the government of the church to be presented at the next meeting for the inspection of the same.

"Also to fix a name for the church to distinguish it from other cross road churches in the State."

The above mentioned committee met at the meeting house on the 14th day of April and agreed on the name of Antioch for the church.

There is in existence no further record of church proceedings until September 1830. Daniel Huff, C. C., John Cogburn, C. C.

William Moss, C. C., from 1833 to 1873; B. T. Mims, C. C., from 1873 to 1877; M. A. Mims, from 1877 to 1886; E. G. Talbert, C. C., from 1886 to 1893.

The Edgefield Baptist Association met here September 6th, 1893, having met with this church only once before since the church was organized. That meeting was held about 40 years before as stated by the oldest members. The church record is silent on the matter.

Two prominent Baptist ministers, Rev. Mark M. Abney and Rev. D. D. Brunson were both members at Antioch and both are buried there.

EPISCOPAL CHURCHES.

There are three Episcopal Churches is the county; one in the town of Edgefield; one in the direction of Ninety-Six, and about twelve miles from that place. This church was erected under the aupices of Mrs. Brooks, the mother of the Hon. P. S. Brooks, and widow of Whitfield Brooks, Esq. One of her sons, Colonel J. H. Brooks, now (1893) owns the property and lives near the church.

There is also one other in the county, situated at Trenton. There is one at Batesburg, on the line.

ROMAN CATHOLIC.

There is only one Catholic Church building in the county, and that is in the town of Edgefield, near and just north of the court house. This house is strong and substantially built of the best and most durable granite. Like all other structures built by Rome from the time Romulus laid her foundation until now, this house was made to outlast the ages. Rome and the Roman Church in the way of building do nothing poor. The Church tries always in material things to realize and make good the truth of the promise that the gates of hell shall not prevail against it.

SECOND ADVENTISTS.

There is only one church of this denomination in the county, and that is situated a few miles from Butler Methodist Church. The congregation used the O'Neall Baptist Church building for some time after their organization, but they set about and soon succeeded in building a house of their own.

The number of members in this church I do not know, nor whether they have a stated pastor.

The church was organized about the year 1883.

THE UNIVERSALISTS.

This denomination has one church and church building in the county. This is at Mount Enon, and has a membership of about three dozen zealous, active, and intelligent members. It was organized about the year 1885 by Rev. D. B. Clayton. There is no regular pastor, but the church is supplied from time to time by Revs. D. B. Clayton, Burruss, Thomas Chapman, and Rev. Mr. Bowers is now pastor.

These are all the denominations I believe. There are no Mennonites, Quakers, Tunkers, Swedenborgians, nor Christians that I can now call to mind.

YOUNG MEN'S CHRISTIAN ASSOCIATION.

With the introduction of the Young Men's Christian Association into Edgefield began a new era. The testimonies of ministers, lawyers, physicians, and business men generally, have been sufficient evidence of this fact.

Such being the case, some facts concerning it will not be out of place in this history.

After two or three unsuccessful attempts at an organization of this kind, the present work was established first with simply a Young Men's Prayer Meeting, organized by seventeen Edgefield boys, January 19th, 1890. So great was the enthusiasm that a public meeting was conducted that night, and after remarks by several of the leaders of the movement, a general hand-shaking followed.

Over thirty public meetings were held during the year for the presentation of the work. Nor was the main object lost sight of, namely, work for young men. The meetings for young men increased in numbers and in influence, daily; and the result can only be appreciated by a former resident of the town. Several conversions were the result during the first year; and when the Association was finally visited by State and international secretaries, it was found, to the astonishment of all, that a *bona fide* "County Association Work" had sprung up unknown to the members themselves. The fact of its being a "County Work" amply justifies the introduction of this sketch into a history of the county. No apologies are necessary for its introducton. This history of the county would be incomplete without it.

Prior to this only three counties in the United States had attempted anything like organizing the Associations by counties, with county conventions, county committees, county secretaries, &c. Here in Edgefield, while the young men were ignorant of what was going on elsewhere, branches had been organized at four country churches, and a constitution, for the government of all under one system, had been adopted.

A county convention, the fifth ever held, was therefore called for February 28th, March 1st and 2nd, 1891. At this convention, besides delegates from the several branches in the county, there were present two international secretaries, one State secretary, three general secretaries, and one president. The convention was characterized by a display of enthusiasm, and yet of sound judgment worthy of any gathering of mere mortals. Indeed, the future outcome forces the belief upon the reflective mind that the Spirit of the Living God was present, quickening and guiding.

The Convention elected a county committee of seven men, namely: A. S. Tomkins, Chairman; James T. Bacon, Secretary; A. J. Norris, Treasurer; Dr. J. W. Hill, W. E. Lynch, R. A. Marsh, and E. J. Mims, all of Edgefield. It was afterwards supplemented by W. Harling, of Meeting Street; J. W. Mitchell, of Batesburg; B. L. Caughman, of Mount Willing;

Dr. J. H. Burkhalter, of Franklin; James L. Andrews, of Kirkseys, and Rev. A. B. Watson, of Edgefield.

To this committee was given the supervision of the work in the county; and on May 1st, 1891, Mr. Mr. John Lake was employed as the only County Secretary then in the South.

Mr. Robert Wiedensall, of Chicago, the oldest Secretary of the International Committee, and the father of nearly all of the leading features of association work, as college work, railroad work, work among German speaking young men, &c., and who first conceived this plan of county work, wrote the the following in his annual report to the International Committee, in New York. It was published in the Year Book for 1891:

"No service during the year afforded me more satisfaction, and promised more for the future, than the County Convention at Edgefield, S. C. It began on Saturday evening with one of the most impressive meetings I ever attended; and in this meeting the most solid testimony was given by responsible business men of the good work that had been done for the young men in the county. The services on Sunday were very complete in their interests and results.

"At the Young Men's Meeting in the afternoon twenty-five fine looking young men rose for prayer; and a number of them accepted Christ in the after meeting. The topics were well discussed. The paper on 'County Work,' read by a lawyer, was excellent, and will be published in the minutes of the Convention, and will be a great help to the work. The Convention seemed like a miniature State Convention. A good county committee was appointed, with headquarters in Edgefield, the county town, where a working quorum, including the officers, resides.

"The author of the paper referred to was made Chairman of the Committee; the strongest financial man of the place was made Treasurer and Chairman of the Finance Committee; and the editor of the county paper was made Secretary. It was determined by the Committee to raise $5,000 to prosecute for the year a true county work.

"This county is noted as one of the most difficult in South Carolina for Christian work; and it is a very significant fact that it should be the first one in the great South to take up this important phase of association effort. The International

Committee's plan of systematic giving for association extension was adopted by the Convention for the Association of the county.   State Secretary Wynne was present at all the sessions of the Convention, and did all he could to make it a success.''

This movement is regarded as one of the most important steps in the work of the Young Men's Christian Association; and Edgefield County, ever forward in such movements as Nullification, Secession, and Red Shirtism in days gone by, has taken the front rank in this.   There are now seven Young Men's Christian Associations fostered by this county organization.

From the Edgefield Chronicle, February 21st, 1894:

The daily papers throughout the State, as well as the local press of Sumter, have given glowing accounts of the recent Convention of South Carolina's Young Men's Christian Associations.   This gathering of eighty or ninety picked men from the Associations of the State was a model of harmony, enthusiasm and spirituality.   The subjects relating to the work were ably discussed; the Bible studies and devotional services were strengthening and ennobling; and everything was conducted in a business-like manner that reflected credit upon all connected with it.

Edgefield was represented by four delegates, and the work in our town and throughout our county made a most encouraging showing when the reports were called for.   County Y. M. C. A. Work, as conducted in our county, is regarded as a model for the other counties of our State, and indeed for the entire nation.

Reports received from various points in the county since the Convention are exceedingly gratifying.   At the last meeting heard from, at Good Hope, about 75 young men were present. Mt. Willing was visited last week, and new life has been infused into the work there.

In our town on Sunday last there were 23 at the young men's meeting, 16 at the boy's meeting, and over two hundred at the public service at night.   During the same day a committee from the Association visited the jail, while a similar committee has been appointed to visit the Poor House at stated periods.   The Bible classes are still doing good work, and everything betokens progress along all lines of Y. M. C. A. work.

XXX.

EDUCATION.

The subject of education has already been mentioned more than once, but the reader will find here the official statement of W. D. Mayfield, Esq., Superintendent of Education, for the year 1891, showing the number of high shools and graded schools in the county, with the number of pupils in attendance, male and female, white and colored.

We find there are four high schools, viz.: Denny's, Emory, Harmony, and Red Hill. Two graded schools, one at Edgefield and one at Johnston.

Number of children that attended school during the scholastic year, 1890-91. This is the total enrolment. Males, white, 2,044; females, white, 1,830; total, 3,874. Males, colored, 2,501; females, colored, 2,907; total, 5,408. Total, males, 4,545; total, females, 4,737; grand total, 9,282.

The average attendance was somewhat less. It is here given:

Males, white, 1,840; females, white, 1,517; total, 3,357; Males, colored, 2,099; females, colored, 2,457; total, 4,556. Total males, 3,939; total females, 3,974; grand total, 7,913. Number of school houses, 169; value, $14,475; 71 log houses, 98 frame; condition good, 90; fair, 43; bad, 36. Owned by school districts, 61; by other parties, 108. Of the students in attendance there were studying the alphabet, 394; spelling, 6,156; reading, 5,527; writing, 4,683; mental arithmetic, 2,342; written arithmetic, 3,367; geography, 2,812; English Grammar, 1,930; History of the United States, 1,771; higher branches, 446. Schools were in session during the year, 3.50 months.

INSTITUTE WORK—TEACHERS IN ATTENDANCE.

Male, white, 5; female, white, 11; total, 16.

Male, colored, 17; female, colored, 16; total, 33.

Total males, 22; total females, 27; grand total, 49.

Amount paid male instructors, $80.00; female $55.00.

Total amount paid instructors, $135.00.

Value of school furniture and apparatus, $300.00.

TEACHERS EMPLOYED IN COMMON SCHOOLS.

Male, white, first grade, 37; female, 51; total, 88.

Male, white, second grade, 2; female, 15; total, 17.

Male white, third grade, 0; female, 2; total, 2.

Male, colored, first grade, 6; female, 3; total, 9.

Male, colored, second grade, 16; female, 10; total, 26.

Male, colored, third grade, 20; female, 25; total, 45.

Licentiate, colored, 4; total, 4.

Males, first grade, 43; females, 54; total, 97.

Males, second grade, 18; female, 25; total, 43.

Males, third grade, 20; females, 27; total; 47.

Males licentiates, 0; females, 4; total, 4.

Total am't paid to teachers during the year 1890-91 $12602 31

SCHOOL FUNDS—EXPENDITURES FOR YEAR 1889-90.

Teachers' salaries $12602 31
School Commissioner's salary 600 00
Traveling expenses of School Commissioner . . .   100 00
Per diem Board of Examiners and mileage   30 00—$13332 31
Money raised for school purposes, 1890, 2-mill tax .   12501 316

AVERAGE MONTHLY WAGES PAID TO TEACHERS.

Male, first grade, $30; female, $20.

Male, second grade, $20; female, $15.

Male, third grade, $18; female, $18.

Licentiates, $12.50; $12.50.

We find from the foregoing statement the total number of children enrolled for instructions in the public schools of the county is 9,282.

At an expense to the county of $13,332.31. For each child enrolled it is $1.436.

Schools are open three and a half months in the year.

From the foregoing statement it is very plain that the education and the amount of instruction to be had in the public schools is not at all sufficient to make one a scholar. Pope, the poet says:

> "A little learning is a dangerous thing;
> Drink deep, or taste not the Pierian Spring."

I am not sure that he is right, but whether he is or not, this is clear, that he who is able to read well, is able to drink deep, is able to store up in his mind the best thoughts of the best and wisest men of all the ages. The public school system lays the foundation and opens the way to the acquisition of knowledge, and the seeker can go on if he wishes. A collegiate training does little more.

The public school system is rather hard on the teachers. Three and a half months' employment during the year is not sufficient, hence the danger is of not being able to find teachers strictly first grade for the public schools. There is great danger of lowering the standard.

In addition to the foregoing mentioned high schools and academies I can add that there is at Ridge Spring a good academy for boys and girls where pupils are prepared for college. Batesburg has two good schools, one under the control of the Baptist denomination, the other under control of the Methodist. Both have good teachers and both do good work. They have good buildings. These schools belong to Lexington as well as Edgefield, as Batesburg is on the line between the two counties. Johnston has already been mentioned. The schools there have been good for a long time. Johnston now has a graded school. Trenton, the old Pine House, has a good academy. At this time, September 1893, the school is under the mastership of M. W. Purifoy—he has just entered upon its duties. He has had some experience and is a good teacher. The school has a competent corps of assistants.

At Edgefield Rev. L. R. Gwaltney has just entered upon his duties as headmaster of the old and venerable Edgefield Academy, where many eminent men were educated in the past, and where one eminent native and citizen of Newberry, James J. Caldwell, taught in the year 1819. Mr. Gwaltney, as pastor of the Baptist Church at Edgefield and a master of the academy, has a fine field for doing good work.

Parksville, Modoc, and Plum Branch, on the Augusta and Knoxville Railroad, have good high schools. And so in every section of the county from Lexington to Abbeville and from the Savannah to the Saluda, education is not neglected anywhere, but from every hamlet and homestead in the land children flock daily to the school houses with their satchels full of books. And all who will may get a good education in the County of Edgefield.

LITERATURE.

Edgefield has been the home, native or adopted, of many eminent men, lawyers, judges, physicians, ministers of the Gospel, statesmen, Governors, and military men, but of few writers and authors of books. The talent and genius have not been wanting; but the atmosphere of Edgefield has always been too intensely active and practical to give a suitable home to the story teller, to the dreaming scholar, or to the poet. There have been men and women both, who, under other auspices, might have developed into poets and writers of general literature. Indeed, the feeling that makes the poet, the scientist, and the scholar is in all lands and in all communities. Circumstances foster, or retard and hinder, the growth of the feeling to the flowering and fruit-bearing age.

In Edgefield the taste and scholarship of Mr. Edmund Bacon were so remarkable that when a boy at school in Augusta and only fifteen years of age, he was selected by the academy to give the address of welcome to Washington on his visit to that city in 1791. Mr. Bacon's wish then was to devote himself to literary pursuits, to which his guardian was favorable. perhaps injudiciously, as his fortune was small. Washington was so well pleased with the address of welcome that he made Mr. Bacon a present of books, and among them were some valuable law books. This present determined him to give his life to the law. He made a good and successful lawyer; but there is little doubt that literature lost a worthy servant. The taste for polite learning (and the love of it) has always been strong in his descendants, but they have produced, so far as is known to this writer, no permanent works. The editor of the Edgefield Chronicle is a graceful and easy writer, of pure taste and is a fine musician. What James T. Bacon might have done had he given himself to letters entirely, I know not; but I feel that he could have done well.

Arthur Simkins, so long the able and popular editor of the Edgefield Advertiser, was a poet and musician of no mean order; but he passed away, leaving no permanent work, except what may be found in the files of the Advertiser. There are others now bearing the name, who might rise to eminence in the world of letters, but the exigencies of life press upon them and force their labors into other channels. Poverty and neglect are too often the portion of the man of letters. When successful the carping critics vex his soul, and he cannot help crying out:

"Tray, Blanche and Sweetheart, see they bark at me."

Mrs. Sophia Lake, born Blocker, the wife of Dr. John Lake, was a good writer; wrote stories and sketches for the Advertiser, and was an occasional contributor to Godey's Lady's Book, and perhaps also to other magazines. She left no book. Had I a specimen of her verse it would afford me pleasure to give one or more here. She was kin by blood to James Beattie, author of the Minstrel.

Why should I write the name of Catherine D. Hammond here? Because she was, or might have been, a writer of verse. She lived and died perhaps a hundred years ago. Hers was a bright, ethereal spirit, the spirit of a poet.

Professor La Borde's History of the South Carolina College is one of the few books, the work of an Edgefield man. The work is very valuable as the history of an institution that has been, and, it is hoped, will long continue to be, of great and lasting benefit to the people of the State. Professor La Borde's work, with Colonel J. P. Thomas' History of the Citadel Academy, should never be permitted to drop into neglect before the sea of oblivion covers all.

William H. Abney had poetical ability of a high order, but no work of his remains, except some few verses which were published in the Advertiser, and which are here given, with remarks of the editor of that paper:

Edgefield Advertiser, January 14th, 1863:

SOMETHING UNIQUE.

W. H. A. sends us from Grahamville, S. C., the following chastely-wrought stanzas, remarking that "although verses of another stripe would be more suited to a time of war like this," yet he does not think "that Melpomene should utterly dethrone her gentler sisters." We decidedly agree to that sentiment, and find room with pleasure for our absent friend's effusion. The ladies will scan its peculiar merits with zest, and, although plain philologists may at first uplift their critical brows against the quaintness of its verbiage, they will, upon examination, find that it stands the test of orthoepy. Only

further premising that we should ourself have preferred that
our classical contributor had furnished a clue to one or two very
pretty phrases which (to be candid) are not entirely within
our ken, we beg leave to introduce to the public:

The Elfin Lake.

A lakelet smiles in yonder druid glen,
  So clipt in roundure that a naiad's hair,
I wis, might shadow it—and one could ken
  No presence but the naiad's presence there.

Innumerous 'quick-freshes,' clear and cold,
  Open their crystal throats, and ever pour
Their bick'ring symphonies, like nerves of gold,
  In the meer's urn with tinkling, doric roar.

A fay-born, grotesque isle, from the lake's eyne,
  Peeps like king-jewel in a carcanet,
Embossed with zimmes and shells of quaint design,
  Whose tints have never blush'd in cabinet.

Eft gossamers elance from spray to spray,
  And weave their lither woofs with subtile powers,
And prank them with the Iris-hues they bray
  With gauzy plumes from ever-blooming flowers.

Here tryst the gentle elves—somewhiles they chase
  The clinquant lake-sprats in their mad-cap mirth;
Somewhiles make periapts that wont to grace
  The necks of ruddy cherubs at their birth.

Edgefield Advertiser, February 25th, 1863:

THORNEY ISLE.

"The sweet loneliness of Thorney Isle pleaseth me more
now." These words are ascribed to Edward III, the Monk-
King, by Sir E. Bulwer Lytton in his powerful romance of
"Harold, the last of the Saxon Kings." They were addressed
to William the Conqueror, as the royal twain rode side by side
to London.

I.

William, I love the Juillet Tower,
  And yon palatial pile;
Yet, o'er me sways a sweeter power,
  The ellinge Thorney Isle.
O Thorney Isle, O Thorney Isle,
  The loneliness so sweet,
Of Thorney Isle, my Thorney Isle,
  Pleaseth me more, I weet!

II.

I love Westminster, my wonne
  Shut out from snare and wile;
And a meet bye for royal mone,
  Is lonely Thorney Isle,
O Thorney Isle, O Thorney Isle,
  The loneliness so sweet,
Of Thorney Isle, my Thorney Isle,
  Pleaseth me more, I weet!

III.

Norman, I love the Palatine, |
  Keep, where I bode erstwhile;
But dear to me in life's decline,
  Is ellinge Thorney Isle.
O Thorney Isle, O Thorney Isle,
  The loneliness so sweet,
Of Thorney Isle, my Thorney Isle,
  Pleaseth me more, I weet!

IV.

Sweet Thorney Isle, to thee I fly
  In these my days senile;
Have off this crown, O let me die
  In lonely Thorney Isle!
O Thorney Isle, O Thorney Isle,
  The loneliness so sweet,
Of Thorney Isle, my Thorney Isle,
  Pleaseth me more, I weet!

Thorney Island was once the seat of Westminster.

W. H. A.

Joseph Abney was a graceful and fluent writer as well as an eloquent speaker. He wrote much for the Advertiser, as he always took a deep interest in the political movements of the times. But he left nothing in the form of book or pamphlet, that I now remember, except an address before Butler Lodge, No. 57, A. F. M., on the Anniversary of St. John, the Baptist, in 1854. Mr. Abney was an ardent and devoted Mason, and in this address he traces the history of the order and shows how strong the tie of brotherhood is amongst all nations and people who have become members of the fraternity. There are some eloquent passages in the address, and if the incidents related are true, and I have no reason to doubt them, Free Masonry is truly a noble order. Like other good things, it is abused sometimes.

Giles Chapman, who was killed at the battle of Buena Vista, soon after the close of his school days wrote and had printed at the office of the Advertiser a poem of three or four hundred lines, descriptive of a trip to the then new country of Texas. It was written before the Texan War of Independence. The poem was inscribed to Charles K. Johnson, for whom the author had great admiration and reverence as a teacher and as a man. Mr. Johnson was then editing and publishing the "Native American" at New Orleans. I transcribe a few lines from the poem:

"O, what a beauteous landscape! Every hill—
  And rising cliff is clothed in evergreen;
And many a rivulet and gushing rill
  Ripples along their verdant sides between.
The plain, arrayed in garb of glorious sheen,
  Arrests by turns the traveller's ardent gaze;
The wild-deer adds fresh beauty to the scene,
  That bounds from cliff to cliff, or on the hillside plays.

"But sadness will at times invade the mind,
  And there are none who can resist the spell;
Pleasure is not to flowery meads confined,
  But oftener haunts the hermit's lonely cell.
And so it was with him, 'tis strange to tell,
  No more this land of beauty charmed his eyes,
Which seemed too bright for men on it to dwell;
  Its beauty seemed to him as borrowed from the skies."

Thomas I. McKie, M. D., of Woodlawn, is a graceful and pleasant writer, and has given to me great assistance in the preparation of this book. His "Medical Biographies," which was printed and published in pamphlet form several years ago, the reader will find incorporated in this book. Dr. McKie was Surgeon in the Tenth Regiment, Gist's Brigade.

The following lines by the author of this book were written and published in the Edgefield Advertiser soon after the decease of the great man whose death they were intended to commemorate:

CALHOUN.

His voice is heard no more,
  Earth's greatest son is gone;
O, weep, fair Carolina, weep!
  But gird thy armor on.

Ah, who shall fill his place?
What mighty man have we,
Whose voice shall, like a trumpet peal,
Make every pulse beat free?

Wail, Carolina, wail;
Put dust upon thy head;—
Thou mournest now thy noblest son,
The mightiest of the dead.

But in thy deepest woe,
Beside his lonely tomb;
When wears the future time for thee
A face of fearful gloom.

Swear that his words shall be
Deep in thy memory set!
Swear in thy grief that thou wilt not
His lessons e'er forget.

Swear with thy hand upraised,
And by his name of might;
That thou wilt still, through weal or woe,
For aye defend the right.

The same writer has also published two small volumes of verse, "The Walk and other Poems," and "Within the Vail," also a "History of South Carolina for use in the common schools." This was adopted in 1893 by the State Board of Education. He has also published Part Second of the Annals of Newberry and this History of Edgefield.

W. C. Moragne was a man of fine education and remarkable for his good literary taste and ability. He made, during his life, several occasional addresses, which were well worthy of preservation, but he did not devote himself to literature as a calling. He was a lawyer, and at the Bar as a practitioner of law he was eminently successful. A sketch of his career is found elsewhere in this book.

There may be others or may have been other workers in the literary field, of whom I know nothing. There may be some now in other States, natives of Edgefield or descendants of natives, whose names I would be glad to record here. Edgefield has produced too few who have devoted themselves to letters, and who have been faithful followers of the muses.

NEWSPAPERS.

The newspapers of the county have always held a good position as papers, pure and hightoned. The Advertiser was the first, and stood alone for many years, published by the elder Mr. W. F. Durisoe as editor and proprietor. Then there was a paper published in Hamburg for some years, the title of which I do not remember, though it seems to me it was the Hamburg Journal by Mr. —— Yarborough as editor. Now there are three weekly papers in the county, two at the Court House—Advertiser and Chronicle, and one, the Monitor, at Johnston. They are all Democratic, though they differ somewhat in their views as to the true policy of the Democratic party. This is but natural and right, so they agree to live, and do live in peace and good fellowship.

Edgefield Advertiser, May 20th, 1869:

LADIES' LIBRARY SOCIETY.

In pursuance of a previous notice, the ladies of Edgefield village and vicinity met on the 17th inst., to organize a Library Society.

On motion of Mrs. Dr. Hill, Mrs. Joseph Abney was called to the Chair, and Mrs. Robert A. Lynch appointed Secretary.

A constitution having been prepared, it was adopted, and the following officers elected, viz.: Mrs. Jos. Abney, President; Mrs. Dr. Hill, Vice-President, and Mrs. Robert A. Lynch, Secretary and Treasurer.

XXXI.

MEDICAL BIOGRAPHIES.

BY THOS. J. MCKIE, M. D., EDGEFIELD, S. C.

"The wind blows out, the bubble dies;
The spring entomb'd in autumn lies;
The dew dries up, the star is shot;
The flight is past, and man forgot."

The laborious and well nigh impossible task assigned me, by this Association at its last meeting, in Aiken, two years ago, of collecting and recording biographical sketches of the medical profession in Edgefield, having been partially and very imperfectly performed, I beg to submit the following brief and barely more than traditional sketches, as a part of that duty, so imperfectly performed. The difficulties which surround this undertaking can only be appreciated by those who have engaged in a similar work, and from such, at least, I hope for the mildest criticism.

As geographers crowd into the edges of their maps parts of the world which they do not know about, adding notes in the margin to the effect that beyond this lies nothing but sandy deserts, Scythian ice or a frozen sea, so would this work be, were more to be said of the few whose names and lives I have attempted to record.

Well may it be said:

"Life's but a walking shadow, a poor player,
That struts and frets his hour upon the stage,
And then is heard no more."

Although the doctor's life is most intimately fraught with that of the human family, from the moment of birth to the hour of death, the first to welcome the new creature into life, and the last to minister to his dying wants, yet he retains not a memory,

"And oft the throng denies its charity."

This much having been said, apologetically, of Edgefield's meagre medical record, the sketches are respectfully submitted:

DR. W. BRAZIER.

Dr. William Brazier, though a native of England, died in Aiken, then a part of Edgefield, in July, 1843, and may be claimed as an Edgefield practitioner, though much of his life was spent elsewhere. Dr. Maximilian Laborde has left us, in an obituary notice, all we know of this rather remarkable character. Born in London about A. D. 1740, (being something like one hundred years old when he died) of highly respectable parentage, one of his cousins, Captain Lambert, of the British Navy, fell at the capture of the Java by the Constitution; another, General Lambert, was in command of the British reserve at the battle of New Orleans; he obtained favor of the British Government, and secured a collectorship at the port of St. Christopher, in the West Indies. Here he turned missionary to the negroes, preaching the doctrine of John Wesley.

About 1791 he was invited to Charleston by a Society of Primitive Wesleyan Methodists, to take charge of their congregation. Here he determined upon the study of medicine, and repaired to Philadelphia for that purpose, a year or two after. Receiving an invitation from Dr. Rush, who discovered rare talent in the student, to go into his office, he prosecuted his studies so successfully as to obtain a license to practice among the inmates of the Philadelphia Almshouse, for six months of the year 1795. He then returned South and practiced medicine at and near Augusta, Ga., and in Edgefield until 1803, when he was again called to Charleston, to take charge of the church, by which he had been invited in 1791. Nine months after he abandoned the pulpit and removed to Columbia, where he practiced medicine a short time; thence he returned to the neighborhood of Edgefield Court House, where he practiced his profession until about 1827. Five or six years were then spent in the valley of the Mississippi.

As a physician, Dr. Brazier stood well with the profession of his day. Between the Shakers, to whom he was at one time strongly attached, Methodists and Baptists, his theological ideas were not always clearly understood, and it is believed he died in the faith of Baron Swedenborg. His intellect was of a high order, but for want of cultivation and discipline, which insure logical precision and perspicuity, and owing to an

ardor of temperament which rendered him impatient of contra-
diction, he was not successful He was an inveterate talker
and a bold listener, so much so that he has been known to talk
his friend into a sound sleep, and then arouse him by a verbal
chastisement for his inattention or want of capacity to understand him.

DR. ELBERT BLAND

Was born near Edgefield, S. C., on the 29th of April, 1823.
Born and reared in affluence, and having a father ambitious for
his son, his educational advantages were of the best.

Nature gifted him with a clear and vigorous intellect, together with an almost unparalleled native energy, and vigorous application capable of rapid and lasting acquirements.
His was a strong, manly, and forcible character, well calculated to carve its way through the deadliest opposition. Having selected medicine for his profession, he properly understood the high requirements of the vocation. He entered the
medical department of the University of New York, and remained there during the sessions of 1843 and '44.

In March, 1844, he graduated with honorable distinction.
Being ardent and ambitious in his profession, he was not satisfied with merely entering upon the threshold of science, but
was desirous of penetrating into the inmost recesses of its mys
teries. He consequently returned to the city of New York,
and spent the greater part of the year 1845 and 1846 attending
the hospitals, and still deriving knowledge from the learned
men of the faculty, among whom he had warm and lasting
friends. His knowledge of the philosophy of medicine was
deep and accurate.

In the captivating and instructive branches of physiology
and anatomy he was exceedingly well versed. But it was in
the specialty of surgery that he rested his hopes for future
eminence. He was singularly fitted by his temperament for
this dignified and important branch of his profession, and it
only needed a longer life to have placed him in the front rank
of American surgeons. On the breaking out of the Mexican
war he applied for and received the appointment of Assistant
Surgeon of the historic Palmetto Regiment, and with them
proceeded to the distant field of action. He passed through
the arduous Mexican campaign with honor and practical im-

provement to himself, with sterling usefulness to his fellow-soldiers, and with the highest intimacy and applause of his commander, the heroic and knightly Colonel P. M. Butler. He returned to Edgefield at the close of the war, in 1848, and resumed the practice of medicine. He was married to Miss Rebecca Griffin, daughter of Honorable Nathan L. Griffin, also of Edgefield, in March, 1854, and from that time until the breaking out of the late war, lived there as a popular, scientific, reliable, fearless, and sympathetic physician. Though actively engaged in arduous professional duties, yet he never ceased to be more or less a student, but with the application of true mental devotion, made himself one of the best informed men of his day.

Unpretentious and unpedantic, he was yet a better scholar than many around him distinguished for high literary and political position. The dark clouds of dissension gathered and the call of an invaded country disturbed the study of scientific pursuits, and with unexampled devotion and patriotism, he exchanged the scalpel for the sword and placed his services and his life upon the altar of his country.

On the 6th of January, 1861, he was commissioned Surgeon of the First Regiment, South Carolina Volunteers, commanded by Colonel Maxey Gregg, and stationed on Morris Island. In this capacity he served but two months, and fired with patriotic ardor and love of martial glory, he resigned this position, determined to seek more active service. He returned home and in March, 1861, was made Captain of the Ninety-six Rifles, one of the best organized, drilled, and equipped companies of the war. This company formed the right, and rifle company of the Seventh Regiment, South Carolina Volunteers. During the first year of the war he led this company through all the marchings and countermarchings of the Army of the Potomac. At Fairfax, at Bull Run, at Manassas, Fall's Church, Munson's Hill, on the retreat to the Peninsula, at Yorktown, and at Williamsburg. In April, 1862, the Seventh Regiment was reorganized and Captain Bland was elected Lieutenant Colonel, and, with the exception of four months, he was in active command of the regiment. In the battles around Richmond, at Savage Station, he received a severe wound in the right arm, from which he never recovered—only a few weeks before his death, a tumor proceeding from this wound, caused him intense suffering. At Fredericksburg, in the terrible battle of December, 1862, he led the Seventh Regiment. In this battle he narrowly escaped death, and was only saved by a spy-glass in his left breast pocket—the cylinder of which was torn and the glass shivered by a minnie ball. At Chancellorsville in May, 1863, he led the regiment. At Gettysburg he led the right wing. In all these battles he was slightly wounded. After his return from Pennsylvania, his health was so shattered. and his wounded arm so troublesome, he determined, very reluctantly, to return home to his profession. The regiment was ordered South, and clamored so loudly for him to lead them that he consented, and on the fatal 20th September, 1863, he marched to the "River of Death," and fell on the bloody field of Chickamauga—shot through the left lung.

He lived three-quarters of an hour, and died in the arms of his devoted Sergeant, Stallworth, and calmly and bravely as became his life, entrusted messages of love and farewell to wife and children.

DR. WILLIAM BUTLER.

Of the distinguished sons of Edgefield who have adorned the medical profession, besides being a rich heritage to the district, State, and county, none are more worthy of record than Dr. William Butler, Jr., who was born in 1792, at Big Creek, near the spot where Butler Church now (1889) stands.

When quite a young man, handsome, tall, (six feet) erect, and graceful, he appears in connection with the medical staff at the battle of New Orleans. From the Navy Department, Bureau of Medicine and Surgery, we obtain the following record of naval service of Dr. William Butler, Jr :

Surgeon's Mate, (equivalent of Assistant Surgeon now) commission dated 10th December, 1814, and handed to him at this Department on the 2nd June, 1815, with an order to report himself to Dr. Cuthbush for duty in the hospital at Washington.

Accepted 2nd June, 1815.

May 14th, 1816, report to Commodore Tingy for duty on board schooner "Non-such."

November 7th, 1817, report to Captain Sinclair for duty on board "Congress," (Norfolk.)

November 25th, 1817, granted furlough, six months.

January 28th, 1818, report to Commodore H. G. Campbell, commanding officer, Charleston, S. C., for duty on Black-beard's Island, under the immediate command of Lieutenant Thomas Newells.

January 9th, 1819, proceed to New York, by water, and report to the commanding naval officer for duty on that station.

June 6th, 1820, resignation accepted.

About this time Dr. Butler was married at Newport, Rhode Island, to Miss Jane Tweedy Perry, daughter of Captain Perry, United States Navy, and sister of the two Commodore Perrys, and seems not to have practiced his profession to any extent afterwards. He settled on his plantation adjoining Saluda Old Town plantation, and devoted himself to agricultural pursuits.

In 1824 he exchanged his plantation for a large body of land in Greenville District, and built on Butler's Hill, near to Lowndes' Hill, four miles from Greenville Court House, where he resided until 1849, when he removed to Arkansas. When Waddy Thompson, his brother-in-law, was appointed Minister to Mexico, Dr. Butler represented the Greenville Congressional District in Congress for the unexpired term. He is represented as being rather stern in manner, at times approaching austerity, distinguished for elevation and integrity of character, with a rigid sense of right, from which nothing could divert or swerve him.

His stay in Arkansas was a brief one. Attacked by gastric disease, he died at Fort Gibson on the 26th of September, 1850, and is buried near Van Buren, Ark.

DR. A. W. BURT.

Dr. Augustus W. Burt at one time enjoyed a large and lucrative practice in the lower Horn's Creek portion of Edgefield, occupying quite an extensive field, often requiring two or more days to make a round of visits. Fevers, mostly of a malarial type, were the prevailing diseases at these busy seasons, and though in the earlier days of quinine in full or even moderate doses, he had a fair degree of success. It is remembered of him that his library was exceedingly small, and his stock of medicine, which every county practitioner was compelled to keep and dispense, was very limited. Mercury, followed by jalap, &c., was the then prevailing fashion of treating fevers. Sulphuric ether was with him a favorite remedy in what he called red tongue fever, a remittent, with excessive gastric irritability.

His death was a tragic one. Perhaps in 1841 or 1842, he was called upon to treat a negro man whose brains had been knocked out with the eye of a weeding hoe, in the hands of another negro on the same plantation. A difficulty arose between them while working in the field together, and the hoe was put to the unlawful use of crushing in the frontal bone, and displacing a considerable quantity of cerebral matter, some of which remained upon the hoe. Shortly after the recovery of this case in the hands of Dr. Burt, both negroes were sold in consequence of the death of the owner, when the Doctor became the purchaser of the assailant. After the close of the sale the Doctor laughingly remarked upon the cheapness of his purchase, the negro having given him a good paying case in thus wounding his fellow servant.

Two years after the purchase, early in 1847, when the Doctor attempted to administer some slight punishment to the negro, while holding a club-axe in his hand, he turned on his owner, and with the axe, treated him as he had before done the negro with the hoe, except that immediate death was the result, the blows being repeated until life was extinct.

Dr. Burt was a tall, commanding figure, with fine face, winning manner and pleasing address. He was popular, and enjoyed the confidence and esteem of a large clientage. He was also a lover of all field sports, in which he freely indulged when the time and opportunity favored, but worked with such assiduous industry as to accumulate quite a competency. His death was a great shock to the entire community, and was deeply regretted by all.

DR. WALL BURT.

Two brothers, both Edgefield practitioners, survived Dr. A. W. Burt. The younger, Dr. William M. Burt, enjoyed a fair practice for several years at Edgefield Court House, where he was well spoken of. But, like many others of Edgefield's sons, thought best to seek fortune in the West, and removed about a quarter of a century ago, to Shreveport, La·, where he practiced till not many years since when he died.

DR. H. BURT.

Dr. Harwood Burt, the eldest of the three, was also the most talented. He was a fine conversationalist, a most popular and successful practitioner, a good speaker, and with all, a metaphysician of no mean order. It is said of him that on one occasion when worsted in an argument by a learned gentleman who opposed him he turned to him and said: "Sir, you remind me of a piney-woods pond—all over creation and ankle deep no where." He stood at the head of the profession in Edgefield and was considered a safe and wise counsellor in all matters pertaining to medicine.

Being a genius, he was also erratic. At times a religious enthusiast, at others an eloquent lecturer on temperance, and at last an industrious and most successful farmer, making an impress of his versatile mind upon agriculture, which redounded to the benefit of his entire section, whose capabilities as an agricultural territory had never before reached such a high state of productiveness as was developed under his skillful hands.

His death was a great loss to his neighborhood, county and State, which he alike adored. He died at his home near Trenton.

DR. M. W. ABNEY.

Dr. Mathew W. Abney was born in the Saluda section of Edgefield in 1814. He was descended from an honored Saluda family, who claim descent from an old English family, members of which still hold honored places in the mother country. Dr. Abney's parents both died when he was young. From early youth, however, he was brave and self-reliant; and in the country schools of his native section, he acquired a fair education. Before reaching manhood's estate he volunteered for the Seminole War under Colonel David Denny, also of the Saluda section. In this campaign his health became impaired.

He travelled in Kentucky and Ohio for the benefits offered by the lime water of those States. While in Cincinnati he became a student of Dr. Curtis, an eminent physician of his day.

Returning home, he continued his medical studies with Dr. John Ready, a prominent physician of the eastern side of Edgefield. He graduated from the South Carolina Medical College in 1838, his thesis having received complimentary notice.

Beginning practice in the Pleasant Lane section of Edgefield he obtained some distinction the following year by his successful management of his cases in an epidemic of typhoid fever which prevailed in his neighborhood.

In 1840 he married Miss Caroline Blocker, a lady whose every quality conspired to bless and brighten the Doctor's whole life—the last thirty years of which was spent in active practice at Edgefield Court House interrupted only by his service as a medical officer in the army of the Confederate States.

This noble gentleman of the old school died at his home in Edgefield village after a lingering and painful illness. Four years before his death he was stricken with paralysis and remained an invalid—the trials of which he bore with such fortitude and courage as to display in an exemplary way his Christian character. For almost half a century, Dr. Abney pursued his work of duty and devotion to his profession and patrons with singular and steadfast earnestness, and died in his seventy-second year.

The following additional tribute to the memory of Dr. M. W. Abney is from the pen and heart of James T. Bacon, Esq., editor of the Edgefield Chronicle:

"This noble gentleman of the old school, of high and honorable Saluda lineage, died at his home in our town on Friday morning, the 20th inst. Four years ago he was stricken with paralysis, since which time he was a helpless, though a cheerful invalid, strong in intellectual keenness and Christian fortitude. And never did mortal man through long years of suffering receive such sublime exemplification of woman's love and truth, and faith, and work, as did our revered and departed townsman.

"His sons gave their lives long ago for the Southern cause,

but his noble wife and daughters will ever wear the crown of duty fulfilled with heavenly completeness. For half a century Dr. Abney was an acknowledged leader in his great humanitarian profession of medicine; a shining light in the scientific world beloved of all, and that grandest of all characters, a genuine Christian.

"We gazed upon his face in death and the clean years of duty showed their impress upon the peaceful countenance, chiseled by thought and tinted with the sweet glow of perennial benevolence.

"Dr. Abney was in the seventy-second year of his age. His busy brain rests now from all its toil and pain."

To this brief biographical sketch of Dr. Abney I do not think it improper to add that at his wedding supper, to which I was an invited guest—he married Miss Caroline Blocker— it was my good fortune to eat off the table cloth, or part of the table cloth that had been used at the entertainment given to Marquis de LaFayette on his visit to Charleston during the administration of Governor Manning.

Mrs. Abney's grandfather was one of the committee whose duty it was to entertain LaFayette on that occasion, and after the feast, as the cloth was very large, the committee divided it among them, and Mrs. Abney's mother used the piece which had come to her at her daughter's wedding feast.

DR. E. J. MIMS.

*Dr. Edward J. Mims, the second son of M. Mims, Esq., one of the oldest settlers of Edgefield village, practiced there almost to the time of his death. He also carried on the first drug store in Edgefield, in partnership with Dr. M. LaBorde. After many years he retired to his plantation, eight miles off, which has since become the site of the flourishing town of Johnston on the Charlotte, Columbia and Augusta Road. He was well educated, kind-hearted, liberal in his views, and a safe and successful practitioner.

DR. J. O. NICHOLSON.

*Dr. John O. Nicholson was the oldest son of Shemuel Nicholson, and located at one time in the village of Edgefield, but

---

*From the Edgefiled Advertiser.

nearly all of his life at the place of his nativity, several miles above, where he practiced with satisfaction to his patrons. In manner he was gentle and dignified. He improved his mind not only in the science of his chosen profession, but in general literature as well. Politics also commanded his attention, he having been chosen a Representative in the State Legislature. He was also a successful farmer, and possessing an able second in the person of his amiable wife, he accumulated a fortune, as fortunes were in those days. He was liberal and kind to the poor. He died comparatively a young man.

DR. JOHN LAKE.

This truly good and able man, Dr. John Lake, was no less a philanthropist than a physician—physician in its broad and true sense. Whenever appealed to he rarely, if ever, said no. And in his special branch, that of obstetrics, he perhaps had no equal in Edgefield County. It is currently said of him that when the first to be called in he never lost a mother in child-birth. He was a firm believer in the necessity of prompt removal of the placenta without the usual waiting taught by the books.

To arrive at any degree of prominence in any special branch of medicine or surgery is rarely to be hoped for by a country practitioner. The duties which devolve upon him are so varied, the amount of physical labor to be performed is so arduous, and the time necessarily consumed in going from house to house, often at long distances from each other, is so great as to preclude the possibility of any specialty without some genius or special adaptation of the individual.

Such fitness Dr. Lake seemed to have possessed.

Though reared in Edgefield he was born in Newberry District, April 28th, 1809, and was educated at Cokesbury, in Abbeville. His father removed to Edgefield when the son was about twelve years of age, and soon afterwards both parents died, leaving the son with three other brothers to carve their way in life.

At the age of twenty-one or two Dr. L. graduated from the University of Pennsylvania, and began the practice of medicine soon after. Two or three years later he was married to Miss Sophia A. Blocker, who was well known in Edgefield as a lady of culture by her frequent contributions to the current literature of her day.

Besides doing a good practice and having a general supervision of his farm upon which he lived, Dr. L. found time to engage in political matters, and represented his district in the State Legislature, having been chosen to that office in 1848 (or thereabout) by a very complimentary vote of 2,300 out of a possible 2,700.

Dr. L. was also active and prominent in his County Medical Society, which lived and flourished most under his able administration as president, which office he filled so ably and acceptably to the members, that the office was thrust upon him against his earnest protest. When well advanced in years, and stricken with the infirmities of age, it is remembered that, in one of his annual addresses before the Society, perhaps the last he ever made, with much feeling and effect he referred to the story of the seven men who agreed among themselves to meet on a given day in each succeeding year, and dine together until the last man was left. He said that, "when I look around me for the associates of my earlier life their seats are all empty. I alone am left to greet you, the rising generation of representatives of Edgefield medicine. I bid you God speed, and I entreat you to foster and perpetuate your Society for your own benefit, for the advancement of your profession and for the good of society."

At one time in its earlier days, Dr. L. was vice-president of this Association. In early life he connected himself with the Baptist denomination, and on January 17th, 1884, in the 75th year of his age, Dr. Lake died as he had lived, a pure and upright man.

DR. W. W. GEIGER.

Dr. William W. Geiger, whose place of nativity is on the Saluda side of Edgefield, came to Cherokee Pond, about eight miles from Hamburg, and began the practice of medicine in 1837 or 1838. He was a graduate of a Kentucky school, Lexington, perhaps, which was a popular resort for students from this section at that time. He enjoyed the confidence and esteem of his community, both as a man and as a physician, doing at one time quite a large and extensive practice. He continued in this field for twelve or fourteen years, and afterwards abandoned the practice for the less laborious business of a commission merchant in the then thriving town of Hamburg. Dr. G. was twice married, and after the second marriage he gave up his business in Hamburg and moved with his family to Florida, where he has since died.

DR. N. MERIWETHER.

Dr. Nicholas Meriwether, another worthy practitioner of Edgefield County, was born August 8th, 1821, near Clark's Hill, a station on the Western Carolina Railway, where he also lived and pursued his work until his health failed.

Like most country doctors, he pursued the double vocation of physician and farmer. The latter was almost a necessity, he having · inherited quite a landed estate and a numerous body of slaves; for none of his school, similarly situated, would willingly part with their slaves, who had been handed down from generations past, however unprofitable they might be, being looked upon as part and parcel of the family household. Having acquired a liberal education, he took up the study of medicine, and graduated at the Georgia Medical College, at Augusta, in 1843. After a few years' practice he abandoned it, and gave most of his time to planting. Like many other Carolinians, at the beginning of hostilities between the States, he took his place in the ranks (Seventh South Carolina Volunteers) as high private, and served until failing health drove him from the field. The close of the war found him broken down in health, and his fortune swept away. Beginning life anew, he found it necessary to resume practice, of which he was never fond, though well versed in medical lore. He was a great reader, and possessed a powerful memory, retaining most of what was found in books or practice. He was not successful financially, and was once heard to say that any moneymaking scheme, undertaken for that purpose, always turned to dust in his hands. He was a Baptist in faith, deeply religions, and scrupulously honest and upright in all the relations of life. His religious duty was his first duty, from which nothing was allowed to divert him. As a neighbor and friend he was faithful and true, as well as hospitable and kind. In practice he somewhat prided himself on his successful management of pneumonic fever, in which he had early resort to blisters. He also thought that the disease was in some way associated with malaria; that is to say, any given case of pneumonia in the spring or winter, is apt to have been preceded by fever in the summer or fall. This view, however, has not been sustained by the experience of another physician in the same locality.

This pious and upright physician, having suffered long and painfully from gastric disease, passed peacefully away on the 18th day of November, 1878.

DR. A. G. TEAGUE.

Dr. Abner Griffin Teague was a native of Laurens District, but practiced for a considerable length of time in that portion of Edgefield known as the Dark Corner. He afterwards removed to Edgefield village, where he also engaged in practice, besides doing a drug business in connection with Dr. T. Jeff. Teague. Dr. T. was a good man, an able physician, and a successful farmer. But, like many others, he grew weary of work, and sought rest on his farm, about three miles from the village of Edgefield, where the evening of his life was passed. He is, therefore, claimed as an Edgefield physician, having spent his professional life in our midst. He died a few years ago, honored and respected by friends and neighbors, who looked upon him as a safe and wise counsellor and upright man.

DR. T. H. PATTISON.

The subject of the following sketch, Dr. Thos. H. Pattison, was born at Old Cambridge, in Edgefield County (then district) in the year 1820. Left an orphan at an early age, he was taken in charge by a maternal uncle, who educated and brought him up to the mercantile business in the city of Augusta, Ga., where he also studied medicine in the office of Dr. L. D. Ford, who was, at that time, professor of the practice of medicine in the Georgia Medical College, which is situated in that city. In 1843, he graduated from that institution, and immediately began the practice of medicine in the neighborhood of Republican Church, in the Martintown section of Edgefield County. Here, by his genial manner and strict attention to duty, he soon acquired a fair practice, which he maintained throughout a long and useful career. As a practitioner, he stood high with his patrons, who were his friends as well. Early in the war between the States, he entered the ranks as a private, and served creditably until discharged, often acting as medical officer to his command, the Seventh South Carolina Volunteers. As a practitioner and farmer, he was fairly successful. Frequent indulgence in his cups—(he was a Bacchanal, and at his own house in one of his bouts, he unfortunately killed Dr. West, another practitioner and drinker)— did not destroy the confidence of patients or friends, or prevent his moderate success as a farmer. In 1845 he married the daughter of Joseph Crafton, a substantial planter, living then between Steven's Creek and Savannah River—a section known as the "Forks."

In the management of malarial fevers, which at certain seasons were rife in his field, he thought mercury a necessity in many cases, in order to prevent recurrence. In such as were of a remittent type, with high fever and gastric irritability, he relied greatly on dram doses of sulphuric ether, to allay the fever and quiet the stomach—a practice he had borrowed from a neighboring physician, Dr. A. W. Burt.

Not many years after the war had closed, by over-exertion in some farm work, the Doctor brought on pulmonary hemorrhage, which was soon followed by a decline in his general health, resulting in death in a few years. None realized more clearly the danger of the situation, and no one ever met the remorseless monster with more heroic courage.

He died March 6th, 1878, in the 58th year of his age.

DR. J. F. ADAMS.

Dr. James F. Adams, the subject of this sketch, was a native of Edgefield County, and fairly exemplified the energy and industry of the people who adorned the age and country in which he lived.

He was born about the year 1790, and began the practice of medicine in his native district, at about the age of twenty-five or thirty years. Of his educational qualifications preparatory to the study of medicine, very little is known. His professional education was obtained at Philadelphia, to which place he journeyed from his home on horseback, consuming almost a month on the road, after having spent some time in the office of Dr. Dent, an eminent practitioner in the city of Augusta, Ga.

Being well equipped, Dr. A. was not long in acquiring an extensive practice, which he maintained to quite the end of his professional life. It is said that ten or twelve doctors occupy the territory at one time exclusively held by himself. Like most country doctors, he was also engaged in planting, to which he gave all of his attention during the latter years, and was quite as successful in this as he had been in medicine.

His forte was in the management of chronic cases, and especially of ulcers. He was a strong believer in the efficacy of calomel in the treatment of malarial fevers, in which he frequently induced ptyalism. Cinchona bark was used not as a tonic after the sufferer had been properly (?) depleted with mercurial purgatives, emetics, bleeding, etc. This was before the introduction into general practice of the cinchona alkaloids.

In the matter of dress, doctor A. acquired some distinction. [In some way the remaining portion of this has been lost, and the manuscript is also out of place.]

Edgefield Chronicle, March 8th, 1893:

W. SCOTT SHEPPARD.

Died at his home on the 27th of January, 1893, Dr. W. Scott Sheppard. He was born April 28th, 1848; baptized into the Bethany Baptist Church by the Rev. John Trapp, 1866; graduated as a physician March, 1869. He was in every sphere of life the true Christian gentleman. In his religion the Word of God was his rule of faith and practice, and while his unusually bright mind was seen in every department of his life's work, in nothing was it more manifest than in attainment in the knowledge of God's precious Word. His conscientious sense of his obligations to that rule, caused his life to conform more and more to its requirements, so that it may be truly said of him, his was the path of the just that shines more and more to the perfect day.

The Master selected him as one who should witness for him under peculiar surroundings that would give no grounds to question the honesty of his testimony.

Stricken with paralysis December 27th, 1876, which gradually grew worse until it terminated in total blindness in April, 1889, in his sense of the Christian privilege to take the promises of God to himself, he was cheerful through all his painful sufferings, counting his afflictions light, however severe, in this life, as working for him a far more exceeding and eternal weight of glory. Nor did his severe afflictions abate his love for and interest in his fellow man, which was ever manifest by his anxiety for their welfare and sympathy for them in trials and afflictions. He had truly a heart to weep with those that weep and rejoice with those that rejoice, yet with perfect resignation to the supreme love and wisdom of God.

As a physician, he was diligent, conscientious, and efficient, having the most implicit confidence of his patients, to which he attributed the blessings asked of God on all his prescriptions. His sympathy with suffering humanity caused him to continue to practice until afflicted with total blindness, and even then his counsel was eagerly sought and cheerfully given.

In his own family, as a loving husband and father, his character and Christian light shone most brightly in his tender love, safe counsel, and earnest prayers. As a son, he was devoted and affectionate; as neighbor and friend, true, kind, and hospitable. As a member of the Mountain Creek Church, his life was read and known with profit to church and community, and especially will his life and memory be cherished by his pastors, who ever had his prayers and co-operation.

He leaves to feel their irreparable loss, a devoted wife, and seven children, with the dying counsel, "go to God for comfort and help, he will ever be true to you," an aged mother, three brothers, and a sister, and a large circle of relatives and friends. Yet they sorrow not as those who have no hope, knowing that the dear one has entered into that rest that remains to the people of God. J. P. M.

Edgefield Advertiser, January 13th, 1897:

DR. WILLIAM D. JENNINGS, SR.

Dr. William D. Jennings, Sr., died on Saturday last, the 9th day of January, at the residence of his life-long friend and kinsman, John R. Blackwell. On Monday his remains were brought to our town and laid to rest by the side of his wife and oldest son. "Old Doctor Bill," as generally called, was

one of our ancient landmarks, as widely known in Edgefield
County, perhaps, as any man living or dead.   For more than
seventy-seven years he has been going in and out among us,
and for only a short period of this long life was he absent from
his beloved old county and people.   (Immediately after the
war he lived in Galveston, Texas, where he was a member of
the faculty of a medical college in that city.)   Dr. Jennings
was noted above all things for his genial disposition; he
"showed himself friendly" to all, and in affliction or distress
was unremitting in his ministrations.   A kinder hearted man
or physician never lived, if we may judge by his acts.   And if
all in Edgefield County who have received kindnesses at his
hands would bring a wreath for his grave it would make a
monument higher than any other in our city of the dead.

DR. GEORGE M. YARBROUGH.

It would please me much to give an extended sketch of the
life of Dr. Yarbrough, but it is out of my power.   I knew him
well for many years; at one time he was a near neighbor and
my family physician, but his life and mine at that time flowed
on in such a calm, uneventful way that there is nothing to relate, unless one had kept a diary, which this writer has never
done.   Sometimes I regret that I have not.

For a good many years Dr. Yarbrough and myself, Dr. William Coleman, Joseph Griffith, Esq., and some others, occasionally met for the purposes of debating any question that
might be chosen for the purpose.   In other words, we formed
a debating society.   We were not mere boys at this time, but
grown men, and thought ourselves competent to discuss almost any question.   One peculiarity, or weakness it might be
called, I discovered in the Doctor's character at that time.   He
often said that it made no difference on which side of any
mooted question he might be chosen to speak, before the discussion was over, he had convinced himself, if no one else,
that he was on the right side.

This is altogether natural.   One who is pledged to maintain
a cause hunts up and gathers together all the evidence that he
can possibly find to sustain it, passing by and ignoring for the
time everything that militates against it.   In this way it is
possible to make a very good argument in order to show that

black is white, and to make the worse appear the better reason.

Dr. Yarbrough was one of the most intelligent, intellectual men I ever knew. He was a good neighbor, a good physician, good company, genial, and kind-hearted. He was born on Big Creek, on the Saluda side of the county, not far from the old Butler homestead, of which family, indeed, he was a connection by blood. After the War of Secession he moved up the country to the neighborhood of Walhalla, where he died about the year 1881 or 1882.

Dr. Yarbrough was twice married. His first wife was the daughter of Bennett Perry, Esq., of Perry's Cross Roads. She brought him one son, whom he named Burr, after his old preceptor in medicine, Dr. Burr Johnstone, of Newberry. His second wife was a widow Coleman and a daughter of Mark Black. She brought him one daughter, Elizabeth, a most lovely and amiable girl.

Dr. Beaufort T. Yarbrough was a brother of the foregoing, and younger by several years. Although I was at school with him—as also with his brother George—for awhile, yet there never was that same degree of intimate acquaintance and association as there was with the elder, though he was a man of fine intelligence and amiable nature. He did not practice his profession long in Edgefield, but went West. He returned towards the close of his life in ill health and died on the 16th of April, 1880, at the house of his sister, Mrs. Culbreath, mother of James Y. Culbreath, Esq., in Edgefield County, and near the place where he was born.

DR. WILLIAM COLEMAN.

Dr. Coleman was born 10th of March, 1820, at Coleman's Cross Roads, Edgefield District, and was the son of Richard Coleman and his wife, Lydia Carson. After graduating in medicine he married Miss Elizabeth Payne, daughter of Mr. David Payne, near Chappell's Ferry on Saluda.

After some years he moved down into Bullock County Georgia, where he farmed and practiced his profession. He died there, leaving some family.

DR. CHARLES M. BURKHALTER IN LIFE AND IN DEATH.

DEAR CHRONICLE: Having been intimately associated with Dr. C. M. Burkhalter for the last four or five years, I feel that I am better qualified, possibly, to write of his true worth than anyone else except his immediate family, whose modesty, as well as great grief, would prevent an expression of the great loss they, as well as the entire community, have sustained in the death of this pure and strong man. Most men, in dealing largely with the public, where almost everybody in the community owes them, will have enemies; yet the concensus of opinion is that Dr. Burkhalter died without an enemy.

John Ploughman says "that when a man owes you a debt, he is more than apt to owe you a grudge, and he is more willing to pay interest on the grudge than the debt." This saying of John Ploughman is true in most instances, but not so in the case of Dr. Burkhalter, for everybody, at some time, in the community, owed him, and still he died without an enemy.

In analyzing his character, I find the explanation of his phenomenal popularity—his kindness of heart, his tenderness. In these regards he was as gentle as a woman; and yet his conscientiousness made him as "true as steel" and as "firm as flint."

Dr. Burkhalter is gone, but he still lives in the hearts of those who were so fortunate as to know him. Truly he left "foot prints on the sands of time" that will be of inestimable value to his children and neighbors, "foot prints" of character, of tenderness, of Christianity, of love, of energy. What more can a man attain in this life? What more need he wish to attain? What more priceless legacy can he leave to his children? "Yea, he rests from his labors, and his works do follow him."

I could fill columns of your paper, Mr. Editor, giving grateful reminiscenses of his life and character, exemplifying his true worth; but to those who knew him, it would be superfluous.

Pope says: "An honest man is the noblest work of God?"; and in these hard times; when men are tempted to take near cuts, and defraud their fellow men, how true and appropriate are these words of Pope's!

Dr. Burkhalter was an honest man in its strictest and broadest sense. His family have lost a true, tender and loving husband, brother and parent. We offer them our sincerest sympathies.
D. A. J. B.

DR. GARRETT.

Among the worthies of Edgefield—Westside—perhaps none stood higher, and none more worthily stood high, than Dr. W. Henry Garrett, who died at Hepzibah, Georgia, in August 1892. From the days of the Revolutionary War, and, doubtless even previous to that time, the name has been an honorable one in the county. His wife was Miss Ann McKie, a sister of Dr. Robert McKie. She, with only one daughter and five sons survives him. Only a few years before his death he had removed from his old home in Collier Township to Georgia for the purpose of educating his sons, Hepzibah affording better facilities for that purpose than the township in which he lived. He was buried at Hepzibah.

The following notice of Dr. Garrett and his death is copied from the Augusta Chronicle:

"HEPZIBAH, Ga., August 25th.

"One of the saddest events that has occurred in the village in a long time occurred this morning about 11 o'clock when the Angel of Death entered the chamber of Dr. H. C. Garrett and touched his eyelids into sleep. He was loved and admired by all who knew him. His family was peculiarly blessed in the light and joy dispensed by him in his happy household. He was endowed with the attribute of a gifted intellect and talents of a high order.

"The Doctor had been sick some time with fever. It was thought, however, he would rally from the attack and this hope reigned from time to time until today when the eyelids closed in death and his spirit went to its eternal reward and heavenly rest.

"We can only commend the bereft wife, the sorrowing daughter and grief-stricken sons to Him that stood by the grave of the one he-loved and wept with the Bethany Sisters."

Is it not true as Young in his Night Thoughts writes?

"Death is the crown of life;
Were death denied, poor man would live in vain;
Were death denied, to live would not be life;
Were death denied, e'en fools would wish to die.
Death wounds to cure; we fall, we rise, we reign!
Spring from our fetters; fasten in the skies;
Where blooming Eden withers in our sight;
Death gives us more than was in Eden lost,
This king of terrors is the prince of peace.
When shall I die to vanity, pain, death?
When shall I die?   When shall I live forever?"

XXXII.

HISTORICAL HINTS OF EDGEFIELD.

The Rev. Dr. George Smith, of the North Georgia Conference, who preached so acceptably in Edgefield a month back, has written the following pleasant letter to the Nashville Christian Advocate:

From Greenville, by way of Augusta, I went to the historic old Town of Edgefield. It is not as old by a hundred years as Charleston, and has been known as Old Edgefield for a long time. Beverly Allen preached in the court house here over a hundred years ago. Lorenzo Dow preached in it near ninety years ago, and years ago the Methodist societies were large and strong. Then came decline, and great changes passed over the country and the Church, and for years Edgefield has barely held her place in the family of the Methodists. The Baptists have been the ruling religious power, and are now much the strongest. With the building of a new railroad the village has taken on new life, and Brother Watson, the faithful pastor, determined on a new church, and by hard work has completed a very handsome brick church. In this beautiful and attractive church I have just conducted a meeting, which was, I hope, profitable.

In Edgefield lived and died "Ned Brace," the "Native Georgian," of the "Georgia Scenes," and his children, grandchildren, and great-grandchildren abide here still. His name was Edmund Bacon, and he was descended from the old Bacon stock of Bacon's rebellion in Virginia. His venerable daughter, Mrs. Wigfall, the widow of an Episcopal minister, a lovely Christian woman, still lives here, and so does his grandson, Colonel James T. Bacon, a charming member of the old noblesse. Among other members of our Church, I met Mrs. General Evans, whose husband was a major-general in the last war. When a young man he was among the Indians, and she showed me a red flag made with eagle feathers and red flannel, which he captured from a Comanche Chief, and one of the arrows from his quiver. General Evans became an earnest Methodist before he died. Edgefield has been the home of many governers and senators. General A. P. Butler lived here, and Senator M. C. Butler still lives here. Preston Brooks died here, and Governors Pickens, Bonham, and Sheppard, and divers and sundry of the great Carolinians have lived here, and still do. It is a pleasant little city to visit, and I much enjoyed my stay.

THE COUNTY AND TOWN OF EDGEFIELD—DESCRIPTIVE.

Although settled some years over a century, the town of Edgefield has never, until recently, improved to any great extent. Though always noted for the culture and refinement of its people it has only recently got into the gulf stream of progress. It may be that the very culture and refinement of its people acted as a bar to what, according to modern ideas, is considered progress. The town now, however, slow as it may have been in the past, is fully up in the march of progress with other parts of the State. It has two banks, about twenty lawyers, half a dozen medical doctors, about fifteen stores, two able and well-edited weekly papers, the Advertiser and Chronicle, a rock quarry, from which granite of the best quality is taken, an oil mill, a few private schools, patronized liberally by both town and country, stores and private dwellings continually in course of erection—besides several churches.

Edgefield is connected with the outside world by railroad. The R. and D. Railroad runs within seven miles of the town; the C. and C. Railroad runs through a portion of the county, and the special pet, Old Cumberland Gap, connects the town directly with Charleston.

On the R. and D. Road, within the County of Edgefield, are the towns of Graniteville, Trenton, Johnston, Ridge Spring, also a part of Batesburg. On the Knoxville Road are Clark's Hill, Woodlawn, Modoc, Parksville, and Plum Branch.

The climate is simply delicious, neither too cold nor too hot. The soil is excellent and produces cotton in perfection, that is the larger part of it. About two-thirds of the county is clay land—oak and hickory—the balance heavily timbered with the yellow pine; is sandy and lying well, produces heavy cotton crops. This is the same land through which Washington passed in May, 1791, and mentioned in his Diary as poor pine barrens of the worst sort. It was so different from his own rich lands on the Potomac that he could not perceive the wealth that lay hidden in the sandy soil requiring only the industrious hand and arm of the laborer to bring it out to view. Indeed it was many years before the people settling there knew and understood its real value.

The rock quarry near the town is daily shipping the best quality of granite to Charleston. An extensive oil mill, ginnery and fertilizer factory, with their large buildings, are all indicative of great life and activity.

The county is well watered, Big Saluda on the one side and the Savannah on the other, with their tributary streams flowing into them—Little Saluda River, Big Stevens' Creek, Shaw's Creek, Turkey Creek, and others, give an abundance of moisture which fertilizes the soil and sustains the growing crops.

The town of Johnston in the County has two banks, four churches and a fine graded school, and is a good market for produce of all kinds. Trenton and Ridge Spring are also good market towns and have good schools, churches, and railroads, and telegraphic communication with the outside world.

I do not know what the mineral wealth of Edgefield County may be, other than the granite and the millstone on Cloud's Creek, and these are inexhaustible. Gold is found in a belt of country running across the county from Saluda to the Savannah River. It touches the Saluda near Higgins' Ferry and runs in a southwestly direction near Richardsonville, crosses Mountain Creek above where Dr. John Lake used to live on to Dorn's Mine in the lower part of Abbeville and crosses the Savannah River into Georgia. It was in this gold belt that Mr. Calhoun's rich mine near Dahlonega, Georgia, was located. In places in the same belt traces of copper very distinctly appear. I have found gold in the rock on the surface simply by breaking them, in an old field once belonging to Mr. William Attaway, afterwards to Mr. John Coleman, afterwards to Edward Coleman, on the road not far from Shiloh Methodist Church. About the year 1886 a piece was picked up on the land of A. P. Coleman, two miles from Higgins'—Kinard's Ferry. The lump was worth about thirty dollars. A small lump worth about two dollars was found in the same neighborhood a great many years ago. Almost anywhere in the belt of country mentioned from the Saluda to the Savannah gold may be found by washing the sand and gravel in the streams or hillsides near or by pounding and washing the rock. Whether any paying working mines can be found is another matter, but the gold is there in very fine grains, and in occasional lumps worth as much as thirty dollars each. I have seen two such. It appears most plentiful on or in the neighborhood of Mountain Creek. In that region also traces of copper show most distinctly.

It was the love of gold that lured De Soto from Florida and finally led him to his death. Early in the spring of 1540 he, with his devoted followers, set out from the head of Appalachee Bay led by an Indian guide towards the gold regions of North Carolina. They passed through middle Georgia, and in April reached the head waters of the Ogeechee, passing still North until they came to the head waters of the Savannah and the Chattahoochee. Finding no gold, though undoubtedly they must have passed through a gold region, they turned southward and southwestwardly, passing through Alabama to Mobile, where they destroyed an Indian village and killed many natives. They then again turned North and Northwest. Crossing the Mississippi at Chickasaw Bluff, in May, they still continued their progress North, until about the last of July, in the neighborhood of the Mississippi, we find them at a place named Pacoha, the site of which is now unknown. From Pacoha they went on North and Northwest, until they reached the highlands of White River, more than two hundred miles from the Mississippi.

In all this time no gold was found. Finally from the heart of the continent west of the Mississippi, they returned down the Washita to that river. Worn out, De Soto died, and to conceal his death, his body was wrapped in his cloak and in the stillness of midnight was sunk in the middle of the stream. The discoverer of the Mississippi slept beneath its waters. He had crossed a large part of the continent in search of gold, and found nothing so remarkable as his burial place. These men knew nothing of the geological indications of gold. They were not miners. They were not men of science and searching for gold as peaceful and peaceable explorers. They were hunting for it as robbers, and as such they meant to take it from those who had already amassed it, as Cortez and Pizarro had done.

There is much gold in Edgefield, but more near the surface of the earth than in its bowels. At any rate, it will pay better to dig it thence.

UNDER THE OAKS AT LANHAM'S.

No excuse nor apology need be given for the insertion in this history of this account of a day "Under the Oaks at Lanham's." It is too well written and describes too vividly some incidents at the battle of Franklin during the war between the States, to be permitted to drop into oblivion as a mere newspaper article. The day was the fourth of September, 1891:

LANHAM'S SPRING, EDGEFIED CO., September 4th.

Under the beautiful oaks and poplars that spread their proteeting boughs over the bold spring which here gushes from the earth to gladden the water drinkers of Edgefield County, there was to-day a notable gathering. The occasion was the inspection by Adjutant General Farley of the Capers Light Infantry, and a reunion of the survivors of Companies I and K of Twenty-fourth South Carolina Volunteers, commanded by General Ellison Capers. The Capers Light Infantry recently organized and named in honor of General Capers, gave a picnic to-day, and the Edgefield Hussars and the Edgefield Light Dragoons were their guests. This a lovely spot, which has been resorted to for many years for the annual picnics of the Edgefield Hussars, and the spacious dancing pavilion owned by that company was used to-day for sheltering a thousand people who had come from every part of Edgefield, and even from distant counties to attend the reunion. But for the weather the attandance would have been doubled, but the rain which had commenced to fall early in the morning continued at intervals during the day, and kept the picnickers under shelter until late in the afternoon.

The scene was a very attractive one. When the representative of the State reached the ground just before noon to-day, there was standing room only under the pavilion. Edgefield County boasts of some exceptionally handsome women, and a hundred or two of them were present. Their fresh summer costumes contrasted prettily with the bright uniforms of the militia and the sober suits of their civilian escorts. Many notables were here. General Capers, ruddy and genial; General Butler, a magnificent looking soldier; Congressman Tillman—Uncle George—as rugged as an oak, and with a look of determination in his steel gray eyes that bodes no good for the purist of the penitentiary when he shall be called upon to sustain the charge made at Greenwood that this "bushy-headed Congressman had been bought up by the money moguls."

Governor Tillman, wearing a natty black suit, standing collar, and white tie, looked little like the "Farmer Ben" of a year ago. He has lost the haunted look that he had during the last campaign, and as he moved through the crowd he seemed thoroughly well pleased with the world and with himself.

Editor Bacon, of the Edgefield Chronicle, tightly wedged in between half a dozen girls, recalled Landseer's "Monarch of the Glen," and was literally "another form gone to press." He pulled the tails of his Prince Albert in out of the rain and scanned the lowering clouds as though beyond them he would seek the sanctuary.

When General Capers arrived within half a mile of Lanham's this morning he was met by the Capers Light Infantry and marched with them to the pavilion under the tattered battle flag of the Twenty-Fourth South Carolina, which, after the war had been sewn together by Mrs. Capers, and was presented by her husband a year ago to the State through Governor Richardson. Secretary of State Tindal had loaned it to the Infantry for this occasion.

About 11:30 o'clock General M. C. Butler eloquently introduced General Capers.

General Butler said: "The pleasant duty devolves upon me of introducing the orator of the day, General Ellison Capers, a gentleman whose gallantry was known and admired by all who were associated with him during that terrible conflict, the war between the States—a man whose conduct, whether on the march, in camp or on the battlefield, was an inspiration to all who came within his influence—the man whose splendid leadership these brave men followed through the trying days of that terrible war—the gentleman, soldier, and Christian, who has always lived up in full measure to the duties of life, wherever they have devolved upon him. A brilliant soldier in battle he is equally a faithful follower of the cross. He has always done his duty to his country and his God, and I welcome him most cordially to the County of Edgefield." [Applause.]

General Capers addressed himself to the Capers Light Infantry; his old comrades and his old friends of Edgefield: "There come," said he, "occasions in a man's life when he finds it difficult to express the conflicting emotions of his mind. This is such an occasion. I am here in the presence of my old comrades and friends, survivors of the gallant company of my regiment. Here are their younger brothers and sons, and, in one or two instances their grandchildren, formed into a military company, with which they have done me the distinguished honor to associate my name. Here before me is a generation who have grown up since the eventful scenes through which we have passed, my old comrades.

"How to speak for the edification of all of you, how to give utterance to the thoughts that throng my mind, is indeed a problem.

"As I marched today under that flag I thought of the noble and heroic founder of the Twenty-Fourth Regiment, Colonel Clement H. Stevens, of Colonel Jesse Jones, Major Appleby, Major Hammond, Major Hill, Adjutant Palmer and all the gallant and heroic dead who have fought under its folds, and by the sacrifice of their lives have built up its glory.

"No regiment had a grander record than the Twenty-Fourth South Carolina. Up to September 1864 out of a total of 1,152 men who marched out under that flag 563 were killed, wounded or captured, and 157 died of disease at home or in camp, making a total of 720 casualties up to that time."

Speaking in this strain, General Capers said he thought he could best serve the young men present by relating incidents of their fathers and elder brothers, and selected those connected with Hood's Tennessee Campaign, and especially of the battle of Franklin.

He described the desperate condition of his men, thirty of whom were without shoes and seventy without blankets in the bitter cold November of that clime when they crossed the

Tennessee River. He described graphically the battle of
Franklin, the advancing lines of Hood's army, the lay of the
field and the position of the enemy, the gallant charge and the
capture of the flag of the Ninety-Seventh Ohio Volunteers by
Lieutenant James Tillman, commanding Company I, Anderson
Walls, Owen Carpenter, and the late J. Press Blackwell.

"General Gist rode up to me in the course of the battle and
called out excitedly—the only time I ever saw him excited on
a battlefield—'Colonel I count on the 24th, today.' I kissed
my hand to him as he rode away to his death. That he could
'count on the 24th' the result showed.

"In front of the enemy they had felled a locust thicket,
making a magnificent abattis. Through those thorns the men
of the 24th gallantly plowed their way, falling like leaves in
the wind.

"In the providence of God, I was shot down. I have always
believed that I owed my life to men of Edgefield, (a voice,
'Here's one of 'em') who seized me by the arm and dragged
me up to a ditch, where I was protected from further fire.

"I did not see one man falter beneath that flag, nor one fail
in the discharge of his full duty.

"While I was lying wounded Jim Tillman came to me and
said 'put your hat on your sword and wave it, and your men
will go over the ditch.' I replied that I was too weak from
the loss of blood to do even that. But Jim Tillman never
wanted inspiration to duty. He led the men over and that
night gave me the flag of the Ninety-Seventh Ohio.

"The man who holds the tattered flag now before you—
Adam Carpenter—defended it gallantly in that battle, in the
absence of the gallant color bearer, Sergeant Hollis, of Company H. When Carpenter, having exhausted his ammunition
was hard pressed by one of the enemy. he picked up a rock
and brained his assailant.

"Was there ever, in the history of a people meeting such
overwhelming defeat as came to Southern armies, such a scene
as is here presented? A meeting to commemorate memories
that were glorious, in spite of defeat, because the examples of
heroism and sacrifice were inspiring."

In conclusion, the speaker addressed himself to Captain
James H. Tillman and the new company, urging them to

emulate the noble deeds of their fathers and elder brothers, and thanking them with much feeling for the honor of associating his name with them and in inviting him to address them today.

General Capers was listened to with great attention throughout, but at times the downpour of rain was so heavy as to almost drown his voice, and the hoarseness caused by speaking against the rain, forced him to shorten his address.

At the conclusion of the address, the centre of the pavilion was cleared and the band began to play. In an instant thirty or forty couples were on the floor, and the dancing was kept up all the afternoon. During the day the Edgefield Hussars, the Edgefield Light Dragoons and the Capers Light Infantry were inspected by General Farley.

The Hussars, thirty-six men, were officered by S. B. Mays, Captain; R. S. Anderson, First Lieutenant; L. A. Brunson, Second Lieutenant; J. J. Holland, Third Lieutenant.

The Light Dragoons, thirty men, W. W. Butler, Captain; J. R. Blocker, First Lieutenant; D. D. Brunson, Second Lieutenant; J. R. Thompkins, Third Lieutenant.

The Capers Light Infantry, thirty-eight men, James H. Tillman, Captain; B. T. Gardner, First Lieutenant; H. H. Townes, Jr., Second Lieutenant; R. L. McKie, Third Lieutenant.

The uniform of the new company is a very striking one, bright red coats with light blue facings, and white pants.

This afternoon a meeting was held of survivors of companies I and H of the Twenty-Fourth South Carolina, at which General Capers presided. A resolution was unanimously passed recommending a reunion of the survivors of the entire regiment at Columbia at some suitable time. Next August was suggested. General Capers was requested to appoint a committee with himself as Chairman, to be composed of one man from each company in the regiment, with whom he should correspond to make arrangements for the reunion.

The utmost good order prevailed during the day, and notwithstanding the rain, the occasion was thoroughly enjoyed by all who were present.

AMBROSE E. GONZALES.

PENN'S DRUG STORE.

In writing of the town of Edgefield and its business, I believe that I did not make that special mention of Penn's Drug Store that an old and honorable institution like that deserves. It is seldom, indeed, that any business in this country where changes are yet so sudden and so rapid, continues for thirty or forty years in the same hands, descending from father to son, as this has done. It started before the war, and was then and for years known as the Drug Store of G. L. Penn. For a long time, I know not how long, the business was conducted by W. B. Penn, the son of G. L. Penn; and now, in August, 1892, I find that the business is again that of G. L. Penn, with the addition of son, making it G. L. Penn & Son.

This is the way that aristocracies are built up. By the transmission of certain noble and superior qualities from father to son, and to son again, there comes a fixity of character and nobility of heart and mind that makes the family *aristos*, the best, for that is all the word means. The best for leadership in war; the best for leadership in the State, and in the councils of the nation. The best scholar; the best teacher; the best statesman, is the greatest aristocrat. And there may and ought to be an aristocracy in business.

WATERS FAMILY.

Philemon B. Waters, son of Philemon B. Waters, who was one time Sheriff of Newberry County, mentioned in O'Neall's Annals, was born September 1st, 1807. He received a good English and classical education—was a lover of literature and was an eloquent and gifted man. He married Martha Caroline Chappell, and soon thereafter moved to Prairie Bluff, Wilcox County, Alabama. During the Seminole War in Florida he served as Captain of the Wilcox Guards. He was much beloved and popular, as is testified by his comrades and neighbors. He died in early manhood, July 30th, 1840. His remains were interred with Masonic honors at Prairie Bluff.

At his death he left surviving him, one daughter, and his widow, who was then *enceinte*. The widow, with her family, subsequently returned to Edgefield, S. C., where she afterwards married Bennett Perry. She is yet living (1893,

February,) nearly eighty years old, near Bouknight's Ferry, in Edgefield County. The daughter, Sarah Gilliam, first married Arthur Dozier, and after his death, John E. Perry. She and Philemon B. Waters, the son born after his father's death, are living at Johnston, S. C. This son is a lawyer in practice at Edgefield, and is also a member of the Legislature from that county. He was also Captain of Company "K," Second Regiment of Artillery, during the War of Secession.

PHILEMON WATERS, A SOLDIER IN WASHINGTON'S FIRST BATTLE.

The New York Times, June 28th, 1891:

Not counting the Jumonville affair, which, nevertheless, cuts quite a figure in French history and literature, the first regular conflict delivered by Washington was the battle of Fort Necessity, in the Great Meadows, now styled the Glades, of the Alleghany Mountains.

A document, yellow and stained with the accidents of a century and more, has recently been found in Virginia, which tells another story of the disappointments of the brave. It proves that to be shot and "have your name spelt wrong in the Gazette" is but one of fame's many mockeries. The soldier whose plaint is here set forth long survived the fight, but failed, as it appears, to secure his share of the reward of land conferred by Virginia upon her soldiers. Led by the current of emigration then settling southward, Philemon Waters became a citizen of South Carolina.

Among the remote hills of Orangeburg, then practically more distant than Oregon is now, he had learned of no limitation of time for the presenting of his claim. Perhaps, thinking it a safe reserve in the way of legacy to his children, he allowed this part of his presumed assets to slumber unrealized for twenty years. Then was informed by a traveler from the rallying ground of the small but famous expedition that his right had probably lapsed, and that for its revival it behooved him to be up and stirring. The steps he took are recorded in three manuscript pages of foolscap, as given below.

The Colonel Hite (misspelled Hight) named in the manuscript was a descendant of Jois Hite, one of the first settlers of Virginia Valley, familiar in history for his legal contest with

Fairfax, which involved the title to 100,000 acres of land, lasted just half a century—from 1736 to 1786—and ended in Hite's favor. The Colonel's visit to South Carolina was probably connected with the running off of some of the family slaves by the Southern Indians in the French War. Hite never recovered his negroes. Possibly their blood might be traced in Tan-le-quah, or among the Cherokee remnant left behind on the Georgia and Carolina uplands.

General Steven, who establishes Water's claim to the first shot, was a man of note in the lower valley. Among his descendants are Virginians highly distinguished in the councils of the State and the Union.

Here is the manuscript:

CHARLESTOWN, S. C., 3rd June, 1772.

HON'D SIR: I am informed by several gentlemen from your parts, and by Colonel Hight particularly, that there is two hundred thousand acres of land laid out on the Ohio River for those men that were in the engagement in the year 1754 with Col. Washington and your honor at the Meadows.

I have therefore taken this opportunity to acquaint your honor, that I am in the Land of the living and to beg you will write me a letter by Col. Hight, or by the post, directed to the post office in Charlestown, in which letter be pleased to inform me whether it is worth my while to come and claim my property in that survey on the Ohio, or whether there is any objections against my receiving it as my dividend in the Land. Your answer to this by Col. Hight or the post office will much oblige.

Hond. Sir,
Your most obdt. huml. Servt.,
PHILEMON WATERS.

To Col. Adam Stephen in Va.

Mr. Philemon Waters:

SIR: I received your favor by Jacob Hite, and had no opportunity of answering before this.

Your are entitled to Six hundred acres of land by your being at the battle of the Meadows, and had it depended upon me you should have had a double share for firing the first gun at the enemy that day, July 3rd, 1754.

That country is settled 100 miles below Fort Pitt, that is 163 miles below Girt's plantation, and there is a great run to it as ever was to Carolina. They could raise about 6000 fighting men over the mountains. They whip the Indians whenever saucy.

It will be an excellent country in a short time, and some spots of land sell at a pound per acre already. I will be glad to hear of your welfare. I am

Dr. Phil.

Your most huml. Serv't,

ADAM STEPHEN.

Berkeley County, Va., July 17, 1773.

I do hereby certify that the bearer, Mr. Philemon Waters, was a Soldier at the battle of the Great Meadows in the year 1754, and that he that day applied to me to receive his claim to land under Mr. Dinwiddie's proclamation of 1745. But as the 200,000 granted by that proclamation hath been long since surveyed, distributed, and patents issued in the names of those who put in their names before Nov., 1773, it is not in my power to give him any relief now.

Given under my hand this 20th day of April, 1775.

GEO. WASHINGTON.

VIRGINIA, PRINCE WILLIAM COUNTY,

Sat., 23 May, 1775.

This day came before me the Subscriber, one of his Majesty's Justices of the Peace for the said County, Philemon Waters, Jr., of Orangeburg District, in the Colony of South Carolina, and made oath on the holy Evangelists of Almighty God that he being a soldier of the battle of the Great Meadows in the year 1754, became entitled to a part of 200,000 acres of land on the Ohio granted by the Hon. Gov. Dinwiddie's proclamation; and this deponent upon his oath had declared that, being a resident of South Carolina, he never heard in any manner whatsoever, until about the middle of April last, that any time was limited for the claimants under the aforesaid procla-

mation to come in and make good their several claims to the
above lands, or he, the said deponent, should have used his
best endeavors to have entered his claim in due time.

HENRY PEYTON.

Whether a real Waters ever got his land there is no information. He stands recorded, however, as the first to fire a
shot in Washington's first battle—the beginning of the long
volley that rolled from the summit of the Alleghanies to
Quebec, Concord, the Brandywine, and Saratoga till it died
out on the beach at Yorktown, and that is some satisfaction
for his descendants.

[Kindly sent the author and compiler by P. B. Waters, Esq.,
of Johnston, S. C., great-grand-son of the hero above named.]

CAPTAIN LEWIS JONES.

In the year 1892 Captain Lewis Jones, at the age of seventy-
seven, after a long illness died at his home in Edgefield. He
was the last of four brothers and of a family that has made
itself historic in the annals of the District and County of
Edgefield. He was Sheriff of the District four years from 1852
to 1856, and he was without a superior in the discharge of the
duties of that important office. After he was Sheriff he was
elected to the Legislature, and faithfully discharged the duties
of a Legislator. At the breaking out of the War of Secession
he raised a company of cavalry and joined the Sixth Regiment.

After the war he was for a number of years President of the
Atlantic and French Broad Railroad, and afterwards of the
Carolina Cumberland Gap, and did as much as any one to give
Edgefield a railroad connection with the outside world.

In private life he was pure. In his dealings with others he
was honest, though he had a somewhat cold and stern appearance, yet it was appearance only. His friends loved him
and were bound to him as closely as friends can be to any one.
He sleeps in the family cemetery on the hill North of the
village and overlooking it.

ROBERT W. JENNINGS.

It is a great pleasure to the writer of this history to trace
the career of the descendants of the primitive settlers of Edgefield and to find that it has been honorable to themselves and

to the land which their forefathers helped to reduce from the condition of wild uncultivated forests to that of blooming fruitful fields. Among the early settlers of Edgefield there were none more honorable and energetic and useful than the Jenningses of Little Saluda. But Edgefield cannot keep all her useful citizens. The same spirit that brought the men of energy here, is still active in the descendants of those men and moves them out and on to other fields of labor and usefulness. A grandson of Edgefield, son of R. W. Jennings, born in Edgefield, and now proprietor of the Jennings Business College of Nashville is rising to distinction, of which he is altogether worthy, in the far off State of Washington on the Pacific Ocean. Recently (1892) he was a candidate for the office of Attorney-General in the District in which he resides, and during the canvas, having been taunted by his opponent with his Southern birth with the intent to excite prejudice against him, he made this eloquent reply:

"Yes, sir, I am from Tennessee, and every foot of her soil is dear to my heart. I love her mountains and her dales. I love her woodlands and her meadows, her rushing rivers and her rippling brooks; I love every leaf upon the trees of her many colored forests; I love every lark, and linnet, and thrush, and golden-throated songster that pipes its morning lay to the rising sun; I love all the daisies on her thousand hills; I love her sunny skies and her starry heavens, and even here, 3,000 miles away, upon the Western Coast of America, on the shores of Puget Sound, looking out across the broad Pacific to the gateways of the day, I fancy, that sometimes upon my cheek, I can feel the soft, warm breath of her perfect June days, and I seem to be once more

Among the fields of yellow corn,
Where the bloom is on the rye.

"I love it all, and if you, sir, think I would deny my birth-right to get this office, for once you mistake your man. I would not do so for the office of Prosecuting Attorney for this or any other county, though it were offered to me upon a golden platter set with diamonds."

Mr. Jennings was elected. He bears the name of his father, who went from Edgefield, Robert W. Jennings.

A GRANDDAUGHTER OF EDGEFIELD DISTINGUISHED IN PARIS.

We copy the following from a late number of the Nashville Banner. The young lady spoken of is a daughter of Prof. R. W. Jennings who lived in our town in his boyhood, and belongs to a branch of the old Jennings family of Saluda. For many years past, he has been at the head of the Jennings Business College of Nashville, one of the leading institutions of the kind in our country.

"It will be gratifying to the friends of Misses Mary and Louise Jennings, the accomplished daughters of Prof. R. W. Jennings, of this city, to learn that these ladies are achieving noteworthy success in art in the Academie Delecluse in Paris which they are attending. The first medal for the best head has been awarded by the academie to Miss Louise in a competition in which there were sixty contestants, representing many schools and nationalities. Some of the contestants had been students of the New York Art League. This achivement of Miss Jennings is not only highly creditable to her, but it also reflects credit upon the Nashville school of Fine Arts, of which she and her sister were pupils."

COLONEL DAVID DENNY.

When the call was made for volunteers for the Seminole War in Florida in the year 1836 David Denny, who was then a young man living near Perry's Cross Roads on the Saluda side of the County, was elected Captain of the company raised in his section. Edgefield furnished three companies; one from the Seventh, one from the Tenth, and one from the Ninth Militia Regiment, besides some from Hamburg. The names of all are given in this connection as taken from the Advertiser of February 11th, 1836, with the introductory remarks of the Editor at that date.

The following incident in the history of that campaign, so honorable to Captain Denny and to the men under his command has never been put on record in any book, nor even the county newspaper. It was told to the present writer by James Y. Culbreath, Esq., son of William Culbreath, who was a member of the company, afterwards confirmed by Mr. Clarke Martin, who was also one of the company and was present and a witness of the fact. Mr. Clarke Martin also gave me the additional information that the fording of the water to reach the hammock was just after Sergeant Nicholas Summer, of Newberry, of Captain Hargrove's mounted men, had received the wound of which he afterwards died at Tampa. An account of that is in the Annals of Newberry.

Near the close of the campaign the Indians were driven into a densely wooded hammock, surrounded, or partially surrounded by water, so that they were, for the time, practically inaccessible in any other way than by fording the intervening water. Mr. Martin tells me that they could see the smoke rising from the Indian camp-fires, and the Indians themselves moving and dodging from place to place. It was necessary to rout them and drive them from their sheltered position, even at the sacrifice of a company. Captain Denny's Company was detailed and ordered forward for the performance of this duty. The water the men had to pass through was not too deep to wade without swimming, but this fact they had to ascertain experimentally. They were ordered forward, and forward they went, completely exposed to any enemy that might be lurking and lying concealed in the swamps beyond. When about half way, or a little more than half way across, Captain Denny faced his men and then called out, "Halt!" With drawn sword, standing waist deep in water, with enemies in front of whose numbers they had little idea; not knowing but that they were all marching to death, Denny says: "Men, remember you are from South Carolina and from Edgefield District! Forward, march!" They went forward, but the enemy fled and disappeared at their approach.

Judge A. P. Butler in speaking of this incident and mentioning that address always characterised it as equal in force, energy, compactness, and effectiveness to any he had ever heard or read, and was worthy of any commanding officer at any time. It was like a solid shot with a true aim and going direct to the mark.

When the War of Secession broke out Colonel Denny again volunteered and was elected Captain of a company—went to Virginia with it, but being too old for active field service he resigned and returned home where he remained performing faithfully all the duties of a farmer citizen until his death.

He was a member of the Baptist Church, a faithful and true man, doing his duty in all stations in life in which he was placed, according to his highest conceptions and perceptions of what those duties might be.

GENERAL JAMES JONES.

This distinguished gentleman, an honor to the State and to the County, was the second son of Colonel Mathias Jones, one of the pioneer settlers of Ridge Spring; and was born October 3rd, 1805. He was educated at the academy at Edgefield Court House, at which institution he was prepared to enter the South Carolina College. He graduated in 1824, in a class of nineteen. In the class were Dr. Josiah C. Nott, Professor R. T. Brumly, and James M. Calhoun, sometimes President of the Alabama Senate. At his graduation Dr. Cooper was President of the South Carolina College. After his graduation he read law at Edgefield and began practice there at a time when that Bar had some of the best and most brilliant lawyers in the State.

In 1827, May 3rd, he married Miss Catherine Louisa Creyon, of Columbia, South Carolina. After his marriage he engaged successfully in his profession at Edgefield. In 1836, in obedience to his military instincts he raised a company of volunteers for the Seminole War. General Milledge L. Bonham, then a young man, was Orderly Sergeant of the company. The reader will find a roll of that company elsewhere in this book. This company formed a part of the regiment of Colonel Abbott H. Brisbane, of which regiment A. G. Magrath, afterwards Governor of South Carolina, was Adjutant. After the expiration of his term of service in Florida Captain Jones became Adjutant and Inspector General of South Carolina, which office he held acceptably for many years. Becoming dissatisfied with the practice of the law he accepted the position of manager of the Vaucluse Factory, which is said to have been the first cotton factory built in South Carolina. The first building was erected by a German named Christian Breithaupt, who settled in Edgefield. This building was destroyed by fire, but was soon rebuilt. He continued some time as Superintendent in partnership with his brother-in-law, William Gregg, but after awhile sold his interest and moved to Columbia in order to assume the duties of the newly created office of Commissioner of the new State Capitol, to which he had been elected by the Legislature. This office he filled to the satisfaction of all until the war came and the work was suspended.

On December 21st, 1842, he was appointed by Governor Hammond to the Chairmanship of the Board of Visitors of the newly created military schools at the Arsenal and the Citadel. No better selection could have been made. For more than twenty-two years, without salary, he gave the necessary time and attention to the cause of the Military Academy. During his time of service here from 1842 to 1865 he had as his colleagues, Jamison, Hanna, Means, Wallace, Wilson, Young, Perrin, Gage, Simms, regular members, and Adjutant Generals Cantey, Dunovant, DeSaussure, Garlington, and Governors Hammond, Aiken, Johnson, Means, Manning, Adams, Allston, Gist, Pickens, Bonham, Magrath, ex-officio members of the Board of Visitors.

In 1861 he became Colonel of the Fourteenth Regiment of South Carolina Volunteers. In 1862–1863 he served in the lower part of the State, when he resigned and was made Quarter-Master General of the State.

After the war was over, Mr. William Gregg, President of the Graniteville Manufacturing Company, being absent for a time in Europe, General Jones was induced to remove to Graniteville and assume entire control of that business and its management. He lived but a short time after this. He died of apoplexy on the 20th of October, 1865, his wife having preceded him to the tomb by about three years. On the day of his death the sun was in eclipse, and on the 20th of October, 1892, just twenty-seven years after his death, the sun was again in eclipse. But no man's life and death can affect the general course of nature. Indeed it seems sometimes that nature does not care whether we live or die.

General Jones and his wife had no children of their own, but out of the kindness of their hearts they adopted two, a son and daughter, of R. H. Nichols and his wife, Susan B. Travis, who were teachers by profession and who died suddenly, leaving these children in distressed circumstances. The children added greatly to the happiness of Mr. and Mrs. Jones, and are both still living (1893).   The daughter is Mrs. U. R. Brooks and the son is a well known citizen of Columbia, Edward Joseph Jones.

General Jones was a believer in the Code Duello and was regarded as high authority on such questions as the Code was expected to determine.   But to his honor be it said, he used the Code as an instrument of peace whenever it was possible for peace to be restored between the parties.

Edgefield may have produced and nourished greater men than General James Jones, but few more useful to the county and to the State than he.   He was captain of a company during the Seminole War in Florida; Adjutant and Inspector General of the State; manufacturer; Commissioner of the new State House; Confederate Colonel; Quarter-Master General of the State, and Chairman of the Board of Visitors of the South Carolina Military Schools for twenty-two years, all which positions he filled with honor.

This sketch of the life and services of General James Jones is drawn from Colonel J. P. Thomas' History of the Citadel Academy of South Carolina.

COLONEL T. P. SHAW.

Colonel Thomas Pickens Shaw was born in Edgefield County, June 10th, 1828; died August 2nd, 1883, at his home near Poverty Hill, S. C., in the same county.

At the commencement of the bloody struggle between the States Colonel Shaw raised a company and was elected its captain.   The company was afterwards known as Company "B," Nineteenth Regiment, South Carolina Volunteers. Colonel Shaw rose by regular promotion, until he became the commander of the gallant regiment.   At the battle of Franklin, Tennessee, Colonel Shaw was severely wounded while at the front in the thickest of the fight, in command of a brigade. Several days after the battle he was captured and remained a prisoner until the close of the war.

He was admired for his chivalry and bravery; esteemed for his ardent patriotism, and loved for his generosity and kindness.   Colonel Shaw was married January 23rd, 1868, to Miss Mattie Lanier, the daughter of the Honorable Silas Lanier, of one of the most prominent families of South Edgefield.

Colonel Shaw was in his 55th year at the time of his death. His remains were laid to rest in Mt. Lebanon cemetery.

> The gallant soldier sleeps in peace,
> To dream no more of battle fields;—
> In his lonely, narrow bed,
> In the still village of the dead.

XXXIII.

THE SCOTT FAMILY, WHO GAVE NAME TO "SCOTT'S FERRY," ON THE WESTSIDE.

Samuel Calliham Scott was born at Scott's Ferry, April 22nd, 1807, and lived in Edgefield District the greater portion of his life. He died in Webster Parish, Louisiana, August 5th, 1873. From him is derived about all we know of the early history of the family

John Scott and his wife, whose maiden name is not known, came to America about the first or middle of the eighteenth century. John Scott was from the North of Ireland—his wife was a Scotch lady.

The names of their children are not all now known, the following only are remembered: Samuel, known as Ready Money Scott, James, William, and Joseph.

They brought with them great wealth in money, how much cannot now be estimated, but enough with their thrift and energy, afterwards, even from one, Samuel, to make at least two of his generations of many families rich.

Robert H. Middleton, the grandson of Ready Money, owns and now resides on a portion of this estate of Ready Money, at Clark's Hill, S. C.

John Scott and sons brought with them letters or documents of credit, or recommendations from the King of Great Britian to the Colonists. Samuel, the eldest son, seemed to be favored with a grant of land in South Carolina from King George II or King George III.

The following letter may be of interest here:

PLUM BRANCH, S. C., Jan. 7th, 1893.

Mr. O. H. P. Scott, Augusta, Ga.:

DEAR SIR: According to promise, have seen Dr. W. D. Jennings, the Encyclopedia, Genealogist, &c., &c., &c. He says your great-grandfather, Samuel (Hard Money) Scott, did own a town and nearly the entire county, or district as then known. He thinks it was Orangeburg City and County. He has seen the deeds and plats to Hard Money Scott, granted by King George. The deeds and plats are made out on sheepskin or parchment. Bob. Middleton's father got them years ago in Charleston, after the death of old Mr. Middleton, who died in Charleston, and was, perhaps, Bob. Middleton's grandfather. He says old John Middleton, the father of Bob., brought the package of papers from Charleston, and it is thought that he never opened the package; nor was it ever opened until after his death. I don't know whether Bob. Middleton or Geo. D. Tillman, son and son-in-law's attorney, have the papers.

He thinks above attorneys will make effort to recover this vast amount of property. Tillman's son-in-law, the lawyer, says that he is satisfied that the property can be recovered. If so, you are undoubtedly an heir to this vast estate. Hoping you complete success in life, that you may enjoy most beautifully the proceeds, &c.

Yours very truly,

[Signed.]   J. H. JENNINGS.

This Scott family first settled on the Georgia side of the Savannah River, but moved over to the Carolina side, prior to the Revolutionary War, and established their homestead at the place then and to-day known as Scott's Ferry.

Here they were resident during the war of independence, and their property continued in the family from Ready Money Scott to his son, Samuel Scott,—from him to his only three children, Elizabeth, John, and Samuel C. Scott. Elizabeth, being the eldest, retained that portion including the ferry.

Elizabeth never married. She willed to Oliver H. P. Scott, and William L. Scott, the eldest son of her brother, &c., &c. The latter two transferred to parties outside the family.

James Scott, the next eldest, moved West, on the Alabama River. William and Joseph Scott moved to the middle or eastern portion of South Carolina. The two latter, being the youngest of the original family, entered the American Army, and were made, one a Captain and the other a Lieutenant. Their names are mentioned in Ramsay's History of South Carolina.

Samuel Scott, (Ready Money) owned and remained at the homestead, Scotts Ferry on the Savannah River. He was married to Miss Joyce Calliham, a brave and plucky lady of a brave, patriotic family of Scotch descent. Her brother, Joel

Calliham, served as a soldier the entire time of the Revolutionary War. Served under Sevier at the battle of Kings Mountain, and is mentioned by L. C. Draper in his history on page 424, as one of the Heroes of Kings Mountain.

Just after the Revolutionary War other records were made of the services of the families of Scott and Calliham; but these remaining in manuscript have become lost or destroyed.

Samuel Scott, Ready Money, was one of the pioneers of Ninety-Six District, being a man of wealth, of education, and a good surveyor, his influence was considerable. He acquired the name of Ready Money by being always prepared to pay cash for what he bought, and by always demanding cash for what he sold. The story is related of him that he once attended a large sale of tobacco at a warehouse in Augusta, Georgia. He was not known to be present. A number of business men of means were there to secure the entire lot at a bargain. The tobacco was sold in small lots with privilege to the purchaser of taking the entire warehouse full if he desired. After a few lots had been sold Ready Money commenced to bid. The capitalists present not knowing the bidder, and hoping to get rid of him permitted the lot on which he had bid to be knocked down to him at a mere nominal price. "How much do you want, sir?" was the question of the auctioneer. "The entire lot," was the ready reponse. "Who's the bidder?" "Ready Money Scott, and here it is; I want the keys, sir." In less than twenty-four hours he realized quite a large profit on his investment selling to these same merchants.

Scott's devotion to the cause of American Independence was proverbial. He was a man deeply interested in the welfare of the country—the owner of large landed estates between Savannah River and Steven's Creek—all his wife's relatives and his own had espoused the cause of the colonies—he lived at a very important crossing of the river, Scott's Ferry, recognized as a point of military importance—the military establishing a fort for its and the country's protection. Pace's Island in Savannah River just above the mouth of Scott's Creek and the ferry was the rendezvous and hiding place of the tories for that portion of Georgia and South Carolina, from which they frequently raided the country on either and both sides, using this Island or German Island below the ferry to store their stolen goods. When the fact was discovered that the Tories were using these islands as places of deposit for their stolen goods none of the neighbors seemed willing to make the trip to Ninety-Six where the American army then was, and Mr. Scott being then too old and infirm, his wife, Joyce, without the knowledge of any one save that of her husband, mounted a fleet horse after sundown and at night rode the whole distance from Scott's Ferry to Ninety-Six and gave the information to the military there. Lieutenant Joel Calliham with a select body of troops was sent down to put a stop to these proceedings. He routed and dispersed the whole camp and force of Tories, and for a time thereafter that part of the country was free from their depredations.

For this act of patriotism Samuel Scott and his wife Joyce were made to suffer at the hands of the detached body of Tarleton's troops who visited the place for plunder. Augusta at the time was in the hands of the enemy.

Mr. Scott at the time of the Revolution was too old to take part in person as a soldier, but he furnished money, raiment, and food, and further encouraged the rebellion by sending and keeping in the service of the continental forces, his brother-in-law, Joel Calliham, Lieutenant in Sevier's Regiment. In consequence of his zeal and patriotism the Tories and British burned and destroyed his dwelling and corn cribs, killed and stole his stock, carried off his slaves, and annoyed him in many other ways; but I think those mentioned above quite enough. It seems, however, that they were not, for his and his wife's feet were burned to make them tell where their money was buried. In addition to this indignity, his wife, with a rope around her waist, was ducked in the Savannah River to make her divulge this secret, but without avail.

The money and plate so buried have not been discovered to this day. Family documents, by which the foregoing statements could be proven, have been lost and destroyed.

The foregoing description seems to have included the destruction of the two raids on this place—Tarleton's, in which the two were treated with indignities by him, destroying the fields of green corn, ripping up feather beds, &c., &c. The other raid will be described further on, which was more destructive and serious and from a different command.

On this raid from Tarleton's command, one of the Callihams, an American soldier, was made prisoner and taken to Augusta, Georgia, and placed in their military prison, the walls of which are occupied to this day and sits on the bank of the Savannah River, according to the recollection of my informant on Reynolds Street.

While in the prison Calliham had learned that they were to be transferred to safer quarters down the river. Knowing the road over which they were to be marched he determined to make his escape. He accordingly divested himself of heavy wearing appeared and with a long Scotch cloak wrapped about his person—having a diagram of the British works which he had already prepared and tightly folded and placed in his mouth, watching his opportunity he suddenly threw off his cloak and leaped into the water under fire from the guards. Swimming and diving alternately he made the Carolina side in safety, calling at the house of an old patriot lady in a nude condition she furnished him a suit of her clothes and he proceeded to rejoin his command which was at the time near Ninety-Six.

The following letter is introduced as corrobatory of the foregoing facts related.

The letter is written to Dr. J. J. Scott, of Shreveport, La., and bears date, Benton, La., December 28th, 1892.

Dear Sir: My father, David Thomas, was born in Edgefield District, S. C., in the year 1775 and died in Louisiana 1849. He was a nephew to Joyce Calliham, the wife of Ready Money Scott, who lived on the Savannah River above Augusta, Ga., and had a ferry that is known to this day as Scott's Ferry. In 1850 I visited among my relatives there and heard much of the family history from old kinspeople who are now dead. Samuel Scott, better known in that country as Ready Money Scott, was a very thrifty farmer. He got his soubriquet from the fact that he always paid the ready money for what he bought, and would not sell unless the ready money was paid to him. This habit obtained for him the reputation of having money, and when the war broke out between the colonies and Great Britian, he, having cast his lot with the colonies and rendered such services as are usually given by patriots to the cause this espousal brought upon him and his family much persecution.

For robbery he was visited from time to time by the Tories and the British. One time they destroyed a field of growing corn by turning their cavalry horses loose in it, while the men plundered the dwelling house and premises.

Failing to find any money, they ripped up with their swords the family featherbeds and gave the feathers to the winds. It is a well authenticated fact that old Ready Money Scott was an intense patriot, and aided the Colonies in their struggle for freedom against Great Britian.

Yours,

[Signed.] SAMUEL M. THOMAS.

At another time a raid was made by the Tories from upper South Carolina and North Carolina, supposed to be a detached body from the noted North Carolina Tory, Colonel Fagan's command, operating principally in that State. Connecting themselves with the Paris Island gang, they visited Scott's Ferry and neighborhood, destroying the place by burning his corn cribs, stables, wagons, vehicles, and killing his stock—taking with them valuable horses and quite a number of his slaves to North Carolina. The latter made their escape near the head waters of the Savannah River, and returned home in canoes down the river, (foraging on the way) to Scott's Ferry.

RECAPITULATION.

John Scott and wife—from Ireland and Scotland. Children: Samuel Scott, the eldest; James Scott, moved to Alabama; William Scott and Joseph, moved to the middle part of South Carolina.

Samuel (Ready Money) Scott married Joyce Jane Calliham. Children: Samuel, Elizabeth, Polly, Joyce, Nancy, Sallie. Elizabeth married John Middleton; Polly married —— Graves; Joyce married —— Martin; Nancy married —— Tate; Sallie married —— Mimms.

Samuel Scott, the only son, married Miss Mary Baker, of Abbeville District, S. C. Children: Elizabeth, the eldest; next John, next and last was Samuel Calliham Scott, father of Dr. J. J. Scott, Shreveport, La. The father of these three children died young, and the widow afterwards married Armistead Burt and had many children, most of whom and their children still live in Edgefield County and Augusta, Ga. Elizabeth, the eldest, heiress of the Scott's Ferry tract, died unmarried, about 30 years of age, willing her property, land, and slaves to her mother, Mrs. Burt, after her death to O. H. P. Scott and a cousin of his.

Samuel Calliham Scott married Miss Martha Collier. Children: O. H. P. Scott, Augusta, Ga.; Hillary Collier Scott; Samuel C. Scott, died young; John Joseph Scott, Shreveport, La.; Mary E. C. Scott; James Oscar, Hugh H., Robert H., Frances Ann, William E.

O. H. P. Scott served in the Confederate States Army, Hillary Collier Scott was living in Philadelphia when the war broke out. He came South and joined the Confederate States Army—was taken prisoner and treated very cruelly—died soon after being exchanged. Hugh H. Scott, of Edgefield, saw service with Hampton. John Joseph was also in the army and is a Confederate Veteran.

Conclusion: Ready Money died in 1808. In what year his wife died is not known.

THE MARTINS OF MARTINTOWN.

The Martin family, of Martintown, in Edgefield County, were prominent, brave, active, and engergetic Whigs during the Revolution, but as Martintown has long since gone to decay, and as the family, from whom the name was derived, is almost or quite extinct in Edgefield, it might please the reader of this book to find here a few items of the family history.

I am indebted to the Honorable John Martin, United States Senator from Kansas, for the following information:

The Martin family was of Scotch-Irish origin. The family emigrated from the North of Ireland somewhere towards the close of the sixteenth century (should be I think seventeenth) and settled originally in Caroline County, Virginia. The family was a large one, there being seven sons and one daughter. The names of the sons were: Abram, John, George, William, Matthew, Barclay, and Edmund. The daughter's name was Letty. They resided in Virginia for many years, and finally scattered to Pennsylvania, Kentucky, Tennessee, North Carolina, Ohio, and South Carolina.

The head of the South Carolina branch of the family, Abram

Martin, was born in Caroline County, Virginia, in the year 1708, and there grew to manhood and married Miss Elizabeth Marshall, of Caroline County, who was said to be a niece of the father of John Marshall, afterwards Chief Justice of the Supreme Court of the United States. Soon after his marriage he moved to South Carolina and located in Edgefield District and there lived and died.

He had eight sons, as follows: William Martin, James Martin, John Martin, George Martin, Barclay Martin, Edmund Martin, Marshall Martin, Matt Martin, and one daughter, Letty Martin.

Of these children, William, the eldest, married Miss Grace Waring and left three children, Robert, Elizabeth, and William. He was captain of artillery and was killed at the siege of Augusta. It was this Mrs. Martin who, in conjunction with Mrs. Barclay Martin, born Rachel Clay, captured the British courier with dispatches while on his way from Augusta to Ninety-Six, as elsewhere related.

The third son, John Martin, was an officer during the Revolution, Brigadier after the war, and served several years in the Legislature.

He was married three times and left many children, one of whom was Judge W D. Martin, of whom something has already been written.

John Martin died in Abbeville District in 1813.

Several of this prolific family rose to distinction. Charles was an officer in the Confederate Army and was killed in the battle of Kennesaw Mountain.

John Martin, Senator from Kansas in 1894, is a grandson of Matthew Martin of the Revolution, who moved to Tennessee and died there in 1846.

Many more names might be added to this roll of the Martins, all worthy, all true men and women; but if all were written that might be written of the children of Edgefield abroad, it would embrace the world, and the book would soon grow to unwieldy size.

WERTS FAMILY.

The Werts family first made its appearance in Newberry in the year 1758, and it was not until nearly one hundred years thereafter that they crossed Saluda into Edgefield.

John Werts, son of John and the grandson of the original John of the American Revolution, moved into Edgefield in the year 1856. He had eight sons and one daughter, Mary. Two sons, Elijah and Jacob, and his daughter died young. The other sons were: J. Wesley, L. Emanuel, J. Noah, A. Calvin, Alfred S., and Andrew A. J. Wesley was a Lutheran minister, whom I used to know very well. His wife was Caroline Derrick. Mr. Werts moved to Orangeburg in 1876, where he died in 1883. His widow and three daughters live near Leesville, in Lexington County. Three sons and one daughter live in Orangeburg County; another son, J. Q. Werts, who married Miss Houseal, of Newberry, is a Lutheran minister in North Carolina. L. Emanuel married Emmaline Wheeler. He was a prosperous farmer on Halfway Swamp, when he and his son James and one daughter, Rosalie, died in 1888 of typhoid fever. They rest at Trinity. His widow, two sons, and two daughters survive him. His son, J. Andrew, married Kittie Long; J. Sidney married Lula Turner; his daughter, Sallie, married Thos. A. Pitts, and Ida, Geo. C. Wheeler. These all married well.

James Noah was twice married, first to Catherine Hipp, who died before the war. He enlisted in Company K Fourteenth Regiment, South Carolina Volunteers, was wounded at Gettysburg, and after the war he married Mary Smith, of Edgefield County. He died in 1874, leaving no children.

Calvin A. went to Mississippi in 1858, but on the breaking out of the war he returned and enlisted in Company K Fourteenth Regiment, South Carolina Volunteers. He served four years under Stonewall Jackson, was wounded at Gettysburg, and was present at the surrender of General Lee. He moved to Florida in 1866. He was twice married, first to Miss Newcome of Florida, second to Miss Boyd of Georgia. His first wife gave him one son and three daughters. He is engaged in the cultivation of oranges.

Alfred S. was a volunteer in Company B Sixth South Carolina Cavalry during the War of Secession. After the war he returned to Edgefield and married Christianah Schumpert. They reared four sons, William F., R. Lee, Eugene, and Julian. William F. married Eva Long; R. Lee, Eugene, and Julian are not married. Their daughters were Nita, who married Jefferson Free—she died in 1895—and Alice, who married Spene Maffett—and Sallie, who is not married.

Andrew A. was quite young when the War of Secession broke out. He volunteered in Company H Third Regiment, South Carolina Volunteers, and was in every battle in which that regiment was engaged. He was wounded at Gettysburg; was in the battle of Chickamauga; was at the seige of Knoxville, thence back to Virginia and the great battle of the Wilderness. Near the close of the war the Third Regiment was sent to Charleston, and Andrew A. then became one of the scouts that waded the swamps near Pocataligo, watching the movements of the enemy and capturing many prisoners. Many a winter night this little band of scouts crossed the Salkehatchie River on the burnt timbers of an old bridge, sometimes wading waist deep in water, feeling their way, and camping without fire, to find their pants frozen stiff the next morning. He was in service till the close of the war.

In 1867 he married Emily May. Eight children were the fruits of this union, three sons, J. Rufus, Forrest E., and Grover C., and five daughters, Lula R., wife of E. J. Mitchell; Minnie L., wife of J. V. Cooper; Dora M., Ella P., and Alma M. are not married.

J. Rufus makes his home at Ninety-Six, the two other sons are with their father.

Andrew Werts, a descendant of Adam Werts, of Newberry, left one son, Levan M., who lives on Cloud's Creek. Simeon O., proprietor of the Johnston Hotel, is a son of Henry Werts, of Newberry County.

Members of this family have long been known to the writer of this book, and it is a source of pleasure to him to be able to say that he has always found them to be strong and true men.

HALTIWANGER FAMILY.

Jacob Haltiwanger was born March 30th, 1785, near Chapin, Lexington County, S. C. He married Elizabeth Feagle and lived for some time in Newberry County. His parents came to this country from Germany, and his father took an active part in the colonial struggle for independence. Jacob had three brothers and two sisters: George, David, William, Nancy, and Christina.

William and David both lived near Spring Hill, Lexington County. Nancy married Henry Eleazer and lived at Spring Hill. Christina married Jacob Huiet and moved to Edgefield, where they lived and died and where some of their descendants still reside. George lived and died in Lexington County. He was a Lutheran minister and also Sheriff of his county at one time.

Jacob lived for a while in the lower section of Newberry County, and moved from there to Edgefield County, in 1820, settling on Big Creek, near Trinity Church. He had ten children, five boys and five girls: George, Nancy, Catharine, Levi, William, Leah, Julia Ann, John Elmore, Emeline, and Isaiah.

George was born May 11th, 1813; married Elizabeth Ann Dreher. He had nine children, five of whom are still living, three having died in their infancy and one in the Confederate War. George graduated at the Lexington (S. C.) Theological Seminary, and afterwards at Gettysburg. He was ordained in 1840 and preached for some time in Lexington. From there he moved to Ebenezer, Ga., where he preached until his death, March 10th, 1862. His gentle and loving disposition won for him friends among people of every faith. He was one of the pioneers of the Lutheran Church in its earlier days. His living children are Abner Daniel, who married Ella Counts, and resides in Columbia; Albert Josiah, married Sallie B. Lipscomb, and resides in Atlanta, Ga.; Paul Hazelius, married Catherine N. Bouknight, and resides in Columbia; Mary Rebecca, married John Luther Fellers, and resides in Columbia; Arthur George, married Laura C. Cole, of Des Moines, Iowa, and resides in Columbia.

Levi was born April 14th, 1819, and married Melvina Attaway. They had nine children. He moved with his family many years ago to Lake City, Fla., where he still lives. One of his sons, Oliver, married Miss Kemp, and lives in Saluda.

William was born November 22nd, 1822, and married Sarah Proctor. He lived in Edgefield near a station on the C. & G.

Railroad, known as Dyson. In sight of his home stood Sister Springs Baptist Church, the oldest church in that section of the country. * He did a prosperous mercantile business before and after the war. In 1878 his people elected him to serve them in the Legislature, where he represented them two years. He died March 7, 1889, and was buried in the old Trinity burying ground. He had ten children, six of whom are still living. Sidney Daniel lives at the old home place in Edgefield. Joseph Johnson and Henry are in Walhalla. J. William is in Oklahoma. Jacob B. is Auditor of Edgefield, and resides there. The only daughter living, Addie, married George Wise, and lives near Edgefield Court House. George, a son who is dead, was a graduate of Newberry College, where he taught for several years. He afterwards practiced law.

Leah was born November 7, 1825, and married first J. Wesley Trotter. They had five children. After his death she married Samuel Dyer, by whom she had two children, James and Alice, who still live at the home place near Trinity Church, in Saluda County. Leah and her husband died and were buried the same day at Trinity Church.

Catherine was born August 16th, 1817, and married Dave Boozer. They moved to Mississippi, where they died. They had several children, who still survive them.

Emeline was born January 3rd, 1835, and first married Jones Rushton near Batesburg, by whom she had one daughter. He was killed in the late war. She then married Mike A. Deloach. They had three children. She now lives at Ninety-Six, Greenwood County.

Isaiah was born May 16th, 1838, and married Fannie Counts. He lives in Lexington County, in what is known as "The Dutch Fork," and has served his county as Clerk of Court. He has a large family.

Julia Ann was born January 11th, 1832, and married Jacob L. Aull, of Newberry County, and moved to Edgefield, now

---

* The Baptist Church, Sister Spring, was overlooked when giving the account of the Baptist Churches in the County. I relied upon others, pastors and clerks, for sketches of the churches. This being one of the oldest it must have been constituted about the year 1800. Chestnut Ridge was constituted in 1809. I regret the oversight, but the brethren may rest assured that it was not done purposely.

Greenwood, near Dyson. She had seven children, six of whom are living, two girls and four boys: Elbert H., a graduate of Newberry College, and printer and publisher, lives in Newberry. Rowena A., a graduate of Columbia Female College, married Rev. W. W. Daniel, a Methodist minister, who resides in Columbia. Nathan E., a graduate of Newberry College, who is teaching in Texas. Eva, who with Wm. B., a graduate of Newberry College, and Luther B., live at the old home in what is now Greenwood.

John Elmore, born November 15th, 1829, and Nancy, born December 25th, 1815, son and daughter of Jacob Haltiwanger, died in early life.

SHEPPARD.

James Sheppard, father of Honorable J. C. Sheppard, was a native of Newberry District, but left there when he was a young man and first settled in Edgefield about two miles from Higgins' Ferry at a place where the old Ninety-Six road crosses the ferry road. He there did business, mercantile, for some years with Mr. William Coleman, father of A. P. Coleman. This was about the year 1825. After awhile he moved out to the place above the Court House where he lived for many years a comfortable and useful life. He continued the mercantile business, and being prudent, energetic and industrious, he naturally prospered. He was not immoderately ambitious of distinction in public life, but was at one time a member of the General Assembly, as Representative. Of his children by his first marriage—he was married twice—I was acquainted only, and that slightly, with his son George. His second wife, the mother of John C. Sheppard, was a Miss Mobley, daughter of Dr. William Mobley. His son George married also a daughter of Dr. Mobley. James Sheppard and his son George both gone long ago.

John C. Sheppard is still a young man, and it is not by any means too late for him to achieve distinction in public life, if he so desires. In 1882, if I mistake not, he was elected Lieutenant Governor, and again in 1884, as there was no opposition to the State officers who were then in office. Hugh S. Thompson was Governor. In July, 1886, Governor Thompson resigned to accept the office of assistant Secretary of the

United States Treasury, and Mr. Sheppard became Governor. In 1892 when Mr. Tillman, who had been elected Governor in 1890, was a candidate for re-election, Mr. Sheppard was put forward by the Conservatives as the opposing candidate. After a very warm contest Mr. Tillman was re-elected. Since the election Mr. Sheppard has been steadily at work at his profession, which is that of law, at Edgefield in company with his brother.

There were other Sheppards also once living in Edgefield County, kinsmen of these. One was a Lutheran minister, and his name appears elsewhere in this book in the brief sketch of the Lutheran Church. The other was Dr. David Sheppard, a practicing physician, who was a surgeon or assistant surgeon of a regiment during the War of Secession. He died about the year 1890 or 1891, not long after his second marriage. He was an amiable, good man. The minister moved West, and I do not known at this time (1893) whether he is living or not.

XXXIV.

RECOLLECTIONS AND REFLECTIONS.

Yesterday, August 3rd, 1892, I met the daughter of a man whom I once knew and loved, and the granddaughter of a man I knew and loved when I was a little boy at school over sixty years ago. He was older than myself by several years, but all the little boys loved him and looked up to him with fond confidence and trust, as he was so gentle in his deportment and bearing towards them; it was impossible for them to do otherwise. I do not now remember who our teacher was, but the school house was in the piney woods, not far from Pine Pleasant Church, but before that church was built, before Mount Enon was founded, just before that great religious revival that swept over the whole country, in which Barnes, Hodges, Worthington, and some others did so great a work.

It is a great pleasure, but at the same time a very sad one, to review the past and to call into active being once more those persons and events, which now live only in the memories of some, or on the pages of the historian. I can see that little log school house, with the writing desk running nearly the whole length of the school room, with a long open window to admit the light. I can see the broad open fire-place, almost as wide as the house itself. I can see the rude benches without backs, and another desk running lengthwise of the house and sloping at both sides with a flat space on top—for the use of the cipherers and other students to rest their books and slates upon. I can hear the children while conning the regular evening spelling lesson—such a noise as they made, loud enough and discordant enough to wake the seven sleepers of Ephesus, if they could be waked at all by discordant noises. I can hear the glad shouts of the boys when school is dismissed and the noise made by a falling bench or two, thrown over by the boys in their wild, mischievous fun. I can see the girls with their bright eyes glancing mischief at the boys. I see distinctly one girl, about twelve years old, who walked with a slight limp, being a little lame in one foot. I see her coming up from the spring with a bottle of milk poised steadily upon her head without holding or touching it with her hands—this she had placed in the morning, in the spring, to keep it cool and sweet until noon. I thought her as sweet and pleasant as the jug of milk she carried. I can see the boys gathered around my friend morning, noon, and afternoon. I can hear him say that it seemed to him that everybody must love him, for that everybody called him "Bud." Yes, everybody did love you, Budd, and they continued to love you until that last sad day when you left, and were no longer here to love or to be loved. All these are gone; all turned long ago to dust and ashes or to spirit, which is more impalpable still. Yes, Budd Bryant, it is your daughter's daughter whom I have just seen, the daughter of Rev. Luther Broaddus, whom to know was to love—whose presence, whose voice, whose smile has called up and made to pass in review the buried memories of over sixty years. She is as good, I hope and believe, as father and grandfather, and I trust that love may wait upon her steps through life. The following lines, written soon after our acquaintance began, when her father was pastor of the Baptist Church at Newberry, aptly express the feelings of the heart:

TO AILEEN.

An old time German story tells
That on the eve before the bells
Of Christmas ring out clear and sweet,
A little child with naked feet,
In tattered garments old and poor,
Goes softly round from door to door,
Low knocking, begging to be let
Within from out the cold and wet.
And if one opens, the tale tells,
Before the ringing of the bells,
That little child, all glorified,
Becomes the Holy Christ who died
To save the world; and then He breaks
The bread and gives; and then He takes
The wine and pours it in the cup,
And blesses ere they drink it up;
And then He passes from their sight
Apparelled in bright robes of light.

That little child, O Aileen dear!
That little child comes every year;
Indeed, indeed He's always near.

And He is softly knocking still,
And you can open if you will,
This holy, blessed Christmas tide,
To Christ, the one-time crucified,
To Christ, the child now glorified,
And say: "Come in, thou heavenly Child!
Abide with me this winter day!
Abide with me, forever stay!
And make me like thyself, holy and meek and mild."
Christmas, 1882.   JOHN A. CHAPMAN.

Miss Aileen Broaddus was married in 1893—may she be happy.

AN ACT OF HEROISM.

The principal actor in the incident I am now about to relate is not a native of Edgefield County, but she married in Edgefield and lived for several years in that county, and still owns a small property there. Her husband was a native of that county, in which he lived his whole life and died, and was buried near the place where he was born. And her father, if I have not been wrongly informed, was born near Saluda Old Town, in Edgefield. The act of heroism itself occurred near Ninety-Six, and in Abbeville County, but near the line. The actor was Mrs. Susan Chapman, *nee* Gaulden, who was born near Ninety-Six, and now, 1892, lives in that town. The hearing of the story moved me so much that I felt bound to record it in the History of Edgefield as one of the heroic deeds of one of her many noble women. Mr. Gaulden was a native of Edgefield.

On Sunday, the first Sunday in June, 1890, Mrs. Chapman was on a visit to her sister (passing the day with her), who lived, if my memory is not at fault here, at their father's old place. The children, and some of the neighbors' children, were playing about in the yard, and, heedless of danger as children always are, were playing about, and running over and upon the well. The well was covered; that is, planks were laid upon, across, and over its mouth. But it appears that the planks were not very strong. At any rate, while Alberta M. Davis, a little girl about eight years old, was upon it, the middle plank broke and she was precipitated to the bottom of the well, a distance of over forty feet. Mrs. Chapman was in the house with her sister, and as soon as they heard the children scream they ran out to see what the trouble was. They lowered a rope immediately, and Mrs. Chapman went down, stepping from stone to stone, with which the well was walled, holding on to the rope to keep from falling, while her sister held the end above. As soon as she reached the bottom she raised and held the child's head above water, until assistance could be had. Fortunately a negro man was living near and in a few minutes he was with them. He descended in the same manner Mrs. Chapman had, and brought the child to the surface. There seems to have been no windlass nor bucket to the well, as Mrs. Chapman ascended holding to the rope and stepping from stone to stone as she had gone down.

The child was insensible when brought up, but recovered consciousness in a few hours, and is now, 1892, a strong, healthy girl.

Mrs. Chapman herself is a very delicate and gentle looking woman, and when asked afterwards how it was that she could go down at once to the rescue of the child: "Why," she replied, "I never thought anything about it at all. The child was in the well and had to be saved and I went. Somebody had to go at once,—that was all."

Mrs. Chapman is the widow of Andrew Chapman, a nephew of the writer. When quite a young man he was rather wild and reckless. This did not last long. He soon became steady and industrious, and was an energetic, upright, honorable, business man. I do not think I have any young relatives to whom it is possible for me to become so warmly and devotedly attached as I was to him. The reader can understand and appreciate his sterling character and the estimation in which he was held by some others who knew him, when he learns that Mrs. C. Mower, who was then a leading merchant at Newberry and a woman of exalted character, wept when she heard of his death.

COLONEL LEWIS ELZEY.

I had heard and read of Colonel Lewis Elzey, but his name had almost entirely faded out from my mind and memory, when I received from a friend a clipping from an old newspaper, which gives an account of an interview with him. He was then living near Aiken. The date of the interview is not

given, nor the date of the publication of the paper in which it
appeared (only slips were sent me), but I think it was in the
year 1875, from the dates of advertisements which appeared in
the same number of the "Advertiser." In giving an account
of this interview I cannot do better than to copy it verbatim.
Who the "reporter" is I have no means of knowing:

Reporter—What is your age, Colonel Elzey?

"I am 83 years old—was born in Virginia before the Revolutionary War—was a lieutenant in the regular army during
the war of 1812—encamped at Lower Sandusky, on Lake Erie,
during the naval fight of Com. Perry—could hear the guns
and see the smoke, but could not·see the vessels."

Reporter—You are not a graduate of West Point, how did
you get a commission in the regular army?

"Well, at that time there were not more than four or five
graduates in the whole army. Scott was not a graduate. I
got my commission by the recommendation of a member of
Congress."

Reporter—Did you return to private life after the close of
the war?

"Yes, I went back to Virginia."

Reporter—You knew many of the celebrated men of your
State?

"I knew Jefferson, Monroe, Chief Justice Marshall, John
Randolph, and others. When President Monroe returned to
Virginia, his term as President having expired, he took the
position of Magistrate in Loudon County, and acted for a good
many years; but the office of Magistrate in those days was always filled by men of talent and eminent character—not like
the d—d Trial Justices of these days, for they are the greatest
curses in the annals of time. The oldest Magistrate of the
county, in those days, became Sheriff, although they never
occupied the position, but farmed it out and gave the proceeds
to charitable purposes. I knew Jefferson by sight; he frequently came up in the country where I lived, near Winchester. He was very popular with the common people. Chief
Justice Marshall was a very plain man in his dress and manner
—very much like Chancellor Harper of this State. I have
often seen him with his knee buckles loose, flapping about his
legs, and sometimes half of his coat tail would be off. We

used to laugh at him about helping an old woman catch her chickens, who had brought them to town for sale. They got out of her basket and Mr. Marshall ran all over the streets to catch them for her."

Reporter—Did Chief Justice Marshall have any brothers?

"Yes, Charles and Jim. Charles was dissipated. Jim was immensely wealthy, but would never hold any office."

Reporter—Was not this plainness of dress affected by Mr. Marshall?

"No, all the Marshalls were that way. Jim Marshall dressed his children so badly that they once complained to my father that they were not dressed as well as the other children in the neighborhood. My father spoke to Jim about it, and he said: 'Captain Elzey, people know that Jim Marshall is rich—very rich—and what is the use for him to dress his children so fine? You can spoil children very easily. When you used to come to my father's house I have many a time hunted eggs for your dinner in my shirt tail.'

"Chief Justice Marshall once sent word to a Mr. Duvall, with whom he was not personally acquainted, that he and family would dine with him on a certain day. When the day arrived, Mr. Marshall rode on before and his carriage with family came on behind. When he reached Mr. Duvall's house, he asked if he could get dinner. Duvall said: 'No, you can't get dinner; I am expecting Judge Marshall and family to dinner, and as they are very fine people I should not like to present you to them.' The Chief Justice responded that he knew Mr. Marshall's family very well and he believed he would stop anyhow. Duvall was very much taken down when he found that the ordinary looking guest was the Chief Justice of the Supreme Court of the United States."

Reporter—When did you come to South Carolina?

"I came to Charleston, S. C., in 1816, with a drove of horses, made lots of money on them, and got on a spree. . Horses were worth more then than they are now, that is, fine horses. Fine horses are worth more in Kentucky than they are here. When I first came to Edgefield, in 1816, there was plenty of game in the woods; we once, in a camp hunt, killed eleven deer on Shaw's Creek. There was a paper published at Edgefield then by Mr. Landrum, called 'The Hive.'"

Reporter—Who were the lawyers at Edgefield in 1816, and what kind of lawyers were they?

"There was Glascock, Edmund Bacon, Jeter, Eldred Simkins, McDuffie. Edmund Bacon was a fine speaker, graceful in manners and gesture, very cunning in his arguments, and had the most musical voice I have ever heard. Eldred Simkins was a book-worm. Jeter was Solicitor, and a very sensible, practical, and short speaker. McDuffie was a great orator, but he was awkward in his manners in private, and got very much excited in speaking—sawed the air with his hands. Glascock was a forcible speaker, but never studied his cases—used frequently to hunt foxes all the morning and make an argument in the evening. I never knew him to study but one case, and that was a case he had in Beaufort, in which he defended a man by the name of Spavins against a man by the name of Spikes. He went down to court three days beforehand, and there he heard for the first time that Petigru and Billy Martin (Judge W. D. Martin) were on the other side, 'and, by G—d,' said he, 'I had to study.' I remember one remark he made to the jury: 'Spikes, gentlemen of the jury, is the plaintiff in this suit, and he has tried to spike this case, not with ten penny nails either, but if you, gentlemen, don't spike Spikes, I am mistaken.' He gained his case.

"Nathan Griffin came to the bar afterwards, about 1824. I think he was in partnership with Judge Butler, and never made a speech until after they dissolved, and they were partners ten or twelve years. Mr. Griffin then became one of the most effective jury lawyers in the State. His style was conversational, which always wins in the long run. Mr. Griffin was a good judge of human nature, and an excellent examiner of witnesses; he was very punctilious and systematic. I was not a great admirer of Mr. Calhoun. Mr. Griffin once said to me: 'Elzey, Calhoun is ten years ahead of his age.' 'Well,' said I, 'if he is that far ahead I shan't try to catch him.' Judge Gant used to hold court in Edgefield when I first came here. He was a fancy man. I remember he once lectured on temperance while he lived at Mt. Vintage—met me the next day—'Elzey,' said he, 'I didn't mean that lecture for you, but for them d—d A's. in your neighborhood; for the drunker they get the more religion they have.'"

NINETY-SIX.

As Edgefield and Saluda Counties were once part of the large District of Ninety-Six, of which the town of Ninety-Six was the capital, I feel that I ought to insert the following legend, which accounts for the origin of the name. This was written for the history of Abbeville, but I feel sure that the reader will not regret its insertion here, as Edgefield and Abbeville were once parts of the same great district.

There is always a reason for the names of places. A place is either named after some eminent man or woman, or it is imported by the settlers of a new place and given to it through a fond recollection of their old home, and a desire to carry the name with them if they cannot carry the place. In this way only recently a Newberry has sprung up in Florida; in this way Newberry itself was brought from England and planted here; in this way Abbeville derived its name, and it is a good one, pleasant in sound, pleasant in fact, and must have been very dear to those good Huguenots who brought it with them from the vine clad hills of France.

There are many Indian names of places, and rivers, and streams, of which Saluda is one, all over the State. I would that there were more; but Ninety-Six is not one, it is very decidedly English. Ramsay does not tell us its origin; nor does any other history with which I am acquainted. I do not think that I have ever seen the story in print, though surely it ought to have been, and may have been long ago. It was told to me as a legend or tradition when I was quite young. I remember crossing Eighteen Mile Creek and, I believe, Twenty-three Mile Creek, and hearing the names of others when they were given to me when the story was told. Shall I tell the story, or try to tell it here? I feel sure that I shall mar it in the telling; but as it gives name to Ninety-Six, as well as other localities on the route, it must be told. It is a story of love, of the love of a beautiful Indian maiden devoted to the welfare and safety of her white lover, who was at that time many miles distant from her. She wanted to give warning of the approach of danger, as Pocahontas gave warning to the English of a threatened attack upon Jamestown. This Indian maiden, whose home was in the neighborhood of Fort Prince George—Keowee—of the tribe of the Cherokees, learning of a contemplated attack upon the white settlements below, which were then very weak, and among whom was her chosen youth, determined to give them warning. Learning of the time fixed for the departure of the braves, she anticipated it by a few hours; passed over the ninety-six miles which lay between Keowee and her destination in less than twenty-four hours, gave the necessary warning, and saved the settlement from destruction. The place at the end of her journey has ever since been called Ninety-Six in commemoration of her heroic deed, and her name is kept alive in the thoughts and memories of men by being used as the name of a hotel, or house of rest for weary travellers at Anderson. It is a soft, sweet name like many others used by the Southern Indians. The very soul of music and of poetry breathes through many of them. Her name was Chiquola, and surely a weary traveller could sleep well in a house having such a euphonious title. Of the after life and fate of this heroic Indian maiden, the story relates nothing.

Such is the sweet poetic legend that I have always heard connected with Ninety-Six, and as having given it name. And yet, in spite of all poetic sentiment, the name was changed by Act of the General Assembly on the 8th of March, 1787, to Cambridge. The words of the Act are as follows:

"*Be it enacted*, That from and immediately after the passing of this Act, the town heretofore called by the name of 96 shall be known and called by the name of Cambridge and no other; any law, usage, or custom to the contrary notwithstanding.   JOHN LLOYD,
                                   President of the Senate.
JOHN JULIUS PRINGLE,
     Speaker of the House of Representatives."

As Cambridge it continued to be the capital and seat of justice of an extensive territory, which continued to be known as Ninety-Six District until it was cut up into the counties of Edgefield, Abbeville, Newberry, Laurens, Spartanburg, and Union. As Cambridge it became a seat of learning (having a chartered college) and intelligence, of wealth and influence. As Cambridge it was the home of some eminent lawyers, who became judges and men of great influence in the State for many years. As Cambridge it was a beautiful and flourishing place for some years. But now, in spite of legislative enactment, it is almost forgotten that the name Cambridge was ever used. The town has vanished, leaving only the fragments of a house or two to mark the spot, and a few large oaks to shade it. These, too, have disappeared, as I have been told, since I wrote the above sentence, and nothing now appears to show that Cambridge ever was. The name Ninety-Six still clings to it, though transferred to the new town on the G. &. C. Railroad, which runs near.

ANNE KENNEDY.

I hope, in fact I know, that the readers of the History of Edgefield will not be sorry to see the following anecdote inserted here. It belongs to the History of the State, but did not come to the knowledge of the writer until about the close of the year 1896, or the beginning of 1897. I hope to see it inserted in a future edition of that work—Chapman's History of South Carolina. The anecdote is related by Mr. D. H. Russell, of Anderson, a great-grandson of the heroine.

At the time the incident occurred Anne Kennedy was about 18 years of age, and lived at Hamilton's Ford, on Broad River, in York District. The Tories came to her father's house to burn it. She was sitting carding wool rolls to make clothes for her father and brothers, who were with Sumter. The band stopped in the yard and one of them went in the house and picked up a chunk of fire to set the house on fire. She seized the intruder and proved to be the stronger and more powerful, and succeeded in forcing him to the edge of the piazza. And getting him by the collar and by the seat of his pants, she threw him headlong into the yard. He was so enraged that he seized his gun to shoot her, but the others were so amused at a woman's handling him so easily that they prevented him from doing it. In the scuffle he pressed the chunk of fire against her left wrist to force her to release her hold, but she would not let go. The scar remained on her wrist through life, and she carried it with her to her grave. She died in 1836, and is buried in Anderson County.

"My great-grandfather," says Mr. Russell, in communicating these facts, "lived until I was 12 years old, and I have often heard him relate the story, and have also frequently heard it from my grandfather. On my way home from the surrender in 1865 I passed through York County and spent a night with her nephew, Kennedy Hamilton, who reported the story to me and the next morning sent his son Robert with me to see the site where the house stood on a high hill overlooking Broad River."

COTTON IN 1808-1818-1819-1820-1822 and 1824.

Here is a copy of an old letter giving price of cotton in 1808. The letter is addressed to Major Zack S. Brooks, Edgefield District, by his negro man, Saint:

"CHARLESTON, 15 Dee'm, 1808.

"Major Zack S. Brooks, Sir:

"We have the pleasure of acknowledging the receipt of yours, dated the 8th instant, consigning us Fifteen Bales of Cotton weighing forty-fix hundred and seventy-nine pounds, and we have herewith enclosed you the weight of each bale of cotton for your information, wherein you will find that we have noted the eight bales of Mrs. Brooks. It being impossible to procure your limits for your cotton at present, for the very primest and best qualities of cotton is selling at eleven cents per ℔., have in consequence thereof put your cotton in store, and shall wait your further instructions as to the sale. We have sent in conformity to your order sundry store goods, amounting to Fifty-five pounds, Eleven Shillings, and Six pence. which is at your debit we wish them safe to hand and that they may be perfectly to your liking. You will find that we omitted sending to you the Six Barrels of Salt, which is in consequence of the advance in price which has taken place on this article. It cannot be procured at present under 5s. 10d. per Barrel in our market. We therefore was of opinion that you would have rather been without this article as we sent you a waggon load not long since. Mr. A. Deliard did not leave a Tobacco not with us as you expected or we should have attended to your instructions.

"We are Respectfully Sir,
"Your Ob't. Servants,
"JOHN AND CHAS. BULOW."

Here is a copy of another old letter giving prices of cotton and other things ten years later. This letter is addressed to Mr. Jonathan Weaver, Edgefield District, S. C.:

"CHARLESTON, Nov. 25th, 1818.

"Mr. Jonathan Weaver.

"DEAR SIR: Within is the sales of your cotton, which we hope will please. We also send you agreeable to your order, as by the within bill, which we hope will also please you.

"The price of West India Rum was One dollar 20 cents, and it being only 3 proof, and 4th Proof Jamaica being only $1.45, we were under the impression that it would suit you best, because in addition to the rum being better than W. I. it is cheaper, because it will bear much more water.

"The balance of two hundred and forty-two 91-100 dollars remains in our hands subject to your order when called for, as we had no instructions what to do with it.

"Cotton is at present 29, but we are not certain how long. It will be lower, as it is continually declining in price.

"We are under the impression that it will come down to 25 or 26 cents, but that it will eventually rise again; we think that it may in the spring command 30, but that is uncertain; it is only our opinion.

"Groceries of almost every description are high: Sugar, 14c. ℔; Molasses, 65c. @ 68; Coffee, 35c., 37½; Coarse woolens are high; Fine woolens and cotton goods much as last season.

"We are, Dear Sir, with sentiments of respect and esteem, your obedient humble servants,

"BOYCE & JOHNSTON."

———

One year later, December 1st, 1819, I find that cotton was considerably lower than the prices paid by Messrs. Boyce & Johnston.

The original bill now lying before me shows that John Abney, on the 1st December, 1819, sold to Charles O'Neale 6 bales of cotton, total weight 1908 pounds, 15⅓ cents per pound, amounting to $295.74. And 5 bales of cotton, total weight, 1574 pounds, at 16 cents per pound, making $244.51½.

The reader will note that the prices paid by John and

Charles Bulow was a few years before the war of 1812 with Great Britian.   After the war prices were high and again went down as with us after the War of Secession.

From a letter from Charles O'Neale to John Abney, Esq., dated Charleston, June 13th, 1820, I learn that cotton at that date was worth in Charleston money 17½, in Bank of Darien Ga., money 18 cents per pound.

And in a letter from the same to the same, dated Charleston, 4th September, 1822, it is stated that "prime old cotton is selling at 12½cts—very good 11cts—inferior 9 @ 10cts—I am under the impression that now if prime will open @ 12½ @ 13cts—perhaps a few bales that first comes in may rate some higher—I do not think it a safe article to deal in without you could lay it down here at 12½cts."

Then follows a bill for bagging and rope:

Mr. John Abney, Jun.
                                   To Charles O'Neale.

To 4 Ps. Cotton Bagging, 42 in
    61—60—60—62, 243 yds., @ 45¾ cts $106.31¼
    1 Coil rope, 69℔ @ 14 . . . .   9.66
                                              $115.97¼

And a little later I find cotton from this part of Edgefied finding a market nearer home than Charleston—price a little better than in September, 1822.

The original bill now lies before me, dated

HAMBURG, JAN. 14, 1824.

Sproull & Pinchback.
                                   Bot of Matthew Coleman.

1 Bal Cotton C. C. 335=2=333℔s. c. 13 77-100 .   . $ 45.85
10 "   "   3249=20=3229=@ 13 77-100 . . . . 444.63
                                          $490.48
Deduct mending   38
                                          $490.10

Hamburg was a new town ten or fifteen years old when this cotton was sold there.   This, I suppose, must be the same William Pinchback mentioned in the Annals of Newberry, page 120, new edition.   Judge O'Neall says of him that he was one of the old inhabitants of Newberry, and that he built the corner house on Caldwell and Boyce streets, once occupied by Mr. Bierfield as a hotel. He came to Newberry from Chester, in 1810 or 1811—was a cabinet maker by trade, but became a merchant, and like Pratt and Boyce, made one or more trips North, carrying out cotton and returning with merchandise. He removed to Charleston and there did business as a cotton speculator and realized a fortune in 1825. He afterwards lived many years in Abbeville District, and there owned a large and valuable plantation. He finally moved to Mississippi, where he died in 1848, leaving neither wife nor children. His large estate went, of course, to the nearest of kin.

PRICES MARCH 3RD, 1821.

And here again is another old bill, the original of which now lies before me, showing the prices of such articles a good many years ago:

AUGUSTA, March 3rd, 1821.

Mr. John Abney.

Bot of Crayton & Sloan.

C Plough Molds, 51 lbs, @ .7	. . $ 3.57
1 Coil rope, 54 lbs, @ .14	7.56
2 Ye planes	1.00
30 lbs Sugar	3.15
20 " Coffee	6.25
2 bags.	25
	$21.78

Recevd Payment,

P. E. DUNCAN.

I hope the reader will not regret the space taken up by these old accounts, nor the time consumed in reading them. I confess that I have a weakness this way, in that I take great pleasure in looking over old letters and papers sixty, seventy, or a hundred years old. I have an old letter written in 1783 to a gentleman in Charlesten about the collection of rent then due on a house in the city, and telling how to proceed.

THE FIRES OF EDGEFIELD.

On the morning of the 30th of October, 1881, the business part of the town of Edgefield was laid in ashes. Just three years thereafter, wanting a few days, October 21st, the same part of the town was again burned. Only one of the new buildings erected after the fire of 1881 was saved. That was Mr. Alvin Hart's.

Again, a little less than eight years, a third fire, the most disastrous and destructive of all swept the town. This last fire occurred on the night of Thursday 21st of January, 1892, at about half past eleven o'clock. The flames were first discovered bursting from the deep and wide basement of the old Masonic Hall, in which was the Advertiser printing and publishing office. Soon almost the entire population of the town, whites and black, male and female, were upon the square. There was but little wind, and the flames from the burning building shot straight upwards towards the sky.

The buildings West of the Hall could not be saved, and all efforts were centered upon saving the Folk law office and the new McHugh building at the lower end of Park Row. These were saved; Park Row was saved—the Farmer's Loan and Savings Bank; the Chronicle office and the two new Butler stores. By half past twelve Dr. Parker's dental office and Abney's old law office, in which this writer has passed many pleasant hours, were entirely gone. And now the flames swept the entire East end of the old Ryan Hotel, which was of wood. The young people were dancing a German in this house, and the young men, as soon as the alarm of fire was raised, and it was known that the hotel would burn set to work and moved out the new and handsome furniture of Major Anderson.

The jail was saved by hard and faithful work, the colored men were ahead in this work and strove with the greatest zeal and intrepidity. Soon the roof was thoroughly wetted and covered with wet blankets, and the jail was saved.

The Ryan Hotel, the old Gray house, the Whittaker Hotel, the contiguous wooden buildings at the corner of the square, the old Bryan brick store (Kearsey saloon), the large brick building, owned by Mr. D. A. Tompkins, were all swept away.

In reading the accounts of this fire, as published in the papers at the time, it is surprising to find so little insurance on the property destroyed. The citizens must have felt that they were surely exempt from the ordinary calamities by fire. On Masonic Hall and the Edgefield Advertiser there was no insurance—loss, $13,000; nothing saved; owned by Thomas J. Adams.

Mr. L. E. Jackson, with a stock of goods valued at $2,500, had insurance for $1,000.

Dr. Parker had no insurance—loss $2,000 or more. Upon the Ryan Hotel there was insurance to the amount of $4,000.

Mrs. Whittaker, the owner of the old Gray House, had no insurance.

Governor J. C. Sheppard, owner of the corner store, had $500 on it.

Major R. S. Anderson of the Hotel had $1,000 on his furniture.

Mr. J. A. Bennett, owner of the old Bryan brick store, had $500 on it.

Upon the large brick building of Mr. D. A. Tomkins near the jail there was no insurance.

J. H. Paul & Co's. saloon lost about $800, no insurance.

The losers went to work immediately and Edgefield will soon be more prosperous and better looking than ever.

THE PINE HOUSE.

The Pine House, or Piney Woods House, is one of those old historical landmarks that has been known in the county for considerably over one hundred years, in fact ever since before the Revolutionary War. It was then called the Piney Woods House. If I am not mistaken it has been in the ownership of the Bettis family ever since a period anterior to the Revolutionary War. They were probably the first settlers and owners. On the 17th of March, 1893, Benjamin W. Bettis, the patriarch of the Pine House passed away at the advanced age of eighty-two years. Surely it must have been a happy home with pleasant surroundings to hold one through a long life of upwards of eighty years. There are very few who pass through so many years and die at the place on which they were born. Life to such fortunate persons must learn at last to glide on like a calm and placid dream and death at the end is a waking up rather than a dropping to sleep. The writer and compiler of this history sometimes grows sentimental and yields placidly to the mood and feels like letting time and tide flow on and on forever and do nothing himself but simply glide along.

Trenton, a railroad town built near the Pine House, is a lively, thrifty little place, but the writer of this book once passed a dreary five hours there waiting for the train from Augusta, and there he avenged himself writing some doggerel verses which he thought of printing here, but does not.

EDGEFIELD VILLAGE.

Pursuant to an Act of the General Assembly, passed the 14th day of March, 1795, establishing county courts and regulating the proceedings therein, the following Justices, appointed and duly qualified, for the County of Edgefield, met at Edgefield Court House on the second Monday, being the 11th day of July, 1785, and proceeded to the appointment of a Clerk as directed by law. Justices present, Leroy Hammond, Arthur Simkins, John Pervis, Benjamin Tutt, John Moore, and William Anderson.

The Justices constituing a quorum, unanimously appointed Robert Stark to be Clerk of the County Court, who took the oath required by law. The County Court continued to hold sessions at Edgefield Court House until abolished by the Act of 1799.

The first court of General Sessions held at Edgefield Court House, as shown by the journal in the Clerk's office for Edgefield, (then District) met agreeable to law on Monday the 24th day of March, 1800. Present his "Honor Lewis Trezevant, Esq."

The Court ordered the commission of his Honor published, read, and to be entered on record. The commissions of Sampson Butler, Sheriff, and Richard Tutt, Clerk, were also read and ordered to be recorded. These officers had pursuant to law drawn on the 22nd day of February, 1800, the grand and petit jurors. Previous to the Act of 1799 the Court of General Sessions was held at Cambridge in the old Ninety-Six District from its establishment in 1769 to 1800.

CLERKS OF COURT FROM 1788 TO 1893.

George Pope . .	. 1788–1800	S. Harrison	1860–1868
R. Tutt	. 1800–1808	A. Ramsy .	1868–1872
Stan. Butler .	1808–1814	W. D. Ramsy .	1872–1874
M. Mims .	1814–1822	Jesse Jones (col.)	. 1874–1876
Daniel Byrd .	1822–1830	O. Y. Cheatham .	1876–1884
J. A. Richardson . . .	1830–1834	B. E. Nicholson, 1884 to Mar., 1885	
H. Boulware .	1834–1836	D. R. Durisoe, March, 1885, to 1888	
George Pope	1836–1844	J. C. Williams 1888–1892	
Thos. G. Bacon	1844–1860	John B. Hill . . .	1892

ORDINARIES AND PROBATE JUDGES FROM 1795 TO 1892.

ORDINARIES.		PROBATE JUDGES.	
R. Tutt	1795–1803	D L. Turner. . . .	1868–1874
John Simkins . .	1803–1833	A. N. Baney (col.)	. . 1875–1876
J. Richardson	1833–1835	L. Charlton	1876–1880
O. Towles .	1835–1844	L. P. Covar	1880–1882
John Hill .	1844–1851	W. F. Roath	1882–1888
H. T. Wright	1851–1855	J. D. Allen .	1888–
W. F. Durisoe .	1855–1868		

SHERIFFS.

The list of Sheriffs as given me is imperfect and imcomplete, nor are the times of service given in all cases. The earlier Sheriffs were Wm. Thurmond, James Butler, Edmund Belcher.

W. H. Moss	1836–1840	James Eidson	1856–1860
S. Christie . .	1840–1844	Wm. Spires .	1860–
H. Boulware	1844–1848	John T. Gaston	1876–1880
S. Christie	1848–1852	W. H. Outzs .	1892–
Lewis Jones	1852–1856		

Isaac Bowles was appointed Sheriff after the war. Hardy Walls succeeded him in 1868. Walls resigned and the negro Coroner named Carroll filled the office until the appointment of J. A. Richardson.

COMMISSIONERS IN EQUITY AND MASTERS.

Whitfield Brooks, James Terry, Arthur Simkins, Z. W. Carwile, S. S. Tomkins—W. F. Roath, Master, who is now, 1892, in office.

XXXV.

The seven company rolls following are from the original rolls as the companies were raised and formed in 1861 and 1862, and were kindly copied and sent to me by Mr. J. R. Wright, of Ninety-Six:

NINETY-SIX RIFLEMEN.

Thomas G. Bacon, Captain; Elbert Bland, First Lieutenant; Stewart Harrison, Second Lieutenant; J. A. Bland, Third Lieutenant; James A. Dozier, First Sergeant; M. B. Weaver, Second Sergeant; H. W. Addison, Third Sergeant; M. Miles, Fourth Sergeant; John Carwile, Fifth Sergeant; Moses Harris, First Corporal; R. Gregory, Second Corporal; T. Vaughn, Third Corporal; R. Cogburn, Fourth Corporal; Daniel Christian, Fifth Corporal; Charles Mathis, Sixth Corporal.

PRIVATES.

J. F. Adams, J. Allman, J. E. Bacon, A. Broadwater, W. S. Boyce, A. Burt, J. Busby, H. Cato, J. Carpenter, L. Clark, W. M. Clark, J. B. Courtney, J. P. Courtney, Wm. Clark, Wardlaw Covar, W. Crawford, G. Crawford, R. M. Cogburn, E. T. Davis, J. Earley, M. Eidson, L. Gomillion, M. Glover, J. Grissom, M. Grice, S. B. Griffin, B. Grice, J. B. Harris, Alfred Hatcher, W. E. Hobbes, E. Holsonbake, L. Holsonbake, J. B. Hodges, J. T. Hagood, L. S. Johnson, G. Johnson, Harmon Kisie, J. Long, W. R. Long, M. B. Lyles, Mike Lebeschultz, W. Lott, W. Littleton, B. F. Lovelace, J. C. Lovelace, B. F. Mayer, P. B. McDaniel, S. McDaniel, J. Mayer, S. Murphy, J. A. Nicholson, J. Oftman, T. D. Padgett, J. H. Prescott, Nat. Ramey, H. Ripley, Simkins Riddle, B. J. Ryan, B. Y. Ryan, J. D. Ramey, John Rinehart, F. E. Randall, E. W. Randall, E. Seibles, Thos. Stevenson, B. F. Smith, J. S. Salter, J. Sherley, L. Sheppard, L. W. Snelgrove, Arthur Swearengin, Eldred Swearengin, John Swearengin, Lark Swearengin, Richard Swearengin, T. Toney, H. Turner, L. B. Wever, R. Willing, J. W. Whitlock, W. Whitlock, H. W. Whitman, J. Woolsey, H. H. Prescott. Privates, 84; officers, 15; total, 99.

CHEROKEE PONDS GUARDS.

Robert Meriwether, Captain; A. P. Butler, First Lieutenant; D. L. Shaw, Second Lieutenant; Jos. Meriwether, Third Lieutenant; W. T. Scott, First Sergeant; M. Medlock, Second Sergeant; J. J. Lanier, Third Sergeant; B. W. Johnson, Fourth Sergeant; J. W. Walker, Fifth Sergeant; George Samuell, First Corporal; J. A. Crowder, Second Corporal; W. T. Gardner, Third Corporal; T. J. Howard, Fourth Corporal; H. N. Blease, Fifth Corporal; C. Pardee, Sixth Corporal.

PRIVATES.

T. L. Anderson, F. M. Brown, Robert Burton, Edward Blease, L. W. Bartee, W. V. Bartee, H. G. Collins, M. Calliham, R. J. Crafton, J. J. Crafton, Thomas Curry, W. L. Curry, J. S. Day, Julius Day, Jr., J. M. Davis, George Delaughter, A. Dow, Gary Floyd, Walker Floyd, Hazel Floyd, T. J. Green, T. W. Green, W. H. Hightower, G. W. Hancock, D. O. Hancock, John Holly, Jasper Holly, Andrew Holly, Calvin Holly, M. G. Hitt, J. F. Johnson, P. B. Kisie, R. J. Lanham, W. O. Morgan, E. O. Morgan, W. J. Morris, W. H. Meriwether, Joel McClendon, Jr., J. M. Marran, J. E. A. Martin, E. McClendon, J. C. Mayes, Whit. Mays, Samuel Mays, R. T. Owen, Thos. Sharpton, W. C. A. Shaw, Robert Samuel, A. Smith, J. M. Thurmond, R. H. Williams. Privates, 51; officers, 15; total, 66.

This company became, I think, Company "G," First Regiment—Colonel Gregg; first Captain, A. P. Butler; last, Captain Holloway.

DENNY COMPANY.

Volunteer company from the lower Battalion, Tenth Regiment, South Carolina Militia:

David Denny, Captain; Thomas L. Smith, First Lieutenant; W. A. Rutland, Second Lieutenant; E. J. Goggans, Third Lieutenant; A. S. Dozier, First Sergeant; J. R. Bouknight, Second Sergeant; J. C. McCelvy, Third Sergeant; Marshal Lott, Fourth Sergeant; B. B. Duke, Fifth Sergeant; James Mitchell, First Corporal; James M. Daniel, Second Corporal; Pinkney Bouknight, Third Corporal; David Padgett, Fourth Corporal; M. W. Coleman, Fifth Corporal; W. G. Denny, Sixth Corporal.

PRIVATES.

G. W. Denny, David Sheppard, J. D. Herlong, S. J. Bouknight, M. D. Padgett, W. W. Smith, Levy Bedenbaugh, William Etheredge, M. B. Watson, J. R. Padgett, Emanuel Padgett, B. F. Sample, Hilary Crouch, Hiram Duncan, Arthur Davis, D. D. W. McCarty, J. C. H. Rauch, W. E. Sample, William Ridlehoover, J. B. Suddath, William Saddler, Edward Mitchell, A. W. Denny, W. A. Watson, J. T. Vansant, J. H. Watson, F. M. Rogers, Paul Mitchell, John Perry, James J. Denny, W. M. Stewart, M. G. McGhee, Eldred Whittle, T. B. Crouch, William Etheredge, George Martin, Noah Etheredge, G. D. Henson, A. L. Wyse, R. T. Jones, A. S. Bouknight, W. L. Parker, E. A. Perry, John Inabenet, James Goodwin, J. T. Bedenbaugh, A. Gibson, T. A. Merchant, Tillman Sawyer, W. J. Cooner, Thomas Whittle, W. D. Cameron, William Leapard, C. W. Hues, J. R. Pou, John McClendon, Benjamin Harris, William Goodwin, Jacob Gibson, Willis Crouch, T. L. Story, J. H. Smith, W. A. Hardy, N. F. Corley, Caleb Etheredge, J. M. Corley, J. B. Ridgwell, P. P. Spann, J. L. Crouch, W. J. Gunter, Joshua Clarke, John Pou, J. H. Spann, L. A. Smith, J. L. Watson, J. A. Clarke, W. Mathis, B. R. Smith, William Sawyer, S. P. Linler, W. A. Mitchell, J. J. Jones, William Harris, E. L. McCarty, M. A. Whittle, Thomas Berry, R. R. Grigsby, Jacob Hirett.   Privates, 88; officers, 15; total, 103.

Captain Denny was too old for active service; in a short time he resigned. His company was too large and was divided into two. Company M Seventh Regiment, E. J. Goggans, Captain, and Company E of the Seventh Regiment, James Mitchell, Captain. The rolls of these companies appear in this book.

EDGEFIELD RIFLEMEN.

Cicero Adams, Captain; H. Rufus Dean, First Lieutenant; W. J. Ready, Second Lieutenant; E. S. Mims, Third Lieutenant; W. H. Brunson, First Sergeant, Orderly; Jacob Youngblood, Second Sergeant; Tillman Watson, Jr., Third Sergeant; Joseph C. Jones, Fourth Sergeant; J. Wade Johnson, Fifth Sergeant; Lewis Coleman, First Corporal; W. P. James, Second Corporal; N. L. Griffin, Third Corporal; W. L. Burt,

Fourth Corporal; A. P. Butler, Fifth Corporal; C. L. Miles, Sixth Corporal.

PRIVATES.

Joseph M. Abney, William H. Abney, O. H. P. Burton, T. H. Bryan, W. D. Bryan, J. J. Bryan, T. C. Banks, John Bridwell, Jas. C. Brooks, Joseph Brunson, R. S. Brunson, J. W. L. Bartley, W. S. Covar, C. L. Covar, C. D. Covar, J. L. Covar, W. A. Christie, Clarke S. Corley, James A. Colgan, C. A. Cheatham, W. H. Casey, J. T. Casey, H. D. Crooker, W. F. Durisoe, Jr., C. L. Durisoe, Preston DeLoach, W. B. Eidson, J. J. Eidson, John T. Gray, C. H. Goodwin, R. B. Hughes, John Jennings, B. A. Jones, T. A. Jones, G. B. Lake, Felix Lake, F. A. Murrell, M. T. McHenry, J. W. McCullough, D. F. McEwen, M. A. Markert, J. P. Moss, Jesse McGhee, J. E. Morgan, B. E. Nicholson, James Paul, A. M. Perrin, Pressley M. Prater, James Ramsay, John A. Rambo, W. D. Ramey, Samuel Ready, J. D. Roper, P. E. B. Bryan, Robert Stalnaker, W. R. Spann, B. T. Swearengin, J. C. Swearengin, S. W. Sullivan, J. A. Sease, Thomas L. Steadhem, J. M. Thurmond, C. W. Winn, H. Winn, S. White, A. G. Woodruff, J. M. Youngblood. Privates, 67; officers, 15; total, 82.

NINTH REGIMENT MILITIA.

Company from Upper Battalion, Ninth Regiment, South Carolina Militia:

B. M. Talbert, Captain; J. F. Burress, First Lieutenant; H. G. Seigler, Second Lieutenant; J. L. Talbert, Third Lieutenant; W. T. West, First Sergeant; O. T. Culbreath, Second Sergeant; W. N. Martin, Third Sergeant; J. W. Cheatham, Fourth Sergeant; W. H. Rush, Fifth Sergeant; C. M. Calhoun, First Corporal; J. W. Franks, Second Corporal; W. M. Reynolds, Third Corporal; John Sentell, Fourth Corporal; T. T. Wilhite, Fifth Corporal; J. H. Sanders, Sixth Corporal.

PRIVATES.

B. O. Adams, C. M. Burress, J. E. Blake, P. Barden, H. J. Bird, R. A. Cochran, W. F. Capeheart, H. H. Clay, John Culbreath, G. R. Coleman, W. L. Coleman, J. A. Cartledge, A. Deal, James Deal, James Devore, E. S. Devore, J. W.

Devore, J. W. Delaughter, John Gable, E. Hamilton, G. A.
Hamilton, William Hollingsworth, E. Hollingsworth, J. T.
Henderson, T. S. Henderson, G. W. Johnson, W. B.
Kemp, L. M. Lanier, O. W. Lanier, C. H. Limbecker,
J. L. Lockridge, E. H. Lagroon, W. Littleton, T. J.
Miller, T. W. Morgan, W. W. McKinnie, Lyles Motes,
James Picket, W. E. Quattlebaum, A. M. Quarles,
J. T. Rampey, J. P. Rush, J. C. Reynolds, J. H. Rutledge,
T. J. Rountree, O. S. Sentell, D. Stalnaker, J. R. Stalnaker,
B. F. Stalnaker, G. S. Stalnaker, G. W. Strom, P. H. Strom,
S. B. Strom, T. W. Shadrack, G. J. Sheppard, T. M. Seigler,
S. D. Shibley, Wiley Timmerman, F. L. Timmerman, G. H.
Timmerman, G. W. Thurmond, John White, Jr., W. G.
White, R. M. Winn, William Yeldell. Privates, 65; officers,
15; total, 80.

NINTH REGIMENT MILITIA.

Company from Lower Battalion, Ninth Regiment, South
Carolina Militia:

W. F. Prescott, Captain; J. P. Nixon, First Lieutenant;
Benjamin Roper, Second Lieutenant; S. B. Blocker, Third
Lieutenant; H. C. Garrett, First Sergeant; Wyat Holmes,
Second Sergeant; Wm. Holmes, Third Sergeant; G. W.
Morgan, Fourth Sergeant; William Holson, Fifth Sergeant;
L. M. Broadwater, First Corporal; L. J. Miller, Second Cor-
poral; J. H. Lanier, Third Corporal; S. G. Merriwether, Fourth
Corporal; N. L. Brunson, Fifth Corporol; Thomas M. Crafton,
Sixth Corporal.

PRIVATES.

James A. Mathis, Charles Hammond, Daniel Briggs, W. A.
Garrett, C. F. Hammond, R. G. Hammond, S. T. Brunson,
P. M. Thurmond, Jos. Holliday, Philip Boyd, E. N. Bartly,
W. G. Coleman, J. C. Strom, David W. Thomas, T. N.
Pressley, W. B. Hughes, Whit. Jennings, Thomas Strom,
A. H. Burt, J. N. Griffin, William Wash, W. A. B. Newson,
A. Howard, R. O. Hovia, N. Merriwether, J. Prince, J. S.
Sharpton, P. B. Hanson, G. W. Holson, James Wood, A.
Holson, T. Irvins, F. W. Treat, L. E. Holmes, Jasper Mc-
Daniel, Thomas M. Colier, James A. Bussey, Sherrad Holmes,
Wm. H. Mathis, Wm. H. Bussey, John Prince, F. Corley,

N. G. Broadwater, John H. Terry, L. F. Sharpton, J. C. Henderson, H. Wood, George Martin, Charles Glanton, John Briggs, T. Halliday, John C. Collins, R. D. Brunson, B. B. Burton, B. B. Johnson, John Cason, Thomas Mathis, Robert Brooks, Roland Terry, J. H. Burdit, S. Stalnaker. Privates, 61; officers, 15; total, 76.

This company is, I suppose, the germ or the original of Company "I," Seventh Regiment, South Carolina Volunteers. In another place appears the roll of that company showing its condition, as reported by Captain Benjamin Roper, July 23rd, 1862, which roll is on file in the office of the Adjutant and Inspector General, Columbia, S. C.

EDGEFIELD HUSSARS.

Attached to the Hampton Legion of South Carolina.

M. C. Butler, Captain; J. J. Bunch, First Lieutenant; J J. Crafton, Second Lieutenant; J. M. Lanham, Third Lieutenant; Thomas W. Glover, First Sergeant; J. M. Wise, Second Sergeant; F. L. Butler, Third Sergeant; A. J. Anderson, Fourth Sergeant; P. M. Butler, Fifth Sergeant; J. B. Ryan, First Corporal; F. B. Walker, Second Corporal; W. A. Glover, Third Corporal; N. L. Griffin, Fourth Corporal; J. L. Nicholson, Fifth Corporal; J. Wesley Barr, Chaplain; Alex. Rutherford, Farrier; M. A. Markert, Bugler.

PRIVATES.

S. D. Adams, W. J. Adams, Wm. Bolton, Wm. A. Batchelor, J. C. Brice, Moses Bruce, A. P. Butler, E. J. Butler, Harrison Butler, J. P. Bryan, F. M. Cheatham, J. W. Chipley, J. S. Cotes, John Colgan, Randal Croft, Robert C. Crafton John Crawford, T. H. Clark, S. C. Deal, S. P. DeLoach, J. J. Eidson, Wm. Frazier, C. B. Glover, M. O. Glover, Wm. Golding, Wade Hampton, Jr., T. P. Hampton, E. W. Henderson, —— Jones, Jno. Kennerly, D. P. Lagrone, John Lyon, J. W. Lagrone, W. W. Lanham, W. P. McKie, Witfield Martin, J. J. Mealing, W. E. Middleton, N. W. Miller, Ruldolphus Niernsee, B. F. Ouzts, —— Oglesby, W. M. Rhine, Jno. Riley, James Robertson, L. L. Roper, J. H. Ross, C. C. Singleton, Richard Singleton, T. L. Stark, J. W. Swearengin, T. N. Talbert, T. H. Thacker, Charles Thomas, T. W. Vaughn, Jas. Wells, Richard Ward, Jno. Ward, M. B.

Ward, H. Winn, Geo. Wise, John B. Watts. Privates, 63; officers, 17; total, 80.

This company was afterwards known as Company "I," Second Regiment Cavalry, the last Captain of which was T. H. Clark. A roll made by Captain Clark since the war is on file in the Adjutant and Inspector General's office, and appears also in this book. Captain Clark, the last captain, is now living at Batesburg. M. C. Butler, first captain, United States Senator,—home at Edgefield.

COMPANY G, FIRST REGIMENT—GREGG'S.

A. P. Butler, Captain; promoted Major 12th May, 1864; Lieutenant Colonel 23rd May, 1864; served through. W. H. Holloway, First Lieutenant; promoted Captain 12th May, 1864; served through. F. W. Andrews, Second Liutenant· resigned December 1861. T. M. Wellborn, Third Lieutenant; promoted Second Lieutenant December, 1861; First Lieutenant 12th May, 1864. J. H. King, First Sergeant; elected Second Lieutenant, April, 1862; resigned 1863. Mark Mathews, Second Sergeant; promoted First Sergeant April, 1862. W. T. Scott, Third Sergeant; promoted Second Sergeant April, 1862; First Sergeant 1862. T. F. Williams. Fourth Sergeant; promoted Third Sergeant April, 1862; died 29th September, 1862, of wounds received at Second Manassas. I. C. Mays, Fifth Sergeant; promoted Fourth Sergeant April, 1862; Second Sergeant 1862; killed in battle at Gettysburg July 3rd, 1863. William J. Delph, First Corporal; promoted Fifth Sergeant April, 1862; Fourth Sergeant 1862; Sergeant Major 1863. D. C. Bullock, Second Corporal; furnished substitute December 14th, 1861. C. H. Gardiner, Third Corporal; promoted First Corporal April, 1862; killed on color guard at Manassas August 29th, 1862. W. L. Durst, Fourth Corporal; promoted Second Corporal April, 1862; Third Sergeant 29th September, 1862; Second Sergeant 3rd July, 1863; served through.

PRIVATES.

P. O. Ranson, promoted Third Corporal April, 1862; Fifth Sergeant September 29th, 1862; died of wounds received at Gettysburg. T. J. Howard, promoted Fourth Corporal April, 1862; discharged 1862. J. C. Tompkins, promoted First Corporal 29th August, 1862; Fourth Sergeant 29th September,

1862; Third Sergeant 3rd July, 1863. J. F. Harling, promoted Second Corporal 29th September, 1862; Fourth Sergeant 3rd July, 1863: lived through—Appomatox. J. T. White, promoted Fourth Corporal September 29th, 1862; Fifth Sergeant 3rd July, 1863; served through. T. M. Wilson, promoted Third Corporal 29th September, 1862. J. B. Rhodes, promoted First Corporal September 29th, 1862; supposed killed at Chancellorsville May 3rd, 1863. H. W. Holloway, promoted First Corporal 3rd July, 1863; supposed killed 1864 at Deep Bottom. G. W. Street, promoted Second Corporal July 3rd, 1863; F. P. Johnson, promoted Third Corporal July 3rd, 1863; L. P. Andrews; Simon Attaway, killed July 3rd, 1863, at Gettysburg; W. W. Bagwell, transferred to Seventh South Carolina Volunteers 1862; L. P. Boone; M. Brewer, surrendered April. 1865; J. W. Bryant; J. C. Bryant, discharged 1862; T. N. Brunson, lost leg at Second Manassas August 29th, 1862—discharged; E. N. Brunson; J. W. Brooks, died of wound received at Second Manassas 1862; L. W. Brooks; M. P. Burnett, died of disease May 18th, 1863; M. C. Burnett, transferred to Seventh South Carolina Volunteers 1862; H. Burnett, transferred to Seventh South Carolina Volunteers 1862; G. W. Blackwell; Peyton Burton; C. L. Burn, missing and supposed killed at Spottsylvania May, 1864; —— Cash, transferred to Company H, First South Carolina Volunteers; I. C. Corley, died of disease May 28th, 1862; W. V. Corley, surrendered at Appomattox 1865; E. W. Corley, died of disease August 16th, 1862; J. H. Carpenter; A. Chapman, surrendered at Appomattox; J. B. Collins, died of disease 27th July, 1862; Irwin Clegg, died 31st May, 1864, of wounds at the Wilderness May 5th, 1864; A. J. Clegg; J. M. Carter, died of disease 1864; J. M. Conally, died of disease December, 1862; W. B. Conally, surrendered at Appomattox; R. W. Conally, surrendered at Appomattox; E. R. Cunningham; Wallace J. Delph, promoted Sergeant Major May 1861; Lieutenant, Company "I," 1863; Captain 23rd May, 1864. R. W. Dorn, killed May 12th, 1864, at Spottsylvania; F. M. L. Duke; J. M. Fry, died of disease 1864; M. Floy, died of disease December 17th, 1863; G. W. Hancock; J. W. Hastings, died of disease July 1st, 1862; W. P. Hastings; John Horten, lost leg at Fredericksburg February 13th, 1863; Thomas Hall, died of disease July 6th, 1862;

Jasper Holly, killed in battle at Second Manassas August 29th, 1862; W. H. Holloway, Jr., killed in battle at Second Manassas August 29th, 1862; R. P. Holloway, surrendered Appomattox 1865; John C. Harris, furnished substitute December, 1861; L. F. Harris, transferred to Second South Carolina Cavalry; A. F. Harris; James Hardy; D. W. Jackson, surrendered April, 1865; S. P. Jones, died of disease June 30th, 1862; William Kennedy; W. G. Kernagham; B. R. Kimbrell, surrendered April, 1865; John Lamb, killed in battle at Fredericksburg February 13th, 1863; Barrel Lamb, killed in battle at Fredericksburg February 13th, 1863; John Lane, died of disease 1864; B. L. Minor; William Magill; George H. Maxwell, died of disease December 23rd, 1861; J. M. Mathews; F. B. Medicis, deserted 1861; Edmond Mills, killed in the battle of the Wilderness May 5th, 1864; R. S. Norris, surrendered April, 1865; Allen Norris, surrendered April, 1865; J. P. Pate, killed in battle at Cold Harbor June 27th, 1862; James Parkman; John Powell, died of disease June 3rd, 1862; B. F. Price, transferred to Seventh South Carolina Volunteers; J. R. Porter, killed at Spottsylvania May 12th, 1864; Samuel Porter, killed at Spottsylvania May 12th, 1864; T. J. Riley, surrendered April, 1865; S. M. Ross, served as Courier for General Wilcox part of 1863 and 1864; appointed Sergeant Signal Corps. James F. Lamb, surrendered Appomattox 1865; E. J. Rhodes; G. W. Richey; John Richardson; W. A. Sale, killed in battle at Gettysburg July 3rd, 1863; J. C. Shafer, killed in battle at Gettysburg July 3rd, 1863; Frank Schwartz, surrendered Appomattox; P. Spinall; P. Sharpton, lost an arm May 3rd, 1863, at Chancellorsville; J. H. Smith, killed at Cold Harbor June 27th, 1862; T. J. Smith, died of disease May 21st, 1862; G. W. Smith, died of wounds received at Chancellorsville May 5th, 1863; Mark Smith; G. W. Stewart, killed at Jerico Ford May 23rd, 1864; J. S. Stewart, killed August 25th, 1864, at Reams' Station; W. W. Stewart; T. J. Styron, died of disease May 28th, 1862; G. W. Seiley, killed at Cold Harbor June 27th, 1862; J. L. Taylor, surrendered Appomattox 1865; J. E. Taylor; Wiley Thompson; S. Thompkins, appointed Hospital Steward 1861; killed at Fredericksburg 1863. J. L. Turner, lost a leg at Gettysburg July 3rd, 1863; T. R. Tate, died April 1st, 1863, of wound received at Fredericksburg 1863;

J. R. Timmerman, died in Federal prison 1865; W. P. Vines; T. A. Walker, died May 31st, 1864, of wounds received at Wilderness May 5th, 1864; M. E. Walker, killed at Wilderness May 5th, 1864; T. M. Walker; J. C. Walker; E. G. Walker; G. M. Walker, died of disease in 1865; James Wooten, died of disease in 1865; Thomas White, died of disease August, 1864; J. C. Williams, killed at Cold Harbor June 27th, 1862; H. J. Williams, kill at Cold Harbor June 27th, 1862; T. H. Williams, killed at Gettysburg July 3rd, 1863; C. H. Wate, killed at Gettysburg July 3rd, 1863; T. A. Wate; David Wate, surrendered April, 1865; William Whatley, killed at Jericho Ford May 23rd, 1864; W. W. Whatley, died September 9th of wound received at Manassas August 29th, 1862; Thomas Weeks, lost a leg at Gettysburg July 3rd, 1863. Total rank and file, 138. Killed in battle, 26; died of wounds, 9; died of disease, 19; in Union prison, 1; total, 55.

Loss very heavy, considerably over one-third. This list was furnished by Colonel A. P. Butler and copied by Sergeant Major William J. Delph.

COMPANY E, FIRST REGIMENT—GREGG'S.

D. B. Goggans last Captain.

Alexander P. McCarty, Corporal; age twenty-five; killed at Chancellorsville May 3rd, 1863. Pinkney Bradley, age forty; discharged at Appomattox. Newton F. Corley, age twenty-three; discharged at Appomattox. William Hyler, age twenty-three; abandoned service without leave. John Perry, age twenty-five; surrendered at Appomattox. Benjamin Perry, age eighteen; surrendered at Appomattox. Peter B. Ramage, age twenty-one; died of disease at Fredericksburg. Virginia, December 1862.

COMPANY H, THIRD REGIMENT.

A. A. Werts, wounded at Savage Station; living. Alfred Werts, wounded. Jesse Werts, discharged; disabled; living.

As instances of the splendid and heroic bravery of the men and boys composing the First South Carolina Regiment, Gregg's, and as facts in its history I insert the following. The writer is Theodore Roosevelt in the Cosmopolitan for December 1892.

GAINES MILL.

"At the battle of Gaines Mill (Cold Harbor) Gregg's First South Carolina Regiment formed part of the attacking force. The resistance was desperate and the fury of the assault unsurpassed. At one point it fell to the lot of this Regiment to bear the brunt of carrying a strong position—moving forward at a run, the South Carolinians were swept by a fierce and consuming fire. Young James Taylor, a lad of sixteen, was carrying the flag, and was killed after being shot down three times, twice rising and struggling on with the colors. The third time he fell the flag was seized by George Cotchett, and when he in turn fell, by Shubrick Hayne. Hayne also was struck down almost immediately; and a fourth lad—for none were over twenty years old—grasped the colors and fell mortally wounded across the body of his friend. The fifth, Gadsden Holmes, was pierced with no less than seven balls. The sixth man, Dominick Spellman, more fortunate, but not less brave, bore the flag throughout the rest of the battle."

COMPANY E, SEVENTH REGIMENT.

Made by J. B. Suddath and J. C. H. Rauch, Sergeants, from memory—November 1893. David Denny, Captain; served one year, resigned; too old. James Mitchell, Captain; served through the war. Lieutenant W. A. Rutland; killed in battle. Lieutenant James Pinson. Lieutenant W. J. Denny, killed in battle. Orderly Sergeant J. C. H. Rauch. Sergeant J. B. Suddath. Sergeant A. W. Denny. Sergeant M. W. Coleman. Sergeant Edward Mitchell, killed in battle. Corporal John Pou, killed in battle. Coporal L. A. Smith, killed in battle. Corporal U. B. McGee, killed in battle. Corporal Emanuel Padgett, killed in battle.

PRIVATES.

Henry Black; Jacob Black, killed in battle; Paul Black, Willis Crouch, T. B. Crouch, Hillery Crouch, J. L. Crouch, Robert Crouch, Milledge Crouch, Eli Crout, J. M. Corley, Jacob Corley; Frank Corley, killed in battle; Wm. M. Cooner, killed in battle; John Chapman; Robert Cash, killed in battle; G. W. Denny, died in hospital; J. O. Denny, J. M. Denny, John Derrick, James Douglas; William Douglas, died during the war; William Etheredge, Sr., William Etheredge, Jr.,

Noah Etheredge, Henry C. Etheredge, Joab Edwards; Joseph Geiger, died during the war; David Geiger, William Goodwin; Joseph Goff, died during the war; Caleb W. Hughes; John Inabnet, died during the war; Wright Little, killed in battle; Alfred Maroney; Luke Lott, died early in the war; Paul Mitchell, killed in battle; W. A. Mitchell, John Mitchell, James Minnick, J. W. Merchant; D. D. W. McCarty, died during the war; John McLendon, killed in battle; Richard Parson, John R. Pinson, J. Robert Pou, Emri Padgett, William Ridlehoover; Frank Rodgers, killed in battle; James C. Ramage, died during the war; William Ridgell, died during the war; John Ridgell, Daniel Ridgell; Thomas Story, died during the war; G. W. Smith, Louis L. Smith; James H. Smith, killed in battle; W. W. Smith, died during the war; John Shealey, died during the war; Abram Shealey, died during the war; Adam Shealy, died during the war; W. E. Sample, died during the war; James Salter, James Thompson; Joseph Thompson, killed in battle; J. T. Vansant, died during the war; Washington Venters, M. B. Watson, J. L. Watson, Nicholas Watson, Riden Walker, William Whittle; John Yarbrough, died during the war; Michel Yarbrough, died during the war. Officers, 15; privates, 73; total, 88; killed in battle, 18; died during the war, 22; total, 40.

This loss is very heavy.

Elsewhere a copy of the original roll of Capt. David Denny's Company is given as it was formed in 1861. At the re-organization at the end of the year, Captain Denny, being too old resigned, and two companies were formed. Company M with E. J. Goggans Captain, and Company E with James Mitchell Captain. Captain Denny died long ago. Captain Mitchell died in 1893; Captain Goggans still lives, November 1893.

COMPANY F, SEVENTH REGIMENT INFANTRY.

This roll was prepared by Lieutenant B. W. Hard, of Graniteville, October 20th, 1883. Many of the names are marked as from "Aiken" County, a county which had no existence during the war, so I am compelled to include all in the roll, whether from Edgefield or elsewhere, as it is impossible for me to tell who in Aiken went from Barnwell and who from Edgefield.

John S. Hard, age 19, Captain,· Edgefield.; promoted·to Major September, 1862, and killed at Chickamauga. James E. Rearden, age 23, Captain, . Edgefield; killed·at Chickamauga; wounded at Sharpsburg; promoted from Third to Second and First Lieutenant and Captain. Warren D. Brooks, age 19, Captain, Edgefield; killed at the Battle of the Wilderness; promoted from Second Sergeant to Third, Second, and First Lieutenant and Captain. Benjamin A. McKibbin, age 21, Captain, Marion; wounded at Cold Harbor; promoted from the ranks to First Sergeant and Third Lieutenant and Captain. Thomas F. Jennings, age 31, First Lieutenant, Edgefield; re-signed at reorganization—living. John B. Gregg, age 22, Second Lieutenant, Edgefield; died of disease at Charlottes-ville. James C. Sentell, age 30, Second Lieutenant, Edgefield; elected at the reorganization; resigned—ill health—living. George W. Baker, age 24, Second Lieutenant, Edgefield; wounded at Sharpsburg in two places; elected Third Lieuten-ant at reorganization and promoted; resigned—ill health—living. Lawrence W. Wise, age 28. Third Lieutenant, Edge-field; killed at home; promoted from Third Sergeant. B. W. Hard, age 28. Third Lieutenant, Edgefield; promoted from the ranks—living. N. D. Matheny, age 42, First Sergeant, Edge-field; discharged at Rocky Run—living. T. Gulledge, age 30, First Sergeant, Edgefield; discharged at Richmond—living. Jefferson Davis, age 25, First Sergeant, Edgefield; died of disease at Richmond. Hampton H. Howard, age 21, First Sergeant, Edgefield; wounded at Sharpsburg; promoted from Corporal—living. Robert J. Cobb, age 21, First Sergeant, Edgefield; wounded at Gettysburg; promoted from the ranks. H. Mandring Stevens, age 19, Corporal, Edgefield; living. William E. Rearden, age 21, Corporal, Edgefield; killed at Sharpsburg. George E. Atkinson, age 24, Corporal, Edge-field; living. Marion Odom, age 27, Corporal, Edgefield; died of disease at Richmond. Robert N. Rearden, age 22, Corporal, Edgefield; wounded at Maryland Heights—lost a finger—living.

PRIVATES.

John L. Atkinson, age 26, Edgefield, died of disease at home; J. Riley Aulmond, age 19, Edgefield, living; Thomas

Aulmond, age 22, Edgefield, living; Mike B. Arthur, age 18, Edgefield, living; Elisha Baggott, age 24, Edgefield, living; William Becks, age 25, Barnwell, living; John Brown, age 24, Spartanburg, living; Jeff Brown, age 22, Spartanburg, living; Milledge Brown, age 23, Spartanburg, living; L. P. Bagwell, age 30, Spartanburg, living; James A. Brewer, age 18, Aiken, living; Isaac Brooks, age 18, Aiken, killed in battle at the Wilderness; Lawrence Bland, age 19, Aiken, living; Robert Brooks, age 32, Aiken, living; Wilson Carroll, age 21, Aiken, wounded at Sharpsburg, living; James A. Cartin, age 30, Aiken, died of disease at home; Robert Cushman, age 22, Barnwell, died of disease at home; Wilson Cash, age 22, Abbeville, wounded at Sharpsburg, living; George Cochràn, age 18, Aiken, living; John Corley, age 19, Aiken, wounded at Wilderness, living; R. J. Cobb, Fifth Sergeant, already named; Hardy Clark, age 19, Aiken, discharged or surrendered at Richmond; Robert Donald, age 21, Aiken, wounded at Winchester, died of disease at home; Edward Dinkins, age 22, Aiken, living; Benjamin Davis, age 32, Aiken, living; John Duncan, age 22, Aiken, living; Reuben Duncan, age 21, Aiken, died of disease at home; Jeff Davis, age 25, Aiken, died of disease at Richmond; Benjamin Duncan, age 18, Aiken, killed at Fredericksburg; William Ellis, age 30, Aiken, died of disease at home, wounded at Fredericksburg; P. A. Friday, age 21, Aiken, wounded at Gettysburg, lost a finger, living; Tillman Faulkner, age 23, Aiken, discharged at Flint Hill, living; William P. Faulkner, age 28, Aiken, discharged at Flint Hill, living; Allen Franklin, age 30, Aiken, discharged at Richmond, living; Peter Fagin, age 29, Aiken, died of disease at Richmond; William German, age 23, Aiken, died of disease at Richmond, wounded at Fredericksburg; Henry Gulledge, age 21, Aiken, living; William Gulledge, age 18, Aiken, living; John Gissue, age 21, Aiken, living; Caloway K. Henderson, age 20, Aiken, living; John C. Hall, age 25, Spartanburg, wounded at Sharpsburg, living; William P. Hammett, age, 24, Spartanburg, living; William Hatcher, age 18, Aiken, living; Seaborn Hamiston, age 31, Aiken, living; Jesse Jackson, age 18, Aiken, discharged at Richmond, living; James Jackson, age 21, Aiken, wounded at Maryland Heights, lost an arm, living; David L. Johnson, age 21, Aiken, living;

Ezekiel Johnson, age 23, Aiken, died of disease at Fredericksburg; Adolphus L. Johnson, age 18, Aiken, wounded at Savage Station, discharged at Richmond, living; William J. Kirksey, age 22, Aiken; James A. Key, age 19, Aiken, wounded at North Anna River, living; James Kadle, age 20, Aiken, died of wounds at Gettysburg; Washington Leach, age 28, Aiken, living; William Leopard, age 29, Aiken, discharged at Richmond, living; Levy Littleton, age 19, Aiken; William Lawrence, age 22, Aiken, living; Elijah Leopard, age 31, Aiken, died of disease at home; John Maddox, age 21, Aiken; Green Maddox, age 20, Aiken, living; John Medlock, age 24, Aiken, died of disease at Richmond; Mark Maddox, age 19, Aiken, wounded at Gettysburg, lost a leg, living; Benjamin Medlock, age 19, Aiken, discharged at Richmond, living; Bogan Maddox, age 18, Aiken; Isaac W. McKee, age 28, Anderson, wounded at Sharpsburg, living; William Myers, age 29; Julius W. McGee, age 19, Anderson, killed at Maryland Heights; Walter McKinsey, age 28, Aiken, died of wounds at Knoxville; Martin Mathis, age 25, Spartanburg, living; Morgan Mathis, age 27, Spartanburg, living; Martin McKinnie, age 31, Spartanburg, living; Judson McGee, age 22, Spartanburg, living; Joseph New, age 20, Aiken, living; Edward New, age 27, Aiken, discharged at Richmond, living; John New, age 18, Aiken, living; Julius Overstreet, age 21, Aiken; John D. Price, age 30, Aiken, wounded at Maryland Heights, died since the war; George W. Platt, age 21, Aiken, living; Arthur Parker, age 18, Aiken, killed at Malvern Hill in battle; Lawrence Prescott, age 24, Aiken; George Perdue, age 29, killed at home since the war; John Parker, age 18, Aiken, died of disease at Richmond; Thomas Price, age 18, Aiken, discharged at Richmond, living; Smith F. Radford, age 19, Aiken, living; James A. Ramsey, age 24, Aiken, died of wounds at North Anna River; Matt Ramsey, age 20, Aiken discharged at Richmond, living; Ed. Rannald, age 21, Aiken, wounded at Cold Harbor; Benjamin Sharpton, age 19, Aiken, died of wounds at Cold Harbor; William Smith, age 19, Aiken; E. Seigler, age 18, Aiken, discharged at Richmond; Edwin Stringfield, age 22, Aiken, discharged at Richmond; Aquilla S. Seigler, age 22, Aiken, living; William B. Sorger, age 21, Aiken, living; Ben. F. Sorger, age 21, Aiken, living; John

Seitzes, age 35, Aiken, died at Frederick City of wounds received at Sharpsburg; Harry Turner, age 20, Aiken, wounded
at Fisherville, died since the war; Thomas P. Tollison, age 29,
Aiken, died since the war; James A. Taylor, age 22, Aiken,
wounded at Chickamauga, living; Benjamin F. Taylor, age 20,
Aiken, killed in battle at Savage Station; Hampton Wade,
died of disease in hospital; W. D. West, died of disease at
home; Wm. A. West, living; William Walker, living; Adolphus
Walker, living. Total rank and file, 123. The name of Jefferson Davis appears twice, once as First Sergeant, once as
private. Killed in battle, 9; died of wounds, 5; died of disease, 18; total, 32.

The name of James Kadle appears on this roll. Is any one
now living in Edgefield named Kadle?

Edgefield Chronicle, March 11th, 1896:

SERGEANT DICK CLARY'S WAR LIST.

DEAR CHRONICLE: The famous old Seventh Regiment, of
which your gallant old uncle, Colonel Thomas G. Bacon, was
the first leader, must always be of deep interest to you, as well
as to all Edgefield and Saluda. Therefore I send you the following list. Let us keep these brave names from being forgotten. I send you a list of soldiers who died or were killed during the late war, from 1861 to 1865, in Company G., Seventh
South Carolina Volunteers:

Died.—George Hudson, Toles Attaway, Fletcher Graddick,
James May, George Clark, George Neal, William Neal, Lieu-
tenant George Strother, Car Williams, Joe Griffin, Robert
Bryan, Carter Burnett, Hix Holloway, Jack Whatley, John
Crouch, William Bagwell, William Burton, Lit Wooten, John
Shafer, Dick Stevens, Frank Dean. Total, 21.

Killed in battle.—Henry Steadham, Jim Steadman, Tink
Williams, William Dees, Captain William Clark, Caleb Walton,
Jim Burnett, Sim Adams, Joe Wright, J. C. Nox, W. Nox,
C. N. Nox, John Turnipseed, John Bolton, Thomas Aiton,
Art Bryant, John Hollingsworth, Tink Jay, Captain John
Kemp, Jim Quattlebaum, Wesley Wright, Wiley Dodgin,
William Coleman, Thomas Burt. Total, 24.

This copy of roll of Company G, Seventh Regiment, is

taken from Edgefield Chronicle of September 13th, 1893.   By whom made and when does not appear:

COMPANY G, SEVENTH SOUTH CAROLINA INFANTRY.

W. E. Clark, Captain; J. W. Kemp, First Lieutenant; J. W. Williams, Second Lieutenant; J. W. Eidson, Third Lieutenant; R. C. Strother, First Sergeant; B. L. Youngblood, Second Sergeant; Artemus Bryant, Third Sergeant; M. Ouzts, Fourth Sergeant; Simeon Adams, Fifth Sergeant; R. C. Clary, First Corporal; J. R. Wright, Second Corporal; T. N. Durst, Third Corporal; D. R. Coleman, Fourth Corporal; J. C. Rambo, Fifth Corporal; Thos. Aiton, Sixth Corporal.

PRIVATES.

J. S. Aiton, W. G. Aiton, B. F. Boone, Wm. Bagwell, L. Berry, J. F. Boulware, H. Burnett, James Burnett, Carter Burnett, W. M. Bolton, D. R. Crouch, John Crouch, William Coleman, V. A. Clark, W. A. Crawford, H. C. Dodgen, Wiley Dodgen, Herlong Dorn, Jesse Duffee, William Leese, Frank Dean, Wm. Eidson, Lark Eidson, G. Ferguson, G. W. Grant, M. A. Griffith, A. B. Griffith, J. B. Gasperson, Abney Hargrove, Joe Hamilton, W. M. Head, J. N. Hollingsworth, Hix Holloway, Dr. D. P. Holloway, John Jay, Fink Jay, Wm. King, W. A. Manus, A. P. Nox, J. B. Nox, T. J. Nox, S. T. Nox, Jas. Quattlebaum, Wm. Rushton, Sr., Wm. Rushton, Jr., G. R. Reeves, Ralph Smith, W. S. Steiffle, J. R. Sentell, F. A. Townsend, Amon Stallworth, Sergeant Major; Henry Steadham, Jas. Steadman, Ira Turner, John Turnipseed, J. Willingham, Pink West, Wm. Wright, Wesley Wright, Joe Wright, Pinkney Williams, Press Williams, Caleb Walton, Jack Whatley.

COMPANY G, SEVENTH REGIMENT

April 1st, 1861, from Upper Battalion, Tenth South Carolina Militia.

J. H. Brooks, Captain; W. E. Clark, First Lieutenant; H. C. King, Second Lieutenant; G. J. Strother, Third Lieutenat; John W. Kemp, First Sergeant; B. L. Youngblood, Second Sergeant; H. C. Culbreath, Third Sergeant; J. W. Griffin, Fourth Sergeant; Carr S. Williams, Fifth Sergeant; M. W. Clary, First Corporal; J. M. Proctor, Second Corporal; J. W. Eidson, Third Corporal; B. G. Smith, Fourth Corporal;

R. H. Holloway, Fifth Corporal; R. S. Burnett, Sixth Corporal.

PRIVATES.

Simeon Adams, Towles Attaway, C. Attaway, W. J. Aiton, T. L. Aiton, J. F. Boleware, T. N. Brunson, A. M. Bryan, L. Brooks, L. J. Brooks, M. P. Burkhalter, J. F. Burnett, George Clark, V. A. Clark, R. C. Clary, John Chaver, O. R. Crouch, J. S. Coleman, M. W. Coleman, A. C. Dees, S. P. DeLoach, William Dogan, H. C. Dogan, T. N. Durst, John F. Frie, J. W. Gentry, Jonathan Gregory, A. B. Griffith, J. P. Hamilton, J. W. Hardy, Isaiah Haltiwanger, D. P. Holloway, J. A. Hollingworth, G. W. Hudson, W. D. King, Levi Koon, Barret Lamb, R. S. Leek, W. Leek, James A. May, B. L. Murrell, J. W. Neill, W. M. Neill, Wm. L. Owdom, G. W. Perdue, W C. Palmer, J. C. Rambo, J. M. Riley, J. B. Rhodes, William Reese, James Robinson, James Roton, Grant Smith, J. W. Smith, S. S. Smith, A. C. Stalworth, Henry Stedham, J. C. Stedham, H. S. Stefle, B. F. Stevens, J. C. Strother, John Thompkins, F. A. Townsend, G. W. Turner, S. Turner, W. S. Wallington, E. P. Walker, James Webb, William Wheeler, J. P. Watley, H. J. Williams, J. C. Williams, W. P. Williams, T. H. Williams, Pinkney Williams, Whit Williams, J. R. Wright, L. Wooten, Densly Youngblood, William Youngblood, J. S. Aiton. Commissioned offices, 4; non-commissioned officers, 11; privates, 82; total, 97.

XXXVI.

On the roll of Company "C," Seventh Regiment, South Carolina Volunteers, I find the names of William Benson, age 18, Edgefield, served to close of the war; James Harrison, age 18, Edgefield.

CAPTAIN BENJAMIN ROPER'S COMPANY I, SEVENTH REGIMENT.

Muster roll of Captain Benjamin Roper's Company I of the Seventh Regiment of South Carolina Volunteers, D. Wyatt, Aiken, Colonel, received at office of Adjutant and Inspector General, April 14th, 1863, showing the condition of the Company, July 23rd, 1862, I have no roll made up since the war.

Benjamin Roper, Captain, entered service 15th April at Charleston, S. C., received by the Authorities of South Carolina for twelve months, absent, sick; B. F. Sharpton, First Lieutenant, entered service 15th April, at Charleston, South Carolina, received by the authorities of South Carolina, was promoted from Second Lieutenant, July 3rd; W. Parkman, Second Lieutenant, entered service 11th September, at Flint Hill, Virginia; received by Colonel Bacon, was promoted from Third Lieutenant, July 3rd; W. E. Middleton, Third Lieutenant, entered service 15th April, at Charleston, South Carolina, received by the authorities of South Carolina, was elected Third Lieutenant July 18th; J. A. Mathis, First Sergeant, same record as W. E. Middleton, absent, sick, furlough; G. W. Holmes, Second Sergeant, same record as W. E. Middleton, present; N. L. Broadwater, Third Sergeant, same record as W. E. Middleton, present; E. J. Anderson, Fourth Sergeant, same record as W. E. Middleton, present; W. W. Bussey, Fifth Sergeant, same record as W. E. Middleton, absent, sick; S. Holmes, First Corporal, same record as W. E. Middleton, present; Thomas Harling, Second Corporal, received 4th June at Butler, S. C., by Major Evans, present; J. S. McKie, Third Corporal, received 15th April at Charleston, S. C., by authorities of South Carolina, present; J. Briggs, Fourth Corporal, same record, present.

PRIVATES.

P. H. Broadwater, same record, but absent on sick furlough; S. Broadwater, same record, present; J. W. Bartley, received June 4th, same authorities, absent sick furlough; M. Calliham, received 6th August, Flint Hill, Va., by Colonel Bacon, present; G. W. Clay, received 4th June, Butler, S. C., by Major Evans, absent without leave; T. G. Green, received 15th April at Charleston, S. C., by authorities of South Carolina, present; W. H. Garrett, received 15th April at Charleston, S. C., by authorities of South Carolina, extra daily duty in Q. M. Department; W. W. Jennings, received 15th April at Charleston, S. C., by authorities South Carolina, present; E. O. Morgan, received 6th August at Flint Hill, Va., by Colonel Bacon, sick at hospital; J. McDaniel, received 15th April at Charleston, S. C., by authorities of South Carolina, present; H. Mathis, received 15th April at Charleston, S. C., by authorities of South Carolina, present; W. A. B. Newson, received 15th April at Charleston, S. C., by authorities of South Carolina, present; A. J. Prince, received 11th September at Flint Hill, Va., by Colonel Bacon, present; P. N. Presley, received 15th April at Charleston, S. C., by authorities of South Carolina, present; J. Roper, received 15th April at Charleston, S. C., by authorities of South Carolina, sick in hospital; J. Sharpton, received same, extra daily duty as teamster; G. W. Vance, received 15th April at Charleston, S. C., by authorities of South Carolina, present; W. W. Wash, received 15th April at Charleston, S. C., by authorities of South Carolina, present; J. Whitcombe, received 15th April at Charleston, S. C., by authorities of South Carolina, present.

The following were entered on the roll as "discharged," and then the entries crossed:

W. F. Prescott, Captain; J. P. Nixon, First Lieutenant; R. H. Middleton, Second Sergeant; Thos. Evans, private; Thos. McKie, private; Charles Wiseman, private; G. W. Morgan, private.

Transferred, also crossed.—T. W. Grafton, private; Thomas Hammond, private; W. L. Holmes, First Sergeant; W. J. Holmes, First Sergeant.

Died, also crossed.—R. Brooks, private; A. J. Briggs, private; J. T. Buse, private.

Total rank and file on the roll, 32; one absent without leave; several sick.

COMPANY K, SEVENTH REGIMENT.

Muster roll of Company "K," John F. Bowers, Captain, showing the condition of the company July 23rd, 1862. At this date, April, 1892, I have no other roll—failed to find any in the office in Columbia:

John F. Bowers, Captain, present; J. L. Talbert, First Lieutenant, absent on furlough; J. M. Berry, Second Lieutenant, absent; wounded at Manchester—hospital. J. A. Cheatham, Third Lieutenant, present; O. T. Culbreath, First Sergeant; received into service April 15th, 1861, for one year by Major Evans; absent on furlough. A. N. Martin, Second Sergeant, absent; wounded at Manchester—hospital. W. M. Reynolds, Third Sergeant, present; L. W. Lanier, Fourth Sergeant, absent; wounded; home on furlough. C. M. Burress, Fifth Sergeant, present; J. W. Reynolds, First Corporal, present; L. D. Shipley, Second Corporal, present; W. G. White, Third Corporal, present; T. R. Williams, Fourth Corporal, present.

PRIVATES.

B. O. Adams, present; J. E. Blake, present; T. A. Cartledge, present; T. M. Crafton, present; W. L. Coleman, present; G. R. Coleman, absent, wounded at Manchester—hospital; John Culbreath, present; Anthony Deal, present; C. L. Devore, present; J. A. Franks, present; C. T. Hammond, present; C. H. Harrison, absent, sick at hospital—unknown; J. T. Henderson, present; J. E. Henderson, present; W. L. Holmes, absent on sick furlough; A. J. Holmes, present; H. Howell, present; T. B. Lanier, absent, wounded, at home on furlough, left arm amputated at shoulder; O. W. Lanier, present; C. H. Limbecker, present; J. L. Lockridge, present; J. H. Mayson, absent, sick at Manchester Hospital; H. M. Quarles, absent on furlough, sick; J. C. Reynolds, present; E. W. Reynolds, absent on furlough, sick; T. J. Rountree, present; F. P. Rush, present; G. S. Stalnaker, absent, wounded, at Manchester Hospital, right arm amputated above elbow; J. R. Stalnaker, present; J. W. Stalnaker, present; G. H. Timmerman, present; J. R. Williams, present; W. B. Wood, absent on sick furlough; W. H. Yeldell, present. Total rank and file, 47.

COMPANY M, SEVENTH REGIMENT.

Muster roll of Company "M," Seventh Regiment, South Carolina Volunteers, showing the condition of the company on July 23rd, 1862, Jerry Goggans, Captain. All were enlisted by Captain Goggans for the period of two years:

Jerry Goggans, Captain, Februarry 11th, McLean's Farm, absent on furlough; J. R. Bouknight, First Lieutenant, February 11th, McLean's Farm, wounded at Richmond; J. C. McCelvey, Second Lieutenant, February 11th, McLean's Farm, present; A. P. Bouknight, Third Lieutenant, February 11th, McLean's Farm, present; T. H. Huiett, First Sergeant, February 11th, McLean's Farm, absent with leave; J. J. McDaniel, Second Sergeant, March 26th, South Carolina, present; W. A. Whittle, Third Sergeant, February 11th, McLean's Farm, present; J. H. Watson, Fourth Sergeant, February 11th, McLean's Farm, present; W. Ruston, Fifth Sergeant, February 11th, McLean's Farm, present; Jacob Huiett, First Corporal, February 11th, McLean's Farm, present; A. L. Wyse, Second Corporal, 11th February, McLean's Farm, wounded at Capital; B. F. Sample, Third Corporal, February 11th, McLean's Farm, present; G. Jennings, Fourth Corporal, February 11th, McLean's Farm, present.

PRIVATES.

H. Barnes, March 17th, South Carolina, present; J. Bedenbaugh, March 17th, South Carolina, present; L. Bedenbaugh, May 1st, Yorktown, sick at Camp Winder; T. Bedenbaugh, May 1st, Yorktown, sick at Brigade Infirmary; A. S. Bouknight, February 11th, McLean's Farm, present; S. J. Bouknight, May 17th, South Carolina, present; N. Bouknight, March 17th, South Carolina, sick at Manchester; J. Buzhardt, March 17th, South Carolina, present; P. Charles, South Carolina, March 17th, present; H. Duffie, March 17th, South Carolina, present; J. Duffie, February 11th, McLean's Farm, present; V. Duffie, February 11th, McLean's Farm, present; A. Duncan, February 11th, McLean's Farm, present; V. Duncan, February 11th, McLean's Farm, present; W. Faban, March 17th, South Carolina, present; R. Gunter, March 17th, South Carolina, sick at Manchester; J. Gunter, February 11th, McLean's Farm, detailed Ordnance Guard; P. Goff, March

17th, South Carolina, present; J. Gibson, March 17th, South Carolina, sick at Petersburg; W. Gibson, March 17th, South Carolina, sick at Petersburg; W. Harris, February 11th, McLean's Farm, present; S. Harris, February 11th, McLean's Farm, present; D. Henson, February 11th, McLean's Farm, present; J. Henson, February 11th, McLean's Farm, present; I. Inabinet, February 11th, McLean's Farm, sick at Manchester; G. Lippard, March 17th, South Carolina, present; J. Lippard, March 17th, South Carolina, sick at Farmville; V. Livingston, March 17th, South Carolina, sick at Petersburg; E. Matthews, March 17th, South Carolina, present; J. Miller, March 17th, South Carolina, sick at Camp Winder; T. Merchant, May 1st, Yorktown, present; M. Mitchell, June 17th, South Carolina, present; G. Martin, February 11th, McLean's, present; A. Padgett, February 11th, McLean's, present; D. Parmer, March 17th, South Carolina, sick at Manchester; J. Rotten, February 11th, McLean's, wounded, gone home on furlough; D. Rushton, February 11th, McLean's, sick at Petersburg; H. Rushton, February 11th, McLean's, present; J. Rushton, April 15th, Yorktown, present; J. Saddler, March 17th, South Carolina, sick at Petersburg; W. Saddler, February 11th, McLean's, present; B. Smith, February 11th, McLean's, present; W. Spann, May 1st, Yorktown, present; P. Spann, February 11th, McLean's, present; M. Shealy, June 1st, South Carolina, present; W. Watson, May 1st, Yorktown, present; J. Wise, February 11th, McLean's, present; W. Wise, March 17th, South Carolina, present; M. Whittle, March 17th, South Carolina, sick at Farmville, Virginia; B. Wright, May 1st, Yorktown, sick at Farmville, Virginia. Total rank and file, 63.

AN OLD CONFEDERATE "FURLOUGH."

Edgefield Chronicle:

Many of our readers have never seen a "furlough" and will no doubt be interested in a perusal of the following. It is a bona fide document, as we have it direct from the hands of the private soldier named in it. The names of all the officers from Longstreet commanding the department to Lieutenant Bouknight commanding the company are quite familiar names to Edgefield people.

FURLOUGH.

To all whom it may concern:

The bearer hereof, B. C. W. Matthews, private of Captain Goggan's company, Infantry, Seventh South Carolina Regiment, aged twenty-nine years, five feet six inches high, light complexion, blue eyes, and dark hair, and by profession a farmer, born in the District of Edgefield, State of South Carolina, and enlisted at Edgefield Court House, July 1st, 1862, to serve for the period of two years, and re-enlisted February, 1864, for the war, is hereby permitted to go to Edgefield District, South Carolina, he having received a furlough from the —— day of —— to the —— day of —— at which period he will rejoin his company or regiment at Bristol, Tenn., or wherever it may be, or be considered a deserter.

Subsistence has been furnished to said B. C. W. Matthews from —— day of —— to the —— day of —— and pay to the first day of November, both inclusive.

Given under my hand at Bristol this 6th day of April, 1864.

A. P. BOUKNIGHT,
Lieut. Com'd'g Co. "M", Seventh South Carolina Reg't.

———

The applicant desires to visit home to look after his family interests, he having a wife and three children who need his attention.

He is also deeply involved in some estates of which he is administrator—they being unsettled and in a state demanding some immediate personal attention.

A better soldier never shouldered a gun. He has not lost a day, or missed a roll call since he has been in the service. His case certainly merits all attention and reward, and I earnestly recommend that this application be granted.

A. P. BOUKNIGHT,
Lieut. Com'd'g Co. "M", Seventh South Carolina Reg't.

———

CAMP SEVENTH SOUTH CAROLINA REG'T,
April 6th, 1864.

Private B. C. W. Matthews, Company "M", Seventh South Carolina Regiment.

Special application for furlough to visit home to attend to

important business. The application is specially recommended on account of his high soldierly qualities, by his company officers.

Approved.

A. P. BOUKNIGHT,
Lieut. Com'd'g Co. "M", Seventh South Carolina Reg't.

HEADQUARTERS SEVENTH SOUTH CAROLINA REG'T, }
April 6th, 1864. }

In consideration of the high character of the soldier, I respectfully forward.

Approved.

BENJAMIN ROPER,
Capt'n. Com'd'g. Reg't.

HEADQUARTERS KERSHAW'S BRIGADE, }
April 6th, 1864. }

Respectfully forwarded.
Approved.

JOHN D. KENNEDY,
Col..Com'd'g Brigade.

DIVISION HEADQUARTERS, }
April 7th, 1864. }

Respectfully forwarded.
Approved.

W. S. WOFFORD,
Brigrdier Com'd'g Div.

HEADQUARTERS DEP'T. EAST TENN., }
April 8th, 1864. }

Respectfully returned, approved, in consideration of the excellent character of this soldier.

By command of

LIEUT. GEN. LONGSTREET.

COMPANY A, NINETEENTH REGIMENT.

Roll of Company "A," Nineteenth Regiment, South Carolina Volunteers:

Tillman Watson, Captain, age —; promoted Major February, 1862. Perry E. Watson, Captain, age 50; promoted from First Lieutenant; was not re-elected at reorganization in 1862. Elijah W. Horne, Captain, age 32; wounded at Atlanta; elected Second Lieutenant February, 1862; elected Captain at reorganization in 1862; retired by his own request 1865. Ezekiel Randall, age 16; promoted from the ranks to Second Lieutenant in 1862, to First Lieutenant 1864, to Captain in 1865. Levi Lybrand, First Lieutenant, age 48; promoted from Second to First Lieutenant February, 1862; resigned 1863. Seaborn E. Watson, Second Lieutenant, age 25; was not re-elected at reorganization 1862. John T. Norris, Second Lieutenant, age 21; wounded at Murfreesboro, Tenn., and died of his wounds at Chattanooga; promoted from ranks 1862. Cornelius J. W. Kreeps; Second Lieutenant, age 22; killed at Atlanta, Ga., July 22nd, 1864; promoted from ranks to Sergeant to Second Lieutenant in 1864. Abe. W. Rutland, Second Lieutenant, age 18; promoted from ranks to Sergeant and to Second Lieutenant 1864. Willis L. Creed, Second Lieutenant, age 24; same record as Rutland. Wyatt H. Haney, age 30, First Sergeant; detached. J. H. A. Williams, age 19, Sergeant. Morgan D. Bodie, age 19, Sergeant; promoted from ranks; died of disease at Knoxville. J. R. Padgett, age 28, Sergeant; promoted from ranks; wounded at Murfreesboro. Hiram Cato, age 20, Sergeant; killed in battle, New Hope Church. James S. A. Satcher, age 18, Sergeant. Alfred A. Pardue, age 35, Sergeant; died of disease in hospital. Henry Dunton, age 50, Sergeant; discharged Tupelo, Miss. J. C. Mitchell, age 18, Sergeant. Lewis V. Claxton, age 21, Sergeant; wounded at Chickamauga; captured at Atlanta. H. Elsey Lybrand, age 22, Sergeant; wounded at Chickamauga; died of the wound in hospital. Solomon Douglass, age 35, Corporal; wounded at Nashville, Tenn. Julius Howard, age 20, Corporal; died of disease in hospital 1862. J. Ellis Creed, age 30, Corporal; promoted from ranks; died of disease in hospital 1862. William Creed, age 32, Corporal; promoted from ranks. Jeter W. Crim, age 23, Corporal; promoted from ranks; captured at Missionary Ridge. Isaac B. Randall, age 30, Corporal; wounded at Atlanta, Ga. George W. Morris, age 20, Corporal. Burton Williams, age 24, Corporal; promoted from ranks; died in hospital 1863.

PRIVATES.

Jefferson J. Asbill, age 30, died of disease at Danville, Kentucky; Loy P. Asbill, age 32, died of disease at Wildcat Mountain, Ky., 1862; Isaac Bush, age 40, discharged at Shelleyville, Tenn.; Washington W. Bush, age 28, wounded at Missionary Ridge, Tenn., died of wounds at Atlanta; Wm. Burges Bush, age 24, died of disease at Chattanooga, Tenn.; John H. Barton, age 26; J. Burgess Barton, age 22, surrendered at Atlanta 1865; James E. Boothe, age 21, surrendered at South Mountain, Ala.; Benjamin Boothe, age 35, surrendered at Atlanta, Ga.; William Braswell, age 23, died of disease at Charleston, S. C.; Peter Brannon, age 40, discharged Lovejoy Station, Ga.; Wiley Bodie, age 40, died of disease at Augusta, Ga.; John M. Cato, age 22, wounded at Chickamauga and Marietta; Whitfield Cato, age 17; J. Preston Cammeron, age 23, captured at Atlanta, not heard from since; James P. Cullum, age 19; William Cullum, age 45, captured at Atlanta, Ga., died in Union prison, Columbus, Ohio; John W. Clark, age 21, wounded at Chickamauga, died in hospital of wounds; Isaac Carroll, age 24, died of disease at Charleston, S. C.; Jesse Couch, age 28; Watson E. Couch, age 24, discharged at Corinth, Miss.; Michael W. Clark, age 16, discharged Shelleyville, Tenn.; Rufus M. Derrick, age 20, captured at Missionary Ridge; John Eidson, age 28, died of disease in hospital, Chattanooga, Tenn.; Robert M. Elsmore, age 45, discharged; Allen Elsmore, age 22, killed in battle at Atlanta, Ga., July 22nd, 1864; William Foley, age 30, discharged; Berry Franklin, age 40; Marshall Franklin, age 29, died of disease in hospital; Henry Grice, age 21, died at Murfreesboro of wounds received there; Benjamin Grice, age 23, died of disease at Charleston, S. C.; Isaac W. Graham, age 30; Noah Goff, age 26; James W. Howard, age 17, died of disease in hospital; William Howard, age 40, died of disease in hospital; Michael Howard, age 38; John Hair, age 20; Hiley Hair, age 16; Jackson Holmes, age 40; Abram F. Hurtt, age 40, killed in battle at Atlanta; Jesse J. Herrin, age 28, died of disease at Enterprise, Miss.; Stanmore Johnson, age 28, killed in battle at Atlanta; Eugene S. Kreeps, age 20; William Kirkland, age 18, wounded at Murfreesboro; John C. Kennerly, age 35, discharged; James Kennerly, age 16, discharged; Elbert L.

Lott, age 28, wounded by railroad; William E. Lott, age 16, wounded at Murfreesboro, Tenn.; John Lott, age 40, died at Chattahoochee of wounds received at Chattahoochee River; Jesse Lott, age 32, died of disease at Enterprise, Miss.; George Lybrand, age 17; Martin Lybrand, age 17, killed in battle at Chickamauga; Wesley A. Lybrand, age 40, wounded at Atlanta, Ga.; George McGeehe, age 30, killed in battle at Atlanta; William A. Mitchell, age 16, killed in battle at Murfreesboro; R. S. Mitchell, age 17; Andrew Mayer, age 18; George W. Neal, age 16; Thomas Odonald, age 45, wounded at Murfreesboro; Wain M. Pasey, age 30; Eldredge Pasey, age 45, discharged; Wilbert Padget, age 25, died of disease at hospital; A. R. Padget, age 26, died of disease at hospital, Va.; Manley Padget, age 33; Josiah Padget, age 16, discharged; Driden Padget, age 22, wounded at Murfreesboro, discharged, lost an arm; Larkin C. Prator, age 28, killed in battle at Atlanta; Jefferson Randall, age 26, killed in battle at Atlanta; Seaborn Randall, age 23, killed in battle at Chickamauga; Lafayette Randall, age 17, killed in battle at Atlanta; Geo. W. Randall, age 30, died of disease at Charleston, S. C.; Mike Rutland, age 16, killed in battle at Kinston, N. C.; Wiley Rhoden, age 35, killed in battle at Atlanta; Robert Satcher, age 28, died of disease at hospital; Henry Satcher, age 17, died of disease at home; Ansel Sawyer, age 28, wounded at Chickamauga; John Simons; James Turner; Thomas H. Williams, age 45, died of disease at Enterprise, Miss.; H. Pickens Williams, age 18, died of disease at Enterprise, Miss.; Isaac B. Williams, age 16, died of disease at home; Joseph Williams, age 30, killed in battle at Chickamauga; Clifton Williams, age 19; A. G. Williams, discharged in 1861; Jefferson Williamson, age 18; Wesley Whittman, age 17; Elijah D. Watson, age 34, discharged; Lewis Yonce, age 20. Commissioned and non-commissioned officers, 29; privates, 88; total, :17.

This roll of Company "A" was prepared by Captains E. W. Horne and L. Lybrand, Ridge Spring, August 7th, 1882—all from Edgefield District.

I observe that some names suffered severely. Three Randalls were killed in battle and one died of disease. Three Williamses died of disease and one was killed in battle.

Casualties.—Killed in battle, 15; mortally wounded, 6; died

of disease, 23; total deaths, 44. Wounds not mortal, 13; total casualties, 57.

The reader will perceive that the total number of deaths in this company was considerably over one-third, which is very great—a little in excess of the average, which is about one-third.

COMPANY B, NINETEENTH REGIMENT.

Roll of Company B, Nineteenth Regiment, South Carolina Volunteers, when first organized:

Thomas P. Shaw, Captain, promoted Lieutenant Colonel and Colonel, wounded and made prisoner at Franklin, Tenn.; Robert G. Lamar, First Lieutenant, promoted Quarter Master Regiment; Matthew H. Hunter, Second Lieutenant; John C. A. Shaw, Third Lieutenant.

Roll of Company as organized at Corinth, May, 1862.

T. W. Getzen, Captain, age 23, wounded at Atlanta, July 28th, 1864, lost a leg 10th of March, 1865, at Bentonville, N. C.; John C. A. Shaw, First Lieutenant, killed in battle at Atlanta; Lewis Hester, Second Lieutenant, killed in battle at Nashville, Tenn.; John H. McDevitt, Third Lieutenant; Franklin Milledge, First Sergeant; James Parker, Second Sergeant, killed in battle at Nashville, Tenn.; Aquilla Mayer, Third Sergeant, wounded at Nashville, Tenn.; David Maver, Sergeant; James Morrison, Corporal; Jesse Mayer, Corporal; George L. Hall, Corporal, age 17, shot accidentally; Christopher Glover, Corporal, age 18; George W. Howard, Corporal, age 15, captured at Glasgow, Tenn., exchanged and discharged as minor at Shelbyville, Tenn.

PRIVATES.

Marshal Arthur, killed at Missionary Ridge; Chapell Attaway, John Brooks; Wm. H. Boulware, age 15; James Broyden, age 15, wounded at Chickamauga; John Bryan, age 18; John Bassell, R. Burkhalter; Francis Clark, captured at Branchville, S. C., and unaccounted for; James Cowan, died of disease; Elbert Doby, wounded at Kingston, N. C.; Henry Doby, Charles Dinkins, Henry Dunn; James Dunn, died of disease at Bardstown, Kentucky; Richard Dunn, died of disease at Atlanta; Robert Day, died of disease at Atlanta; James Davis, wounded at Atlanta; Thomas Franklin, killed in battle at

Chickamauga; Robert Foster, discharged at Saltillo, Miss., consumptive; Fletcher Goff, Colleton Glover; John Green, killed in battle at Chickamauga; William Gullege, Henry Gullege; John Horn, died of disease in Mississippi; Samuel Horn, killed in battle at Kingston, N. C ; Peter G. Horn, wounded at Altanta, arm amputated; Milledge Horn, wounded at Bentonville, N. C.; William Horn, killed in battle at Chickamauga; Elijah Horn, died of disease at Rome, Ga.; Absalom Horn, wounded at Murfreesboro, Tenn.; J. A. Horn, wounded at Atlanta; John Harden, George Harden, Frank B. Henderson, John Hester, Robert Hatcher; John Hatcher, killed in battle at Chickamauga; Mark Hilborn, wounded at Chickamauga; James Henderson; William Jones, wounded; Thomas Kernaghan, wounded in battle at Murfreesboro; Joseph Kennedy, died of disease; Joel McClendon; Drury Mealing, died of disease at Enterprise, Miss.; Joseph Napper; William Napper, died of disease; William Noble, died of disease; Thomas Peay, discharged at Saltillo, Miss.; Joseph Powell; Thomas Page, wounded at Atlanta; John W. Roper, killed in battle at Chickamauga; Joseph Ryan, Elbert Ryan, Edward Ripley, Ephriam Rhodes, Henry Rhodes, Benjamin Smith; George Samuel, wounded at Atlanta; Leonidas Sego; John Slaton, wounded at Atlanta; William Sharpton, died of disease at Lauderdale Springs, Miss.; William Treadaway, Edward Toney, James M. Turner, James H. Webb; Hiram Webb, wounded at Farmington, Tenn., accidental discharge of his gun; William Whitehead, wounded at Atlanta, Ga.; George Wise, wounded at Shelbyville, Tenn., arm amputated; Robert I. Walker, died of disease in Mississippi. Commissioned and non-commissioned officers after reorganization, May 1862, 13; privates, 71; total rank and file, 84.

This roll was prepared by Captain Thomas W. Getzen, of Lake City, Fla. I have two copies before me, both prepared by Captain Getzen, and they do not correspond with each other absolutely in all particulars, nor does the copy from the office in Columbia entirely correspond with either, though very nearly.

There were killed in battle, 10; mortally wounded, o; died of disease, 12; total deaths, 22; wounds received not mortal, 20; total casualties, 42; deaths only one over one-fourth.

As matter of history, I copy the following memoranda, which
I find upon the roll of Company "B," Nineteenth South Carolina Volunteers:

Thomas W. Getzen "entered company at organization as a
private; elected Third Lieutenant vice R. G. Lamar appointed
Quarter-Master of regiment; elected Captain of Company 'B' at
reorganization at Corinth, Miss., May, 1862; commanded regiment at the battle of Murfreesboro, Tenn., after the wounding
of Colonel and Major; acted as Major until the 22nd July at Atlanta, when Major White, commanding, was wounded; commanded regiment on 28th July on the left at Atlanta, was
wounded and furloughed 60 days; returned to regiment and
commanded it at Nashville, Tenn., Kingston, and Bentons-
ville, N. C.; lost a leg at the latter place; paroled at Highpoint,
N. C " No signature.

I think Captain Thomas P. Shaw has rather hard measure
dealt him. According to one copy of the roll which lies before
me he was promoted from Coporal to Captain; was wounded at
Franklin, Tenn., and died from his wound at that place.
Another copy says he was wounded at Franklin, but says
nothing of his promotion from Corporal, nor of his death;
while still another copy says he died of wounds at Franklin,
making no mention of promotion. On the copy, however,
which does not mention his death at Franklin, there is written
in pencil on the line with his name, "Promoted Colonel", no
date. This, no doubt, was read by the clerk in the Adjutant
General's office, "promoted from Corporal." I do not know
when he was promoted Colonel. I only know that when I
joined the Regiment, Company "D", in March or February
1864, while they were still in winter quarters at Dalton, Ga.,
Shaw was Colonel or Lieutenant Colonel commanding the
Regiment. He was in command as Colonel until after I was
wounded and carried to the rear. I saw him under fire more
than once, but especially at New Hope church, and he was as
cool and collected as though he were receiving welcome guests
at his own home. He was in command of the Regiment at
Franklin, Tenn., was wounded there, shot through the body,
the ball striking centrally in the upper part of the chest, but
he did not die at Franklin; he was taken prisoner, but how
long he remained in the hands of the enemy I do not know.

He lived until some time after the war I know, for I saw him once since, and I hope he is living yet. He died in 1883.

His brother, Lieutenant Shaw, was killed in battle at Atlanta in 1864.

COMPANY C, NINETEENTH REGIMENT.

Roll of Company "C", Nineteenth Regiment, South Carolina Volunteers, prepared by Lieutenant James R. Faulkner, Kirksey's, September 11th, 1884. I copy the roll in full, though all the men were not from Edgefield. Those not from Edgefield their county is mentioned:

John Quattlebaum, Captain, resigned at reorganization in 1862; H. Rufus Dean, wounded at Franklin, promoted from ranks at reorganization in July 1862, promoted in 1864 and served as Inspector General on General Manigault's Staff, was with army at surrender in 1865; W. Marion Dean, First Lieutenant, died of wounds at Chickamauga, September 27th, 1863; John B. Harris, First Lieutenant, died of disease at hospital, April 1863, promoted from ranks at reorganization in 1862; Joseph T. Buzhardt, First Lieutenant, killed in battle at Chickamauga, September 20th, 1863, promoted from Corporal in 1862 at reorganization; William Quattlebaum, Second Lieutenant, resigned at re organization in 1862; James R. Faulkner, Second Lieutenant, promoted from ranks at reorganization 1862, living; W. D. Rountree, Third Lieutenant, resigned at re-organization in 1862; E. W. Eidson, Third Lieutenant, wounded at Chickamauga, with army at surrender in 1865, promoted from ranks to Corporal, July 1862, and to Third Lieutenant March, 1865; Wm. H. Burkhalter, First Sergeant, wounded at Chickamauga, disabled for life; Harman D. Quattlebaum, Second Sergeant, died of disease at home in 1862, on sick furlough; Newton C. Harling, Second Sergeant, killed in battle at Chickamauga; Hiram L. Adams, Second Sergeant, died of wounds at Nashville, May 1865, was wounded December 16th, 1864, promoted from the ranks; J. Bruntley Ouzts, Third Sergeant, killed in battle at Murfreesboro, December 31st, 1862; W. Frank May, Third Sergeant, died of wounds at Chickamauga, September 30th, 1863, wounded September 20th, 1863, promoted from ranks July 1862; Edward H. Lagrone, Fourth Sergeant, with army at

surrender in 1865, promoted from ranks to Corporal in 1862
and to Sergeant in 1865; James M. Rambo, Fourth Sergeant,
same record as Lagrone; Robert W. Connolly, Fifth Sergeant,
wounded in railroad collision in 1862 and disabled for life;
John W. Devore, First Corporal, captured May 1864; John
Ouzts, Second Corporal, transferred at re-organization; Alfred
Hart, Third Corporal, died of disease at Shelbyville, Tenn.,
April 1863; Wiley T. Adams, Fourth Corporal, died of disease
at Charleston, S. C., February 7th, 1862, promoted from the
ranks; Charles Haney, from Laurens.

PRIVATES.

Robert Aiton, died of disease in hospital in 1862; Pickens
M. Adams, transferred in 1862; Richard W. Adams, died of
wounds at Atlanta, August 1864; Robert Anderson, Laurens,
killed at Atlanta, July 22nd, 1864; Robert Baysworth, with
army at surrender in 1865, detached as teamster; William
Brooks, wounded at Murfreesboro in 1862, discharged under
conscript act, January 20th, 1863; J. Pinckney Burnet, transferred to Second Artillery, April 1862; Isaac Cross, died of
disease at Charleston, S. C., March 22nd, 1862; John H.
Devore, died of disease at Charleston, S. C., February 13th,
1862; Newton P. Devore, discharged under conscript act,
January 20th, 1862; Herlong Dorn, transferred in 1862; John
H. Ellenberg, discharged under conscript act, January 20th,
1862; Martin Ellenberg, transferred 1862; Jack F. Faulkner,
transferred 1862; W. Talbert Faulkner, wounded at Chick-
amanga, September 1863; John Franklin, died of disease at
Enterprise, Miss., June 20th, 1862; John Goleman, captured
October 1862, Union prison war; W. H. Gray, killed in battle
at Chickamauga, September 20th, 1863; Jesse M. Hart, transferred April, 1862. William M. Hamilton, died in Union
prison at Rock Island, February 1865; Lafayette P. Harling,
with army at surrender in 1865; Tillman Harling, with army
at surrender in 1865; John M. Harling, discharged January
20th, 1863, under conscript act; Bud Horn, died of disease at
Enterprise, Miss., June 1862; Madison Horn, wounded at
Missionary Ridge in leg November 25th, 1863, disabled remainder of the war; L. Simps Horn, killed in battle at Chicka-
manga September 20th, 1863; Douglas W. Holloway, trans-

ferred April, 1862; William P. Lipford, discharged June, 1862;
A. J. Langley, discharged June, 1862; Frank Lovelace, transferred April, 1862; Mark Matthews, died of disease at Enter-
prise, Miss., July 18th, 1862; Simeon Matthews, died of
disease at Charleston, S. C., March 10th, 1862; Samuel Mc-
Manus, captured at Atlanta, Ga., August 31st, 1864; William
T. McManus, wounded in railroad collision April, 1862, discharged; Thomas McManus, died of disease in Union Prison,
Rock Island, Ill., December, 1863; Abner Mays, wounded at
Nashville, Tenn., December 16th, 1864; John F. Marbut,
wounded at Chickamauga in jaw and thigh, disabled for life;
John Motes, discharged January 20th, 1863, conscript act;
Wiley Miller, died of disease at Charleston, S. C., February
4th, 1863; John H. Miller, disabled in railroad collision April,
1862, discharged; Daniel McDowell, died of disease at Coving-
ton, Ga., June, 1864; James M. McCrelus, died of disease at
Charleston, S. C., February 9th, 1862; James Mills, captured
February, 1865; W. A. Owdom, transferred April, 1862; Peter
D. Ouzts, captured at Atlanta, Ga., July 22nd, 1864; John
Parkman, with army at surrender 1865, teamster, war; Simeon
Parkman, killed in battle at Murfreesboro December 31st,
1862; Thomas Parkman, with army at surrender 1865; William
D. Padgett, transferred to Company "K," Nineteenth South
Carolina Volunteers, February, 1862; James M. Polatty, died
in Union Prison at Rock Island January, 1865; William Pat-
terson, Laurens, killed in battle at Atlanta, Ga., July 22nd,
1864; John D. Quattlebaum, killed in battle at Murfreesboro
December 31st, 1862; James M. Roberson, died of disease in
hospital, Mississippi, 1863; Higdon Roberson, died of disease
in hospital Enterprise, Miss., July 1862; H. A. Roberson, died
of disease at Enterprise, Miss., July, 1862; John Roberson, transferred April, 1862; John Rambo, captured at Egypt Station,
Miss., July, 1864; James Roberson, captured at Pulaski, Tenn.,
December, 1864; John M. Schenk, died in Union Prison, Rock
Island, December, 1863; William Still, wounded at Chickamauga; with army at surrender 1865; William A. Still, transferred to Hampton Legion 1863; John B. Timmerman, transferred to Company "K," Nineteenth South Carolina Volunteers, January, 1862; N. Douglas Timmerman, discharged
March, 1862; William S. Terry, died of wounds at Chicka-

mauga October 1st, 1863; W. Talbert Timmerman, died of disease at Enterprise, Miss., June, 1863; Robert A. Watkins, with army at surrender in 1865; Milton Walker, killed in railroad collision Enterprise, Miss., April, 1862; James M. Wiseman, died in Union Prison, Rock Island, Ill.; James H. Wrenn, wounded at Chickamauga September 20th, 1863, in elbow and groin, at Nashville December 16th, 1864, in thigh. Luke G. Williams, wounded at Chickamauga, disabled for life. Total privates, 70; officers commissioned and non-commissioned, 23; total rank and file, 93. Killed in battle, 10; died of disease, 17; died of wounds, 6; died in Union Prison, 5; killed by railroad, 1; total deaths, 39. Wounds in battle not mortal, 13; wounded in railroad collision, 2; total wounds not mortal, 15.

The reader will perceive that the losses by death in this company were very great, unusually so. Thirty-nine deaths out of ninety-three men is largely over one-third, which I have found to be the average.

The company suffered greatly from sickness. The number of accidents is also somewhat unusual. There must have been several awkward squads in the company. There appears also to have been a fatality attending certain names. There were five Robersons in the company; three died of disease in Mississippi, and one was captured at Pulaski, Tenn.; the other was transferred in April, 1862, before the deaths of these, or he, too, might have died. There were three McManuses; one died in Union Prison, December, 1863; another was captured at Atlanta in August, 1864, and the other was wounded in a railroad collision in April, 1862, and discharged. There were two Matthewses; both died of disease in 1862, one at Charleston, S. C., March 10th, the other at Enterprise, Miss., July 18th. I observe a similar fatality attending certain name in Company "B." There were eight Horns in that company, every one of whom suffered; two were killed in battle, four were wounded, and two died of disease.

Nor is this all; there were three Horns in Company "C," and every one of them also suffered. One died of disease in June, 1862. One was wounded and disabled in November, 1863. One was killed in battle in September, 1863. Of eleven men named Horn in these two companies, three were killed in battle, five were wounded, and three died of disease.

Nor is this all yet; Captain Elijah W. Horne, of Company "A," was wounded at Atlanta, making twelve of the name, every one of whom were sufferers. I observe, however, the "e" as the final letter in Captain Horne's name, which the others have not.

COMPANY D, NINETEENTH REGIMENT.

Roll of Company "D," Nineteenth Regiment, South Carolina Volunteers:

This roll was prepared by Captain J. W. Denny, (who was the last Captain commanding,) in 1882. I do not copy it verbatim as I find it in the Adjutant General's office, but take the liberty of making corrections where I know there are errors.

Ira Cromley, age 38, Captain, discharged at Corinth, Miss., over age. William Spencer Peterson, Captain, killed in battle at Atlanta, Ga., July 28th, 1864, elected Captain May, 1862. John W. Denny, age 30, Captain, promoted from Sergeant to First Lieutenant May, 1862, Captain July 28th, 1864. John A. Crowder, age 29, First Lieutenant, died of wounds January, 1863, wounded at Murfreesboro, promoted Major May, 1862. Elzey B. Forrest, age 37, Second Lieutenant, discharged at Corinth, Miss., over age. Isaac Edwards, age 38, Second Lieutenant, discharged at Corinth, Miss., over age. Basil Peterson, age 29, Second Lieutenant, promoted from Sergeant August, 1864. James H. Lagrone, age 20, promoted from ranks to Sergeant in 1864, to Second Lieutenant in 1865. Henry E. Vansant, age 22, First Lieutenant, promoted from ranks to Second Lieutenant May, 1862, to First Lieutenant in 1864. Theophilus Wright, age 34, Sergeant. Samuel T. Edwards, age 27, Sergeant, wounded at Atlanta, Ga., July 28th, 1864. J. D. Smith Livingston, age 23, Sergeant, wounded at Atlanta, Ga., July 28th, 1864. Thomas E. Chapman, age 32, Sergeant, died at home August, 1864, of wound received at Atlanta July 28th, 1864, promoted Sergeant May, 1862. William G. Matthews, age 27, promoted Sergeant September, 1863. John C. Wheeler, age 25, ensign, killed in battle at Atlanta, Ga., July 28th, 1864, promoted from ranks 1862. Rowland Eidson, age 26, Corporal, killed in battle at Atlanta, Ga., July 22nd, 1864. Levi M. Crouch,

age 25, Corporal, died of disease in Kentucky 1862. James
M. Abney, age 33, Corporal, wounded at Atlanta July 28th,
1864. John D. Eidson, age 15, Corporal, discharged at Shelbyville, Tenn , January, 1863. William E. Reese, age 31, Corporal, promoted from ranks 1864. Amos W. Satcher, age 20,
Corporal, promoted from ranks May, 1862.

PRIVATES.

John P. Abney, age 25, killed Columbia, S. C., January,
1865; James C. Abney, age 20; Ezra Abney, age 23; D. Sumter
Adams, age 30, died of disease at Charleston, S. C.; Wesley
A. Black, age 19, killed in battle Nashville, Tenn., December,
1864, wounded at Atlanta, Ga., July 26th, 1864; Henry S.
Black, age 17; William H. Banks, age 16, discharged at Shelbyville, Tenn., January, 1863; John D. Bruce, age 19, died of
disease at Enterprise, Miss., May, 1862; John A. Chapman,
age 41, Newberry, wounded near New Hope Church, Ga.,.
May 30th, 1864; Charles Carson, age 16, discharged at Shelbyville, Tenn., January, 1863; Zedekiah Crouch, age 16, discharged at Shelbyville, Tenn., January, 1863; Larkin Crouch,
age 33; Jacob Crouch, age 30, killed in battle at Atlanta July
22nd, 1864; James B. Crouch, age 18; James R. Crouch, age
19; Sion Corley, age 16, discharged at Shelbyville, Tenn.,
January, 1863; William Corley, age 31; Arthur Davis, age 24,
killed in battle at Bentonville, N. C., 1865; John Davis, age
22; Pinckney D. Denny, age 16, died of disease at Enterprise,
Miss., May, 1862; Pickens Dean, age 37; Julius Eason, age
22, killed in battle at New Hope Church, Ga., May, 1864;
John D. Eidson; William Gentry, age 28, killed in battle at
Franklin, Tenn., December, 1864; Lewis C. Goff, age 23;
William C. Goff, age 21; Jonathan N. Gregory, age 20; Daniel
Havird, age 22, died of disease at Charleston, S. C., January,
1862; Franklin J. Havird, age 20, died of disease at Charles-
ton, S. C., January, 1862; Israel P. Hartzoge, age 27, killed
in battle Chickamauga, Tenn., September 20th, 1863; ———
Holden, age 18, Chester, killed in battle at Franklin, Tenn.;
Jesse Jay, age 30; Irvin G. Jones, age 32, killed in battle at
Nashville, Tenn., December, 1864; Henry P. Jones, age 34;
Brown Jennings, age 32, wounded at Chickamauga, Tenn.,
September 20th, 1863; Philip Jennings, age 35; ——— Lang-

ston, age 20, Sumter, lost; George Little, age 25, killed in battle at Chickamauga, Tenn., September 20th, 1863; Wm. McCarty, age 28; Isaac McCarty, age 26, discharged Charleston, S. C., December, 1861; John Mannel, age 30, Chester, killed in battle at Atlanta, Ga., July 22nd, 1864; Simeon Morse, age 26, wounded—thumb—near New Hope, Ga., May, 1864; George W. Matthews, age 25; William Matthews, age 18; Sulton J. Mills, age 40; Jake Nelson, age 16, Union; Moses New, age 24, wounded at Murfreesboro, Tenn., January, 1863; Edward G. New, age 29; Jackson J. Odom, age 40; Lawson Padgett, age 16; Samuel Padgett, age 31, died of disease at Atlanta, Ga.; Armstead Parish, age 28, died of disease in Mississippi; Wesley Parish, age 23; Cornelius E. Rowe, age 31; John Rushton, age 20, captured at Missionary Ridge November, 1863; Wm. M. Raborn, age 33, died of wounds January, 1863, wounded December 31st, 1862, at Murfreesboro, Tenn.; Josiah Dodgen, age 27, died of disease at Chattanooga 1863; Lemuel Salter, age 37; John C. Salter, age 31, killed in battle at Franklin, Tenn.; William Salter, age 29, killed in battle at Franklin, Tenn.; L. Gideon Salter, age 24; Geo. A. Schumpert, age 18, killed in battle at Chickamauga September 20th, 1863; James Speer, age 32; Jasper Story, age 33; A. M. Smith, age 40, Fairfield; James Vines, age 25; William A. Watson, age 23, killed in battle at Murfreesboro, Tenn., December 31st, 1862; Milledge Watson, age 20, discharged at Charleston January, 1862; Patrick Wages, age 20, died of disease at Charleston January, 1862; Eldred J. Wills, age 32; H. Lafayette Winn, age 16, discharged at Shelbyville, Tenn., January, 1863; John W. Whittle, age 31, died of disease at Chattanooga 1863; Henry A. Williams, age 18; Burr J. Yarbrough, age 16, died of disease on retreat from Corinth, Miss. Commissioned officers, 9; non-commissioned officers, 12; privates, 73; total, 94. Killed in battle, 16; died of wounds received in battle, 3; died of disease, 12; total deaths, 31. Discharged, 9; captured, 1; lost, 1.

The number mortally wounded is small, but the whole loss is about the average. Deducting the number discharged the loss of the remainder is a little over one-third.

In the roll on file in the Adjutant General's office John A. Chapman is entered as having been wounded at Atlanta in

August, 1864; but in point of fact, as Judge O'Neall used to express it, he was wounded about two o'clock at night, on the night of Sunday, May 29th, 1864. Being after midnight would make it May 30th. Captain Robert N. Chatham, commanding Company "G," who was killed by the same ball, is entered on the roll of his company as having been killed by accident near New Hope, in June, 1864. This entry is only a few days wrong. Whether he was killed by accident, or by the discharge of an enemy's gun, can never be known with certainty. Occasional firing was going on all that night, and, in fact, nearly all the time, day and night, for we were nearly always in the presence of the enemy. We were lying, at the time Captain Chatham was fatally wounded, in line of battle. I was in the rear rank lying upon my left side with my right leg a little drawn up, so that the foot rested upon the left just above the ankle. Captain Chatham, a little in the rear of the rear rank, was lying upon his right side within a few feet of me. I was about half asleep when suddenly a gun fired, which seemed to be very near. The ball passed through my right leg about an inch above the ankle, tearing out the smaller bone without touching the larger, and struck Captain Chatham in the stomach and lodged in his body. We were both carried together to a little house not far away. On the afternoon of Monday, May 30th, I was lifted into a wagon and transported to Marietta over the roughest road, it seemed to me then, that ever wagon travelled over. Captain Chatham was alive when I left him, but he died that afternoon, as I was told afterwards. He was an amiable and good man, a brave and good officer, and loved by his men. I saw Colonel Shaw at Newberry in 1867, and, talking about the events of that night, he said he had come to the conclusion, and the general conclusion was, that the gun was fired by the enemy. I thought at the time that, being so near, it must have been the accidental discharge of one of our own guns, but the ball passed diagonally across our line, so that the man who fired the gun must have been in our front, though near.

On the last day of May I was lodged in hospital at Atlanta, where I remained all through that rainy month of June, 1864. Early in July, as Sherman began to draw near, the hospital was moved to Forsyth, Ga. There I remained until August

10th, when I was furloughed for sixty days. I arrived at home safely August 13th, 1864,—found all well, and never saw the army any more, except some of General Cheatham's at Newberry and some of Stewart's, a few miles below Chappells, in Edgefield. My fighting days were over. Very often during those four years I thought it a little strange and singular that men could not find something better to do than to make it a regular daily business to try to kill one another. However, I suppose it is all right. Fighting great battles and gaining great victories is glory; shooting and killing birds is sport.

XXXVII.

COMPANY "F," NINETEENTH REGIMENT.

Muster roll of Company "F," Nineteenth Regiment, South Carolina Volunteers, from the 18th day of December, 1861. Copy of T. D. Villard, Ridge Spring, April 25th, 1886. This company was enlisted for 12 months:

Wade Holstein was first Captain; resigned February 15th, 1862. W. H. Norris, Captain, December, 1862; promoted to Captain by resignation of Captain Holstein February 15th, 1862. M. N. Holstein, First Lieutenant; promoted to First Lieutenant by promotion of Norris to Captain. Hiram Holstein, Second Lieutenant, promoted to Second Lieutenant by promotion of M. N. Holstein to First Lieutenant. J. W. Turner, promoted Second Lieutenant; elected February 15th, 1862. W. K. Smith, First Sergeant. E. M. Corder, promoted Second Sergeant February 29th, vice J. W. Holstein, discharged. M. B. Asbill, Sergeant; left camp February 20th; unable to return on account of sickness. Irving M. Norris, Sergeant; left camp February 20th; unable to return on account of sickness. Lorenzo Feaster, Corporal. J. W. Hartley, Corporal; absent for 10 days. M. C. Corder, Corporal; absent for 10 days. Wm. Hartley, Corporal; appointed Fourth Corporal vice Jacob Busby, absent.

PRIVATES.

Wesley Autrey, Henry Anderson, Abijah Anderson; S. Anderson, left camp February 14th for seven days, sick, unable to return; Barney Anderson, left camp February 11th for ten days, sick, unable to return; H. Asbill; A. B. Asbill, left camp February 26th for 30 days; Thomas Busby, lost a leg at Franklin, Tenn.; Jacob Busby, transferred to cavalry and killed in Virginia; John Britt, Sam. Bloodsworth, Geo. Cockrill; P. B. DeMedicis, Camp Hampton, left camp 3rd February for 10 days, after that absent without leave; Wm. Daniel, discharged January 10th for disability; G. W. Fallaw, Abraham Gossett, James Goodwyn; Mayne Hale, sick in Soldiers' Relief Hospital; H. Hall; Irvin Hall, Camp Wappo;

Willis Hartley, E. F. Hartley, B. Hite; S. Hite, left 15th February for 10 days, too sick to return in time; H. Hallman, A. Kneece, L. D. Landrum; J. B. Holstein, Sergeant, discharged February 19th; S. F. Lowman, left 1st February for 15 days, too sick to return in time; A. M. Lott, J. Pylant, E. Padgett; D. A. Prater, appointed Fifth Sergeant vice E. M. Corder, promoted February 24th; P. N. Ridgell; Ira Reynolds, left 11th February for 10 days, too sick to return in time; I. M. Reynolds, David Stone; John Stone, January 20th seven days furlough, absent without leave; J. P. Sawyer; S. W. Smith, February 19th furlough for 30 days; J. Sanguinnett, February 27th furlough for 5 days; T. D. Villard, Camp Wappo; J. Wells; Jas. Warren, left 1st February for 15 days, too sick to return in time; William Warren, deserted on 19th February from Camp Wappo, recaptured 3rd March, placed under arrest; J. D. Waddell, B. T. Walker, T. Whittle; M. M. Whittle, left February 1st for 10 days, too sick to return in time; E. D. Watson, Camp Wappo, transferred from Company "A" February 6th; furloughed seven days; S. Senterfit; Jacob Mabar, discharged February 26th for disability; J. Duffie, died February 21st in Soldiers' Relief Hospital—pneumonia. Commissioned officers, 5; non-commissioned officers, 8; total, 13; privates, 33; total rank and file, 46.

The reader will perceive that this is an army muster roll, showing the condition of the company on the first day of March, 1862, with a few casualties of a later date. One was transferred to cavalry and killed in battle. One lost a leg at Franklin. One died in hospital. Two discharged for disability. One deserted, but I hope he behaved better afterwards. All, I believe, both officers and men, were from Edgefield.

COMPANY K, NINETEENTH REGIMENT.

Roll of Campany "K," Nineteenth Regiment, South Carolina Volunteers, prepared by Captain J. B. Courtney, Trenton, July 2nd, 1882:

A. Jones, age 55, Captain; promoted from Captain to Major. William Gregg, age 28, Captain; promoted; resigned. W. H. Timmerman, age 32, Captain; promoted from First Lieutenant; resigned. J. B. Courtney, age 34, Captain; wounded on railroad Georgia 1862; Nashville, Tenn., December 15th, 1864, promoted from Second Lieutenant. C. W. Randall, age 32, Second Lieutenant; wounded on M. & O. R. R. April 24th, 1862. A. L. Holley, age 32, Second Lieutenant; wounded at Murfreesboro December 31st, 1863; promoted from Sergeant. John B. Timmerman, age 33, Sergeant; killed on M. & O. R. R. April 24th, 1862. Mose Harris, age 39, Sergeant. E. Jones, age 38, Sergeant; died of disease. G. W. Dooley, age 55, Sergeant. Wilson Haney, age 40, Sergeant; killed on M. & O. R. R. April 24th, 1862. Martin Yonce, age —, Sergeant; wounded at Bentonville, N. C., March 19th, 1865. J. C. Holley, age 23, Sergeant; wounded at Murfreesboro, Tenn., December 31st, 1863; by M. & O. R. R. April 24th, 1862; promoted from the ranks. Wm. Glaze, age 23, Sergeant; died of wounds at Franklin, Tenn., November 30th, 1864; promoted from the ranks. John R. Sneed, age 25, Sergeant; wounded at Atlanta, Ga., July 22nd, 1864; promoted from ranks. Grice Ambers, age 40, Corporal. William Turner, age 24, Corporal; killed at Murfreesboro, Tenn., December 31st, 1863. J. S. Williams, age 32, Corporal. J. H. Osburn, age 25, Corporal. M. Hainey, age —, Corporal; killed at Franklin, Tenn., November 30th, 1864. Charles T. Stvran, age 23, Corporal; killed at Atlanta, Ga., July 28th, 1864; promoted from ranks.

PRIVATES.

F. M. Arthur, age 28; Wm. Augustine, age 21, wounded on railroad in Georgia; C. T. Barton, age 22; Robert Barton, age 68, discharged April 24th, 1862; John Broglen, age 28, killed by M. & O. R. R.; John Busbee, age 35; Allen Busbee, age 24; Martin Burton, age 16; Stephen Cockran, age 25; Joe Cockran, age 16; Jabez Courtney, age 16; Wm. Cameron, age —; Henry Day, age 28; Samuel Ergles, age 20; Daniel Ergles, age 16; B. Z. Fowler, age 21; Thomas Faulkner, age 20; Wm. Glaze, age 23; John Gregory, age 35, discharged; J. H. Gerkin, age 25, Germany, wounded by M. & O. R. R., first man wounded in regiment—in engagement at Corinth, Miss.; G. W. Giles, age 25; Sam. Green, age 28; James Green, age 32; Jackson Green, age 27; Wm. Goings, age 30, wounded at Franklin, Tenn., November 3rd, 1864; Ulysses Guantt, age 25,

Lexington, captured at Atlanta, Ga.; Jasper Howard, age 25; John Hatcher, age 16, transferred to Company "B"; James Hutto, age 23; Marion Hutto, age 16; S. Holesenbake, age 45, discharged; John Jackson, age 25, wounded by M. & O. R. R., discharged on account of it; F. Jackson, age 21; Richard Johnson, age 23; Middleton Koon, age 45; Louis Koon, age 36; James Long, age 30, Abbeville; M. Long, age 21, Abbeville; Wm. Martin, age 30; John Mobley, age 45, discharged; Luther Mills, age 21, died of disease; James Mills, age 44, died of disease; Joseph Nobles, age 36; Joseph New, age 35; George Overstreet, age 33, wounded by M. & O. R. R., Enterprise, Miss., April 24th, 1862; Henry Overstreet, age 28; Tillman Padget, age 29, wounded by M. & O. R. R., April 24th, 1862; M. Posey, age 45; Holden Posey, age 23; Wm. Parker, age 25; John Piper, age 32; Noah Plindell, age 25, died in hospital; Robert Patterson, age 22, Abbeville, wounded; Thomas Patterson, age 19, Abbeville, captured at Atlanta; R. P. Pinson, age 18, Abbeville; H. G. Randall, age 40, discharged; E. Randall, age 44; John Rowe, age 25; Miles Rhoden, age 17, died of disease, Charleston, S. C., March, 1862; Wm. Randall, age 30, killed at Snake Creek Gap, Ga.; Joseph Steel, age 23; James Steel, age 17; James Snipes, age 24; Sam. Simons, age 40, wounded by M. & O. R. R. and discharged; Wade Samuels, age 24; M. Samuels, age 20; Milledge Smith, age 18; Bennet Smith, age 44, discharged; Martin Turner, age 22; Darling Turner, age 16; John Turner, age 23; Dowlas Timmerman, age 28; B. Turner, age 25; J. D. Turner, age 47; Peter Trimmons, age 19; James Walker, age 28; Wm. Wever, age 40, wounded M. & O. R. R. April 24th, 1862; J. P. Wages, age —, wounded at Atlanta, lost a leg; Allen Yonce, age 25, wounded M. & O. R. R. April 24th, 1862. Commissioned officers, 6; non-commissioned officers, 15; total, 21; privates, 79; total rank and file, 100. Killed in battle, 4; killed by railroad, 3; died of wounds, 1; died of disease, 4; total deaths, 12.

All were from Edgefield except a few, whose counties I have named. The losses in this company were very light—barely one-eighth from all causes.

COMPANY B, SIXTH REGIMENT.

Roll of Company "B," Sixth Regiment, Cavalry:

Lewis Jones, Captain; resigned 1863. James J. Gregg, Captain; served to end of war; promoted from Second to First Lieutenant in 1862; to Captain 1863. Z. W. Carwile, First Lieutenant; resigned 1862. John M. Ward, First Lieutenant, served to end of war; promoted to Second Lieutenant 1862; from Second to First Lieutenant 1863. John Bauskett, Second Lieutenant, Richland; served to end of war. J. J. Bunch, Second Lieutenant; served to end of war. Samuel G. Cothran Sergeant, Abbeville; killed near Fayetteville, N. C., March, 1865. W. H. Winn, Sergeant; killed near Columbia, S. C., 1865. Andrew Giles, Sergeant; died of wounds near Richmond, Va., 1864; wounded near Travillian Station, Va. T. Shelton Fox, Sergeant, Lexington; served to end of war; appointed Assistant Surgeon 1863; J. L. Addison, Sergeant; served to end of war. John Briggs, Sergeant; served to end of war; promoted from Corporal 1865. Wm. C. Hart, Sergeant; served to end of war; promoted from Corporal 1865. B. W. Hard, Sergeant; served to end of war; promoted from Corporal 1865. James Quattlebaum, Corporal; served to end of war. M. W. Clark, Corporal; promoted from ranks 1864. Mark Crouch, Corporal; promoted from ranks 1864.

PRIVATES.

John B. Abney, served through the war, died in 1865; C. M. Adams, killed in a skirmish February, 1865; Geo. B. Addison, surrendered April, 1865; W. D. H. Allen, surrendered April, 1865; Mat. Abney, Pickens Adams; Eldred N. Bartley, surrendered April, 1865; Richard M. Berry, wounded at Travillian Station, Va., served through; A. F. Broadwater, served through war; Geo. W. Broadwater, wounded at Rock Fish Creek, served through war; Robert E. Broadwater, served through war; Robert S. Brunson, served through war; N. L. Brunson, served through the war; Wm. H. Briggs, served through the war; James M. Briggs, died of disease in 1864 in Virginia; C. M. Burkhalter, appointed Assistant Surgeon in 1864; William Busby, transferred in 1864 to another command, afterwards wounded; Whitfield B. Brooks, killed in battle at Travillian Station, Va.; U. R. Brooks; Isaacs Bush, served through the war; Samuel Blackwell, died of disease in Virginia 1864; Edward Bush; Wm. L. Claxton, killed in battle at Travillian Station, Va.; Lafayette Cogburn, killed in a skirmish; L. R. Cogburn, served through the war; Wm. B. Crane, discharged 1862; Geo. W. Crouch, served through the war; Watson E. Crouch, served through the war; Mike W. Clark; Sam. Cochran, killed in battle at Rock Fish Creek, N. C.; J. Pickens Denny, served through the war; Henry W. Dobey, served through the war; John D. Eidson, served through the war; Henry W. Eubanks, served through the war; J. H. Ellis; Archy Fundyburg, died of disease July, 1863; Watson Fundyburg, surrendered April, 1865; Wm. R. Forrest, surrendered April, 1865; Jesse M. Fountaine, surrendered April, 1865; Adam Fulman, surrendered April, 1865; John A. Green, surrendered April, 1865; Benj. F. Glanton, surrendered April, 1865; J. Wm. Glanton, surrendered April, 1865; Charles R. Glanton, died of disease at Richmond, Va., 1864; Lewis Glanton, died of disease at home 1863; David M. Glover, surrendered April, 1865; Franklin Harris, surrendered April, 1865; John W. Harris, surrendered April, 1865; Jesse M. Hart, surrendered April, 1865; Wm. Head, surrendered at Appomattox 1865, transferred May, 1864, to another command; James M. Holden, surrendered at Appomattox 1865; B. O. Hernden, Marlboro, surrendered at Appomattox 1865, transferred May, 1864, to another command; Lewis W. Holmes, surrendered April, 1865; E. Holsenbake, surrendered April, 1865; John Howard, surrendered April, 1865; W. J. Holloway, surrendered April, 1865; John Hatcher, Tillman S. Hudson; M. Johnson, surrendered April, 1865; David Kisick, surrendered April, 1865; John F. Kenny, transferred May, 1864, to another command; James Kimbrell, transferred May, 1864, to another command; Stanmore Kirkland, transferred May, 1864, to another command; J. Felder Kirkland, surrendered April, 1865; Abner Kirkland, surrendered April, 1865; Wm. E. Kilcrease, surrendered April, 1865; Abram Kilcrease, surrendered April, 1865; Thomas Lanham, surrendered April, 1865; G. Lewis, surrendered April, 1865; L. W. Mays, died of disease at home 1864; Wm. H. Mays, wounded at Travillian Station 1864, discharged, leg amputated; Samuel E. Mays, wounded at Travillian Station 1864, discharged, leg amputated; Washington O. Morgan, surrendered April, 1865; Charles R. Montague, surrendered April, 1865; Wm. Mc-Manus, surrendered April, 1865; E. J. Miller, surrendered April, 1865; David Myers, surrendered April, 1865; M. Robert Munalu, surrendered April, 1865; John H. Moss, killed in battle at Travillian Station June, 1864; Matt. Moss, killed in battle at Travillian Station June, 1864; J. Wiley Mayers, killed in battle at Travillian Station June, 1864; John Mitchell, transferred to another command May, 1864; W. E. Middleton; James Nappier, killed in battle at Hatcher's Run; John R. Niernsee, age 18, surrendered April, 1865; Frank Niernsee, age 14, surrendered April, 1865; Geo. T. Piper, wounded in Virginia 1864, surrendered April, 1865; L. C. Prater, transferred to another command; E. Padgett, killed in battle at Fayetteville, N. C.; David Plunkett, killed at Travillian Station in 1864; John B. Presley, surrendered April, 1865; David Quarles, died of disease at Kilpatrick (Union) Camp; Wm. Quarles, surrendered April, 1865; Henry R. Quattlebaum; P. Randall, died of disease in Virginia 1864, transferred to another command 1864; Reuben Richardson, transferred to another command 1864; David Reynolds, died of disease in Virginia 1864, transferred to another command 1864; W. D. Rountree, surrendered April, 1865; Charles Roper, died of disease at home 1864; George Rump, Colleton, surrendered April, 1865; John M. Scott, surrendered April, 1865, transferred to another command 1864; John Scott, surrendered April, 1865, transferred to another command 1864; Milton Scott, surrendered April, 1865, transferred to another command 1864; Jesse Scott, surrendered April, 1865, transferred to another command 1864; L. G. Spradley, surrendered April, 1865, transferred to another command 1864; Thomas Sego, died of disease in 1865; E. V. Steadman, Lexington, surrendered April, 1865; Starling Turner, surrendered April, 1865; Wm. H. Turner, surrendered April, 1865; Sumpter Turner, surrendered April, 1865; Robert Turner, surrendered April, 1865, transferred to another command 1864; Wm. Timmerman, surrendered April, 1865, transferred to another command 1864; John N. Perry, surrendered April, 1865, transferred to another command 1864; Geo. P. Trotter, surrendered April, 1865; Thomas D. Villard, surrendered April, 1865; S. B. Whatley, died of disease at home 1864; Thomas R. Williams, died of disease at Petersburg September, 1864; A. G. Williams, surrendered April, 1865; Pressley M. Williams, surrendered April, 1865; Calvil Watson, surrendered April, 1865; E. D. Watson, surrendered April, 1865; John P. Wages, surrendered April, 1865, tranferred to another command in 1864; A. S. W. West, surrendered April, 1865; Hezekiah Woods, surrendered April, 1865. Commissioned officers, 6; non-commissioned officers, 11; total, 17; privates, 124; total rank and file, 141. Killed in battle, 11; died of wounds, 2; died of disease, 11; died in Kilpatrick Union Camp, 1; total deaths, 25. Wounds not mortal, 5.

Losses killed in battle in this troop were rather heavier than usual with cavalry. I have observed that cavalry seldom suffers as much in battle as infantry.

COMPANY I, STATE TROOPS.

Roll of Company "I," South Carolina State Troops—Station Pocotaligo—February, 1864:

J. C. Brooks, Captain: L. S. Johnson, First Lieutenant; C. H. Plunkett, Second Lieutenant; J. A. Bland, Third Lieutenat; W. P. Delph, First Sergeant; G. W. Thurmond, Second Sergeant; S. V. Johnson, Third Sergeant; W. L. Anderson, Fourth Sergeant; Wm. Culham, First Corporal; J. P. Courtney, Second Corporal; Stephen Mays, Third Corporal; Robert D. Bryant, Fourth Corporal.

PRIVATES.

A. Adams, H. Adams, G. A. Addison, T. Broadwater, W. Cartledge, W. H. Cumbee, M. Coon, B. Davis, W. B. Elsmore, B. Franklin, M. Franklin, W. Grice, W. Glover, S. Glover, J. Glover, M. D. Green, Wm. Hill, T. Hitt, S. Herndon, S. Hendrix, J. Jones, R. E. Kenney, W. Lippard, M. Lebeschultz, W. E. Legg, A. Lewis, R. Merriwether, A. Miles, W. L. Murrell, W. D. McGhee, J. C. Mills, W. B. Mays, L. Mayer, A. Numberger, M. J. Palmer, El. Posey, Jesse Satcher for E. M. Posey, B. M. Posey for Jacob Mayer, W. Powell, James Powell, John Rhinehart, C. L. Refoe, E. Randall, Jno. Rossan, J. Rice, Jacob Mayer, Julius Satcher, Joe. Saunders, S. M. Williamson, Jacob Wise, Joseph D. Turner, H. Gulledge, Wm. P. Butler, Ed. Tankersly, M. De-

Medicis, George Miller, Timothy Thomas, J. C. Kennedy. Total, 71.

COMPANY B, SECOND REGIMENT.

Roll of Company "B," Second Regiment, State Troops, Colonel William Fort, commanding, Pocotaligo, S. C., September, 1863, to February, 1864:

George D. Huiett, Captain; Thomas Jones, First Lieutenant; Joseph Wyse, Second Lieutenant; Thomas Carson, Second Lieutenant; Ira Cromley, Orderly Sergeant—Clerk.

PRIVATES.

H. H. Mays, T. J. Burnett, John Pardue, Holloway Claig, Leuellen Matthews, Allen Kemp, David Holloway, Mike Riley, Joseph Berry, Sam Dyer, Whitfield Smith, Henry Griffith, Rufus Jones, Henry Jones, Benjamin Lewis, Isham Culbreath, John Griffith, L. E. Holloway, H. Hair, D. A. J. Bell, Lewis Bean, Lod Hill, J. Weaver, G. Dorn, John Eidson, N. A. Burton, A. S. Powell, Dan'l Ridgell, Henry Hart, P. L. Wright, James Smyley, E. J. Amaker, Andrew Cromer.

COMPANY B, FOURTEENTH INFANTRY REGIMENT.

Roll of Company "B," Fourteenth Infantry Regiment, South Carolina Volunteers:

The whole company, officers and men, were from Edgefield, so I need not repeat that statement.

Pinckney A. West, age 32, Captain; wounded at Ox Hill; discharged at Camp Gregg in consequence of wound. James Boatwright, age 28, Captain; wounded at Port Royal; discharged at Appomattox; promoted from Second Lieutenant. Ezekiel W. Rutland, age 35, First Lieutenant; died of disease at Camp Butler October 16th, 1861. Robert B. Watson, age 23, First Lieutenant; wounded at Frazier's Farm and at Gettysburg; discharged from Appomattox; promoted from Second Lieutenant. John W. Bell, age 21, Second Lieutenant; wounded at Gettysburg; promoted from Fifth Sergeant. Ervin A. Roach, Jr., age 22, Second Lieutenant; wounded at Gettysburg; promoted from the ranks. Henry Ranch, Jr., age 19, Second Lieutenant; killed in battle at Gettysburg 1863; promoted from the ranks. Francis W. Gibson, age 21, First Sergeant; wounded at Gaines' Mill; transferred. James H. White, age 25, First

Sergeant; killed at Petersburg in 1864; promoted from First Corporal. Woodruff W. Holston, age 17, First Sergeant; discharged at Hart's Island, N. Y.; promoted from the ranks. John M. Corley, age 23, Second Sergeant; discharged at Appomattox. John M. Lott, age 20, Third Sergeant; discharged at Point Lookout. Joseph R. Huiett, age 19, Fourth Sergeant; killed at Frazier's Farm 1862. George Y. Langford, age 20, Fourth Sergeant; discharged Hart's Island, N. Y. William W. Chapman, age 30, First Corporal; discharged Hart's Island, N. Y. William D. L. Miller, age 21, Second Corporal, killed at Deep Bottom July 28th, 1864. Jesse Jennings, age 21, Third Corporal, died of disease at Richmond 1862. Robert Brooks, age 25, Fourth Corporal; died since the war. John E. Grice, age 18, Fifth Corporal; wounded Gaines' Mill; died of disease at Columbia, S. C. Nathan N. Burton, age 18, Sixth Corporal; wounded at Deep Bottom; discharged from Hart's Island, N. Y.

PRIVATES.

Levi W. Addy, age 20, discharged at Appomattox; David S. Bodie, age 23, killed at Petersburg April 2nd, 1865; Felix Bodie, age 45, died of disease at Richmond 1864; Andrew Bartley, age 23, killed at Port Royal January 1st, 1861; Westley Bartley, age 22, wounded at Second Manassas, discharged at Appomattox; Samuel Bartley, age 16, discharged at Appomattox; Daniel Berry, age 19, discharged at Appomattox; Nathan Bodie, age 25, discharged at Appomattox; Daniel Busby, age 18, discharged at Appomattox, died since the war; William Busby, age 18, wounded at Port Royal, discharged at Appomattox, transferred to Seventh Infantry; George Black, age 19, discharged at Appomattox; Jesse Black, age 21, wounded at Ox Hill and Second Manassas, discharged at Appomattox; Mark P. Black, age 17, wounded at Second Manassas and at Chancellorsville, discharged at Appomattox; Pressley Buzzard, age 20, died of disease at Richmond 1862; John Brown, age 25, killed at Gettysburg July 2nd, 1863; James M. Brown, age 19, wounded at Gaines' Mill, discharged at Appomattox; Jesse Brown, age 21, wounded at Chancellorsville and discharged at Appomattox; Obidiah Bodie, age 30, died of disease at Richmond 1862; Tillman

Brown, age 18, discharged at Appomattox; Hilary A. Clark, age 28, discharged at Appomattox; Joseph A. Clark, age 17, discharged at Appomattox; John Crouch, age 30, wounded at Chancellorsville and died of his wounds since the war; William Crouch, age 28, wounded at Second Manassas and at Deep Bottom, discharged at Appomattox; Jacob W. Crouch, age 18, discharged at Appomattox; J. Jackson Chapman, age 28, wounded at Chancellorsville and at Gaines' Mill, discharged at Appomattox; George W. Chapman, age 20, discharged at Appomattox; Adam Chapman, age 18, wounded at Second Manassas, discharged at Appomattox; Adam D. Corley, age 20, wounded at Deep Bottom, discharged at Appomattox; Uriah Etheridge, age 18, wounded twice at Gaines' Mill, discharged at Appomattox; Guildford Etheridge, age 25, killed at Gettysburg June 2nd, 1862; Caleb Etheridge, age 21, discharged at Appomattox; Robert V. Faulkner, age 18, discharged at Appomattox; Larkin Faulkner, age 20, discharged at Appomattox, died since the war; John R. Gibson, age 23, discharged at Appomattox; Ambrose Gibson, age 18, wounded at Petersburg and Second Manassas, discharged at Appomattox, died since; Pressley W. Gillion, age 25, discharged at Appomattox, died since; John R. Gillion; age 19, wounded at Chancellorsville and at Gettysburg, discharged at Appomattox; Allen Gillion, age 31, discharged at Appomattox; Guildford A. Gilder, age 18, died in Union Prison at David's Island —supposed in 1863; Joseph P. Hewson, age 17, wounded at Port Royal, transferred to Seventh South Carolina Infantry; William P. Havird, age 18, wounded at Gettysburg, discharged at Appomattox; Andrew Hargit, age 25, killed at Deep Bottom July 28th, 1864; George Harris, age 25, wounded at Gettysburg and discharged at Appomattox; Caleb Hare, age 17, killed at Chancellorsville May 3rd, 1863; James Hare, age 19, wounded at Deep Bottom and at Gaines' Mill, discharged at Appomattox; Pinckney W. Harris, age 17, wounded at Chancellorsville, discharged at Appomattox; William A. Hardy, age 18, wounded at Gaines' Mill, discharged at Appomattox; Philip Jennings, age 21, discharged at Appomattox; Henry Jennings, age 18, wounded at Gaines' Mill, lost a leg, discharged at Richmond; Matthew W. Jennings, age 17, died in Union Prison; Lot Jennings, age 31, discharged at Appomattox; James J. Jones, age 29, discharged at Appomattox; Robert T. Jones, age 31, killed at Petersburg in 1864; Warren Laidler, age 25, transferred to Seventh Infantry; Hezekiah K. Laidler, age 17; P. J. Lankford, age 17, died of wounds at Port Royal 1862; Lewis M. Lankford, age 19, died of wounds at Port Royal 1862; General McHare, age 18, discharged at Appomattox; Joseph F. McHare, age 35, wounded at Spottsylvania, discharged at Appomattox; William McHare, age 19, discharged at Appomattox, died since; John Mathis, age 20, wounded at Gettysburg, discharged at Appomattox; Bailey Matthews, age 16, discharged at Appomattox; Andrew G. McGee, age 21, died of disease at Port Royal 1862; William D. McGee, age 15, wounded at Second Manassas and at Chancellorsville, discharged at Appomattox; Joseph McGee, age 18, killed at Deep Bottom July 28th, 1864; Alfred Maroney, age 18, transferred to Seventh Infantry; William T. Minick, age 27, discharged at Hart's Island; Joel Minick, age 21, wounded at Port Royal and at Gettysburg, discharged at Appomattox; Jacob Minick, age 22, wounded at Spottsylvania, discharged at Appomattox; Thomas H. Miller, age 18, killed at Gettysburg July 2nd, 1863; George W. McCarthy, age 26, died at Richmond of wounds 1862; Henry McCullough, age 30, discharged at Appomattox, died since; Edgar Merchant, age 18, killed at Port Royal January 1st, 1862; Joseph Outz, age 18, wounded at Frazier's Farm seven times in one battle; John H. Outz, age 20, killed in battle near Petersburg; Thomas Outz, age 23, died of disease at Malvern Hill, wounded at Chancellorsville; George Outz, age 16, wounded at Second Manassas, discharged at Appomattox; Lawson Padgett, age 17, killed at Petersburg 1864; Wesley P. Padgett, age 18, killed at Gettysburg July 3rd, 1863; Henry H. Padgett, age 18, wounded at Deep Bottom, discharged at Appomattox; Emri Padgett, age 17, transferred to Seventh Infantry; Nat. Y. Padget, age 15, wounded at Chancellorsville, paroled from Elmira Prison; Mahlon Padgett, age 17; died of disease at Orange Court House, Va., 1863; M. Turner Parker, age 22, died of disease at Bowling Green 1862; Ezekiel A. Perry, age 20, wounded at Second Manassas, discharged at Appomattox; Thomas Perry, age 18, killed at Spottsylvania May, 1862; John L. Perry, age 16, wounded near James River, discharged

at Appomattox; Michael Plymale, age 23, killed at Port Royal
January 1st, 1862; Augustus M. Rogers, age 30, discharged at
Chimborazo Hospital; James Rogers, age 25, discharged at
Appomattox; Martin Rogers, age 18, discharged at Appomat-
tox; Gonan Richardson, age 20, killed by train at Petersburg;
James R. Rivers, age 23, wounded at Deep Bottom, discharged
at Appomattox; Samuel N. Rauch, age 20, wounded at Get
tysburg, discharged at Appomattox; James F. Rutherford,
age 17, wounded at Gettysburg, discharged at Appomattox;
Mastin Rowe, age 18, wounded at Gettysburg, discharged at
Appomattox; Francis M. Riser, age 18. killed at Port Royal
January 1st, 1862; Jacob I. Ranch, age 25, discharged at Ap-
pomattox; John Rowe, age 16, discharged at Appomattox;
William H. Stone, age 24, wounded at Gaines' Mill, discharged at Appomattox; John Stone, age 20, killed at Gaines'
Mill; Jackson Snipes, age 23, died of disease at Richmond
1863; Richard W. Smith, age 19, died in Union Prison, David's
Island, 1863; J. M. Salter, age 25, transferred to Peagram's
Battery; James Salter, age 18, transferred to Seventh Infantry; Francis M. Snelgrove, age 20, killed at Gettysburg
July 2nd, 1863; Luther Snelgrove, age 18, discharged at Appomattox; William Sawyer, age 23, died of disease at Richmond; James P. Thompson, age 25; Jesse W. Vincent, age 23,
died of disease at Richmond 1862; Jacob W. Whittle, age 17,
discharged at Point Lookout; Malachi Whittle, age 18,
wounded at Frazier's Farm, discharged at Appomattox; Joel
M. Whittle, age 16, died of disease in Union Prison at Chester,
Penn., wounded at Harper's Ferry in 1863; Hamer Whittle,
age 18, wounded at Gettysburg four times in the same battle,
discharged at Appomattox; Ira Whittle, age 35, died of
disease at Baltimore in 1863; Wesley Whittle, age 37, died of
disease at Richmond in 1862; Hezekiah Whittle, age 20, discharged at Appomattox; William J. Wise, age 20, died of
disease at Petersburg in 1863; Calhoun Wise, age 18, wounded
at Wilderness, lost a leg; Tyre Wise, age 16, died of disease at
Petersburg in 1863; Andrew M. Whitman, age 18, died in
Union Prison, Chester, Penn., 1862 or 1863; Larkin W. Warren, age 15, wounded at Chancellorsville and at Gaines' Mill,
discharged at Appomattox; Rhyder Walker, age 18, transferred to Seventh Infantry; Henry C. White, age 20, wounded

at Second Manassas and at Chancellorsville, discharged at Appomattox; Michael J. Watson, age 17, discharged at Appomattox; John Wilson, age 40, discharged at Appomattox; John Waits, age 16, killed near Petersburg April 2nd, 1865. Officers commissioned and non-commissioned, 20; privates, 127; total rank and file, 147. Killed in battle, 23; killed by railroad accident, 1; died of wounds, 3; died of disease, 17; died in prison, 5; total deaths, 49.

The number killed in battle in this company is rather above the average—died of wounds below the average.

The whole loss is precisely one third during the war, which I have found to be the average loss of all the companies, the rolls of which I have copied. Some went a little over, some a little under. This company is the first one which I have found to be exact. If the Confederate States had in actual service in the field during the war as many as 240,000 men, then the actual number of deaths in battle and from the casualties of the war, was not less than 80,000. It is true, however, that some of the 80,000 would have died during that time; but it is true, nevertheless, that the war slaughtered in the Southern States 60,000 able-bodied men besides rendering many others cripples for life. "Lord, what fools these mortals be."

From the Baltimore Sun.

"THE CONFEDERATE FLAG."

The quarterly meeting of the Baltimore Chapter, United Daughters of Confederacy, was marked yesterday by the reading of an original poem on the Confederate flag composed and read by the President, Mrs. D. Giraud Wright. The poem is as follows:

"THE CONFEDERATE FLAG."

"The hands of our women made it,
    Baptized in our mothers tears
And drenched with the blood of our kindred
    With hope for those four long years,
Across vale and plain we watched it
    While the tide of battle rolled,
And with streaming eyes have we followed
    The wave of each soft silken fold.

"As high over our hosts it floated,
    Through dust and din of the fight,
We could catch the glint of spearhead
    And the flash of crimson light;
While the blood of men who bore it
    Flowed fast on the reddened plain,
And our cry went up in anguish
    To our God for our martyred slain.

"And we went and watched and waited
    By our lonely household fire,
For the mother gave her firstborn
    And the daughter gave her sire,
But the wife sent forth her husband
    The maiden her lover sweet,
And hearts kept time in the silence
    To the rhythmic tread of their feet.

"As they marched o'er vale and mountains,
    While our banners rose and fell,
Though victory often crowned it
    As the Northern hosts can tell.
But the whole world was against us;
    Our battle we fought alone,
Till the conquerors —want and famine—
    Bade us lay our colors down.

"Cold are the loved hands that bore it,
    Stilled are the brave hearts and true,
Watching nor waiting can bring them,
    Weeping is all we can do.
Light from our banner has faded,
    We, in its shadow forlorn,
Have only our mem'ries left us,
    And our battle flag drooping and torn.

"No hand of vandal shall touch it.
    'Tis shrined in our heart of hearts
With dearest, holiest mem'ries;
    And the burning tear drops starts,
While laurel we weave and cypress
    For the fair, the brave, the good;
The only stain on our banner
    Is the stain of our heroes' blood."

The poem by Mrs. D. Giraud Wright, of this c
Confederate flag, read yesterday at the meeting of
ters of the Confederacy, will touch many hearts.
struggle of which the Confederate flag is the symb

noble qualities it called forth in a brave, conscientious and chivalric people, must ever command the interest and respect of all generous minds. All the world honors the magnificent efforts of the South in behalf of what it deemed right and expedient, though all the world may not view its failure with regret. The sentiment of loyalty with which ex-Confederates regard their flag is intelligible and commands the deference, if not sympathy, of those who upheld the stars and stripes. There is much that is pathetic in the memories the sight of the flag of the Confederacy invokes, and it has inspired many poems, of which Mrs. Wright's is one of the best.

COMPANY D, FOURTEENTH REGIMENT INFANTRY.

Roll of Company "D," Fourteenth Regiment Infantry, South Carolina Volunteers,—all from Edgefield:

Abner Perrin, Captain; promoted Major, Colonel, and Brigadier General; killed at Spottsylvania. E. H. Youngblood, Captain; wounded at Ox Hill; promoted from First Lieutenant; appointed Enrolling Officer in 1863. E. S. Mims, Captain; wounded at Malvern Hill; promoted from Second and First Lieutenant. W. H. Brunson, First Lieutenant; wounded at Cold Harbor, Gettysburg, and Petersburg; promoted from Third Lieutenant. H. D. Crooker, Second Lieutenant; killed at Gettysburg, promoted from First Sergeant; W. E. Durisoe, Second Lieutenant; wounded at Noel's Station; promoted from ranks. L. W. Youngblood, Second Lieutenant; promoted from Sergeant; transferred to Enrolling Department. T. W. Carwile, Sergeant Major; wounded at Chancellorsville; promoted from the ranks. J. B. Wallace, First Sergeant; wounded at Chancellorsville; promoted from the ranks. B. A. Jones, First Sergeant; wounded at Chancellorsville, Cold Harbor, and at Petersburg. Lewis Coleman; First Sergeant; killed at Manassas. C. L. Durisoe, First Sergeant; promoted from Corporal. Joe Brunson, First Sergeant; wounded at Gettysburg and at the Wilderness; promoted from the ranks; J. T. Gray, First Sergeant; wounded at Chancellorsville; promoted from the ranks. James Paul, First Sergeant; promoted from the ranks. Jackson Covar, Commanding Sergeant; promoted from the ranks. M. T. McHenry, Corporal; wounded at Cold Harbor; promoted Ensign. B. T. Swearengen, Corporal; died of disease in hospital in 1862. John Roper, Corporal; transferred to the Seventh Infantry May, 1862. W. S. Covar, Corporal; wounded at Spottsylvania; promoted from ranks. J. A. Colgan, Corporal; killed at Malvern Hill; wounded at Manassas and Gettysburg; promoted from ranks. T. P. DeLoach, Corporal; wounded at Gettysburg and Noel's Station; promoted from the ranks.

PRIVATES.

W. H. Atkinson, age 33, from Aiken; T. C. Banks, age 36, died of disease in hospital in 1864; W. V. Bartee, age 26, died of disease in hospital in 1864; M. L. Bartley, age 17, wounded at Gettysburg; N. L. Bartley, age 32, killed at Gettysburg; T. W. Bartley, age 30, furnished substitute January, 1863; James Boyd, age 44, killed at Noel's Station; John Bridwell, age 21; killed at Gettysburg; G. M. Broadwater, age 29; R. H. Broadwater, age 25, wounded at Chancellorsville; J. F. Burton, age 33, discharged March 15th, 1863; L. R. Boyce, age 17, died of disease in hospital in 1863; L. H. Bryan, age 22, Musician; W. D. Bryan, age 18, Musician; J. O. Brunson, age 16, wounded at Cold Harbor; C. A. Cheatham, age 18, wounded at Manassas, transferred to Second Infantry in 1864; J. H. Cheatham, age 17, wounded at Cold Harbor and Gettysburg; Oscar Cheatham, age 16, wounded at Cold Harbor and Spottsylvania; M. A. Christie, age 22, wounded Cold Harbor; B. W. Christian, age 28, wounded at Gettysburg; John Cockrell, age 14, wounded at Petersburg; Enos Clark, age 60, discharged November, 1861; W. L. Clark, age 22, killed at Cold Harbor; William Clark, age 20, killed at Cold Harbor; W. L. Coleman, age 35; L. P. Collum, age 20, wounded at Wilderness and Petersburg; J. M. Collum, age 17, wounded at Petersburg; A. Collum, age 22; B. Corley, age 26, wounded at Wilderness and Gettysburg; C. S. Corley, age 22, died of disease in hospital 1862; F. H. Corley, age 20, killed at Gettysburg; W. Corley, age 18, wounded at Cold Harbor, discharged February, 1863; C. L. Covar, age 23, died of disease in hospital 1862; J. W. Covar, age 25; L. P. Covar, age 16, wounded at Chancellorsville; John Cosey, age 20, wounded at Chancellorsville; J. E. Colgan, age 17, wounded at Gettysburg; J. C. DeLoach, age 30, killed at the Wilderness; Jabez DeLoach, age 20, wounded at Gettysburg and Noel's Station; E. M. Dinkins, age 24, wounded at Chancellorsville and Gettysburg; G. R. Durisoe, age 17, killed at Petersburg; David Etheridge, age 18, wounded at Gettysburg, Joseph Gray, age 16, wounded at Cold Harbor; W. B. Griffin, age 18, wounded at Gettysburg; A. Grice, age 16, died of disease in hospital 1862; John Gregory, age 18, discharged November 23rd, 1861; W. P. Goodman, age 15, discharged April 22nd, 1864; W. W. Goodman, age 40, appointed Sutler October, 1861; L. D. Hagood, age 26; L. D. Hickson, age 16, wounded at Cold Harbor and Wilderness; John Hatcher, age 26, died of disease in hospital January, 1863; John Harrison, age 22, killed at Cold Harbor; H. B. Harrison, age 17, wounded at Cold Harbor and Petersburg; John Hostillo, age 52, discharged April 30th, 1864; P. B. Kissie, age 24, killed at Noel's Station, wounded at Culpepper; H. G. Kissie, age 22, died of disease in hospital May, 1863; M. Lott, age 22, wounded at Chancellorsville and Wilderness; W. M. Lott, age 26, Musician; S. P. Lott, age 24, discharged November 22nd, 1863; Paul Mapuss, age 25, wounded at Chancellorsville; W. D. McCarty, age 17, wounded at Cold Harbor; W. H. McClintock, age 17, discharged December 19th, 1861; J. P. Moss, age 20, wounded at Frazier's Farm and Chancellorsville, transferred to Second Infantry; F. A. Murrell, age 22, wounded at Frazier's Farm; G. W. Murrell, age 16, wounded at Boteler's Ford and Spottsylvania; J. W. McCullough, age 20; William McGee, age 19; F. M. Nicholas, age 43, discharged January 25th, 1863; A. R. Nicholas, age 16; Samuel Overstreet, age 24, wounded at Chancellorsville, Gettysburg, and Noel's Station; P. P. Posey, age 28, wounded at Gettysburg, Malvern Hill, Peterburg; W. H. Posey, age 21, died of disease in hospital 1863, wounded at Chancellorsville; W. C. Prater, age 48, discharged March 10th, 1863; P. M. Prater, age 21, died in Union Prison, wounded at Cold Harbor and at Gettysburg; N. P. Raimey, age 23; W. D. Raimey, age 21, wounded at Malvern Hill; Felix Ridgell, age 17, killed at Gettysburg; T. T. Ridgell, age 20, killed at Petersburg, wounded at Cold Harbor and Gettysburg; Cullen Rowe, age 17; Simpson Rowe, age 20; W. P. Ryan, age 16, wounded at Noel's Station; P. B. Ryan, age 45, discharged April, 1863; T. M. Sawyer, age 35, killed at Cold Harbor; J. T. Sawyer, age 17, wounded at Cold Harbor,

Chancellorsville; J. A. Sease, age 26; J. D. Smitherman, age 28, killed at Frazier's Farm; H. A. Strom, age 17, killed at Noel's Station, wounded at Manassas; T. C. Strom, age 17, wounded at Chancellorsville; T. J. Strom, age 20, killed at Petersburg, wounded at Cold Harbor; D. W. Thomas, age 25; G. J. Toney, age 30; A. S. Walker, age 23, Hospital Steward; W. S. Walker, age 21, wounded at Cold Harbor, Gettysburg O. P. Walker, age 19, killed at Chancellorsville; William Wal ton, age 17; John Williams, age 26, died of disease in hospital 1862; S. M. Williams, age 21; Steel White, age 45, killed at Cold Harbor; A. G. Woodruff, age 18; John Whittle, age 42, wounded at Gettysburg; A. W. Youngblood, age 25, pro- moted Assistant Surgeon September 10th, 1861; J. A. Young blood, age 17, died of diseases in hospital in 1865, wounded at Manassas and Chancellorsville; J. M. Youngblood, age 20, wounded at Gettysburg. Officers commissioned and non-com- missioned, 22; privates, 103; total rank and file, 125. Killed in battle, 21; died of disease in hospital, 12; died in Union Prison, 1; total deaths, 34.

Total loss from all causes a little less than one-third of the whole number, but the number killed in battle is a fraction greater than the usual rate, being a little over one-sixth of the whole.

COMPANY G, FOURTEENTH REGIMENT

Company "G," Fourteenth Regiment South Carolina Vol- unteers. The following members of this company and regi- ment were from Edgefield County·

J. T. Gordon, age 27, Second Lieutenant; died at Gettys burg of wounds; wounded at Gaines' Mill; promoted from First Sergeant to Second Lieutenant March 20th, 1863. J. M. Dyson, age 20, Second Lieutenant; promoted from ranks to Second Lieutenant February 17th, 1864.

PRIVATES.

John L. Bussey, age 18, killed at Gaines Mill; T. R. Cole- man, age 22, surrendered April 9th, 1865; T. J. Coleman, age 18, died of disease February 9th, 1862; James E. Goff, age 18, wounded at Fredericksburg and Petersburg; Seaborn Stalna- ker, age 18, paroled from prison; Samuel Stalnaker, age 25, died of wounds at Gettysburg July 10th, 1863.

XXXVIII.

COMPANY K, FOURTEENTH REGIMENT.

Roll of Company "K," Fourteenth Regiment South Carolina Volunteers:

D. C. Tomkins, Captain, resigned in 1862. O. W. Allen, First Lieutenant; resigned in 1862. W. L. Stevens, Second Leutenant; resigned in 1863. James H. Allen, Third Lieutenant; promoted to Captain in 1863. J. A. Landrum, First Sergeant; killed in battle May 12th, 1864, at Spottsylvania C. H., Va. B. B. Bryan, Second Sergeant; made Second Lieutenant; disabled in battle 3rd of May, 1864. Simeon Cogburn, Third Sergeant; made Second Lieutenant; severely wounded at Gettysburg July 1st, 1863. E. L. Strother, Fourth Sergeant; wounded near Richmond, Va., detailed to Pioneer Company. E. R. Mobley, Fifth Sergeant; killed at Gettysburg, Pa., July 3rd, 1863. J. R. Hill, Sixth Sergeant; wounded. R. G. Johnson, First Corporal; wounded in battle—discharged. F. L. Harling, Second Corporal; killed at Fredericksburg, Va., 13th December, 1863. E. M. Outzs, Third Corporal; killed at Fredericksburg, Va., 13th December, 1863. J. C. Buzhardt, 4th Corporal; severely wounded at Gettysburg, Pa., July 3rd, 1863. R. S. Tombs, Fifth Corporal; wounded at Gettysburg, 1st July, 1863. J. U. Werts, Sixth Corporal; died since the war.

PRIVATES.

A. B. Adams, killed at Gettysburg, Pa., 1st July, 1863; W. H. W. Adams; W. J. Adams, wounded near Richmond—transferred to supporting force at home; W. S. Allen, appointed Second Lieutenant for distinguished valor at Spottsylvania C. H., May 12th, 1864, and assigned to Company "K," Fourteenth, South Carolina Volunteers, as Brevet Captain; A. B. Amaker, wounded near Richmond, 1862, discharged 28th December, 1864; R. D. Amaker, wounded; Alex Adkins, died since the war; Oliver Adkins, eye shot out near Richmond, Va., discharged; H. R. Adkins, recruit; Jesse Berry, died of disease at Richmond; J. P. Berry, died of wounds near Richmond; A. M. Buzhardt, died of wounds in hands of enemy;

J. W. Buzhardt, discharged; Wm. Bledsoe; V. B. Bledsoe, died of disease at Richmond, 1862; Benj. Busby; D. P. Butler; Goodwin Bryan, killed in battle near Richmond; Lewis Bledsoe, died at home of measles; J. H. Cogburn, died of disease in hospital at Richmond, 1862; Charbar Dean, severely wounded; J. L. Dobey, killed at Gettysburg July 1st, 1863; Wm. Dodgen; Wm. Durst; Benedict Dean, died at home of measles; A. B. Dean, received in place of Peter Rogers; Joshua Edwards; J. H. Edwards, detailed to Pioneer Company; Gibson P. Faulkner, severely wounded near Richmond; G. W. Free killed at Gettysburg 3rd July, 1863; L. M. Free, detailed to Pioneer Company; John Faulkner, severely wounded and captured at Gettysburg 1st July, 1863; Thos. Faulkner; Whit Glauzier, severely wounded—Wilderness, 1864; J. M. Goleman, killed near Richmond; U. J. Goleman, severely wounded near Richmond; W. J. Graham, killed near Richmond; W. D. Graddick; Jno. A. Green, wounded and transferred to cavalry; H. F. Green, detailed to brass band; Joseph Harling, died at hospital; Lemuel Harling; James Harling, died at hospital; Rufus Harling, wounded at Gettysburg July 1st, 1863, also at Wilderness; T. B. Harvey, died of wounds in hospital; Whit Harvely; Milledge Hall, died of disease at hospital; W. M. Harris, wounded; P. B. Head, wounded and discharged; B. R. Hill; Mahlon Hearn, killed at Second Manassas; W. F. Horn, died after war from old wounds; Cornelius Horn; D. B. Johnston, died of disease at hospital; Allen King, killed at Gettysburg July 1st, 1863; M. C. Little, killed at Chancellorsville, Va.; L. O. Lovelace, belonged to brass band; E. M. Martin, belonged to brass band; B. W. Mayson; J. M. May, killed near Richmond, Va.; Silas Morse, furnished a substitute; Solomon Morse, joined Laurens Artillery without leave; W. H. Monce, deserted in Battle of the Wilderness; E. V. Mobley, discharged and joined cavalry; John Malay, substitute for Stevens Tompkins—deserted; Willis Neal, died of wounds at hospital; W. H. Neal, died of wounds at hospital; John Ouzts; Martin Ouzts; Andrew Ouzts, killed near Richmond; John W. Ouzts; James Ouzts, killed at Gettysburg; Marion Ouzts; F. M. Ouzts; W. H. Ouzts, severely wounded; J. L. Ouzts, killed at Wilderness; J. H. Ouzts; B. F. Ouzts; George Ouzts, killed at Gettysburg 1st July, 1863; Franklin Ouzts, lost an arm at Spottsylvania

C. H. 12th May, 1864; Jesse Parkman, killed near Richmond; J. S. Poliattie, left command without leave; H. D. Quattlebaum, died of disease at hospital; Larkin Rice, wounded at Noel Station; James Riley, discharged; Williamson Rice, killed at Gettysburg 1st July, 1863; Peter Rodgers, exchanged for A. B. Dean; J. L. Russell; Martin Rodgers; A. J. Rome; J. Asa Stevens, wounded; Lafayette Stevens, severely wounded; M. W. Stevens, killed at Gettysburg 1st July, 1863; Thos. Steedhan, died of disease at hospital; John Sheppard; B. N. Strother; J. L. Timmerman, killed near Richmond; A. J. Timmerman; B. M. Timmerman, died of disease in hospital; B. W. Timmerman, discharged; E. Timmerman, severely wounded at Gettysburg 1st July, 1863; G. M. Timmerman, severely wounded at Gettysburg 1st July, 1863; J. H. Timmerman; J. L. Timmerman, died of disease in hospital; R. W. Timmerman, died of disease in hospital; F. Timmerman, killed; W. E. Timmerman; Jno. Tompkins, died of wounds; Stevens Thompkins, furnished Jno. Malay substitute; W. H. Turner exchanged for Franklin Ouzts; George Turner; James Taylor; A. C. Werts; M. W. Wooten, killed at the Wilderness. Total, officers, 16; privates, 114; total, rank and file, 130. Killed in battle, 22; died of disease, 14; died of wounds, one since the war, 7; total number of deaths, 43. Wounds received, not fatal, 26.

The deaths in this company is thus seen to be about one-third of the whole number of enlisted men in it. This I find to be above the average—it is rarely greater—sometimes less.

As part of the history of Company "K" and of the Fourteenth Regiment, I insert the following, clipped from the Charleston News and Courier:

CLARK'S HILL, S. C., July 30th, 1891.
To the Editor of the News and Courier:

As a subscriber to your valuable paper, I ask the favor of you to publish my letter of inquiry as to the whereabouts of the colors of the Fourteenth South Carolina Regiment. I was a member of that regiment and feel interested as to final disposal of its colors. By complying with the above you will confer a favor. Respectfully,
RUFUS HARLING.

In the early days of 1865 McGowan's Brigade was holding the right wing of General Lee's army. Early in the morning we were ordered to move out of our works, by the right flank,. in the direction of the South Side Railroad, to cover the retreating and shattered forces of Lee's army, and soon after we had gotten on the march Captain Dunlap's Battalion of sharpshooters was ordered to the rear, deployed, and ordered to fall back in rear of the brigade. Soon after crossing a small stream we heard the roaring as that of distant thunder, which we soon discovered to be the mighty host of Sheridan's Cavalry in hot pursuit, and each cavalryman seemed to have a man behind him. As soon as they would come within range, the men behind would dismount and fire on us. We would return the fire as often as possible. Thus for some distance we were hotly pursued.

As soon as the brigade reached the South Side Railroad it halted, and formed a line of battle. Hastily piling up some rails as a protection from the advancing foe, which was a welcome cover to the hard pressed sharp-shooters, we fell in with the brigade as we found it, but not long to rest, for soon the enemy emerged from the woods into the open field in a splendid line of infantry to charge a little remnant of men. As they advanced across an open field they were allowed to come within easy range of our rifles. It then seemed that every man was determined to make his shots count, for after two or three volleys the enemy fell back in disorder to the woods from where they came. Receiving reinforcements, rapidly formed and moved to our left, and with their overwhelming forces we were compelled to retreat in disorder.

After crossing the railroad in the direction of the Appomattox River, I came up with the Color-Bearer of the Fourteenth South Carolina Regiment, and around him were about twenty-five men of the First, Eleventh, Twelfth, Thirteenth, and Fourteenth Regiments. Not having time to consult as to the better way of safety, we moved hastily on to the Appomattox River, thinking we might cross and join Longstreet's Corps, which was thought to be retreating up the river from Richmond. Finding the river considerably swollen and no way of crossing, we made our way up the river as best we could. Night coming on, we lay our wornout selves down to sleep, and a glorious sleep it was, such as we had not had in several nights. Next morning we were up early, ate a scanty breakfast, and continued to move up the river, thinking perhaps we might find some way of escape. On reaching a hill we found the enemy had gotten ahead of us, and that we must soon be made prisoners We then collected around the Color-Bearer, and determined to conceal the colors of the Fourteenth South Carolina Regiment. Then I, assisted by two others, raised a large, flat rock, under which our Color-Bearer placed the colors of the Fourteenth Regiment.

Captain W. L. Delph, now of Augusta, Ga., recently informed me that a gentleman by the name of Bunch, from the lower part of this State, was sent back to Virginia after the colors of the First South Carolina Regiment, which were placed with the colors of the Fourteenth South Carolina Regiment, under the same rock, and that Bunch also got the colors of the Fourteenth Regiment. If so, where are they? Any information respecting them will be thankfully received.

RUFUS HARLING,
Clark's Hill, S. C.

ATTENTION, COMPANY K, FOURTEENTH REGIMENT, SOUTH CAROLINA VOLUNTEERS.

CLARK, S. C., June 6th, 1896.

Editor Edgefield Chronicle:

DEAR SIR: The casualties of my company were published when you were editor of the Advertiser, A. Simkins, D. R. Durisoe, and E. Keese, proprietors. I would like to say something about my dear old captain's gallantry on this bloody occasion, but incompetency will not allow me.

The first day of July this year falls on Wednesday, the same day of the week and the month on which was fought the bloody battle of Gettysburg, the most eventful and disastrous battle of the war. I have in my scrap book a clipping from the Edgefield Advertiser of 1863, giving the casualties of our company in that battle. I copy the list of killed and wounded. Ponder over the list, dear old survivors and comrades, and remember the dear boys who fell on this memorable day.

"Killed.—Sergeant E. R. Mobley, G. W. Free, James Ouzts, Jesse Parkman, Wilkerson Rice, M. W. Stevens.

"Wounded.—Lieutenant S. Cogburn, foot severe; Sergeant J. C. Buzzard, arm severe; Corporal J. N. Werts, shoulder slight; Corporal W. D. Gradick, thigh severe; W. H. Ouzts, head slight; privates A. B. Adams, back severe; W. H. W. Adams, leg severe; R. D. Amaker, head slight; John L. Doby, thigh severe; Joshua Edwards, thigh slight; John Faulkner, head and shoulder severe; T. B. Harvey, leg slight; Whit Harvley, neck severe; James Harling, thigh severe; Rufus Harling, face severe; Allen King, left arm amputated; B. W. Mason, thigh severe; Martin Ouzts, thigh severe; Franklin Ouzts, leg slight; George Ouzts, head mortally; Larkin Rice, side slight; B. M. Timmerman, hand slight; Edward Timmerman, face severe; G. M. Timmerman, head slight; Geo. Taylor, shocked with shell; James Taylor, back slight; R. S. Towles, leg severe; A. C. Werts, arm slight.

"Missing.—Marion Ouzts and J. T. Timmerman.

"Killed, 6; wounded, 29; missing, 2; total, 37.

"[Signed.]   J. H. ALLEN,

"Lieutenant Commanding Company K."

This was the most disastrous battle of the war to our company. Its casualties on that day were equal to all the rest from that time to the close of the war. As well as my memory serves me, we went into the battle with 43 men. Thirty-seven were killed and wounded, only six being able to march back to old Virginia. Well do I remember our orders from the brave Query, "Hold your fire men and close in on the enemy."

RUFUS HARLING,

Company K, Fourteenth South Carolina Volunteers.

HISTORY OF THE COMPANY.

For the following brief sketch of the history of Company "K," Fourteenth Regiment, South Carolina Volunteers, I am indebted to the graphic pen of Mr. Rufus Harling, who was a member of the company:

Company K was organized in 1861, under command of the following officers: D. C. Tompkins, Captain; O. W. Allen, First Lieutenant; W. L. Stevens, Second Lieutenant; Jos. H. Allen, Third Lieutenant.

This company was organized from that portion of Edgefield

County commonly known as the "Dutch Settlement," situated on old Sleepy Creek, whose fore-parents were from the "Old Country"—there were no aristocrats among them. They owned but few slaves, but were sturdy yeomen, and did their own work. Always had plenty of "hog and hominy" at home, as the result of their own labor. Their time for schooling was from January till planting time; and from laying by till gathering time. Their chief amusements were going to corn-shuckings, log-rollings, and quiltings; but the happiest time for them was when on Christmas eve, with their "little brown jug," they went serenading, and "ate, drank, and were merry," till Christmas was over. Early in 1861 some of them began to go to Edgefield Court House, and there they heard some of the fiery speeches about the "infernal Yankees" trying to rob us of our rights. They saw other men called "Minute Men" wearing a badge, commonly known as a cockade. Some of them got a badge and wore it home, it being looked upon by many with amazement, as being something very honorable to wear the red cockade. Soon thereafter this company was formed and organized. Being supplied with the general parapharnalia which go to make up a soldier's outfit, they were bid by their dear mothers and wives to go to the front and to do their duty for their country.

Soon letters came from the dear boys from the Camp of Instruction at Pole Cat. Next came letters from Pocotaligo, saying "we are expecting a fight soon," and, as was expected, the Yankees landed and a fight occurred, in which this company took part. After the battle was over two privates of this company went out on the battle field and captured a prisoner, the first captured in South Carolina. These two privates, Lemuel Harling and Russell Rhodes, went through the war and are still living, August, 1892. Really some of these men thought the war was about over, as they had whipped the Yankees; but they soon learned that they had turned up in Virginia and that they must go there.

I, being at that time a fifteen-year-old boy, at home, trying to help my father make bread and meat for these men, will leave the history of Company "K" blank up to April 12th, 1863.

During all this time I was miserable for fear the war would terminate before I would take a hand in the struggle. I could hear of the battles of Manassas and around Richmond, all resulting in victories for the Confederates. I then would have been glad to have heard of a defeat, because I thought it would prolong the struggle and give me an opportunity to take a hand. After awhile the welcome news came that Captain Stevens and Lieutenant Allen were at home on furlough and would return to the army early in 1863. Being anxious to return with them I feared my father would not let me go, as he had already sent four sons to the front. Besides, being only seventeen years of age, which was unfavorable to me.

On Sunday, the 12th of April, 1863, father and myself went to church at Little Steven's Creek. There we met Captain W. L. Stevens and Lieutenant Jim Allen, who informed us that they would leave next morning for Virginia. After a short conversation father took Lieutenant Allen aside, and I heard him say: "Jim, take care of my boy," and at the same time wiping his eyes with his handkerchief. Lieutenant Allen said: "Have your boy to meet us at Chappells to-morrow morning." We returned home and heartily ate dinner. Mother soon got my bundle ready, which consisted of two suits of clothes, needles, and darning thread, and plenty of victuals, well cooked, to last me a week. About 3 o'clock father had two horses saddled and at the gate, one for me and one for the servant, who was to take me to the neighborhood of Ninety-Six, so as to be convenient to take the train next morning for Columbia. I did but little sleeping for fear the train would leave me; but I was there in good time, and as soon as the train rolled up I got aboard for the first time, still holding to my bundle. As the train moved off I looked to see the last of the negro and the horses. Then for the first time tears came to my eyes, because it first dawned upon me that I was in reality leaving home and all that was dear to me, perhaps never more to return. When we reached Chappells, Captain Stevens and Lieutenant Allen boarded the train. I then felt perfectly safe. It was but a few hours run from there to Columbia, the Capital of the State, which I had never before seen. We spent the night there; next morning took the train for Charlotte, N. C.; changed cars there for Raleigh;

then Weldon; there to Petersburg, Virginia; from there to Richmond, where we spent the night. Next day boarded the train for Guinea Station, which ended our journey on the train. We then set out to find the Fourteenth South Carolina Regiment, which was camped at a place called Camp Gregg. It took its name from the brave General Gregg, who was killed at Fredericksburg in 1862. He was Brigadier-General and was commanding the First, Eleventh, Twelfth, Thirteenth, and Fourteenth South Carolina Regiments. After three miles' walk we found our Company "K" in high spirits, flushed with the victory gained at Fredericksburg. This was April 18th, 1863, that I spent my first night in camp. Next day my name was enrolled as a member of Company "K," and with the regiment I went to do picket duty on the Rappahannock. Remained on picket twenty-four hours—was then relieved and we returned to camp. We did not remain there three days, for about the 25th of April, early in the morning, the sullen booming of cannon in the direction of Fredericksburg was a signal that the enemy were crossing the river.

Soon everything was astir. Orders had been issued to be ready with three days' rations to move at a moment's notice. Soon the long roll began to beat, and the hurried orders were to "fall in." We moved in the direction of Fredericksburg, and soon learned that Joe Hooker had crossed the river in heavy force. Before night set in we were in line of battle fronting the enemy, awaiting their advance. We remained fronting them for two days without any fighting, save a few artillery shots exchanged at long range. Early in the morning about the last of April orders came to move again. We learned the enemy had made a feint at Fredericksburg and had crossed the river about twelve miles higher up. We found them strongly fortified at a place called Chancellorsville. We bivouacked in front of them the first night, and about 9 o'clock next morning, being a part of General Jackson's command, we moved off as though we were on the retreat, but before sunset we found ourselves completely in rear of the enemy, whipping them most desperately and putting them in wild confusion. Night coming on, and General Jackson being mortally wounded, put a stop to the career of his victorious troops until the next morning.

At daylight we advanced again under command of J. E. B. Stuart, who was singing, "Old Joe Hooker, get out of the Wilderness!" and the boys shouting: "Remember Jackson!" It seemed that every man bent forward and did his whole duty. The enemy was moved from their strong breastworks into the tangled thickets of the wilderness, and such destruction I hope never to see again. Men fell almost in heaps. The woods being dry, caught fire from the bursting of shells, and I saw many men with every remnant of clothing burnt off, presenting the most sickening appearance imaginable—this being a memorable picture of the first Sabbath in May, 1863.

Night coming on, the enemy having been whipped, both seemed content to remain quiet—but there was not much sleep for fear of a surprise. The next day it began to rain and continued to do so all day. No regular engagement took place,—only sharp picket firing. By the next morning the enemy had recrossed the river, leaving many thousands of their dead in the hands of the victorious Confederates. We all returned to Camp Gregg, leaving many of our brave boys and messmates sleeping their last sleep. We remained in camp perhaps a month unmolested. During this time Company "K" was getting in fresh troops from the hospital and other sources, until we about regained our loss at Chancellorsville.

About the first of June the booming of cannon was again heard in the direction of Fredericksburg. Couriers again began to dart up to our Field Officers' tent with dispatches. Many men began to pack up to move, even without further orders. Soon the long roll beat again and we took up the march towards Fredericksburg. We were now leaving Camp Gregg never more to return to it.

Soon we found ourselves occupying the same ground as formerly fronting the enemy at Fredericksburg. We remained there several days. The enemy were at bay and did not advance. It seemed that Gen. Lee got restless for a fight and moved his army around the right wing of Hooker's, and of course the enemy withdrew from Fredericksburg. We moved on for several days without coming in contact with them. We found ourselves on the borders of the Potomac River, and it was then even known by the privates that another great battle would be fought north of the Potomac. The whole army crossed over, the bands playing: "Maryland, my Maryland!" The troops were in the highest spirits—flushed by the victory they had won at Chancellorsville. Shouting and yelling almost continually, they did not seem to think of defeat.

We still moved north—had not as yet seen the foe. We then found we had marched through Maryland and were in Pennsylvania. We rested for a day or so and then moved again. Across the Blue Ridge Mountains, and then we bivouacked in the Cumberland Valley. And sad, sad indeed that it was the last before the last sleep of so many of our brave boys.

Early in the morning of July 1st we were ordered to "fall in," and we hastily moved in the direction of Gettysburg. It was not long before we heard an occasional roar of the cannon, and it then became known that our advance lines had at last found the enemy, and that we, too, would soon be engaged in battle. As we came nearer the more constant and rapid could the firing be heard. About 10 o'clock we came in sight of the enemy. Without halting we filed out of the road to the right and formed line of battle in the edge of the roads. There we saw the wounded who had been engaged with the enemy returning —some stating they had been cut up badly and a great many had been captured. Col. Perrin commanded McGowan's brigade, to which the Fourteenth South Carolina belonged. Col. J. M. Brown commanding the Regiment, ordered the Regiment to lie down until other Regiments could form on our left. We could see the enemy just in the edge of the town behind a strong rock fence waiting for us to advance. The ground over which we had to advance was open—nothing to shield us from the shot of the enemy. At the word "Attention" we formed in open field, in plain view of the enemy. The orders were, "hold your fire men, and close in with the enemy." We advanced in splendid order and when in 200 yards of the enemy they opened a terrific fire on us with both artillery and musketry, sending the missiles of death into our faces and plowing great gaps through our ranks. Still we obeyed orders to hold our fire. We advanced—filling up the space made by our fallen, and when we had gotten within about fifty yards where the enemy were posted, our lines wavered, caused by filling up the spaces, and it now seemed that

our thin lines were destined to almost complete annihilation.
We were fired upon from right, left, and centre, and to retreat
would have been complete destruction. Just at this time Col.
Perrin, seeing our situation, came charging through our lines
and at a time when it seemed that no living being could escape
the thick flying missiles of death. But the brave Colonel
dashed along our thin lines, waving and pointing his sword at
the enemy. The men redoubled their resolutions and made a
dash for and captured the rock fence. The enemy fled in disorder. Then came our time for sending the death-dealing
shots into their broken ranks,—equally as they had of pouring
it into our unfortunate faces as we had advanced.

Soon the town of Gettysburg was in our possession. Mc-
Gowan's brigade, under the command of the brave Perrin, had
won the day, but at a great sacrifice. At least one-half his
command had been killed or wounded and was compelled to
halt. Had another as equally good brigade then come up to
follow the pursuit of the flying enemy, the three days battle at
Gettysburg would have ended in a complete victory to the
Confederates.

Just here let me say in honor to the brave Colonel Perrin,
that his dashing through our lines at its most critical period,
was the most daring and gallant act I have ever seen executed.
And to him your humble writer gives credit for the victory
won on the first day of July at Gettysburg. He was complimented by Gen. Lee and on the field made Brigadier-General.

I will now close my chapter and give the record of Company
"K" from Dutch settlement, which belonged to the Fourteenth
South Carolina Regiment. It was then commanded by Capt.
J. H. Allen, and, as well as I remember, the strength of his company at Gettysburg was 43; and I am in possession of the list
of casualties sent by him to the Edgefield Advertiser. It read
thus: killed, 6; wounded, 29; missing, 2; total, 37—leaving
only 6 to march back in ranks to Virginia. Besides the 6 killed,
I remember 3, at least, died of their wounds at the Field Hospital in less than 26 hours.

The above casualties will show something of the severity of
the battle of Gettysburg. But this little remnant of Company
"K" safely retreated with the Army of Virginia, and finally
winter-quartered in 1863, at Orange Court House, on the banks

of the Rapidan; and had comparatively a good long rest. And then we had preaching and prayer-meetings in camp.

During the winter our company recruited to almost its former strength, and we afterwards took part in all the important battles under Gen. Lee. There were the Battle of the Wilderness, Battle of the Horseshoe or Spottsylvania C. H., Noel's Station, Second Cold Harbor, Ridley's Shops, Deep Bottom, New Market Heights, around Petersburg, Jones' House, Reams' Station, Hatcher's Run, and on the South Side Railroad at Trevillian Station. But in all these close regular engagements Company "K's" losses did not exceed that of the battle of Gettysburg.

The small remnant of this company surrendered at Appomattox under command of Captain W. S. Allen. Then, in their well-worn old uniforms, came to their homes on Sleepy Creek without a penny with which to begin the battle of life. But they had not forgotten their former occupations, and any one visiting them now would not find men of fine dress, but sit down to dine with them you would be filled with home-raised ham and plenty of other good things to make any one content and happy.

Dear reader, the writer of this is quietly and comfortably at home, with his wife and little boys, striving to serve the Master in remembrance of His goodness to me, and praying that I may meet my dear unfortunate comrades gone before.

R. H.

MRS. LUCINDA HORNE.

The History of Edgefield cannot be complete without some notice of Mrs. Lucinda Horne, and I feel that I could never forgive myself were I to send this book into the world without her name in it.

In 1861 Cornelius Horne and his wife Lucinda were living in Edgefield County near Kirksey's. They had only one child, William F. Horne, who was grown up. Husband and son both enlisted in Company "K," Fourteenth South Carolina Volunteers, and as they had no home or other children, and her whole life being wrapped up in the lives of her husband and son, she also volunteered and went to the front with them. She remained with them until the close of the war, undergoing all the hardships incident to a soldier's life. She was loved and respected by every member of McGowan's Brigade. She was with her husband and son in all of General Jackson's hard marches always on hand when the regiment went into camp and prepared their scanty meals. When in winterquarters she took in washing besides her own, thus making some money, which added to their supplies. Her husband and son wore cleaner clothes and which were nicely patched by her industry through her love for them. Always just before a battle she would find out where the field hospital would be and she was always there to minister to the wounded and dying. "I remember," writes Mr. Rufus Harling to me, "while we were in line of battle near Petersburg in September, 1864, we had a fight at a place called Jones' Farm, and in this battle her son William was wounded, and then the kind hearted mother was ready to wait on her only son. She went with him to the hospital in Richmond and nursed him so as to be able to return home with him. Her son lived, I think, about 12 years after the war and then died of the wound received at the battle of Jones' Farm. After the son's death she travelled with her husband in a small covered wagon, peddling until just before her death, which was early in March, 1896.

"Mrs. Horne met with a reunion of the old Fourteenth Regiment at Greenwood, S. C., in August, 1891, and she was unanimously elected an honorary member of the same (the Veterans Association) and was carried to dinner by our old surviving Colonel J. N. Brown. I have often thought that had it not been for this good woman I might have been numbered with the many whose bones have been left in Virginia, as she gave me some good soup when I was sick, which seemed to revive me after a spell of sickness."

In their journeys through the country this loving and devoted couple, whom only death could part, sometimes ran great risks from high water. On one occasion they undertook to cross Half Way Swamp Creek when the water was too deep and they came very near drowning. Providentially they escaped with their lives and but little damage to their goods.

This couple, whose love and devotion to each other no words can express, were scarcely ever apart from the beginning of the war until the death of Mrs. Horne.

"She was buried at Chestnut Hill beside the son she followed so faithfully throughout the war. She was eighty-two years old, and has left her husband behind to mourn her loss."

After the war Mr. and Mrs. Horne and their son were living happily together when the son was so unfortunate as to be thrown by a mule he was riding, and the fall so injured his wound as to cause his death. The son had married some time before his death.

I feel that this brief record has not done justice to this heroic woman's career, but I have not the material to write more, and I could not do less.

COMPANY I, TWENTY-FOURTH REGIMENT.

Roll of Company "I," Twenty-fourth Regiment, South Carolina Volunteers. I am indebted to Rev. E. Capers, Colonel commanding Twenty-fourth Regiment, for kindly copying and sending me this roll:

A. J. Hammond, Captain; L. B. Weber, First Lieutenant; Jas. M. Lanham, Second Lieutenant; R. S. Key, Third Lieutenant; Thos. J. Adams, Orderly; J. H. Adams, Second Sergeant; B. U. Lanham, Third Sergeant; T. H. Curry, Fifth Sergeant; S. B. Lanham, First Corporal; J. H. Yeldell, Second Corporal; T. L. Tucker, Third Corporal; J. S. Reynolds, Fourth Corporal.

PRIVATES.

M. Medlock, J. W. Carpenter, J. M. Lanham, T. P. Anderson, John A. Mays, A. Sharpton, Jr., J. Kimbrell, Ezra Moore, Samuel Cook, John Bryant, H. A. Drasing, George R. Morgan, Wm. Grisham, J. Grisham, Jno. Miles, G. W. King, J. M. Riley, Jno. Shippe, John Mallet, L. H. Keitt, S. W. Sullivan, E. Reese, S. J. W. Clarke, D. Y. Clarke, W. L. Coleman, James F. Burton, J. E. Muse, Wm. Quarles, Robert Breckenridge, Jas. Larke, Jas. Padgett, John Leigh, Jno. Mays, James Howard, Wm. Harden, F. M. Coleman, W. P. Delph, R. A. Adams, W. E. Rodgers, Wm. Bryant, Wm. Clarke, S. Clarke, Jere. Cartledge, Samuel Cartledge, W. L. Miles, R. H. Williams, Jno. Hardy, J. Moore, Nicholas Bodie, Jno. Duncan, J. W. Buff, George Allen, Jno. Permenter, Benj. Burton, Charlie Burton, R. Murrall, Adam E. Carpenter. Total, 69.

NOTE:—This is a copy of the original muster roll on file in the office of the Adjutant General.   E. C.

COMPANY K, TWENTY-FOURTH REGIMENT.

Roll of Company "K," Twenty-fourth Regiment, South Carolina Volunteers, prepared by Lieutenant R. A. Cochran, commanding company at surrender at Greensboro, N. C., 1865:

S. S. Tomkins, Captain; resigned 1862. T. C. Morgan, Captain; promoted to Lieutenant Colonel; severely wounded at Calhoun and Decatur; surrendered at Greensboro. Jas. A. Dozier, First Lieutenant; resigned 1862. F. W. Andrews, Second Lieutenant; severely wounded at Nashville; promoted to First Lieutenant. G. W. Talbert, Second Lieutenant; resigned 1863. J. E. Morgan, Second Lieutenant; killed at Chickamauga while attempting to rally a Georgia regiment. T. M. Seigler, Second Lieutenant; surrendered at Greensboro; promoted to First Lieutenant. R. M. Winn, Second Lieutenant; killed in battle at Peach Tree Creek. R. A. Cochran, Second Lieutenant; in command of Company K at surrender; twice wounded; promoted to First Lieutenant. G. McWeaver, First Sergeant; lost a leg at Peach Tree Creek. J. A. Reynolds, First Sergeant; surrendered at Greensboro. G. W. Burton, Sergeant; severely wounded at Secessionville; P. M. Williams, Sergeant; transferred to Gregg's Cavalry. W. E. Hobbs, Sergeant; killed at Atlanta 1864. J. E. Holmes, Sergeant; surrendered at Greensboro. G. W. Andrews, Sergeant; severely wounded at Decatur; surrendered at Greensboro. L. H. Kemp, Corporal; surrendered at Greensboro. P. H. Strom, Corporal; surrendered at Greensboro. H. S. Seigler, Corporal; killed at Jonesborough, Ga. W. W. McDowell, Corporal; wounded at Franklin.

PRIVATES.

T. J. Adams; E. Bussey, killed at Secessionville 1862; D. W. Christian; Tom Collins, died in hospital 1863; J. J. Dorn, surrendered at Greensboro; John Dorn, died in hospital August 7th, 1863; W. P. Dorn, died in hospital October 15th, 1863; George Dorn, killed at Jonesborough; James Dorn, surrendered at Greensboro; J. R. Ellenberger, surrendered at Greensboro; R. P. Geoman, surrendered at Greensboro; R.

Glaze, died in hospital August 4th, 1863; Wm. Glaze, severely wounded at Decatur, Ga.; D. J. Gilchrist; William Harrison, died 1863; E. M. Holmes, wounded at Franklin, Tenn.; Tom Holiday, died in camp at Dalton, Ga.; William Hollings-worth; P. Hamilton, died in hospital 1863; E. Harling, honorably discharged; James Horn, severely wounded at Secessionville; Rit Horn, deserted at Dalton, Ga.; Wm. Kidd, deserted in route to Chickamauga; Jobe Martin, surrendered at Jonesboro; Whitfield Martin, killed at Peach Tree Creek; Lafayette Martin, died in hospital December 12th, 1863; W. T. Mathis, Joseph Morris; Dave Morgan, died in camp at Dalton January 9th, 1864; T. W. Morgan, severely wounded at Franklin, Tenn.; Pick New; Ben New, deserted 1863; Ned New, died 1862; J. T. Ouzts, surrendered at Greensboro; S. W. Ouzts, died May 30th, 1863, from wounds received in battle at Calhoun, Ga.; T. J. Ouzts; Peter Ouzts, surrenderrd at Greensboro; Isaac Ouzts, surrendered at Greensboro; Ab Ouzts, died in hospital 1862; Marion Ouzts, honorably discharged 1862; John Pardue, deserted at Dalton, Ga., 1864; D. Pardue, died in hospital; Abram Price; L. Parkman, surrendered at Greensboro· W. H. Rush; W. T. Robertson, surrendered at Greensboro; E. H. Reynolds; Alex Reynolds, honorably discharged 1864; A. W. Reel, surrendered at Greensboro; John Shaffer, died in hospital 1863; W. T. Stillman, died May 20th, 1863, from wounds received at Calhoun, Ga.; G. H. Seigler, severely wounded at Chickamauga; S. B. Strom, died at home while on furlough; J. P. Strom, wounded at Franklin, surrendered at Greensboro; W. S. Strom, killed at Franklin, Tenn.; Hag. Strom; G. W. Strom, surrendered at Greensboro; J. E. Strom, surrendered at Greensboro; W. H. Strom, T. Strom; George Timmerman, killed at Jonesboro; F. A. Timmerman, died in hospital January 20th, 1864; Wm. Timmerman, surrendered at Greensboro; G. H. Timmerman, died in hospital November 8th, 1863; Dave Timmerman; S. Thomas, severely wounded near Kenesaw Mountain; John Taylor, surrendered at Greensboro; G. W. Thurmond, lost his right arm and two fingers of left hand at Franklin, Tenn.; John Williams, killed at Atlanta; William White, killed at Chickamauga; W. A. Winn, died in hospital May 11th, 1864; E. C. Winn, severely wounded at Decatur, Ga.; Henry Timmerman, killed at Chickamauga.

Commissioned officers, 9; non-commissioned officers, 11; privates, 73; total rank and file, 93.   Killed in battle, 11; died of wounds, 2; died in hospital, 12; died at home on furlough, 1; died in camp, 2; total deaths, 28.   Wounded not mortal, 14; deserted, 4.

Deaths and wounded about the average.   Desertions unusually great.

COMPANY F, TWENTY-SEVENTH REGIMENT INFANTRY.

Roll of Company "F," Twenty-seventh Regiment, South Carolina Volunteers—Infantry.   I find the following names from Edgefield in this regiment, which I give with casualties:

Jacob Staubs, age 31, Third Sergeant; killed in battle at Cold Harbor June 6th, 1864. Jacob Boozer, age 21, Fourth Sergeant; died of disease at Danville September 5th, 1864; named in official reports for gallantry. W. L. Stone, age 40, First Corporal, died of disease at home July 4th, 1863. T. G. Attaway, age 23, Third Corporal.

PRIVATES.

William Page, age 19, (from Company "B"); J. A. Attaway, age 19, wounded at Pocotaligo and died of his wound at home December 21st, 1862; T. J. Bladon, age 35; J. W. D. Bowen, age 25, wounded at Petersburg; J. T. Bryant, age 25; C. W. Burder, age 17; Wesley Cockerill, age 24; George De-Loach, age 24, captured Weldon R. R.; Caleb DeLoach, age 20; Allen DeLoach, age 29; William DeLoach, age 23, killed in battle Weldon R. R. August 21st, 1864; Milledge DeLoach, age 18; John Dean, age 37, transferred to Second Artillery; W. T. Fulmer, age 20; J. H. Goodman, age 37, wounded at Drewry's Bluff; H. W. Griffith, age 35; P. B. McDaniel, age 37, killed in battle at Pocotaligo October 22nd, 1862; B. L. Murrell, age 19; D. Proctor, age 20; Ezekiel Rutland, age 16, transferred to Second Artillery; James Smith, age 25; George W. Seay, age 25, wounded in the trenches at Richmond June, 1864, and died at Richmond June 30th, 1864; G. W. Turner, age 21, transferred; J. P. Weaver, age 16, killed in battle at Drewry's Bluff May 16th, 1864; W. S. Wightman, age 17. Total—28 in Company F and 1 in Company B.

Company F was commanded by Captain Joseph Blythe Allston and Company B by Captain Thomas Y. Simons.

On the roll of Company "G," Twenty-seventh Regiment, in the Adjutant General's office I find the following written endorsement:

"N. B.—Company G, Twenty-seventh Regiment, South Carolina Volunteers, was Company C, Battalion South Carolina Volunteers, commanded by Major Joseph Abney. The Charleston Battalion, South Carolina Volunteers, and Abney's Battalion, South Carolina Volunteers, were united in 1863, and formed the Twenty-Seventh Regiment, South Carolina Volunteers."

Henry Buist was Captain of Company "G," which was made up of men from different parts of the State, Laurens, Spartanburg, Union, Orangeburg, Charleston, &c., but none from Edgefield.

XXXIX.

COMPANY E, SEVENTH REGIMENT CAVALRY.

J. Wash Williams, Captain; W. P. Burkhalter, age 21, died of disease at home 1864; H. M. Burkhalter, age 19; A. J. Coleman, age 30; A. P. Coleman, age 26, wounded at Deep Bottom; L. E. Ferguson, age 26; J. R. Fox, age 19, died of disease at home; W. T. Golding, age 24, wounded near Barnville, scouting; W. S. Golding, age 22; F. G. Holloway, age 27; B. F. Payne, age 26, dead; J. W. Payne, age 21; W. B. Pulley, age 22, died since the war; D. Proctor, age 21, killed at Cold Harbor May 31st, 1864; J. M. Proctor, age 23; B. G. Smith, age 23; W. S. Smith, age 28; G. S. Smith, age 21, died since the war; Fred Scurry, age 30, died since the war.

The following were in Company "C," Holcombe Legion, commanded by Captain J. R. Spearman, which company was merged in Company "E," Seventh Cavalry:

George P. Abney, died at Adams' Run of measles; Nichols Burkhalter, Harry Coleman, Adolphus Gregory, Kit Gregory, B. F. Gregory, Augustus Mason, R. W. Payne, Garlen Smith, Jacob Smith.

COMPANY I, SECOND CAVALRY.

Roll of Company "I," Second Cavalry, prepared by Captain T. H. Clark, Trenton, Edgefield County, S. C.:

Names only of those men from Edgefield are here given, except officers:

M. C. Butler, Captain; promoted Colonel August, 1861, afterwards Brigadier-General. J. J. Bunch, Captain; left after reorganization April, 1862. T. H. Clark, Captain; wounded at Culpepper, Va.; served through war. Joseph Crafton, First Lieutenant; left after reorganization April, 1862. P. M. Butler, First Lieutenant; wounded at Culpepper; served through war. M. A. Markert, Second Lieutenant; served through the war. James M. Lanham, Second Lieutenant from June, 1861, to January, 1862. R. G. Fleming, Second Lieutenant, Richland, from January to April, 1862. John R. Tolbert, Second Lieutenant, Abbeville; wounded at Culpepper,

Va.; served from April, 1862, to surrender. J. Munroe Wise, First Sergeant from August, 1861, to surrender. John D. Reilly, Second Sergeant, Augusta, Ga., dead. Benj. F. Ouzts, Third Sergeant. Samuel D. Adams, Fourth Sergeant; dead. J. Marion Shirer, Fourth Sergeant, St. Matthew's; Regimental Color-Bearer. Thos. L. Butler, Third Sergeant; killed at Gettysburg. Andrew Anderson, Fourth Sergeant; discharged; furnished substitute. C. W. Winn, Fourth Sergeant; wounded at Baconhall, Va. F. P. Walker, Corporal. Augustus W. Glover, Corporal. T. N. Talbert, Corporal, Abbeville. J. J. Eidson, Corporal. M. H. Mims, Corporal. Jabez Ryan, Corporal; died at Manassas of disease. J. N. Griffin, Corporal.

PRIVATES.

W. J. Adams, George B. Addison; John F. Bates, died at Green Pond, S. C.—disease—detailed as Ordinance Sergeant; Andrew Bates, killed at John's Island, S.C., July 5th, 1863; J. Wesley Barr, discharged 1862, (The originator of Barr's legion); D. C. Bullock, W. N. Burnett, Harrison Butler; O. N. Butler, transferred to M. C. Butler's staff, dead; Sampson Butler, died at Martinsburg, Va., disease; Seth G. Butler, G. B. Blocker; Moses Bruce, killed in battle at John's Island, S. C., July 5th, 1864; James P. Bryan; Wm. H. Bolton, killed at John's Island in battle; C. A. Cheatham, wounded at Catawba River, dead; Wm. H. Cogburn; Randall Croft, transferred 1862 to Sixth Regiment of Cavalry, dead; J. F. Cole, transferred to Quarter Master's department, dead; John A. Crawford, dead; R. F. Coleman; Geo. M. Crafton, dead; Robt. J. Crafton; Thomas M. Crafton, killed at John's Island, 5th July, 1864, in battle; Reuben P. DeLoach, Elijah Dorn, John B. Etheredge, Isaac Edwards; Joab Edwards, transferred 1863; ——— Evans, Pennsylvania, enrolled on the march to Gettysburg and lost; James H. Eidson; Avery Franklin, transferred; E. B. Forrest, James M. Forrest, J. N. Fowler; N. L. Griffin, died of wounds at Poheek Church, Va.; F. B. Griffin; John Goode, died of wounds at John's Island; T. W. Glover, died of disease at Baconhall, Va.; M. O. Glover, dead; C. B. Glover, transferred; P. B. Hanson, died at home; A. G. Hackett; Douglas Holloway, died of disease at home; Laurence Harris;

Wade Hampton, Jr., promoted on General J. E. Johnston's Staff, dead; Preston T. Hampton, promoted on General Wade Hampton's Staff and killed; J. P. Hamilton, Greene Hamilton, Lewis E. Holmes, W. A. Hamlee, E. N. Henderson, T. J. Hibler, M. B. Johnson, John D. Johnson, M. W. Johnson, Jesse Jay; D. P. Lagrone, commissioned assistant Surgeon; John W. Lagrone, dead; Walter W. Lanham, John S. Lyon; Joshua McKie, discharged in 1861; John W. Mays, killed in battle at John's Island, July 5th, 1864; E. A. Mims, Abney Mims, R. F. Matthews, E. G. Morgan, D. F. McEwen, H. E. Mealing; James P. Moss, died of wounds received at Malvern Hill; E. V. Mobley; J. L. Nicholson, discharged; Serene Parkman, James G. Prim, James W. Quarles, James H. Ross, Samuel L. Roper, Hugh H. Scott; George W. Talbert, dead; James H. Taylor, killed in battle at John's Island; Mack Toney, N. D. Timmerman; T. W. Vaughan, died at home, sickness; M. B. Ward, transferred, dead; F. R. Warren. Total from Edgefield rank and file, 103; killed in battle—all at John's Island, 7; died of wounds, 3; died of disease, 7; total, 17.

Total loss from Edgefield only one-sixth.

COMPANY K, SECOND REGIMENT ARTILLERY.

Roll of Company "K," Second Regiment Artillery, Lamar's, as furnished me by Captain P. B. Waters, January 24th, 1893, written by him from memory:

H. C. Culbreath, Captain, resigned; Philemon B. Waters, Captain, served through war; J. Crawford Perry, Lieutenant, resigned; Edward H. Addy, Lieutenant; J. A. Pitts, Lieutenant; Felix Lake, Lieutenant; R. M. Scurry, Lieutenant, resigned; Wilson Abney, Sergeant; Joel R. Abney, Sergeant; William Webb, Sergeant; J. H. Williams, Sergeant; Joseph Watkins, Orderly Sergeant; William A. Culbreath, Sergeant; George Berry, Corporal, wounded; George W. Mack, Corporal; Joseph Ridlehoover, Corporal; Malachi M. Pitts, Assistant Surgeon; W. C. Barber, Sergeant Major; William Abney, Ordinance Sergeant.

PRIVATES.

James Adams; William Arander, wounded; Lewis Arander, transferred; Solomon Auttman, Joseph W. Banks, Wilson Barnes,

Jacob J. Barnes, William Barnes, B. W. Bledsoe; L. W. Bledsoe, wounded; W. F. Boyd, Whitfield Brooks, William Brooks, A. Pickens Burnett, J. P. Burnett, Ralp S. Burnett; Joseph Buffington, died 1893; J. Oliver Berry, wounded; Elijah Berry; William Berry, died; Steven A. Campbell, died; John C. Chapman, William E. Clark; Andrew T. Coleman, Company Clerk; Jacob Corley, lost arm; John A. Corley, West Corley, Hardy Crouch, Noel Crouch, W. S. Crouch; V. L. Crouch, wounded; William Crouch, H. Pope Culbreath; Ira P. Culbreath, color bearer; J. H. Cambee; Frank Cockerel, transferred; William Davis; Lewis Davis, died; Daniel C. Glenn, James Goodwin, James Gosset, Crawford Griffith, George Griffith, M. C. Gant, John Goggans; West Gentry, transferred; George Havird, L. J. Havird, Z. C. Havird, Winfield Havird, John Oliver Havird, T. W. Halman, Milledge Halman, Calvin Halman, L. Berry Hazle, William Hazle; John B. Hill, wounded; W. R. Hunter, Tillman Jennings, Spencer Jennings, Philip Jennings, M. H. Kempson; J. S. Kennerly, died; Levi Koon, transferred; M. R. Lowrey, Frank Lowrey, Joseph M. Long; George W. Long, company commissary; George W. Long, Sr., killed; Leontine Mack, Solomon Morse; Sret Mills, transferred; Wade Mills, killed; William Mills, died during the war; Job McGee, transferred; West McGee, Reuben McCarty; J. Mack McCarty, wounded; M. C. Nichols Wat Nichols; J. J. Odom, transferred; Willis A. Odom, J. P. Owens, David W. Padget; West Parish, transferred; M. B. Perry, wounded; Wesley Perry, Oliver B. Perry, Bennet Perry; Milledge Pitts, killed; James S. Pou, William B. Powel, W. M. Prather; Albert Reams, wounded; Ridley Reams, Jordan Reams; John B. Riley, died; Derrick Riley, Samuel Riley, T. E. Rinehart, West Rinehart, Sumter Ridlehoover, B. F. Sample; Walter D. Spann, died; George W. Spearman, J. F. Spearman, W. B. Stevens; David R. Strother, wounded; William A. Strother, L. M. Smith, William Martin Stewart, Larkin Snelgrove; T. L. Smith, transferred; William Salter, transferred; Willis Stone, transferred; D. R. Thomas, James Thomas, J. Pinckney Trotter, Jesse Turner, George W. Turner, Ralph Turner, Samuel Webb, Daniel Whittle; Willis Whittle, discharged; W. W. Williams; Calvin Watson, transferred; Tillman Watson regimental commissary; Frank M.

Yarbrough, Jesse Riddle, L. Riddle, Benjamin Watkins. Total rank and file, 149.

This number is not more than half of those who were actually connected with the company during the war.

Of these were killed, 4; wounded, 10; died of disease, 8.

ADDITIONAL NAMES.

John Aughtry, Charles Aughtry; Elisha Attaway, wounded; A. J. Cobler, Henry Butler, Chesley Butler, Silas Butler, Presley Butler, Milledge Bledsoe, R. W. Bledsoe, Peter Duffy, A. E. Dorn, George DeLoach, Caleb DeLoach; Jeremiah Morgan; Ralph Morris, killed; Brown Jennings; Adam C. Ripley, wounded; Richard Ripley, Henry Ripley, Sumter Ridlehoover, Henry Waits, Alley Ridlehoover, Samuel Waits; Peter Schumpert, died; Jefferson Reams, James P. Merchant, James D. B. Miller, John B. W. Miller. Total, 30; making a grand total of 179.

There were several from Laurens County who were members of this company, but their names are not given here. Perhaps they should be, as they were in an Edgefield company, but Edgefield should have credit only for the men who went from that county.

Wade Mills was killed by the bursting of a siege gun at Battery Reid, on James Island, while firing on the "Swamp Angel."

This company was enlisted in August, 1861, and went into service at Camp Butler, near Aiken. After the organization the command was transferred to Fort Johnson, on James Island, and served in the defence of Charleston until the evacuation of that city in February, 1865. The company was the nucleus of Colonel T. G. Lamar's Battalion and subsequent regiment, the Second of Artillery. In the battle of Secessionville—the capture of the Isaac P. Smith, a Federal gunboat, and in other engagements and skirmishes on James Island—this command was an active participant. After the evacuation of Charleston, which city this command had held safe from the enemy for four long years by arduous labor on her defences and exhausting exposure, night after night, under an almost continual fire of the enemies guns, the command was attached to the army of General Johnston and served as infantry until the

surrender. There was no finer body nor better drilled company in the Army of the South. The company suffered heavy
loss in the battles of Averysboro and Bentonville in North
Carolina. This Veteran command surrendered with General
Joe Johnston at Greensboro, N. C., in 1865.

THE CITADEL ACADEMY.

In Colonel J. P. Thomas' History of the South Carolina
Military Academy, I find the name of J. A. Crooker, from
Edgefield, as a graduate in 1850; Civil Engineer; Adjutant
Twenty-second South Carolina Volunteers in 1862; Lieutenant
Twenty-seventh South Carolina Volunteers in 1863, in what
company is not stated. He was not, however, in either Com-
pany F or B; or if he was he is not so marked as from Edge-
field.

E. J. Walker, from Edgefild, graduated in 1851; lawyer in
Georgia; Captain Georgia Volunteers in 1861; Colonel of
Georgia Regiment, and was severely wounded at Manassas
Gap in 1863.

E. Croft, Edgefield, graduated in 1856; planter in Edgefield
District; Captain in Fourteenth Regiment, South Carolina
Volunteers, in 1861; in battles around Richmond and Fredericksburg, and skirmishes; severely wounded at battle of Cold
Harbor; promoted Major; severely wounded at battle of Gettysburg; promoted Lieutenant Colonel Fourteenth Regiment.
After the war lawyer at Greenville Court House; Trial Justice;
member of Board of Visitors South Carolina Military Academy;
died in 1892.

A. J. Norris, Edgefield, graduated with distinction in 1860;
Instructor in Citadel Academy, resigned April, 1861; Captain
Confederate States Army 1861, resigned December, 1862;
Professor Belles Letters and History, A. A., and Second Lieu-
tenant Battalion Cadets. After the war lawyer at Edgefield;
President of the Bank; President of the Factory.

P. S. Norris, graduated with distinction in 1864; Lieutenant and Assistant Professor in Hillsboro Military Academy,
N. C.; merchant in 1872; died in 1874.

J. H Bouknight, graduated in 1865; farmer.

O. Sheppard, graduated in 1865; lawyer.

T. G. Croft, cadetship from 1862 to 1865; University of Virginia 1866-67; in business in Georgia 1867-73; physician 1875-92, established at Aiken with a lucrative practice.

P. N. Zimmerman, graduated in 1886; farmer.

J. W. Outz, graduated in 1886; Civil Engineer and contractor; Chief Engineer Atlanta Iron and Steel Company.

J. H. Brooks, graduated in 1886; with the maintenance of Way Department of the A. & C. Division of the R. & D. R. R.

B. L. Clark, graduated with distinction in 1888; Civil Engineer; died in 1891.

B. S. Cogburn, graduated in 1890; Principal of Long Branch School, Edgefield County.

A. G. Etheredge, graduated in 1892; teacher.

A very interesting chapter might be given here of the services of the cadets of the Military Academy during the War of Secession, but that chapter belongs to the general history of the State, and it is perhaps enough to insert here what Major J. B. White says, closing his report of the operations of the Battalion of State Cadets from November, 1864, to April, 1865:

"I regret to report the deaths of the following cadets, all of whom died from diseases induced by the exposure and hardship of service, viz.: R. F. Nichols and John Culbreath, Company A, [Culbreath was from Edgefield]; G. O. Buck, T. A. Johnson, and R. Noble, of Company B." John Culbreath died at home.

James Y. Culbreath, now a lawyer at Newberry, brother to John, was at that time also a cadet in the Academy, and was several times sent as a guard with prisoners to Andersonville.

Major White thus closes: "I would take this opportunity to express my obligations to the officers under my command for the zeal, ability, and alacrity with which they discharged their duties, nor can I fail to call your attention to those young but noble sons of our beloved State, the Cadets of the Military Academy of South Carolina. Upon the battlefield, in camp, on the march, on picket, or working upon defences, they were ready for every emergency, manifesting at all times, and under the most trying circumstances, a manly and soldierly aspect, not finding fault with those in authority, but doing their duty cheerfully and well."

Colonel Thomas supplements the report of Major White

with an account of the services of the cadets from the beginning of the war to the close—services honorable to themselves,
to the Academy, and to the State. Mention has been made
here, if we mistake not, of all the officers, graduates, and
cadets who were from Edgefield. Less I could not do, and
more is beyond the scope of this work.

THE CONFEDERATE FLAG.

It is with great pleasure that I am able to introduce among
the rolls of the Confederate soldiers from Edgefield a poem
(see page 471) on the Confederate flag. The author of the
poem is a daughter of the late Colonel Louis T. Wigfall, of
Texas, who was born at Edgefield. Some years before Secession Colonel Wigfall moved to Texas and was Confederate
States Senator from that State during the four years of struggle and trial.

Of his career in life I know but little, but I was very deeply
impressed by reading a speech he made while in the Confederate Senate. I think the speech was on a resolution to suspend
the operation of the writ of *habeas corpus*; and Colonel Wigfall
opposed with all the zeal and strength of a great mind the
passage of the resolution. He showed with all the energy
possible the evil effects that would follow and what a horrible
thing it was to take away at one stroke all the rights of a citizen and all the rights of the States and reduce the whole country to the condition of a military despotism and subject to the
arbitrary will of one man.

It was a strong plea for individual and personal rights, and
for the rights of the individual States. And his plea was successful.

"The Confederate Flag" is copied from the Edgefield
Chronicle of April 28th, 1897.

HALTIWANGER.

In a notice of the Haltiwanger family on page 395 it is said
that the father of Jacob Haltiwanger, who was born March
30th, 1785, came from Germany, and that he took an active
part in the colonial struggle for Independence. He was indeed
an ardent Whig and fought bravely for the success of the cause
which he so ardently espoused.

Tradition has given me only one incident of his career as a

soldier illustrating the narrow escape he had from captivity or death, and perhaps both. On one occasion the party of Whigs to which he belonged had been attacked, routed, and dispersed. In making his escape he ran through a field which had been only recently cleared and there were many piles of brush in the field. Into one of these piles of brush he was able to crawl and hide himself without being seen by the enemy. The Tories, however, knew that he was of the party, for he had been seen, and they knew that he was lying somewhere about hidden in the brush. They made a diligent search, even surrounded the pile in which he was concealed and thrust their swords into the brush, by some of which thrusts he was severely cut; but he had fortitude enough to bear the pain without crying out. And so he escaped without serious hurt.

This reminds me of a story very much like it in the Annals of Newberry (page 595), where it is related that the house of a Mr. Townsend was burned and he barely escaped with his life. He had just time to hide himself without having been seen by his enemies in a pile of brush near the house. While the house was burning the heat was so intense where he lay concealed as to be almost unbearable. In fact, it is said that his back was blistered by the intense heat. But he was enabled to bear it, and so escaped with his life. This incident occurred, I think, in the upper part of Edgefield, that part which now forms part of the new County of Greenwood.

Descendants of both these men are now living in Saluda and adjoining counties, and I have no doubt that many of them are known to each other, but they may not know of the facts here related until they read them in this book.

From the Youth's Companion:

BUTLER AND FARLEY.

"The bravest are the tenderest, the loving are the daring."

General Maury tells a story, worthy of everlasting remembrance, about a South Carolina soldier, Colonel Haskell, whose arm was shattered so that amputation at the shoulder was necessary. The surgeon was about to administer chloroform when Haskell said: "Stop, doctor! You must have very little chloroform, since the enemy has declared it contraband of war. Is it not so?" "Yes, Colonel." "Then keep it for some poor soldier who needs it. I can do without." Another anecdote of a similar kind is thus related by General Maury:

General M. C. Butler, of South Carolina, was seriously wounded and maimed for life at the battle of Brandy Station. He and a young captain named Farley had just come out of action in the early morning and were laughing together over some amusing incident they had noticed. At that moment a cannon ball came bounding at them. It struck Butler's leg above the ankle, tore through his horse, and cut off Farley's leg above the knee.

Down they all went. Butler began to stanch the blood with his handkerchief and advised Farley how to do the same. Captain Chestnut, Lieutenant Rhett, and other officers came running to Butler's help; but at that moment he observed that Farley's dying horse was struggling and seemed likely to crush its rider.

"Go at once to Farley!" cried Butler. "He needs you more than I do."

They did as they were bidden, and Farley was placed in a litter. He asked them to bring his leg and put it, too, in the litter. Then he said:

"Now, gentlemen, you have done all for me that is possible. I shall be dead in an hour. God bless you for your kindness. I bid you all an affectionate farewell. Go at once to Butler."

That evening Butler's leg was dressed in the hospital just as poor Farley breathed his last. The two men had never seen each other till that morning.

"Henceforth," says General Maury, "we shall not need to go to Sir Philip Sidney for an example of noble self-sacrifice."

XL.

TROOPS FOR FLORIDA.

From the Edgefield Advertiser, February 11th, 1836:

"Our readers are informed that an express reached Governor McDuffie eight or ten days ago, requiring two regiments of men from the State, for the Florida service. A requisition of three companies was made upon this District. The Tenth Regiment was immediately assembled, and it is highly gratifying for us to record that the draft was superceded by the prompt volunteering of the men. In all the Regiments more men tendered their services than were required and the officers of the respective companies were compelled to refuse many. And as strange as it may sound to the ears of some, it is nevertheless true, that we saw men with tears in their eyes, begging that they should be received. On Thursday last the three companies were assembled at this place by order of the Governor to be reviewed and ordered to their place of destination. A fine band of music attended from Hamburg, and never did we see at this place a larger throng of our citizens. His Excellency made a short, but animating address to the respective companies—he told them they were charged with the honor of South Carolina, and said he had no fears that honor was safe. We looked at the officers and we looked at the men again and again, and we will venture to say without intending a boast that the volunteers of Edgefield, come what may, will nobly do their duty.

In the evening they took up the march to Aiken, under an escort of Captain Griffin's Troop of Cavalry. They are destined for Charleston, and finally, we understand, for Picalati, Florida.

It may be important to observe that a fund of upward of $5,000 was subscribed by our citizens for these brave volunteers—and that the ladies of our village, with a patriotism and public spirit highly commendable were most busily engaged up to the very moment of their departure, in the making of uniforms for Captain Jones' Company, of this Regiment and providing otherwise for their comfort.

We have the pleasure of laying before our readers the names of the officers and privates.

SEVENTH REGIMENT.

James Jones, Captain; Eldred Simkins, First Lieutenant; Edmund L. Penn, Second Lieutenant; John W. Wimbush, Ensign; Milledge L. Bonham, First Sergeant; Charles K. Johnson, Second Sergeant; Giles Mims, Third Sergeant; Aquilla Miles, Fourth Sergeant; W. P. Delph, First Corporal; Arthur Simkins, Second Corporal; Bartley M. Mims, Third Corporal; John M. Prothro, Fourth Corporal; Julius C. Perdue, Fifth Corporal.

PRIVATES.

Thomas G. Bacon, Wilson Bartlet, Thomas Bird, John Bradley, B. C. Bryan, Wm. H. Bunch, Richard J. Burton, Wm. M. Burt, Edward Butler, Dennis Carpenter, Noah Corley, Enos Clark, Sherry Covar, Wincey Dorton, Ephr'm Franklin, Casper Gallman, Milledge Galphin, William Q. Gardner, Wm. G. Gilliam, Edmund Glascock, John Grice, Eldred Grice, Jeremiah Hall, James Hagood, Lucius L. Hall, Leroy H. Hall, Isham Carpenter, Thos. J. Hamilton, Isham Haney, William Harris, Benjamin Harrison, Henry Ward, William Jackson, Robert Kenny, Stewart Long, William Lyles, Sampson B. Mays, Henry Mays, Stephen Mays, Wm. H. Mears, George Miller, John Mims, John W. Mundy, David Murphy, Joseph Nobles, Feb. Nifholas, William Pierce, Smith Radford, Richard Ripley, Stanmore B. Ryan, Benjamin I. Ryan, Lewis Satcher, Ab. Swearingen, Davis Tissick, James Swearingen, Edward Trailer, Enoch Walker, Herbert Elder, Samuel L. Ward, R. Weatherford, J. Weatherford, William Whitlock.

TENTH REGIMENT.

David Denny, Captain; Jesse Schumpert, First Lieutenant; W. T. Abney, Second Lieutenant; John Johns, Ensign; Thos. Scurry, First Sergeant; Abner Hearn, Second Sergeant; John Smith, Third Sergeant; O. Ramage, Fourth Sergeant.

PRIVATES.

Allen Vaughn, Willis Rotton, James Edwards, A. H. Patrick, George Gilman, George Heuson, Caleb Inabnet, Joel

Merchant, Wesley Barnes, William Culbreath, Simpson Corley, James Powell, A. G. McCarty, Jesse Augustine, Benjamin Abney, Peter Berry, Arch'd Jenning, H. Raiborn, J. P. Duffy, Jonathan Row, George Long, Benjamin Neal, J. B. Smith, Benjamin Raiborn, J. Hughes, H. Culbreath, Lewis Watson, A. Clark, A. Whittle, William Christian, S. Edson, William Foy, W. Wheeler, R. Humphries, Jacob Trotter, W. Barker, Thomas Jennings, Elisha Barker, H. Arnold, William Corley, H. C. Etheredge, Andrew Harter, Prince Little, W. L. Coleman, James Norrel, Alexander Stewart, Elisha Ataway, Clark Martin, William Abney, John Perry, Jr., Walter Brown, Charles O'Neal, Grant Scurry, A. Martin, W. G. Salter, B. Merchant, Luber Taylor, P. McCarty, David Long, F. Massey, Joseph Gaston, George Lacook, J. W. Holly, West Culbreath, M. Graham, M. W. Abney.

NINTH REGIMENT.

Thomas J. Hibbler, Captain; R. P. Brunson, First Lieutenant; James Yeldell, Second Lieutenant; L. G. Holloway, Ensign; Elbert Devore, First Sergeant; John B. Holmes, Second Sergeant; Edward Morris, Third Sergeant; Wm. H. Adams, Fourth Sergeant.

PRIVATES.

Thomas S. Adams, John Kilcrease, Robert Burton, Joseph Lantern, D. Holsonback, Seaton Mootry, George Bussey, George Martin, William Bowling, Hugh Moseley, Arthur Grice, Robert Meriwether, William Bush, James Martin, James Buffington, Joel McClendon, Edward Collier, Henry M. Nix, Luke Corley, John North, Cartlet Corley, John Prince, Thomas Corley, Terry Quinn, John Cox, Francis Reynolds, James Creymore, J. M. Reynolds, David Johnson, Reuben Reynolds, Russell Doolittle, J. W. Radcliffe, James Davis, Henry Reel, Saborn Doolittle, E. P. Spivy, Wdooly, William Street, Solomon Eikner, Archy Smith, John Evans, Wiley G. Spencer, Thomas Edwards, John Stedham, David Ferguson, John Syms, Wiley Freeman, James J. Spivy, Yancy Freeman, Amos Smith, Spencer Elmore, A. W. Shannon, William Holmes, J. P. Terry, Lewis Hill, J. Timmerman, William Y. Hitt, George Thurmond, H. Holsonback, Peter Williams,

Wash C. Hall, Mitchell Wells, Minor Kilcrease, Henry Winn, George Kilcrease, Chas. G. Wallace.

After the above was in type a friend handed us the names of the "Hamburg Volunteers," which makes our list of volunteers from this District complete.

HAMBURG VOLUNTEERS.

S. W. Cunningham, Captain; M. Penworth, First Lieutenant; Beverly A. Mann, First Sergeant; W. Ladson Smith, Third Sergeant.

PRIVATES.

D. S. Bobb, N. B. Wise, Larkin Anderson, Washington Floyd, J. D. Atterberry, J. C. Mayson, R. S. Butler, Thomas M. Anderson, M. F. D. Roddy, Charles C. Spann, W. Drake, W. H. Cox, James Meelin, J. Jeanerett, S. Hyams, George H. Fraser, John W. Yarborough, E. C. Rice, Tucker, G. W. Chamberlin, Robert Quian.

XLI.

WAR WITH MEXICO.

I am proud and happy that I am able to introduce in this History of Edgefield the following documents, viz.: Abstract of the last muster roll of Captain Brooks, Company of old Ninety-Six Boys, Company D, Palmetto Regiment, showing all the casualties. Letter from the officers of the company to the Clerk of the Court accompanying the flag, under which it appears that 108 men were enrolled, of whom only 28 returned with it from Mexico. The presentation of a sword to Lieutenant Joseph Abney by the Saluda (Tenth) Regiment, with the speeches on the occasion.

The whole, taken together, reads like a chapter from the old days of chivalry and romance. Copied and sent to me by John R. Abney, Esq., of New York.

These, with the rolls of the troops engaged in the Seminole War, make a proper and fitting close of the history.

Edgefield Advertiser, October 11th, 1848:

MUSTER ROLL OF CAPTAIN BROOKS' COMPANY.

Abstract of the last muster roll of Captain Brooks' Company of old Ninety-Six Boys (Company D, Palmetto Regiment,) showing all the casualties and changes which have occurred in said company during the Mexican Campaign:

Preston S. Brooks, Captain; Joseph Abney, Second Lieutenant; Lafayette Wever, Second Lieutenant; Richard S. Key, First Sergeant; Eldred Simkins, Second Sergeant; Cary W. Styles, Third Sergeant; Hillery Cooper, Fourth Sergeant; Jefferson P. Nixon, First Corporal; Wm. B. Galphin, Second Corporal; Charles Kenny, Third Corporal; Robert Slowman, Fourth Corporal.

PRIVATES.

John A. Addison, Leonard P. Andrews; Thomas Anderson, transferred from Company L to Company D; John W. Arnold, transferred from Company E to Company D; Willis Brannon, left sick in Hamburg, afterwards joined the regiment, never having heard of the order, discharging the sick left behind;

Horatio Blease, Wm. Betsil, Wm. Burrell, John Cureton, Geo. W. Durst, Jasper Devore, James Goff, David Hopkins, Wiley Holsonback, Robert E. Kenny, Edmund Melton, Alex. McKenzie, James Marony; Henry Mallon, substitute for J. C. Larke; Thomas B. Norvel, recruit; Elbert Padgett; Nelson D. Philips, recruit; Alex. Sharpton; Wm. S. Smith, transferred from Company K to Company D; Godfrey Strobel, Wm. F. Uuthank; John A. Walsingham, recruit; Jeptha L. Wikle, recruit. Total, 28.

RESIGNED.

Wm. C. Moragne, First Lieutenant, resigned 1848; Wm. P. Jones, Second Lieutenant, resigned 1847.

KILLED IN BATTLE.

David Adams, Second Lieutenant, killed at Churubusco August 20th, 1847, promoted from First Sergeant to Second Lieutenant July 8th; Wm. Butler Blocker, Sergeant, killed at Garita de Belin September 13th, while in command of company; Lewellen Goode, Corporal, killed at Garita de Belin September 13th, 1847; Turner Crooker, private, killed at Garita de Belin September 13th, 1847; Henry Callahan, killed at Garita de Belin September 13th, 1847; Thomas M. Lyles, killed at Garita de Belin September 13th, 1847; Mathew L Martin, killed at Garita de Belin September 13th, 1847; Thomas F. Tillman, killed at Churubusco August 20th, 1847. Total, including Corporal Brooks, 9.

DIED.

Lemons Abney, died on march to Perote August 8th, 1847; Malachi Bettis, died at Puebla August 1st, 1847; John A. Blankenship, died at Vera Cruz June, 1847; William H. Cobb, died at Puebla June 3rd, 1847; Nathan DeLoach, died at Puebla June 3rd, 1847; Wm. B. Davis, recruit, died at Jalapa May, 1848; James Duncan, died at Vera Cruz December 16th, 1847; James Fitzsimmons, transferred from Company H to Company D—died or deserted at San Angel 12th January, 1847; John T. Gassaway, died at Puebla September 8th, 1847; Julius N. Glover, died at San Angel September 20th, 1847; Jesse Hill, at Puebla September 15th, 1847; Reub. Jarral, at Atlanta January 14th, 1846; Bolivar Jones, at Puebla July

2nd, 1847; John Johnson, Vera Cruz May 16th, 1847; Hugh McMahon, San Angel December 27th, 1847; Moody McDaniel, City of Mexico October 20th, 1847; Thomas H. Nixon, City of Mexico October 17th, 1847; Reuben Newman, substitute for C. Ardis, at Puebla August, 1847; John Proctor, Perote June 21st, 1847; Wm. F. Reynolds, Vera Cruz April 4th, 1847; Wiley Robinson, Puebla June 18th, 1847; Edward Ramsay, died at sea February 10th, 1847; Benj. Tillman, Perote September, 1847; Paschal Tillman, Perote August, 1847; Benj. G. Tillman, killed accidentally at City of Mexico November 6th, 1847; John Wells, Jalapa June 8th, 1848; Jeff. Williamson, Perote June 16th, 1847; Toliver Youngblood, Puebla October 7th, 1847. Total, 28; deserters, 5.

DISCHARGED.

Vincent Cogburn, Sergeant, discharged on certificate of disability November 1st, 1847; Lewis Covar, Corporal, discharged on certificate of disability June 1st, 1847; Christopher Ardis, private, discharged on certificate June 25th, 1847, at Puebla, by substitute; James M. Addison, on certificate of disability at Puebla December 2nd, 1847; Henry W. Barham, by general order from Washington April 26th, 1847; Joshua Broome, by surgeon's certificate of disability November 27th, 1847; Anthony Delorea, on pension certificate October 27th, 1847; James D. Davis, on certificate of disability at Puebla October 30th, 1847; Joseph H. Gassaway, on certificate of disability at Puebla November 2nd, 1847; Wm. T. Gafford, on certificate of disability at Puebla 1847; Benj. Gill, on certificate of disability at Puebla December 30th, 1847; John Gill, by general order from Washington April 26th, 1847; Joel P. Hill, on certificate of disability at Perote November 2nd, 1847; Anderson Howard, on certificate of disability at City of Mexico December 7th, 1847; Joseph A. Jones, on certificate of disability at Puebla December 2nd, 1847; Thomas G. Key, by order of Secretary of War at San Angel March 10th, 1848; James C. Lark, by substitute at City of Mexico December 7th, 1847; Wm. E. Murphy, certificate of disability at Mexico November 27th, 1847; Frederick Morgan, discharged on disability at Mexico December 27th, 1847; Joseph C. Payne, on account of mental incapacity at Griffin January 8th; Francis Posey, on pension certificate at Mexico October 27th, 1847; Christopher Pryor, by general order from Washington at Hamburg April 26th, 1847; Pickens B. Ryan, by general order from Washington at Hamburg April 27th, 1847; Jeff Whitaker, on pension certificate at Mexico October 27th, 1847. Total, 22.

TRANSFERRED.

John C. Simkins, Sergeant, promoted to First Lieutenant Twelfth Infantry July, 1847; Whitfield B. Brooks, promoted to Second Lieutenant Twelfth Infantry October, 1847, died of wound received in Battle Churubusco October, 1847.

LETTER FROM THE OFFICERS ACCOMPANYING THE FLAG.

Edgefield Advertiser, October 18th, 1848:

We subjoin a letter from the officers of the Company of "Ninety-Six Boys" to Thos. G. Bacon, Esq. It will be seen that these gentlemen have deposited the company flag for safe keeping in the office of the Clerk of the Court of Common Pleas. Under this flag 108 men were enrolled, and only 28 returned with it from Mexico.

EDGEFIELD C. H., October 16th, 1848.
Thos. G. Bacon, Esq., C. C. P.:

DEAR SIR: As the representatives of Company "D," "Ninety-Six Boys," Palmetto Regiment, we have the honor to place into your keeping and that of your successors in office, the accompanying "battle flag," presented to our corps by one of our own fair countrywomen and baptized in the purest of Carolina's best blood.

We present it to the people of Edgefield District as a voucher of the patriotism and gallantry of her children, devoutly hoping that mild vizaged peace will long permit it to remain a district record, and in full confidence that should South Carolina be called again to the field it will have "a place in the picture."

Respectfully your ob't serv'ts,

P. S. BROOKS.
WM. C. MORAGNE.
JOS. ABNFY.
L. B. WEAVER.

Edgefield Advertiser, November 15th, 1848:

PRESENTATION OF A SWORD

To Lieutenant Joseph Abney, of the old Ninety-Six Boys:

The citizens of the Saluda Regiment, Edgefield, at their parade of the 31st ult., presented to the above named officer of the Palmetto Regiment, the sword which had been agreed upon at a previous meeting for that purpose. The sword is a highly finished one, from the Manufactory of Gregg & Haden, Charleston, with inscriptions denoting the cause and purpose of the gift. Col. Arthur Simkins, who was requested to act on the part of the regiment, accompanied the presentation with the following address:

Lieutenant Abney: I have the honor to discharge at this moment what is to me a very pleasing duty. I hold in my hand a sword intended by the citizens of your native regiment, as a mark of the high appreciation with which we have all regarded your very handsome conduct during the recent war with Mexico. Permit me to say that many of your fellow-citizens, and especially your early associates, watched your individual progress through the perilous scenes to which that war gave rise, with much more than ordinary interest. It was expected, sir, that you would be found on all occasions fearlessly discharging the high duties of a soldier good and true, and these expectations (I speak not for any purpose of flattery) have been most fully realized. We have indeed been gratified to recognize in your name that of a worthy representative from Old Saluda, who bore himself wherever danger was most imminent with a gallantry equalled by few, surpassed by none. We were not disappointed in the confident belief we entertained from the beginning, that your generous enthusiasm could result in naught, but honor to yourself and to the "home of your nativity." That it has done so is doubtless, as it should be, a source of honest pride to you and is certainly cause of congratulation, to your immediate fellow-citizens. As an evidence of our feelings towards you in this matter, I now, in behalf of the Saluda Regiment, deliver to you this sword. Accept it, sir, in the sense in which it is meant to be given, as a brave soldier's guerdon. And if in the progress of the ill boding events which thicken around us, it shall become necessary to raise the cry "to arms for the defence of Southern rights," we know full well that this bright blade will be among the first to leap from its scabbard, obedient to the impulsive grasp of one who has already been tried and found faithful.

Lieutenant Abney, with an unaffected fervor, which is one of his highest characteristics, replied as follows:

Sir: I receive through you, the representative of the Saluda Regiment, this elegant and costly sword, with the deepest feelings of gratitude. The handsome manner in which you have spoken the wishes and sentiments of your people, enhances if possible, the value of the gift.

This testimonial of the good will of "Old Saluda," the land famous for warriors and brave men, and this high, public manifestation of her appreciation of my services to the country, is the most grateful reward I could ask, for all the sufferings and privations I have endured in the camp and on the battle field. It is an offering, too, by the friends of my boyhood and by my father's friends—by those who knew me at an age when the mind has no concealment, and who have a right to know me better than all others could know. I have the honor this day, and it is my glory and pride to receive from the associates of my early youth, and from those who have observed me from the cradle, "the plaudit of well done thou good and faithful servant." In the sincerity of my nature, I thank you—I thank you all for your uniform kindness in all the trials and difficulties of my life. In sickness, in affliction and in battle, your warm sympathies have ever animated my heart and invigorated my feeble body. Without this, sir, I should not have been spared by providence to meet with you on an occasion so full of feeling and interest.

My absence from home was attended by every anguish that the body or the mind could bear. Health was a blessing, by the inscrutable will of Heaven, wholly denied me; and the wounds inflicted by the enemy had scarcely ceased to bleed, when my bosom was made desolate by the intelligence of the death of an only parent, of one of the kindest and noblest and best of mothers. Though it may indulge somewhat too fondly, yet the heart must speak. She was the embodiment of all the loveliness, affection, purity, and dignity of woman;

516 HISTORY OF EDGEFIELD.

and to be a solace and an honor to her declining years, had been the chief aim and ambition of my life; and when she was so suddenly torn from me, I felt that the great object for which I lived and labored had been removed. The prospect before me was as blank as despair, as dark as the grave.

You must pardon me for alluding to a subject that you can only contemplate with pain, but which I dwell upon with melancholy fondness. It was suggested by the presence of my old neighbors who know so well how to appreciate the warmth of my feelings.

You have been pleased to speak in kind and complimentary terms of my conduct in battle, and of my bearing in all the appalling and exciting scenes of the great campaign of General Scott. In every situation in which I was called upon to act, I did endeavor faithfully to discharge my duty as a soldier, and as a citizen of our great Republic. I could scarcely have done less than I did do.

How could I have failed to fight while representing the honor of my country, the character of my State, the spirit of my District and the renowned courage of the people of my birth-place? When we were children, we were taught to revere the honored scars of our fathers, received in the achievement of our national Independence—we were taught their tales of suffering, and their heroic fortitude was ever present to our minds. If I had passed through the world without bearing on my body some evidence of my devotion to the Union, I should have felt that I had not completed my whole task—that I was unequal to those who went before me.

By an accident in the transmission of the orders for raising the Palmetto Regiment, this portion of the District was deprived of an opportunity of bearing her full share in the dangers of the war, and as one of the few young soldiers she had in battle, I was impelled by every feeling to endeavor to perform the part of a man. Do you think, sir, that you could have shrunk from danger or death, when you were the proud representative of the spirit of the gallant men who are now around us—when you were the champion of the noble regiment formed on my left? No, sir, deeply alive to the responsibility of your position, and animated by that high spirit which God has given you, you could have felt no fear in dis charging your obligations to your friends, your neighbors, and your country.

If I had been disposed to protect myself from the hazards of the fight, the brilliant examples of the young men whom you did send to the field, would have shamed my weakness, and would have raised me above my fears. Of the twelve heroic spirits besides him you honor to-day, who went from your midst to vindicate our national rights, one-fourth were slain in battle, and of the remaining number, there were only two that passed unscathed through the perilous conflicts in which they were engaged; and I am sure that those two, in the hour of strife, never retired for a moment from their posts. I say it with pleasure and with pride, that some one from Saluda was amongst the foremost in the trench in every engagement of the war. On that bloody day when the mettle of South Carolina was taxed to its utmost—when the spirit of death walked through the field, and when our glorious Palmetto floated so gallantly amid the tumult and blaze of battle—if you had witnessed the behaviour of your boys, you would have been proud to call them your children. Though I was the humblest amongst them, I have reason to declare to you that they were ever with the first in the onset. I had determined, and I think we had all determined, never to let our banner fall. We would have preferred to perish under the flag, which bore on its folds the blended ensigns of our State and Union.

But, sir, the great and honored leader of the Palmetto Regiment was born and brought up only a few miles from where I now stand, and was constantly before us, a model of virtue and courage worthy of the proudest days of Greece and Rome. Whilst he was bleeding in the field, how could a man of the Tenth Regiment refuse to bleed? Whilst he was cheering his gallant men to the charge, who could have been a laggard? If I could have faltered for an instant in the contest, whilst my noble commander was dying by the hand of the enemy, I would have been no son of yours—no son of "Saluda."

I reiterate to you my thanks for this most appropriate mark of the approbation of my fellow citizens. It is the richest reward that could have been bestowed upon one whose efforts to serve you have been feeble, but sincere. I requested the committee who consulted me in regard to it, to have an eye mainly to the metal and temper of the blade. My wishes have been fully complied with. I shall preserve this sword with sacred care, and if it should become necessary, I will try to use it well in the defence of my country—in the defence of our own institutions, and to the vindication of justice and honor.

The serious and respectful attention of the large assembly indicated even more forcibly than the loud shouts of applause raised by a thousand voices at the close of the ceremony, that the transaction was regarded by all much more as a matter of feeling than of form.

XLII.

SALUDA COUNTY.

Since I began to write the History of Edgefield the County has been shorn of its fair proportions. I congratulated it upon the loss of Hamburg, but I do not congratulate it upon the loss of that portion which has been cut off and named Saluda County. The people of Saluda may be greatly benefited, indeed. I hope they may, but Edgefield's loss is very great. There is no finer region of country in the State than that which lies on Big Saluda, and which is traversed by Little Saluda and Red Bank and other streams.

I give here the Ordinance establishing the County of Saluda, and close the History of Edgefield with the beginning of the history of Saluda:

AN ORDINANCE

To establish a new judicial and election County from a portion of the territory of Edgefield County, to be called Saluda with boundaries as hereinafter described.

We, the people of South Carolina, by our delegates in convention assembled, do ordain:

SECTION 1. That a new judicial and election county, which shall be known as Saluda County, shall be formed and is hereby authorised to be formed with the following boundaries, to wit: Beginning at the centre of Big Saluda River at a point opposite the corner of Edgefield and Lexington Counties, thence the Edgefield and Lexington line to the corner of Lexington and Aiken Counties, thence the Edgefield and Aiken line to a point three miles North of where the public road crosses said line near Lybrand's old mill, thence a straight line to ten mile post on public highway leading from Edgefield to Columbia near the residence of J. W. L. Bartley, thence a straight line to the junction of the public road leading from Pleasant Lane with the Long Cane road near William Lott's, thence by the Long Cane road to Matt Mathis' Cross Roads, thence a straight line to Owdom's Post Office, thence a straight line to Little Red School House near Dr. Landrum's old place,

thence a straight line to a point on the Northwestern line of
Pine Grove Township one mile North of Double Bridges, thence
along the Northwestern boundary of Pine Grove Township to
the point on the old Charleston and Cambridge road where it
crosses Halfway Swamp Creek, thence down the middle of
Halfway Swamp Creek to a point in the middle of Saluda River
opposite the mouth of said creek, thence down the middle of
Big Saluda River to the initial point; and the territory embraced within the said lines shall be known as the County of
Saluda.

Done in Columbia the Sixteenth day of October, in the
year of our Lord One Thousand Eight Hunded and Ninety-
Five.

_____

The Convention met September 10th, 1895, and continued
to December 4th, 1895, when it adjourned *sine die.*

The delegates from Edgefield were B. R. Tillman, W. J.
Talbert, W. H. Timmerman, G. D. Tillman, J. C. Sheppard,
and R. B. Watson.

Mr. G. D. Tillman, as we have seen, was a member of the
Convention of 1865, which framed a constitution, which never
became the organic law, as the State had not then passed
through the throes of Revolution and Reconstruction. Are we
throu:h yet?

_____

The upper part of Edgefiel: above Saluda County was cut
off, joined to a part of Abbeville, and made into the County of
Greenwood, with County Seat at Greenwood, January, 1897.

Poor old Edgefield! dreadfully shrunk since 1817.

A PARTING WORD.

It is with a feeling of sadness, not unmingled with a sense
of relief, that I close my labors on the History of Edgefield.
The work is not perfect, no human production is, nor can be.
Still I hope that I have done something to perpetuate the
memory of some events and facts in history which should not
be forgotten. And I hope that the work will not be altogether
unacceptable to those for whom it was written—the children
of old Edgefield, whether at home or abroad.

It is easy to find fault with any work, for faults do exist in all. I can find defects in the plot and in the execution of Milton's Paradise Lost, though it is impossible for me to write a poem equal to that immortal work. And so with all the productions of all writers who have ever lived. He is a very vain and conceited individual who thinks that what he has done is so very nearly perfect as to be above criticism. At the same time the critic, when he sees a defect in the work of a writer or other artist, unless he knows the work is evil in purpose and intent, should endeavor to put himself in the place of the writer and consider whether he could have done any better. Where the purpose of the book is evil no castigation can be too severe.

Children of Edgefield, it may be that this is the last work, historical or other, that you will ever see from my pen. If it should be so, let us in love and peace greet each other with hail and farewell!

Newberry, S. C., May 13th, 1897.

ERRATA.

On page 198 for "Rev. Wm. M. Wood," read "Rev. Wm. M. Mood."

Page 200 in two places for "Captain David Bird," read "Captain Daniel Bird."

On page 176 for "Harry Fall, term," read "Horry, Fall Term."

INDEX.

INDEX.

84688009R00294

Made in the USA
Lexington, KY
24 March 2018